T0355595

Ford Mondeo
Service and Repair Manual

A K Legg LAE MIMI and Peter T Gill

Models covered

(3990 - 1AR2 - 384)

Ford Mondeo Hatchback, Saloon and Estate models, including special/limited editions;
Petrol engines: 1.8 litre (1798 cc) and 2.0 litre (1999 cc) four-cylinder engines, and 2.5 litre (2544 cc*) V6 engine
Turbo-diesel engines: 2.0 litre (1998 cc)

* also listed as 2495 cc and 2499 cc

Does not cover 3.0 litre V6 ST220 models
Does not cover 'facelifted' range introduced July 2003

© Haynes Group Limited 2012

A book in the **Haynes Service and Repair Manual Series**

ISBN **978 1 78521 521 6**

British Library Cataloguing in Publication Data
A catalogue record for this book is available from the British Library.

Haynes Group Limited
Haynes North America, Inc

www.haynes.com

Contents

LIVING WITH YOUR FORD MONDEO

MAINTENANCE

Routine maintenance and servicing

Contents

Originally introduced in March 1993, Ford Mondeo models are available in four-door Saloon, five-door Hatchback and five-door Estate configurations. This manual covers the New Ford Mondeo models manufactured from October 2000-on. All models feature a high standard of equipment, with driver/passenger safety in accidents being a particularly high design priority. The New Mondeo has a restyled 'sleeker' exterior with front driver and passenger airbags, and all-round disc brakes. Side curtain airbags are fitted to some models.

The new range of engines includes 1.8 and 2.0 litre Duratec-HE petrol, 2.5 litre V6 Duratec-VE petrol, and 2.0 litre Duratorq-Di and Duratorq-DCi turbo-diesel. All of these engines are fitted with timing chains, and, with the exception of the 24-valve V6, have 16 valves. All engines are fitted with sophisticated engine management systems; petrol engines are fitted with the Ford Black Oak system, and diesel engines are fitted with the Bosch VP44 system. The transversely-mounted engine drives the front roadwheels through a 5-speed manual transmission or a 4- or 5-speed automatic transmission. The clutch is hydraulically-operated.

The ABS braking system incorporates discs all-round, and the power-assisted steering is of the 'speed-sensitive' type.

The fully-independent suspension is by MacPherson strut on all four roadwheels, located by transverse lower arms at the front, and by transverse and trailing arms at the rear; anti-roll bars are fitted at the front and rear. The Estate rear suspension is of a different design, to give maximum loadspace inside the vehicle, with self-levelling suspension units available as an option.

The steering is power-assisted, the pump being belt-driven from the engine, and the rack-and-pinion steering gear mounted behind the engine.

Provided that regular servicing is carried out in accordance with the manufacturer's recommendations, the Mondeo should prove a reliable and economical car. The engine compartment is well-designed, and most of the items needing frequent attention are easily accessible.

Your Ford Mondeo manual

The aim of this manual is to help you get the best value from your vehicle. It can do so in several ways. It can help you decide what work must be done (even should you choose to get it done by a garage). It will also provide information on routine maintenance and servicing, and give a logical course of action and diagnosis when random faults occur. However, it is hoped that you will use the manual by tackling the work yourself. On simpler jobs it may even be quicker than booking the car into a garage and going there twice, to leave and collect it. Perhaps most important, a lot of money can be saved by avoiding the costs a garage must charge to cover its labour and overheads.

The manual has drawings and descriptions to show the function of the various components so that their layout can be understood. Tasks are described and photographed in a clear step-by-step sequence. The illustrations are numbered by the Section number and paragraph number to which they relate – if there is more than one illustration per paragraph, the sequence is denoted alphabetically.

References to the 'left' or 'right' of the vehicle are in the sense of a person in the driver's seat, facing forwards.

Acknowledgements

Certain illustrations are the copyright of the Ford Motor Company, and are used with their permission. Thanks are due to Draper Tools Limited, who provided some of the workshop tools, and to all those people at Sparkford who helped in the production of this manual.

We take great pride in the accuracy of information given in this manual, but vehicle manufacturers make alterations and design changes during the production run of a particular vehicle of which they do not inform us. No liability can be accepted by the authors or publishers for loss, damage or injury caused by any errors in, or omissions from, the information given.

Working on your car can be dangerous. This page shows just some of the potential risks and hazards, with the aim of creating a safety-conscious attitude.

General hazards

Scalding

• Don't remove the radiator or expansion tank cap while the engine is hot.
• Engine oil, automatic transmission fluid or power steering fluid may also be dangerously hot if the engine has recently been running.

Burning

• Beware of burns from the exhaust system and from any part of the engine. Brake discs and drums can also be extremely hot immediately after use.

Crushing

• When working under or near a raised vehicle, always supplement the jack with axle stands, or use drive-on ramps. *Never venture under a car which is only supported by a jack.*

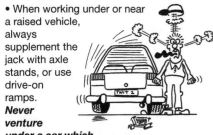

• Take care if loosening or tightening high-torque nuts when the vehicle is on stands. Initial loosening and final tightening should be done with the wheels on the ground.

Fire

• Fuel is highly flammable; fuel vapour is explosive.
• Don't let fuel spill onto a hot engine.
• Do not smoke or allow naked lights (including pilot lights) anywhere near a vehicle being worked on. Also beware of creating sparks (electrically or by use of tools).
• Fuel vapour is heavier than air, so don't work on the fuel system with the vehicle over an inspection pit.
• Another cause of fire is an electrical overload or short-circuit. Take care when repairing or modifying the vehicle wiring.
• Keep a fire extinguisher handy, of a type suitable for use on fuel and electrical fires.

Electric shock

• Ignition HT voltage can be dangerous, especially to people with heart problems or a pacemaker. Don't work on or near the ignition system with the engine running or the ignition switched on.

• Mains voltage is also dangerous. Make sure that any mains-operated equipment is correctly earthed. Mains power points should be protected by a residual current device (RCD) circuit breaker.

Fume or gas intoxication

• Exhaust fumes are poisonous; they often contain carbon monoxide, which is rapidly fatal if inhaled. Never run the engine in a confined space such as a garage with the doors shut.
• Fuel vapour is also poisonous, as are the vapours from some cleaning solvents and paint thinners.

Poisonous or irritant substances

• Avoid skin contact with battery acid and with any fuel, fluid or lubricant, especially antifreeze, brake hydraulic fluid and Diesel fuel. Don't syphon them by mouth. If such a substance is swallowed or gets into the eyes, seek medical advice.
• Prolonged contact with used engine oil can cause skin cancer. Wear gloves or use a barrier cream if necessary. Change out of oil-soaked clothes and do not keep oily rags in your pocket.
• Air conditioning refrigerant forms a poisonous gas if exposed to a naked flame (including a cigarette). It can also cause skin burns on contact.

Asbestos

• Asbestos dust can cause cancer if inhaled or swallowed. Asbestos may be found in gaskets and in brake and clutch linings. When dealing with such components it is safest to assume that they contain asbestos.

Special hazards

Hydrofluoric acid

• This extremely corrosive acid is formed when certain types of synthetic rubber, found in some O-rings, oil seals, fuel hoses etc, are exposed to temperatures above 400°C. The rubber changes into a charred or sticky substance containing the acid. *Once formed, the acid remains dangerous for years. If it gets onto the skin, it may be necessary to amputate the limb concerned.*
• When dealing with a vehicle which has suffered a fire, or with components salvaged from such a vehicle, wear protective gloves and discard them after use.

The battery

• Batteries contain sulphuric acid, which attacks clothing, eyes and skin. Take care when topping-up or carrying the battery.
• The hydrogen gas given off by the battery is highly explosive. Never cause a spark or allow a naked light nearby. Be careful when connecting and disconnecting battery chargers or jump leads.

Air bags

• Air bags can cause injury if they go off accidentally. Take care when removing the steering wheel and/or facia. Special storage instructions may apply.

Diesel injection equipment

• Diesel injection pumps supply fuel at very high pressure. Take care when working on the fuel injectors and fuel pipes.

⚠️ *Warning: Never expose the hands, face or any other part of the body to injector spray; the fuel can penetrate the skin with potentially fatal results.*

Remember...

DO

• Do use eye protection when using power tools, and when working under the vehicle.

• Do wear gloves or use barrier cream to protect your hands when necessary.

• Do get someone to check periodically that all is well when working alone on the vehicle.

• Do keep loose clothing and long hair well out of the way of moving mechanical parts.

• Do remove rings, wristwatch etc, before working on the vehicle – especially the electrical system.

• Do ensure that any lifting or jacking equipment has a safe working load rating adequate for the job.

DON'T

• Don't attempt to lift a heavy component which may be beyond your capability – get assistance.

• Don't rush to finish a job, or take unverified short cuts.

• Don't use ill-fitting tools which may slip and cause injury.

• Don't leave tools or parts lying around where someone can trip over them. Mop up oil and fuel spills at once.

• Don't allow children or pets to play in or near a vehicle being worked on.

The following pages are intended to help in dealing with common roadside emergencies and breakdowns. You will find more detailed fault finding information at the back of the manual, and repair information in the main chapters.

If your car won't start and the starter motor doesn't turn

☐ If it's a model with automatic transmission, make sure the selector is in P or N.
☐ Open the bonnet and make sure that the battery terminals are clean and tight.
☐ Switch on the headlights and try to start the engine. If the headlights go very dim when you're trying to start, the battery is probably flat. Get out of trouble by jump starting (see next page) using a friend's car.

If your car won't start even though the starter motor turns as normal

☐ Is there fuel in the tank?
☐ Is there moisture on electrical components under the bonnet? Switch off the ignition, then wipe off any obvious dampness with a dry cloth. Spray a water-repellent aerosol product (WD-40 or equivalent) on ignition and fuel system electrical connectors like those shown in the photos. Pay special attention to the ignition coil wiring connector and HT leads. (Note that Diesel engines don't normally suffer from damp.)

A Check the condition and security of the battery connections.

B Check that the HT leads are securely connected to the spark plugs and coils (petrol models).

C Check the engine wiring loom multi-plugs for security.

Check that electrical connections are secure (with the ignition switched off) and spray them with a water dispersant spray like WD40 if you suspect a problem due to damp

D Check that the fuel cut-off switch has not been activated (diesel models).

E Check that none of the engine compartment fuses have blown.

Jump starting

When jump-starting a car using a booster battery, observe the following precautions:

✔ Before connecting the booster battery, make sure that the ignition is switched off.

✔ Ensure that all electrical equipment (lights, heater, wipers, etc) is switched off.

✔ Take note of any special precautions printed on the battery case.

✔ Make sure that the booster battery is the same voltage as the discharged one in the vehicle.

✔ If the battery is being jump-started from the battery in another vehicle, the two vehicles MUST NOT TOUCH each other.

✔ Make sure that the transmission is in neutral (or PARK, in the case of automatic transmission).

Jump starting will get you out of trouble, but you must correct whatever made the battery go flat in the first place. There are three possibilities:

1 *The battery has been drained by repeated attempts to start, or by leaving the lights on.*

2 *The charging system is not working properly (alternator drivebelt slack or broken, alternator wiring fault or alternator itself faulty).*

3 *The battery itself is at fault (electrolyte low, or battery worn out).*

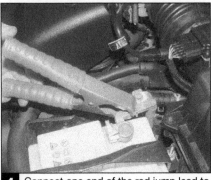

1 Connect one end of the red jump lead to the positive (+) terminal of the flat battery.

2 Connect the other end of the red lead to the positive (+) terminal of the booster battery.

3 Connect one end of the black jump lead to the negative (-) terminal of the booster battery.

4 Connect the other end of the black jump lead to a bolt or bracket on the engine block, well away from the battery, on the vehicle to be started.

5 Make sure that the jump leads will not come into contact with the fan, drive-belts or other moving parts of the engine.

6 Start the engine using the booster battery and run it at idle speed. Switch on the lights, rear window demister and heater blower motor, then disconnect the jump leads in the reverse order of connection. Turn off the lights etc.

Wheel changing

 Warning: Do not change a wheel in a situation where you risk being hit by another vehicle. On busy roads, try to stop in a lay-by or a gateway. Be wary of passing traffic while changing the wheel - it is easy to become distracted by the job in hand.

Preparation

☐ When a puncture occurs, stop as soon as it is safe to do so.
☐ Park on firm level ground, if possible, and well out of the way of other traffic.
☐ Use hazard warning lights if necessary.

☐ If you have one, use a warning triangle to alert other drivers of your presence.
☐ Apply the handbrake and engage first or reverse gear (or Park on models with automatic transmission).

☐ Chock the wheel diagonally opposite the one being removed – a couple of large stones will do for this.
☐ If the ground is soft, use a flat piece of wood to spread the load under the jack.

Changing the wheel

1 The spare wheel and tools are stored in the luggage compartment. Fold back the floor covering and lift up the cover panel, then unscrew the retainer, and lift the spare wheel out.

2 Unscrew the retainer, and lift the jack and wheel brace out of the wheel well. The screw-in towing eye is also provided in the wheel well.

3 Where applicable, using the flat end of the wheelbrace, prise off the centre cover or wheel trim for access to the wheel nuts. Slacken each wheel nut by a half turn, using the wheelbrace. If the bolts are too tight, DON'T stand on the wheel brace to undo them – call for assistance from one of the motoring organisations.

4 On models with side skirts, remove the jacking point covers by pressing upwards and outwards. The front jacking point is located approximately 27 cm (height of a Haynes Manual) from the front end of the sill, and the rear jacking point is located approximately 10 cm (half the width of a Haynes Manual) from the rear end of the sill. Use the jacking point nearest the punctured wheel. Locate the jack head in the jacking point (don't jack the vehicle at any other point of the sill). Turn the jack handle clockwise until the wheel is raised clear of the ground.

5 Unscrew the wheel nuts, noting which way round they fit (tapered side inwards), and remove the wheel. Where a locking wheel nut is fitted, use the special adapter.

7 Lower the vehicle to the ground and fully tighten the wheel nuts, then refit the wheel trim or centre cover, as applicable. Have the wheel nuts tightened to the correct torque at the earliest opportunity.

6 Fit the spare wheel, and screw on the nuts. Lightly tighten the nuts with the wheelbrace.

Caution: If a temporary space-saving spare wheel is fitted, do not exceed 50 mph and do not drive through an automatic car wash.

Finally...

☐ Remove the wheel chocks.
☐ Stow the jack and tools in the correct locations in the car.
☐ Check the tyre pressure on the wheel just fitted. If it is low, or if you don't have a pressure gauge with you, drive slowly to the nearest garage and inflate the tyre to the right pressure.
☐ Have the damaged tyre or wheel repaired as soon as possible.

Identifying leaks

Puddles on the garage floor or drive, or obvious wetness under the bonnet or underneath the car, suggest a leak that needs investigating. It can sometimes be difficult to decide where the leak Is coming from, especially if the engine bay is very dirty already. Leaking oil or fluid can also be blown rearwards by the passage of air under the car, giving a false impression of where the problem lies.

 Warning: Most automotive oils and fluids are poisonous. Wash them off skin, and change out of contaminated clothing, without delay.

 The smell of a fluid leaking from the car may provide a clue to what's leaking. Some fluids are distinctively coloured. It may help to clean the car carefully and to park it over some clean paper overnight as an aid to locating the source of the leak.
Remember that some leaks may only occur while the engine is running.

Sump oil

Engine oil may leak from the drain plug...

Oil from filter

...or from the base of the oil filter.

Gearbox oil

Gearbox oil can leak from the seals at the inboard ends of the driveshafts.

Antifreeze

Leaking antifreeze often leaves a crystalline deposit like this.

Brake fluid

A leak occurring at a wheel is almost certainly brake fluid.

Power steering fluid

Power steering fluid may leak from the pipe connectors on the steering rack.

Towing

When all else fails, you may find yourself having to get a tow home – or of course you may be helping somebody else. Long-distance recovery should only be done by a garage or breakdown service. For shorter distances, DIY towing using another car is easy enough, but observe the following points:

☐ Use a proper tow-rope – they are not expensive. The vehicle being towed must display an ON TOW sign in its rear window.

☐ Always turn the ignition key to the 'on' position when the vehicle is being towed, so that the steering lock is released, and that the direction indicator and brake lights will work.

☐ The front towing eye is of the screw-in type, and is stored in the spare wheel well. The towing eye screws into the threaded hole below the right-hand headlight, accessible

after prising out a cover in the bumper, and has a left-hand thread – ie, it screws in anti-clockwise **(see illustration)**. A similar arrangement is used for the rear towing eye on models with the standard rear bumper. On models with the Sports rear bumper, the rear towing eye is located on the right-hand side of the air vent slot.

☐ Before being towed, release the handbrake and make sure the transmission is in neutral. On models with automatic transmission, special precautions apply. If in doubt, do not tow, or transmission damage may result.

☐ Note that greater-than-usual pedal pressure will be required to operate the brakes, since the vacuum servo unit is only operational with the engine running.

☐ The driver of the car being towed must

keep the tow-rope taut at all times to avoid snatching.

☐ Make sure that both drivers know the route before setting off.

☐ Only drive at moderate speeds and keep the distance towed to a minimum. Drive smoothly and allow plenty of time for slowing down at junctions.

Introduction

There are some very simple checks which need only take a few minutes to carry out, but which could save you a lot of inconvenience and expense.

These *Weekly checks* require no great skill or special tools, and the small amount of time they take to perform could prove to be very well spent, for example;

☐ Keeping an eye on tyre condition and pressures, will not only help to stop them wearing out prematurely, but could also save your life.

☐ Many breakdowns are caused by electrical problems. Battery-related faults are particularly common, and a quick check on a regular basis will often prevent the majority of these.

☐ If your car develops a brake fluid leak, the first time you might know about it is when your brakes don't work properly. Checking the level regularly will give advance warning of this kind of problem.

☐ If the oil or coolant levels run low, the cost of repairing any engine damage will be far greater than fixing the leak, for example.

Underbonnet check points

◀ 4-cylinder 1.8 litre petrol

A *Engine oil level dipstick*

B *Engine oil filler cap*

C *Coolant reservoir (expansion tank)*

D *Brake fluid reservoir*

E *Washer fluid reservoir*

F *Battery*

G *Power steering fluid reservoir*

◀ V6 2.5 litre petrol

A *Engine oil level dipstick*

B *Engine oil filler cap*

C *Coolant reservoir (expansion tank)*

D *Brake fluid reservoir*

E *Washer fluid reservoir*

F *Battery*

G *Power steering fluid reservoir*

◀ **2.0 litre turbo-diesel**

A *Engine oil level dipstick*
B *Engine oil filler cap*
C *Coolant reservoir (expansion tank)*
D *Brake fluid reservoir*
E *Washer fluid reservoir*
F *Battery*
G *Power steering fluid reservoir*

Engine oil level

Before you start

✔ Make sure that your car is on level ground.
✔ Check the oil level before the car is driven, or at least 5 minutes after the engine has been switched off.

 If the oil is checked immediately after driving the vehicle, some of the oil will remain in the upper engine components, resulting in an inaccurate reading on the dipstick.

The correct oil

Modern engines place great demands on their oil. It is very important that the correct oil for your car is used (See *Lubricants and fluids*).

Car Care

● If you have to add oil frequently, you should check whether you have any oil leaks. Place some clean paper under the car overnight, and check for stains in the morning. If there are no leaks, the engine may be burning oil.

● Always maintain the level between the upper and lower dipstick marks (see photo 3). If the level is too low severe engine damage may occur. Oil seal failure may result if the engine is overfilled by adding too much oil.

1 The dipstick is located on the front of the engine (see *Underbonnet Check Points* for exact location). Withdraw the dipstick.

2 Using a clean rag or paper towel remove all oil from the dipstick. Insert the clean dipstick into the tube as far as it will go, then withdraw it again.

3 Note the oil level on the end of the dipstick, which should be between the upper (MAX) mark and lower (MIN) mark.

4 Oil is added through the filler cap. Rotate the cap through a quarter-turn anti-clockwise and withdraw it. Top-up the level. A funnel may help to reduce spillage. Add the oil slowly, checking the level on the dipstick often. Do not overfill.

Coolant level

Warning:
• **DO NOT attempt to remove the expansion tank pressure cap when the engine is hot, as there is a very great risk of scalding.**
• **Do not leave open containers of coolant about, as it is poisonous.**

Car Care

● With a sealed-type cooling system, adding coolant should not be necessary on a regular basis. If frequent topping-up is required, it is likely there is a leak. Check the radiator, all hoses and joint faces for signs of staining or wetness, and rectify as necessary.

● It is important that antifreeze is used in the cooling system all year round, not just during the winter months. Don't top-up with water alone, as the antifreeze will become too diluted.

1 The coolant level varies with the temperature of the engine, and is visible through the expansion tank. When the engine is cold, the coolant level should be between the MAX mark on the side . . .

2 . . . and the MIN mark on the front of the reservoir. When the engine is hot, the level may rise slightly above the MAX mark.

3 If topping-up is necessary, **wait until the engine is cold**. Slowly unscrew the expansion tank cap, to release any pressure present in the cooling system, and remove it.

4 Add a mixture of water and antifreeze to the expansion tank until the coolant level is halfway between the level marks. Refit the cap and tighten it securely.

Power steering fluid level

Before you start

✔ Park the vehicle on level ground.
✔ Set the steering wheel straight-ahead.
✔ The engine should be turned off.

HAYNES HiNT *For the check to be accurate, the steering must not be turned once the engine has been stopped.*

Safety First!

● The need for frequent topping-up indicates a leak, which should be investigated immediately.

1 The fluid level is visible through the reservoir body. When the system is at operating temperature, the level should be up to the MAX mark on the side of the reservoir.

2 If topping-up is required, wipe clean the area around the reservoir filler neck and unscrew the filler cap from the reservoir.

3 When topping-up, use the specified type of fluid and do not overfill the reservoir. When the level is correct, securely refit the cap.

Tyre condition and pressure

It is very important that tyres are in good condition, and at the correct pressure - having a tyre failure at any speed is highly dangerous. Tyre wear is influenced by driving style - harsh braking and acceleration, or fast cornering, will all produce more rapid tyre wear. As a general rule, the front tyres wear out faster than the rears. Interchanging the tyres from front to rear ("rotating" the tyres) may result in more even wear. However, if this is completely effective, you may have the expense of replacing all four tyres at once! Remove any nails or stones embedded in the tread before they penetrate the tyre to cause deflation. If removal of a nail does reveal that the tyre has been punctured, refit the nail so that its point of penetration is marked. Then immediately change the wheel, and have the tyre repaired by a tyre dealer.

Regularly check the tyres for damage in the form of cuts or bulges, especially in the sidewalls. Periodically remove the wheels, and clean any dirt or mud from the inside and outside surfaces. Examine the wheel rims for signs of rusting, corrosion or other damage. Light alloy wheels are easily damaged by "kerbing" whilst parking; steel wheels may also become dented or buckled. A new wheel is very often the only way to overcome severe damage.

New tyres should be balanced when they are fitted, but it may become necessary to re-balance them as they wear, or if the balance weights fitted to the wheel rim should fall off. Unbalanced tyres will wear more quickly, as will the steering and suspension components. Wheel imbalance is normally signified by vibration, particularly at a certain speed (typically around 50 mph). If this vibration is felt only through the steering, then it is likely that just the front wheels need balancing. If, however, the vibration is felt through the whole car, the rear wheels could be out of balance. Wheel balancing should be carried out by a tyre dealer or garage.

1 *Tread Depth - visual check*
The original tyres have tread wear safety bands (B), which will appear when the tread depth reaches approximately 1.6 mm. The band positions are indicated by a triangular mark on the tyre sidewall (A).

2 *Tread Depth - manual check*
Alternatively, tread wear can be monitored with a simple, inexpensive device known as a tread depth indicator gauge.

3 *Tyre Pressure Check*
Check the tyre pressures regularly with the tyres cold. Do not adjust the tyre pressures immediately after the vehicle has been used, or an inaccurate setting will result.

Tyre tread wear patterns

Shoulder Wear

Underinflation (wear on both sides)
Under-inflation will cause overheating of the tyre, because the tyre will flex too much, and the tread will not sit correctly on the road surface. This will cause a loss of grip and excessive wear, not to mention the danger of sudden tyre failure due to heat build-up.
Check and adjust pressures
Incorrect wheel camber (wear on one side)
Repair or renew suspension parts
Hard cornering
Reduce speed!

Centre Wear

Overinflation
Over-inflation will cause rapid wear of the centre part of the tyre tread, coupled with reduced grip, harsher ride, and the danger of shock damage occurring in the tyre casing.
Check and adjust pressures

If you sometimes have to inflate your car's tyres to the higher pressures specified for maximum load or sustained high speed, don't forget to reduce the pressures to normal afterwards.

Uneven Wear

Front tyres may wear unevenly as a result of wheel misalignment. Most tyre dealers and garages can check and adjust the wheel alignment (or "tracking") for a modest charge.
Incorrect camber or castor
Repair or renew suspension parts
Malfunctioning suspension
Repair or renew suspension parts
Unbalanced wheel
Balance tyres
Incorrect toe setting
Adjust front wheel alignment
Note: *The feathered edge of the tread which typifies toe wear is best checked by feel.*

Brake (and clutch) fluid level

Warning:
● Brake fluid can harm your eyes and damage painted surfaces, so use extreme caution when handling and pouring it.

● Do not use fluid that has been standing open for some time, as it absorbs moisture from the air, which can cause a dangerous loss of braking effectiveness.

HAYNES HiNT
• Make sure that your car is on level ground.
• The fluid level in the reservoir will drop slightly as the brake pads wear down, but the fluid level must never be allowed to drop below the MIN mark.

Safety First!
● If the reservoir requires repeated topping-up this is an indication of a fluid leak somewhere in the system, which should be investigated immediately.

● If a leak is suspected, the car should not be driven until the braking system has been checked. Never take any risks where brakes are concerned.

1 The brake fluid reservoir is located on the left-hand side of the engine compartment.

2 The MAX and MIN marks are indicated on the side of the reservoir. The fluid level must be kept between the marks at all times.

3 If topping-up is necessary, first wipe clean the area around the filler cap to prevent dirt entering the hydraulic system, then unscrew and remove the reservoir cap. Inspect the reservoir; if the fluid is dirty, the hydraulic system should be drained and refilled (see Chapter 1A or 1B).

4 Carefully add fluid, taking care not to spill it onto the surrounding components. Use only the specified fluid; mixing different types can cause damage to the system. After topping-up to the correct level, securely refit the cap and wipe off any spilt fluid.

Screen washer fluid level

Note: *The underbonnet reservoir also serves the tailgate washer, and the headlight washers, where fitted.*
Screenwash additives not only keep the windscreen clean during foul weather, they also prevent the washer system freezing in cold weather - which is when you are likely to need it most. Don't top up using plain water as the screenwash will become too diluted, and will freeze during cold weather. *On no account use coolant antifreeze in the washer system - this could discolour or damage paintwork.*

1 The screen washer fluid reservoir filler neck is located in the right-hand front corner of the engine compartment, behind the headlight. The fluid level is checked by removing the filler cap and checking the dipstick which is attached to the cap.

2 When topping-up the reservoir, add a screenwash additive in the quantities recommended on the bottle.

Wiper blades

1 Check the condition of the wiper blades; if they are cracked or show any signs of deterioration, or if the glass swept area is smeared, renew them. Wiper blades should be renewed annually.

2 To remove a wiper blade, pull the arm fully away from the glass until it locks. Swivel the blade through 90°, then squeeze the locking clip, and detach the blade from the arm. When fitting the new blade, make sure that the blade locks securely into the arm, and that the blade is orientated correctly.

3 Don't forget to check the tailgate wiper blade as well (where applicable). Remove the blade using a similar technique to the windscreen wiper blades.

Battery

Caution: Before carrying out any work on the vehicle battery, read the precautions given in 'Safety first' at the start of this manual.

✔ Make sure that the battery tray is in good condition, and that the clamp is tight. Corrosion on the tray, retaining clamp and the battery itself can be removed with a solution of water and baking soda. Thoroughly rinse all cleaned areas with water. Any metal parts damaged by corrosion should be covered with a zinc-based primer, then painted.

✔ Periodically (approximately every three months), check the charge condition of the battery as described in Chapter 5A.

✔ If the battery is flat, and you need to jump start your vehicle, see *Roadside Repairs*.

1 The battery is located in the left-hand front corner of the engine compartment. The exterior of the battery should be inspected periodically for damage such as a cracked case or cover.

2 Check the tightness of battery clamps (A) to ensure good electrical connections. You should not be able to move them. Also check each cable (B) for cracks and frayed conductors.

Battery corrosion can be kept to a minimum by applying a layer of petroleum jelly to the clamps and terminals after they are reconnected.

3 If corrosion (white, fluffy deposits) is evident, remove the cables from the battery terminals, clean them with a small wire brush, then refit them. Automotive stores sell a tool for cleaning the battery post . . .

4 . . . as well as the battery cable clamps

Electrical systems

✔ Check all external lights and the horn. Refer to the appropriate Sections of Chapter 12 for details if any of the circuits are found to be inoperative.

✔ Visually check all accessible wiring connectors, harnesses and retaining clips for security, and for signs of chafing or damage.

HAYNES HiNT *If you need to check your brake lights and indicators unaided, back up to a wall or garage door and operate the lights. The reflected light should show if they are working properly.*

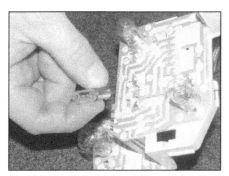

1 If a single indicator light, stop-light or headlight has failed, it is likely that a bulb has blown and will need to be renewed. Refer to Chapter 12 for details. If both stop-lights have failed, it is possible that the switch has failed (see Chapter 9).

2 If more than one indicator light or headlight has failed, it is likely that either a fuse has blown or that there is a fault in the circuit (see Chapter 12). The main fusebox is located below the facia panel on the passenger's side, and is accessed by a lever behind the glovebox. The auxiliary fusebox is located next to the battery – unclip and remove the cover for access.

3 To renew a blown fuse, remove it, where applicable, using the plastic tool provided. Fit a new fuse of the same rating, available from car accessory shops. It is important that you find the reason that the fuse blew (see *Electrical fault finding* in Chapter 12).

Lubricants and fluids

Engine (petrol and diesel)	Multigrade engine oil, viscosity range SAE 5W/30, 5W/40 or 10W/40 to ACEA-A3/B3
Cooling system	Motorcraft Super Plus 2000 antifreeze to Ford specification WSS-M97B44-D
Manual gearbox	Gear oil to Ford specification WSD-M2C200C
Automatic transmission	Automatic transmission fluid to Ford specification ESP-M2C 166-H
Power steering reservoir	Hydraulic fluid to Ford specification WSA-M2C195-A
Brake fluid reservoir	Hydraulic fluid to Ford specification ESD-M6C57-A, Super DOT 4

Choosing your engine oil

Engines need oil, not only to lubricate moving parts and minimise wear, but also to maximise power output and to improve fuel economy.

HOW ENGINE OIL WORKS

• *Beating friction*

Without oil, the moving surfaces inside your engine will rub together, heat up and melt, quickly causing the engine to seize. Engine oil creates a film which separates these moving parts, preventing wear and heat build-up.

• *Cooling hot-spots*

Temperatures inside the engine can exceed 1000° C. The engine oil circulates and acts as a coolant, transferring heat from the hot-spots to the sump.

• *Cleaning the engine internally*

Good quality engine oils clean the inside of your engine, collecting and dispersing combustion deposits and controlling them until they are trapped by the oil filter or flushed out at oil change.

Note: It is illegal and anti-social to dump oil down the drain. To find the location of your local oil recycling bank, call 08708 506 506 or visit www.oilbankline.org.uk.

Tyre pressures (cold)

	Front	Rear
Normally-laden (up to 3 people)	2.1 bar (30 psi)	2.1 bar (30 psi)
Fully-laden	2.4 bar (35 psi)	2.8 bar (41 psi)
Emergency **temporary** spare tyre (only 16 x 4 inch)	4.2 bars (61 psi)	4.2 bars (61 psi)

Note 1: *Pressures apply to original-equipment tyres, and may vary if any other make of tyre is fitted; check with the tyre manufacturer or supplier for the correct pressures if necessary.*

Note 2: *For sustained high speeds above 100 mph (160 km/h), increased pressures are necessary. Consult the driver's handbook supplied with the vehicle.*

Chapter 1 Part A:
Routine maintenance and servicing – petrol engine models

Contents

Degrees of difficulty

Easy, suitable for novice with little experience

Fairly easy, suitable for beginner with some experience

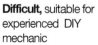

Fairly difficult, suitable for competent DIY mechanic

Difficult, suitable for experienced DIY mechanic

Very difficult, suitable for expert DIY or professional

Lubricants and fluids

Refer to the end of *Weekly checks* on page 0•18

Capacities

Engine oil:
With filter:	
1.8 and 2.0 litre engines	4.3 litres
2.5 litre V6 engine	5.5 litres
Without filter:	
1.8 and 2.0 litre engines	3.9 litres
2.5 litre V6 engine	5.0 litres
Difference between dipstick minimum and maximum marks	0.75 to 1.0 litre

Cooling system:
1.8 litre engine	8.3 litres
2.0 litre engine	8.1 litres
2.5 litre V6 engine:	
Manual transmission	9.5 litres
Automatic transmission	9.7 litres
Fuel tank	58.5 litres
Manual transmission	1.9 litres

Automatic transmission:
4-speed transmission (CD4E):	
1.8 and 2.0 litre engines:	
Total, including fluid cooler	7.5 litres
Drain and refill	6.0 litres
2.5 litre V6 engine:	
Total, including fluid cooler	9.6 litres
Drain and refill	6.3 litres
5-speed transmission (Durashift 5-tronic)	8.8 litres

Cooling system

Coolant protection at 40% antifreeze/water mixture ratio:
Slush point	–25°C (–13°F)
Solidifying point	–30°C (–22°F)

Ignition system

Firing order:
1.8 and 2.0 litre engines	1-3-4-2
2.5 litre V6 engine	1-4-2-5-3-6
No 1 cylinder position	Timing chain end of engine

Spark plugs:

	Type	Electrode gap
1.8 and 2.0 litre engines	Motorcraft AGFS 22FE1	1.3 mm
V6 engine	Bosch HR 8 DPP 15 V	1.3 mm
	Motorcraft AWSF 32F	1.3 mm

Braking system

Note: *No minimum lining thicknesses are given by Ford – the following is given as a general recommendation.*

Minimum front or rear brake pad lining thickness .... 1.5 mm

Torque wrench settings

	Nm	lbf ft
Automatic transmission drain plug:		
4-speed	27	20
5-speed	45	33
Automatic transmission filler plug (5-speed)	45	33
Automatic transmission selector lever cable cover (5-speed)	22	16
Automatic transmission test plug (5-speed)	15	11
Engine oil drain plug:		
1.8 and 2.0 litre engines	28	21
2.5 litre V6 engine	26	19
Manual transmission filler/level/drain plug	45	33
Roadwheel nuts	85	63
Spark plugs:		
1.8 and 2.0 litre engines	15	11
2.5 litre V6 engine	14	10

The maintenance intervals in this manual are provided with the assumption that you, not the dealer, will be carrying out the work. These are the minimum maintenance intervals recommended by us for vehicles driven daily. If you wish to keep your vehicle in peak condition at all times, you may wish to perform some of these procedures more often. We encourage frequent maintenance, because it enhances the efficiency, performance and resale value of your vehicle.

If the vehicle is driven in dusty areas, used to tow a trailer, or driven frequently at slow speeds (idling in traffic) or on short journeys, more frequent maintenance intervals are recommended.

When the vehicle is new, it should be serviced by a factory-authorised dealer service department, in order to preserve the factory warranty.

Every 250 miles (400 km) or weekly

☐ Refer to *Weekly checks*

Every 6250 miles or 6 months, whichever occurs first

☐ Renew the engine oil and filter (Section 3)

Note: *Frequent oil and filter changes are good for the engine. We recommend changing the oil at the mileage specified here, or at least twice a year if the mileage covered is a less.*

Every 12 500 miles or 12 months, whichever occurs first

In addition to the item listed in the previous service, carry out the following:

☐ Check the battery and clean the terminals (Section 4)
☐ Check the auxiliary drivebelt (Section 5)
☐ Check the electrical system (Section 6)
☐ Check under the bonnet for fluid leaks and hose condition (Section 7)
☐ Check the condition of all engine compartment wiring (Section 8)
☐ Check the condition of all air conditioning system components (Section 9)
☐ Check the seat belts (Section 10)
☐ Check the antifreeze concentration (Section 11)
☐ Check the steering, suspension and roadwheels (Section 12)
☐ Check the driveshaft rubber gaiters and CV joints (Section 13)
☐ Check the exhaust system (Section 14)
☐ Check the underbody, and all fuel/brake lines (Section 15)
☐ Check the braking system (Section 16)
☐ Check the doors and bonnet, and lubricate their hinges and locks (Section 17)
☐ Renew the ventilation system pollen filter (Section 18)
☐ Check the security of all roadwheel nuts (Section 19)
☐ Road test (Section 20)

Every 25 000 miles or 2 years, whichever occurs first

In addition to the relevant items listed in the previous services, carry out the following:

☐ Check the automatic transmission fluid level (Section 21)

Every 37 500 miles or 3 years, whichever occurs first

In addition to the relevant items listed in the previous services, carry out the following:

☐ Renew the spark plugs (Section 22)
☐ Renew the air filter element (Section 23). Note that this task must be carried out at more frequent intervals if the vehicle is used in dusty or polluted conditions
☐ Check the manual transmission oil level (Section 24)
☐ Renew the automatic transmission fluid (Section 25). Note that this task applies to vehicles used in severe conditions only (short trips of less than 10 miles in freezing conditions, extensive idling, towing a trailer, operating off-road)

Every 3 years (regardless of mileage)

☐ Renew the brake fluid (Section 26)
☐ Renew the coolant (Section 27)

Every 50 000 miles or 4 years, whichever occurs first

In addition to the relevant items listed in the previous services, carry out the following:

☐ Renew the fuel filter (Section 28)
☐ Check the valve clearances – 1.8 and 2.0 litre only (Section 29)
☐ Renew the auxiliary drivebelts (Section 30)

Underbonnet view of a 2.0 litre engine model

1 Engine oil filler cap
2 Engine oil dipstick
3 Power steering hydraulic fluid reservoir
4 Washer fluid reservoir
5 Coolant expansion tank filler cap
6 Front suspension strut upper mounting
7 Spark plugs and HT leads
8 Ignition coil
9 Brake and clutch hydraulic fluid reservoir
10 Air cleaner
11 Battery

Underbonnet view of a 2.5 litre V6 engine model

1 Engine oil filler cap
2 Engine oil dipstick
3 Power steering hydraulic fluid reservoir
4 Washer fluid reservoir
5 Coolant expansion tank filler cap
6 Front suspension strut upper mounting
7 Upper inlet manifold
8 Ignition coil
9 Brake and clutch hydraulic fluid reservoir
10 Air cleaner
11 Battery

Front underbody view of a 2.0 litre engine model

1 Engine oil drain plug
2 Oil filter
3 Manual transmission filler/level plug
4 Fuel and brake lines
5 Exhaust pipe
6 Steering track rods
7 Front suspension lower arms
8 Rear engine mounting link
9 Driveshaft
10 Front brake calipers
11 Manual transmission
12 Front subframe
13 Air conditioning compressor

Front underbody view of a 2.5 litre V6 engine model

1 Engine oil drain plug
2 Oil filter
3 Manual transmission filler/level plug
4 Fuel and brake lines
5 Exhaust pipe
6 Steering track rods
7 Front suspension lower arms
8 Rear engine mounting link
9 Driveshaft
10 Front brake calipers
11 Manual transmission
12 Front subframe
13 Air conditioning compressor

Rear underbody view - Saloon and Hatchback models

1 Fuel tank
2 Exhaust pipe
3 Handbrake cables
4 Rear anti-roll bar
5 Rear suspension front
   lower arm
6 Rear suspension rear
   lower arm
7 Rear suspension
   crossmember
8 Spare wheel well

Rear underbody view - Estate models

1 Fuel tank
2 Rear suspension brace
3 Rear suspension tie
   bar/knuckle
4 Handbrake cables
5 Rear suspension front
   lower arms
6 Rear suspension struts
7 Rear suspension lower
   arms
8 Rear anti-roll bar
9 Rear anti-roll bar link
   lower mountings
10 Rear suspension
   crossmember
11 Rear exhaust system
12 Spare wheel well

1 General information

1 This Chapter is designed to help the home mechanic maintain his/her vehicle for safety, economy, long life and peak performance.

2 The Chapter contains a master maintenance schedule, followed by Sections dealing specifically with each task in the schedule. Visual checks, adjustments, component renewal and other helpful items are included. Refer to the accompanying illustrations of the engine compartment and the underside of the vehicle for the locations of the various components.

3 Servicing your vehicle in accordance with the mileage/time maintenance schedule and the following Sections will provide a planned maintenance programme, which should result in a long and reliable service life. This is a comprehensive plan, so maintaining some items but not others at the specified service intervals, will not produce the same results.

4 As you service your vehicle, you will discover that many of the procedures can – and should – be grouped together, because of the particular procedure being performed, or because of the proximity of two otherwise-unrelated components to one another. For example, if the vehicle is raised for any reason, the exhaust can be inspected at the same time as the suspension and steering components.

5 The first step in this maintenance programme is to prepare yourself before the actual work begins. Read through all the Sections relevant to the work to be carried out, then make a list and gather all the parts and tools required. If a problem is encountered, seek advice from a parts specialist, or a dealer service department.

2 Regular maintenance

1 If, from the time the vehicle is new, the routine maintenance schedule is followed closely, and frequent checks are made of fluid levels and high-wear items, as suggested throughout this manual, the engine will be kept in relatively good running condition, and the need for additional work will be minimised.

2 It is possible that there will be times when the engine is running poorly due to the lack of regular maintenance. This is even more likely if a used vehicle, which has not received regular and frequent maintenance checks, is purchased. In such cases, additional work may need to be carried out, outside of the regular maintenance intervals.

3 If engine wear is suspected, a compression test (refer to the relevant Part of Chapter 2) will provide valuable information regarding the overall performance of the main internal components. Such a test can be used as a basis to decide on the extent of the work to be carried out. If, for example, a compression test indicates serious internal engine wear,

conventional maintenance as described in this Chapter will not greatly improve the performance of the engine, and may prove a waste of time and money, unless extensive overhaul work is carried out first.

4 The following series of operations are those most often required to improve the performance of a generally poor-running engine:

Primary operations

a) Clean, inspect and test the battery (See 'Weekly checks' and Section 4).
b) Check all the engine-related fluids (See 'Weekly checks').
c) Check the condition and tension of the auxiliary drivebelt (Section 5).
d) Renew the spark plugs (Section 22).
e) Check the condition of the air filter, and renew if necessary (Section 23).
f) Renew the fuel filter (Section 28).
g) Check the condition of all hoses, and check for fluid leaks (Sections 7 and 15).

5 If the above operations do not prove fully effective, carry out the following secondary operations:

Secondary operations

All items listed under *Primary operations*, plus the following:
a) Check the charging system (Chapter 5A).
b) Check the ignition system (Chapter 5B).
c) Check the fuel system (see Chapter 4A or 4B).
d) Renew the ignition HT leads (see Chapter 5B).

Every 6250 miles or 6 months

3 Engine oil and filter renewal

1 Frequent oil changes are the most important preventive maintenance the DIY home mechanic can give the engine, because ageing oil becomes diluted and contaminated, which leads to premature engine wear.

2 Before starting this procedure, gather together all the necessary tools and materials. Also make sure that you have plenty of clean rags and newspapers handy, to mop up any spills. Ideally, the engine oil should be warm, as it will drain more easily and more built-up sludge will be removed with it. Take care not to touch the exhaust or any other hot parts of the engine when working under the vehicle. To avoid any possibility of scalding and to protect yourself from possible skin irritants and other harmful contaminants in used engine oils, it is advisable to wear gloves when carrying out this work.

3 Firmly apply the handbrake then jack up the front of the car and support it on axle stands (see *Jacking and vehicle support*). Where

applicable, remove the engine undershield.

4 Remove the oil filler cap, then unscrew the engine oil drain plug (located at the rear of the sump) about half a turn. Position the draining container under the drain plug, then remove the plug completely – recover the sealing washer (see illustration and Haynes Hint).

5 Allow some time for the oil to drain, noting that it may be necessary to reposition the container as the oil flow slows to a trickle.

6 After all the oil has drained, wipe off the drain plug with a clean rag, and fit a new

3.4 Removing the engine oil drain plug (2.0 litre engine)

sealing washer. Clean the area around the drain plug opening, and refit the plug. Tighten the plug to the specified torque.

7 Move the container into position under the oil filter, which is located on the front side of the cylinder block.

HAYNES HiNT

Keep the plug pressed into the sump while unscrewing it by hand the last couple of turns. As the plug releases from the threads, move it away sharply, so the stream of oil issuing from the sump runs into the pan, not up your sleeve.

3.8a Unscrew the oil filter plastic cover . . .

3.8b . . . then remove and discard the paper element (2.0 litre engine)

3.9 Removing the O-ring seal from the bottom cover (2.0 litre engine)

3.10 Lubricate the new O-ring seal with a little engine oil (2.0 litre engine)

3.11 Oil filter location (2.0 litre engine)

All engines

15 Remove the old oil and all tools from under the car, then lower the car to the ground.
16 Remove the dipstick, then unscrew the oil filler cap from the cylinder head cover. Fill the engine, using the correct grade and type of oil (*see Weekly checks*). An oil can spout or funnel may help to reduce spillage. Pour in half the specified quantity of oil first, then wait a few minutes for the oil to fall to the sump. Continue adding oil a small quantity at a time until the level is up to the lower mark on the dipstick. Adding approximately 1.0 litre will bring the level up to the upper mark on the dipstick. Refit the filler cap.
17 Start the engine and run it for a few minutes; check for leaks. Note that there may be a delay of a few seconds before the oil pressure warning light goes out when the engine is first started, as the oil circulates through the engine oil galleries and the new oil filter before the pressure builds-up.
18 Switch off the engine, and wait a few minutes for the oil to settle in the sump once more. With the new oil circulated and the filter completely full, recheck the level on the dipstick, and add more oil as necessary.
19 Dispose of the used engine oil safely, with reference to *General Repair Procedures*.

1.8 and 2.0 litre engines

8 Unscrew the oil filter plastic cover from the bottom of the oil filter housing, then remove and discard the paper element **(see illustrations)**.
9 Remove the O-ring seal and obtain a new one **(see illustration)**. Clean the filter housing and cover.
10 Fit the new O-ring seal onto the cover and lubricate it with a little engine oil **(see illustration)**.
11 Locate the new paper element on the cover, then screw the assembly into the filter housing and tighten securely by hand **(see illustration)**. Where necessary, refit the splash guard under the engine.

2.5 litre V6 engine

12 Use an oil filter removal tool to slacken the filter initially, then unscrew it by hand the rest of the way **(see illustration)**. Empty the oil in the old filter into the container.
13 Use a clean rag to remove all oil, dirt and sludge from the filter sealing area on the engine. Check the old filter to make sure that the rubber sealing ring hasn't stuck to the engine. If it has, carefully remove it.
14 Apply a light coating of clean engine oil to the sealing ring on the new filter, then screw it into position on the engine **(see illustration)**. Tighten the filter firmly by hand only – **do not** use any tools. Where necessary, refit the splash guard under the engine.

3.12 Using a chain-type wrench to remove the oil filter (2.5 litre V6 engine)

3.14 Lubricate the filter's sealing ring with clean engine oil before installing the filter on the engine (2.5 litre V6 engine)

Every 12 500 miles or 12 months

4 Battery maintenance and charging

⚠️ *Warning: Certain precautions must be followed when checking and servicing the battery. Hydrogen gas, which is highly flammable, is always present in the battery cells, so keep lighted tobacco and all other open flames and sparks away from the battery. The electrolyte inside the battery is actually dilute sulphuric acid, which will cause injury if splashed on your skin or in your eyes. It will also ruin clothes and painted surfaces. When disconnecting the battery, always detach the negative (earth) lead first and connect it last.*

Note: *Before disconnecting the battery, refer to 'Disconnecting the battery' at the end of this manual.*

General

1 A routine preventive maintenance programme for the battery in your vehicle is the only way to ensure quick and reliable starts. For general maintenance, refer to *Weekly checks* at the start of this manual. Also at the front of the manual is information on jump starting. For details of removing and installing the battery, refer to Chapter 5A.

Battery electrolyte level

2 On models not equipped with a sealed or 'maintenance-free' battery, check the electrolyte level of all six battery cells.

3 The level must be approximately 10 mm above the plates; this may be shown by maximum and minimum level lines marked on the battery's casing.

4 If the level is low, use a coin or screwdriver to release the filler/vent cap, and add distilled water. To improve access to the centre caps, it may be helpful to remove the battery hold-down clamp.

5 Install and securely retighten the cap, then wipe up any spillage.

Caution: Overfilling the cells may cause electrolyte to spill over during periods of heavy charging, causing corrosion or damage.

Charging

⚠️ *Warning: When batteries are being charged, hydrogen gas, which is very explosive and flammable, is produced. Do not smoke, or allow open flames, near a charging or a recently-charged battery. Wear eye protection when near the battery during charging. Also, make sure the charger is unplugged before connecting or disconnecting the battery from the charger.*

6 Slow-rate charging is the best way to restore a battery that's discharged to the point where it will not start the engine. It's also a good way to maintain the battery charge in a vehicle that's only driven a few miles between starts. Maintaining the battery charge is particularly important in winter, when the battery must work harder to start the engine, and electrical accessories that drain the battery are in greater use.

7 Check the battery case for any instructions regarding charging the battery. Some maintenance-free batteries may require a particularly low charge rate or other special conditions, if they are not to be damaged.

8 It's best to use a one- or two-amp battery charger (sometimes called a 'trickle' charger). They are the safest, and put the least strain on the battery. They are also the least expensive. For a faster charge, you can use a higher-amperage charger, but don't use one rated more than 1/10th the amp/hour rating of the battery (ie, no more than 5 amps, typically). Rapid boost charges that claim to restore the power of the battery in one to two hours are hardest on the battery, and can damage batteries not in good condition. This type of charging should only be used in emergency situations.

9 The average time necessary to charge a battery should be listed in the instructions that come with the charger. As a general rule, a trickle charger will charge a battery in 12 to 16 hours.

5 Auxiliary drivebelt check

Note: *The work in this Section is not a Ford recommendation at this time interval, however, we recommend renewing the drivebelt at 50 000 miles.*

General

1 The main auxiliary drivebelt is of flat, multi-ribbed type, and is located on the right-hand end of the engine. It drives the alternator, water pump (1.8 and 2.0 litre engines), power steering pump and the air conditioning compressor from the engine's crankshaft pulley **(see illustrations)**.

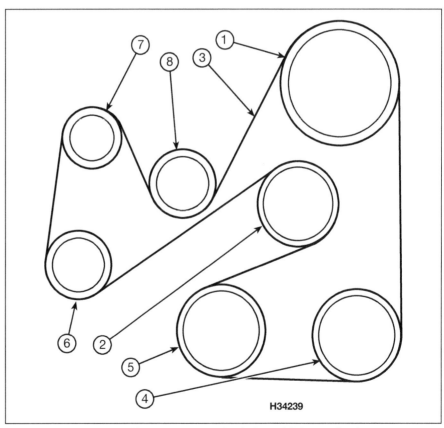

5.1a Auxiliary drivebelt routing (1.8 and 2.0 litre engines)

1 Power steering pump pulley	5 Crankshaft pulley
2 Water pump pulley	6 Tensioner pulley
3 Auxiliary drivebelt	7 Alternator pulley
4 Air conditioning compressor pulley	8 Idler pulley

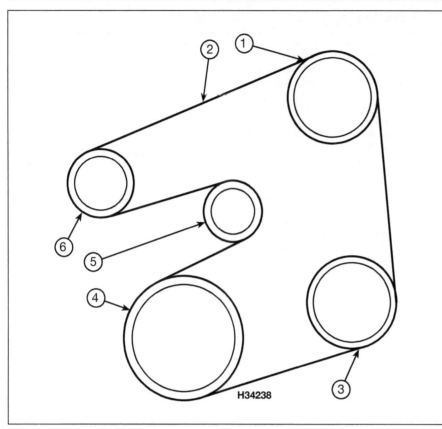

5.1b Auxiliary drivebelt routing (2.5 litre V6 engine)

1 Power steering pump pulley
2 Auxiliary drivebelt
3 Air conditioning compressor pulley
4 Crankshaft pulley
5 Tensioner pulley
6 Alternator pulley

2 On V6 engine models, the water pump is driven by an additional drivebelt at the left-hand end of the engine. The belt is of the multi-ribbed type, and is driven by the front inlet camshaft.

3 The good condition and proper tension of the auxiliary drivebelt is critical to the operation of the engine. Because of their composition and the high stresses to which they are subjected, drivebelts stretch and deteriorate as they get older. They must, therefore, be regularly inspected.

Check

4 With the engine switched off, open and support the bonnet. For improved access to the right-hand end of the engine, first loosen the right-hand front wheel nuts, then jack up the front right-hand side of the vehicle and support it securely on an axle stand. Remove the roadwheel, then remove the auxiliary drivebelt cover (two fasteners) from inside the wheel arch. Remove the engine undertray. If necessary, also remove the rear section of the inner wheel arch liner, which is secured by two further bolts.

5 Using an inspection light or a small electric torch, and rotating the engine with a spanner applied to the crankshaft pulley bolt, check the whole length of the drivebelt for cracks,

separation of the rubber, and torn or worn ribs. Also check for fraying and glazing, which gives the drivebelt a shiny appearance.

6 Both sides of the drivebelt should be inspected, which means you will have to twist the drivebelt to check the underside. Use your fingers to feel the drivebelt where you can't see it. If you are in any doubt as to the condition of the drivebelt, renew it as described below.

7 In addition on models with the V6 engine, remove the water pump drivebelt cover from the top of the engine. Inspect the drivebelt as described in paragraphs 5 and 6.

5.13 Removing the water pump drivebelt (2.5 litre V6 engine)

Drivebelt tension

8 The auxiliary drivebelt is tensioned by an automatic tensioner; regular checks are not required, and manual 'adjustment' is not possible.

9 If you suspect that the drivebelt is slipping and/or running slack, or that the tensioner is otherwise faulty, it must be renewed. Refer to Chapter 2A or 2B.

Drivebelt renewal

10 Gain access to the drivebelt as described in paragraph 4 or 7, as applicable.

11 If the existing drivebelt is to be refitted, mark it, or note the maker's markings on its flat surface, so that it can be installed the same way round.

12 Rotate the tensioner pulley clockwise to release its pressure on the drivebelt. Depending on model and equipment, the tensioner will either have a hex fitting for a spanner or socket, or a square hole into which a ratchet handle from a socket set can be fitted.

13 Slip the drivebelt off the drive pulley, and release the tensioner again (see illustration). Working from the wheel arch or engine compartment as necessary, and noting its routing, slip the drivebelt off the remaining pulleys and withdraw it.

14 Check all the pulleys, ensuring that their grooves are clean, and removing all traces of oil and grease. Check that the tensioner works properly, with strong spring pressure being felt when its pulley is rotated clockwise, and a smooth return to the limit of its travel when released.

15 If the original drivebelt is being refitted, use the marks or notes made on removal, to ensure that it is installed to run in the same direction as it was previously. To fit the drivebelt, arrange it on the grooved pulleys so that it is centred in their grooves, and not overlapping their raised sides (note that the flat surface of the drivebelt is engaged on one or more pulleys) and routed correctly. Start at the top, and work down to finish at the bottom pulley; rotate the tensioner pulley clockwise, slip the drivebelt onto the bottom pulley, then release the tensioner again.

16 Using a spanner applied to the crankshaft pulley bolt, rotate the crankshaft through at least two full turns clockwise to settle the drivebelt on the pulleys, then check that the drivebelt is properly installed.

17 Refit the components removed for access, then lower the vehicle to the ground. Refit the roadwheel and tighten the wheel nuts to the specified torque.

6 Electrical system check

1 Check the operation of all external lights and indicators (front and rear).

2 Check for satisfactory operation of the instrument panel, its illumination and warning lights, the switches and their function lights.
3 Check the horn(s) for satisfactory operation.
4 Check all other electrical equipment for satisfactory operation.

7 Underbonnet check for fluid leaks and hose condition

1 Visually inspect the engine joint faces, gaskets and seals for any signs of water or oil leaks. Pay particular attention to the areas around the cylinder head cover, cylinder head, oil filter and sump joint faces. Bear in mind that, over a period of time, some very slight seepage from these areas is to be expected – what you are really looking for is any indication of a serious leak. Should a leak be found, renew the offending gasket or oil seal by referring to the appropriate Chapters in this manual.
2 Also check the security and condition of all the engine-related pipes and hoses, and all braking system pipes and hoses and fuel lines. Ensure that all cable ties or securing clips are in place, and in good condition. Clips which are broken or missing can lead to chafing of the hoses, pipes or wiring, which could cause more serious problems in the future.
3 Carefully check the radiator hoses and heater hoses along their entire length. Renew any hose which is cracked, swollen or deteriorated. Cracks will show up better if the hose is squeezed. Pay close attention to the hose clips that secure the hoses to the cooling system components. Hose clips can pinch and puncture hoses, resulting in cooling system leaks. If the crimped-type hose clips are used, it may be a good idea to replace them with standard worm-drive clips.
4 Inspect all the cooling system components (hoses, joint faces, etc) for leaks **(see Haynes Hint)**.
5 Where any problems are found on system components, renew the component or gasket with reference to Chapter 3.
6 With the vehicle raised, inspect the fuel tank and filler neck for punctures, cracks and other damage. The connection between the filler neck and tank is especially critical. Sometimes a rubber filler neck or connecting hose will leak due to loose retaining clamps or deteriorated rubber.
7 Carefully check all rubber hoses and metal fuel lines leading away from the fuel tank. Check for loose connections, deteriorated hoses, crimped lines, and other damage. Pay particular attention to the vent pipes and hoses, which often loop up around the filler neck and can become blocked or crimped. Follow the lines to the front of the vehicle, carefully inspecting them all the way. Renew damaged sections as necessary. Similarly, whilst the vehicle is raised, take the opportunity to inspect all underbody brake fluid pipes and hoses.

8 From within the engine compartment, check the security of all fuel, vacuum and brake hose attachments and pipe unions, and inspect all hoses for kinks, chafing and deterioration.
9 Check the condition of the power steering and, where applicable, the automatic transmission fluid pipes and hoses.

8 Engine compartment wiring check

1 With the vehicle parked on level ground, apply the handbrake firmly and open the bonnet. Using an inspection light or a small electric torch, check all visible wiring within and beneath the engine compartment.
2 What you are looking for is wiring that is obviously damaged by chafing against sharp edges, or against moving suspension/transmission components and/or the auxiliary drivebelt, by being trapped or crushed between carelessly-refitted components, or melted by being forced into contact with the hot engine castings, coolant pipes, etc. In almost all cases, damage of this sort is caused in the first instance by incorrect routing on reassembly after previous work has been carried out.
3 Depending on the extent of the problem, damaged wiring may be repaired by rejoining the break or splicing-in a new length of wire, using solder to ensure a good connection, and remaking the insulation with adhesive insulating tape or heat-shrink tubing, as appropriate. If the damage is extensive, given the implications for the vehicle's future reliability, the best long-term answer may well be to renew that entire section of the loom, however expensive this may appear.
4 When the actual damage has been repaired, ensure that the wiring loom is rerouted correctly, so that it is clear of other components, and not stretched or kinked, and is secured out of harm's way using the plastic clips, guides and ties provided.
5 Check all electrical connectors, ensuring that they are clean, securely fastened, and

A leak in the cooling system will usually show up as white – or rust-coloured deposits on the area adjoining the leak.

that each is locked by its plastic tabs or wire clip, as appropriate. If any connector shows external signs of corrosion (accumulations of white or green deposits, or streaks of 'rust'), or if any is thought to be dirty, it must be unplugged and cleaned using electrical contact cleaner. If the connector pins are severely corroded, the connector must be renewed; note that this may mean the renewal of that entire section of the loom – see your local Ford dealer for details.
6 If the cleaner completely removes the corrosion to leave the connector in a satisfactory condition, it would be wise to pack the connector with a suitable material which will exclude dirt and moisture, preventing the corrosion from occurring again; a Ford dealer may be able to recommend a suitable product.
7 Check the condition of the battery connections – remake the connections or renew the leads if a fault is found (see Chapter 5A). Use the same techniques to ensure that all earth points in the engine compartment provide good electrical contact through clean, metal-to-metal joints, and that all are securely fastened.

9 Air conditioning system check

1 The following maintenance checks will ensure that the air conditioner operates at peak efficiency:
   a) Check the auxiliary drivebelt (see Section 5).
   b) Check the system hoses for damage or leaks.
   c) Inspect the condenser fins for leaves, insects and other debris. Use a clean paint brush to clean the condenser.
   d) Check that the drain tube from the front of the evaporator is clear – note that it is normal to have clear fluid (water) dripping from this while the system is in operation, to the extent that quite a large puddle can be left under the vehicle when it is parked.
2 It's a good idea to operate the system for about 30 minutes at least once a month, particularly during the winter. Long term non-use can cause hardening, and subsequent failure, of the seals.
3 Because of the complexity of the air conditioning system and the special equipment necessary to service it, in-depth fault diagnosis and repairs are not included in this manual.
4 The most common cause of poor cooling is simply a low system refrigerant charge. If a noticeable drop in cool air output occurs, the following quick check will help you determine if the refrigerant level is low.
5 Warm the engine up to normal operating temperature.
6 Place the air conditioning temperature selector at the coldest setting, and put the

blower at the highest setting. Open the doors – to make sure the air conditioning system doesn't cycle off as soon as it cools the passenger compartment.

7 With the compressor engaged – the clutch will make an audible click, and the centre of the clutch will rotate – feel the inlet and outlet pipes at the compressor. One side should be cold, and one hot. If there's no perceptible difference between the two pipes, there's something wrong with the compressor or the system. It might be a low charge – it might be something else. Take the vehicle to a dealer service department or an automotive air conditioning specialist.

10 Seat belt check

1 Check the seat belts for satisfactory operation and condition. Inspect the webbing for fraying and cuts. Check that they retract smoothly and without binding into their reels.
2 Check that the seat belt mounting bolts are tight, and if necessary tighten them to the specified torque wrench setting (Chapter 11).

11 Antifreeze concentration check

1 The cooling system should be filled with the recommended antifreeze and corrosion protection fluid. Over a period of time, the concentration of fluid may be reduced due to topping-up (this can be avoided by topping-up with the correct antifreeze mixture) or fluid loss. If loss of coolant has been evident, it is important to make the necessary repair before adding fresh fluid. The exact mixture of antifreeze-to-water which you should use depends on the relative weather conditions. The mixture should contain at least 40% antifreeze, but not more than 70%. Consult the mixture ratio chart on the antifreeze container before adding coolant. Use antifreeze which meets the vehicle manufacturer's specifications.
2 With the engine **cold**, carefully remove the cap from the expansion tank. If the engine is not completely cold, place a cloth rag over the cap before removing it, and remove it slowly to allow any pressure to escape.
3 Antifreeze checkers are available from car accessory shops. Draw some coolant from the expansion tank and observe how many plastic balls are floating in the checker. Usually, 2 or 3 balls must be floating for the correct concentration of antifreeze, but follow the manufacturer's instructions.
4 If the concentration is incorrect, it will be necessary to either withdraw some coolant and add antifreeze, or alternatively drain the old coolant and add fresh coolant of the correct concentration.

12 Steering, suspension and roadwheel check

Front suspension and steering

1 Raise the front of the vehicle, and securely support it on axle stands (see *Jacking and vehicle support*).
2 Visually inspect the balljoint dust covers and the steering rack-and-pinion gaiters for splits, chafing or deterioration. Any wear of these components will cause loss of lubricant, together with dirt and water entry, resulting in rapid deterioration of the balljoints or steering gear.
3 Check the power steering fluid hoses for chafing or deterioration, and the pipe and hose unions for fluid leaks. Also check for signs of fluid leakage under pressure from the steering gear rubber gaiters, which would indicate failed fluid seals within the steering gear.
4 Grasp the roadwheel at the 12 o'clock and 6 o'clock positions, and try to rock it **(see illustration)**. Very slight free play may be felt, but if the movement is appreciable, further investigation is necessary to determine the source. Continue rocking the wheel while an assistant depresses the footbrake. If the movement is now eliminated or significantly reduced, it is likely that the hub bearings are at fault. If the free play is still evident with the footbrake depressed, then there is wear in the suspension joints or mountings.
5 Now grasp the wheel at the 9 o'clock and 3 o'clock positions, and try to rock it as before. Any movement felt now may again be caused by wear in the hub bearings or the steering track rod balljoints. If the outer balljoint is worn, the visual movement will be obvious. If the inner joint is suspect, it can be felt by placing a hand over the rack-and-pinion rubber gaiter and gripping the track rod. If the wheel is now rocked, movement will be felt at the inner joint if wear has taken place.
6 Using a large screwdriver or flat bar, check for wear in the suspension mounting bushes by levering between the relevant suspension component and its attachment point. Some movement is to be expected, as the mountings

12.4 Checking for wear in the front suspension and hub bearings

are made of rubber, but excessive wear should be obvious. Also check the condition of any visible rubber bushes, looking for splits, cracks or contamination of the rubber.
7 With the car standing on its wheels, have an assistant turn the steering wheel back-and-forth, about an eighth of a turn each way. There should be very little, if any, lost movement between the steering wheel and roadwheels. If this is not the case, closely observe the joints and mountings previously described. In addition, check the steering column universal joints for wear, and also check the rack-and-pinion steering gear itself.

Rear suspension

8 Chock the front wheels, then jack up the rear of the vehicle and support securely on axle stands (see *Jacking and vehicle support*).
9 Working as described previously for the front suspension, check the rear hub bearings, the suspension bushes and the strut or shock absorber mountings (as applicable) for wear.

Shock absorber

10 Check for any signs of fluid leakage around the shock absorber body, or from the rubber gaiter around the piston rod. Should any fluid be noticed, the shock absorber is defective internally, and should be renewed. **Note:** *Shock absorbers should always be renewed in pairs on the same axle.*
11 The efficiency of the shock absorber may be checked by bouncing the vehicle at each corner. Generally speaking, the body will return to its normal position and stop after being depressed. If it rises and returns on a rebound, the shock absorber is probably suspect. Also examine the shock absorber upper and lower mountings for any signs of wear.

Roadwheels

12 Periodically remove the roadwheels, and clean any dirt or mud from the inside and outside surfaces. Examine the wheel rims for signs of rusting, corrosion or other damage. Light alloy wheels are easily damaged by 'kerbing' whilst parking, and similarly, steel wheels may become dented or buckled. Renewal of the wheel is very often the only course of remedial action possible.
13 The balance of each wheel and tyre assembly should be maintained, not only to avoid excessive tyre wear, but also to avoid wear in the steering and suspension components. Wheel imbalance is normally signified by vibration through the vehicle's bodyshell, although in many cases it is particularly noticeable through the steering wheel. Conversely, it should be noted that wear or damage in suspension or steering components may cause excessive tyre wear. Out-of-round or out-of-true tyres, damaged wheels and wheel bearing wear/maladjustment also fall into this category. Balancing will not usually cure vibration caused by such wear.

14 Wheel balancing may be carried out with the wheel either on or off the vehicle. If balanced on the vehicle, ensure that the wheel-to-hub relationship is marked in some way prior to subsequent wheel removal, so that it may be refitted in its original position.

15 At this time, also check the spare wheel for damage.

13 Driveshaft rubber gaiter and CV joint check

1 The driveshaft rubber gaiters are very important, because they prevent dirt, water and foreign material from entering and damaging the constant velocity (CV) joints. External contamination can cause the gaiter material to deteriorate prematurely, so it's a good idea to wash the gaiters with soap and water occasionally.

2 With the vehicle raised and securely supported on axle stands, turn the steering onto full-lock, then slowly rotate each front wheel in turn. Inspect the condition of the outer constant velocity (CV) joint rubber gaiters, squeezing the gaiters to open out the folds **(see illustration)**. Check for signs of cracking, splits, or deterioration of the rubber, which may allow the escape of grease, and lead to the ingress of water and grit into the joint. Also check the security and condition of the retaining clips. Repeat these checks on the inner CV joints. If any damage or deterioration is found, the gaiters should be renewed as described in Chapter 8.

3 At the same time, check the general condition of the outer CV joints themselves, by first holding the driveshaft and attempting to rotate the wheels. Repeat this check on the inner joints, by holding the inner joint yoke and attempting to rotate the driveshaft.

4 Any appreciable movement in the CV joint indicates wear in the joint, wear in the drive-shaft splines, or a loose driveshaft retaining nut.

14 Exhaust system check

1 With the engine cold, check the complete exhaust system, from its starting point at the engine to the end of the tailpipe. If necessary, raise the front and rear of the vehicle and support it on axle stands (see *Jacking and vehicle support*). Remove any engine undershields as necessary for full access to the exhaust system.

2 Check the exhaust pipes and connections for evidence of leaks, severe corrosion, and damage **(see illustration)**. Make sure that all brackets and mountings are in good condition and that all relevant nuts and bolts are tight. Leakage at any of the joints or in other parts of the system will usually show up as a black sooty stain in the vicinity of the leak.

13.2 Check the driveshaft gaiters by hand for cracks and/or leaking grease

3 Rattles and other noises can often be traced to the exhaust system, especially the brackets and rubber mountings. Try to move the pipes and silencers. If the components are able to come into contact with the body or suspension parts, secure the system with new mountings. Otherwise separate the joints (if possible) and twist the pipes as necessary to provide additional clearance.

15 Underbody and fuel/brake line check

1 With the vehicle raised and supported on axle stands (see *Jacking and vehicle support*), thoroughly inspect the underbody and wheel arches for signs of damage and corrosion. In particular, examine the bottom of the side sills, and any concealed areas where mud can collect.

2 Where corrosion and rust is evident, press and tap firmly on the panel with a screwdriver, and check for any serious corrosion which would necessitate repairs.

3 If the panel is not seriously corroded, clean away the rust, and apply a new coating of underseal. Refer to Chapter 11 for more details of body repairs.

4 At the same time, inspect the PVC-coated lower body panels for stone damage and general condition.

5 Inspect all of the fuel and brake lines on the underbody for damage, rust, corrosion and leakage. Also make sure that they are correctly supported in their clips. Where

16.2 Check the thickness of the pad friction material through the caliper inspection window

14.2 Check the condition of the exhaust system

applicable, check the PVC coating on the lines for damage.

16 Braking system check

Front disc brakes

1 Apply the handbrake, then jack up the front of the vehicle and support it on axle stands (see *Jacking and vehicle support*). For better access to the brake calipers, remove the wheels.

2 Look through the inspection window in the caliper, and check that the thickness of the friction lining material on each of the pads is not less than the recommended minimum thickness given in the Specifications **(see illustration)**.

3 If it is difficult to determine the exact thickness of the pad linings, or if you are at all concerned about the condition of the pads, then remove them from the calipers for further inspection (refer to Chapter 9) **(see illustration)**.

4 Check the caliper on the other side in the same way.

5 If any one of the brake pads has worn down to, or below, the specified limit, *all four* pads at that end of the car must be renewed as a set.

6 Check both front brake discs with reference to Chapter 9.

7 Before refitting the wheels, check all brake lines and flexible hoses with reference to

16.3 Checking the thickness of the pad linings with a steel rule

16.7 Checking the condition of a flexible brake hose

18.4a Release the retaining clips . . .

18.4b . . . and withdraw the pollen filter from its housing

Chapter 9. In particular, check the flexible hoses in the vicinity of the calipers, where they are subjected to most movement. Bend them between the fingers and check that this does not reveal previously-hidden cracks, cuts or splits **(see illustration)**.

8 On completion, refit the wheels and lower the car to the ground. Tighten the wheel nuts to the specified torque.

Rear disc brakes

9 Chock the front wheels then jack up the rear of the vehicle and support on axle stands (see *Jacking and vehicle support*). Remove the rear wheels.

10 The procedure for checking the rear brakes is much the same as described in paragraphs 1 to 8 above.

Handbrake

11 With the vehicle on a slight slope, firmly apply the handbrake lever, and check that it holds the vehicle stationary, then release the lever and check that there is no resistance to movement of the vehicle. The handbrake lever incorporates a self-adjusting mechanism which automatically adjusts its total travel.

17 Door and bonnet check and lubrication

1 Check that the doors, bonnet and tailgate/boot lid close securely. Check that the bonnet safety catch operates correctly. Check the operation of the door check straps.

2 Lubricate the hinges, door check straps, the striker plates and the bonnet catch sparingly with a little oil or grease.

18 Ventilation system pollen filter renewal

1 The air entering the vehicle's ventilation system is passed through a very fine pleated-paper air filter element, which removes particles of pollen, dust and other airborne foreign matter. To ensure its continued effectiveness, this filter's element must be renewed at regular intervals. Failure to renew

the element will also result in reduced airflow into the passenger compartment, reducing demisting and ventilation.

2 Remove the windscreen wiper arms as described in Chapter 12.

3 Unclip and remove the cowl sections from in front of the windscreen.

4 Release the retaining clips and withdraw the pollen filter from its housing **(see illustrations)**.

5 Wipe clean the housing, then insert the new filter and check that the clips are correctly engaged.

6 Refit the cowl sections and wiper arms with reference to Chapter 12.

19 Roadwheel nut tightness check

1 Apply the handbrake, chock the wheels, and engage 1st gear (or P).

2 Remove the wheel cover (or wheel centre cover), using the flat end of the wheel brace supplied in the tool kit.

3 Check the tightness of all wheel nuts using a torque wrench (refer to the Specifications).

20 Road test

Instruments and electrical equipment

1 Check the operation of all instruments and electrical equipment.

2 Make sure that all instruments read correctly, and switch on all electrical equipment in turn, to check that it functions properly.

Steering and suspension

3 Check for any abnormalities in the steering, suspension, handling or road 'feel'.

4 Drive the vehicle, and check that there are no unusual vibrations or noises.

5 Check that the steering feels positive, with no excessive 'sloppiness', or roughness, and check for any suspension noises when cornering and driving over bumps.

Drivetrain

6 Check the performance of the engine, clutch, transmission and driveshafts.

7 Listen for any unusual noises from the engine, clutch and transmission.

8 Make sure that the engine runs smoothly when idling, and that there is no hesitation when accelerating.

9 Check that, where applicable, the clutch action is smooth and progressive, that the drive is taken up smoothly, and that the pedal travel is not excessive. Also listen for any noises when the clutch pedal is depressed.

10 Check that all gears can be engaged smoothly without noise, and that the gear lever action is smooth and not abnormally vague or 'notchy'.

11 On automatic transmission models, make sure that all gearchanges occur smoothly, without snatching, and without an increase in engine speed between changes. Check that all of the gear positions can be selected with the vehicle at rest.

12 Listen for a metallic clicking sound from the front of the vehicle, as the vehicle is driven slowly in a circle with the steering on full-lock. Carry out this check in both directions. If a clicking noise is heard, this indicates wear in a driveshaft joint (see Chapter 8).

Braking system

13 Make sure that the vehicle does not pull to one side when braking, and that the wheels do not lock when braking hard.

14 Check that there is no vibration through the steering when braking.

15 Check that the handbrake operates correctly, without excessive movement of the lever, and that it holds the vehicle stationary on a slope.

16 Test the operation of the brake servo unit as follows. Depress the footbrake four or five times to exhaust the vacuum, then start the engine. As the engine starts, there should be a noticeable 'give' in the brake pedal as vacuum builds-up. Allow the engine to run for at least two minutes, and then switch it off. If the brake pedal is now depressed again, it should be possible to detect a hiss from the servo as the pedal is depressed. After about four or five applications, no further hissing should be heard, and the pedal should feel considerably harder.

21.4 Removing the automatic transmission dipstick from its tube (4-speed)

H34242

21.6 Transmission fluid dipstick MIN and MAX marks (4-speed)

1 MAX mark
2 MIN mark
3 Lower hole mark (DO NOT DRIVE)

21.7 Adding automatic transmission fluid through the dipstick tube (4-speed)

Every 25 000 miles or 2 years

21 Automatic transmission fluid level check

4-speed transmission

1 The level of the automatic transmission fluid should be carefully maintained. Low fluid level can lead to slipping or loss of drive, while overfilling can cause foaming, loss of fluid and transmission damage.
2 The transmission fluid level should only be checked when the transmission is hot (at its normal operating temperature). If the vehicle has just been driven over 10 miles (15 miles in cold weather), the transmission is hot. **Note:** *If the vehicle has just been driven for a long time at high speed or in city traffic in hot weather, or if it has been pulling a trailer, an accurate fluid level reading cannot be obtained. In these circumstances, allow the fluid to cool down for about 30 minutes.*
3 Park the vehicle on level ground, apply the handbrake firmly, and start the engine. While the engine is idling, depress the brake pedal and move the selector lever through all the positions three times, beginning and ending in P.
4 Allow the engine to idle, and remove the dipstick from its tube **(see illustration)**. Note the condition and colour of the fluid on the dipstick.
5 Wipe the fluid from the dipstick with a clean rag, and re-insert it into the filler tube until the cap seats.
6 Pull out the dipstick again, and note the fluid level. The level should be between the MIN and MAX marks **(see illustration)**.
7 If the level is on the MIN mark, stop the engine, and add the specified automatic transmission fluid through the dipstick tube, using a clean funnel if necessary **(see**

illustration). It is important not to introduce dirt into the transmission when topping-up.
8 Add the fluid a little at a time, and keep checking the level as previously described until it is correct.
9 The need for regular topping-up of the transmission fluid indicates a leak, which should be found and rectified without delay.
10 The condition of the fluid should also be checked along with the level. If the fluid at the end of the dipstick is black or a dark reddish-brown colour, or if it has a burned smell, the fluid should be changed. If you are in doubt about the condition of the fluid, purchase some new fluid, and compare the two for colour and smell.

5-speed transmission

11 To accurately check the fluid level on 5-speed automatic transmissions, a Ford diagnostic tool is necessary. The following paragraphs describe the procedure for the DIY home mechanic who has access to this tool. First connect the tool to the diagnostic socket.
12 The transmission fluid temperature must initially be below 30°C.
13 Apply the handbrake, then jack up the front of the vehicle and support it on axle stands (see *Jacking and vehicle support*). Unbolt the selector lever cable cover for access to the test plug, then lower the vehicle to the ground.
14 Start the engine. While the engine is idling, depress the brake pedal and move the selector lever through all the positions three times, beginning and ending in P. Leave the engine idling until while the fluid level is being checked.
15 When the fluid temperature reaches 30°C, move the selector lever from P to D, and back again to P.
16 With the handbrake applied, jack up the

front and rear of the vehicle and support it on axle stands (see *Jacking and vehicle support*). **Note:** *The vehicle must be level for an accurate check.*
17 Check that the fluid temperature is between 35°C and 45°C.
18 Position a suitable container beneath the transmission, then unscrew and remove the test plug **(see illustration)**. The test plug is located in the middle of the drain plug, and incorporates a tube extension to the fluid level height inside the transmission. Remove and discard the plug seal.
Caution: Wear suitable gloves as protection against scalding.
19 If no fluid escapes from the test plug, unscrew the filler plug from the top of the transmission and add fresh fluid until it emerges from the test hole. When the fluid ceases to drain, the level is correct.
20 Refit the filler and test plugs together with new seals and tighten to the specified torque. Refit the selector lever cable cover and tighten the bolts to the specified torque.
21 Switch off the engine and lower the vehicle to the ground.
22 Disconnect the diagnostic tool.

H34243

21.18 Test plug (5-speed)

22.2 Removing the engine top cover (2.0 litre engine)

22.4 Disconnecting the HT leads from the spark plugs

22.5a Tools required for spark plug removal, gap adjustment and refitting

Every 37 500 miles or 3 years

22 Spark plug renewal

1 The correct functioning of the spark plugs is vital for the correct running and efficiency of the engine. It is essential that the plugs fitted are appropriate for the engine; suitable types are specified at the beginning of this Chapter, or in the vehicle's Owner's Handbook. If the correct type is used and the engine is in good condition, the spark plugs should not need attention between scheduled replacement intervals. Spark plug cleaning is rarely necessary, and should not be attempted unless specialised equipment is available, as damage can easily be caused to the firing ends.

22.5b Removing the spark plugs

22.11b ... or a wire gauge ...

2 Remove the engine top cover, with reference to Chapter 2A or 2B if necessary **(see illustration)**.
3 On 2.5 litre V6 models, carry out the following:
   a) *Remove the water pump drivebelt cover from the top and front of the engine – the cover is secured by three bolts.*
   b) *Remove the upper section of the inlet manifold as described in Chapter 2B.*
   c) *To gain access to the plugs on the front bank of cylinders, unscrew the retaining bolts from the Inlet Manifold Runner Control (IMRC) motor. Place the motor out of the way – there is no need to disconnect the wiring or operating cable.*
   d) *The spark plugs are numbered from the timing chain end of the engine – 1 to 3 along the rear bank, and 4 to 6 along the front.*

22.11a If single electrode plugs are being fitted, check the electrode gap using a feeler gauge ...

22.12 ... and if necessary adjust the gap by bending the electrode

4 Carefully disconnect the HT leads from the spark plugs **(see illustration)**. The original leads are marked for position, however, if they have been previously renewed, mark them to correspond to the cylinder the lead serves.
5 Unscrew the spark plugs from the cylinder head using a spark plug spanner, suitable box spanner or a deep socket and extension bar **(see illustrations)**. Keep the socket aligned with the spark plug – if it is forcibly moved to one side, the ceramic insulator may be broken off.
6 Examination of the spark plugs will give a good indication of the condition of the engine. As each plug is removed, examine it as follows. If the insulator nose of the spark plug is clean and white, with no deposits, this is indicative of a weak mixture or too hot a plug (a hot plug transfers heat away from the electrode slowly, a cold plug transfers heat away quickly).
7 If the tip and insulator nose are covered with hard black-looking deposits, then this is indicative that the mixture is too rich. Should the plug be black and oily, then it is likely that the engine is fairly worn, as well as the mixture being too rich.
8 If the insulator nose is covered with light tan to greyish-brown deposits, then the mixture is correct and it is likely that the engine is in good condition.
9 Where multi-electrode plugs are fitted, the electrode gaps are all preset and no attempt should be made to bend the electrodes.
10 If standard single electrode plugs are fitted, the spark plug electrode gap is of considerable importance. If the gap is too large or too small, the size of the spark and its efficiency will be seriously impaired and it will not perform correctly under all engine speed and load conditions. The gap should be set to the value specified by the manufacturer.
11 To set the gap, measure it with a feeler blade or spark plug gap gauge and then carefully bend the outer plug electrode until the correct gap is achieved. The centre electrode should never be bent, as this may crack the insulator and cause plug failure, if nothing worse. If using feeler blades, the gap is correct when the appropriate-size blade is a firm sliding fit **(see illustrations)**.
12 Special spark plug electrode gap

It is very often difficult to insert spark plugs into their holes without cross-threading them. To avoid this possibility, fit a short length of rubber hose over the end of the spark plug. The flexible hose acts as a universal joint to help align the plug with the plug hole. Should the plug begin to cross-thread, the hose will slip on the spark plug, preventing thread damage to the aluminium cylinder head.

adjusting tools are available from most motor accessory shops, or from some spark plug manufacturers **(see illustration)**.
13 Before fitting the spark plugs, check that the threaded connector sleeves are tight, and that the plug exterior surfaces and threads are clean **(see Haynes Hint)**.
14 Remove the rubber hose (if used), and tighten the plug to the specified torque using the spark plug socket and a torque wrench. Refit the remaining spark plugs in the same manner.
15 Connect the HT leads to the spark plugs in their correct order, then refit the engine top cover.

23 Air filter element renewal

1 The air filter element is located in the air cleaner assembly on the left-hand side of the engine compartment, behind the battery. Undo the screws and lift up the air cleaner cover **(see illustrations)**.
2 If additional working clearance is required,

24.3a Using a suitable Allen key or socket, unscrew . . .

23.1a Air cleaner assembly location (2.5 litre V6 engine)

remove the cover completely; on 1.8 and 2.0 litre models, unclip the cover from the air mass meter, while on the V6 engine, slacken the air inlet hose clip and detach it from the air mass meter.
3 Lift out the element, noting its direction of fitting, and wipe out the housing **(see illustration)**.
4 If carrying out a routine service, the element must be renewed regardless of its apparent condition.
5 On four-cylinder engine models, note that the small foam filter in the rear right-hand corner of the air cleaner housing must be cleaned whenever the air filter element is renewed.
6 If you are checking the element for any other reason, inspect its lower surface; if it is oily or very dirty, renew the element. If it is only moderately dusty, it can be re-used by blowing it clean with compressed air.
7 Fit the new element using a reversal of the removal procedure.

24 Manual transmission oil level check

Note: *The work in this Section is not a Ford recommendation.*
1 The manual transmission does not have a dipstick. To check the oil level, raise the vehicle and support it securely on axle stands, making sure that the vehicle is level.
2 Remove the engine undershields as necessary for access to the front of the transmission.

24.3b . . . and remove the transmission oil filler/level plug

23.1b Undo the screws and lift the cover . . .

23.3 . . . then remove the air filter element

3 The filler/level plug is located on the lower front side of the transmission housing. Using a suitable Allen key or socket, unscrew and remove it – take care, as it will probably be very tight **(see illustrations)**.
4 If the lubricant level is correct, the oil should be up to the lower edge of the hole.
5 If the transmission needs more lubricant (if the oil level is not up to the hole), use a syringe, or a plastic bottle and tube, to add more **(see illustration)**.
6 Stop filling the transmission when the lubricant begins to run out of the hole, then wait until the flow of oil ceases.
7 Refit the filler/level plug, and tighten it to the specified torque wrench setting. Drive the vehicle a short distance, then check for leaks.
8 A need for regular topping-up can only be due to a leak, which should be found and rectified without delay.

24.5 Topping-up the manual transmission oil

25 Automatic transmission fluid renewal

1 Park the car on level ground, and switch off the engine. Apply the handbrake, and engage P. Jack up the front of the car and support on axle stands. Remove the transmission fluid dipstick on 4-speed transmissions.

2 Depending on model, it may be necessary to remove the engine undershield for access to the transmission drain plug. The plug is fitted on the base of the transmission housing.

3 Taking adequate precautions against burning or scalding if the engine and transmission are hot (wear gloves), position a suitable container below the transmission drain plug.

4 Loosen and remove the drain plug (see illustration), and allow the fluid to drain into the container. On 5-speed transmissions, remove the seal from the plug and also unscrew the filler plug from the top of the transmission.

5 Clean the drain plug thoroughly, then when the flow of fluid has ceased, refit the plug and tighten it to the specified torque. Fit a new seal on 5-speed transmissions.

6 Remove the fluid container from under the car.

7 The transmission is filled through the dipstick tube on 4-speed transmissions and through the filler plug aperture on 5-speed transmissions. Use a narrow funnel, and take great care to avoid introducing any kind of dirt into the transmission as it is filled.

8 After about half the specified 'drain and refill' quantity of fluid has been added, refer to

25.4 Automatic transmission fluid drain plug (4-speed)

Section 21 and complete the level checking procedure.

9 Refit the engine undershield (where removed), then lower the car to the ground.

Every 3 years (regardless of mileage)

26 Brake fluid renewal

The procedure is similar to that for the bleeding of the hydraulic system as described in Chapter 9, except that the brake fluid reservoir should be emptied by syphoning, and allowance should be made for the old fluid to be removed from the circuit when bleeding a section of the circuit.

27 Coolant renewal

Note: *If the antifreeze used is Ford's own, or of similar quality, Ford state that the coolant need not be renewed for the life of the vehicle. If the vehicle's history is unknown, if the antifreeze is of lesser quality, or if you prefer to follow conventional servicing intervals, the coolant should be changed as follows.*

⚠️ *Warning: Refer to Chapter 3 and observe the warnings given. In particular, never remove the*

27.3 Radiator drain plug (shown with radiator removed)

expansion tank filler cap when the engine is running, or has just been switched off, as the cooling system will be hot, and the consequent escaping steam and scalding coolant could cause serious injury. If the engine is hot, the electric cooling fan may start rotating even if the engine is not running, so be careful to keep hands, hair and loose clothing well clear when working in the engine compartment.

Cooling system draining

⚠️ *Warning: Wait until the engine is cold before starting this procedure.*

1 To drain the system, first remove the expansion tank filler cap. Place a thick cloth over the expansion tank cap, then turn the cap anti-clockwise as far as the first stop and wait for any pressure to be released, then depress it and turn it further anti-clockwise to remove it.

2 If additional working clearance is required, apply the handbrake, then jack up the front of the vehicle and support it on axle stands (see *Jacking and vehicle support*).

3 Remove the radiator undershield, then place a large drain tray underneath, and unscrew the radiator drain plug (see illustration). Allow the coolant to drain into the tray. On completion, retighten the drain plug and refit the undershield. Where necessary, lower the vehicle to the ground.

Cooling system flushing

4 If coolant renewal has been neglected, or if the antifreeze mixture has become diluted, then in time, the cooling system may gradually lose efficiency, as the coolant passages become restricted due to rust, scale deposits, and other sediment. The cooling system efficiency can be restored by flushing the system clean.

5 The radiator should be flushed

independently of the engine, to avoid unnecessary contamination.

Radiator flushing

6 Disconnect the top and bottom hoses and any other relevant hoses from the radiator, with reference to Chapter 3.

7 Insert a garden hose into the radiator top inlet. Direct a flow of clean water through the radiator, and continue flushing until clean water emerges from the radiator bottom outlet.

8 If after a reasonable period, the water still does not run clear, the radiator can be flushed with a good proprietary cleaning agent. It is important that the manufacturer's instructions are followed carefully. If the contamination is particularly bad, remove the radiator, insert the hose in the radiator bottom outlet, and reverse-flush the radiator.

Engine flushing

9 Remove the thermostat as described in Chapter 3 then, if the radiator top hose has been disconnected from the engine, temporarily reconnect the hose.

10 With the top and bottom hoses disconnected from the radiator, insert a garden hose into the radiator top hose. Direct a clean flow of water through the engine, and continue flushing until clean water emerges from the radiator bottom hose.

11 On completion of flushing, refit the thermostat and reconnect the hoses with reference to Chapter 3.

Cooling system filling

12 Before attempting to fill the cooling system, make sure that all hoses and clips are in good condition, and that the clips are tight. Note that an antifreeze mixture must be used all year round, to prevent corrosion of the engine components.

13 Slowly fill the system until the coolant level reaches the MAX mark on the side of the expansion tank.

1.8 and 2.0 litre engine models

14 With the filler cap not fitted, start the engine and run it at 2500 rpm for 10 seconds – this will prime the heater circuit.

15 Switch off the engine, then fill the expansion tank to 15 mm over the MAX mark.

16 Refit the filler cap, then start the engine and run it at 2500 rpm for 8 minutes, or until the engine reaches normal operating temperature.

17 Maintain the engine speed at 2500 rpm for a further 3 minutes, then increase the engine speed to 4000 rpm for 5 seconds.

18 Decrease the engine speed to 2500 rpm for 3 minutes and switch off the engine.

19 Check the cooling system for leaks, then allow the engine to cool for at least 30 minutes.

20 Remove the filler cap and top-up the coolant level to the MAX mark on the expansion tank.

2.5 litre V6 engine models

21 Refit expansion tank filler cap.

22 Start the engine and allow it to idle until it reaches its normal operating temperature.

23 Allow the engine to idle for a further 5 minutes, then switch it off.

24 Allow the engine to cool for at least 30 minutes.

25 Remove the filler cap and top-up the coolant level to the MAX mark on the expansion tank.

Antifreeze mixture

26 Ford state that, if the only antifreeze used is the type with which the system was first filled at the factory (see *Lubricants and fluids*) it will last the lifetime of the vehicle. This is subject to it being used in the recommended concentration, unmixed with any other type of antifreeze or additive, and topped-up when necessary using only that antifreeze mixed with clean water. If any other type of antifreeze is added, the lifetime guarantee no longer applies; to restore the lifetime protection, the system must be drained and thoroughly reverse-flushed before fresh coolant mixture is poured in.

27 If the vehicle's history (and therefore the quality of the antifreeze in it) is unknown, owners who wish to follow Ford's recommendations are advised to drain and thoroughly reverse-flush the system, before refilling with fresh coolant mixture. If the appropriate quality of antifreeze is used, the coolant can then be left for the life of the vehicle.

28 If any antifreeze other than Ford's is to be used, the coolant must be renewed at regular intervals to provide an equivalent degree of protection; the conventional recommendation is to renew the coolant every three years.

29 If the antifreeze used is to Ford's specification, the levels of protection it affords are indicated in the Specifications Section of this Chapter. To give the recommended

standard mixture ratio for this antifreeze, 40% (by volume) of antifreeze must be mixed with 60% of clean, soft water; if you are using any other type of antifreeze, follow its manufacturer's instructions to achieve the correct ratio.

30 It is best to make up slightly more than the system's specified capacity, so that a supply is available for subsequent topping-up. However, note that you are unlikely to fully drain the system at any one time (unless the engine is being completely stripped), and the capacities quoted are therefore slightly academic for routine coolant renewal.

31 Before adding antifreeze, the cooling system should be completely drained, preferably flushed, and all hoses checked for condition and security. Fresh antifreeze will rapidly find any weaknesses in the system.

32 After filling with antifreeze, a label should be attached to the expansion tank, stating the type and concentration of antifreeze used, and the date installed. Any subsequent topping-up should be made with the same type and concentration of antifreeze. If topping-up using antifreeze to Ford's specification, note that a 50/50 mixture is permissible, purely for convenience.

33 Do not use engine antifreeze in the windscreen/tailgate washer system, as it will damage the vehicle's paintwork. A screenwash additive should be added to the washer system in its maker's recommended quantities.

Every 50 000 miles or 4 years

28 Fuel filter renewal

Note: The work in this Section is not a Ford recommendation.

⚠️ **Warning: Before carrying out the following operation, refer to the precautions given in 'Safety first!' at the beginning of this manual and follow them implicitly. Petrol is a highly dangerous and volatile liquid and the precautions necessary when handling it cannot be overstressed.**

1 The fuel filter is located by the front right-hand corner of the fuel tank, just forward of the vehicle's right-hand rear jacking point **(see illustration)**. The filter performs a vital role in keeping dirt and other foreign matter out of the fuel system, and so must be renewed at regular intervals, or whenever you have reason to suspect that it may be clogged.

2 Before disturbing any fuel lines, which may contain fuel under pressure, any residual pressure in the system must be relieved as follows.

3 With the ignition switched off, open the engine compartment fusebox and remove the fuel pump fuse.

4 Start the engine, if possible – if the engine will not start, turn it over on the starter for a few seconds.

5 If the engine starts, allow it to idle until it stalls. Turn the engine over once or twice on the starter, to ensure that all pressure is released, then switch off the ignition.

⚠️ **Warning: This procedure will merely relieve the increased pressure necessary for the engine to run – remember that fuel will still be present in the system components, and take precautions accordingly before disconnecting any of them.**

6 Disconnect the battery negative lead (refer to *Disconnecting the battery* at the end of this manual).

7 Jack up the rear right-hand side of the vehicle, and support it securely on an axle stand.

8 Using rag to soak up any spilt fuel, release the fuel feed and outlet pipe unions from the filter, by squeezing together the protruding locking lugs on each union, and carefully pulling the union off the filter stub **(see illustration)**. Where the unions are colour-coded, the feed and outlet pipes cannot be confused; where both unions are the same colour, note carefully which pipe is connected to which filter stub, and ensure that they are correctly reconnected on refitting.

28.1 Fuel filter location in front of the right-hand side of the fuel tank

28.8 Disconnecting the fuel lines from the fuel filter

28.9a Fuel filter bracket mounting bolts

28.9b Fuel filter clamp bolt

9 Noting the arrows and/or other markings on the filter showing the direction of fuel flow (towards the engine), unscrew the filter bracket to underbody bolts, withdraw the bracket, then slacken the clamp bolt and slide out the filter **(see illustrations)**. Note that the filter will still contain fuel; care should be taken, to avoid spillage and to minimise the risk of fire.

10 On installation, slide the filter into its clamp so that the arrow marked on it faces the same direction as noted when removing the old filter. Tighten the clamp bolt until the filter is just prevented from moving, then refit the bracket to the underbody and tighten the mounting bolts.
11 Slide each pipe union onto its (correct) respective filter stub, and press it down until the locking lugs click into their groove.
12 Refit the fuel pump fuse and reconnect the battery earth terminal, then switch the ignition on and off five times, to pressurise the system. Check for any sign of fuel leakage around the filter unions before lowering the vehicle to the ground and starting the engine.

29 Valve clearance check

Note: *This work applies to the 1.8 and 2.0 litre engines only.*
Refer to Chapter 2A.

30 Auxiliary drivebelt renewal

Refer to Section 5.

Chapter 1 Part B:
Routine maintenance and servicing – diesel engine models

Contents

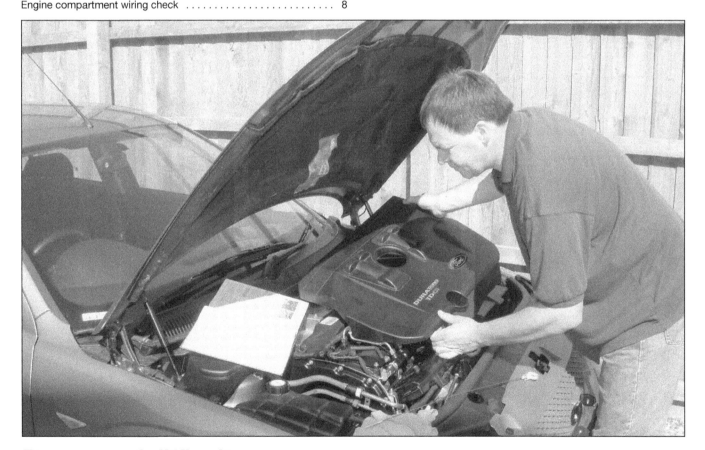

Degrees of difficulty

Easy, suitable for novice with little experience	**Fairly easy,** suitable for beginner with some experience	**Fairly difficult,** suitable for competent DIY mechanic	**Difficult,** suitable for experienced DIY mechanic	**Very difficult,** suitable for expert DIY or professional

Lubricants and fluids

Refer to the end of *Weekly checks* on page 0•18

Capacities

Engine oil:

With filter	6.01 litres
Without filter	5.81 litres
Difference between dipstick minimum and maximum marks	2.0 litres

Cooling system (including heating):

With standard heater	10.4 litres
With auxiliary heater	10.6 litres
Fuel tank	58.5 litres
Manual transmission	1.9 litres

Automatic transmission:

4-speed transmission (CD4E):

Total, including fluid cooler	7.5 litres
Drain and refill	6.0 litres
5-speed transmission (Durashift 5-tronic)	8.8 litres

Cooling system

Coolant protection at 40% antifreeze/water mixture ratio:

Slush point	–25°C (–13°F)
Solidifying point	–30°C (–22°F)

Braking system

Note: *No minimum lining thicknesses are given by Ford – the following is given as a general recommendation.*

Minimum front or rear brake pad lining thickness .... 1.5 mm

Torque wrench settings

	Nm	lbf ft
Automatic transmission drain plug:		
4-speed	27	20
5-speed	45	33
Automatic transmission filler plug (5-speed)	45	33
Automatic transmission selector lever cable cover (5-speed)	22	16
Automatic transmission test plug (5-speed)	15	11
Engine oil drain plug	23	17
Manual transmission filler/level/drain plug	45	33
Roadwheel nuts	85	63

The maintenance intervals in this manual are provided with the assumption that you, not the dealer, will be carrying out the work. These are the minimum maintenance intervals recommended by us for vehicles driven daily. If you wish to keep your vehicle in peak condition at all times, you may wish to perform some of these procedures more often. We encourage frequent maintenance, because it enhances the efficiency, performance and resale value of your vehicle.

If the vehicle is driven in dusty areas, used to tow a trailer, or driven frequently at slow speeds (idling in traffic) or on short journeys, more frequent maintenance intervals are recommended.

When the vehicle is new, it should be serviced by a factory-authorised dealer service department, in order to preserve the factory warranty.

Note that the service interval for vehicles manufactured up to (and including) 07/2001 is 10 000 miles, whereas for vehicles manufactured from 08/2001-on, the interval is 12 500 miles.

Models manufactured up to (and including) 07/2001 *

* Refer to the service schedule supplied with the car handbook if in doubt as to the month of manufacture which, in most cases, will be different to the date of registration. If the schedule has been mislaid, then contact your local Ford dealer with the 17 digit VIN (Vehicle Identification Number) and they will be able to tell you the exact month your vehicle was built. See page REF•3 for details of where to find the VIN.

Every 250 miles (400 km) or weekly
☐ Refer to *Weekly checks*

Every 5000 miles or 6 months, whichever occurs first
☐ Renew engine oil and filter (Section 3)
Note: *Frequent oil and filter changes are good for the engine. We recommend changing the oil at the mileage specified here, or at least twice a year if the mileage covered is a less.*

Every 10 000 miles or 12 months, whichever occurs first
In addition to the item listed in the previous service, carry out the following:
☐ Check the battery and clean the terminals (Section 4)
☐ Check the auxiliary drivebelt (Section 5)
☐ Check the electrical system (Section 6)
☐ Check under the bonnet for fluid leaks and hose condition (Section 7)
☐ Check the condition of all engine compartment wiring (Section 8)
☐ Check the condition of all air conditioning system components (Section 9)
☐ Check the seat belts (Section 10)
☐ Check the antifreeze concentration (Section 11)
☐ Check the steering, suspension and roadwheels (Section 12)
☐ Check the driveshaft rubber gaiters and CV joints (Section 13)
☐ Check the exhaust system (Section 14)
☐ Check the underbody, and all fuel/brake lines (Section 15)
☐ Check the braking system (Section 16)
☐ Check the doors and bonnet, and lubricate their hinges and locks (Section 17)
☐ Renew the ventilation system pollen filter (Section 18)
☐ Check the security of all roadwheel nuts (Section 19)
☐ Road test (Section 20)

Every 20 000 miles or 2 years, whichever occurs first
In addition to the relevant items listed in the previous services, carry out the following:
☐ Check the automatic transmission fluid level (Section 21)
☐ Renew the fuel filter (Section 22)

Every 30 000 miles or 3 years, whichever occurs first
☐ Check the glow plugs (Section 23)
☐ Renew the air filter element (Section 24). Note that this task must be carried out at more frequent intervals if the vehicle is used in dusty or polluted conditions
☐ Check the manual transmission oil level (Section 25)
☐ Renew the automatic transmission fluid (Section 26). Note that this task applies to vehicles used in severe conditions only (short trips of less than 10 miles in freezing conditions, extensive idling, towing a trailer, operating off-road)

Every 3 years (regardless of mileage)
☐ Renew the brake fluid (Section 27)
☐ Renew the coolant (Section 28)

Every 50 000 miles
In addition to the relevant items listed in the previous services, carry out the following:
☐ Renew the auxiliary drivebelt (Section 29)

Models manufactured from 08/2001-on *

* Refer to the service schedule supplied with the car handbook if in doubt as to the month of manufacture which, in most cases, will be different to the date of registration. If the schedule has been mislaid, then contact your local Ford dealer with the 17 digit VIN (Vehicle Identification Number) and they will be able to tell you the exact month your vehicle was built. See page REF•3 for details of where to find the VIN.

Every 250 miles (400 km) or weekly
☐ Refer to *Weekly checks*

Every 6250 miles or 6 months, whichever occurs first
☐ Renew the engine oil and filter (Section 3)
Note: *Frequent oil and filter changes are good for the engine. We recommend changing the oil at the mileage specified here, or at least twice a year if the mileage covered is a less.*

Every 12 500 miles or 12 months, whichever occurs first
In addition to the item listed in the previous service, carry out the following:
☐ Check the battery and clean the terminals (Section 4)
☐ Check the auxiliary drivebelt (Section 5)
☐ Check the electrical system (Section 6)
☐ Check under the bonnet for fluid leaks and hose condition (Section 7)
☐ Check the condition of all engine compartment wiring (Section 8)
☐ Check the condition of all air conditioning system components (Section 9)
☐ Check the seat belts (Section 10)
☐ Check the antifreeze concentration (Section 11)
☐ Check the steering, suspension and roadwheels (Section 12)
☐ Check the driveshaft rubber gaiters and CV joints (Section 13)
☐ Check the exhaust system (Section 14)
☐ Check the underbody, and all fuel/brake lines (Section 15)
☐ Check the braking system (Section 16)
☐ Check the doors and bonnet, and lubricate their hinges and locks (Section 17)
☐ Renew the ventilation system pollen filter (Section 18)
☐ Check the security of all roadwheel nuts (Section 19)
☐ Road test (Section 20)

Every 25 000 miles or 2 years, whichever occurs first
In addition to the relevant items listed in the previous services, carry out the following:
☐ Check the automatic transmission fluid level (Section 21)
☐ Renew the fuel filter (Section 22)

Every 37 500 miles or 3 years, whichever occurs first
In addition to the relevant items listed in the previous services, carry out the following:
☐ Check the glow plugs (Section 23)
☐ Renew the air filter element (Section 24). Note that this task must be carried out at more frequent intervals if the vehicle is used in dusty or polluted conditions
☐ Check the manual transmission oil level (Section 25)
☐ Renew the automatic transmission fluid (Section 26). Note that this task applies to vehicles used in severe conditions only (short trips of less than 10 miles in freezing conditions, extensive idling, towing a trailer, operating off-road)

Every 3 years (regardless of mileage)
☐ Renew the brake fluid (Section 27)
☐ Renew the coolant (Section 28)

Every 50 000 miles
In addition to the relevant items listed in the previous services, carry out the following:
☐ Renew the auxiliary drivebelt (Section 29)

Underbonnet view of a 2.0 litre turbocharged diesel

1 Engine oil filler cap
2 Engine oil dipstick
3 Power steering hydraulic
   fluid reservoir
4 Washer fluid reservoir
5 Coolant expansion tank
   filler cap
6 Front suspension strut
   upper mounting
7 Fuel filter
8 Fuel injectors
9 Common fuel rail
10 Brake fluid reservoir
11 Air mass meter
12 Air cleaner
13 Battery
14 Brake vacuum pump

Front underview of a 2.0 litre turbocharged diesel

1 Engine oil filter
2 Engine oil drain plug
3 Manual transmission filler
   plug
4 Brake lines
5 Fuel supply and return
   lines
6 Front subframe
7 Steering track rods
8 Front suspension lower
   arms
9 Front brake calipers
10 Driveshafts
11 Manual transmission
12 Engine rear
   mounting/torque link
13 Front exhaust pipe
14 Cooling system auxiliary
   heater

Rear underbody view - Saloon and Hatchback models

1 Fuel tank
2 Exhaust pipe
3 Handbrake cables
4 Rear anti-roll bar
5 Rear suspension front lower arm
6 Rear suspension rear lower arm
7 Rear suspension crossmember
8 Spare wheel well

Rear underbody view - Estate models

1 Fuel tank
2 Rear suspension brace
3 Rear suspension tie bar/knuckle
4 Handbrake cables
5 Rear suspension front lower arms
6 Rear suspension struts
7 Rear suspension lower arms
8 Rear anti-roll bar
9 Rear anti-roll bar link lower mountings
10 Rear suspension crossmember
11 Rear exhaust system
12 Spare wheel well

1 General information

1 This Chapter is designed to help the home mechanic maintain his/her vehicle for safety, economy, long life and peak performance.

2 The Chapter contains a master maintenance schedule, followed by Sections dealing specifically with each task in the schedule. Visual checks, adjustments, component renewal and other helpful items are included. Refer to the accompanying illustrations of the engine compartment and the underside of the vehicle for the locations of the various components.

3 Servicing your vehicle in accordance with the mileage/time maintenance schedule and the following Sections will provide a planned maintenance programme, which should result in a long and reliable service life. This is a comprehensive plan, so maintaining some items but not others at the specified service intervals, will not produce the same results.

4 As you service your vehicle, you will discover that many of the procedures can – and should – be grouped together, because of the particular procedure being performed, or because of the proximity of two otherwise-unrelated components to one another. For example, if the vehicle is raised for any reason, the exhaust can be inspected at the same time as the suspension and steering components.

5 The first step in this maintenance programme is to prepare yourself before the actual work begins. Read through all the Sections relevant to the work to be carried out, then make a list and gather all the parts and tools required. If a problem is encountered, seek advice from a parts specialist, or a dealer service department.

2 Regular maintenance

1 If, from the time the vehicle is new, the routine maintenance schedule is followed closely, and frequent checks are made of fluid levels and high-wear items, as suggested throughout this manual, the engine will be kept in relatively good running condition, and the need for additional work will be minimised.

2 It is possible that there will be times when the engine is running poorly due to the lack of regular maintenance. This is even more likely if a used vehicle, which has not received regular and frequent maintenance checks, is purchased. In such cases, additional work may need to be carried out, outside of the regular maintenance intervals.

3 If engine wear is suspected, a compression test or leakdown test (refer to Chapter 2C) will provide valuable information regarding the overall performance of the main internal components. Such a test can be used as a basis to decide on the extent of the work to be carried out. If, for example, a compression or leakdown test indicates serious internal engine wear, conventional maintenance as described in this Chapter will not greatly improve the performance of the engine, and may prove a waste of time and money, unless extensive overhaul work is carried out first.

4 The following series of operations are those most often required to improve the performance of a generally poor-running engine:

Primary operations

a) Clean, inspect and test the battery (See 'Weekly checks' and Section 4).
b) Check all the engine-related fluids (refer to 'Weekly checks').
c) Check the condition and tension of the auxiliary drivebelt (Section 5).
d) Check the condition of all hoses, and check for fluid leaks (Sections 7 and 15).
e) Renew the fuel filter (Section 22).
f) Check the glow plugs (Section 23).
g) Check the condition of the air filter, and renew if necessary (Section 24).

5 If the above operations do not prove fully effective, carry out the following secondary operations:

Secondary operations

All items listed under *Primary operations*, plus the following:

a) Check the charging system (refer to Chapter 5A).
b) Check the preheating system (refer to Chapter 5C).
c) Check the fuel system (refer to Chapter 4B).

Every 5000 miles (6250 from 08/2001) or 6 months

3 Engine oil and filter renewal

1 Frequent oil changes are the most important preventive maintenance the DIY home mechanic can give the engine, because ageing oil becomes diluted and contaminated, which leads to premature engine wear.

2 Before starting this procedure, gather together all the necessary tools and materials. Also make sure that you have plenty of clean rags and newspapers handy, to mop up any spills. Ideally, the engine oil will be warm, as it will drain more easily and more built-up sludge will be removed with it. Take care not to touch the exhaust or any other hot parts of the engine when working under the vehicle. To avoid any possibility of scalding and to protect yourself from possible skin irritants and other harmful contaminants in used engine oils, it is advisable to wear gloves when carrying out this work.

3 Firmly apply the handbrake then jack up the front of the car and support it on axle stands (see *Jacking and vehicle support*). Where applicable, remove the engine undershield.

4 Remove the oil filler cap, then unscrew the engine oil drain plug (located at the lowest point of the sump) about half a turn. Position the draining container under the drain plug, then remove the plug completely – recover the sealing washer **(see illustration and Haynes Hint)**.

5 Allow some time for the oil to drain, noting that it may be necessary to reposition the container as the oil flow slows to a trickle.

6 After all the oil has drained, wipe off the drain plug with a clean rag, and fit a new sealing washer. Clean the area around the drain plug opening, and refit the plug. Tighten the plug to the specified torque.

3.4 Removing the engine oil drain plug

Keep the plug pressed into the sump while unscrewing it by hand the last couple of turns. As the plug releases from the threads, move it away sharply, so the stream of oil issuing from the sump runs into the pan, not up your sleeve.

3.8a Unscrew the oil filter housing cover . . .

3.8b . . . and discard the paper element

3.9 Removing the O-ring seal

7 Move the container into position under the oil filter, which is located on the front side of the cylinder block.

8 Unscrew the oil filter plastic cover from the bottom of the oil filter housing, then remove and discard the paper element **(see illustrations)**.

9 Remove the O-ring seal and obtain a new one **(see illustration)**. Clean the filter housing and cover.

10 Fit the new O-ring seal onto the cover and lubricate it with a little engine oil.

11 Locate the new paper element on the cover, then screw the assembly into the filter housing and tighten securely by hand. Where necessary, refit the splash guard under the engine.

12 Remove the old oil and all tools from under the car, then lower the car to the ground.

13 Remove the dipstick, then unscrew the oil filler cap from the cylinder head cover. Fill the engine, using the correct grade and type of oil (*see Weekly checks*). An oil can spout or funnel may help to reduce spillage. Pour in half the specified quantity of oil first, then wait a few minutes for the oil to fall to the sump. Continue adding oil a small quantity at a time until the level is up to the lower mark on the dipstick. Refit the filler cap.

14 Start the engine and run it for a few minutes; check for leaks. Note that there may be a delay of a few seconds before the oil pressure warning light goes out when the engine is first started, as the oil circulates through the engine oil galleries and the new oil filter before the pressure builds-up.

15 Switch off the engine, and wait a few minutes for the oil to settle in the sump once more. With the new oil circulated and the filter completely full, recheck the level on the dipstick, and add more oil as necessary.

16 Dispose of the used engine oil safely, with reference to *General Repair Procedures*.

Every 10 000 miles (12 500 from 08/2001) or 12 months

4 Battery maintenance and charging

> ⚠ *Warning: Certain precautions must be followed when checking and servicing the battery. Hydrogen gas, which is highly flammable, is always present in the battery cells, so keep lighted tobacco and all other open flames and sparks away from the battery. The electrolyte inside the battery is actually dilute sulphuric acid, which will cause injury if splashed on your skin or in your eyes. It will also ruin clothes and painted surfaces. When disconnecting the battery, always detach the negative (earth) lead first and connect it last.*

Note: *Before disconnecting the battery, refer to 'Disconnecting the battery' at the end of this manual.*

General

1 A routine preventive maintenance programme for the battery in your vehicle is the only way to ensure quick and reliable starts. For general maintenance, refer to *Weekly checks* at the start of this manual. Also at the front of the manual is information on jump starting. For details of removing and installing the battery, refer to Chapter 5A.

Battery electrolyte level

2 On models not equipped with a sealed or 'maintenance-free' battery, check the electrolyte level of all six battery cells.

3 The level must be approximately 10 mm above the plates; this may be shown by maximum and minimum level lines marked on the battery's casing.

4 If the level is low, use a coin or screwdriver to release the filler/vent cap, and add distilled water. To improve access to the centre caps, it may be helpful to remove the battery hold-down clamp.

5 Install and securely retighten the cap, then wipe up any spillage.

Caution: Overfilling the cells may cause electrolyte to spill over during periods of heavy charging, causing corrosion or damage.

Charging

> ⚠ *Warning: When batteries are being charged, hydrogen gas, which is very explosive and flammable, is produced. Do not smoke, or allow open flames, near a charging or a recently-charged battery. Wear eye protection when near the battery during charging. Also, make sure the charger is unplugged before connecting or disconnecting the battery from the charger.*

6 Slow-rate charging is the best way to restore a battery that's discharged to the point where it will not start the engine. It's also a good way to maintain the battery charge in a vehicle that's only driven a few miles between starts. Maintaining the battery charge is particularly important in winter, when the battery must work harder to start the engine, and electrical accessories that drain the battery are in greater use.

7 Check the battery case for any instructions regarding charging the battery. Some maintenance-free batteries may require a particularly low charge rate or other special conditions, if they are not to be damaged.

8 It's best to use a one- or two-amp battery charger (sometimes called a 'trickle' charger). They are the safest, and put the least strain on the battery. They are also the least expensive. For a faster charge, you can use a higher-amperage charger, but don't use one rated more than 1/10th the amp/hour rating of the battery (ie, no more than 5 amps, typically). Rapid boost charges that claim to restore the power of the battery in one to two hours are hardest on the battery, and can damage batteries not in good condition. This type of charging should only be used in emergency situations.

9 The average time necessary to charge a battery should be listed in the instructions that come with the charger. As a general rule, a trickle charger will charge a battery in 12 to 16 hours.

5 Auxiliary drivebelt check

Note: *The work in this Section is not a Ford recommendation at this time interval, however, we recommend renewing the drivebelt at 50 000 miles.*

General

1 The main auxiliary drivebelt is of flat, multi-ribbed type, and is located on the right-hand end of the engine. It drives the alternator and air conditioning compressor from the engine's crankshaft pulley. A separate multi-ribbed drivebelt drives the water pump from the left-hand end of the inlet camshaft **(see illustrations)**.
2 The good condition and proper tension of the auxiliary drivebelt(s) is critical to the operation of the engine. They must, therefore, be regularly inspected.

Check

3 With the engine switched off, open and support the bonnet. For improved access to the right-hand end of the engine, first loosen the right-hand front wheel nuts, then jack up the front right-hand side of the vehicle and support it securely on an axle stand. Remove the roadwheel, then remove the auxiliary drivebelt cover (two fasteners) from inside the wheel arch. Remove the engine undertray. If necessary, also remove the front section of the inner wheel arch liner, which is secured by two further bolts.
4 Using an inspection light or a small electric torch, and rotating the engine with a spanner applied to the crankshaft pulley bolt, check the whole length of the drivebelt for cracks, separation of the rubber, and torn or worn ribs. Also check for fraying and glazing, which gives the drivebelt a shiny appearance.
5 Both sides of the drivebelt should be inspected, which means you will have to twist the drivebelt to check the underside. Use your fingers to feel the drivebelt where you can't see it. If you are in any doubt as to the condition of the drivebelt, renew it as described below.
6 In addition, remove the water pump drivebelt cover from the top of the engine. Inspect the drivebelt as described in paragraphs 4 and 5.

Drivebelt tension

7 The auxiliary drivebelt is tensioned by an automatic tensioner; regular checks are not required, and manual 'adjustment' is not possible.
8 If you suspect that the drivebelt is slipping and/or running slack, or that the tensioner is otherwise faulty, it must be renewed.

Drivebelt renewal

Note: *The alternator and bracket will have to be unbolted and moved to allow the belt to be removed.*

9 Gain access to the drivebelt as described in paragraph 3 or 6, as applicable.
10 If the existing drivebelt is to be refitted, mark it, or note the maker's markings on its flat surface, so that it can be installed the same way round.
11 Rotate the tensioner pulley clockwise to release its pressure on the drivebelt. Depending on model and equipment, the tensioner will either have a hex fitting for a spanner or socket, or a square hole into which a ratchet handle from a socket set can be fitted.
12 Slip the drivebelt off the drive pulley, and release the tensioner again. Working from the wheel arch or engine compartment as necessary, and noting its routing, slip the drivebelt off the remaining pulleys and withdraw it.
13 Check all the pulleys, ensuring that their grooves are clean, and removing all traces of oil and grease. Check that the tensioner works properly, with strong spring pressure being felt when its pulley is rotated clockwise, and a smooth return to the limit of its travel when released.

5.1a Main auxiliary drivebelt routing

1 Idler pulley	4 Air conditioning	6 Crankshaft pulley
2 Tensioner pulley	compressor pulley	7 Alternator pulley
3 Idler pulley	5 Auxiliary drivebelt	

5.1b Water pump drivebelt routing

1 Tensioner pulley	3 Auxiliary drivebelt
2 Camshaft pulley	4 Power steering pump pulley

A leak in the cooling system will usually show up as white- or rust-coloured deposits on the area adjoining the leak.

14 If the original drivebelt is being refitted, use the marks or notes made on removal, to ensure that it is installed to run in the same direction as it was previously. To fit the drivebelt, arrange it on the grooved pulleys so that it is centred in their grooves, and not overlapping their raised sides (note that the flat surface of the drivebelt is engaged on one or more pulleys) and routed correctly. Start at the top, and work down to finish at the bottom pulley; rotate the tensioner pulley clockwise, slip the drivebelt onto the bottom pulley, then release the tensioner again.

15 Using a spanner applied to the crankshaft pulley bolt, rotate the crankshaft through at least two full turns clockwise to settle the drivebelt on the pulleys, then check that the drivebelt is properly installed.

16 Refit the components removed for access, then lower the vehicle to the ground. Refit the roadwheel and tighten the wheel nuts to the specified torque.

6 Electrical system check

1 Check the operation of all external lights and indicators (front and rear).
2 Check for satisfactory operation of the instrument panel, its illumination and warning lights, the switches and their function lights.
3 Check the horn(s) for satisfactory operation.
4 Check all other electrical equipment for satisfactory operation.

7 Underbonnet check for fluid leaks and hose condition

1 Visually inspect the engine joint faces, gaskets and seals for any signs of water or oil leaks. Pay particular attention to the areas around the cylinder head cover, cylinder head, oil filter and sump joint faces. Bear in mind that, over a period of time, some very slight seepage from these areas is to be expected – what you are really looking for is any indication of a

serious leak. Should a leak be found, renew the offending gasket or oil seal by referring to the appropriate Chapters in this manual.
2 Also check the security and condition of all the engine-related pipes and hoses, and all braking system pipes and hoses and fuel lines. Ensure that all cable ties or securing clips are in place, and in good condition. Clips which are broken or missing can lead to chafing of the hoses, pipes or wiring, which could cause more serious problems in the future.
3 Carefully check the radiator hoses and heater hoses along their entire length. Renew any hose which is cracked, swollen or deteriorated. Cracks will show up better if the hose is squeezed. Pay close attention to the hose clips that secure the hoses to the cooling system components. Hose clips can pinch and puncture hoses, resulting in cooling system leaks. If the crimped-type hose clips are used, it may be a good idea to replace them with standard worm-drive clips.
4 Inspect all the cooling system components (hoses, joint faces, etc) for leaks **(see Haynes Hint)**.
5 Where any problems are found on system components, renew the component or gasket with reference to Chapter 3.
6 With the vehicle raised, inspect the fuel tank and filler neck for punctures, cracks and other damage. The connection between the filler neck and tank is especially critical. Sometimes a rubber filler neck or connecting hose will leak due to loose retaining clamps or deteriorated rubber.
7 Carefully check all rubber hoses and metal fuel lines leading away from the fuel tank. Check for loose connections, deteriorated hoses, crimped lines, and other damage. Pay particular attention to the vent pipes and hoses, which often loop up around the filler neck and can become blocked or crimped. Follow the lines to the front of the vehicle, carefully inspecting them all the way. Renew damaged sections as necessary. Similarly, whilst the vehicle is raised, take the opportunity to inspect all underbody brake fluid pipes and hoses.
8 From within the engine compartment, check the security of all fuel, vacuum and brake hose attachments and pipe unions, and inspect all hoses for kinks, chafing and deterioration.
9 Check the condition of the power steering and, where applicable, the automatic transmission fluid pipes and hoses.

8 Engine compartment wiring check

1 With the vehicle parked on level ground, apply the handbrake firmly and open the bonnet. Using an inspection light or a small electric torch, check all visible wiring within and beneath the engine compartment.
2 What you are looking for is wiring that is

obviously damaged by chafing against sharp edges, or against moving suspension/transmission components and/or the auxiliary drivebelt, by being trapped or crushed between carelessly-refitted components, or melted by being forced into contact with the hot engine castings, coolant pipes, etc. In almost all cases, damage of this sort is caused in the first instance by incorrect routing on reassembly after previous work has been carried out.
3 Depending on the extent of the problem, damaged wiring may be repaired by rejoining the break or splicing-in a new length of wire, using solder to ensure a good connection, and remaking the insulation with adhesive insulating tape or heat-shrink tubing, as appropriate. If the damage is extensive, given the implications for the vehicle's future reliability, the best long-term answer may well be to renew that entire section of the loom, however expensive this may appear.
4 When the actual damage has been repaired, ensure that the wiring loom is rerouted correctly, so that it is clear of other components, and not stretched or kinked, and is secured out of harm's way using the plastic clips, guides and ties provided.
5 Check all electrical connectors, ensuring that they are clean, securely fastened, and that each is locked by its plastic tabs or wire clip, as appropriate. If any connector shows external signs of corrosion (accumulations of white or green deposits, or streaks of 'rust'), or if any is thought to be dirty, it must be unplugged and cleaned using electrical contact cleaner. If the connector pins are severely corroded, the connector must be renewed; note that this may mean the renewal of that entire section of the loom – see your local Ford dealer for details.
6 If the cleaner completely removes the corrosion to leave the connector in a satisfactory condition, it would be wise to pack the connector with a suitable material which will exclude dirt and moisture, preventing the corrosion from occurring again; a Ford dealer may be able to recommend a suitable product.
7 Check the condition of the battery connections – remake the connections or renew the leads if a fault is found (see Chapter 5A). Use the same techniques to ensure that all earth points in the engine compartment provide good electrical contact through clean, metal-to-metal joints, and that all are securely fastened.

9 Air conditioning system check

1 The following maintenance checks will ensure that the air conditioner operates at peak efficiency:
  a) *Check the auxiliary drivebelt (see Section 5).*

b) *Check the system hoses for damage or leaks.*

c) *Inspect the condenser fins for leaves, insects and other debris. Use a clean paint brush to clean the condenser.*

d) *Check that the drain tube from the front of the evaporator is clear – note that it is normal to have clear fluid (water) dripping from this while the system is in operation, to the extent that quite a large puddle can be left under the vehicle when it is parked.*

2 It's a good idea to operate the system for about 30 minutes at least once a month, particularly during the winter. Long term non-use can cause hardening, and subsequent failure, of the seals.

3 Because of the complexity of the air conditioning system and the special equipment necessary to service it, in-depth fault diagnosis and repairs are not included in this manual.

4 The most common cause of poor cooling is simply a low system refrigerant charge. If a noticeable drop in cool air output occurs, the following quick check will help you determine if the refrigerant level is low.

5 Warm the engine up to normal operating temperature.

6 Place the air conditioning temperature selector at the coldest setting, and put the blower at the highest setting. Open the doors – to make sure the air conditioning system doesn't cycle off as soon as it cools the passenger compartment.

7 With the compressor engaged – the clutch will make an audible click, and the centre of the clutch will rotate – feel the inlet and outlet pipes at the compressor. One side should be cold, and one hot. If there's no perceptible difference between the two pipes, there's something wrong with the compressor or the system. It might be a low charge – it might be something else. Take the vehicle to a dealer service department or an automotive air conditioning specialist.

10 Seat belt check

1 Check the seat belts for satisfactory operation and condition. Inspect the webbing for fraying and cuts. Check that they retract smoothly and without binding into their reels.

2 Check that the seat belt mounting bolts are tight, and if necessary tighten them to the specified torque wrench setting (Chapter 11).

11 Antifreeze concentration check

1 The cooling system should be filled with the recommended antifreeze and corrosion protection fluid. Over a period of time, the concentration of fluid may be reduced due to topping-up (this can be avoided by topping-up

with the correct antifreeze mixture) or fluid loss. If loss of coolant has been evident, it is important to make the necessary repair before adding fresh fluid. The exact mixture of antifreeze-to-water which you should use depends on the relative weather conditions. The mixture should contain at least 40% antifreeze, but not more than 70%. Consult the mixture ratio chart on the antifreeze container before adding coolant. Use antifreeze which meets the vehicle manufacturer's specifications.

2 With the engine **cold**, carefully remove the cap from the expansion tank. If the engine is not completely cold, place a cloth rag over the cap before removing it, and remove it slowly to allow any pressure to escape.

3 Antifreeze checkers are available from car accessory shops. Draw some coolant from the expansion tank and observe how many plastic balls are floating in the checker. Usually, 2 or 3 balls must be floating for the correct concentration of antifreeze, but follow the manufacturer's instructions.

4 If the concentration is incorrect, it will be necessary to either withdraw some coolant and add antifreeze, or alternatively drain the old coolant and add fresh coolant of the correct concentration.

12 Steering, suspension and roadwheel check

Front suspension and steering

1 Raise the front of the vehicle, and securely support it on axle stands (see *Jacking and vehicle support*).

2 Visually inspect the balljoint dust covers and the steering rack-and-pinion gaiters for splits, chafing or deterioration. Any wear of these components will cause loss of lubricant, together with dirt and water entry, resulting in rapid deterioration of the balljoints or steering gear.

3 Check the power steering fluid hoses for chafing or deterioration, and the pipe and hose unions for fluid leaks. Also check for signs of fluid leakage under pressure from the steering gear rubber gaiters, which would indicate failed fluid seals within the steering gear.

4 Grasp the roadwheel at the 12 o'clock and 6 o'clock positions, and try to rock it **(see illustration)**. Very slight free play may be felt, but if the movement is appreciable, further investigation is necessary to determine the source. Continue rocking the wheel while an assistant depresses the footbrake. If the movement is now eliminated or significantly reduced, it is likely that the hub bearings are at fault. If the free play is still evident with the footbrake depressed, then there is wear in the suspension joints or mountings.

5 Now grasp the wheel at the 9 o'clock and 3 o'clock positions, and try to rock it as before. Any movement felt now may again be

caused by wear in the hub bearings or the steering track rod balljoints. If the outer balljoint is worn, the visual movement will be obvious. If the inner joint is suspect, it can be felt by placing a hand over the rack-and-pinion rubber gaiter and gripping the track rod. If the wheel is now rocked, movement will be felt at the inner joint if wear has taken place.

6 Using a large screwdriver or flat bar, check for wear in the suspension mounting bushes by levering between the relevant suspension component and its attachment point. Some movement is to be expected, as the mountings are made of rubber, but excessive wear should be obvious. Also check the condition of any visible rubber bushes, looking for splits, cracks or contamination of the rubber.

7 With the car standing on its wheels, have an assistant turn the steering wheel back-and-forth, about an eighth of a turn each way. There should be very little, if any, lost movement between the steering wheel and roadwheels. If this is not the case, closely observe the joints and mountings previously described. In addition, check the steering column universal joints for wear, and also check the rack-and-pinion steering gear itself.

Rear suspension

8 Chock the front wheels, then jack up the rear of the vehicle and support securely on axle stands (see *Jacking and vehicle support*).

9 Working as described previously for the front suspension, check the rear hub bearings, the suspension bushes and the strut or shock absorber mountings (as applicable) for wear.

Shock absorbers

10 Check for any signs of fluid leakage around the shock absorber body, or from the rubber gaiter around the piston rod. Should any fluid be noticed, the shock absorber is defective internally, and should be renewed. **Note:** *Shock absorbers should always be renewed in pairs on the same axle.*

11 The efficiency of the shock absorber may be checked by bouncing the vehicle at each corner. Generally speaking, the body will return to its normal position and stop after being depressed. If it rises and returns on a rebound,

12.4 Checking for wear in the front suspension and hub bearings

13.2 Check the driveshaft gaiters by hand for cracks and/or leaking grease

the shock absorber is probably suspect. Also examine the shock absorber upper and lower mountings for any signs of wear.

Roadwheels

12 Periodically remove the roadwheels, and clean any dirt or mud from the inside and outside surfaces. Examine the wheel rims for signs of rusting, corrosion or other damage. Light alloy wheels are easily damaged by 'kerbing' whilst parking, and similarly, steel wheels may become dented or buckled. Renewal of the wheel is very often the only course of remedial action possible.
13 The balance of each wheel and tyre assembly should be maintained, not only to avoid excessive tyre wear, but also to avoid wear in the steering and suspension components. Wheel imbalance is normally signified by vibration through the vehicle's bodyshell, although in many cases it is particularly noticeable through the steering wheel. Conversely, it should be noted that wear or damage in suspension or steering components may cause excessive tyre wear. Out-of-round or out-of-true tyres, damaged wheels and wheel bearing wear/malad-justment also fall into this category. Balancing will not usually cure vibration caused by such wear.
14 Wheel balancing may be carried out with the wheel either on or off the vehicle. If balanced on the vehicle, ensure that the wheel-to-hub relationship is marked in some way prior to subsequent wheel removal, so that it may be refitted in its original position.
15 At this time, also check the spare wheel for damage.

14.2 Check the condition of the exhaust system

13 Driveshaft rubber gaiter and CV joint check

1 The driveshaft rubber gaiters are very important, because they prevent dirt, water and foreign material from entering and damaging the constant velocity (CV) joints. External contamination can cause the gaiter material to deteriorate prematurely, so it's a good idea to wash the gaiters with soap and water occasionally.
2 With the vehicle raised and securely supported on axle stands, turn the steering onto full-lock, then slowly rotate each front wheel in turn. Inspect the condition of the outer constant velocity (CV) joint rubber gaiters, squeezing the gaiters to open out the folds **(see illustration)**. Check for signs of cracking, splits, or deterioration of the rubber, which may allow the escape of grease, and lead to the ingress of water and grit into the joint. Also check the security and condition of the retaining clips. Repeat these checks on the inner CV joints. If any damage or deterioration is found, the gaiters should be renewed as described in Chapter 8.
3 At the same time, check the general condition of the outer CV joints themselves, by first holding the driveshaft and attempting to rotate the wheels. Repeat this check on the inner joints, by holding the inner joint yoke and attempting to rotate the driveshaft.
4 Any appreciable movement in the CV joint indicates wear in the joint, wear in the driveshaft splines, or a loose driveshaft retaining nut.

14 Exhaust system check

1 With the engine cold, check the complete exhaust system, from its starting point at the engine to the end of the tailpipe. If necessary, raise the front and rear of the vehicle and support it on axle stands (see *Jacking and vehicle support*). Remove any engine undershields as necessary for full access to the exhaust system.
2 Check the exhaust pipes and connections for evidence of leaks, severe corrosion, and damage **(see illustration)**. Make sure that all brackets and mountings are in good condition and that all relevant nuts and bolts are tight. Leakage at any of the joints or in other parts of the system will usually show up as a black sooty stain in the vicinity of the leak.
3 Rattles and other noises can often be traced to the exhaust system, especially the brackets and rubber mountings. Try to move the pipes and silencers. If the components are able to come into contact with the body or suspension parts, secure the system with new mountings. Otherwise separate the joints (if possible) and twist the pipes as necessary to provide additional clearance.

15 Underbody and fuel/brake line check

1 With the vehicle raised and supported on axle stands (see *Jacking and vehicle support*), thoroughly inspect the underbody and wheel arches for signs of damage and corrosion. In particular, examine the bottom of the side sills, and any concealed areas where mud can collect.
2 Where corrosion and rust is evident, press and tap firmly on the panel with a screwdriver, and check for any serious corrosion which would necessitate repairs.
3 If the panel is not seriously corroded, clean away the rust, and apply a new coating of underseal. Refer to Chapter 11 for more details of body repairs.
4 At the same time, inspect the PVC-coated lower body panels for stone damage and general condition.
5 Inspect all of the fuel and brake lines on the underbody for damage, rust, corrosion and leakage. Also make sure that they are correctly supported in their clips. Where applicable, check the PVC coating on the lines for damage.

16 Braking system check

Front disc brakes

1 Apply the handbrake, then jack up the front of the vehicle and support it on axle stands (see *Jacking and vehicle support*). For better access to the brake calipers, remove the wheels.
2 Look through the inspection window in the caliper, and check that the thickness of the friction lining material on each of the pads is not less than the recommended minimum thickness given in the Specifications **(see illustration)**.
3 If it is difficult to determine the exact thickness of the pad linings, or if you are at all concerned about the condition of the pads, then remove them from the calipers for further

16.2 Check the thickness of the pad friction material through the caliper inspection window

inspection (refer to Chapter 9) **(see illustration)**.

4 Check the caliper on the other side in the same way.

5 If any one of the brake pads has worn down to, or below, the specified limit, *all four* pads at that end of the car must be renewed as a set.

6 Check both front brake discs with reference to Chapter 9.

7 Before refitting the wheels, check all brake lines and flexible hoses with reference to Chapter 9. In particular, check the flexible hoses in the vicinity of the calipers, where they are subjected to most movement. Bend them between the fingers and check that this does not reveal previously-hidden cracks, cuts or splits **(see illustration)**.

8 On completion, refit the wheels and lower the car to the ground. Tighten the wheel nuts to the specified torque.

Rear disc brakes

9 Chock the front wheels then jack up the rear of the vehicle and support on axle stands (see *Jacking and vehicle support*). Remove the rear wheels.

10 The procedure for checking the rear brakes is much the same as described in paragraphs 1 to 8 above.

Handbrake

11 With the vehicle on a slight slope, firmly apply the handbrake lever, and check that it holds the vehicle stationary, then release the lever and check that there is no resistance to movement of the vehicle. The handbrake lever incorporates a self-adjusting mechanism which automatically adjusts its total travel.

17 Door and bonnet check and lubrication

1 Check that the doors, bonnet and tailgate/boot lid close securely. Check that the bonnet safety catch operates correctly. Check the operation of the door check straps.

2 Lubricate the hinges, door check straps, the striker plates and the bonnet catch sparingly with a little oil or grease.

18 Ventilation system pollen filter renewal

1 The air entering the vehicle's ventilation system is passed through a very fine pleated-paper air filter element, which removes particles of pollen, dust and other airborne foreign matter. To ensure its continued effectiveness, this filter's element must be renewed at regular intervals. Failure to renew the element will also result in reduced airflow into the passenger compartment, reducing demisting and ventilation.

16.3 Checking the thickness of the pad linings with a steel rule

2 Remove the windscreen wiper arms as described in Chapter 12.

3 Unclip and remove the cowl sections from in front of the windscreen.

4 Release the retaining clips and withdraw the pollen filter from its housing **(see illustrations)**.

5 Wipe clean the housing, then insert the new filter and check that the clips are correctly engaged.

6 Refit the cowl sections and wiper arms with reference to Chapter 12.

19 Roadwheel nut tightness check

1 Apply the handbrake, chock the wheels, and engage 1st gear (or P).

2 Remove the wheel cover (or wheel centre cover), using the flat end of the wheel brace supplied in the tool kit.

3 Check the tightness of all wheel nuts using a torque wrench (refer to the Specifications).

20 Road test

Instruments and electrical equipment

1 Check the operation of all instruments and electrical equipment.

2 Make sure that all instruments read

18.4a Release the retaining clips . . .

16.7 Checking the condition of a flexible brake hose

correctly, and switch on all electrical equipment in turn, to check that it functions properly.

Steering and suspension

3 Check for any abnormalities in the steering, suspension, handling or road 'feel'.

4 Drive the vehicle, and check that there are no unusual vibrations or noises.

5 Check that the steering feels positive, with no excessive 'sloppiness', or roughness, and check for any suspension noises when cornering and driving over bumps.

Drivetrain

6 Check the performance of the engine, clutch, transmission and driveshafts.

7 Listen for any unusual noises from the engine, clutch and transmission.

8 Make sure that the engine runs smoothly when idling, and that there is no hesitation when accelerating.

9 Check that, where applicable, the clutch action is smooth and progressive, that the drive is taken up smoothly, and that the pedal travel is not excessive. Also listen for any noises when the clutch pedal is depressed.

10 Check that all gears can be engaged smoothly without noise, and that the gear lever action is smooth and not abnormally vague or 'notchy'.

11 On automatic transmission models, make sure that all gearchanges occur smoothly, without snatching, and without an increase in engine speed between changes. Check that all of the gear positions can be selected with the vehicle at rest.

18.4b . . . and withdraw the pollen filter from its housing

12 Listen for a metallic clicking sound from the front of the vehicle, as the vehicle is driven slowly in a circle with the steering on full-lock. Carry out this check in both directions. If a clicking noise is heard, this indicates wear in a driveshaft joint (see Chapter 8).

Braking system

13 Make sure that the vehicle does not pull to one side when braking, and that the wheels do not lock when braking hard.
14 Check that there is no vibration through the steering when braking.
15 Check that the handbrake operates correctly, without excessive movement of the lever, and that it holds the vehicle stationary on a slope.
16 Test the operation of the brake servo unit as follows. Depress the footbrake four or five times to exhaust the vacuum, then start the engine. As the engine starts, there should be a noticeable 'give' in the brake pedal as vacuum builds up. Allow the engine to run for at least two minutes, and then switch it off. If the brake pedal is now depressed again, it should be possible to detect a hiss from the servo as the pedal is depressed. After about four or five applications, no further hissing should be heard, and the pedal should feel considerably harder.

Every 20 000 miles (25 000 from 08/2001) or 2 years

21 Automatic transmission fluid level check

4-speed transmission

1 The level of the automatic transmission fluid should be carefully maintained. Low fluid level can lead to slipping or loss of drive, while overfilling can cause foaming, loss of fluid and transmission damage.
2 The transmission fluid level should only be checked when the transmission is hot (at its normal operating temperature). If the vehicle has just been driven over 10 miles (15 miles in cold weather), the transmission is hot. **Note:** *If the vehicle has just been driven for a long time at high speed or in city traffic in hot weather, or if it has been pulling a trailer, an accurate fluid level reading cannot be obtained. In these circumstances, allow the fluid to cool down for about 30 minutes.*
3 Park the vehicle on level ground, apply the handbrake firmly, and start the engine. While the engine is idling, depress the brake pedal and move the selector lever through all the positions three times, beginning and ending in P.
4 Allow the engine to idle, and remove the dipstick from its tube **(see illustration)**. Note the condition and colour of the fluid on the dipstick.
5 Wipe the fluid from the dipstick with a clean rag, and re-insert it into the filler tube until the cap seats.
6 Pull out the dipstick again, and note the fluid level. The level should be between the MIN and MAX marks **(see illustration)**.
7 If the level is on the MIN mark, stop the engine, and add the specified automatic transmission fluid through the dipstick tube, using a clean funnel if necessary **(see illustration)**. It is important not to introduce dirt into the transmission when topping-up.
8 Add the fluid a little at a time, and keep checking the level as previously described until it is correct.
9 The need for regular topping-up of the transmission fluid indicates a leak, which should be found and rectified without delay.
10 The condition of the fluid should also be checked along with the level. If the fluid at the end of the dipstick is black or a dark reddish-brown colour, or if it has a burned smell, the fluid should be changed. If you are in doubt about the condition of the fluid, purchase some new fluid, and compare the two for colour and smell.

5-speed transmission

11 To accurately check the fluid level on 5-speed automatic transmissions, a Ford diagnostic tool is necessary. The following paragraphs describe the procedure for the DIY home mechanic who has access to this tool. First connect the tool to the diagnostic socket.
12 The transmission fluid temperature must initially be below 30°C.
13 Apply the handbrake, then jack up the front of the vehicle and support it on axle stands (see *Jacking and vehicle support*). Unbolt the selector lever cable cover for access to the test plug, then lower the vehicle to the ground.
14 Start the engine. While the engine is idling, depress the brake pedal and move the selector lever through all the positions three times, beginning and ending in P. Leave the engine idling until while the fluid level is being checked.
15 When the fluid temperature reaches 30°C, move the selector lever from P to D, and back again to P.
16 With the handbrake applied, jack up the front and rear of the vehicle and support it on axle stands (see *Jacking and vehicle support*). **Note:** *The vehicle must be level for an accurate check.*
17 Check that the fluid temperature is between 35°C and 45°C.
18 Position a suitable container beneath the transmission, then unscrew and remove the test plug **(see illustration)**. The test plug is

21.4 Removing the automatic transmission dipstick from its tube (4-speed)

H34242

21.6 Transmission fluid dipstick MIN and MAX marks (4-speed)

| 1 | MAX mark | 3 | Lower hole mark |
| 2 | MIN mark | | (DO NOT DRIVE) |

21.7 Adding automatic transmission fluid through the dipstick tube (4-speed)

H34243

21.18 Test plug (5-speed)

22.1 The fuel filter is located in the right-hand rear corner of the engine compartment

22.3 Fuel filter quick-release fittings

22.4 Fuel filter retaining spring clip

located in the middle of the drain plug, and incorporates a tube extension to the fluid level height inside the transmission. Remove and discard the plug seal.
Caution: Wear suitable gloves as protection against scalding.
19 If no fluid escapes from the test plug, unscrew the filler plug from the top of the transmission and add fresh fluid until it emerges from the test hole. When the fluid ceases to drain, the level is correct.
20 Refit the filler and test plugs together with new seals and tighten to the specified torque. Refit the selector lever cable cover and tighten the bolts to the specified torque.
21 Switch off the engine and lower the vehicle to the ground.

22 Disconnect the diagnostic tool.

22 Fuel filter renewal

Note: *Before carrying out the following procedure, read carefully the precautions given in the appropriate Part of Chapter 4.*
1 The fuel filter is located in a mounting bracket on the right-hand rear corner of the engine compartment, next to the front suspension strut tower **(see illustration)**.
2 Note the location of the supply and return hoses on the filter, then place some cloth rags beneath it to catch any spilled fuel.

3 Disconnect the quick-release fittings from the filter and position them to one side **(see illustration)**. Be prepared for some loss of fuel.
4 Push back the spring clip from the top of the filter and remove it from the mounting bracket **(see illustration)**. The fuel filter is supplied as a single renewable unit, and cannot be dismantled.
5 Insert the new filter in the mounting bracket with its stubs in the previously-noted positions, then reconnect the hoses. Make sure that the quick-release fittings have engaged securely.
6 Wipe away any spilled fuel, then prime and bleed the fuel system with reference to Chapter 4B.

Every 30 000 miles (37 500 from 08/2001) or 3 years

23 Glow plug check

Refer to Chapter 5C.

24 Air filter element renewal

1 The air filter element is located in the air cleaner assembly on the left-hand side of the engine compartment, behind the battery. Undo the screws and lift up the air cleaner cover **(see illustration)**. If additional working clearance is required, remove the cover completely with reference to Chapter 4B.
2 Lift out the element, noting its direction of fitting, and wipe out the housing **(see illustration)**.
3 If carrying out a routine service, the element must be renewed regardless of its apparent condition.
4 If you are checking the element for any other reason, inspect its lower surface; if it is oily or very dirty, renew the element. If it is

only moderately dusty, it can be re-used by blowing it clean with compressed air.
5 Fit the new element using a reversal of the removal procedure.

25 Manual transmission oil level check

Note: *The work in this Section is not a Ford recommendation.*

1 The manual transmission does not have a dipstick. To check the oil level, raise the vehicle and support it securely on axle stands, making sure that the vehicle is level.
2 Remove the engine undershields as necessary for access to the front of the transmission.
3 The filler/level plug is located on the lower front side of the transmission housing. Using a suitable Allen key or socket, unscrew and remove it – take care, as it will probably be very tight **(see illustrations)**.

24.1 Remove the cover . . .

24.2 . . . then lift out the element

25.3a Using a suitable Allen key or socket, unscrew . . .

25.3b . . . and remove the transmission oil filler/level plug

25.5 Topping-up the manual transmission oil

4 If the lubricant level is correct, the oil should be up to the lower edge of the hole.
5 If the transmission needs more lubricant (if the oil level is not up to the hole), use a syringe, or a plastic bottle and tube, to add more **(see illustration)**.
6 Stop filling the transmission when the lubricant begins to run out of the hole, then wait until the flow of oil ceases.
7 Refit the filler/level plug, and tighten it to the specified torque wrench setting. Drive the vehicle a short distance, then check for leaks.
8 A need for regular topping-up can only be due to a leak, which should be found and rectified without delay.

26 Automatic transmission fluid renewal

1 Park the car on level ground, and switch off the engine. Apply the handbrake, and engage P. Jack up the front of the car and support on axle stands. Remove the transmission fluid

dipstick on 4-speed transmissions.
2 Depending on model, it may be necessary to remove the engine undershield for access to the transmission drain plug. The plug is fitted on the base of the transmission housing.
3 Taking adequate precautions against burning or scalding if the engine and transmission are hot (wear gloves), position a suitable container below the transmission drain plug.
4 Loosen and remove the drain plug **(see illustration)**, and allow the fluid to drain into the container. On 5-speed transmissions, remove the seal from the plug and also unscrew the filler plug from the top of the transmission.
5 Clean the drain plug thoroughly, then when the flow of fluid has ceased, refit the plug and tighten it to the specified torque. Fit a new seal on 5-speed transmissions.
6 Remove the fluid container from under the car.
7 The transmission is filled through the dipstick tube on 4-speed transmissions and through the filler plug aperture on 5-speed

26.4 Automatic transmission fluid drain plug (4-speed)

transmissions. Use a narrow funnel, and take great care to avoid introducing any kind of dirt into the transmission as it is filled.
8 After about half the specified 'drain and refill' quantity of fluid has been added, refer to Section 21 and complete the level checking procedure.
9 Refit the engine undershield (where removed), then lower the car to the ground.

Every 3 years

27 Brake fluid renewal

The procedure is similar to that for the bleeding of the hydraulic system as described in Chapter 9, except that the brake fluid reservoir should be emptied by syphoning, and allowance should be made for the old fluid to be removed from the circuit when bleeding a section of the circuit.

28 Coolant renewal

Note: *If the antifreeze used is Ford's own, or*

of similar quality, Ford state that the coolant need not be renewed for the life of the vehicle. If the vehicle's history is unknown, if the antifreeze is of lesser quality, or if you prefer to follow conventional servicing intervals, the coolant should be changed as follows.

⚠ *Warning: Refer to Chapter 3 and observe the warnings given. In particular, never remove the expansion tank filler cap when the engine is running, or has just been switched off, as the cooling system will be hot, and the consequent escaping steam and scalding coolant could cause serious injury. If the engine is hot, the electric cooling fan may start rotating even if the engine is not running, so be careful to keep hands, hair and loose clothing well clear when working in the engine compartment.*

Cooling system draining

⚠ *Warning: Wait until the engine is cold before starting this procedure.*

1 To drain the system, first remove the expansion tank filler cap. Place a thick cloth over the expansion tank cap, then turn the cap anti-clockwise as far as the first stop and wait for any pressure to be released, then depress it and turn it further anti-clockwise to remove it.
2 If additional working clearance is required, apply the handbrake, then jack up the front of the vehicle and support it on axle stands (see *Jacking and vehicle support*).
3 Remove the radiator undershield, then place a large drain tray underneath, and unscrew the radiator drain plug **(see**

28.3 Radiator drain plug (shown with radiator removed)

28.9 Cylinder block drain plug

28.13 Bleed valve located on the top of the water pump

illustration). Allow the coolant to drain into the tray. On completion, retighten the drain plug and refit the undershield. Where necessary, lower the vehicle to the ground.

Cooling system flushing

4 If coolant renewal has been neglected, or if the antifreeze mixture has become diluted, then in time, the cooling system may gradually lose efficiency, as the coolant passages become restricted due to rust, scale deposits, and other sediment. The cooling system efficiency can be restored by flushing the system clean.
5 The radiator should be flushed independently of the engine, to avoid unnecessary contamination.

Radiator flushing

6 Disconnect the top and bottom hoses and any other relevant hoses from the radiator, with reference to Chapter 3.
7 Insert a garden hose into the radiator top inlet. Direct a flow of clean water through the radiator, and continue flushing until clean water emerges from the radiator bottom outlet.
8 If after a reasonable period, the water still does not run clear, the radiator can be flushed with a good proprietary cleaning agent. It is important that the manufacturer's instructions are followed carefully. If the contamination is particularly bad, remove the radiator, insert the hose in the radiator bottom outlet, and reverse-flush the radiator.

Engine flushing

9 Remove the thermostat as described in Chapter 3 then, if the radiator top hose has been disconnected from the engine, temporarily reconnect the hose. The cylinder block may also be drained by removing the drain plug located on the rear left-hand side (see illustration).
10 With the top and bottom hoses disconnected from the radiator, insert a garden hose into the radiator top hose. Direct a clean flow of water through the engine, and continue flushing until clean water emerges from the radiator bottom hose.
11 On completion of flushing, refit the thermostat and reconnect the hoses with reference to Chapter 3.

Cooling system filling

12 Before attempting to fill the cooling system, make sure that all hoses and clips are in good condition, and that the clips are tight. Note that an antifreeze mixture must be used all year round, to prevent corrosion of the engine components.
13 Loosen the bleed valve located on the top of the water pump (see illustration).
14 Slowly fill the system through the expansion tank until coolant emerges from the water pump bleed valve. Tighten the bleed valve.
15 Continue to fill the system until the coolant level reaches the MAX mark on the side of the expansion tank.
16 Start the engine and increase its speed to 1500 rpm for 20 seconds. Switch off the engine.
17 Top-up the coolant in the expansion tank to 15 mm above the MAX mark, then refit the filler cap.
18 Start the engine and allow it to idle for 2 minutes.
19 Increase the engine speed to 3000 rpm and hold it at this speed until the electric cooling fan operates. Allow the engine to idle for a further 5 minutes.
20 Switch off the engine and allow it to cool for at least 30 minutes.
21 Remove the filler cap and top-up the coolant level to the MAX mark on the expansion tank. Refit and tighten the cap.

Antifreeze mixture

22 Ford state that, if the only antifreeze used is the type with which the system was first filled at the factory (see *Lubricants and fluids*) it will last the lifetime of the vehicle. This is subject to it being used in the recommended concentration, unmixed with any other type of antifreeze or additive, and topped-up when necessary using only that antifreeze mixed with clean water. If any other type of antifreeze is added, the lifetime guarantee no longer applies; to restore the lifetime protection, the system must be drained and thoroughly reverse-flushed before fresh coolant mixture is poured in.
23 If the vehicle's history (and therefore the quality of the antifreeze in it) is unknown,

owners who wish to follow Ford's recommendations are advised to drain and thoroughly reverse-flush the system, before refilling with fresh coolant mixture. If the appropriate quality of antifreeze is used, the coolant can then be left for the life of the vehicle.
24 If any antifreeze other than Ford's is to be used, the coolant must be renewed at regular intervals to provide an equivalent degree of protection; the conventional recommendation is to renew the coolant every three years.
25 If the antifreeze used is to Ford's specification, the levels of protection it affords are indicated in the Specifications Section of this Chapter. To give the recommended *standard* mixture ratio for this antifreeze, 40% (by volume) of antifreeze must be mixed with 60% of clean, soft water; if you are using any other type of antifreeze, follow its manufacturer's instructions to achieve the correct ratio.
26 It is best to make up slightly more than the system's specified capacity, so that a supply is available for subsequent topping-up. However, note that you are unlikely to fully drain the system at any one time (unless the engine is being completely stripped), and the capacities quoted are therefore slightly academic for routine coolant renewal.
27 Before adding antifreeze, the cooling system should be completely drained, preferably flushed, and all hoses checked for condition and security. Fresh antifreeze will rapidly find any weaknesses in the system.
28 After filling with antifreeze, a label should be attached to the expansion tank, stating the type and concentration of antifreeze used, and the date installed. Any subsequent topping-up should be made with the same type and concentration of antifreeze. If topping-up using antifreeze to Ford's specification, note that a 50/50 mixture is permissible, purely for convenience.
29 Do not use engine antifreeze in the windscreen/tailgate washer system, as it will damage the vehicle's paintwork. A screen wash additive should be added to the washer system in its maker's recommended quantities.

Every 50 000 miles

29 Auxiliary drivebelt renewal

Refer to Section 5.

Chapter 2 Part A:
1.8 and 2.0 litre petrol engine in-car repair procedures

Contents

Degrees of difficulty

Easy, suitable for novice with little experience	**Fairly easy,** suitable for beginner with some experience	**Fairly difficult,** suitable for competent DIY mechanic	**Difficult,** suitable for experienced DIY mechanic	**Very difficult,** suitable for expert DIY or professional

Specifications

General

Engine type	Four-cylinder, in-line, double overhead camshafts
Engine code:	
1.8 litre models	CGBA and CHBA
2.0 litre models	CJBA
Capacity:	
1.8 litre models	1798 cc
2.0 litre models	1999 cc
Bore:	
1.8 litre models	83.0 mm
2.0 litre models	87.5 mm
Stroke – all models	83.1 mm
Compression ratio – all models	10.8:1
Power output:	
1.8 litre models:	
CGBA	81 kW at 5500 rpm
CHBA	92 kW at 6000 rpm
2.0 litre models	107 kW at 6000 rpm
Compression pressure	Not available
Firing order	1-3-4-2 (No 1 cylinder at timing chain end)
Direction of crankshaft rotation	Clockwise (seen from right-hand side of vehicle)

Camshafts

Camshaft endfloat	0.09 to 0.24 mm
Exhaust lobe lift	7.7 mm
Intake lobe lift :	
1.8 litre:	
CGBA	7.4 mm
CHBA	8.5 mm
2.0 litre	8.8 mm
Camshaft bearing journal diameter	24.96 to 24.98 mm
Camshaft bearing running clearance	0.055 to 0.060 mm

Tappets

Valve clearances (cold):	
Inlet	0.22 to 0.28 mm
Exhaust	0.27 to 0.33 mm

Lubrication

Engine oil capacity (including filter)	See Chapter 1A
Engine oil pressure	3.5 bar @ 2000 rpm
Engine oil type/specification	See end of *Weekly checks*

Torque wrench settings

	Nm	lbf ft
Alternator upper bolt	25	18
Auxiliary drivebelt idler pulley	25	18
Camshaft bearing cap bolts:		
Stage 1	7	5
Stage 2	16	12
Camshaft cover bolts	10	7
Camshaft position sensor retaining bolt	6	4
Camshaft sprocket retaining bolts	65	48
Coolant pump pulley bolts	25	18
Crankshaft oil seal carrier bolts	10	7
Crankshaft position sensor retaining bolts	7	5
Crankshaft pulley bolt:		
Stage 1	100	74
Stage 2	Angle-tighten a further 90°	
Cylinder block timing peg blanking plug	20	15
Cylinder head bolts:		
Stage 1	5	4
Stage 2	15	11
Stage 3	45	33
Stage 4	Angle-tighten a further 90°	
Stage 5	Angle-tighten a further 90°	
Driveshaft support bearing bracket-to-cylinder block bolts	48	35
Engine rear mounting retaining nut	80	59
Engine right-hand top mounting:		
Mounting-to-inner wing bolts	80	59
Mounting-to-engine nuts	80	59
Engine/transmission left-hand mounting:		
Bracket-to-transmission nuts	90	66
Mounting centre bolt	133	98
Exhaust front pipe to manifold	46	34
Exhaust manifold bracket-to-cylinder block bolts	25	18
Exhaust manifold heat shield bolts	10	7
Exhaust manifold retaining nuts	55	41
Flywheel/driveplate bolts:		
Stage 1	50	37
Stage 2	80	59
Stage 3	112	83
Intake manifold retaining bolts	18	13
Knock sensor bolt	20	15
Oil filter housing bolts	25	18
Oil pressure warning light switch	15	11
Oil pump chain guide bolts	10	7
Oil pump chain tensioner bolt	10	7
Oil pump sprocket bolt	25	18
Oil pump-to-cylinder block bolts:		
Stage 1	10	7
Stage 2	23	17
Oil separator-to-cylinder block bolts	10	7
Power steering pump-to-cylinder block bolts	18	13
Sump bolts	25	18
Sump oil drain plug	28	21
Sump-to-transmission bolts	40	30
Timing chain cover:		
Lower blanking plug	12	9
Upper blanking plug	10	7
Timing chain cover bolts:		
Bolts 9, 20, 21 & 22	48	35
All other bolts	10	7
Timing chain guide retaining bolts	10	7
Timing chain tensioner bolts	10	7
Torque converter to driveplate	36	27
Transmission-to-engine bolts	44	32

1 General information

How to use this Chapter

This Part of Chapter 2 is devoted to repair procedures possible while the engine is still installed in the vehicle, and includes only the Specifications relevant to those procedures. Since these procedures are based on the assumption that the engine is installed in the vehicle, if the engine has been removed from the vehicle and mounted on a stand, some of the preliminary dismantling steps outlined will not apply.

Information concerning engine/transmission removal and refitting, and engine overhaul, can be found in Part D of this Chapter, which also includes the Specifications relevant to those procedures.

Engine

This is a new engine which has been developed in Japan along with Mazda. Its main objectives were to reduce fuel consumption, engine weight, noise emissions and pollutant levels, It also has increased torque and power output.

The engine, known by Ford's internal code name Duratec-HE (which replaces the Zetec-E range of engines), is of four-cylinder, in-line type, mounted transversely at the front of the vehicle, with the (clutch and) transmission on its left-hand end.

Apart from the plastic intake manifold, the complete engine castings are of aluminium alloy. This is to help reduce engine weight and noise, it will also increase the torque and power output.

The main bearing caps are built into a frame, which holds the crankshaft in the cylinder block to help strengthen the assembly and reduce engine vibration. There are no service operations allowed on the crankshaft assembly, as there is a fine tolerance in the bearing clearances and bearing shells. If there is any reason for repair in this area then the complete cylinder block and crankshaft assembly must be renewed as a unit.

Both camshafts are driven by the same low-noise, maintenance-free, pinned-link timing chain. Each camshaft operates eight valves via conventional bucket/tappets without adjusting shims. If there is wear, and the valve clearances require adjustment, then new bucket tappets are available in different sizes to reach the correct clearance.

Each camshaft rotates in five bearings that are line-bored directly in the cylinder head and the (bolted-on) bearing caps; this means that the bearing caps are not available separately from the cylinder head, and must not be interchanged with caps from another engine.

The water pump is bolted to the right-hand end of the cylinder block, and is driven with the power steering pump, air conditioning compressor (where fitted) and alternator by a flat 'polyvee' type auxiliary drivebelt from the crankshaft pulley.

Lubrication system

Lubrication is by means of an eccentric-rotor pump, which is mounted under the right-hand end of the cylinder block, and is driven via a chain from the crankshaft and draws oil through a pick-up pipe located in the sump. The pump forces oil through an externally-mounted element type filter – on some versions of the engine, an oil cooler is fitted to the oil filter mounting, so that clean oil entering the engine's galleries is cooled by the main engine cooling system. From the filter, the oil is pumped into a main gallery in the cylinder block/crankcase, from where it is distributed to the crankshaft (main bearings) and cylinder head.

The big-end bearings are supplied with oil via internal drillings in the crankshaft. While the crankshaft and camshaft bearings and the tappets receive a pressurised supply, the camshaft lobes and valves are lubricated by splash, as are all other engine components.

2 Repair operations possible with the engine in the vehicle

The following major repair operations can be accomplished without removing the engine from the vehicle. However, owners should note that any operation involving the removal of the sump requires careful forethought, depending on the level of skill and the tools and facilities available; refer to the relevant text for details.

a) Compression pressure – testing.
b) Cylinder head valve cover – removal and refitting.
c) Timing chain covers – removal and refitting.
d) Timing chain – renewal.
e) Timing chain tensioner and sprockets – removal and refitting.
f) Camshafts and tappets – removal and refitting.
g) Cylinder head – removal, overhaul and refitting.
h) Cylinder head and pistons – decarbonising.
i) Sump – removal and refitting.
j) Crankshaft oil seals – renewal.
k) Oil pump – removal and refitting.
l) Flywheel/driveplate – removal and refitting.
m) Engine/transmission mountings – removal and refitting.

Clean the engine compartment and the exterior of the engine with some type of degreaser before any work is done. It will make the job easier, and will help to keep dirt out of the internal areas of the engine.

Depending on the components involved, it may be helpful to remove the bonnet, to improve access to the engine as repairs are performed (refer to Chapter 11 if necessary). Cover the wings to prevent damage to the paint; special covers are available, but an old bedspread or blanket will also work.

If vacuum, exhaust, oil or coolant leaks develop, indicating a need for component/gasket or seal renewal, the repairs can generally be made with the engine in the vehicle. The intake and exhaust manifold gaskets, sump gasket, crankshaft oil seals and cylinder head gasket are all accessible with the engine in place.

Exterior components such as the intake and exhaust manifolds, the sump, the oil pump, the water pump, the starter motor, the alternator and the fuel system components can be removed for repair with the engine in place.

Since the cylinder head can be removed without lifting out the engine, camshaft and valve component servicing can also be accomplished with the engine in the vehicle, as can renewal of the timing chain and sprockets.

3 Compression test – description and interpretation

1 When engine performance is down, or if misfiring occurs which cannot be attributed to the ignition or fuel systems, a compression test can provide diagnostic clues as to the engine's condition. If the test is performed regularly, it can give warning of trouble before any other symptoms become apparent.

2 The engine must be fully warmed-up to normal operating temperature, the oil level must be correct, the battery must be fully charged, and the spark plugs must be removed. The aid of an assistant will be required also.

3 Disable the ignition system by unplugging the ignition coil's electrical connector.

4 Referring to Chapter 12, identify and remove the fuel pump fuse from the fusebox. Now start the engine and allow it to run until it stalls. If the engine will not start, at least keep it cranking for about 10 seconds. The fuel system should now be depressurised, preventing unburnt fuel from soaking the catalytic converter as the engine is turned over during the test.

5 Fit a compression tester to the No 1 cylinder spark plug hole – the type of tester which screws into the plug thread is to be preferred.

6 Have the assistant hold the throttle wide open and crank the engine on the starter motor; after one or two revolutions, the compression pressure should build-up to a maximum figure, and then stabilise. Record the highest reading obtained.

7 Repeat the test on the remaining cylinders, recording the pressure developed in each.

4.7 TDC sensor (arrowed) under the right-hand wheel arch

4.8a Remove the timing hole plug . . . .

4.8b . . . and insert the timing peg

8 Due to the variety of testers available, and the fluctuation of starter motor speed when cranking the engine, different readings are often obtained when carrying out the compression test. For this reason, specific compression pressure figures are not quoted by Ford. However, all cylinders should produce very similar pressures; any difference greater than 10% indicates the existence of a fault.

9 If the pressure in any cylinder is considerably lower than the others, introduce a teaspoonful of clean oil into that cylinder through its spark plug hole, and repeat the test.

10 If the addition of oil temporarily improves the compression pressure, this indicates that bore or piston wear is responsible for the pressure loss. No improvement suggests that leaking or burnt valves, or a blown head gasket, may be to blame.

11 A low reading from two adjacent cylinders is almost certainly due to the head gasket having blown between them; the presence of coolant in the engine oil will confirm this.

12 If one cylinder is about 20 percent lower than the others and the engine has a slightly rough idle, a worn camshaft lobe could be the cause.

13 If the compression is unusually high, the combustion chambers are probably coated with carbon deposits. If this is the case, the cylinder head should be removed and decarbonised.

14 On completion of the test, refit the spark plugs, then reconnect the ignition system coil and refit the fuel pump fuse.

4 Top Dead Centre (TDC) for No 1 piston – locating

Note: *Only turn the engine in the normal direction of rotation – clockwise from the right-hand side of the vehicle.*

General

1 Top Dead Centre (TDC) is the highest point in its travel up-and-down its cylinder bore that each piston reaches as the crankshaft rotates. While each piston reaches TDC both at the top of the compression stroke and again at the top of the exhaust stroke, for the purpose of timing the engine, TDC refers to the No 1 piston position at the top of its compression stroke.

2 It is useful for several servicing procedures to be able to position the engine at TDC.

3 No 1 piston and cylinder are at the right-hand (timing chain) end of the engine (right-and left-hand are always quoted as seen from the driver's seat).

Locating TDC

4 Remove all the spark plugs, this will make it easier to turn the engine (Chapter 1A).

5 Disconnect the battery negative (earth) lead (refer to *Disconnecting the battery* at the end of this manual).

6 Apply the handbrake, then jack up the front of the vehicle and support it on axle stands (see *Jacking and vehicle support*). Remove the right-hand front roadwheel.

7 Remove the cover from under the right-

hand front wheel arch to expose the crankshaft pulley and TDC sensor (see illustration).

8 There is a timing hole provided on the rear of the cylinder block (below the alternator) to position the crankshaft at TDC (see illustrations). Unscrew the timing hole plug and insert a timing peg (obtainable from Ford dealers (303-507) – or a tool supplier).

9 Using a spanner or socket on the crankshaft pulley bolt, rotate the crankshaft clockwise until it stops against the timing peg.

10 There is a bolt hole in the crankshaft pulley which should align with the thread in the timing chain cover, insert a bolt (M6 x 18 mm) to locate the pulley at TDC (see illustration).

11 Number 1 and 4 pistons are now at TDC, one of them on the compression stroke. To determine which cylinder is on the compression stroke the camshaft cover will need to be removed (as described in Section 5).

12 Obtain Ford service tool 21-162B, or fabricate a substitute from a strip of metal 5 mm thick (while the strip's thickness is critical, its length and width are not, but should be approximately 180 to 230 mm by 20 to 30 mm). If number 1 cylinder is on the compression stroke – rest the tool on the cylinder head mating surface, and slide it into the slot in the left-hand end of both camshafts (see illustration). The tool should slip snugly into both slots while resting on the cylinder head mating surface; if one camshaft is only slightly out of alignment, it is permissible to use an open-ended spanner to rotate the camshaft gently and carefully until the tool will fit.

13 If both camshaft slots (they are machined significantly off-centre) are below the level of the cylinder head mating surface, rotate the crankshaft through one full turn clockwise and fit the tool again; it should now fit as described in the previous paragraph. **Note:** *The timing peg and crankshaft pulley locking bolt will have to be removed before turning the engine.*

14 Do not use the locked camshafts to prevent the crankshaft from rotating – use only the locking methods described in Section 8 for removing the crankshaft pulley.

15 Once No 1 cylinder has been positioned at TDC on the compression stroke, TDC for any of the other cylinders can then be located

4.10 Insert an M6 bolt through the pulley to align for TDC

4.12 Slide the tool/metal bar into the slots in the end of the camshafts

5.2 Unclip the hose and remove the engine upper cover

5.3 Disconnect the wiring connector from the camshaft sensor

5.4 Unclip the wiring harness from the camshaft cover

5.5 Using a pair of pliers to remove the crankcase ventilation hose from the rocker cover

5.9 Check the rubber seal (arrowed) on the camshaft cover retaining bolts for damage

5.11 Insert the retaining bolts into the camshaft cover gasket, ensuring the gasket is located correctly in groove

by rotating the crankshaft clockwise 180° at a time and following the firing order (see Specifications).

16 Before turning the engine again, make sure that the timing peg and crankshaft pulley locating bolt have been removed.

5 Camshaft cover – removal and refitting

Removal

1 Disconnect the battery negative (earth) lead (refer to *Disconnecting the battery* at the end of this manual).

2 Unclip the breather hose from the engine upper plastic cover, then unclip the cover from the top of the engine **(see illustration)**.

3 Disconnect the electrical connector from the camshaft position sensor **(see illustration)**.

4 Detach the wiring harness from the camshaft cover **(see illustration)**.

5 Disconnect the positive crankcase ventilation (PCV) hose from the camshaft cover **(see illustration)**.

6 Unscrew the three engine upper plastic cover retaining pegs from the camshaft cover retaining studs, note the position of the retaining studs.

7 Carefully unplug the HT leads from the spark plugs and withdraw them, unclipping the leads from the cover.

8 Working progressively, unscrew the cylinder head cover retaining bolts and withdraw the cover.

9 Discard the cover gasket; this must be renewed whenever it is disturbed. Check that the sealing faces are undamaged, and that the rubber seal at each retaining bolt is serviceable **(see illustration)**; renew any worn or damaged seals.

Refitting

10 On refitting, clean the cover and cylinder head gasket faces carefully, then fit a new gaskets to the cover, ensuring that they locate correctly in the cover grooves.

11 Insert the retaining bolts, complete with rubber seals and spacer at each bolt location then refit the cover to the cylinder head **(see illustration)**. Start all bolts finger-tight, ensuring that the gasket remains seated in its groove.

12 Working in the sequence shown **(see illustration)**, tighten the cover bolts to the specified torque wrench setting. Refit the three engine upper plastic cover retaining pegs to the cover retaining studs noted on removal.

5.12 Sequence for tightening the camshaft cover

6.4 Intake manifold lower retaining bolt (arrowed)

6.5 Release the securing clip and remove the air intake pipe

6.6 Twist the outer cable to release it from the mounting bracket

13 The remainder of reassembly is the reverse of the removal procedure. Make sure the HT leads are clipped into place and are correctly routed; each is numbered, and can also be identified by the numbering on its respective coil terminal.

6 Intake manifold – removal and refitting

⚠️ *Warning: Petrol is extremely flammable, so take extra precautions when disconnecting any part of the fuel system. Don't smoke, or allow naked flames or bare light bulbs in or near the work area. Don't work in a garage where a natural gas appliance (such as a clothes dryer or water heater) is installed. If you spill petrol on your skin, rinse it off immediately. Have a fire extinguisher rated for petrol fires handy, and know how to use it.*

Removal

1 Park the vehicle on firm, level ground, apply the handbrake, then jack up the front of the vehicle and support it on axle stands (see *Jacking and vehicle support*).
2 Disconnect the battery negative (earth) lead (refer to *Disconnecting the battery* at the end of this manual).
3 Unclip the breather hose from the engine upper plastic cover, then unclip the cover from the top of the engine.
4 From underneath the vehicle, remove the oil

level dipstick tube lower retaining bolt, and the intake manifold lower retaining bolt **(see illustration)**.
5 Release the securing clip and detach the air intake pipe from the throttle body **(see illustration)**.
6 Unclip the accelerator inner cable from the throttle linkage, then twist the outer cable to release it from the bracket **(see illustration)**.
7 Unplug the two electrical connectors from the throttle position (TP) sensor and the idle air control (IAC) valve **(see illustrations)**.
8 Carefully pull the vacuum hoses (for the brakes, the fuel pulse damper and the purge valve) to release them from the intake manifold.
9 Detach the wiring harness from across the top of the intake manifold (releasing it from any relevant connectors and retaining clips, marking or labelling them as they are unplugged), then move the wiring loom to one side of the engine bay.
10 Remove the upper retaining bolt **(see illustration)** and withdraw the oil level dipstick tube out from the engine. Renew the O-ring at the bottom of the dipstick tube on reassembly.
11 Unscrew the bolts securing the intake manifold to the cylinder head and withdraw it. Take care not to damage vulnerable components such as the EGR pipe and valve as the manifold assembly is manoeuvred out of the engine compartment.

Refitting

12 Refitting is the reverse of the removal procedure, noting the following points:

a) When using a scraper and solvent to remove all traces of old gasket material and sealant from the manifold and cylinder head, be careful to ensure that you do not scratch or damage the material of either; the cylinder head is of aluminium alloy, while the manifold is a plastic moulding – any solvents used must be suitable for this application. If the gasket was leaking, have the mating surfaces checked for warpage at an automotive machine shop. While it may be possible to have the cylinder head gasket surface skimmed if necessary, to remove any distortion, the manifold must be renewed if it is found to be warped, cracked – check with special care around the mounting points for components such as the idle speed control valve and EGR pipe – or otherwise faulty.
b) Provided the relevant mating surfaces are clean and flat, a new gasket will be sufficient to ensure the joint is gas-tight. **Do not** use any kind of silicone-based sealant on any part of the fuel system or intake manifold.
c) Fit new gaskets to the four intake ports and one to the EGR port in the manifold **(see illustrations)**, then locate the manifold on the head and install the retaining bolts.
d) Tighten the bolts evenly to the torque listed in the Specifications at the beginning of this Chapter. Work from the centre outwards, to avoid warping the manifold.
e) Refit the remaining parts in the reverse order of removal – tighten all fasteners to

6.7a Disconnect the wiring connector from the throttle position (TP) sensor . . .

6.7b . . . and the idle air control (IAC) valve

6.10 Remove the oil level dipstick tube upper retaining bolt (arrowed)

the torque wrench settings specified and fit a new O-ring seal to the bottom of the dipstick tube.

f) Make sure the wiring loom is routed correctly and the connections fitted as labelled up on removal.

g) Before starting the engine, check the accelerator cable for correct adjustment and the throttle linkage for smooth operation.

h) When the engine is fully warmed-up, check for signs of fuel, intake and/or vacuum leaks.

i) Road test the vehicle, and check for proper operation of all disturbed components.

7 Exhaust manifold – removal, inspection and refitting

Warning: The engine must be completely cool before beginning this procedure.

Removal

1 Park the vehicle on firm, level ground, apply the handbrake, then jack up the front of the vehicle and support it on axle stands (see *Jacking and vehicle support*).

2 Disconnect the battery negative (earth) lead (refer to *Disconnecting the battery* at the end of this manual).

3 Unclip the breather hose from the engine upper plastic cover, then unclip the cover from the top of the engine.

6.12a Fitting one of the four intake manifold gaskets . . .

4 Undo the six retaining bolts and withdraw the upper part of the heat shield, then undo the two lower retaining bolts and remove the lower part from the exhaust manifold **(see illustrations)**.

5 Trace the wire back from the oxygen sensor in the manifold downpipe and disconnect the electrical connector. From under the vehicle unscrew the two retaining nuts to disconnect the exhaust system front down pipe from the manifold **(see illustration)**.

6 Undo the four securing bolts and remove the exhaust manifold lower retaining bracket **(see illustration)**.

7 Remove the nuts and detach the exhaust manifold and gasket. Take care not to damage vulnerable components as the manifold assembly is manoeuvred out of the engine compartment. When removing the manifold with the engine in the vehicle, additional clearance can be obtained by

6.12b . . . and the EGR gasket to the intake manifold

unscrewing the studs from the cylinder head; a female Torx-type socket will be required **(see illustration)**.

Inspection

8 When using a scraper to remove all traces of old gasket material and carbon deposits from the manifold and cylinder head mating surfaces, be careful to ensure that you do not scratch or damage the material of either component – any solvents used must be suitable for this application. If the gasket was leaking, check the manifold and cylinder head for warpage, this may need to be done at an automotive machine shop, resurface if necessary.

Caution: When scraping, be very careful not to gouge or scratch the delicate aluminium alloy cylinder head.

9 Provided both mating surfaces are clean and flat, a new gasket will be sufficient to ensure the joint is gas-tight. Do not use any kind of exhaust sealant upstream of the catalytic converter.

Refitting

10 Refitting is the reverse of the removal procedure, noting the following points:

a) Fit a new manifold gasket over the cylinder head studs.

b) Refit the manifold, and tighten the nuts to the torque listed in the Specifications at the beginning of this Chapter.

c) Fit a new gasket to the front pipe (where fitted).

d) Run the engine, and check for exhaust leaks.

7.4a Remove the upper part of the exhaust manifold heat shield . . .

7.4b . . . then remove the lower heat shield retaining bolts (one side – arrowed)

7.5 Undo the two retaining bolts (arrowed) from the exhaust front pipe

7.6 Undo the four bolts (arrowed) to remove the manifold lower retaining bracket

7.7 The studs can be unscrewed using a Torx socket, for additional clearance

8.3 Using a locking tool to hold the flywheel

8 Crankshaft pulley – removal and refitting

Note: *Only turn the engine in the normal direction of rotation – clockwise from the right-hand side of the vehicle.*
Caution: The pulley and crankshaft timing gear are not on a keyway, they are held in place by the crankshaft retaining bolt. Make sure the engine is set at TDC (see Section 4) before the pulley is removed.
Note: *The crankshaft pulley retaining bolt is very tight and Ford use a special tool (205-072/15-030A) to lock the pulley to prevent it from turning. A new pulley retaining bolt will be required on refitting.*

Removal

1 Remove the auxiliary drivebelt – either

9.3 Slacken the three retaining bolts (arrowed)

9.9 Undo the retaining bolts and move the coolant expansion tank to one side

8.6 Use a new retaining bolt when refitting the pulley

remove the drivebelt completely, or just secure it clear of the crankshaft pulley, depending on the work to be carried out (see Chapter 1A).
2 Set the engine to TDC (see Section 4).
3 The crankshaft must now be locked to prevent its rotation while the pulley bolt is unscrewed. If the Ford Special tool is not available proceed as follows:
a) *Remove the rubber plug from the transmission bellhousing or, on automatics, unbolt the small metal cover plate from the sump, and use a large screwdriver or similar to lock the flywheel/driveplate ring gear teeth while an assistant slackens the pulley bolt; take care not to damage the teeth or the surrounding castings when using this method.*
b) *If the engine/transmission has been removed and separated, lock the flywheel/driveplate using a locking tool (see illustration).*

9.7 Disconnect the wiring connector from the crankshaft position sensor

9.10 Unscrew the engine mounting nuts and bolts (arrowed) and remove the engine mounting

4 Unscrew the pulley bolt and remove the pulley.

Refitting

5 Refitting is the reverse of the removal procedure; making sure the engine has not moved from its setting at TDC (see Section 4).
6 Ensure that a new retaining bolt is used **(see illustration)**, and tightened to the torque specified at the beginning of this Chapter.

9 Timing chain cover – removal and refitting

Note: *Only turn the engine in the normal direction of rotation – clockwise from the right-hand side of the vehicle.*

Removal

1 Remove the camshaft cover as described in Section 5.
2 Apply the handbrake, then jack up the front of the vehicle and support it on axle stands (see *Jacking and vehicle support*). Remove the right-hand front road wheel and remove the cover from under the right-hand front wheel arch.
3 Slacken the water pump pulley retaining bolts by approximately three turns **(see illustration)**.
4 Remove the auxiliary drivebelt (Chapter 1A).
5 Remove the power steering pump as described in Chapter 10.
6 Remove the crankshaft pulley (Section 8).
7 Disconnect the crankshaft position (CKP) sensor wiring connector **(see illustration)**.
8 Unscrew the retaining bolts and remove the water pump pulley.
9 Undo the retaining bolts and move the coolant expansion tank to one side, disconnect the lower coolant hose if required **(see illustration)**.
10 Support the engine using a trolley jack and block of wood beneath the sump, then unscrew the nuts/bolts securing the engine/transmission right-hand mounting bracket and remove the mounting from the engine **(see illustration)**.
11 Unbolt and remove the auxiliary drivebelt idler **(see illustration)**.

9.11 Undo the retaining bolt (arrowed) and remove the idler pulley

9.13a Apply a 3.0 mm bead of sealant around the timing chain cover, including the inner bolt holes

12 Unscrew the timing chain cover retaining bolts (noting their positions for refitting) and withdraw the cover from the engine.

Refitting

13 Refitting is the reverse of the removal procedure (using the relevant Sections); Note the following points:

a) *Clean the sealant from the timing cover, cylinder block and cylinder head mating surfaces. When using a scraper and solvent to remove all traces of old gasket/sealant from the mating surfaces, be careful to ensure that you do not scratch or damage the material of either component – any solvents used must be suitable for this application. If the gasket was leaking, have the mating surfaces checked for warpage – this may need to be done at an automotive machine shop.*

b) *Provided the relevant mating surfaces are clean and flat, apply a (3.0mm) bead of silicone sealant around the timing chain cover and the inner bolt holes (see illustration). Note: The cover must be fitted within 10 minutes of applying the sealant.*

c) *Tighten the timing chain cover bolts to the specified torque settings at the beginning of this Chapter, following the sequence shown (see illustration).*

10 Timing chain, tensioner and guides – removal, inspection and refitting

Note: *Only turn the engine in the normal direction of rotation – clockwise from the right-hand side of the vehicle.*

Removal

1 Remove the camshaft cover as described in Section 5.

2 Set the engine to TDC as described in Section 4.

3 Remove the timing chain cover as described in Section 9.

4 Slacken the timing chain tensioner by inserting a small screwdriver into the access hole in the tensioner and releasing the pawl mechanism. Press against the timing chain guide to depress the piston into the tensioner

9.13b Tightening sequence for the timing chain cover

housing, when fully depressed, insert a locking pin (approximately 1.5 mm) to lock the piston in its compressed position **(see illustration)**.

5 Hold the camshafts by the hexagon on the shafts to prevent them from turning, using an open-ended spanner.

6 With the camshafts held in position, undo the camshaft sprocket retaining bolts and remove the camshaft sprockets and timing chain. Do not rotate the crankshaft until the timing chain is refitted **(see illustration)**.

7 If required, unbolt the fixed timing chain guide and withdraw the tensioner timing chain guide from its pivot pin on the cylinder head **(see illustrations)**.

10.4 Press against the timing chain guide and insert a locking pin (approximately 1.5 mm)

10.6 Using a spanner to hold the camshafts, while undoing the retaining bolts

10.7a Withdraw the tensioner guide from the pivot pin . . .

10.7b ... then undo the retaining bolts (arrowed) to remove the fixed guide

10.8 Undo the two retaining bolts (arrowed) and remove the tensioner, take care not to remove the locking pin (drill bit)

10.16 Refit the timing chain tensioner (still in the locked position) to the cylinder block

8 To remove the tensioner, undo the two retaining bolts and remove the timing chain tensioner from the cylinder block, taking care not to remove the locking pin **(see illustration)**.

9 To remove the timing chain sprocket from the crankshaft, the oil pump drive chain will need to be removed as described in Section 15, of this Chapter. Note which way round it is fitted, mark the sprocket to ensure it is refitted the same way round.

Inspection

Note: *Keep all components identified for position to ensure correct refitting.*

10 Clean all components thoroughly and wipe dry.

11 Examine the chain tensioner and tensioner guide for excessive wear or other

damage. Check the guides for deep grooves made by the timing chain.

12 Examine the timing chain for excessive wear. Hold it horizontally and check how much movement exists in the chain links. If there is any doubt, compare it to a new chain. Renew as necessary.

13 Examine the teeth of the camshaft and crankshaft sprockets for excessive wear and damage.

14 Before refitting the timing chain tensioner, the piston must be compressed and locked until refitted (if not already done on removal). To do this, insert a small screwdriver into the access hole in the tensioner and release the pawl mechanism. Now lightly clamp the tensioner in a soft-jawed vice and slowly compress the piston. Do not apply excessive force and make sure that the piston remains

aligned with its cylinder. When completely compressed, insert a locking pin/1.5 mm diameter wire rod into the special hole to lock the piston in its compressed position.

Refitting

15 If not already fitted, slide the crankshaft drive sprocket (and washer, where fitted) onto the crankshaft. Ensure it is refitted the same way round as noted on removal (see Section 15, for further information on refitting the oil pump drive chain).

16 Refit the tensioner to the cylinder block and tighten the retaining bolts to the specified torque setting. Take care not to remove the locking pin **(see illustration)**.

17 Refit the fixed timing chain guide and tighten the two retaining bolts, then slide the tensioner timing chain guide back into place on the upper pivot pin **(see illustration)**.

18 Refit the intake camshaft sprocket onto the camshaft, DO NOT tighten the retaining bolt at this stage.

19 With the timing chain around the exhaust camshaft sprocket refit the timing chain and sprocket, feeding the timing chain around the crankshaft drive sprocket and intake camshaft sprocket **(see illustration)**.

20 With the timing chain in place, hold pressure against the tensioner guide and withdraw the tensioner locking pin. This will then tension the timing chain **(see illustration)**.

21 Check that the engine is still set to TDC (as described in Section 4).

22 Tighten the both camshaft retaining bolts, to the torque setting specified in the Specifications at the beginning of this Chapter. **Note:** *Use an open-ended spanner on the hexagon on the camshafts to stop them from turning* **(see illustration)**.

23 Refit the timing chain cover as described in Section 9.

24 Remove the camshaft locking plate and crankshaft timing peg and turn the engine (in the direction of engine rotation) two full turns. Refit the camshaft locking plate and crankshaft timing peg to make sure the engine is still set at TDC (see Section 4 for further information).

25 Refit the camshaft cover as described in Section 5.

10.17 Refitting the timing chain guides to the engine

10.19 Refit the camshaft sprockets into position, complete with timing chain

10.20 Hold pressure against the tensioner guide and withdraw the tensioner locking pin (arrowed)

10.22 Use an open-ended spanner on the hexagon on the camshafts to stop them from turning

11.3a Remove the timing chain cover lower . . .

11.3b . . . and upper blanking plugs

11.4 Inserting a small screwdriver into the lower access hole, to release the timing chain tensioner

11 Camshafts and tappets –
removal, inspection and refitting

Note: *Only turn the engine in the normal direction of rotation – clockwise from the right-hand side of the vehicle.*

Removal

1 Remove the camshaft cover as described in Section 5.

2 Remove the timing hole plug and insert a timing peg to position the crankshaft at TDC (obtainable from Ford dealers (303-507) – or a tool supplier). For further information on setting the engine to TDC, see Section 4.

3 Remove the timing chain cover lower and upper blanking plugs, to gain access to the timing chain tensioner and guide **(see illustrations)**.

4 Slacken the timing chain tensioner by inserting a small screwdriver into the lower access hole in the timing chain cover and releasing the pawl mechanism in the tensioner **(see illustration)**.

5 Carefully turn the exhaust camshaft (by using an open-ended spanner on the hexagon on the shaft) in the normal direction of rotation, to slacken the timing chain tensioner **(see illustration)**.

6 Holding the exhaust camshaft in position, insert a bolt (M6x18mm) into the upper access hole in the timing chain cover to lock the tensioner guide rail in position **(see illustration)**.

7 With the camshafts held in position (by using an open-ended spanner on the hexagon on the shaft), slacken the camshaft sprocket retaining bolts.

8 Using a cable tie or similar, fasten the timing chain to the camshaft sprockets.

9 Remove the camshaft sprocket retaining bolts and remove the sprockets, complete with timing chain, away from the camshafts. Using a suitable piece of wire secure the sprockets and timing chain to prevent them dropping into the timing cover.

10 Working in the sequence shown **(see illustration)**, slacken the camshaft bearing cap bolts progressively by half a turn at a

11.5 Carefully turn the exhaust camshaft in the direction of the arrow, to slacken the timing chain tensioner

time. Work only as described, to release gradually and evenly the pressure of the valve springs on the caps.

11 Withdraw the camshaft bearing caps, noting their markings, then remove the camshafts. The intake camshaft can be identified by the reference lobe for the camshaft position sensor; therefore, there is

11.6 While holding the exhaust camshaft in position, insert a bolt (M6x18mm) to lock the tensioner guide rail

no need to mark the camshafts **(see illustrations)**.

12 Obtain sixteen small, clean containers, and number them 1 to 16. Using a rubber sucker, withdraw each bucket tappet in turn and place them in the containers. Do not interchange the bucket tappets as they are of different sizes; the shim is part of the bucket

11.10 Sequence for slackening the camshaft bearing cap bolts

11.11a Note the identification markings (arrowed) on the camshaft bearing caps . . .

11.11b . . . and the reference lobe (arrowed) on the intake camshaft for the position sensor

11.12a Removing the bucket tappet using a rubber sucker

11.12b Note the thickness number under the bucket tappet, different sizes are available

11.14 Use a micrometer to measure diameter of tappets

11.15 Check the cam lobes for pitting, wear and score marks – if scoring is excessive, as shown here, renew the camshaft

tappet **(see illustrations)**. Different sizes of bucket tappets are available in the event of wear on the valves or repair on the cylinder head assembly.

Inspection

13 With the camshafts and tappets removed, check each for signs of obvious wear (scoring, pitting, etc) and for ovality, and renew if necessary.

14 Measure the outside diameter of each tappet **(see illustration)** – take measurements at the top and bottom of each tappet, then a second set at right-angles to the first; if any measurement is significantly different from the others, the tappet is tapered or oval (as applicable) and must be renewed. If the necessary equipment is available, measure the inside diameter of the corresponding

cylinder head bore. If the tappets or the cylinder head bores are excessively worn, new tappets and/or a new cylinder head will be required.

15 Visually examine the camshaft lobes for score marks, pitting, galling (wear due to rubbing) and evidence of overheating (blue, discoloured areas). Look for flaking away of the hardened surface layer of each lobe **(see illustration)**. If any such signs are evident, renew the component concerned.

16 Examine the camshaft bearing journals and the cylinder head bearing surfaces for signs of obvious wear or pitting. If any such signs are evident, renew the component concerned.

17 Using a micrometer, measure the diameter of each journal at several points **(see illustration)**. If any measurement is

significantly different from the others, renew the camshaft.

18 To check the bearing journal running clearance, remove the tappets, use a suitable solvent and a clean lint-free rag to clean carefully all bearing surfaces, then refit the camshafts and bearing caps with a strand of Plastigauge across each journal **(see illustration)**. Tighten the bearing cap bolts to the specified torque wrench setting (do not rotate the camshafts), then remove the bearing caps and use the scale provided to measure the width of the compressed strands **(see illustration)**. Scrape off the Plastigauge with your fingernail or the edge of a credit card – don't scratch or nick the journals or bearing caps.

19 If the running clearance of any bearing is found to be worn to beyond the specified

11.17 Measure each journal diameter with a micrometer

11.18a Lay a strip of Plastigauge on each camshaft journal

11.18b Compare the width of the crushed Plastigauge to the scale on the envelope to determine the running clearance

service limits, fit a new camshaft and repeat the check; if the clearance is still excessive, the cylinder head must be renewed.

20 To check camshaft endfloat, remove the tappets, clean the bearing surfaces carefully, and refit the camshafts and bearing caps. Tighten the bearing cap bolts to the specified torque wrench setting, then measure the endfloat using a DTI (Dial Test Indicator, or dial gauge) mounted on the cylinder head so that its tip bears on the camshaft right-hand end.

21 Tap the camshaft fully towards the gauge, zero the gauge, then tap the camshaft fully away from the gauge, and note the gauge reading. If the endfloat measured is found to be at or beyond the specified service limit, fit a new camshaft and repeat the check; if the clearance is still excessive, the cylinder head must be renewed.

Refitting

22 On reassembly, liberally oil the cylinder head tappet bores and the tappets **(see illustration)**. Carefully refit the tappets to the cylinder head, ensuring that each tappet is refitted to its original bore. Some care will be required to enter the tappets squarely into their bores.

23 Turn the engine back approximately 45° so that there are no pistons at the top of the cylinders.

24 Liberally oil the camshaft bearings and lobes **(see illustration)**. Ensuring that each camshaft is in its original location, refit the camshafts, locating each so that the slot in its left-hand end is approximately parallel to, and just above, the cylinder head mating surface.

25 All camshaft bearing caps have an identifying number and letter etched on them. The exhaust camshaft's bearing caps are numbered in sequence E1 to E5 and the inlet camshaft's bearing caps I1 to I5 **(see illustration 11.11a)**.

26 Ensuring that each cap is kept square to the cylinder head as it is tightened down, and working in the sequence shown **(see illustration)**, tighten the camshaft bearing cap bolts slowly and by one turn at a time, until each cap touches the cylinder head. Next, go round again in the same sequence, tightening the bolts to the first stage torque wrench setting specified, then once more, tightening them to the second stage setting. Work only as described, to impose gradually and evenly the pressure of the valve springs on the caps.

27 Fit the camshaft aligning tool; it should slip into place as described in Section 4, paragraph 12 **(see illustration)**.

28 Refit the camshaft sprockets, complete with timing chain to the ends of the camshafts. DO NOT tighten the camshaft sprocket retaining bolts at this stage. Remove the cable ties from the timing chain and camshaft sprockets.

29 Remove the tensioner guide rail locking bolt (M6x18mm) from the upper access hole in the timing chain cover. It may be necessary

11.22 Oil liberally when refitting hydraulic tappets

11.24 Apply clean engine oil to the cam lobes and journals before refitting a camshaft

11.26 Sequence for tightening the camshaft bearing cap bolts

to hold some pressure against the tensioner guide rail to remove the locking bolt.

30 Turn the engine (in the direction of rotation) approximately 45° to TDC. For further information on setting the engine to TDC, see Section 4.

31 With the camshafts held in position (by using an open-ended spanner on the hexagon on the shaft), tighten the camshaft sprocket retaining bolts to the specified torque.

11.27 Fit the camshaft aligning tool to set TDC position

32 Remove the camshaft locking plate and crankshaft timing peg and turn the engine (in the direction of engine rotation) two full turns. Refit the camshaft locking plate and crankshaft timing peg to make sure the engine is still set at TDC (see Section 4 for further information).

33 Refit the timing chain cover upper and lower blanking plugs, coat the blanking plug threads with a suitable sealant to prevent leaks.

34 Refit the camshaft cover as described in Section 5.

12 Valve clearances – checking and adjustment

Note: *Only turn the engine in the normal direction of rotation – clockwise from the right-hand side of the vehicle.*

Checking

1 Remove the camshaft cover as described in Section 5.

12.3 Measure the clearance between the base of the cam lobe and the bucket using feeler blades

12.6 The bucket tappet has a number engraved on the inside

13 Cylinder head – removal and refitting

Note: *The following text assumes that the cylinder head will be removed with both intake and exhaust manifolds attached; this simplifies the procedure, but makes it a bulky and heavy assembly to handle – an engine hoist will be required, to prevent the risk of injury, and to prevent damage to any delicate components as the assembly is removed and refitted. If it is wished first to remove the manifolds, proceed as described in Sections 6 and 7 of this Chapter; amend the following procedure accordingly.*

Note: *Only turn the engine in the normal direction of rotation – clockwise from the right-hand side of the vehicle.*

Removal

1 With the vehicle parked on firm level ground, open the bonnet and disconnect the battery negative (earth) lead (refer to *Disconnecting the battery* at the end of this manual).

2 Whenever you disconnect any vacuum lines, coolant and emissions hoses, wiring loom connectors, earth straps and fuel lines as part of the following procedure, always label them clearly, so that they can be correctly reassembled.

> **HAYNES HiNT**
> *Masking tape and/or a touch-up paint applicator work well for marking items. Take instant photos, or sketch the locations of components and brackets.*

3 Drain the cooling system as described in Chapter 1A.

4 Remove the intake manifold as described in Section 6.

5 Remove the exhaust manifold and heat shields as described in Section 7.

6 Remove the camshaft cover as described in Section 5.

7 Remove the timing chain and sprockets as described in Section 10.

8 Release the pressure in the fuel system by following the first procedure in Chapter 4A, Section 2.

9 Release the fuel feed pipe from the fuel injector rail **(see illustration)**, see Chapter 4A for more information. Plug or cap all open fittings, to prevent any ingress of dirt etc.

10 Disconnect the coolant hoses from the coolant housing on the left-hand end of the cylinder head **(see illustration)**.

11 Slacken and remove the upper retaining bolt from the alternator assembly **(see illustration)**.

2 Set the engine to TDC on cylinder No 1 as described in Section 4. The inlet and exhaust cam lobes of No 1 cylinder will be pointing upwards (though not vertical) and the valve clearances can be checked.

3 Working on each valve, measure the clearance between the base of the cam lobe and the bucket tappet using feeler blades **(see illustration)**. Record the thickness of the blade required to give a firm sliding fit on all the valves of No 1 cylinder. The desired clearances are given in the Specifications. Note that the clearances for inlet and exhaust valves are different. The intake camshaft is at the front of the engine and the exhaust camshaft at the rear. Record all four clearances.

4 Now turn the crankshaft clockwise through 180° so that the valves of cylinder No 3 are pointing upwards. Check and record the four valve clearances for cylinder No 3. The clearances for cylinders 4 and 2 can be checked after turning the crankshaft through 180° each time.

Adjustment

5 If adjustment is required, the bucket tappets must be changed by removing the camshafts as described in Section 11.

6 If the valve clearance was too small, a thinner bucket tappet must be fitted. If the clearance was too large, a thicker bucket tappet must be fitted. The bucket tappet has a number engraved on the inside **(see**

illustration), if the marking is missing or illegible, a micrometer will be needed to establish bucket tappet thickness.

7 When the bucket tappet thickness and the valve clearance are known, the required thickness of the new bucket tappet can be calculated as follows:

Sample calculation – clearance too small
Desired clearance (A)	= 0.25 mm
Measured clearance (B)	= 0.20 mm
Tappet thickness found (C)	= 2.55 mm
Thickness required (D)	= C + B – A = 2.50 mm

Sample calculation – clearance too large
Desired clearance (A)	= 0.30 mm
Measured clearance (B)	= 0.36 mm
Tappet thickness found (C)	= 2.19 mm
Thickness required (D)	= C + B – A = 2.25 mm

8 With the correct thickness bucket tappets fitted in the cylinder head, refit the camshafts as described in Section 11.

9 Check the valve clearances are now correct, as described in paragraphs 2 to 4. If any clearances are still not within specification then carry out the adjustment procedure again.

10 It will be helpful for future adjustment if a record is kept of the thickness of bucket fitted at each position. The buckets required can be purchased in advance once the clearances and the existing bucket thicknesses are known.

11 When all the clearances are correct, refit the camshaft cover as described in Section 5.

13.9 Release the fuel feed pipe from the fuel injector rail

13.10 Disconnect the hoses from the coolant housing

12 Undo the securing bolt and disconnect the earth lead from the cylinder head above the alternator assembly **(see illustration)**.

13 Remove the camshafts and tappets as described in Section 11.

14 Working in the sequence shown **(see illustration),** slacken the ten cylinder head bolts progressively and by one turn at a time. Remove each bolt in turn, and ensure that new ones are obtained for reassembly; these bolts are subjected to severe stresses and so must be renewed, regardless of their apparent condition, whenever they are disturbed.

15 Lift the cylinder head away; use assistance if possible, as it is a heavy assembly. Remove the gasket and discard it, note the position of the dowels.

Refitting

16 The mating faces of the cylinder head and cylinder block must be perfectly clean before refitting the head. Use a hard plastic or wood scraper to remove all traces of gasket and carbon; also clean the piston crowns. Take particular care, as the soft aluminium alloy is easily damaged. Also, make sure that the carbon is not allowed to enter the oil and water passages – this is particularly important for the lubrication system, as carbon could block the oil supply to any of the engine's components. Using adhesive tape and paper, seal the water, oil and bolt holes in the cylinder block. Clean all the pistons in the same way.

 HAYNES HiNT *To prevent carbon entering the gap between the pistons and bores, smear a little grease in the gap. After cleaning each piston, use a small brush to remove all traces of grease and carbon from the gap, then wipe away the remainder with a clean rag.*

17 Check the mating surfaces of the cylinder block and the cylinder head for nicks, deep scratches and other damage. If excessive, machining may be the only alternative to renewal.

18 If warpage of the cylinder head gasket surface is suspected, use a straight-edge to check it for distortion. Refer to Part D of this Chapter, if necessary.

13.20 Note the trapezoidal tooth (arrowed) on the rear of the head gasket (2.0 litre engine)

13.11 Remove the upper retaining bolt from the alternator bracket

13.12 Disconnect the earth lead from the cylinder head

13.14 Sequence for slackening the cylinder head bolts

19 Wipe clean the mating surfaces of the cylinder head and cylinder block. Check that the locating dowels are in position in the cylinder block, and that all cylinder head bolt holes are free from oil.

20 Position a new gasket over the dowels on the cylinder block surface, making sure it is fitted the correct way around. The trapezoidal tooth (2.0 litre engines) or two trapezoidal teeth (1.8 litre engines) protruding from one edge of the gasket point to the rear of the vehicle **(see illustration)**.

21 Rotate the crankshaft anti-clockwise so

that No 1 cylinder's piston is lowered to approximately 20 mm before TDC, thus avoiding any risk of valve/piston contact and damage during reassembly.

22 Refit the cylinder head, locating it on the dowels. Fit the new cylinder head bolts; carefully enter each into its hole and screw it in, by hand only, until finger-tight.

23 Working progressively and in the sequence shown, use first a torque wrench, then an ordinary socket extension bar and an angle gauge to tighten the cylinder head bolts **(see illustrations)**. This is completed in

13.23a Tighten the cylinder head bolts in the sequence shown

13.23b Use an angle gauge for the final stages

stages given in the Specifications Section at the beginning of this Chapter. **Note:** *Once tightened correctly, following this procedure, the cylinder head bolts do not require check-tightening, and must not be retorqued.*

24 Refit the bucket tappets, the camshafts, and the timing chain as described in Sections 10 and 11.

25 The remainder of reassembly is the reverse of the removal procedure, noting the following points:
a) *See the refitting procedures in the relevant Sections and tighten all nuts and bolts to the torque wrench settings specified.*

14.3 Equipment must be available to raise and support engine/transmission unit while vehicle is raised, to allow sump removal

b) *Refill the cooling system, and top-up the engine oil.*
c) *Check all disturbed joints for signs of oil or coolant leakage, once the engine has been restarted and warmed-up to normal operating temperature.*

14 Sump –
removal and refitting

Note: *To carry out this task with the engine/transmission installed in the vehicle it requires the assistance of at least one person,*

plus the equipment necessary to raise and support the front of the vehicle (high enough that the sump can be withdrawn from underneath). It will also need a support bar across the top of the engine bay to hold the complete engine/transmission unit in place, while the vehicle is raised. Precise details of the procedure will depend on the equipment available – the following is typical.

Removal

1 Apply the handbrake, then jack up the front of the vehicle and support it on axle stands (see *Jacking and vehicle support*).

2 Drain the engine oil, then clean and refit the engine oil drain plug, tightening it to the specified torque wrench setting. **Note:** *If the drain plug seal is damaged, a new drain plug will be required.* Although not strictly necessary as part of the dismantling procedure, owners are advised to remove and discard the oil filter, so that it can be renewed with the oil (see Chapter 1A).

3 Remove the timing chain cover as described in Section 9. **Note:** *When supporting the engine/transmission, it will need to be held up using a support bar across the top of the engine, using the lifting eyes provided on the cylinder head* **(see illustration).** *Not by using a jack under the sump.*

4 Unscrew and remove the sump-to-transmission bolts **(see illustration).**

5 Progressively unscrew the sump retaining bolts **(see illustration).** Use a scraper to break the sealant around the sump, taking care not to damage the mating surfaces of the sump and cylinder block. Lower the sump and withdraw it with the engine/transmission.

Refitting

6 On reassembly, thoroughly clean and degrease the mating surfaces of the cylinder block/crankcase and sump, then use a clean rag to wipe out the sump.

7 Apply a 3.0 mm bead of sealant to the sump flange so that the bead is around the inside edge of the bolt holes **(see illustration).** **Note:** *The sump must be refitted within 10 minutes of applying the sealant.*

8 Offer up the sump and insert the retaining bolts, do not tighten them at this stage.

14.4 Remove the sump-to-transmission retaining bolts

14.5 Unscrew the retaining bolts (arrowed)

14.7 Apply a 3.0 mm bead of sealant to the sump flange

14.9a Using a straight-edge to align the sump to the cylinder block

9 Using a straight-edge, align the sump to the cylinder block on the timing chain end. With the sump held in position, progressively tighten the retaining bolts to the specified torque in the sequence shown **(see illustrations)**.

10 Refit the sump-to-transmission bolts and tighten them to the specified torque.

11 Refit the timing chain cover as described in Section 9.

12 Refit the camshaft cover as described in Section 5.

13 Lower the car to the ground and refill the engine with oil (and fit new oil filter) and the cooling system with coolant (see Chapter 1A).

14 Check for signs of oil or coolant leaks once the engine has been restarted and warmed-up to normal operating temperature.

15 Oil pump –
removal, inspection and refitting

Note: *While this task is theoretically possible when the engine is in place in the vehicle, in practise, it requires so much preliminary dismantling, and is so difficult to carry out due to the restricted access, that owners are advised to remove the engine from the vehicle first. All the illustrations used in this Section are with the engine out of the vehicle and the engine upside down on a work bench.*

Note: *In addition to the new pump gasket and other replacement parts required, read through Section 14, and ensure that the necessary tools and facilities are available.*

Removal

1 Remove the timing chain as described in Section 10.

2 Remove the sump as described in Section 14.

3 Undo the two bolts securing the oil pump pick-up pipe to the pump **(see illustration)**. Discard the O-ring/gasket.

4 Undo the two retaining bolts and remove the oil pump chain guide, then undo the retaining bolt and remove the oil pump chain tensioner **(see illustration)**.

5 Hold the oil pump drive sprocket to prevent it from turning and slacken the sprocket retaining bolt **(see illustration)**.

6 Undo the bolt and remove the oil pump sprocket complete with the oil pump drive chain.

7 Unbolt the pump from the cylinder block/crankcase **(see illustration)**. Withdraw and discard the gasket.

Inspection

8 At the time of writing there was no information on the stripdown of the oil pump, if there is any doubt in the operation of the oil pump, then the complete pump assembly should be renewed.

14.9b Sump bolt tightening sequence

Refitting

9 Thoroughly clean and degrease all components, particularly the mating surfaces of the pump, the sump, and the cylinder block/crankcase. When using a scraper and solvent to remove all traces of old gasket/sealant from the mating surfaces, be careful to ensure that you do not scratch or damage the material of either component – any solvents used must be suitable for this application.

10 The oil pump must be primed on installation, by pouring clean engine oil into it, and rotating its inner rotor a few turns.

11 Fit the new gasket in place on the oil pump using one of the retaining bolts to locate it, refit the pump to the cylinder

15.3 Remove the two bolts securing the oil pump pick-up pipe to the pump

15.4 Undo the retaining bolts (arrowed), then remove the chain guide and tensioner

15.5 Holding the oil pump drive sprocket, while undoing the sprocket retaining bolt

15.7 Undo the four retaining bolts (arrowed) to remove the oil pump

15.11 Using one of the retaining bolts to locate the new gasket in place on the oil pump

15.12 Fit a new O-ring (arrowed) to the oil pump pick-up pipe

3 Disconnect the wiring connector from the oil pressure switch on the filter housing. **Note:** *On some models, a separate oil cooler may be bolted to the top of the oil filter housing, it has two coolant hoses going to it. If required, disconnect the two coolant hoses from the oil cooler, undo the retaining bolt and remove the oil cooler from the top of the filter housing. Renew the o-ring seal on refitting.*

4 Unscrew the four retaining bolts from the filter housing and withdraw the housing from the cylinder block **(see illustration)**, be prepared for coolant loss. Discard the gasket.

5 On reassembly, thoroughly clean any gasket or sealant from the mating surfaces of the cylinder block and oil filter housing.

6 Refitting is the reverse of the removal procedure, noting the following points:

a) *Renew all gaskets* **(see illustration)**, *O-rings and seals disturbed on removal.*

b) *Tighten the housing retaining bolts to the specified torque wrench setting.*

c) *Refill the cooling system (see Chapter 1A).*

d) *Refit (or renew) the oil filter, then check the engine oil level, and top-up as necessary (see 'Weekly checks').*

e) *Check for signs of oil or coolant leaks once the engine has been restarted and warmed-up to normal operating temperature.*

15.13 Align the flats (arrowed) on the oil pump driveshaft and oil pump sprocket when refitting

15.14 Make sure the spring on the tensioner is hooked behind the bolt (arrowed) to tension the chain

17 Oil pressure warning light switch – removal and refitting

block/crankcase and insert the retaining bolts, tightening them to the specified torque wrench setting **(see illustration)**.

12 Fit the new O-ring/gasket in place and refit the pump pick-up pipe to the pump, tightening its retaining bolts securely **(see illustration)**.

13 Refit the oil pump drive chain complete with oil pump sprocket **(see illustration)** and tighten the retaining bolt to the specified torque setting. Hold the oil pump drive sprocket (using the same method as removal) to prevent it from turning when tightening the sprocket retaining bolt.

14 Refit the oil pump chain tensioner to the cylinder block, making sure the spring is located correctly **(see illustration)**. Tighten the retaining bolt to its specified torque setting.

15 Refit the oil pump chain guide to the cylinder block, tightening the two retaining bolts to their specified torque setting.

16 Refit the timing chain as described in Section 10.

17 Refit the sump as described in Section 14.

16 Oil filter housing – removal and refitting

Note: *The oil filter has coolant passing through its housing to help cool the engine oil.*

1 Drain the cooling system (see Chapter 1A).

2 If the oil filter element requires renewal, unscrew the oil filter cap from the filter housing (see Chapter 1A) – catch any escaping oil in a drip tray.

Removal

1 The switch is screwed into the oil filter housing on the front of the cylinder block **(see illustration)**.

2 With the vehicle parked on firm level ground, open the bonnet and disconnect the battery negative (earth) lead (refer to *Disconnecting the battery* at the end of this manual).

3 If required, raise the front of the vehicle, and support it securely on axle stands, this will give better access to the switch.

4 Disconnect the wiring connector from the switch, and unscrew it; be prepared for some oil loss.

16.4 Undo the retaining bolts and withdraw the filter housing from the cylinder block

16.6 Using one of the retaining bolts to locate the new gasket in place on the filter housing

17.1 The oil pressure switch (arrowed) is screwed into the oil filter housing

Refitting

5 Refitting is the reverse of the removal procedure; apply a thin smear of suitable sealant to the switch threads, and tighten it to the specified torque wrench setting. Check the engine oil level, and top-up as necessary (see *Weekly checks*). Check for signs of oil leaks once the engine has been restarted and warmed-up to normal operating temperature.

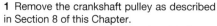

18 Crankshaft oil seals – renewal

18.4a Make sure the oil seal remains square as it is being inserted into the cover

18.4b A socket of the correct size can be used for fitting of the new seal

Timing chain end oil seal

1 Remove the crankshaft pulley as described in Section 8 of this Chapter.
2 Using a screwdriver, prise the old oil seal from the timing cover. Take care not to damage the surface of the timing cover and crankshaft. If the oil seal is tight, carefully drill two holes diagonally opposite each other in the oil seal, then insert self-tapping screws and use a pair of pliers to pull out the oil seal.
3 Wipe clean the seating in the timing cover and the nose of the crankshaft.
4 Smear clean engine oil on the outer periphery and sealing lips of the new oil seal, then start it into the timing cover by pressing it in squarely. Using a large socket or metal tubing, drive in the oil seal until flush with the outer surface of the timing cover. Make sure the oil seal remains square as it is being inserted. Wipe off any excess oil **(see illustrations)**.
5 Refit the crankshaft pulley as described in Section 8 of this Chapter.

Transmission end oil seal

Note: *At the time of writing the oil seal could not be purchased as a separate item, therefore the seal and oil seal carrier will have to be renewed as a complete unit.*

6 Remove the transmission (see the relevant Part of Chapter 7).
7 On manual models, remove the clutch assembly (see Chapter 6).
8 Unbolt the flywheel/driveplate (Section 19).
9 Remove the sump (see Section 14).
10 Undo the six retaining bolts and remove the oil seal carrier from the cylinder block. Where applicable, remove and discard its gasket.
11 Clean the seal housing and crankshaft, polishing off any burrs or raised edges, which may have caused the seal to fail in the first place. Where applicable, clean also the mating surfaces of the cylinder block/crankcase, using a scraper to remove all traces of the old gasket/sealant – be careful not to scratch or damage the material of either – then use a suitable solvent to degrease them.
12 Use a special sleeve to slide the seal over the crankshaft, if this is not available, make up a guide from a thin sheet of plastic or similar,

18.13 Tightening sequence for the oil seal carrier retaining bolts

lubricate the lips of the new seal and the crankshaft shoulder with oil, then offer up the oil seal carrier, with the guide feeding the seal's lips over the crankshaft shoulder.
13 Being careful not to damage the oil seal, move the carrier into the correct position, and tighten its bolts in the correct sequence to the specified torque wrench setting **(see illustration)**.
14 Wipe off any surplus oil or grease; the remainder of the reassembly procedure is the reverse of dismantling, referring to the relevant text for details where required. Check for signs of oil leakage when the engine is restarted.

19 Flywheel/driveplate – removal, inspection and refitting

Removal

1 Remove the transmission (see the relevant Part of Chapter 7). Now is a good time to check components such as oil seals and renew them if necessary.
2 Where appropriate, remove the clutch

(Chapter 6). Now is a good time to check or renew the clutch components.
3 Use a centre-punch or paint to make alignment marks on the flywheel/driveplate and crankshaft, to ensure correct alignment during refitting.
4 Prevent the flywheel/driveplate from turning by locking the ring gear teeth, or by bolting a strap between the flywheel/driveplate and the cylinder block/crankcase **(see illustration)**. Slacken the bolts evenly until all are free.

19.4 Lock the flywheel/driveplate while the bolts (arrowed) are removed

19.10 Apply suitable locking fluid to the threads of the new bolts on refitting

19.11 Tighten the new bolts, using the method used on dismantling for locking the flywheel/driveplate

5 Remove each bolt in turn, and ensure that new ones are obtained for reassembly; these bolts are subjected to severe stresses, and so must be renewed, regardless of their apparent condition, whenever they are disturbed.

6 Withdraw the flywheel/driveplate from the end of the crankshaft. **Note:** *Take care when removing the flywheel/driveplate as it is a very heavy component.*

Inspection

7 Clean the flywheel/driveplate to remove grease and oil. Inspect the surface for cracks, rivet grooves, burned areas and score marks. Light scoring can be removed with emery cloth. Check for cracked and broken ring gear teeth. Lay the flywheel/driveplate on a flat surface, and use a straight-edge to check for warpage.

8 Clean and inspect the mating surfaces of the flywheel/driveplate and the crankshaft. If the crankshaft left-hand oil seal is leaking, renew it (see Section 18) before refitting the flywheel/driveplate.

9 While the flywheel/driveplate is removed, clean carefully its inboard (right-hand) face. Thoroughly clean the threaded bolt holes in the crankshaft – this is important, since if old sealer remains in the threads, the bolts will settle over a period and will not retain their correct torque wrench settings.

Refitting

10 On refitting, fit the flywheel/ driveplate to the crankshaft so that all bolt holes align – it will fit only one way – check this using the

20.10a Remove the two locking nuts and the three retaining bolts (arrowed) . . .

marks made on removal. Apply suitable sealer to the threads of the new bolts then insert them **(see illustration)**.

11 Lock the flywheel/driveplate by the method used on dismantling. Working in a diagonal sequence to tighten them evenly, and increasing to the final amount in three stages, tighten the new bolts to the specified torque wrench setting **(see illustration)**.

12 The remainder of reassembly is the reverse of the removal procedure, referring to the relevant text for details where required.

---

20 Engine/transmission mountings –
inspection and renewal

General

1 The engine/transmission mountings seldom require attention, but broken or deteriorated mountings should be renewed immediately, or the added strain placed on the driveline components may cause damage or wear.

2 While separate mountings may be removed and refitted individually, if more than one is disturbed at a time – such as if the engine/transmission unit is removed from its mountings – they must be reassembled and their fasteners tightened in the position marked on removal.

3 On reassembly, the complete weight of the engine/transmission unit must not be taken by the mountings until all are correctly aligned with the marks made on removal. Tighten the

20.10b . . . and withdraw the mounting from the vehicle

engine/transmission mounting fasteners to their specified torque wrench settings.

Inspection

4 During the check, the engine/transmission unit must be raised slightly, to remove its weight from the mountings.

5 Raise the front of the vehicle, and support it securely on axle stands. Position a jack under the sump, with a large block of wood between the jack head and the sump, then carefully raise the engine/transmission just enough to take the weight off the mountings.

⚠ *Warning: DO NOT place any part of your body under the engine when it is supported only by a jack.*

6 Check the mountings to see if the rubber is cracked, hardened or separated from the metal components. Sometimes the rubber will split right down the centre.

7 Check for relative movement between each mounting's brackets and the engine/ transmission or body (use a large screwdriver or lever to attempt to move the mountings). If movement is noted, lower the engine and check-tighten the mounting fasteners.

Renewal

Note: *The following paragraphs assume the engine is supported beneath the sump as described earlier.*

Right-hand mounting

8 Remove the coolant expansion bottle from the right-hand inner wing, as described in Chapter 3.

9 Mark the position of the mounting on the vehicle, right-hand inner wing panel.

10 With the engine/transmission supported, unscrew the two locking nuts from the engine casing, then undo the three retaining bolts to the vehicle inner wing panel and withdraw the mounting from the vehicle **(see illustrations)**.

11 On refitting, tighten all fasteners to the torque wrench settings specified. Tighten the two locking nuts to the engine casing first, then release the hoist or jack to allow the mounting bracket to rest on the vehicle inner wing panel. Re-align the marks made on removal, then tighten the three mounting bracket-to-inner wing retaining bolts.

Left-hand mounting

Note: *The mounting securing nuts are self-locking, and must therefore be renewed whenever they are disturbed.*

12 Undo the retaining clip from the air intake hose **(see illustration)**, then lift the complete air cleaner assembly and remove it from the vehicle (see Chapter 4A).

13 With the transmission supported, note the position of the mounting then unscrew the centre retaining nut to release the mounting from the transmission **(see illustration)**.

14 Unscrew the four outer retaining nuts to dismantle the mounting from the mounting bracket **(see illustration)**. To remove the

20.12 Undo the retaining clip and remove the air intake hose

20.13 Unscrew the centre retaining nut

20.14 Unscrew the four mounting outer retaining nuts (arrowed)

mounting bracket, undo the retaining bolts and remove the bracket from the left-hand inner wing panel.

15 On refitting, renew the self-locking nuts. Re-align the mounting in the position noted on removal, then tighten all fasteners to the specified torque wrench settings.

Rear mounting (roll restrictor)

16 Unbolt the mounting from the subframe and the transmission by unscrewing the mounting's centre bolts **(see illustrations)**.

17 On refitting, ensure that the bolts are securely tightened to the specified torque wrench setting.

20.16a Unscrew the rear mounting's centre bolts (arrowed) . . .

20.16b . . . and remove the mounting from the subframe and the transmission

Notes

Chapter 2 Part B:
2.5 litre petrol engine in-car repair procedures

Contents

Degrees of difficulty

Easy, suitable for novice with little experience	Fairly easy, suitable for beginner with some experience	Fairly difficult, suitable for competent DIY mechanic	Difficult, suitable for experienced DIY mechanic	Very difficult, suitable for expert DIY or professional

Specifications

General

Engine type	Six-cylinder, V6 24-valve, in two banks of three cylinders, double overhead camshafts on each bank (4 camshafts in total)
Engine code	LCBD
Capacity	2544 cc
Bore	81.66 mm
Stroke	79.5 mm
Compression ratio	9.7 : 1
Power output	125 kW at 6250 rpm
Firing order	1-4-2-5-3-6 (No 1 cylinder at timing chain end of rear bank)
Direction of crankshaft rotation	Clockwise (seen from right-hand side of vehicle)

Cylinder head

Camshaft bearing diameter	26.987 to 27.012 mm
Hydraulic tappet bore diameter	16.018 to 16.057 mm
Cylinder head gasket thickness	1.0 mm
Cylinder head warp (maximum)	0.08 mm

Camshafts

Camshaft bearing journal diameter	26.926 to 26.936 mm
Camshaft bearing journal-to-cylinder head running clearance	0.0125 to 0.038 mm
Camshaft endfloat	0.025 to 0.165 mm

Lubrication

Engine oil capacity (including filter)	See Chapter 1A
Oil pressure	3.1 bars @ 1500 rpm
Oil pump clearances (inner to outer rotor max.)	0.18 mm

Torque wrench settings

	Nm	lbf ft
Big-end bolts:		
Stage 1	23	17
Stage 2	43	32
Stage 3	Angle-tighten a further 90°	
Camshaft bearing cap	10	7
Camshaft oil seal housing to front cylinder head	10	7
Camshaft position sensor	10	7
Centre bolt to rear engine roll restrictor	80	59
Coolant pipe to cylinder head	10	7
Coolant transfer pipe to cylinder head	6	4
Crankshaft position sensor to timing cover	10	7
Crankshaft pulley/vibration damper centre bolt:		
Stage 1	120	89
Stage 2	Loosen 360°	
Stage 3	50	37
Stage 4	Angle-tighten a further 90°	
Cylinder head bolts:		
Stage 1	40	30
Stage 2	Angle-tighten a further 90°	
Stage 3	Loosen 360°	
Stage 4	40	30
Stage 5	Angle-tighten a further 90°	
Stage 6	Angle-tighten a further 90°	
Cylinder head valve cover	10	7
Earth cable-to-transmission bolt	25	18
Engine mounting bracket to cylinder block	47	35
Exhaust front pipe to manifold	40	30
Exhaust manifold	20	15
Fixed timing chain guide to cylinder block	25	18
Flywheel/driveplate to crankshaft	80	59
Front engine roll restrictor to subframe	48	35
Knock sensor to cylinder head	34	25
Left-hand engine mounting:		
Automatic transmission models	48	35
Manual transmission models	90	66
Left-hand transmission mounting retaining nut	133	98
Lower crankcase to block*:		
Stage 1 (bolts 1 to 8)	25	18
Stage 2 (bolts 9 to 16)	40	30
Stage 3 (bolts 1 to 16)	Angle-tighten a further 90°	
Stage 4 (bolts 17 to 22)	25	18
Lower intake manifold	10	7
Oil baffle to crankcase	10	7
Oil baffle to sump	10	7
Oil cooler pipe to transmission	23	17
Oil cooler to cylinder block	57	42
Oil dipstick tube to transfer pipe	10	7
Oil pressure switch	14	10
Oil pump cover	10	7
Oil pump intake pipe to crankcase:		
M6	10	7
M8	25	18
Oil pump to cylinder block	11	8
Oil separator to cylinder block	10	7
Rear engine roll restrictor to subframe	48	35
Right-hand engine mounting	83	61
Sump oil drain plug	26	19
Sump	25	18
Timing chain cover to cylinder block	25	18
Timing chain tensioner to cylinder block	25	18
Torque converter to driveplate	36	27
Transmission-to-engine bolts	44	32
Upper intake manifold	10	7
Wheel nuts	85	63

* **Note:** *Bolts 1 to 16 are torque-to-yield bolts and must be renewed whenever removed.*

1 General information

How to use this Chapter

This Part of Chapter 2 is devoted to in-car repair procedures for the engine. All procedures concerning engine removal and refitting, and engine block/cylinder head overhaul can be found in Chapter 2D.

The operations included in this Part are based on the assumption that the engine is still installed in the car. Therefore, if this information is being used during a complete engine overhaul, with the engine already removed, many of the steps included here will not apply.

Engine

The engine, also known by Ford's internal code name Duratec (DURAble TECHnique), is of V6 type, mounted transversely at the front of the vehicle, with the transmission on its left-hand end. The engine is of all-aluminium construction, incorporating two banks of three cylinders each. Each cylinder has four valves, two intake and two exhaust, making a total of 24 valves.

The crankshaft runs in four main bearings, the bearing at the flywheel/driveplate end incorporates thrustwashers at each side of the bearing shell to control crankshaft endfloat. The connecting rods rotate on horizontally-split bearing shells at their big-ends. The pistons are attached to the connecting rods by fully-floating gudgeon pins which are retained by circlips in the pistons. The aluminium alloy pistons are fitted with three piston rings: two compression rings and an oil control ring. After manufacture, the cylinder bores and piston skirts are measured and classified into three grades, which must be carefully matched together, to ensure the correct piston/cylinder clearance; no oversizes are available to permit reboring.

The intake and exhaust valves are closed by coil springs; they operate in guides which are shrink-fitted into the cylinder heads, as are the valve seat inserts.

The camshafts on each bank are driven by a twin-row timing chain (one to the front bank and another to the rear bank), each operating the twelve valves on each bank via self-adjusting hydraulic tappets, thus eliminating the need for routine checking and adjustment of the valve clearances. Except for the front bank intake camshaft which rotates in five bearings, the remaining camshafts rotate in four bearings which are line-bored directly in the cylinder head and bearing caps; the bearing caps are not available separately from the cylinder head, and must not be interchanged with caps from another engine.

The water pump is bolted to the left-hand end of the cylinder block, and is driven by drivebelt from a pulley attached to the left-hand end of the front bank intake camshaft.

Lubrication

Lubrication is by means of an eccentric-rotor trochoidal pump, which is mounted on the crankshaft right-hand end, and draws oil through a strainer located in the sump. The pump forces oil through an externally-mounted full-flow cartridge-type filter – on some versions of the engine, an oil cooler is fitted to the oil filter mounting, so that clean oil entering the engine's galleries is cooled by the main engine cooling system. From the filter, the oil is pumped into a main gallery in the cylinder block/crankcase, from where it is distributed to the crankshaft (main bearings) and cylinder head.

The engine covered in this Chapter employs hydraulic tappets which use the lubricating system's oil pressure to take up the clearance between each rocker tip and its respective valve stem. Therefore, there is no need for regular checking and adjustment of the valve clearances, but it is essential that only good-quality oil of the recommended viscosity and specification is used in the engine, and that this oil is always changed at the recommended intervals. On starting the engine from cold, there will be a slight delay while full oil pressure builds-up in all parts of the engine, especially in the tappets; the valve components, therefore, may well 'rattle' for about 10 seconds or so, and then quieten. This is a normal state of affairs, and is nothing to worry about, provided that all tappets quieten quickly and stay quiet.

After the vehicle has been standing for several days, the valve components may 'rattle' for longer than usual, as nearly all the oil will have drained away from the engine's top end components and bearing surfaces. While this is only to be expected, care must be taken not to damage the engine under these circumstances – avoid high speed running until all the tappets are refilled with oil and operating normally. With the vehicle stationary, hold the engine at no more than a fast idle speed (maximum 2000 to 2500 rpm) for 10 to 15 seconds, or until the noise ceases. *Do not run the engine at more than 3000 rpm until the tappets are fully recharged with oil and the noise has ceased.*

2 Repair operations possible with the engine in the vehicle

1 The following repair operations can be accomplished without removing the engine from the vehicle.

a) *Intake and exhaust manifolds – removal and refitting.*
b) *Timing chains, tensioners and guide – removal and refitting s.*
c) *Camshafts and hydraulic tappets – removal and refitting.*
d) *Cylinder heads – removal and refitting.*
e) *Sump – removal and refitting.*

f) *Oil pump – removal and refitting.*
g) *Crankshaft oil seals – renewal.*
h) *Flywheel/driveplate – removal and refitting.*
i) *Engine/transmission mounting – removal and refitting s.*

2 Although it is possible to remove the pistons and connecting rods with the engine installed in the car after removal of the sump, it is better for the engine to be removed, in the interests of cleanliness and improved access. For this reason, the procedure is described in Chapter 2D.

3 Compression test – description and interpretation

1 When engine performance is down, or if misfiring occurs which cannot be attributed to the ignition or fuel systems, a compression test can provide diagnostic clues as to the engine's condition. If the test is performed regularly, it can give warning of trouble before any other symptoms become apparent.

2 The engine must be fully warmed-up to normal operating temperature, the oil level must be correct, the battery must be fully charged, and the spark plugs must be removed. The aid of an assistant will be required also.

3 Disable the ignition system by unplugging the ignition coil or DIS unit electrical connector.

4 Referring to Chapter 12, identify and remove the fuel pump fuse from the fusebox. Now start the engine and allow it to run until it stalls. If the engine will not start, at least keep it cranking for about 10 seconds. The fuel system should now be depressurised, preventing unburnt fuel from soaking the catalytic converter as the engine is turned over during the test.

5 Fit a compression tester to the No 1 cylinder spark plug hole – the type of tester which screws into the plug thread is to be preferred.

6 Have the assistant hold the accelerator wide open and crank the engine on the starter motor; after one or two revolutions, the compression pressure should build-up to a maximum figure, and then stabilise. Record the highest reading obtained.

7 Repeat the test on the remaining cylinders, recording the pressure developed in each.

8 Due to the variety of testers available, and the fluctuation of starter motor speed when cranking the engine, different readings are often obtained when carrying out the compression test. For this reason, specific compression pressure figures are not quoted by Ford. However, all cylinders should produce very similar pressures; any difference greater than 10% indicates the existence of a fault.

9 If the pressure in any cylinder is considerably lower than the others, introduce

4.6a TDC mark on the timing cover

4.6b Timing marks on the timing cover

4.7 With No 1 piston at TDC on compression, these marks must point to each other

a teaspoonful of clean oil into that cylinder through its spark plug hole, and repeat the test. If the addition of oil temporarily improves the compression pressure, this indicates that bore or piston wear is responsible for the pressure loss. No improvement suggests that leaking or burnt valves, or a blown head gasket, may be to blame.

10 A low reading from two adjacent cylinders is almost certainly due to the head gasket having blown between them; the presence of coolant in the engine oil will confirm this.

11 On completion of the test, refit the spark plugs, then reconnect the ignition system coil and refit the fuel pump fuse.

4 Top Dead Centre (TDC) for No 1 piston – locating

⚠️ **Warning: When turning the engine to locate TDC, always turn it in the normal direction of rotation.**

1 Top Dead Centre (TDC) is the highest point in the cylinder that each piston reaches as it travels up-and-down when the crankshaft rotates. Each piston reaches TDC on the compression stroke and again on the exhaust stroke, but TDC generally refers to piston position on the compression stroke. The timing marks on the vibration damper fitted to the front of the crankshaft refer to the number one piston at TDC on the compression stroke.

2 No 1 piston is at the right-hand end of the rear bank, with pistons 2 and 3 on the same bank. No 4 piston is at the right-hand end of the front bank, with pistons 5 and 6 on the same bank.

3 Remove all the spark plugs (Chapter 1A). This will make turning the engine easier. For better access to the crankshaft pulley, the front wheel and wheel arch liner can be removed if preferred.

4 The engine may be turned using a socket on the crankshaft pulley centre bolt. Alternatively on a manual transmission model, it may be turned by jacking up the right-hand side of the car so that the wheel is just clear of the ground, and turning the wheel with 4th gear engaged.

5 Turn the engine clockwise and feel for compression from the No 1 spark plug hole. To do this, temporarily insert a suitable plug (such as the handle of a screwdriver) over the spark plug hole. It is important that compression is felt, otherwise the following procedure will position the No 1 piston at TDC on the exhaust stroke instead of the compression stroke.

6 Continue to turn the engine until the crankshaft pulley keyway on the crankshaft is at the 11 o'clock position. The timing mark on the edge of the pulley must be exactly in line with the TDC arrow on the timing cover. **Note:** *On some models, there may be two other timing marks on the timing cover, indicating 10° and 30° before top dead centre (see illustrations).*

7 If necessary, for a further check, the cylinder head covers may be removed (see Section 5) and the position of the timing marks on the rear of the camshaft sprockets checked. With No 1 piston at TDC on compression, the marks must point to each other **(see illustration)**.

8 Once the engine has been positioned at TDC for No 1 piston, TDC for any of the remaining cylinders can be located by turning the crankshaft 120° and following the firing order (refer to the Specifications). Mark the crankshaft pulley at 120° intervals past the TDC notch. Turning the engine to the first mark past the No 1 TDC position, will locate No 4 piston at TDC. Another 120° will locate No 2 piston at TDC.

5 Cylinder head cover – removal and refitting

Front cylinder head cover

Removal

1 Remove the upper intake manifold as described in Section 6 of this Chapter.

2 Unscrew the bolts securing the intake manifold runner control actuator (IMRC) to the front cylinder head cover and unclip the wiring and cable and position to one side. Disconnect the wiring if necessary **(see illustrations)**.

3 Note the location of the HT leads and if necessary identify them. Disconnect the HT

5.2a Unscrew the bolts (arrowed) and remove the IMRC actuator from the valve cover . . .

5.2b . . . then release the cable from the clips near the water pump pulley

5.2c If necessary disconnect the wiring from the IMRC actuator

5.3a Disconnect the HT leads from the spark plugs . . .

5.3b . . . and remove the lead support from the top of the right-hand engine mounting

5.4 Disconnect the crankcase ventilation hose from the top of the valve cover

5.6 Removing the front valve cover

5.8a Locate new spark plug hole gaskets in the cylinder head cover . . .

5.8b . . . then fit the outer gasket in the groove

leads from the spark plugs and remove the lead support from the right-hand engine mounting **(see illustrations)**.

4 Release the crankcase ventilation hose from the top of the valve cover **(see illustration)**.

5 At both ends of the cylinder head cover, unclip the wiring harness bracket from the cylinder head cover retaining studs.

6 Using the reverse of the sequence shown **(see illustration 5.8c)**, progressively unscrew the cylinder head cover bolts. With all the bolts removed, lift off the cover and remove the gaskets **(see illustration)**.

Refitting

7 Make sure the mating faces of the cover and cylinder head are perfectly clean. Apply an 8 mm diameter bead of suitable sealer to the joints between the timing cover and cylinder head, and the water pump drive pulley housing and cylinder head. Observe the instructions with the sealer, as normally the fitting procedure must be completed within a few minutes of applying the sealer.

8 Locate new spark plug hole gaskets in the cylinder head cover, then fit the outer gasket in the groove **(see illustrations)**. Fit the cylinder head cover and tighten the mounting

bolts to the specified torque in the sequence shown **(see illustration)**. Make sure the O-ring seals are correctly fitted to the bolts.

9 Clip the wiring loom to the cylinder head cover retaining studs.

10 Reconnect the HT leads to the spark plugs and to the lead support on the right-hand engine mounting.

11 Refit the intake manifold runner control actuator (IMRC) wiring and support.

12 Refit the upper intake manifold together with new gaskets as described in Section 6 of this Chapter. Tighten the retaining bolts in the sequence shown **(see illustration)**.

5.8c Tightening sequence for the front cylinder head cover bolts

5.12 Tightening sequence for the upper inlet manifold bolts

5.15 Remove the ignition coil assembly along with the earth cable and suppressor

5.18 Removing the wiring harness support bracket from the right-hand side of the rear cylinder head cover

5.19 Unscrew the bolts and lift off the rear cylinder head cover

5.21a Tightening sequence for the rear cylinder head cover bolts

5.21b Note the O-ring seals on the cover mounting bolts

Rear cylinder head cover

Removal

13 Remove the upper intake manifold as described in Section 6 of this Chapter.

14 Note the location of the HT leads and if necessary identify them. Disconnect the HT leads from the spark plugs and from the lead support on the right-hand engine mounting.

15 Unscrew the bolts and remove the ignition coil assembly, also removing the earth cable and suppressor **(see illustration)**.

16 Disconnect the wiring connectors and move the coil and suppressor to one side.

17 At both ends of the cylinder head cover, unclip the wiring harness bracket from the cylinder head cover retaining studs.

18 Disconnect the wiring then unbolt the wiring harness bracket from the rear cylinder head cover **(see illustration)**.

19 Using the reverse of the sequence shown **(see illustration 5.21a)**, progressively unscrew the cylinder head cover bolts. With all the bolts removed, lift off the cover and remove the gasket **(see illustration)**.

Refitting

20 Make sure the mating faces of the cover and cylinder head are perfectly clean. Apply an 8 mm diameter bead of suitable sealer to

the joints between the timing cover and cylinder head. Observe the instructions with the sealer, as normally the fitting procedure must be completed within a few minutes of applying the sealer.

21 Locate new spark plug hole gaskets in the cylinder head cover, then fit the outer gasket in the groove. Fit the cylinder head cover and tighten the mounting bolts to the specified torque in the sequence shown **(see illustration)**. Make sure the O-ring seals are correctly fitted to the mounting bolts **(see illustration)**.

22 Refit the wiring harness rail to the rear of

6.2a One of the cover bolts secures a coolant hose clip

the cylinder head cover and tighten the bolt(s).

23 Refit the front wiring harness bracket to the both ends of the cylinder head cover retaining studs.

24 Refit the ignition coil/suppressor assembly and tighten the bolts. Reconnect the wiring and refit the earth cable.

25 Reconnect the HT leads to the spark plugs and to the lead support on the right-hand engine mounting.

26 Refit the upper intake manifold together with new gaskets and tighten the retaining bolts in the sequence shown, as described in Section 6 of this Chapter.

6 Intake manifolds – removal and refitting

Upper manifold

Removal

1 Disconnect the battery negative (earth) lead (refer to *Disconnecting the battery* at the end of this manual).

2 Undo the three retaining bolts and remove the plastic cover from the top of the front cylinder bank **(see illustrations)**.

6.2b Undo the bolts (arrowed) and lift the plastic cover from the top of the front cylinder bank

6.3a Disconnecting the crankcase ventilation hoses from the front of the air duct . . .

6.3b . . . and the rear of the air duct

6.5 Disconnecting the vacuum hose from the upper manifold

6.6a Disconnecting the retaining clip . . .

6.6b . . . withdraw the locking clip . . .

3 Disconnect the crankcase ventilation hoses from each side of the air intake duct leading from the air cleaner to the throttle body **(see illustrations)**.
4 Loosen the two clips and disconnect the air intake duct from the throttle body and air cleaner. Remove the duct.
5 Disconnect the brake vacuum servo hose from the upper intake manifold **(see illustration)**.

6 Use a screwdriver to prise off the retaining clips, then disconnect the accelerator and speed control cables from the mounting bracket **(see illustrations)**.
7 Unbolt and remove the accelerator cable mounting bracket.
8 Disconnect the wiring from the idle air control (IAC) valve and throttle position (TP) sensor **(see illustrations)**.
9 Where applicable, disconnect the vacuum hose from the EGR valve, then unscrew the valve mounting bolts and recover the gasket. If necessary, remove the valve from the tube **(see illustrations)**.
10 Disconnect the positive crankcase ventilation (PCV) hose from the intake manifold stub **(see illustration)**.
11 Where applicable, disconnect the wiring and vacuum hoses from the EGR vacuum regulator **(see illustrations)**.

6.6c . . . and remove the accelerator cable

6.8a Disconnecting the wiring from the idle air control valve . . .

6.8b . . . and throttle position sensor

6.9a Disconnecting the vacuum hose from the EGR valve

6.9b Unscrew the bolts . . .

6.9c ... and recover the gasket from the EGR valve

6.10 Disconnecting the positive crankcase ventilation (PCV) hose from the upper inlet manifold

6.11a Disconnect the wiring ...

6.11b ... and vacuum hoses from the EGR vacuum regulator

12 Progressively unscrew the upper intake manifold mounting bolts in the reverse order to that shown **(see illustration 5.12)** , then remove the upper manifold. Recover the gaskets from the lower intake manifold. Recover the rubber insulators from the mounting bolts and inspect them – if they are not serviceable, renew them **(see illustrations)**.

6.12a Upper inlet manifold mounting bolts (arrowed)

6.12b Mounting bolts and rubber insulators

6.12c Removing the upper inlet manifold ...

6.12d ... and gaskets

Refitting

13 Clean the mating surfaces of the upper and lower intake manifolds.
14 Locate new gaskets on the lower manifold, then refit the upper manifold. Insert the bolts and tighten to the specified torque in the sequence shown **(see illustration 5.12)**.
15 Reconnect the vacuum hose and wiring to the EGR vacuum regulator.
16 Reconnect the PCV hose to the intake manifold stub.
17 Refit the EGR valve together with a new gasket and tighten the bolts. Reconnect the vacuum hose.
18 Reconnect the wiring to the throttle position sensor and idle air control valve.
19 Reconnect the accelerator and speed control cables to the mounting bracket and retain with the clip.
20 Reconnect the brake vacuum servo hose(s) to the upper intake manifold.
21 Refit the air intake duct and tighten the securing clips.
22 Reconnect the idle air control valve hose to the air intake duct.
23 Reconnect the crankcase ventilation hoses each side of the air intake duct.
24 Refit the plastic cover to the top of the front cylinder bank and tighten the retaining bolts.
25 Reconnect the battery negative (earth) lead. **Note:** *After the battery has been disconnected, the engine management system requires approximately 10 miles of driving to relearn its optimum settings. During this period, the engine may not perform normally.*

Lower manifold

Removal

26 Depressurise the fuel system as described in Chapter 4A.
27 Disconnect the battery negative (earth) lead (refer to *Disconnecting the battery* at the end of this manual).
28 Remove the upper intake manifold as described earlier in this Section.
29 Disconnect the fuel feed and return lines. For further information on fuel lines and fittings see Chapter 4A, Section 3.
30 Disconnect the wiring harness from across the top of the fuel rail and the injectors.
31 Disconnect the vacuum hose from the fuel pressure regulator.
32 Disconnect the intake manifold runner control (IMRC) actuator rod or cable from the stud and bracket on the front cylinder head cover, and disconnect the vacuum hose from the IMRC vacuum solenoid.
33 Progressively unscrew the lower intake manifold mounting bolts in the reverse sequence to that shown **(see illustration 6.38)**.
34 With all the bolts removed, lift the lower intake manifold from the cylinder heads and recover the gaskets **(see illustrations)**.

6.34a Unscrew and remove the bolts . . .

6.34b . . . then remove the lower inlet manifold from the cylinder heads . . .

6.34c . . . and recover the gaskets

35 Clean the mating surfaces of the manifold and cylinder head taking care not to damage the aluminium surfaces.

Refitting

36 Place the new gaskets on the cylinder head, making sure that the they are located correctly.

37 Carefully position the lower intake manifold on the gaskets making sure that the gaskets are not displaced.

38 Insert the bolts and progressively tighten them to the specified torque in the sequence shown **(see illustration)**.

39 Reconnect the IMRC vacuum hose or actuator rod.

40 Reconnect the vacuum hose to the fuel pressure regulator.

41 Reroute the wiring across the top of the fuel rail and connect the wiring plugs to the injectors, reconnect any other connectors that have been disconnected.

42 Reconnect the fuel line.

43 Reconnect the battery negative (earth) lead. **Note:** *After the battery has been disconnected, the engine management system requires approximately 10 miles of driving to relearn its optimum settings. During this period, the engine may not perform normally.*

6.38 Tightening sequence for the lower inlet manifold bolts

4 If necessary for additional working room, drain the cooling system and remove the radiator bottom hose.

5 Unbolt the exhaust front pipe (Y-pipe) from the exhaust manifolds.

6 Unscrew the mounting nuts and withdraw the exhaust manifold from the studs on the cylinder head. Remove the gasket and discard it along with the retaining nuts **(see illustrations)**.

7 If necessary, unscrew the oxygen sensor with reference to Chapter 4A.

8 Clean the mating surfaces of the exhaust manifold and cylinder head.

Refitting

9 If removed, refit the oxygen sensor and

tighten to the specified torque with reference to Chapter 4A.

10 Position a new gasket on the cylinder head studs.

11 Refit the exhaust manifold and progressively tighten the new mounting nuts to the specified torque.

12 Reconnect the exhaust front pipe (Y-pipe) to the exhaust manifolds and tighten the bolts to the specified torque.

13 Where removed, reconnect the radiator bottom hose and tighten the clip. Refill the cooling system with reference to Chapter 1A.

14 Where applicable, reconnect the EGR transfer tube and tighten the union nut.

15 Reconnect the oxygen sensor wiring, then refit the plastic cover to the top of the front cylinder bank and tighten the retaining bolts.

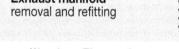

7 Exhaust manifold –
removal and refitting

⚠ *Warning: The engine must be completely cold before starting this procedure.*

Front exhaust manifold

Removal

1 Disconnect the battery negative (earth) lead (refer to *Disconnecting the battery* at the end of this manual).

2 Undo the three retaining bolts and remove the plastic cover from the top of the front cylinder bank, then disconnect the oxygen sensor wiring connector located on the engine lifting eye bracket.

3 Where fitted, unscrew the union nut and disconnect the EGR transfer tube from the exhaust manifold.

7.6a Remove the front exhaust manifold . . .

7.6b . . . and remove the gasket

7.24a Remove the rear exhaust manifold . . .

7.24b . . . and remove the gasket

16 Reconnect the battery negative (earth) lead. **Note:** *After the battery has been disconnected, the engine management system requires approximately 10 miles of driving to relearn its optimum settings. During this period, the engine may not perform normally.*

Rear exhaust manifold

Removal

17 Disconnect the battery negative (earth) lead (refer to *Disconnecting the battery* at the end of this manual).

18 Apply the handbrake, then jack up the front of the vehicle and support it on axle stands (see *Jacking and vehicle support*). Remove the right-hand front wheel.

19 Remove the alternator as described in Chapter 5A. Also unbolt and remove the alternator mounting bracket from the cylinder block.

8.5 Hold the crankshaft stationary using a scissor bar while the pulley bolt is loosened

20 With reference to Chapter 4C, remove the catalytic converter from the exhaust system. Also remove the exhaust front pipe (Y-pipe) from the bottom of the exhaust manifolds.

21 Unscrew and remove the oxygen sensor from the manifold with reference to Chapter 4A.

22 Where fitted, unscrew the union nut and disconnect the EGR transfer tube from the exhaust manifold.

23 Undo the bolt securing the rear engine/transmission mounting roll restrictor and move the engine forward slightly, supporting it with a block of wood. **Note:** *Take care not to damage any components when moving the engine forward.*

24 Unscrew the mounting nuts and withdraw the exhaust manifold from the studs on the cylinder head. Remove the gasket and discard it along with the retaining nuts **(see illustrations)**.

25 Clean the mating surfaces of the exhaust manifold and cylinder head.

Refitting

26 Position a new gasket on the cylinder head studs.

27 Refit the exhaust manifold and progressively tighten the new mounting nuts to the specified torque.

28 Remove the block of wood, then refit the bolt securing the rear engine/transmission mounting roll restrictor.

29 Where applicable, reconnect the EGR transfer tube and tighten the union nut.

30 Refit the oxygen sensor to the manifold with reference to Chapter 4A.

31 Refit the exhaust front pipe (Y-pipe) and

catalytic converter with reference to Chapter 4A and 4C.

32 Refit the alternator mounting bracket and tighten the bolts, then refit the alternator with reference to Chapter 5A.

33 Refit the right-hand wheel and lower the car to the ground.

34 Reconnect the battery negative (earth) lead. **Note:** *After the battery has been disconnected, the engine management system requires approximately 10 miles of driving to relearn its optimum settings. During this period, the engine may not perform normally.*

8 Crankshaft pulley – removal and refitting

Removal

1 Disconnect the battery negative (earth) lead (refer to *Disconnecting the battery* at the end of this manual).

2 Apply the handbrake, then jack up the front of the vehicle and support it on axle stands (see *Jacking and vehicle support*). Remove the right-hand wheel.

3 Remove the right-hand wheel arch liner with reference to Chapter 11.

4 Using a socket in the square provided, turn the main auxiliary drivebelt tensioner clockwise and slip the belt from the pulleys on the right-hand end of the engine. Carefully release the tensioner.

5 The crankshaft pulley must now be held stationary while the bolt is loosened. On manual transmission models have an assistant engage 4th gear and firmly depress the footbrake pedal. On automatic transmission models, remove the cover from the transmission bellhousing and have an assistant engage a wide-blade screwdriver with the teeth of the starter ring gear. Alternatively, the pulley can be held stationary by bolting a length of metal bar to it using the threaded holes provided, or by using a scissor bar **(see illustration)**.

6 Loosen the bolt then unscrew it completely and remove the washer **(see illustration)**. When fitted, the bolt is torqued-to-yield, and a new bolt must therefore be used on refitting.

8.6 Removing the crankshaft pulley bolt and washer

8.7a Using a puller to remove the crankshaft pulley from the end of the crankshaft

8.7b Removing the crankshaft pulley

7 Using a suitable puller, draw the crankshaft pulley from the end of the crankshaft. If the Woodruff key is loose, remove it from the groove in the crankshaft and keep it in a safe place **(see illustrations)**.

8 Clean the crankshaft pulley and the end of the crankshaft.

Refitting

9 Apply suitable sealer to the key groove on the inside of the pulley. If removed, locate the Woodruff key in the crankshaft groove, making sure that it is parallel with the surface of the crankshaft.

10 Locate the pulley on the crankshaft and engage it with the key. Use the old pulley bolt and washer to draw the pulley fully onto the crankshaft. Unscrew the old bolt and discard it.

11 Insert the new bolt together with the washer, and tighten it to the specified torque and angle while holding the crankshaft stationary using the method described in paragraph 5. Note that the bolt is tightened in four stages as described in the Specifications **(see illustrations)**.

12 Remove the holding tool, and on automatic transmission models refit the cover to the transmission bellhousing.

13 Refit the main auxiliary drivebelt to the right-hand end of the engine with reference to Chapter 1A.

14 Refit the right-hand wheel arch liner with reference to Chapter 11.

15 Refit the right-hand wheel and lower the car to the ground.

8.11a Using a torque wrench to tighten the crankshaft pulley bolt

9 Timing chain cover – removal and refitting

Removal

1 Disconnect the battery negative (earth) lead (refer to *Disconnecting the battery* at the end of this manual). Apply the handbrake, then jack up the front of the vehicle and support it on axle stands (see *Jacking and vehicle support*). Remove the right-hand wheel.

2 Drain the engine oil (see Chapter 1A).

3 Remove both cylinder head covers as described in Section 5.

4 Remove the alternator as described in Chapter 5A. Also unbolt the alternator mounting bracket from the cylinder block and timing cover.

8.11b Using an angle disc to tighten the crankshaft pulley bolt to the specified angle

5 Remove the crankshaft pulley as described in Section 8.

6 Support the weight of the engine with a hoist or engine support bar. If the timing cover is being removed in order to remove the cylinder heads, the hoist must be attached to the right-hand mounting bracket on the cylinder block **(see illustration)**.

7 Disconnect the wiring from the low coolant warning switch (where fitted), then undo the coolant expansion tank mounting screws and position the tank to one side. If the timing cover is being removed in order to remove the cylinder heads, drain the cooling system and remove the expansion tank completely after disconnecting the hoses **(see illustrations)**.

8 Mark the position of the right-hand engine mounting, then unscrew the nuts and bolts and remove the mounting and bracket, noting the location of any earth cables.

9 Loosen only the bolts securing the pulley to the power steering pump.

10 Using a socket in the square provided, turn the main auxiliary drivebelt tensioner clockwise and slip the belt from the pulleys. Carefully release the tensioner.

11 Fully unscrew the bolts and remove the pulley from the power steering pump, then remove the pump with reference to Chapter 10 but do not disconnect the hydraulic fluid hoses. Position the pump together with the hydraulic lines on the bulkhead **(see illustrations)**.

12 Disconnect the wiring from the camshaft position sensor on the upper part of the timing cover. If necessary, the sensor can be removed at this stage **(see illustration)**.

9.6 Engine support bar attached to the right-hand mounting bracket on the cylinder block

9.7a Disconnecting the low coolant warning switch wiring

9.7b Coolant hoses on the expansion tank

9.7c Expansion tank front mounting bolt

9.7d Removing the expansion tank

9.11a Using a strap wrench to hold the pulley while the bolts are unscrewed

9.11b Removing the power steering pump pulley

9.11c Withdrawing the power steering pump with the hydraulic lines still connected

9.12 Disconnect the wiring connector from the camshaft position sensor (arrowed)

9.16 Stud bolts at the top of the timing cover (power steering pump mounting)

9.17 Removing the timing cover bolts

13 Remove the sump with reference to Section 14.

14 Disconnect the wiring from the crankshaft position sensor on the lower part of the timing cover. If necessary, the sensor can be removed at this stage.

15 If necessary for improved working room, unbolt the air conditioning compressor and position it to one side. Do not disconnect the refrigerant lines from the compressor.

16 Note the location of the bolts and stud bolts on the timing cover to ensure correct refitting. If necessary, make a drawing of the bolt positions **(see illustration)**.

17 Progressively unscrew the bolts from the timing cover in the reverse sequence to that shown **(see illustration and illustration 9.23)**.

18 Remove the timing cover from the location dowels on the engine and withdraw it over the nose of the crankshaft. Carefully remove the cover from the engine compartment, taking care not to damage it as there is very little room to manœuvre it between the engine and inner wing panel. Remove the gaskets from the cover **(see illustration)**.

19 Clean the contact surfaces of the timing cover, cylinder block and head, taking care not to damage the aluminium faces.

20 If necessary, renew the crankshaft oil seal as described in Section 18. Alternatively, it can be fitted after the timing cover is in position **(see illustration)**. Also if necessary, remove the auxiliary drivebelt tensioner from the timing cover.

9.18 Removing the timing cover from the engine

9.20 Fitting a new crankshaft oil seal with the timing cover on the bench

Refitting

21 Apply suitable sealer as beads, 6.0 mm long, at the joints between the cylinder head and block, and between the main bearing ladder and cylinder block **(see illustration)**.

22 Locate new gaskets in the timing cover grooves **(see illustration)**.

23 Refit the timing cover with gaskets,

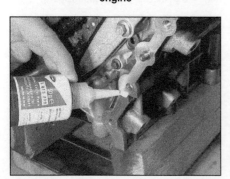

9.21 Apply sealer at the joints between the main bearing ladder and block

9.22 Locate a new gasket in the timing cover grooves

making sure that it locates correctly on the dowels. Insert the bolts and stud bolts in their original positions, and first tighten them by hand only. Finally, progressively tighten the bolts to the specified torque in the sequence shown **(see illustration)**.

24 If removed, refit the auxiliary drivebelt tensioner to the timing cover **(see illustrations)**.

25 If removed, refit the air conditioning compressor with reference to Chapter 3 and tighten the bolts.

26 Refit the sump with reference to Section 14.

27 Refit the crankshaft position sensor and the camshaft position sensor, and reconnect the wiring.

28 Refit the power steering pump with reference to Chapter 10 and tighten the bolts to the specified torque. Refit the pulley and tighten the bolts.

29 Locate the main auxiliary drivebelt on its pulleys and release the tensioner with reference to Chapter 1A.

30 Refit the right-hand engine mounting and bracket in their previously noted positions and tighten the nuts and bolts to the specified torque. Make sure that any earth cables that have been removed are refitted back to the engine mounting bracket. Refit the expansion tank and tighten the mounting screws.

31 Remove the engine lifting hoist.

32 Refit the crankshaft pulley with reference to Section 8.

33 Refit the alternator bracket and alternator with reference to Chapter 5A.

34 Refit the cylinder head covers with reference to Section 5.

35 Reconnect the battery negative (earth) lead. **Note:** *After the battery has been disconnected, the engine management system requires approximately 10 miles of driving to relearn its optimum settings. During this period, the engine may not perform normally.*

36 Refit the right-hand wheel and lower the car to the ground.

37 Refill the engine with oil (see Chapter 1A).

---

10 Timing chains, tensioners and guides – removal, inspection and refitting

Removal

1 Set the engine to TDC on No 1 cylinder as described in Section 4.

2 Remove the timing cover as described in Section 9.

3 Slide the crankshaft position sensor pulse ring from the front of the crankshaft noting which way round it is fitted. Mark the sensor to ensure it is refitted correctly **(see illustration)**.

4 Temporarily screw the crankshaft pulley bolt in the end of the crankshaft so the crankshaft can be turned with a socket.

9.23 Tightening sequence for the timing cover bolts/studs

J34911

5 Note that the timing chain for a particular bank must be removed with the crankshaft at the relevant removal position for that bank. This ensures the camshafts have even valve spring pressure along their lengths. To remove the rear timing chain, turn the crankshaft until the crankshaft pulley keyway is at the 3 o'clock position.

6 If there are no markings on the timing chain, mark the links in relation to the sprocket timing marks with dabs of paint as an aid to refitting. If there are markings on the chain, it is unlikely that they will be aligned with the sprocket marks, however they may be used when refitting the chains. The original marks may be in the form of copper links or white painted dots.

7 Unbolt the rear timing chain tensioner, then

9.24a Refit the auxiliary drivebelt tensioner . . .

9.24b . . . and secure with the special bolt

9.24c Refitting the auxiliary drivebelt idler

10.3 Slide the crankshaft position sensor pulse ring from the front of the crankshaft

10.7a Unscrew the bolts . . .

10.7b . . . and remove the rear timing chain
tensioner

10.7c Removing the rear timing chain
tensioner guide

10.8 Removing the fixed timing chain
guide for the rear timing chain

10.9a Disconnecting the rear timing chain
from the crankshaft sprocket . . .

10.9b . . . and camshaft sprockets

remove the tensioner guide from its pivot **(see
illustrations)**.
8 Unbolt the fixed timing chain guide for the
rear timing chain **(see illustration)**.
9 Disengage the rear timing chain from the

crankshaft and camshaft sprockets and
remove from the engine **(see illustrations)**. If
it is to be re-used, make sure it is identified for
the correct fitted position.
10 Remove the crankshaft pulley bolt, then

slide the rear timing chain sprocket from the
crankshaft, noting which way round it is fitted.
Mark the sprocket to ensure it is refitted the
same way round **(see illustration)**.
11 Remove the intake and exhaust
camshafts from the rear engine bank as
described in Section 12. This is to prevent
valve damage when rotating the engine.
12 To remove the front timing chain, first refit
the crankshaft pulley bolt, then turn the
crankshaft forward one and three quarter
turns until the crankshaft pulley keyway is at
the 11 o'clock position.
13 If there are no markings on the timing
chain, mark the links in relation to the
sprocket timing marks with dabs of paint as
an aid to refitting. If there are markings on the
chain, it is unlikely that they will be aligned
with the sprocket marks, however they may
be used when refitting the chains. The original
marks may be in the form of copper links or
white painted dots.
14 Unbolt the front timing chain tensioner,
then remove the tensioner guide from its pivot
(see illustrations).
15 Disengage the front timing chain from the
crankshaft and camshaft sprockets and
remove from the engine **(see illustrations)**. If
it is to be re-used, make sure it is identified for
the correct fitted position.
16 Unbolt the fixed timing chain guide for the
front timing chain **(see illustration)**.
17 Slide the front timing chain sprocket from
the crankshaft, noting which way round it is
fitted. Mark the sprocket to ensure it is refitted
the same way round **(see illustration)**.

10.10 Removing the rear timing chain
crankshaft sprocket

10.14a Unscrew the bolt . . .

10.14b . . . and remove the front timing
chain tensioner . . .

10.14c . . . and tensioner guide

Inspection

Note: *Keep all components identified for position to ensure correct refitting.*

18 Clean all components thoroughly and wipe dry.

19 Examine the chain tensioners and tensioner guides for excessive wear or other damage. Check the guides for deep grooves made by the timing chains.

20 Examine the timing chains for excessive wear. Hold them horizontally and check how much movement exists in the chain links. If there is any doubt, compare them to new chains. Renew as necessary.

21 Examine the teeth of the camshaft and crankshaft sprockets for excessive wear and damage. Note that the sprockets are integral with the camshafts, and if worn excessively, the complete camshaft must be renewed.

22 Before refitting the timing chain tensioners, their pistons must be compressed and locked until refitted. To do this, insert a small screwdriver into the access hole in the tensioner and release the pawl mechanism. Now lightly clamp the tensioner in a soft-jawed vice and slowly compress the piston. Do not apply excessive force and make sure that the piston remains aligned with its cylinder. When completely compressed, insert a paper clip or similar 1.5 mm diameter wire rod into the special hole to lock the piston in its compressed position.

Refitting

23 If necessary, turn the crankshaft so that the crankshaft pulley keyway is in the 11 o'clock position. This is the position for refitting the front timing chain. **Note:** *The engine should still be in this position, as the front timing chain was the last to be removed.*

24 Refit the fixed timing chain guide for the front timing chain and tighten the mounting bolts.

25 Engage the front timing chain with the

10.15a Disengage the front timing chain from the crankshaft sprocket . . .

10.15b . . . and camshaft sprocket

10.16 Fixed timing chain guide for the front timing chain

10.17 Slide the front timing chain sprocket from the crankshaft

camshaft sprockets, making sure that the paint marks/copper links on the timing chain are aligned with the timing marks on the outside of the camshaft sprockets **(see illustration)**.

26 Locate the crankshaft sprocket in the timing chain making sure that the timing marks are correctly aligned, then fit the sprocket onto the crankshaft and engage it with the key **(see illustration)**. The front run of the chain must be against the fixed guide, but the rear run will be loose at this stage.

27 Refit the tensioner guide on its pivot, then refit the tensioner (and adapter plate if fitted) and tighten the mounting bolts to the specified

torque. Check that the position marks are still aligned, then remove the 1.5 mm wire rod to release the tensioner. The internal spring is very strong, and it is preferable to hold the chain guide against the tension and release it slowly **(see illustrations)**.

28 Turn the crankshaft clockwise so that the crankshaft pulley key groove is in the 3 o'clock position. This is the position for refitting the rear timing chain.

29 Refit the intake and exhaust camshafts to the rear engine bank as described in Section 12.

30 Slide the rear timing chain sprocket onto the crankshaft.

10.25 Engage the front timing chain with the camshaft sprockets, making sure that the timing marks are correctly aligned

10.26 Locate the sprocket on the front of the crankshaft, making sure that the timing marks are correctly aligned

10.27a Locate the timing chain tensioner on the block. Note the welding rod holding the tensioner plunger

10.27b Tightening the tensioner mounting bolts

10.27c Hold the chain guide against the spring tension when removing the locking wire rod

31 Refit the fixed timing chain guide for the rear timing chain and tighten the mounting bolts.

32 Engage the rear timing chain with the camshaft and crankshaft sprockets, making sure that the paint marks/copper links are aligned with the timing marks on the outside of the sprockets. The front run of the chain must be against the fixed guide, but the rear run will be loose at this stage.

33 Refit the tensioner guide on its pivot, then refit the tensioner (and adapter plate if fitted) and tighten the mounting bolts to the specified torque. Check that the timing marks are still aligned then remove the wire to release the tensioner.

34 Slide the crankshaft position sensor pulse ring onto the front of the crankshaft making sure that the key groove with the blue painted mark is engaged with the key. The ring may be marked 2.5L and FRONT **(see illustration)**.

35 Temporarily refit the crankshaft pulley bolt, and rotate the engine clockwise two complete turns so that the crankshaft key is located at the 11 o'clock position. **Note:** *After turning the engine, the timing chain timing marks will no longer align with the marks on the sprockets, but the timing marks on the rear of the camshaft sprockets must face each other.*

36 Refit the timing cover with reference to Section 9.

10.34 The crankshaft position sensor pulse ring has a FRONT mark on it

11 Camshaft oil seal – renewal

Note: *There is only one camshaft oil seal located on the left-hand end of the front intake camshaft. This is because this camshaft drives the water pump by means of a drivebelt. The sprockets at the timing end of the camshafts are enclosed within the timing cover.*

Note: *Check the availability of parts, as the seal may be sold as part of the housing, and not be available as a separate item.*

1 Disconnect the battery negative (earth) lead (refer to *Disconnecting the battery* at the end of this manual).

2 Undo the three retaining bolts and remove the plastic cover from the top of the front cylinder bank.

3 Remove the water pump drivebelt by moving the tensioner towards the camshaft. Remove the drivebelt from the pulleys, then carefully release the tensioner.

4 The pulley must now be removed from the camshaft. To do this, use a suitable puller.

5 If the seal is available separately, use a screwdriver to carefully prise the oil seal from its bore, taking care not to damage the camshaft or bore.

6 If the seal is supplied together with the housing, it will be necessary to unbolt the housing from the cylinder head and remove the gasket.

7 Wipe clean the camshaft and bore in oil seal housing, or cylinder head face for oil seal housing.

8 Where the seal is available separately, smear clean engine oil on the new oil seal outer periphery and sealing lip, then use a suitable socket or metal tube to drive the oil seal into its bore in the housing, making sure it is kept square. Wipe clean any surplus engine oil.

9 Where the seal is supplied together with the housing, fit a new gasket to the oil seal housing, then smear clean engine oil on the sealing lip of the oil seal. Fit the housing to the cylinder head, while guiding the oil seal onto the end of the camshaft. Then insert and tighten the retaining bolts to the specified torque.

10 Press the pulley onto the camshaft using a bolt screwed into the centre hole, together with a nut and washers. The pulley outer face must be flush with the end of the camshaft to ensure correct alignment with the water pump pulley and tensioner. If the pulley is very tight, preheat it with a heat gun before fitting it.

11 Move the tensioner towards the camshaft and refit the water pump drivebelt on the pulleys. Release the tensioner and make sure that the drivebelt is correctly engaged with the pulleys.

12 Refit the plastic cover to the front cylinder bank and tighten the retaining bolts.

13 Reconnect the battery negative (earth) lead. **Note:** *After the battery has been disconnected, the engine management system requires approximately 10 miles of driving to relearn its optimum settings. During this period, the engine may not perform normally.*

12 Camshafts, hydraulic tappets and rocker arms – removal, inspection and refitting

Note: *All camshafts, bearing caps, hydraulic tappets and rocker arms must be marked with their locations, to make sure they are assembled in the original locations in the cylinder head.*

Removal

1 Remove the cylinder head covers and timing cover as described in Sections 5 and 9.

2 Temporarily screw the crankshaft pulley bolt in the end of the crankshaft so the crankshaft can be turned with a socket.

3 Remove the timing chains as described in Section 10. Note that the camshafts for a particular bank must be removed with the crankshaft at the relevant removal position for that bank. This ensures the camshafts have even valve spring pressure along their lengths. If the procedure described in Section 10 is followed correctly, then the camshafts will be at the correct positions.

4 If removing the front bank intake camshaft, move the water pump drivebelt tensioner towards the camshaft and remove the

12.4a Removing the water pump pulley drivebelt

12.4b Unbolt the housing from the left-hand end of the front cylinder head

12.4c Use a puller to pull off the water pump pulley . . .

12.4d . . . then unbolt the housing

12.5a The camshaft bearing caps are numbered from the timing chain end of the engine . . .

12.5b . . . with corresponding numbers on the cylinder head

drivebelt. Also unscrew and remove the bolts securing the housing to the left-hand end of the front cylinder head – the water pump pulley may remain in position **(see illustrations)**. Alternatively, pull the water pump pulley from the camshaft, then unbolt the housing **(see illustrations)**.

5 Check that the camshaft bearing caps are marked to indicate their positions. The numbers have the letter R or L to indicate the bank they are fitted to. The 'right-hand' bank is the rear bank, and the 'left-hand' bank is the front bank **(see illustrations)**.

6 Working on one bank at a time, remove the thrust bearing caps first – they are numbered 1L and 5L (or 1R and 5R). These caps must be completely removed before loosening the remaining cap bolts. Unscrew the bolts and remove the thrust bearing caps **(see illustration)**.

7 Using the sequence given, progressively unscrew the bolts securing the camshaft bearing caps to the cylinder head. Make sure the bearing caps lift evenly with the camshafts, then with all the bolts loose, remove the bearing caps **(see illustrations)**. **Note:** *If the bearing caps are tight, tap them*

lightly with a soft-faced mallet as they are on dowels in the cylinder head.

8 Identify the camshafts (intake and exhaust/front or rear engine bank) and lift them directly from the cylinder head **(see illustrations)**.

9 Note the fitted positions of the rocker arms.

12.6 Removing a camshaft bearing cap

12.7a Loosening sequence for the rear (right-hand) camshaft bearing cap bolts

12.7b Loosening sequence for the front (left-hand) camshaft bearing cap bolts

12.7c Unscrewing the camshaft bearing cap bolts

12.8a Front exhaust camshaft sprocket marking

12.8b Rear inlet camshaft sprocket marking

12.8c Removing the front inlet camshaft . . .

12.8d . . . and front exhaust camshaft

12.9 Removing the rocker arms

Remove the rocker arms from the head, keeping them identified for position by placing them in a container marked with their locations **(see illustration)**.

10 Remove the hydraulic tappets from their bores in the cylinder head, and place them in a container marked with their locations **(see illustration)**.

Inspection

11 With the camshafts and hydraulic tappets removed, check each for obvious wear (scoring, pitting and out-of-round). Renew if necessary.

12 Using a micrometer, measure the outside diameter of each tappet – take measurements at the top and bottom of each tappet, then a second set at right-angles to the first. If any measurement is significantly different from the others, the tappet is tapered or out-of-round and must be

renewed. If the necessary equipment is available, measure the inside diameter of the corresponding cylinder head bore. Compare the measurements obtained to those given in the Specifications. If the tappets or the cylinder head bores are excessively worn, new tappets and/or a new cylinder head will be required.

13 If a top-end noise is evident, particularly if the noise persists after initial start-up from cold, there is reason to suspect a faulty hydraulic tappet. However, this is best checked with the engine running.

14 Visually examine the camshaft lobes for score marks, pitting, and evidence of overheating. Look for flaking away of the hardened surface layer of each lobe. If necessary renew the camshaft.

15 Examine the camshaft bearing journals and the cylinder head bearing surfaces for obvious wear or pitting. If excessive wear is

evident, it may be necessary to obtain a new or reconditioned cylinder head.

16 Using a micrometer, measure the diameter of each journal at several points. If the diameter of any one journal is less than the specified amount, renew the camshaft. If an internal micrometer is available, measure the internal diameters of the bores in the cylinder head and caps.

17 The camshaft endfloat can be checked using a dial gauge in contact with the end of the camshaft. Move the camshaft fully one way and zero the gauge, then move it fully the other way and check the endfloat. If excessive, new thrust caps must be fitted to the relevant camshaft.

Refitting

18 Working on the front bank, lubricate the hydraulic tappets and locate them in their relevant bores in the cylinder head.

19 Lubricate the rocker arms and locate them in their relevant positions in the cylinder head.

20 Lubricate the journals of the intake and exhaust camshafts, then locate the camshafts in the cylinder head in their relevant positions. Make sure the crankshaft pulley keyway is in the 11 o'clock position before fitting the camshaft bearing caps.

21 Locate the bearing caps in their correct positions on the cylinder head. Insert the bolts and progressively hand-tighten them initially, until they are fully seated. Finally, tighten all the bearing cap bolts to the specified torque in the sequence given **(see illustrations)**.

12.10 Removing the hydraulic tappets

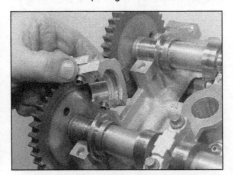

12.21a Refitting the camshaft bearing caps

12.21b Tightening sequence for the front (left-hand) camshaft bearing cap bolts

12.26 Tightening sequence for the rear (right-hand) camshaft cap bolts

12.29a Refitting the housing and new gasket to the front inlet camshaft

12.29b Using a threaded rod and nut to press on the water pump pulley

22 Refit the front timing chain as described in Section 10.

23 Working on the rear bank, lubricate the hydraulic tappets and locate them in their relevant bores in the cylinder head.

24 Lubricate the rocker arms and locate them in their relevant positions in the cylinder head.

25 Lubricate the journals of the intake and exhaust camshafts, then locate the camshafts in the cylinder head in their relevant positions. Make sure the crankshaft pulley keyway is in the 3 o'clock position before fitting the camshaft bearing caps.

26 Locate the bearing caps in their correct positions on the cylinder head. Insert the bolts and progressively hand-tighten them initially, until they are fully seated. Finally, tighten all the bearing cap bolts to the specified torque in the sequence given **(see illustration)**.

27 Refit the rear timing chain as described in Section 10.

28 Refit the timing cover and cylinder head covers as described in Sections 9 and 5.

29 If removed, refit the housing to the front intake camshaft together with a new gasket, then press on the water pump pulley **(see illustrations)**.

13 Cylinder heads –
removal and refitting

Removal

1 Disconnect the battery negative (earth) lead (refer to *Disconnecting the battery* at the end of this manual). To provide additional working room, remove the battery and the air cleaner assembly.

2 Drain the cooling system as described in Chapter 1A.

3 Remove the upper and lower intake manifolds as described in Section 6.

4 Drain the engine oil (see Chapter 1A).

5 Remove the timing chains as described in Section 10. **Note:** *If only the rear cylinder head is to be removed, it is only necessary to remove the rear timing chain. If the front cylinder head is to be removed, it is still necessary to remove the rear timing chain.*

6 Temporarily refit the right-hand engine mounting (removed in paragraph 5), and remove the hoist.

7 Remove the camshafts, hydraulic tappets and rocker arms as described in Section 12.

Rear cylinder head

8 Unscrew and remove the oxygen sensor from the rear exhaust manifold (refer to Chapter 4A). Also unbolt the rear engine lifting eye and exhaust gas pressure sensor and bracket from the cylinder head **(see illustration)**.

9 Disconnect the EGR valve back pressure transducer hoses from the EGR valve-to-exhaust manifold tube.

10 Disconnect the wiring from the EGR valve back pressure transducer and from the EGR unit.

11 Unscrew the union nut and detach the EGR valve tube from the rear exhaust manifold.

12 Loosen the clips and disconnect the hoses from the coolant connecting pipe at the left-hand end of the cylinder heads. Also disconnect the wiring from the temperature sensors on the pipe.

13 Unscrew the bolts and remove the coolant connecting pipe from the rear cylinder head. Withdraw the pipe from the front cylinder head and recover the O-rings. Note that the upper bolt has a stud extension.

14 The rear exhaust manifold can be removed at this stage, or alternatively it can be removed together with the rear cylinder head and separated on the bench (see Section 7).

15 Loosen each cylinder head bolt, one turn at a time, following the order shown **(see illustration)**. With all the head bolts loose, remove them together with their washers. It is recommended that the head bolts are renewed as a matter of course.

16 Carefully lift the rear cylinder head from the cylinder block and place it on the bench. Recover the gasket from the block.

17 Unbolt the exhaust manifold from the cylinder head and recover the gasket.

13.8 Removing the exhaust gas pressure sensor and bracket from the rear cylinder head

J34916

13.15 Loosening sequence for the rear cylinder head bolts

J34917

13.24a Loosening sequence for the front cylinder head bolts

13.18a Removing the water pump

13.19 Disconnecting the hoses from the coolant connecting pipe

13.18b Removing the thermostat housing and hoses

13.20 Removing the coolant connecting pipe

Front cylinder head

18 Remove the water pump with reference to Chapter 3. If necessary, also remove the thermostat housing and hoses **(see illustrations)**.
19 Loosen the clips and disconnect the hoses from the coolant connecting pipe at the left-hand end of the cylinder heads. Also disconnect the wiring from the temperature sensors on the pipe **(see illustration)**.
20 Unscrew the bolts and remove the coolant connecting pipe from the rear cylinder head. Withdraw the pipe from the front cylinder head and recover the O-rings. Note that the upper bolt has a stud extension **(see illustration)**.
21 Loosen the clip and disconnect the radiator bottom hose from the elbow on the front cylinder head, then unbolt the elbow.
22 Pull out the engine oil level dipstick tube.
23 The front exhaust manifold can be

removed at this stage, or alternatively it can be removed together with the front cylinder head and separated on the bench (see Section 7). If it is decided to remove the head together with the manifold, unbolt the air conditioning compressor from the engine block and place it on the front crossmember, and also remove the oil filter. This will provide additional room for the exhaust downpipe to be lifted from the engine compartment.
24 Loosen each cylinder head bolt, one turn at a time, following the order shown **(see illustration)**. With all the head bolts loose, remove them together with their washers and check them for damage **(see illustrations)**. It is recommended that the head bolts are renewed as a matter of course.
25 Carefully lift the front cylinder head from the cylinder block and place it on the bench. Recover the gasket from the block **(see illustrations)**.

13.24b Unscrew the cylinder head bolts . . .

13.24c . . . and remove them together with their washers

13.25a Lifting the front cylinder head from the cylinder block

13.25b Engine with the front cylinder head and gasket removed

26 Unbolt the exhaust manifold from the cylinder head and recover the gasket.

Refitting

27 The mating faces of the cylinder heads and cylinder blocks must be perfectly clean before refitting the heads. Use a hard plastic or wood scraper to remove all traces of gasket and carbon; also clean the piston crowns. Take particular care, as the soft aluminium alloy is easily damaged. Also, make sure that the carbon is not allowed to enter the oil and water passages – this is particularly important for the lubrication system, as carbon could block the oil supply to any of the engine's components. Using adhesive tape and paper, seal the water, oil and bolt holes in the cylinder block. Clean all the pistons in the same way.

 HAYNES HiNT *To prevent carbon entering the gap between the pistons and bores, smear a little grease in the gap. After cleaning each piston, use a small brush to remove all traces of grease and carbon from the gap, then wipe away the remainder with a clean rag.*

28 Check the mating surfaces of the cylinder block and the cylinder head for nicks, deep scratches and other damage. If slight, they may be removed carefully with a fine file, but if excessive, machining may be the only alternative to renewal.

29 If warpage of the cylinder head gasket surface is suspected, use a straight-edge to

13.31 Locating the front cylinder head gasket on the cylinder block

check it for distortion. Refer to Part D of this Chapter if necessary.

30 Wipe clean the mating surfaces of the cylinder heads and cylinder block. Check that the locating dowels are in position in the cylinder block, and that all cylinder head bolt holes are free from oil.

Front cylinder head

31 Locate the front cylinder head gasket on the cylinder block **(see illustration)**.

32 Clean the surfaces of the exhaust manifold and cylinder head, then refit the manifold together with a new gasket and tighten the bolts (see Section 7). Alternatively, the exhaust manifold can be refitted after refitting the cylinder head on the cylinder block.

33 Carefully lower the front cylinder head onto the gasket, making sure that it is aligned with the locating dowels.

34 Insert the head bolts together with washers, and initially hand-tighten them.

35 Using a torque wrench, tighten the head bolts to the Stage 1 torque in the sequence shown **(see illustrations)**.

36 Tighten the bolts in the remaining stages given in the Specifications. For the angle-tightening, use an angle disc socket attachment to ensure the correct angle **(see illustration)**.

37 If applicable, refit the exhaust manifold together with a new gasket.

38 Insert the engine oil level dipstick.

39 Refit the elbow to the front cylinder head together with a new gasket, and tighten the bolts. Reconnect the radiator bottom hose and tighten the clip.

J34918

13.35a Tightening sequence for the cylinder head bolts (front shown, rear similar)

40 Refit the coolant connecting pipe together with a new gasket and O-rings, and tighten the bolts. Reconnect the hoses and tighten the clips. Reconnect the wiring to the temperature sensors, then refit the water pump with reference to Chapter 3.

Rear cylinder head

41 Note: *If this procedure is being used during an engine overhaul, make sure that the right-hand engine mounting bracket is bolted in position on the cylinder block before refitting the rear cylinder head, as it will be impossible to fit the bracket between the front and rear cylinder heads with them already fitted* **(see illustration).**

42 Locate the rear cylinder head gasket on the cylinder block **(see illustration)**.

43 Clean the surfaces of the exhaust manifold and cylinder head, then refit the manifold together with a new gasket and tighten the bolts (see Section 7). Alternatively, the exhaust manifold can be refitted after refitting the cylinder head on the cylinder block.

13.35b Tightening the head bolts with a torque wrench

13.36 Using an angle disc socket attachment to angle-tighten the cylinder head bolts

13.41 The right-hand engine mounting bracket must be fitted before fitting the rear cylinder head

13.42 Locating the rear cylinder head gasket on the cylinder block

44 Carefully lower the rear cylinder head onto the gasket, making sure that it is aligned with the locating dowels.

45 Insert the head bolts together with washers, and initially hand-tighten them.

46 Using a torque wrench, tighten the head bolts to the Stage 1 torque in the sequence shown **(see illustration 13.35a)**.

47 Tighten the bolts in the remaining stages given in the Specifications. For the angle-tightening, use an angle disc socket attachment to ensure the correct angle.

48 If applicable, refit the exhaust manifold together with a new gasket.

49 Refit the coolant connecting pipe together with a new gasket and O-rings, and tighten the bolts. Reconnect the hoses and tighten the clips. Reconnect the wiring to the temperature sensors.

50 Refit the EGR valve tube to the rear exhaust manifold and tighten the union nut.

51 Reconnect the wiring to the EGR valve back pressure transducer.

52 Reconnect the EGR valve back pressure transducer hoses to the EGR valve-to-exhaust manifold tube.

53 Refit the oxygen sensor to the rear exhaust manifold (refer to Chapter 4A).

Front and rear cylinder heads

54 Refit the camshafts, hydraulic tappets and rocker arms as described in Section 12.

55 Support the weight of the engine with the hoist, then remove the right-hand engine mounting in order to refit the timing chains and timing cover.

56 Refit the timing chains and cover as described in Section 10, then refit the engine mounting and remove the hoist.

57 Refit the upper and lower intake manifolds as described in Section 6.

58 If removed, refit the battery and air cleaner. Reconnect the battery negative (earth) lead.

59 Refill the engine with oil with reference to Chapter 1A.

60 Refill the cooling system with reference to Chapter 1A.

61 Start the engine and run to normal operating temperature. Check for coolant and oil leaks. **Note:** *After the battery has been disconnected, the engine management system requires approximately 10 miles of driving to relearn its optimum settings. During this period, the engine may not perform normally.*

14 Sump –
removal and refitting

Removal

1 Apply the handbrake, then jack up the front of the vehicle and support it on axle stands (see *Jacking and vehicle support*).

2 Drain the engine oil as described in Chapter 1A. On completion, clean the drain plug and threaded hole, then refit the plug and tighten to the specified torque. If necessary, renew the drain plug and sealing washer.

3 Unscrew the nuts and bolts and remove the exhaust Y-pipe from the bottom of the front downpipes and intermediate exhaust section.

4 Unbolt the exhaust support bracket from the studs on the rear of the sump **(see illustrations)**.

5 Unscrew and remove the lower flange bolts securing the sump to the transmission.

6 Note the location of the stud bolts on the sump, then unscrew and remove the bolts, leaving two opposite ones in place. Finally support the sump, and remove the last two bolts. Lower the sump from the engine. Remove the gasket and discard it **(see illustrations)**.

Refitting

7 Thoroughly clean the contact surfaces of the sump and cylinder block. Also clean the inside of the sump. If necessary, unbolt and remove the baffle plate **(see illustration)**. After cleaning, refit the baffle plate and tighten the bolts.

8 Apply a bead of sealant to the joints between the timing cover and cylinder block, on the bottom of the block.

9 Locate a new gasket on the sump **(see illustration)**. Retain it with a little grease if necessary.

10 Raise the sump and gasket onto the bottom of the cylinder block and insert several bolts to hold it in position. Make sure the gasket remains in position. Insert the remaining bolts then hand-tighten all the bolts.

11 Tighten the bolts to the specified torque, in the sequence shown **(see illustration)**.

14.4a Removing the exhaust Y-piece from under the sump

14.4b Exhaust support bracket on the rear of the sump

14.6a Unscrew the bolts . . .

14.6b . . . and lower the sump from the cylinder block

14.7 Removing the baffle plate from the sump

14.9 Locating a new gasket on the sump

12 Insert and tighten the lower flange bolts securing the sump to the transmission.
13 Refit the exhaust support bracket to the rear of the sump and tighten the bolts **(see illustration)**.
14 Refit the exhaust Y-pipe to the bottom of the front downpipes and intermediate exhaust section and tighten the new nuts and bolts.
15 Lower the vehicle to the ground, then fill the engine with fresh oil as described in Chapter 1A.

15 Oil pump – removal, inspection and refitting

Removal

1 Remove the timing chains and sprockets as described in Section 10. This procedure

14.11 Tightening sequence for the sump bolts

includes the removal of the sump as described in Section 14.
2 Unscrew the flange bolts and support nut, and remove the oil pump pick-up tube and filter. Recover the O-ring from the pump.
3 Although not essential at this stage, undo the screws and remove the oil baffle from the crankcase.
4 Progressively loosen the mounting bolts one at a time in the reverse sequence to that

14.13 Refitting the exhaust support bracket

shown **(see illustration 15.11)**. With all of the bolts removed, withdraw the oil pump from the cylinder block **(see illustrations)**.

Inspection

5 Using a Torx key, undo the screws and remove the cover from the oil pump **(see illustration)**.
6 Note the location of the identification marks on the inner and outer rotors, then remove the rotors. The dot on the outer rotor faces the cover, but the dot on the inner rotor faces the body **(see illustrations)**.
7 Unscrew the plug and remove the pressure relief valve, spring and plunger **(see illustration)**.
8 Clean all the components and examine them for wear and damage. If the rotors or body are excessively scored or damaged, the complete oil pump must be renewed. If the components are still serviceable, first refit the

15.4a Unscrew the bolts . . .

15.4b . . . and withdraw the oil pump from the cylinder block

15.5 Removing the cover from the oil pump

15.6a Oil pump and rotors with the cover removed

15.6b Removing the inner rotor . . .

15.6c . . . and outer rotor

15.7 Pressure relief valve components

15.8 Lubricate the rotors with clean engine oil before fitting the cover

15.9 Tightening the oil pump cover screws

J34920

15.11 Tightening sequence for the oil pump mounting bolts

pressure relief valve components and tighten the plug. Lubricate the rotors with fresh engine oil and insert them in the body making sure that the identification marks are position as noted on removal **(see illustration)**.
9 Refit the pump cover and tighten the screws to the specified torque **(see illustration)**.
10 Before refitting the oil pump, prime it by pouring fresh engine oil into the pick-up tube flange port. Turn the rotors by hand so that the oil enters the internal cavities.

Refitting

11 Position the inner rotor so that it will align with the flat on the crankshaft, then locate the oil pump on the cylinder block. Insert the bolts and tighten to the specified torque in the sequence shown **(see illustration)**.
12 If removed, refit the baffle to the crankcase and tighten the bolts.

16.5 Removing the oil cooler and O-ring

13 Locate the oil pump pick-up tube and filter in the oil pump together with a new O-ring, then insert the flange bolts and tighten to the specified torque. Refit and tighten the support nut.
14 Refit the timing chains and sprockets as described in Section 10, and the sump as described in Section 14.

16 Oil cooler – removal and refitting

Removal

1 The oil cooler is located on the front of the cylinder block between the oil filter and cylinder block. First drain the cooling system as described in Chapter 1A.
2 Apply the handbrake, then jack up the front of the vehicle and support it on axle stands (see *Jacking and vehicle support*). Remove the splash shield from the bottom of the radiator.
3 Loosen the clips and disconnect the coolant hoses from the oil cooler.
4 Position a container beneath the oil filter, then unscrew and remove the oil filter. Keep the oil filter upright to prevent oil spillage.
5 Note the position of the oil cooler stubs, then unscrew the nut and withdraw the oil cooler from the mounting stud. Recover the O-ring **(see illustration)**. Be prepared for loss of oil and coolant.

Refitting

6 Wipe clean the cylinder block and contact surfaces of the oil cooler and oil filter.

7 Locate the oil cooler onto the mounting stub together with a new O-ring. Position the coolant stubs as noted on removal, then tighten the nut to the specified torque.
8 Smear some fresh engine oil onto the sealing ring of the oil filter, then screw it onto the stud and tighten firmly using only the hands. Wipe clean the oil filter and cooler.
9 Reconnect the hoses and tighten the clips.
10 Refit the splash shield to the bottom of the radiator, and lower the vehicle to the ground.
11 Refill the cooling system with reference to Chapter 1A.
12 Check and if necessary top-up the engine oil level with reference to *Weekly checks*.

17 Oil pressure warning light switch – removal and refitting

Removal

1 The oil pressure warning light switch is located on the front of the cylinder block next to the oil filter.
2 Apply the handbrake, then jack up the front of the vehicle and support it on axle stands (see *Jacking and vehicle support*). Remove the splash shield from the bottom of the radiator.
3 Disconnect the wiring, then unscrew the switch from the cylinder block.

Refitting

4 Insert the switch and tighten to the specified torque.
5 Reconnect the wiring.
6 Refit the splash shield to the bottom of the radiator, and lower the vehicle to the ground.
7 Check and if necessary top-up the engine oil level as described in *Weekly checks*.

18 Crankshaft oil seals – renewal

Timing chain end oil seal

1 Remove the crankshaft pulley as described in Section 8 of this Chapter.
2 Using a screwdriver, prise the old oil seal from the timing cover. Take care not to damage the surface of the timing cover and crankshaft. If the oil seal is tight, carefully drill two holes diagonally opposite each other in the oil seal, then insert self-tapping screws and use a pair of pliers to pull out the oil seal.
3 Wipe clean the seating in the timing cover and the nose of the crankshaft.
4 Smear clean engine oil on the outer periphery and sealing lips of the new oil seal, then start it into the timing cover by pressing it in squarely. Using a large socket or metal tubing, drive in the oil seal until flush with the outer surface of the timing cover. Make sure

19.4 Remove the flywheel bolts . . .

19.5 . . . then lift the flywheel from the crankshaft

19.6 Removing the adapter plate

the oil seal remains square as it is being inserted. Wipe off any excess oil.

5 Refit the crankshaft pulley as described in Section 8 of this Chapter.

Transmission end oil seal

6 Remove the transmission as described in Chapter 7A or 7B.

7 Remove the flywheel or driveplate (as applicable) as described in Section 19.

8 Remove the adapter plate from the engine.

9 Using a screwdriver, prise the old oil seal from the cylinder block. Take care not to damage the surface of the oil seal seating and crankshaft. If the oil seal is tight, carefully drill two holes diagonally opposite each other in the oil seal, then insert self-tapping screws and use a pair of pliers to pull out the oil seal.

10 Wipe clean the seating in the block and the crankshaft.

11 Smear clean engine oil on the outer periphery and sealing lips of the new oil seal, then start it into the cylinder block by pressing it in squarely. Using a large socket or metal tubing, drive in the oil seal until flush with the outer surface of the cylinder block. Make sure the oil seal remains square as it is being inserted. Wipe off any excess oil.

12 Locate the adapter plate on the dowels in the cylinder block.

13 Refit the flywheel or driveplate (as applicable) with reference to Section 19.

14 Refit the transmission as described in Chapter 7A or 7B.

19 Flywheel/driveplate – removal, inspection and refitting

Removal

1 Remove the transmission as described in Chapter 7A or 7B. Now is a good time to check components such as oil seals and renew them if necessary.

2 On manual transmission models, remove the clutch as described in Chapter 6. Now is a good time to check or renew the clutch components.

3 Make alignment marks on the flywheel/ driveplate and crankshaft as an aid to refitting.

4 Prevent the flywheel/driveplate from turning by locking the ring gear teeth, or by bolting a strap between the flywheel/driveplate and the cylinder block/crankcase. Unscrew and remove the bolts **(see illustration)**.

5 Withdraw the flywheel/driveplate from the crankshaft, taking care not to drop it – it is very heavy **(see illustration)**.

6 If necessary, remove the adapter plate from the dowels on the cylinder block **(see illustration)**.

Inspection

7 Clean the flywheel/driveplate to remove grease and oil. Inspect the surface for cracks, rivet grooves, burned areas and score marks. Light scoring can be removed with emery cloth. Check for cracked and broken ring gear teeth. Lay the flywheel/driveplate on a flat surface, and use a straight-edge to check for warpage.

8 Clean and inspect the mating surfaces of the flywheel/driveplate and the crankshaft. If the crankshaft left-hand oil seal is leaking, renew it (see Section 18) before refitting the flywheel/driveplate.

9 While the flywheel/driveplate is removed, clean carefully its inner face. Thoroughly clean the threaded bolt holes in the crankshaft, and also clean the threads of the bolts – this is important, since if old sealer remains in the threads, the bolts will settle over a period and will not retain their correct torque wrench settings.

Refitting

10 Locate the adapter plate on the cylinder block dowels.

11 Refit the flywheel/driveplate on the crankshaft and align the previously made marks (the bolt holes are arranged so that the flywheel/driveplate will only fit in one position). Apply suitable sealer to the threads of the bolts then insert them and progressively tighten to the specified torque while holding the flywheel/driveplate stationary using the method described in paragraph 4.

12 On manual transmission models, refit the clutch with reference to Chapter 6.

13 Refit the transmission with reference to Chapter 7A or 7B (as applicable).

20 Engine/transmission mountings – inspection and renewal

1 The engine/transmission mountings seldom require attention, but broken or deteriorated mountings should be renewed immediately, otherwise the added strain placed on the transmission components may cause damage or wear.

2 While separate mountings may be removed and refitted individually, if more than one is disturbed at a time – such as if the engine/transmission unit is removed – they must be reassembled and tightened in the sequence described in Chapter 2D for engine refitting.

Inspection

3 For access to the right-hand engine mounting, undo the screws securing the coolant expansion tank to the right-hand inner wing panel and temporarily position the tank to one side. For access to the left-hand engine mounting, remove the battery (Chapter 5A) and air cleaner (Chapter 4A). For access to the front and rear engine roll restrictors, apply the handbrake, then jack up the front of the vehicle and support it on axle stands (see *Jacking and vehicle support*). The use of a mirror will help to view the engine mounting from all angles.

4 Check the mounting rubber to see if it is cracked, hardened or separated from the metal at any point; renew the mounting if any such damage or deterioration is evident.

5 Check that all the mounting nuts/bolts are securely tightened; use a torque wrench to check if possible.

6 Using a large screwdriver or lever, check for wear in the mounting by carefully levering against it to check for free play; where this is not possible, enlist the aid of an assistant to move the engine/transmission unit back-and-forth, or from side-to-side, while you watch the mounting. While some free play is to be expected even from new components, excessive wear should be obvious. If excessive free play is found, check first that the nuts/bolts are correctly tightened, then renew any worn components as described below.

20.10a Unscrew the right-hand engine mounting bracket nuts and bolts . . .

20.10b . . . noting the location of the earth cable

20.10c Removing the right-hand engine mounting brackets

Renewal

Right-hand engine mounting

7 Undo the three retaining bolts and remove the plastic cover from the top of the front cylinder bank.

8 Undo the screws and position the coolant expansion tank to one side.

9 Support the weight of the engine using a suitable hoist. Alternatively, if only the right-hand engine mounting is to be renewed, it is acceptable to carefully support the weight of the engine using a trolley jack and piece of wood beneath the engine sump.

10 Mark the position of the engine mounting bracket for correct refitting, then unscrew the

nuts and remove the bracket. Where applicable, note the position of the earth cable **(see illustrations)**. **Note:** *The nuts are self-locking and must be renewed.*

11 Unbolt the mounting from the body panel.

12 Fit the new mounting to the body panel and tighten the bolts to the specified torque.

13 Locate the bracket on the mounting and engine and position it as noted before removal. Fit the new nuts and tighten to the specified torque. Where applicable, make sure the earth cable is refitted in its correct position.

14 Lower the engine and remove the hoist.

15 Refit the coolant expansion tank and tighten the screws.

16 Refit the plastic cover to the top of the front cylinder bank and tighten the retaining bolts.

Left-hand engine mounting

17 Remove the battery as described in Chapter 5A.

18 Remove the air filter and housing as described in Chapter 4A.

19 Undo the three retaining bolts and remove the plastic cover from the top of the front cylinder bank.

20 Support the weight of the transmission using a suitable hoist. Alternatively, if only the left-hand engine mounting is to be renewed, it is acceptable to carefully support the weight of the transmission using a trolley jack and piece of wood.

21 Mark the position of the engine mounting bracket for correct refitting, then unscrew the nuts securing the mounting to the studs on the transmission **(see illustration)**. **Note:** *The nuts are self-locking and must be renewed.*

22 Unscrew the bolts and remove the mounting from the body panel **(see illustration)**.

23 Fit the new mounting to the body panel and tighten the bolts to the specified torque.

24 Locate the bracket on the mounting and transmission and position it as noted before removal. Fit the new nuts and tighten to the specified torque.

25 Lower the transmission and remove the hoist.

26 Refit the plastic cover to the top of the front cylinder bank and tighten the retaining bolts.

J35111

20.21 Left-hand engine/transmission mounting (manual transmission shown – automatic transmission similar)

1 *Body bracket*	3 *Transmission*	5 *Plate (if fitted)*
2 *Transmission bracket*	4 *Studs*	

20.22 Left-hand engine mounting body bracket bolt

20.30 Front roll restrictor

| 1 Transmission | 2 Mounting bracket | 3 Mounting | 4 Subframe | 5 Centre bolt |

27 Refit the air filter and housing with reference to Chapter 4A.
28 Refit the battery with reference to Chapter 5A. **Note:** *After the battery has been disconnected, the engine management system requires approximately 10 miles of driving to relearn its optimum settings. During this period, the engine may not perform normally.*

Front roll restrictor

29 Apply the handbrake, then jack up the front of the vehicle and support it on axle stands (see *Jacking and vehicle support*).
30 Unscrew the bolts securing the front roll

restrictor to the subframe, and also unscrew the centre bolt. Remove the roll restrictor **(see illustration)**.
31 If necessary, unbolt the bracket from the transmission.
32 Refit the bracket to the transmission and tighten the bolts to the specified torque.
33 Locate the new front roll restrictor in the bracket and insert the centre bolt.
34 Insert the bolts securing the front roll restrictor to the subframe, and tighten to the specified torque.
35 Tighten the centre bolt to the specified torque.
36 Lower the vehicle to the ground.

Rear roll restrictor

37 Apply the handbrake, then jack up the front of the vehicle and support it on axle stands (see *Jacking and vehicle support*).
38 Unscrew the nuts/bolts and centre bolt, and remove the rear roll restrictor from its bracket **(see illustrations)**. If necessary, use a trolley jack and block of wood to slightly raise the transmission. Note on certain automatic transmission models, an additional rubber damper is fitted in a bracket below the subframe.
39 If necessary, unbolt the bracket from the transmission **(see illustration)**.

20.38a Rear roll restrictor viewed from under the car

20.38b Removing the rear roll restrictor centre bolt

20.38c Removing the rear roll restrictor

J35113

20.38d Rear roll restrictor (manual transmission type)

1 Transmission	3 Front subframe	5 Centre bolt
2 Mounting bracket	4 Mounting	

20.39 Removing the rear roll restrictor bracket from the transmission

40 Refit the bracket to the transmission and tighten the bolts to the specified torque.

41 Locate the rear roll restrictor in its bracket and tighten the nuts/bolts to the specified torque. On automatic transmission models, locate a new rubber damper to the bracket on the subframe and tighten the nuts to the specified torque.

42 Insert the centre bolt and tighten to the specified torque.

Chapter 2 Part C:
Diesel engine in-car repair procedures

Contents

Degrees of difficulty

Easy, suitable for novice with little experience	**Fairly easy,** suitable for beginner with some experience	**Fairly difficult,** suitable for competent DIY mechanic	**Difficult,** suitable for experienced DIY mechanic	**Very difficult,** suitable for expert DIY or professional 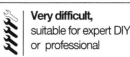

Specifications

General

Engine type	Four-cylinder, in-line, double overhead camshaft
Designation	Duratorq-DI and DCI
Engine codes:	
Duratorq-DI (66 kW – direct injection)	D5BA
Duratorq-DI (85 kW – direct injection)	D6BA
Duratorq-DCI (85 kw – common rail)	H7BA, BB or BC
Duratorq-DCI (96 kW – common rail)	FMBA
Capacity	1998 cc
Bore	86.0 mm
Stroke	86.0 mm
Compression ratio	19 :1
Power output:	
D5BA	66 kW at 4000 rpm
D6BA	85 kW at 4000 rpm
FMBA	96 kW at 3800 rpm
Firing order	1-3-4-2 (No 1 cylinder at timing chain end)
Direction of crankshaft rotation	Clockwise (seen from right-hand side of vehicle)

Camshaft

Camshaft bearing journal diameter	26.450 mm
Camshaft bearing journal-to-cylinder head running clearance	0.065 mm
Camshaft endfloat	0.125 mm

Cylinder head

Piston protrusion:	**Thickness of cylinder head gasket**
D5BA (66kW) engine:	
0.310 to 0.400 mm	1.10 mm (1 hole/tooth)
0.401 to 0.450 mm	1.15 mm (2 hole/teeth)
0.451 to 0.500 mm	1.20 mm (3 hole/teeth)
All other engines:	
0.430 to 0.520 mm	1.10 mm (1 hole/tooth)
0.521 to 0.570 mm	1.15 mm (2 hole/teeth)
0.571 to 0.620 mm	1.20 mm (3 hole/teeth)
Maximum permissible gasket surface distortion	0.10 mm

Lubrication

Engine oil capacity	See Chapter 1B
Oil pressure – maximum (engine at operating temperature):	
At idle	1.25 bars
At 2000 rpm	2.00 bars

Torque wrench settings

	Nm	lbf ft
Auxiliary drivebelt idler pulley bolt	43	32
Auxiliary drivebelt tensioner mounting nuts	23	17
Big-end bearing cap bolts:		
Stage 1	30	22
Stage 2	Angle-tighten a further 80°	
Camshaft carrier bolts		
Stage 1 – bolts 1 to 22	23	17
Stage 2 – bolts 23 to 25	10	7
Camshaft cover	10	7
Camshaft position sensor	10	7
Camshaft sprocket bolts	33	24
Common rail studs (FMBA/96kW engines)	23	17
Coolant pipe bracket to transmission	40	30
Coolant pump	23	17
Crankshaft oil seal carrier	10	7
Crankshaft position sensor	7	5
Crankshaft pulley bolt:		
Stage 1	30	22
Stage 2	Angle-tighten a further 90°	
Cylinder head bolts:		
Stage 1 – bolts 1 to 10	10	7
Stage 2 – bolts 11 to 18	5	4
Stage 3 – bolts 1 to 10	20	15
Stage 4 – bolts 11 to 18	10	7
Stage 5 – bolts 1 to 10	40	30
Stage 6 – bolts 11 to 18	20	15
Stage 7 – bolts 1 to 10	Angle-tighten a further 180°	
Stage 8 – bolts 11 to 18	Angle-tighten a further 180°	
Earth cable-to-transmission bolt	40	30
EGR cooler-to-exhaust manifold bolts	37	27
EGR cooler securing nut and bolt	10	7
EGR pipe union	23	17
Engine/transmission mountings:		
Left-hand mounting:		
Centre nut	133	98
To subframe	80	59
To transmission	90	66
Right-hand mounting bolts	80	59
Exhaust manifold and turbocharger nuts and bolts	40	30
Exhaust manifold bracket to block	46	34
Exhaust manifold heat shield	10	7
Exhaust manifold to catalytic converter	46	34
Flywheel/driveplate bolts:		
Stage 1	15	11
Stage 2	30	22
Stage 3	75	55
Stage 4	Angle-tighten a further 45°	
Fuel injection pump mounting bolts	23	17
Fuel injection pump sprocket	32	24
Fuel injectors:		
D5BA (66kW) and D6BA (85kW) engines	52	38
All other engines	47	35
Fuel pressure line unions:		
D5BA (66kW) and D6BA (85kW) engines	35	26
All other engines	40	30
Fuel return line unions	8	6
Glow plugs	13	10
Intake manifold	16	12
Knock sensor	20	15
Lower crankcase/ladder to cylinder block	23	17

Torque wrench settings (continued)

	Nm	lbf ft
Main bearing cap bolts:		
Stage 1	45	33
Stage 2	80	59
Stage 3	Angle-tighten a further 80°	
Oil filter cooler	23	17
Oil pump bolts	10	7
Oil pump chain tensioner	16	12
Oil pump pick-up pipe	10	7
Power steering pump	18	14
Power steering pump bracket to block	23	17
Power steering pump belt pulley	64	47
Rocker shaft bolts:		
Stage 1	13	10
Stage 2	Angle-tighten a further 45°	
Starter motor	25	18
Sump bolts:		
Stage 1	7	5
Stage 2	14	10
Sump oil drain plug	23	17
Thermostat housing to cylinder head	23	17
Timing chain cover:		
Nuts	10	7
Bolts	14	10
Timing chain guide retaining bolts	15	11
Timing chain tensioner	15	11
Transmission-to-engine bolts	44	32
Turbocharger oil feed pipe union	14	10
Turbocharger oil return pipe bolts	10	7
Wheel nuts	85	63

1 General information

How to use this Chapter

This Part of Chapter 2 is devoted to repair procedures possible while the engine is still installed in the vehicle. Since these procedures are based on the assumption that the engine is installed in the vehicle, if the engine has been removed from the vehicle and mounted on a stand, some of the preliminary dismantling steps outlined will not apply.

Information concerning engine/transmission removal and refitting and engine overhaul, can be found in Part D of this Chapter.

Engine

The diesel engines covered in this manual are an in-line four-cylinder, turbocharged unit. There are three variations of the 2.0 litre, 16-valve, double overhead camshaft (DOHC) engines. They are of the direct fuel injection type, with the DCI engine being a common rail design. The engine is mounted transversely at the front of the vehicle, with the transmission on its left-hand end.

The engine cylinder block casting is of cast-iron and has a lower aluminium crankcase which is bolted to the underside of the cylinder block, with an aluminium sump bolted under that. This arrangement offers greater rigidity than the normal sump arrangement, and helps to reduce engine vibration.

The crankshaft runs in five main bearings, the centre main bearing's upper half incorporating thrust washers to control crankshaft endfloat. The connecting rods rotate on horizontally-split bearing shells at their big-ends. The pistons are attached to the connecting rods by gudgeon pins which are a floating fit in the connecting rod small-end eyes, secured by circlips. The aluminium alloy pistons are fitted with three piston rings: two compression rings and an oil control ring.

The inlet and exhaust valves are each closed by coil springs; they operate in guides which are shrink-fitted into the cylinder head, as are the valve seat inserts.

The double overhead camshaft sprockets and the fuel injection pump are driven by a twin chain from a sprocket on the crankshaft. The camshaft operates the sixteen valves via rockers which are mounted on rocker shafts that run parallel with the camshafts. Each camshaft rotates in five bearings that are machined directly in the cylinder head and the (bolted-on) bearing caps; this means that the bearing caps are not available separately from the cylinder head, and must not be interchanged with caps from another engine.

The vacuum pump (used for the brake servo and other vacuum actuators) is located on the transmission end of the cylinder head, driven by a slot in the end of the exhaust camshaft.

When working on this engine, note that Torx-type (both male and female heads) and hexagon socket (Allen head) fasteners are widely used; a good selection of bits, with the necessary adapters, will be required so that these can be unscrewed without damage and, on reassembly, tightened to the torque wrench settings specified.

Lubrication

Lubrication is by means of a chain driven oil pump driven from a sprocket on the crankshaft. The oil pump is mounted below the lower crankcase, and draws oil through a strainer located in the sump. The pump forces oil through an externally-mounted full-flow cartridge-type filter. From the filter, the oil is pumped into a main gallery in the cylinder block/crankcase, from where it is distributed to the crankshaft (main bearings) and cylinder head. On some models, an oil cooler is fitted next to the oil filter, at the rear of the block. The cooler is supplied with coolant from the engine cooling system.

While the crankshaft and camshaft bearings receive a pressurised supply, the camshaft lobes and valves are lubricated by splash, as are all other engine components. The undersides of the pistons are cooled by oil, sprayed from nozzles fitted above the upper main bearing shells. The turbocharger receives its own pressurised oil supply.

Repairs with engine in car

The following major repair operations can

be accomplished without removing the engine from the vehicle. However, owners should note that any operation involving the removal of the timing chain, camshafts or cylinder head require careful forethought, depending on the level of skill and the tools and facilities available; refer to the relevant text for details.

a) *Compression pressure – testing.*
b) *Camshaft cover – removal and refitting.*
c) *Timing chain cover – removal and refitting.*
d) *Timing chain – renewal.*
e) *Timing chain tensioner and sprockets – removal and refitting.*
f) *Camshaft oil seal – renewal.*
g) *Camshaft and hydraulic rockers – removal and refitting.*
h) *Cylinder head – removal, overhaul and refitting.*
i) *Crankshaft pulley – removal and refitting.*
j) *Sump – removal and refitting.*
k) *Crankshaft oil seals – renewal.*
l) *Oil pump – removal and refitting.*
m) *Flywheel – removal and refitting.*
n) *Engine/transmission mountings – removal and refitting.*
o) *Intake manifold – removal and refitting.*
p) *Exhaust manifold – removal and refitting.*

Clean the engine compartment and the exterior of the engine with some type of degreaser before any work is done (and/or clean the engine using a steam cleaner). It will make the job easier and will help to keep dirt out of the internal areas of the engine.

Depending on the components involved, it may be helpful to remove the bonnet, to improve access to the engine as repairs are performed (refer to Chapter 11 if necessary). Cover the wings to prevent damage to the paint; special covers are available, but an old bedspread or blanket will also work.

2 Compression and leakdown tests –
description and interpretation

Compression test

Note: *A compression tester suitable for use with diesel engines will be required for this test.*

1 When engine performance is down, or if misfiring occurs which cannot be attributed to the fuel or emissions systems, a compression test can provide diagnostic clues as to the engine's condition. If the test is performed regularly, it can give warning of trouble before any other symptoms become apparent.

2 The engine must be fully warmed-up to normal operating temperature, the battery must be fully-charged and the glow plugs must be removed. The aid of an assistant will be required.

3 Make sure that the ignition is switched off (take out the key). Disconnect the wiring plug from the stop solenoid on the fuel injection pump, and place the wiring to one side. While

the plug is disconnected, cover each half of the plug to keep the pins clean, and to prevent any static discharge, which may damage the pump electronic control unit.

4 Remove the glow plugs as described in Chapter 4B.

5 Fit a compression tester to the No 1 cylinder glow plug hole. The type of tester which screws into the plug thread is preferred.

6 Crank the engine for several seconds on the starter motor. After one or two revolutions, the compression pressure should build up to a maximum figure and then stabilise. Record the highest reading obtained.

7 Repeat the test on the remaining cylinders, recording the pressure in each.

8 The cause of poor compression is less easy to establish on a diesel engine than on a petrol engine. The effect of introducing oil into the cylinders (wet testing) is not conclusive, because there is a risk that the oil will sit in the recess on the piston crown, instead of passing to the rings. However, the following can be used as a rough guide to diagnosis.

9 All cylinders should produce very similar pressures. Any difference greater than that specified indicates the existence of a fault. Note that the compression should build-up quickly in a healthy engine. Low compression on the first stroke, followed by gradually increasing pressure on successive strokes, indicates worn piston rings. A low compression reading on the first stroke, which does not build-up during successive strokes, indicates leaking valves or a blown head gasket (a cracked head could also be the cause).

10 A low reading from two adjacent cylinders is almost certainly due to the head gasket having blown between them and the presence of coolant in the engine oil will confirm this.

11 On completion, remove the compression tester, and refit the glow plugs, with reference to Chapter 4B.

12 Take out the ignition key, then reconnect the injection pump wiring connector.

Leakdown test

13 A leakdown test measures the rate at which compressed air fed into the cylinder is lost. It is an alternative to a compression test, and in many ways it is better, since the escaping air provides easy identification of

3.10 Undo the retaining bolt and withdraw the crankshaft position sensor

where pressure loss is occurring (piston rings, valves or head gasket).

14 The equipment required for leakdown testing is unlikely to be available to the home mechanic. If poor compression is suspected, have the test performed by a suitably-equipped garage.

3 Engine timing – setting

Note: *Only turn the engine in the normal direction of rotation – clockwise from the right-hand side of the vehicle.*

General information

1 Top Dead Centre (TDC) is the highest point in the cylinder that each piston reaches as it travels up and down when the crankshaft turns. Each piston reaches TDC at the end of the compression stroke and again at the end of the exhaust stroke, but TDC generally refers to piston position on the compression stroke. No 1 piston is at the timing chain end of the engine.

2 On the 2.0 litre diesel engine, setting No 1 piston at 50° before top dead centre (BTDC) is an essential part of many procedures, such as timing chain removal, cylinder head removal and camshaft removal.

3 The design of the engines covered in this Chapter is such that piston-to-valve contact may occur if the camshaft or crankshaft is turned with the timing chain removed. For this reason, it is important to ensure that the camshaft and crankshaft do not move in relation to each other once the timing chain has been removed from the engine.

Setting

Note: *Ford service tool 303-675 or 303-698 – depending on engine type - obtainable from Ford dealers or a tool supplier will be required to set the timing at 50° BTDC - a tool can be fabricated to set the timing, using a piece of metal bar (see illustrations 3.11a and 3.11b).*

4 Disconnect the battery negative (earth) lead (refer to *Disconnecting the battery*).

5 Loosen the right-hand front wheel nuts, then firmly apply the handbrake. Jack up the front of the car, and support on axle stands (see *Jacking and vehicle support*). Remove the right-hand front wheel.

6 Loosen and remove the retaining screws securing the engine undershield, lower the shield, and remove it.

7 The engine can now be rotated using the crankshaft pulley.

8 A timing hole is provided on the top of the transmission, to permit the crankshaft position sensor to be located.

9 Remove the air cleaner assembly as described in Chapter 4B.

10 Disconnect the wiring connector from the crankshaft position sensor, undo the retaining bolt and withdraw the sensor from the bellhousing **(see illustration)**.

3.11a Ford timing tool inserted into the crankshaft sensor bracket . . .

11 The special tool can now be inserted into the sensor hole to set the timing at 50° BTDC **(see illustrations)**.
12 Turn the crankshaft in the direction of engine rotation, until the end of the tool drops into a recess in the outer toothed part of the flywheel, this will be in the 50° BTDC position.
13 If the engine is being set to 50° BTDC as part of the timing chain removal/renewal procedure, further confirmation of the position can be gained once the timing chain outer cover has been removed. At 50° BTDC, 6 mm timing pins are inserted into the camshaft and fuel pump sprockets, see Section 7.
14 If the holes in the camshaft sprockets do not align, remove the timing pin from the crankshaft and rotate the engine one full turn and re-install the timing pin.
15 Before rotating the crankshaft again, make sure that the timing pin and where fitted the camshaft sprocket timing pins are

3.11b . . . a fabricated tool can be used (gearbox removed for clarity)

removed. When operations are complete, refit the crankshaft sensor. **Do not** use the crankshaft timing setting tool to prevent the crankshaft from rotating.

4 Camshaft cover – removal and refitting

Caution: Do not carry out any work on the fuel system with the engine running. Wait for at least 2 minutes after the engine has been stopped before any work is carried out on the fuel system, to make sure the fuel pressure and temperature has dropped sufficiently. Make sure that all the fuel lines are kept clean. Fit blanking plugs to the end of the fuel lines when they are disconnected, to prevent foreign matter entering the components.

Removal

D5BA and D6BA engines

1 Remove the intake manifold as described in Section 19.
2 Using a spanner to hold the injectors in position, slacken the fuel supply pipes. Note the position of the fuel supply pipes before removal.
3 Slacken the fuel supply pipes from the fuel injection pump, then disconnect the fuel supply pipes and discard them. New supply pipes will be required on refitting. Fit blanking plugs to the injectors and fuel pump unions, to prevent dirt ingress.
4 Disconnect the fuel injector return pipe from the fuel injection pump.
5 Release the retaining clips and disconnect the fuel return lines from the injectors. Discard the return pipe and sealing washers, new ones will be required on refitting.
6 Disconnect the crankcase ventilation hose from the rear of the camshaft cover.
7 Unscrew the retaining bolts and lift the camshaft cover off the cylinder head. Recover the gasket and discard it – a new gasket and seals will be required on refitting.

All other engines

8 Disconnect the battery negative (earth) lead (refer to *Disconnecting the battery*).
9 Remove the oil level dipstick and unclip the engine upper cover.
10 Disconnect the electrical connectors from the fuel injectors **(see illustration)**, make sure the wiring connectors are kept clean.
11 Release the retaining clips and disconnect the fuel return lines from the injectors. Discard the O-ring seals, new ones will be required on refitting. **Note:** *On later models, the collar around the injector is removed with the return pipe (see illustrations)*.
12 Using a spanner to hold the injectors in position, slacken the fuel supply pipes **(see illustration)**. Note the position of the fuel supply pipes before removal.
13 Slacken the fuel supply pipes from the supply manifold **(see illustration)**, then disconnect the fuel supply pipes and discard them. New supply pipes will be required for refitting. Fit blanking plugs to the injectors and supply manifold unions, to prevent dirt ingress.

4.10 Disconnecting the electrical connectors from the fuel injectors

4.11a Release the retaining clips and pull the fuel return lines from the injectors

4.11b On later models, release the collar around the injector . . .

4.11c . . . and withdraw the return pipe

4.12 Using two spanners, one to hold the injectors in position

4.13 Slacken the fuel supply pipes from the supply manifold

4.14 Where applicable, withdraw the fuel return pipe collars

4.15a Prise out the four valve cover fuel injector seals

4.15b Unclip the wiring loom from across the top of the camshaft cover

4.16 Disconnect the crankcase ventilation hose from the camshaft cover

4.17 Remove the securing brackets from the camshaft cover

14 Temporarily remove the blanking plugs from the injectors and withdraw the fuel return pipe collars (early models) from the injectors **(see illustration)**. Refit the blanking plugs.
15 Carefully prise out the four valve cover fuel injector seals from the camshaft cover. Discard the seals, new ones will be required on refitting. Unclip the wiring loom from across the top of the camshaft cover **(see illustrations)**.
16 Disconnect the crankcase ventilation hose from the rear of the camshaft cover **(see illustration)**.
17 Unscrew the retaining bolts and remove the two supply manifold securing brackets from the camshaft cover **(see illustration)**.
18 Unscrew the retaining bolts and lift the camshaft cover off the cylinder head **(see illustration)**. Recover the gasket and discard it – a new gasket and seals will be required on refitting.

4.18 Remove the camshaft cover

Refitting

19 Clean the sealing surfaces of the cover and the head, and check the condition of the rubber seals fitted to the cover bolts.
20 Refitting is a reversal of removal. Noting the following points:
a) Renew all seals, gaskets and supply pipes as noted on removal.
b) Ensure the gasket is correctly seated on the cylinder head, and take care to avoid displacing it as the camshaft cover is lowered into position.
c) Ensure that the supply pipes are routed as noted on removal.
d) Check the ventilation hose is securely reconnected.
e) Tighten the camshaft cover retaining bolts to the specified torque setting.
21 When the engine has been run for some time, check for signs of oil leakage from the gasket joint.

5 Timing chain cover –
removal and refitting

Note: To carry out this task with the engine/transmission installed in the vehicle it requires the equipment necessary to raise and support the front of the vehicle. Ford technicians use an engine support bar, which locates in the channels at the top of each inner wing, and a further beam attached to this, which rests on the front crossmember. If such an arrangement is not available, use an engine

crane; either way, use a suitable length of chain and hooks to attach the lifting gear to the engine lifting eye. If the engine must be supported from below, use a large piece of wood on a trolley jack to spread the load and reduce the chance of damage to the sump. Precise details of the procedure will depend on the equipment available – the following is typical.
Note: Ford use special tools for removing the oil seal and aligning the timing chain cover – see text. A new timing chain cover will be required on refitting, as the cover will be distorted on removal.

Removal

1 Disconnect the battery negative (earth) lead (refer to Disconnecting the battery).
2 Loosen the right-hand front wheel nuts, then firmly apply the handbrake. Jack up the front of the car, and support on axle stands (see Jacking and vehicle support). Remove the right-hand front wheel.
3 Remove the auxiliary drivebelt as described in Chapter 1B.
4 Remove the crankshaft pulley as described in Section 6.
5 Remove the crankshaft timing chain end oil seal as described in Section 16.
6 Remove the retaining bolts and nuts from the lower part of the timing chain cover.
7 Undo the retaining bolts and remove the auxiliary drivebelt tensioner bracket.
8 Working from inside the engine compartment, undo the retaining bolts and move the coolant expansion tank to one side **(see illustration)**.

5.8 Undo the retaining bolts and move the coolant expansion tank to one side

5.9a Disconnect the fuel lines (blanking off the open ends) . . .

5.9b . . . undo the retaining nut and bolt and detach the fuel line bracket from the cylinder head

5.11 Undo the retaining bolts/nuts (arrowed) and remove the engine mounting

5.12 Undo the retaining nut (arrowed) and slide the idler pulley away from the engine

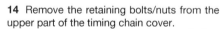

Note: It cannot be removed at this point

5.13a Undo the retaining bolts, including the one (arrowed) behind the idler pulley . . .

9 Disconnect the fuel lines, then undo the retaining nut and bolt and detach the fuel line bracket from the cylinder head **(see illustrations)**.

10 Depending on the equipment available, support the engine either from the top using a support bar or from underneath the sump using a suitable jack.

11 Undo the retaining bolts and nuts, then remove the engine mounting from the right-hand inner front wing panel **(see illustration)**.

12 Undo the retaining nut and slide the idler pulley from the mounting bracket **(see illustration)**. **Note:** *This will not come all the way off the stud at this point.*

13 Undo the retaining bolts, and remove the mounting bracket, complete with idler pulley from the timing chain cover **(see illustrations)**.

14 Remove the retaining bolts/nuts from the upper part of the timing chain cover.

15 Using a couple of scrapers or similar, carefully work your way around the timing chain cover and prise it away from the engine. The cover will become distorted on removal, discard it, as a new cover must be used on refitting.

Refitting

16 Make sure that the mating surfaces of the cover and the engine casing are clean. Apply a 3 mm bead of sealant around the outer mating surface of the engine casing **(see illustration)**.

Caution: Install the timing chain cover within 5 minutes of applying the sealer to the engine casing. Make sure the casing does not come into contact with the

engine casing, until the correct position for fitting is obtained.

17 Fit the timing chain cover and install the retaining nuts and bolts hand tight.

18 Using a cover aligning tool (Ford special tool 303-682), insert the tool over the end of the crankshaft to align the cover **(see illustration)**, then tighten all the timing chain cover retaining nuts and bolts to the specified torque. Remove the tool once the cover is in position.

19 Further refitting is a reversal of removal. Noting the following points:
  a) Fit a new crankshaft oil seal as described in Section 16.
  b) Refit the crankshaft pulley as described in Section 6.
  c) Refit the auxiliary drivebelt as described in Chapter 1B.

5.13b . . . and remove the mounting bracket, complete with idler pulley

5.16 Apply a 3 mm bead of sealant around the mating surface of the engine casing

5.18 Insert the tool over the end of the crankshaft to align the cover, before tightening the retaining bolts

6.7 Unscrew the bolts and remove the crankshaft pulley

6 Crankshaft pulley – removal and refitting

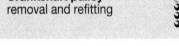

Removal

1 Disconnect the battery negative (earth) lead (refer to *Disconnecting the battery* at the end of this manual).

2 Loosen the right-hand front road wheel nuts, then raise the front of the vehicle, and support securely on axle stands (see *Jacking and vehicle support*). Remove the roadwheel.

3 Remove the retaining screws and withdraw the engine undershield from under the car.

4 Remove the auxiliary drivebelt, as described in Chapter 1B.

5 The three bolts which secure the crankshaft pulley must now be slackened. Ensure that the car is adequately supported, as considerable effort may be needed to slacken the bolts.

6 Ford technicians use a special holding tool (205-072) which locates in the outer holes of the pulley and prevents it from turning. If this is not available, select a gear, and have an assistant firmly apply the handbrake and footbrake as the bolts are loosened. If this method is unsuccessful, and on automatic

6.8 Check the crankshaft oil seal for signs of oil leakage

transmission models, remove the starter motor as described in Chapter 5A, and jam the flywheel ring gear, using a suitable tool, to prevent the crankshaft from rotating.

7 Unscrew the bolts securing the pulley to the crankshaft, and remove the pulley **(see illustration)**.

8 With the pulley removed, it is advisable to check the crankshaft oil seal for signs of oil leakage **(see illustration)**. If necessary, fit a new seal as described in Section 16.

Refitting

9 Refit the pulley to the end of the crankshaft, then fit the pulley securing bolts and tighten them as far as possible before the crankshaft starts to rotate.

10 Holding the pulley against rotation as for removal, first tighten the bolts to the specified Stage 1 torque.

11 Stage 2 involves tightening the bolts though an angle, rather than to a torque. The bolts must be rotated through the specified angle – special angle gauges are available from tool outlets. As a guide, a 90° angle is equivalent to a quarter-turn, and this is easily judged by assessing the start and end positions of the socket handle or torque wrench.

12 Refit and tension the auxiliary drivebelt as described in Chapter 1B.

13 Refit the auxiliary drivebelt lower cover, and where removed, the engine undershield(s) and wheel arch liner panels.

14 Refit the road wheel, lower the vehicle to the ground, and reconnect the battery negative lead. Tighten the wheel nuts to the specified torque.

7 Timing chain – removal inspection and refitting

Note: *Only turn the engine in the normal direction of rotation – clockwise from the right-hand side of the vehicle.*

Removal

1 Remove the timing chain cover, as described in Section 5.

2 Referring to the information in Section 3, set the engine to 50° BTDC on No 1 cylinder. In this position, insert a 6 mm timing pin (6 mm drill bit) in each camshaft sprocket and one in the fuel pump sprocket **(see illustration)**.

3 If the timing chain is not being fitted straight away (or if the chain is being removed as part of another procedure, such as cylinder head removal), temporarily refit the engine right-hand mounting and tighten the bolts securely **(see illustration)**.

4 Slacken the timing chain tensioner by inserting a small screwdriver into the access hole in the tensioner and releasing the pawl mechanism. Press against the timing chain guide to depress the piston into the tensioner housing, when fully depressed, insert a locking pin (approximately 1.5 mm) to lock the piston in its compressed position **(see illustration)**.

5 To remove the tensioner, undo the two retaining bolts and remove the timing chain tensioner from the cylinder block, taking care not to remove the locking pin **(see illustration)**.

7.2 Insert 6 mm timing pins (6 mm drill bits), to align the camshaft sprockets

7.3 Temporarily refit the engine mounting to support the engine

7.4 Insert a pin (arrowed) to lock the piston in its compressed position

7.5 Remove the timing chain tensioner from the cylinder block, taking care not to remove the locking pin

7.6a Undo the retaining bolts and remove the tensioner timing chain guide . . .

7.6b . . . the upper fixed chain guide bolts (arrowed) . . .

7.6c . . . the middle fixed chain guide . . .

7.6d . . . and the lower fixed timing chain guide

6 Undo the retaining bolts and remove the tensioner timing chain guide and the fixed timing chain guides from the cylinder block (see illustrations).

7 Holding the fuel injection pump sprocket in position, slacken the retaining bolts and remove the sprocket (see illustration). Note: Do not rely on the timing pin (6 mm drill bit) to hold the sprocket in position.

8 With the camshafts held in position, undo the camshaft sprocket retaining bolts and remove the camshaft sprockets and timing chain. Do not rotate the crankshaft until the timing chain is refitted. Note: Do not rely on the timing pins (6 mm drill bit) to hold the sprockets in position.

9 Check the condition of the timing chain, tensioner and guides before refitting them. When fitting a new timing chain, a new tensioner should be fitted as a matter of

course, especially if the engine has completed a large mileage.

10 To remove the timing chain sprocket from the crankshaft, the oil pump drive chain will need to be removed first, hold the tensioner in and insert a locking pin (approximately 1.5 mm) to lock the piston in its compressed position (see illustration). Undo the two retaining bolts and remove the oil pump drive chain tensioner from the engine. The chain can now be removed from the sprocket. Undo the retaining bolt and withdraw the sprocket from the crankshaft (see illustration).

Inspection

Note: Keep all components identified for position to ensure correct refitting.

11 Clean all components thoroughly and wipe dry.

12 Examine the chain tensioner and

tensioner guide for excessive wear or other damage. Check the guides for deep grooves made by the timing chain.

13 Examine the timing chain for excessive wear. Hold it horizontally and check how much movement exists in the chain links. If there is any doubt, compare it to a new chain. Renew as necessary.

14 Examine the teeth of the camshaft and crankshaft sprockets for excessive wear and damage.

15 Before refitting the timing chain tensioner, the piston must be compressed and locked until refitted (if not already done on removal). To do this, insert a small screwdriver into the access hole in the tensioner and release the pawl mechanism. Now lightly clamp the tensioner in a soft-jawed vice and slowly compress the piston. Do not apply excessive force and make sure that the piston remains

7.7 Remove the fuel pump sprocket

7.10a Insert a locking pin (drill bit) to lock the piston in its compressed position

7.10b Undo the retaining bolt and withdraw the sprocket from the crankshaft

7.19 Refit the timing chain and sprockets

7.20a With the timing pins/6 mm drill bits (arrowed) inserted into the sprockets . . .

7.20b . . . re-align the copper links on the timing chain with the timing mark (arrowed) on the camshaft sprockets . . .

7.20c . . . and the timing mark (arrowed) on the fuel pump sprocket

aligned with its cylinder. When completely compressed, insert a locking pin/1.5 mm diameter wire rod into the special hole to lock the piston in its compressed position.

Refitting

16 Ensure that the crankshaft and camshaft are still set to 50° BTDC on No 1 cylinder, as described in Section 3.

17 If not already fitted, refit the crankshaft drive sprocket onto the crankshaft. Refit the oil pump drive chain and tensioner, hold pressure against the tensioner guide and withdraw the tensioner locking pin. (see Section 13, for further information on refitting the oil pump).

18 Refit the fuel pump sprocket and the exhaust camshaft sprocket, DO NOT tighten the retaining bolts at this stage.

7.22 Hold pressure against the tensioner guide (arrowed) and withdraw the locking pin

19 With the timing chain around the intake camshaft sprocket, refit the timing chain and sprocket, feeding the timing chain around the crankshaft drive sprocket, fuel pump sprocket and exhaust camshaft sprocket **(see illustration)**.

20 With the timing pins (6 mm drill bits) inserted into the sprockets to re-align them, the copper links on the timing chain must line up with the timing marks on the sprockets **(see illustrations)**.

21 Refit the tensioner to the cylinder block and tighten the retaining bolts to the specified torque setting. Take care not to remove the locking pin.

22 Refit the timing chain tensioner guide on the upper pivot pin and tighten the retaining bolt to the specified torque setting. Hold pressure against the bottom of the tensioner guide and withdraw the tensioner locking pin. This will then tension the timing chain **(see illustration)**.

23 Refit the three fixed timing chain guides and tighten the retaining bolts to the specified torque setting.

24 Tighten the camshaft sprocket retaining bolts and the fuel injection pump sprocket retaining bolts, to the specified torque setting shown at the beginning of this Chapter. **Note:** *Do not rely on the timing pins (6 mm drill bits) to hold the sprockets in position.*

25 Check that the engine is still set to 50° BTDC (as described in Section 3), and remove the timing pins (6 mm drill bits) from the sprockets and the timing peg from the crankshaft sensor hole.

26 Turn the engine (in the direction of engine rotation) two full turns. Refit the timing pins and crankshaft timing peg to make sure the engine timing is still set at 50° BTDC (see Section 3 for further information).

27 Check the tension of the chain then remove the timing pins (6 mm drill bits) from the sprockets and the timing peg from the crankshaft sensor hole. Refit the crankshaft sensor.

28 Refit the timing chain cover as described in Section 5.

8 Timing chain tensioner and sprockets – removal, inspection and refitting

Timing chain tensioner

1 The timing chain tensioner is removed as part of the timing chain renewal procedure, in Section 7.

Camshaft sprocket

2 The camshaft sprocket is removed as part of the timing chain renewal procedure, in Section 7.

Fuel injection pump sprocket

3 Removal of the injection pump sprocket is described as part of the timing chain renewal procedure, in Section 7

9 Camshaft and hydraulic rockers – removal and refitting

Note: *A new camshaft oil seal and suitable sealant will be required on refitting. New rocker shaft retaining bolts will also be required.*
Note: *Only turn the engine in the normal direction of rotation – clockwise from the right-hand side of the vehicle.*

Removal

1 Remove the timing chain cover, as described in Section 5.

2 Referring to the information in Section 3, set the engine to 50° BTDC on No 1 cylinder. In this position, insert a 6 mm timing pin (6 mm drill bit) in each camshaft sprocket and one in the fuel injection pump sprocket (see Section 7).

3 Remove the camshaft cover, as described in Section 4.

4 Remove the power steering belt as described in Chapter 10, Section 33. Undo the retaining bolt and remove the power steering pump pulley from the end of the camshaft, see Section 10.

5 Undo the retaining bolts and remove the brake vacuum pump from the transmission end of the exhaust camshaft, as described in Chapter 9.

6 Slacken and remove the rocker shaft retaining bolts, discard them as new ones will be required on refitting. Lift out the rocker shafts, complete with rocker arms and store them in a clean and safe area. **Note:** *They are marked at the timing chain end of the shaft, IN for intake shaft and EX for exhaust shaft* **(see illustration)**.

7 Slacken the timing chain tensioner and remove the tensioner timing chain guide, the upper timing chain guide and the camshaft sprockets **(see illustration)** as described in Section 7.

8 Slacken the camshaft carrier retaining bolts in the sequence shown **(see illustration)**, then lift the camshaft carrier from the cylinder head.

9 Carefully lift out the camshafts, and place them somewhere clean and safe – the lobes must not be scratched. Remove the camshaft oil seals from the transmission end of the camshafts and discard them, new ones will be required for refitting.

10 Before removing the hydraulic rocker arms from the rocker shaft, first mark the rockers so that they are fitted in the same position on re-assembly. The rocker arms can then be withdrawn from the rocker shaft along with the springs.

Refitting

11 Make sure that the top surfaces of the cylinder head, and in particular the camshaft bearing surfaces and the mating surfaces for the camshaft carrier, are completely clean.

12 Lubricate the camshafts and cylinder head bearing journals with clean engine oil, then carefully lower the camshafts into position in the cylinder head **(see illustrations)**.

13 Apply a 2.5 mm bead of sealant around the outer mating surface of the camshaft carrier **(see illustration)**.

Caution: Install the timing camshaft carrier within 5 minutes of applying the sealer to the mating surface. Make sure the carrier does not come into contact with the cylinder head, until the correct position for fitting is obtained.

14 Install the camshaft carrier retaining bolts and tighten them in the **opposite** sequence to that shown **(see illustration 9.8)**.

15 Refit the timing chain, sprockets, guides and tensioner as described in Section 7.

16 Install the rocker shafts using new

9.6 Marked at the timing chain end of the shafts: IN for intake shaft

9.7 Removing the upper timing chain guide

9.8 Slackening sequence for the camshaft carrier retaining bolts

retaining bolts, making sure they are fitted in the correct position as noted on removal (see paragraph 6). Tighten the retaining bolts to the specified torque setting.

17 Fit a new oil seal **(see illustration)**, then refit the brake vacuum pump to the transmission end of the exhaust camshaft, as described in Chapter 9.

9.12a Lubricating the cylinder head bearing journals with clean engine oil . . .

9.12b . . . then carefully lower the camshafts into position

9.13 Apply a 2.5 mm bead of sealant around the outer mating surface of the camshaft carrier

9.17 Fit a new oil seal before refitting the brake vacuum pump

18 Fit a new camshaft oil seal and refit the power steering pump pulley to the end of the camshaft as described in Section 10.
19 Refit the camshaft cover, as described in Section 4.
20 Refit the timing chain cover, as described in Section 5.

10 Camshaft oil seal – renewal

1 Remove the plastic cover from the power steering belt and slacken the pulley retaining bolt **(see illustration)**.
2 Remove the power steering pump belt as described in Chapter 10, Section 33.
3 Undo the retaining bolt and remove the power steering pump pulley from the end of the camshaft **(see illustration)**.

4 Remove the camshaft oil seal. Ford dealers have a special seal extractor for this (tool No 303-293). In the absence of this tool, do not use any removal method which might damage the sealing surfaces, or a leak will result when the new seal is fitted **(see Haynes Hint)**.

> *One of the best ways to remove an oil seal is to carefully drill or punch two holes through the seal, opposite each other (taking care not to damage the surface behind the seal as this is done). Two self-tapping screws are then screwed into the holes; by pulling on the screw heads alternately with a pair of pliers, the seal can be extracted.*

5 Clean out the seal housing and the sealing surface of the camshaft by wiping it with a lint-free cloth. Remove any swarf or burrs that may cause the seal to leak.
6 Apply a little oil to the new camshaft oil seal, and fit it over the end of the camshaft, using the sleeve supplied with the new oil seal **(see illustration)**. If a sleeve is not supplied, to avoid damaging the seal lips, wrap a little tape over the end of the camshaft.
7 Ford dealers have a special tool for pressing the seal into the cylinder head, but if this is not available, a deep socket of suitable size can be used. **Note:** *Select a socket that bears only on the hard outer surface of the seal, not the inner lip which can easily be damaged. It is important that the seal is fitted square to the shaft, and is fully seated.*
8 Refitting is a reversal of removal.

11 Cylinder head – removal, inspection and refitting

Removal

1 Disconnect the battery negative (earth) lead (refer to *Disconnecting the battery* at the end of this manual).
2 Drain the cooling system as described in Chapter 1B.
3 Remove the alternator as described in Chapter 5A.
4 Remove the camshafts and hydraulic rockers as described in Section 9.
5 Remove the exhaust manifold as described in Section 20.
6 Remove the air cleaner housing assembly, as described in Chapter 4B.
7 Undo the retaining nut and disconnect the bracket for the cylinder head temperature sensor wiring block connector. Unclip the wiring from the end of the cylinder head **(see illustration)**.
8 Undo the retaining bolt and detach the power steering high pressure pipe upper bracket from the engine lifting eye **(see illustration)**.
9 Undo the retaining bolts and detach the power steering high pressure pipe lower bracket and release the wiring loom securing clip **(see illustration)**.
10 On Common Rail diesel engines, disconnect the wiring connector from the end of the fuel supply rail and the camshaft position sensor **(see illustrations)**. Also disconnect the wiring connector from the

10.1 Undo the retaining nut (arrowed) and remove the pulley plastic cover

10.3 Undo the retaining bolt and remove the power steering pump pulley

10.6 Fitting the oil seal over the end of the camshaft, using the sleeve supplied with the new oil seal

11.7 Undo the retaining nut (arrowed) and remove the bracket for the wiring block connector

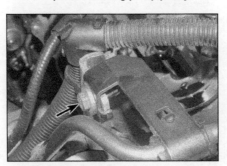

11.8 Undo the retaining bolt (arrowed) and detach the bracket from the engine lifting eye

11.9 Undo the retaining bolts (arrowed) and detach the lower bracket

11.10a Disconnect the wiring connector (common rail diesel engines) from the end of the fuel supply rail

11.10b Disconnect the wiring connector from the camshaft position sensor

11.11 Unclip the coolant hose (arrowed) from under the front of the intake manifold

11.13 Undo the retaining nut (arrowed) and disconnect the glow plug wiring connector

11.14a On Common Rail diesel engines, remove the clamp bolt (arrowed) and slacken the fuel supply pipe union . . .

11.14b . . . then slacken the fuel supply pipe at the fuel rail

intake manifold sensor and the vacuum hose from the intake manifold.

11 Unclip the coolant hose from under the front of the intake manifold (see illustration).

12 Undo the retaining bolts and remove the intake manifold.

13 Undo the retaining nut and disconnect the glow plug wiring connector (see illustration).

14 On Common Rail diesel engines, remove the fuel supply pipe clamp and slacken the supply line at the fuel pump (see illustrations). Slacken the fuel supply pipe at the fuel supply rail then remove and discard (see illustration), a new pipe will be required on refitting. Install blanking plugs to the open ports on the fuel pump and supply rail to prevent dirt ingress. Release the retaining clip and disconnect the return pipe from the fuel injection pump, discard the return pipe as a new one will be required on refitting.

15 On engines without Common Rail, undo

the retaining bolts and remove the fuel supply and return pipes from the fuel pump (see illustration).

16 Slacken the fuel injector locking sleeves and remove the fuel injectors, for further information see Chapter 4B.

17 Check around the head and the engine bay that there is nothing still attached to the cylinder head, nor anything which would prevent it from being lifted away.

18 Working in the reverse order of the tight-ening sequence (see illustration 11.42), loosen the cylinder head bolts by half a turn at a time, until they are all loose. Remove the head bolts, and discard them – Ford state that they must not be re-used, even if they appear to be serviceable.

19 Lift the cylinder head away; use assistance if possible, as it is a heavy assembly. Do not, under any circumstances, lever the head between the mating surfaces,

as this will certainly damage the sealing surfaces for the gasket, leading to leaks.

20 Once the head has been removed, recover the gasket from the two dowels, discard the gasket, a new one will be required on refitting, see paragraph 22.

Inspection

21 If required, dismantling and inspection of the cylinder head is covered in Part D of this Chapter.

Cylinder head gasket selection

22 Examine the old cylinder head gasket for manufacturer's identification markings. These will be in the form of teeth (one, two or three) on the front edge of the gasket and/or holes in the gasket, which indicate the gasket's thickness (see illustration).

23 Unless new components have been fitted, or the cylinder head has been machined

11.14c Release the retaining clip (arrowed) and disconnect the return pipe from the fuel injection pump

11.15 Remove the fuel supply and return pipes (arrowed) from the fuel pump

11.22 Teeth and holes in the gasket (arrowed), which indicate the gasket's thickness

11.25 Using a dial test indicator to measure the piston protrusion

11.38 Locate the new cylinder head gasket over the dowels correctly

(skimmed), the new cylinder head gasket must be of the same type as the old one. Purchase the required gasket, and proceed to paragraph 29.

24 If the head has been machined, or if new pistons have been fitted, it is likely that a head gasket of different thickness to the original will be needed. Gasket selection is made on the basis of the measured piston protrusion above the cylinder head gasket surface (the protrusion must fall within the range specified at the start of this Chapter).

25 To measure the piston protrusion, anchor a dial test indicator (DTI) to the top face (cylinder head gasket mating face) of the cylinder block, and zero the gauge on the gasket mating face **(see illustration)**.

26 Rest the gauge probe above No 1 piston crown, and turn the crankshaft slowly by hand until the piston reaches TDC (its maximum height). Measure and record the maximum piston projection at TDC.

27 Repeat the measurement for the remaining pistons, and record the results.

28 If the measurements differ from piston to piston, take the highest figure, and use this to determine the thickness of the head gasket required. See Specifications at the start of this Chapter.

Preparation for refitting

29 The mating faces of the cylinder head and cylinder block must be perfectly clean before refitting the head. Use a hard plastic or wooden scraper to remove all traces of gasket and carbon; also clean the piston crowns. **Note:** *The new head gasket has rubber-coated surfaces, which could be damaged from sharp edges or debris left by a metal scraper.*

30 Take particular care when cleaning the piston crowns, as the soft aluminium alloy is easily damaged.

31 Make sure that the carbon is not allowed to enter the oil and water passages – this is particularly important for the lubrication system, as carbon could block the oil supply to the engine's components. Using adhesive tape and paper, seal the water, oil and bolt holes in the cylinder block.

32 To prevent carbon entering the gap between the pistons and bores, smear a little grease in the gap. After cleaning each piston, use a small brush to remove all traces of grease and carbon from the gap, then wipe away the remainder with a clean rag. Clean all the pistons in the same way.

33 Check the mating surfaces of the cylinder block and the cylinder head for nicks, deep scratches and other damage (refer to the Note in paragraph 29). If slight, they may be removed carefully with a file, but if excessive, machining may be the only alternative to renewal.

34 If warpage of the cylinder head gasket surface is suspected, use a straight-edge to check it for distortion. Refer to Part D of this Chapter if necessary.

35 Ensure that the cylinder head bolt holes in the crankcase are clean and free of oil. Syringe or soak up any oil left in the bolt holes. This is most important in order that the correct bolt tightening torque can be applied, and to prevent the possibility of the block being cracked by hydraulic pressure when the bolts are tightened.

Refitting

36 Make sure the timing is still set at 50° BTDC (see Section 3). This will eliminate any risk of piston-to-valve contact as the cylinder head is refitted.

37 To guide the cylinder head into position, screw two long studs (or old cylinder head bolts with the heads cut off, and slots cut in the ends to enable the bolts to be unscrewed) into the end cylinder head bolt locations on the manifold side of the cylinder block.

38 Ensure that the cylinder head locating dowels are in place in the cylinder block, then fit the new cylinder head gasket over the dowels **(see illustration)**. The gasket can only be fitted one way, with the teeth to determine the gasket thickness at the front **(see illustration 11.22)**. Take care to avoid damaging the gasket's rubber coating.

39 Lower the cylinder head into position on the gasket, ensuring that it engages correctly over the guide studs and dowels.

40 Fit the new cylinder head bolts to the remaining bolt locations and screw them in as far as possible by hand.

41 Unscrew the two guide studs from the cylinder block, then screw in the two remaining new cylinder head bolts as far as possible by hand.

42 Working in the sequence shown **(see illustration)**, tighten the cylinder head bolts to the specified Stage 1 torques.

43 Again working in the sequence shown, tighten all the cylinder head bolts through the specified Stages as shown in the specifications at the beginning of this Chapter.

11.42 Tightening sequence for the cylinder head bolts

44 The last Stages involve tightening the bolts through an angle, rather than to a torque. Each bolt in sequence must be rotated through the specified angle – special angle gauges are available from tool outlets. As a guide, a 90° angle is equivalent to a quarter-turn, and this is easily judged by assessing the start and end positions of the socket handle or torque wrench.

45 The remainder of the refitting procedure is a reversal of the removal procedure, bearing in mind the following points:
 a) *Refit the timing chain with reference to Section 7.*
 b) *Refit the camshafts and hydraulic rockers with reference to Section 9.*
 c) *Refit the fuel injectors with reference to Chapter 4B.*
 d) *Reconnect the exhaust manifold with reference to Section 20.*
 e) *Refit the cylinder head cover with reference to Section 4.*
 f) *Refit the alternator with reference to Section 5A.*
 g) *Refit the air cleaner assembly with reference to Chapter 4B.*
 h) *Refill the cooling system with reference to Chapter 1B.*
 i) *Check and if necessary top-up the engine oil level and power steering fluid level as described in 'Weekly checks'.*
 j) *Before starting the engine, read through the section on engine restarting after overhaul, at the end of Chapter 2D.*

12 Sump – removal and refitting

Removal

1 Apply the handbrake, then jack up the front of the vehicle and support it on axle stands (see *Jacking and vehicle support*). Remove the engine undershield.

2 Drain the engine oil, then clean and refit the engine oil drain plug. Inspect the seal for damage, fit a new drain plug and seal if required. Tighten the drain plug to the specified torque wrench setting. Although not strictly necessary as part of the dismantling procedure, owners are advised to remove and discard the oil filter, so that it can be renewed with the oil. Refer to Chapter 1B if necessary.

3 A conventional sump gasket is not used, and sealant is used instead.

4 Progressively unscrew the sump retaining bolts and nuts, break the joint by striking the sump with the palm of the hand, then lower the sump away, turning it as necessary.

5 Unfortunately, the use of sealant can make removal of the sump more difficult. If care is taken not to damage the surfaces, the sealant can be cut around using a scraper or a sharp knife. On no account lever between the mating faces, as this will almost certainly damage them, resulting in leaks when finished.

HAYNES HiNT *If the sump is particularly difficult to remove, extracting the studs may prove useful – if a Torx socket is not available, thread two nuts onto the stud, tightening them against each other, then use a spanner on the inner nut to unscrew the stud. Note the locations of the studs for refitting.*

Refitting

6 On reassembly, thoroughly clean and degrease the mating surfaces of the cylinder block/crankcase and sump, removing all traces of sealant, then use a clean rag to wipe out the sump and the engine's interior.

7 If the studs have been removed, they must be refitted before the sump is offered up, to ensure that it is aligned correctly. If this is not done, some of the sealant may enter the blind holes for the sump bolts, preventing the bolts from being fully fitted.

8 Apply a 3 mm bead of sealant to the sump flange, making sure the bead is around the inside edge of the bolt holes **(see illustration). Note:** *The sump must be refitted within 5 minutes of applying the sealant.*

9 Fit the sump over the studs, and insert the sump bolts and nuts, tightening them by hand only at this stage.

10 Tighten all the bolts and nuts in the sequence shown **(see illustration).**

11 Lower the car to the ground, and refill the

12.8 Apply a 3 mm bead of sealant (arrowed) to the lower casing

engine with oil. If removed, fit a new oil filter with reference to Chapter 1B.

13 Oil pump – removal and refitting

Note: *The following procedure is for removing and refitting of the oil pump. If the oil pump drive chain or tensioner requires renewing, the engine timing chain will need to be removed (see Section 7).*

Removal

1 Remove the sump as described in Section 12.
2 Carefully pull on the oil pump drive chain, to push the oil out of the chain tensioner.
3 Ford special tool (303-705) is used to align

12.10 Tightening sequence for the sump retaining bolts

13.3 Aligning the oil pump sprocket using a plate bolted to the lower crankcase

the oil pump sprocket, bolt the tool/plate to the sump flange so that it sits flush with oil pump drive sprocket **(see illustration)**.

4 Undo the retaining bolts and remove the pick-up pipe from the oil pump **(see illustration)**.

5 Undo the retaining bolts and remove the oil pump from the lower crankcase, withdraw the chain from the sprocket on removal.

Caution: The oil pump sprocket and crankshaft sprocket must be kept in line with each other, so that the chain runs straight. Use Ford's special tool or a DTI gauge to make sure they are aligned correctly.

Refitting

6 Refit the oil pump to the lower crankcase, installing the drive chain to the sprocket on the oil pump. Only finger-tighten the oil pump retaining bolts at this stage.

14.1 The oil pressure switch (arrowed) is screwed into the oil filter housing

15.1 The oil cooler (arrowed) is mounted next to the oil filter

13.4 Removing the oil pick-up pipe from the oil pump

7 Slide the oil pump until the drive sprocket sits flush with the special tool, as aligned on removal **(see illustration 13.3)**. With the oil pump in position, tighten the retaining bolts to the specified torque setting.

8 Ensuring that the alignment of the pump is correct, undo the retaining bolts and remove the special tool from the sump flange.

9 Refit the pick-up pipe to the oil pump.

10 Refit the sump with reference to Section 12.

14 Oil pressure warning light switch – removal and refitting

Removal

1 The switch is screwed into the upper part of the oil filter housing **(see illustration)**.

2 To improve access to the switch, it may be necessary to apply the handbrake, then jack up the front of the vehicle and support it on axle stands (see *Jacking and vehicle support*). Remove the engine undershield.

3 Unplug the wiring from the switch and unscrew it from the filter housing; be prepared for some oil loss.

Refitting

4 Refitting is the reverse of the removal procedure; apply a thin smear of suitable sealant to the switch threads, and tighten it securely.

5 Check the engine oil level and top-up as necessary (see *Weekly checks*).

6 Check for correct warning light operation, and for signs of oil leaks, once the engine has

15.4 Unscrew the four bolts and withdraw the oil cooler from the oil filter housing (shown removed for clarity)

been restarted and warmed-up to normal operating temperature.

15 Oil cooler – removal and refitting

Note: *New sealing rings will be required on refitting.*

Removal

1 The oil cooler is mounted next to the oil filter on the front of the cylinder block **(see illustration)**. Access to the oil cooler is best obtained from below – apply the handbrake, then jack up the front of the car and support it on axle stands (see *Jacking and vehicle support*). Remove the engine undershield.

2 Position a container beneath the oil filter to catch escaping oil and coolant.

3 Clamp the oil cooler coolant hoses to minimise spillage, then remove the clips, and disconnect the hoses from the oil cooler. Be prepared for coolant spillage.

4 Unscrew the four securing bolts and withdraw the oil cooler from the oil filter housing, recover the gasket (a new gasket must be used on refitting) **(see illustration)**.

Refitting

5 Refitting is a reversal of removal, bearing in mind the following points:
  a) Use a new gasket.
  b) Fit the oil cooler mounting bolts, and tighten them securely.
  c) On completion, lower the car to the ground. Check and if necessary top-up the oil and coolant levels, then start the engine and check for signs of oil or coolant leakage.

16 Crankshaft oil seals – renewal

Timing chain end seal

1 Remove the crankshaft pulley with reference to Section 6.

2 Ford technicians use a special seal-removing and refitting tool (303-679), but an adequate substitute can be achieved using a three-legged puller and three bolts **(see illustrations)**. Turn the seal anti-clockwise, using the tool, to remove the crankshaft oil seal from the timing chain cover.

3 Wipe clean the oil seal contact surfaces and seating, and clean up any sharp edges or burrs which might damage the new seal as it is fitted, or which might cause the seal to leak once in place.

4 The new oil seal may be supplied fitted with a locating sleeve, which must **not** be removed prior to fitting.

5 Locate the new seal (lips facing inwards) over the end of the crankshaft, and press the seal squarely and fully into position in the

16.2a Tool for removing the oil seal, using a three-legged puller and three bolts . . .

16.2b . . . insert the bolts into the recesses (arrowed) in the seal . . .

16.2c . . . and rotate the seal anti-clockwise to remove

16.5a Locate the new seal over the end of the crankshaft using the locating sleeve . . .

16.5b . . . remove the locating sleeve

16.12 A locating/centring sleeve (arrowed) is supplied with the new oil seal

cover, remove the locating sleeve **(see illustrations)**.

6 Using the special tool used on removal, turn the seal clockwise until it is located securely into the timing chain cover.

7 Refit the crankshaft pulley with reference to Section 6.

Flywheel end seal

8 Remove the transmission as described in the appropriate Part of Chapter 7, and the clutch assembly as described in Chapter 6 on manual transmission models.

9 Unbolt the flywheel (see Section 17).

10 Unbolt and remove the oil seal carrier; the seal is renewed complete with the carrier, and is not available separately. A complete set of new carrier retaining bolts should also be obtained for reassembly.

11 Clean the end of the crankshaft, polishing off any burrs or raised edges, which may have caused the seal to fail in the first place. Clean also the seal carrier mating face on the engine block, using a suitable solvent for degreasing if necessary.

12 The new oil seal is supplied fitted with a locating sleeve, which must **not** be removed prior to fitting **(see illustration)**. It should also have a centring sleeve supplied with the seal.

13 Offer up the carrier into position, feeding the locating sleeve over the end of the crankshaft **(see illustrations)**. Insert the new seal carrier retaining bolts, and tighten them all by hand. Remove the locating sleeve.

14 Using the special centring sleeve supplied with the seal, centre the oil seal carrier around the end of the crankshaft **(see illustration)**.

15 Ensuring that the correct alignment of the carrier is maintained, work in a diagonal sequence, tightening the retaining bolts to the specified torque **(see illustration)**. Remove the seal centring sleeve.

16 The remainder of the reassembly procedure is the reverse of dismantling, referring to the relevant text for details where required. Check for signs of oil leakage when the engine is restarted.

16.13a Locate the new seal over the end of the crankshaft using the locating sleeve . . .

16.13b . . . remove the locating sleeve

16.14 Use the centring sleeve to centre the oil seal carrier

16.15 With the oil seal carrier centred around the crankshaft, tighten the retaining bolts

17.3 Locating dowel (arrowed) to align the flywheel when refitting

17.4 Special tool (arrowed) used to lock the flywheel, while the retaining bolts are slackened

though an angle, rather than to a torque. Each bolt must be rotated through the specified angle – special angle gauges are available from tool outlets.

15 The remainder of reassembly is the reverse of the removal procedure, referring to the relevant text for details where required.

17 Flywheel/driveplate – removal, inspection and refitting

Removal

1 Remove the transmission as described in the appropriate Part of Chapter 7. Now is a good time to check components such as oil seals and renew them if necessary.

2 On manual transmission models, remove the clutch as described in Chapter 6. Now is a good time to check or renew the clutch components and release bearing.

3 There is a locating dowel in the end of the crankshaft, to ensure correct alignment during refitting **(see illustration)**.

4 Prevent the flywheel from turning by locking the ring gear teeth, or by bolting a strap between the flywheel and the cylinder block/crankcase **(see illustration)**. Slacken the bolts evenly until all are free.

5 Remove each bolt in turn and ensure that new replacements are obtained for reassembly; these bolts are subjected to severe stresses and so must be renewed, regardless of their apparent condition, whenever they are disturbed.

6 Withdraw the flywheel, remembering that it is very heavy – do not drop it.

Inspection

7 Clean the flywheel to remove grease and oil. Inspect the surface for cracks, rivet grooves, burned areas and score marks. Light

scoring can be removed with emery cloth. Check for cracked and broken ring gear teeth. Lay the flywheel on a flat surface and use a straight-edge to check for warpage.

8 Clean and inspect the mating surfaces of the flywheel and the crankshaft. If the crankshaft seal is leaking, renew it (see Section 16) before refitting the flywheel. If the engine has covered a high mileage, it may be worth fitting a new seal as a matter if course, given the amount of work needed to access it.

9 While the flywheel is removed, clean carefully its inboard (right-hand) face, particularly the recesses which serve as the reference points for the crankshaft speed/position sensor. Clean the sensor's tip and check that the sensor is securely fastened.

10 Thoroughly clean the threaded bolt holes in the crankshaft, removing all traces of locking compound.

Refitting

11 Fit the flywheel to the crankshaft so that all bolt holes align – it will fit only one way – check the dowel is located correctly. Apply suitable locking compound to the threads of the new bolts, then insert them.

12 Lock the flywheel by the method used on dismantling. Working in a diagonal sequence, tighten the bolts to the specified Stage 1 torque wrench setting.

13 Then working in the same diagonal sequence, tighten them to the specified Stage 2 torque wrench setting.

14 Stage 3 involves tightening the bolts

18 Engine/transmission mountings – inspection and renewal

Refer to Chapter 2A, Section 20.

19 Intake manifold – removal and refitting

Removal

1 Disconnect the battery negative (earth) lead (refer to *Disconnecting the battery* at the end of this manual).

2 Remove the oil level dipstick, then unclip the engine upper plastic cover from the top of the engine.

3 Unclip the coolant hose from under the front of the intake manifold **(see illustration)**.

4 Release the securing clip and detach the turbocharger outlet pipe from the end of the intake manifold **(see illustration)**.

5 Where applicable, detach any wiring or vacuum hoses from across the intake manifold (releasing it from any relevant connectors and retaining clips, marking or labelling them as they are unplugged), then move the wiring loom to one side of the engine bay.

6 Unscrew the bolts securing the intake manifold to the cylinder head and withdraw it. Take care not to damage vulnerable components as the manifold is being removed.

Refitting

7 Refitting is the reverse of the removal procedure, noting the following points:

  a) *If using a scraper or solvent to remove any traces of old gasket material and sealant from the manifold and cylinder head, be careful to ensure that you do not scratch or damage the material of either; the cylinder head is of aluminium alloy, while the manifold is a plastic moulding – any solvents used must be suitable for this application. If the gasket was leaking, have the mating surfaces checked for warpage at an automotive machine shop. While it may be possible to have the cylinder head gasket surface skimmed if necessary, to remove any distortion, the manifold must be renewed if it is found to be warped or cracked – check with special care around the mounting points.*

  b) *Provided the relevant mating surfaces are clean and flat, a new gasket will be*

19.3 Unclip the coolant hose (arrowed) from under the intake manifold

19.4 Release the securing clip (arrowed) and detach the outlet pipe from the turbocharger

19.7 Fit new gaskets to the intake ports in the manifold

sufficient to ensure the joint is gas-tight. **Do not** use any kind of silicone-based sealant on any part of the fuel system or intake manifold.

c) Fit new gaskets to the intake ports in the manifold **(see illustration)**, then locate the manifold on the head and install the retaining bolts.

d) Tighten the bolts evenly to the torque listed in the Specifications at the beginning of this Chapter. Work from the centre outwards, to avoid warping the manifold.

e) Refit the remaining parts in the reverse order of removal – tighten all fasteners to the torque wrench settings specified.

f) If removed, make sure any vacuum hoses and wiring are routed correctly and the connections fitted as labelled up on removal.

g) When the engine is fully warmed-up,

check for signs of fuel, intake and/or vacuum leaks.

h) Road test the vehicle, and check for proper operation of all disturbed components.

20 Exhaust manifold –
removal, inspection
and refitting

 Warning: The engine must be completely cool before beginning this procedure.

Removal

1 Disconnect the battery negative (earth) lead (refer to Disconnecting the battery at the end of this manual).

2 Park the vehicle on firm, level ground, apply the handbrake, then jack up the front of the vehicle and support it on axle stands (see Jacking and vehicle support). Remove the engine undershield.

3 Remove the catalytic converter as described in Chapter 4C.

4 Release the securing clip and detach the turbocharger intake pipe from the turbocharger **(see illustration)**.

5 Release the securing clip and detach the charger air cooler intake pipe from the turbocharger **(see illustration)**.

6 Undo the two retaining bolts and disconnect the oil return tube from under the turbocharger **(see illustration)**. Discard the gasket.

20.4 Release the securing clip (arrowed) and detach the intake pipe from the turbocharger

7 Remove the oil return tube lower retaining bolt and withdraw it from the engine **(see illustration)**. Discard the O-ring.

8 Undo the retaining bolt and disconnect the oil supply tube from the turbocharger **(see illustration)**. Discard the sealing washers.

9 Undo the two retaining bolts and disconnect the EGR cooler from the exhaust manifold **(see illustration)**. Discard the gasket.

10 Slacken and remove the retaining nut and bolt to disconnect the other end of the EGR cooler from the exhaust manifold **(see illustration)**.

11 Where applicable, disconnect the vacuum pipe from the vacuum diaphragm unit **(see illustration)**.

12 Undo the two retaining bolts and detach the heat shield from the top of the exhaust manifold **(see illustration)**. **Note:** This cannot completely be removed, until the manifold is withdrawn.

20.5 Release the securing clip and detach the charger air cooler intake pipe (arrowed)

20.6 Undo the retaining bolts (arrowed) and disconnect the oil return tube

20.7 Remove the oil return tube lower retaining bolt (arrowed)

20.8 Disconnect the oil supply tube from the turbocharger (renew the washers on refitting)

20.9 Undo the retaining bolts (arrowed) and disconnect the EGR cooler

20.10 Remove the nut and bolt (arrowed) to disconnect the EGR cooler from the exhaust manifold

20.11 Disconnecting the vacuum pipe from the vacuum diaphragm unit

20.12 Remove the heat shield retaining bolts (arrowed)

13 Slacken and remove the retaining bolts along the top of the bulkhead at the back of the engine bay, then withdraw the grille brace bar. This will give more room at the rear of the engine to remove the exhaust manifold.

14 Remove the retaining nuts and bolts from the exhaust manifold. When removing the manifold with the engine in the vehicle, additional clearance can be obtained by unscrewing the studs from the cylinder head; a female Torx-type socket will be required. Discard the nuts and studs, new ones will be required for refitting.

15 Slide the exhaust manifold/turbocharger away from the engine and withdraw the heat shield from the top of the manifold.

16 Rotate the assembly through 180° to remove it, discard the gasket. Take care not to damage vulnerable components as the manifold assembly is manoeuvred out of the engine compartment.

Inspection

17 If using a scraper to remove all traces of old gasket material and carbon deposits from the manifold and cylinder head mating surfaces, be careful to ensure that you do not scratch or damage the material of either

component – any solvents used must be suitable for this application. If the gasket was leaking, check the manifold and cylinder head for warpage, this may need to be done at an automotive machine shop, resurface if necessary.

Caution: When scraping, be very careful not to gouge or scratch the delicate aluminium alloy cylinder head.

18 Provided both mating surfaces are clean and flat, a new gasket will be sufficient to ensure the joint is gas-tight. Do not use any kind of exhaust sealant upstream of the catalytic converter.

Refitting

19 Refitting is the reverse of the removal procedure, noting the following points:
 a) *Fit a new manifold gasket and cylinder head studs and nuts.*
 b) *Refit the manifold, and tighten the nuts to the torque listed in the Specifications at the beginning of this Chapter.*
 c) *Fit new gaskets, O-rings and sealing washers where required.*
 d) *Refit the catalytic converter with reference to Chapter 4C.*
 e) *Run the engine, and check for exhaust leaks.*

Chapter 2 Part D:
Engine removal and overhaul procedures

Contents

Degrees of difficulty

Easy, suitable for novice with little experience		Fairly easy, suitable for beginner with some experience		Fairly difficult, suitable for competent DIY mechanic		Difficult, suitable for experienced DIY mechanic		Very difficult, suitable for expert DIY or professional	

Specifications

Engine codes

Petrol engines

1.8 litre	CGBA (81 kW) and CHBA (92 kW)
2.0 litre	CJBA (107 kW)
2.5 litre	LCBD (125 kW)

Diesel engines

Duratorq-DI direct injection	D5BA (66 kW)
Duratorq-DI direct injection	D6BA (85 kW)
Duratorq-DCI common rail	H7BA, BB or BC (85 kW)
Duratorq-DCI common rail	FMBA (96 kW)

4-cylinder petrol engines

Note: *Because of the fine tolerances in the bearing shells, no service operations are permitted on the cylinder block/crank assembly. In the event of any failure, the complete cylinder block, pistons and crank assembly must be renewed as a unit.*

Valves – general	Inlet	Exhaust
Valve lift:		
1.8 litre:		
CGBA	7.4 mm	7.7 mm
CHBA	8.5 mm	7.7 mm
2.0 litre	8.8 mm	7.7 mm
Valve stem-to-guide clearance (engine cold)	0.22 to 0.28 mm	0.27 to 0.33 mm
Valve stem diameter	5.465 to 5.480 mm	5.470 to 5.485 mm

V6 petrol engine

Note: *On the V6 petrol engine, Ford say that the cylinder bores cannot be rebored or honed, the crankshaft cannot be reground, the main bearings cannot be renewed, and the lower crankcase cannot be re-used once removed.*

Cylinder head

Hydraulic tappet clearance in bore	0.018 0.069 mm
Hydraulic tappet diameter	15.988 to 16.000 mm
Maximum permissible gasket surface distortion	0.10 mm
Valve seat angle	45.5°
Valve seat included angle	90°
Valve seat width, inlet	1.1 to 1.4 mm
Valve seat width, exhaust	1.4 to 1.7 mm

Valves	Inlet	Exhaust
Valve head diameter	32.0 mm	26.0 mm
Valve stem-to-guide clearance	0.020 to 0.069 mm	0.045 to 0.094 mm

V6 petrol engine (continued)

Cylinder block
Number of main bearings 4
Cylinder bore diameter:
  Class 1 .... 81.640 to 81.650 mm
  Class 2 .... 81.651 to 81.660 mm
  Class 3 .... 81.661 to 81.670 mm

Pistons and piston rings
Piston diameter:
  Class A .... 81.630 to 81.650 mm
  Class B .... 81.638 to 81.662 mm
  Class C .... 81.650 to 81.670 mm
Piston protrusion at TDC .... 0.415 to 0.115 mm
Piston clearance in bore:
  Coated .... 0.012 to 0.022 mm
  Uncoated .... 0.018 to 0.042 mm
Piston ring end gaps*:
  Top compression ring .... 0.10 to 0.25 mm
  Second compression ring .... 0.27 to 0.42 mm
  Oil control ring .... 0.15 to 0.65 mm
*Note: *Piston ring end gaps should be offset at 120° to one another when fitted*

Connecting rod
Connecting rod endfloat .... 0.10 to 0.30 mm
Small end bore diameter .... 21.071 to 21.032 mm
Connecting rod length .... 138.06 to 138.40 mm

Gudgeon pin
Gudgeon pin length .... 55.05 to 55.47 mm
Gudgeon pin bore diameter .... 21.011 to 21.013 mm
Gudgeon pin clearance in piston .... −0.005 to +0.001 mm
Gudgeon pin clearance in connecting rod .... 0.004 to 0.020 mm

Crankshaft and bearings
Crankshaft endfloat .... 0.135 to 0.255 mm
Main bearing journal diameter – rear .... 62.968 to 62.992 mm
Main bearing bore diameter .... 68.998 to 69.002 mm

Diesel engines

Valves – general	Inlet	Exhaust
Valve stem-to-guide clearance	0.045 mm	0.055 mm

Cylinder block
Cylinder bore diameter:
  Class 1 .... 86.000 to 86.010 mm
  Class 2 .... 86.010 to 86.020 mm
  Class 3 .... 86.020 to 86.030 mm

Pistons and piston rings
Piston diameter:
  Class A .... 85.94 to 85.95 mm
  Class B .... 85.95 to 85.96 mm
  Class C .... 85.96 to 85.97 mm
Piston-to-cylinder bore clearance .... 0.05 to 0.07 mm
Piston ring end gaps*:
  Top compression ring .... 0.25 to 0.50 mm
  Second compression ring .... 0.50 to 0.75 mm
  Oil scraper ring .... 0.25 to 0.50 mm
*Note: *Piston ring end gaps should be offset at 120° to one another when fitted*

Gudgeon pin
Length .... 66.700 mm
Diameter .... 30.000 mm
Clearance in piston .... 0.002 to 0.012 mm
Small-end bore (inside connecting rod) diameter .... 30.010 to 30.018 mm

Diesel engines (continued)

Crankshaft and bearings

Big-end bearing shell standard inside diameter – installed . . . .   56.004 to 56.032 mm
Big-end bearing shell running clearance . . . .   0.034 mm to 0.100 mm
Big-end bearing journal standard diameter . . . .   52.980 to 53.000 mm
Big-end bearing endfloat . . . .   0.100 to 0.320 mm
Big-end bore (inside connecting rod) diameter . . . .   55.096 to 56.015 mm
Crankshaft endfloat . . . .   0.090 to 0.305 mm
Main bearing journals standard diameter:
    1 to 4 . . . .   64.950 to 64.970 mm
    5 . . . .   69.950 to 69.970 mm
Main bearing shells – installed:
    1 to 4 inside diameter . . . .   65.003 to 65.030 mm
    5 inside diameter . . . .   70.004 to 70.033 mm
Main bearing journal-to-shells – running clearance:
    1 to 4 . . . .   0.333 to 0.080 mm
    5 . . . .   0.034 to 0.083 mm

Torque wrench settings

Refer to Chapter 2A , 2B or 2C Specifications

---

1 General information and precautions

How to use this Chapter

This Part of Chapter 2 is devoted to engine/transmission removal and refitting, to those repair procedures requiring the removal of the engine/transmission from the vehicle, and to the overhaul of engine components. It includes only the Specifications relevant to those procedures. Refer to Part A, B or C (depending on engine type) for additional Specifications and for all torque wrench settings.

General information

The information ranges from advice concerning preparation for an overhaul and the purchase of new parts, to detailed step-by-step procedures covering removal and installation of internal engine components and the inspection of parts.

The following Sections have been written based on the assumption that the engine has been removed from the vehicle. For information concerning in-vehicle engine repair, as well as removal and installation of the external components necessary for the overhaul, see Part A, B or C of this Chapter.

When overhauling the engine, it is essential to establish first exactly what parts are available. At the time of writing, very few under- or oversized components are available for engine reconditioning. In many cases, it would appear that the easiest and most economically-sensible course of action is to use an exchange unit.

Caution: Although it is possible to remove the pistons and crankshaft on the 4-cylinder petrol engine, at the time of writing it is not possible to carry out any work on the cylinder block. Because of the fine tolerances in the bearing shells, no service operations are permitted on the cylinder block/crank assembly. In the event of any failure, the complete cylinder block, pistons and crank assembly must be renewed as a unit.

Caution: Although it is possible to remove the pistons and crankshaft on the V6 petrol engine, at the time of writing it is not possible to carry out any work on the cylinder block. Ford say that the cylinder bores cannot be rebored or honed, the crankshaft cannot be reground, the main bearings cannot be renewed, and the lower crankcase cannot be re-used once removed.

2 Engine overhaul – general information

It's not always easy to determine when, or if, an engine should be completely overhauled, as a number of factors must be considered.

High mileage is not necessarily an indication that an overhaul is needed, while low mileage doesn't preclude the need for an overhaul. Frequency of servicing is probably the most important consideration. An engine that's had regular and frequent oil and filter changes, as well as other required maintenance, will most likely give many thousands of miles of reliable service. Conversely, a neglected engine may require an overhaul very early in its life.

Excessive oil consumption is an indication that piston rings, valve seals and/or valve guides are in need of attention. Make sure that oil leaks aren't responsible before deciding that the rings and/or guides are worn. Perform a cylinder compression check (Part A, B or C of this Chapter) to determine the extent of the work required.

Loss of power, rough running, knocking or metallic engine noises, excessive valve train noise and high fuel consumption rates may also point to the need for an overhaul, especially if they're all present at the same time. If a full service doesn't remedy the situation, major mechanical work is the only solution.

An engine overhaul involves restoring all internal parts to the specification of a new engine. **Note:** *Always check first what parts are available before planning any overhaul operation; refer to Section 1. Ford dealers, or a good engine reconditioning specialist/ automotive parts supplier may be able to suggest alternatives which will enable you to overcome the lack of parts.*

During an overhaul, it is usual to renew the piston rings, and to rebore and/or hone the cylinder bores; where the rebore is done by an automotive machine shop, new oversize pistons and rings will also be installed – all these operations, of course, assume the availability of suitable replacement parts. The main and big-end bearings are generally renewed and, if necessary, the crankshaft may be reground to restore the journals.

Note: *On the V6 petrol engine, Ford say that the cylinder bores cannot be rebored or honed, the crankshaft cannot be reground, the main bearings cannot be renewed, and the lower crankcase cannot be re-used once removed.*

Note: *On the 4-cylinder petrol engines, because of the fine tolerances in the bearing shells, no service operations are permitted on the cylinder block/crank assembly. In the event of any failure, the complete cylinder block, pistons and crank assembly must be renewed as a unit.*

Generally, the valves are serviced as well during an overhaul, since they're usually in less-than-perfect condition at this point. While the engine is being overhauled, other components, such as the starter and alternator, can be renewed as well, or rebuilt, if the necessary parts can be found. The end result should be an as-new engine that will give many trouble-free miles. **Note:** *Critical cooling system components such as the hoses, drivebelt, thermostat and water pump MUST have new parts when an engine is overhauled. The radiator should be checked carefully, to ensure that it isn't clogged or leaking (see Chapter 3). Also, as a general rule, the oil pump should be renewed when an engine is rebuilt.*

Before beginning the engine overhaul, read through the entire procedure to familiarise yourself with the scope and requirements of the job. Overhauling an engine isn't difficult, but it is time-consuming. Plan on the vehicle being off the road for a minimum of two weeks, especially if parts must be taken to an automotive machine shop for repair or reconditioning. Check on availability of parts, and make sure that any necessary special tools and equipment are obtained in advance. Most work can be done with typical hand tools, although a number of precision measuring tools are required, for inspecting parts to determine if they must be renewed. Often, an automotive machine shop will handle the inspection of parts, and will offer advice concerning reconditioning and replacement. **Note:** *Always wait until the engine has been completely dismantled, and all components, especially the cylinder block/crankcase, have been inspected, before deciding what service and repair operations must be performed by an automotive machine shop. Since the block's condition will be the major factor to consider when determining whether to overhaul the original engine or buy a rebuilt one, never purchase parts or have machine work done on other components until the cylinder block/crankcase has been thoroughly inspected.* As a general rule, time is the primary cost of an overhaul, so it doesn't pay to install worn or sub-standard parts.

As a final note, to ensure maximum life and minimum trouble from a rebuilt engine, everything must be assembled with care, in a spotlessly-clean environment.

3 Engine/transmission removal – methods and precautions

If you've decided that an engine must be removed for overhaul or major repair work, several preliminary steps should be taken.

Locating a suitable place to work is extremely important. Adequate work space, along with storage space for the vehicle, will be needed. If a workshop or garage isn't available, at the very least, a flat, level, clean work surface made of concrete or asphalt is required.

Cleaning the engine compartment and engine/transmission before beginning the removal procedure will help keep tools clean and organised.

The engine can be withdrawn by removing it complete with the transmission; Ford recommend that the vehicle's body is raised and supported securely, sufficiently high that the engine/transmission can be unbolted as a single unit and lowered to the ground; the engine/transmission unit can then be withdrawn from under the vehicle and separated. An engine hoist or A-frame will therefore be necessary. Make sure the equipment is rated in excess of the combined weight of the engine and transmission. Safety is of primary importance, considering the potential hazards involved in removing the engine/transmission from the vehicle.

If this is the first time you have removed an engine, a helper should ideally be available. Advice and aid from someone more experienced would also be helpful. There are many instances when one person cannot simultaneously perform all of the operations required when removing the engine/transmission from the vehicle. Safety is of primary importance, considering the potential hazards involved in this kind of operation. A second person should always be in attendance to offer help in any emergency.

Plan the operation ahead of time. Arrange for, or obtain, all of the tools and equipment you'll need prior to beginning the job. Some of the equipment necessary to perform engine/transmission removal and installation safely and with relative ease, and which may have to be hired or borrowed, includes (in addition to the engine hoist) a heavy-duty trolley jack, a strong pair of axle stands, some wooden blocks, and an engine dolly (a low, wheeled platform capable of taking the weight of the engine/transmission, so that it can be moved easily when on the ground). A complete set of spanners and sockets (as described in the rear of this manual) will obviously be needed, together with plenty of rags and cleaning solvent for mopping-up spilled oil, coolant and fuel. If the hoist is to be hired, make sure that you arrange for it in advance, and perform all of the operations possible without it beforehand. This will save you money and time.

Plan for the vehicle to be out of use for quite a while. A machine shop will be required to perform some of the work which the do-it-yourselfer can't accomplish without special equipment. These establishments often have a busy schedule, so it would be a good idea to consult them before removing the engine, to accurately estimate the amount of time required to rebuild or repair components that may need work.

When removing the engine from the vehicle, be methodical about the disconnection of external components. Labelling cables and hoses as they are removed will greatly assist the refitting process.

Always be extremely careful when removing and installing the engine/transmission. Serious injury can result from careless actions. If help is required, it is better to wait until it is available rather than risk personal injury and/or damage to components by continuing alone. By planning ahead and taking your time, the job (although a major task) can be accomplished successfully and without incident.

4 Engine/transmission – removal, separation and refitting

⚠️ *Warning: Petrol is extremely flammable, so take extra precautions when disconnecting any part of the fuel system. Don't smoke, or allow naked flames or bare light bulbs in or near the work area, and don't work in a garage where a natural gas appliance (such as a clothes dryer or water heater) is installed. If you spill petrol on your skin, rinse it off immediately. Have a fire extinguisher rated for petrol fires handy, and know how to use it.*

Note: *Read through the entire Section, as well as reading the advice in the preceding Section, before beginning this procedure. The engine and transmission are removed as a unit, lowered to the ground and removed from underneath, then separated outside the vehicle.*

Removal

1 Park the vehicle on firm, level ground, apply the handbrake firmly, and slacken the nuts securing both front roadwheels.
2 Place protective covers on the wings and engine compartment front crossmember. For better access to the engine for the engine hoist, remove the bonnet as described in Chapter 11.
3 Disconnect the battery negative (earth) lead (refer to *Disconnecting the battery* at the end of this manual). For better access, the battery may be removed completely (see Chapter 5A).
4 Depressurise the fuel system pressure (see the relevant Part of Chapter 4).
5 Whenever you disconnect any vacuum lines, coolant and emissions hoses, wiring loom connectors, earth straps and fuel lines as part of the following procedure, always label them clearly, so that they can be correctly reassembled **(see illustration)**.

4.5 Label the wiring and hoses as they are disconnected (TPS – Throttle Position Sensor)

HAYNES HiNT *Whenever any wiring is disconnected, mark or label it, to ensure correct reconnection . . . vacuum hoses and pipes should be similarly marked. Masking tape and/or a touch-up paint applicator work well for marking items. Take instant photos, or sketch the locations of components and brackets.*

6 Where applicable, unclip the breather hose from the engine upper plastic cover, then unclip/unbolt the cover from the top of the engine.

7 Unclip the plastic covers from the top of the suspension struts on both sides of the vehicle, then slacken the top mounting retaining nuts by approximately four turns each **(see illustration)**.

8 Drain the cooling system as described in the relevant Part of Chapter 1.

⚠️ *Warning: Make sure the engine is cold before draining any of the fluids, since it may be very hot.*

9 Remove the air cleaner assembly and intake ducting with reference to the relevant part of Chapter 4.

10 On diesel models, undo the retaining clips and remove the turbocharger air intake hose with reference to Chapter 4B.

11 On V6 petrol engines, undo the retaining bolts and remove the ignition coil from the rear camshaft cover, also unclip the evaporative emissions (EVAP) solenoid valve from the retaining bracket **(see illustration)**.

12 Disconnect the accelerator cable from the throttle linkage as described in Chapter 4A – where fitted, also disconnect the cruise control actuator cable (see Chapter 12). Secure the cable(s) clear of the engine/transmission.

13 Label all the vacuum hoses, wiring connections, and coolant hoses to ensure correct refitment. Follow the engine/transmission hoses and wiring loom unclipping them from any retaining clips, then disconnect them. Pieces of masking tape with numbers or letters written on them work well. If there is a possibility of confusion regarding connections or routing, make a sketch or notes.

14 On V6 petrol models, unbolt the engine wiring harness earth cable from the left-hand inner wing panel, behind the headlight. The engine wiring harness must now be disconnected from the powertrain control module (PCM). It will be necessary to drill out the rivets in order to lift the cover from the module. Unscrew the bolt and disconnect the multi-plug. To prevent entry of dust and dirt, cover the multi-plug and PCM with polythene sheeting or place it in a polythene bag. Withdraw the wiring harness onto the engine.

15 On diesel models, undo the retaining bolt and disconnect the engine wiring loom block connector from the left-hand front suspension turret, in front of the brake master cylinder **(see illustration)**.

4.7 Unclip the plastic covers and slacken the top mounting retaining nuts

16 On 4-cylinder petrol models, detach the power steering line bracket from the camshaft cover. On V6 petrol models, disconnect the power steering line from by the right-hand engine mounting. On diesel models, detach the power steering line brackets from the transmission end of the cylinder head.

17 Undo the retaining bolts and withdraw the coolant expansion tank from the inner wing panel.

18 With the fuel pressure released (see paragraph 4), disconnect the fuel supply line connection to the engine (see Chapter 4A or 4B). Plug or cap all open fittings **(see illustration)**.

19 Remove the cooling fan motor and shroud as described in Chapter 3.

20 Where the vehicle is fitted with manual transmission, mark their positions, then disconnect the gearchange linkage cables from the transmission (see Chapter 7A for details). Also prise out the spring clip and disconnect the clutch hydraulic pipe (see Chapter 6), release the pipe from the bracket and plug the pipe opening to prevent dirt ingress and fluid loss.

21 Where the vehicle is fitted with an automatic transmission, disconnect the selector cable, wiring connectors and the fluid cooler pipe(s) from the transmission with reference to Chapter 7B.

22 On petrol models, disconnect the wiring connector for the oxygen sensor.

23 Unbolt the engine/transmission-to-body earth lead(s) from the transmission's top surface. Disconnect the wiring connector from the reversing light switch in the top of the

4.15 Undo the retaining bolt and disconnect the engine wiring loom block connector (diesel models)

4.11 Remove the ignition coil from the rear camshaft cover (V6 models)

transmission and the wiring connector(s) from the vehicle speed sensor(s) – refer to Chapter 7A or 7B.

24 Raise the vehicle and support it securely on axle stands, there must be sufficient clearance below the vehicle for the engine/transmission to be lowered and removed. Remove both front roadwheels and where fitted the engine undertray. If the engine is to be dismantled, drain the engine oil and remove the oil filter (see the relevant Part of Chapter 1). Also drain the transmission as described in the relevant Part of Chapter 7.

25 Remove the front Section of the exhaust system with reference to Chapter 4A or 4B.

26 Remove the front subframe with reference to Chapter 10.

27 Remove the driveshafts with reference to Chapter 8. Unbolt the right-hand driveshaft centre bearing bracket, from the rear of the cylinder block.

Caution : Make sure the inner joints of the driveshaft do not bend more than 18° and the outer joints do not bend more than 45° when removing the driveshafts.

28 Remove the auxiliary drivebelt (see the relevant Part of Chapter 1).

29 Where the vehicle is fitted with air conditioning, unplug the compressor's electrical connector, and unbolt the compressor from the engine. Secure it as far as possible (without disconnecting the system's hoses) clear of the engine/transmission.

⚠️ *Warning: Do not disconnect the refrigerant hoses.*

4.18 Note colour-coding on the fuel supply and return lines when disconnecting

4.32 Attach the chains/straps to the lifting eyes on the cylinder head

30 Unbolt the power steering pump (see Chapter 10); secure it as far as possible (without disconnecting the system's hoses – where possible) clear of the engine/transmission.

31 The engine/transmission unit should now be hanging on the right- and left-hand mountings only, with all components which connect it to the rest of the vehicle disconnected or removed and secured well clear of the unit. Make a final check that this is the case, then ensure that the body is securely supported, high enough to permit the withdrawal of the engine/transmission unit from underneath; allow for the height of the engine lift, if used.

32 Attach lifting chains/straps to the lifting eyes provided on the cylinder head and take the weight of the engine/transmission unit **(see illustration)**. Unscrew the nuts and bolts securing the right-hand mounting bracket and left-hand bracket to the vehicle inner wing panels and remove the mountings from the engine/transmission unit (see the relevant Part of Chapter 2).

33 If available, a low trolley should be placed under the engine/transmission assembly, to facilitate its easy removal from under the vehicle. Make a final check to ensure that nothing else remains connected to the engine/transmission. Lower the engine/transmission to the ground, making sure nothing is trapped, taking great care not to damage the radiator assembly. Enlist the help of an assistant during this procedure, as it may be necessary to tilt the assembly slightly to clear the underbody. Great care must be taken to ensure that no components are trapped and damage during the removal procedure.

34 Detach the hoist and withdraw the engine/transmission from under the vehicle.

Separation

35 With the engine/transmission assembly removed, support the assembly on suitable blocks of wood, on a work bench (or failing that, on a clean area of the workshop floor).

36 On automatic transmission models, remove the blanking plug to access the torque converter retaining nuts/bolts. Turn the crankshaft to align each one in turn through the access hole – see Chapter 7B.

37 Ensure that engine and transmission are adequately supported, then slacken and remove the remaining bolts securing the transmission housing to the engine. Note the correct fitted positions of each bolt (and relevant brackets) as they are removed, to use as a reference on refitting. Refer to the relevant Part of Chapter 7, when separating the transmission from the engine.

38 Carefully withdraw the transmission from the engine, ensuring that on manual transmission models, the weight of the transmission is not allowed to hang on the input shaft while it is engaged with the clutch friction disc – see Chapter 7A. On automatic models, make sure the torque converter withdraws from the engine with the transmission – see Chapter 7B.

39 While the engine/transmission is removed, check the mountings; renew them if they are worn or damaged. Similarly, check the condition of all coolant and vacuum hoses and pipes (see the relevant Part of Chapter 1); components that are normally hidden can now be checked properly, and should be renewed if there is any doubt at all about their condition. Where the vehicle is fitted with manual transmission, take the opportunity to overhaul the clutch components (see Chapter 6). It is regarded by many as good working practice to renew the clutch assembly as a matter of course, whenever major engine overhaul work is carried out. Check also the condition of all components (such as the transmission oil seals) disturbed on removal, and renew any that are damaged or worn.

Refitting

40 Refitting is the reverse of the removal procedure, noting the following points.

a) *Tighten all fasteners to the torque wrench settings given; where settings are not quoted in the Specifications Sections of Chapter 2A, 2B or 2C, refer to the Specifications Section of the relevant Chapter of this manual.*

b) *In addition to the points noted in paragraph 39 above, always renew any circlips and self-locking nuts disturbed on removal.*

c) *Where wiring, etc, was secured by cable ties which had to be cut on removal, ensure that it is secured with new ties on refitting.*

d) *With all overhaul operations completed, refit the transmission to the engine as described in Chapter 7A or 7B.*

e) *Manoeuvre the engine/transmission unit under the vehicle, attach the hoist, and lift the unit into position until the right- and left-hand mountings can be reassembled; tighten the (new) nuts only lightly at this stage. Do not yet release the hoist; the weight of the engine/transmission unit must not be taken by the mountings until all are correctly aligned.*

f) *Refit, and where applicable adjust, all engine related components and systems*

with reference to the Chapters concerned.

g) *Add coolant, engine oil and transmission fluids as needed (see 'Weekly checks' and the relevant Part of Chapter 1).*

h) *Run the engine, and check for proper operation and the absence of leaks. Shut off the engine, and recheck the fluid levels.*

Note: *Remember that, since the front suspension subframe and steering gear have been disturbed, the wheel alignment and steering angles must be checked fully and carefully as soon as possible, with any necessary adjustments being made. This operation is best carried out by an experienced mechanic, using proper checking equipment; the vehicle should therefore be taken to a Ford dealer or similarly-qualified person for attention.*

5 Engine overhaul – dismantling sequence

Caution: Refer to the Caution and Note in Sections 1 and 2 on models fitted with petrol engines.

1 It is much easier to dismantle and work on the engine if it is mounted on a portable engine stand. These stands can often be hired from a tool hire shop. Before the engine is mounted on a stand, the flywheel/driveplate should be removed so that the stand bolts can be tightened into the end of the cylinder block/crankcase.

2 If a stand is not available, it is possible to dismantle the engine with it mounted on blocks, on a sturdy workbench or on the floor. Be extra-careful not to tip or drop the engine when working without a stand.

3 If you are going to obtain a reconditioned engine, all external components must be removed first, to be transferred to the new engine (just as they will if you are doing a complete engine overhaul yourself). **Note:** *When removing the external components from the engine, pay close attention to details that may be helpful or important during refitting. Note the fitted position of gaskets, seals, spacers, pins, washers, bolts and other small items. These external components include the following:*

a) *Alternator, starter and mounting brackets (Chapter 5A).*

b) *The ignition system, HT leads and spark plugs, etc – petrol models (Chapters 1A and 5B).*

c) *The glow plug/preheating system components – diesel models (see Chapter 5C).*

d) *Cooling system/thermostat housings (Chapter 3).*

e) *Oil level dipstick and dipstick tube.*

f) *All fuel injection system components (Chapter 4A – petrol models, 4B – diesel models).*

g) *Brake vacuum pump – diesel models (Chapter 9).*
h) *All electrical switches and sensors and engine wiring harness (Chapters 4 and 5).*
i) *Inlet and exhaust manifolds (Part A, B or C of this Chapter).*
j) *Engine/transmission mounting brackets (Part A, B or C of this Chapter).*
k) *Flywheel/driveplate (Part A, B or C of this Chapter).*

4 If you are obtaining a 'short' engine (which consists of the engine cylinder block/crankcase, crankshaft, pistons and connecting rods all assembled), then the cylinder head, sump, oil pump, oil filter cooler/housing and timing chains will have to be removed also.

5 If you are planning a complete overhaul, the engine can be dismantled and the internal components removed in the following order.
a) *Inlet and exhaust manifolds (Part A, B or C of this Chapter).*
b) *Timing chains and toothed pulleys (Part A, B or C of this Chapter).*
c) *Cylinder head(s) (Part A, B or C of this Chapter).*
d) *Flywheel/driveplate (Part A, B or C of this Chapter).*
e) *Sump (Part A, B or C of this Chapter).*
f) *Oil pump (Part A, B or C of this Chapter).*
g) *Piston/connecting rod assemblies (Section 9).*
h) *Crankshaft (Section 10).*

6 Before beginning the dismantling and overhaul procedures, make sure that you have all of the correct tools necessary. Refer to the introductory pages at the beginning of this manual for further information.

6 Cylinder head – dismantling

Note: *New and reconditioned cylinder heads are available from the manufacturers, and from engine overhaul specialists. Due to the fact that some specialist tools are required for the dismantling and inspection procedures, and new components may not be readily available (refer to Section 1), it may be more practical and economical for the home mechanic to purchase a reconditioned head, rather than to dismantle, inspect and recondition the original head.*

1 Remove the cylinder head(s) from the engine cylinder block, then remove the camshafts and tappets (Part A, B or C of this Chapter).

2 On diesel models, remove the injectors and glow plugs (see Chapters 4B and 5C).

3 Where applicable, remove the rear coolant outlet housing together with its gasket/O-ring.

4 With the cylinder head resting on one side, using a valve spring compressor, compress each valve spring in turn until the split collets can be removed. A special valve spring compressor will be required, to reach into the

6.4 Compress the valve springs using a spring compressor tool

6.6b . . . and the valve springs

deep wells in the cylinder head without risk of damaging the tappet bores; such compressors are now widely available from most good motor accessory shops. Release the compressor, and lift off the spring upper seat and spring **(see illustration)**.

5 If, when the valve spring compressor is screwed down, the spring upper seat refuses to free and expose the split collets, gently tap the top of the tool, directly over the upper seat, with a light hammer. This will free the seat to remove the collets.

6 Release the valve spring compressor and remove the upper spring seat, and valve spring **(see illustrations)**.

7 Withdraw the valve through the combustion chamber. If it binds in the guide (won't pull through), push it back in, and deburr the area around the collet groove with a fine file or whetstone; on 4-cylinder petrol engines, take care not to mark the tappet bores.

6.8b . . . then remove the lower spring seat (where applicable)

6.6a Remove the upper spring seat . . .

6.8a Use a removal tool to extract the stem oil seal . . .

8 Use a pair of pliers or a special tool to extract the valve spring lower seat/stem oil seals from the valve guide **(see illustrations)**. **Note:** *On some models, the seal and lower spring seat are a complete assembly.*

9 It is essential that the valves are kept together with their collets, spring seats and springs, and in their correct sequence (unless they are so badly worn that they are to be renewed). If they are going to be kept and used again, place them in a labelled polythene bag or similar small container **(see illustration)**.

7 Cylinder head and valve components – cleaning and inspection

1 Thorough cleaning of the cylinder head and valve components, followed by a detailed

6.9 Use clearly marked containers to identify components and to keep matched assemblies together

7.7 Check the cylinder head surface for warpage, in the planes indicated. Using feeler blades under the straight-edge

7.13 Measure the diameter of the valve stems with a micrometer

inspection, will enable you to decide how much valve service work must be carried out during the engine overhaul. **Note:** *If the engine has been severely overheated, it is best to assume that the cylinder head is warped, and to check carefully for signs of this.*

Cleaning

2 Using a suitable degreasing agent, remove all traces of oil deposits from the cylinder head, paying particular attention to the journal bearings, cam follower/bucket tappet bores, valve guides, oilways and where applicable, hydraulic tappet bores.

3 Scrape away all traces of old gasket material and sealing compound from the cylinder head, taking great care not to score or gouge the surfaces.

4 Scrape away the carbon from the combustion chambers and ports, then wash the cylinder head thoroughly with paraffin or a suitable solvent to remove the remaining debris.

5 Scrape off any heavy carbon deposits that may have formed on the valves, then use a power-operated wire brush to remove deposits from the valve heads and stems.

Inspection

Note: *Be sure to perform all the following inspection procedures before concluding that the services of a machine shop or engine overhaul specialist are required. Make a list of all items that require attention.*

Cylinder head

6 Inspect the head very carefully for cracks, evidence of coolant leakage, and other damage. If cracks are found, a new cylinder head should be obtained.

7 Use a straight-edge and feeler blade to check that the cylinder head gasket surface is not distorted, check the head across a number of different ways to find any distortion **(see illustration)**. If it is, it may be possible to resurface it.

8 Examine the valve seats in each of the combustion chambers. If they are severely pitted, cracked or burned, then they will need to be renewed or recut by an engine overhaul specialist. If they are only slightly pitted, this can be removed by grinding-in the valve heads and seats with fine valve-grinding compound, as described below.

9 If the valve guides are worn, indicated by a side-to-side motion of the valve, new guides must be fitted. Measure the diameter of the existing valve stems (see below) and the bore of the guides, then calculate the clearance, and compare the result with the specified value; if the clearance is excessive, renew the valves or guides as necessary.

10 The renewal of valve guides is best carried out by an engine overhaul specialist.

11 If the valve seats are to be recut, this must be done only after the guides have been renewed.

Valves

12 Examine the head of each valve for pitting, burning, cracks and general wear, and check the valve stem for scoring and wear ridges. Rotate the valve, and check for any obvious indication that it is bent. Look for pits and excessive wear on the tip of each valve stem. Renew any valve that shows any such signs of wear or damage.

7.16 Grind-in the valves with a reciprocating rotary motion

13 If the valve appears satisfactory at this stage, measure the valve stem diameter at several points, using a micrometer **(see illustration)**. Any significant difference in the readings obtained indicates wear of the valve stem. Should any of these conditions be apparent, the valve(s) must be renewed.

14 If the valves are in satisfactory condition, they should be ground (lapped) into their respective seats, to ensure a smooth gas-tight seal. If the seat is only lightly pitted, or if it has been recut, fine grinding compound only should be used to produce the required finish. Coarse valve-grinding compound should not be used unless a seat is badly burned or deeply pitted; if this is the case, the cylinder head and valves should be inspected by an expert, to decide whether seat recutting, or even the renewal of the valve or seat insert, is required.

15 Valve grinding is carried out as follows. Place the cylinder head upside-down on a bench, with a block of wood at each end to give clearance for the valve stems.

16 Smear a trace of (the appropriate grade of) valve-grinding compound on the seat face, and press a suction grinding tool onto the valve head. With a semi-rotary action, grind the valve head to its seat, lifting the valve occasionally to redistribute the grinding compound **(see illustration)**. A light spring placed under the valve head will greatly ease this operation.

17 If coarse grinding compound is being used, work only until a dull, matt even surface is produced on both the valve seat and the valve, then wipe off the used compound, and repeat the process with fine compound. When a smooth unbroken ring of light grey matt finish is produced on both the valve and seat, the grinding operation is complete. Do not grind in the valves any further than absolutely necessary, or the seat will be prematurely sunk into the cylinder head.

18 When all the valves have been ground-in, carefully wash off all traces of grinding

7.19 Measure the free length of each valve spring

7.20 Checking the squareness of the valve springs

Warning: Wear eye protection when using compressed air.

compound, using paraffin or a suitable solvent, before reassembly of the cylinder head.

Valve components

19 Examine the valve springs for signs of damage and discolouration, and also measure their free length by comparing each of the existing springs with a new component **(see illustration)**.
20 Stand each spring on a flat surface, and check it for squareness **(see illustration)**. If any of the springs are damaged, distorted, or have lost their tension, obtain a complete set of new springs.
21 Check the spring upper seats and collets for obvious wear and cracks. Any questionable parts should be renewed, as extensive damage will occur if they fail during engine operation. Any damaged or excessively-worn parts must be renewed; the

valve spring lower seat/stem oil seals must be renewed as a matter of course whenever they are disturbed.
22 Check the tappets (hydraulic or conventional) as described in Part A, B or C of this Chapter.

8 Cylinder head – reassembly

1 Regardless of whether or not the head was sent away for repair work of any sort, make sure that it is clean before beginning reassembly. Be sure to remove any metal particles and abrasive grit that may still be present from operations such as valve grinding or head resurfacing. Use compressed air, if available, to blow out all the oil holes and passages.

2 Beginning at one end of the head, lubricate and install the first valve. Apply molybdenum disulphide-based grease or clean engine oil to the valve stem, and refit the valve **(see illustration)**. Where the original valves are being re-used, ensure that each is refitted in its original guide. If new valves are being fitted, insert them into the locations to which they have been ground.
3 Where applicable, fit the plastic protector supplied with new valve spring lower seat/stem oil seals to the end of the valve stem. Dip a new valve stem oil seal in clean engine oil, then put the new seal squarely on top of the guide – take care not to damage the stem seal as it passes over the valve end face. Use a suitable long reach socket or special installer to press it firmly into position **(see illustrations)**, remove the protective sleeve.
4 Refit the valve spring and upper seat **(see illustration)**.
5 Compress the spring with a valve spring compressor, and carefully install the collets in the stem groove. Apply a small dab of grease to each collet to hold it in place if necessary. Slowly release the compressor, and make sure the collets seat properly **(see illustration)**.
6 When the valves are installed, use a hammer and interposed block of wood (to prevent the end of the valve stem being damaged), tap the end of the valve stem gently, to settle the components.

8.2 Oil the valve stems before refitting them

8.3a Fit a protective sleeve over the valve stem before fitting the stem seal

8.3b Push the stem seal over the valve and onto the top of the valve guide . . .

8.3c . . . then use a long reach socket to seat the seal

8.4 Fitting the valve spring and upper seat

8.5 Use grease to hold the two halves of the split collet in the groove

9.4a On the V6 engine, unscrew the flange bolts . . .

9.4b . . . and support nuts . . .

9.4c . . . remove the oil pump pick-up tube and filter

9.4d . . . recover the flange O-ring . . .

9.4e . . . then unscrew the nuts and remove and remove the oil baffle

9.5 Note the markings (arrowed) on each part of the connecting rod and cap

7 Repeat the procedure for the remaining valves. Be sure to return the valve assembly components to their original locations – don't mix them up!

8 Refit the tappets and camshafts as described in Part A, B or C of this Chapter.

9 Piston/connecting rod assemblies – removal and inspection

Caution: Refer to the Caution and Notes in Sections 1 and 2 on models fitted with petrol engines.

Note: *While this task is theoretically possible when the engine is in place in the vehicle, in practise, it requires so much preliminary dismantling, and is so difficult to carry out due to the restricted access, that owners are advised to remove the engine from the vehicle*

first. *The following paragraphs assume the engine is removed from the car.*

Removal

1 Remove the cylinder head(s) and sump with reference to Part A, B or C of this Chapter.

2 Unbolt the oil pump pick-up tube and filter, and recover the O-ring from the pump.

3 Where applicable, unscrew the bolts securing the lower crankcase to the cylinder block. Loosen the bolts gradually and evenly, then separate the lower crankcase from the cylinder block.

4 On V6 engines, undo the nuts and remove the oil baffle from the crankcase **(see illustrations)**.

5 On diesel engines, the connecting rods and caps are of 'cracked' design. During production, the connecting rod and cap are forged as one piece, then the cap is broken apart from the rod using a special technique.

Because of this design, the mating surfaces of each cap and rod is unique and, therefore, nearly impossible to mix up **(see illustration)**.

6 Temporarily refit the crankshaft pulley, so that the crankshaft can be rotated. Note that each piston/connecting rod assembly can be identified by its cylinder number (counting from the timing chain end of the engine) etched into the flat-machined surface of both the connecting rod and its cap. Furthermore, each piston has an arrow stamped into its crown, pointing towards the timing chain end of the engine. If no marks can be seen, make your own before disturbing any of the components, so that you can be certain of refitting each piston/connecting rod assembly the right way round, to its correct (original) bore, with the cap also the right way round **(see illustration)**.

7 Use your fingernail to feel if a ridge has formed at the upper limit of ring travel (about 6 mm down from the top of each cylinder). If carbon deposits or cylinder wear have produced ridges, they must be completely removed with a special tool called a ridge reamer **(see illustration)**. Follow the manufacturer's instructions provided with the tool.

Caution: Failure to remove the ridges before attempting to remove the piston/connecting rod assemblies may result in piston ring breakage.

8 Slacken each of the big-end bearing cap bolts half a turn at a time, until they can be removed by hand. Remove the No 1 cap and bearing shell. Don't drop the shell out of the cap.

9.6 Make your own marks (arrowed) to correspond with the connecting rod location

9.7 A ridge reamer may be required, to remove the ridge from the top of each cylinder

9.11a Remove the piston cooling jet retaining screws . . .

9.11b . . . and remove the jets from their mounting holes

9 Remove the upper bearing shell, and push the connecting rod/piston assembly out through the top of the cylinder block. Use a wooden hammer handle to push on the connecting rod's bearing recess. If resistance is felt, double-check that all of the ridge was removed from the cylinder. Repeat the procedure for the remaining cylinders.

10 After removal, reassemble the big-end bearing caps and shells on their respective connecting rods, and refit the bolts finger-tight. Leaving the old shells in place until reassembly will help prevent the bearing recesses from being accidentally nicked or gouged. New shells should be used on reassembly.

11 If applicable, remove the retaining screws and withdraw the piston cooling jets from the bottom of the cylinder bores **(see illustrations)**.

Inspection

12 Before the inspection process can be carried out, the piston/connecting rod assemblies must be cleaned, and the original piston rings removed from the pistons. The rings should have smooth, polished working surfaces, with no dull or carbon-coated sections (showing that the ring is not sealing correctly against the bore wall, so allowing combustion gases to blow by) and no traces of wear on their top and bottom surfaces. The end gaps should be clear of carbon, but not polished (indicating a too-small end gap), and all the rings (including the elements of the oil control ring) should be free to rotate in their grooves, but without excessive up-and-down movement. If the rings appear to be in good condition, they are probably fit for further use; check the end gaps (in an unworn part of the bore) as described in Section 14. If any of the rings appears to be worn or damaged, or has an end gap significantly different from the specified value, the usual course of action is to renew all of them as a set. **Note:** *While it is usual to renew piston rings when an engine is overhauled, they may be re-used if in acceptable condition. If re-using the rings, make sure that each ring is marked during removal to ensure that it is refitted correctly.*

13 Using a piston ring removal tool, carefully remove the rings from the pistons. Be careful not to nick or gouge the pistons in the

process, and mark or label each ring as it is removed, so that its original top surface can be identified on reassembly, and so that it can be returned to its original groove. Take care also with your hands – piston rings are sharp! (see **Tool Tip**).

 TOOL TiP *If a piston ring removal tool is not available, the rings can be removed by hand, expanding them over the top of the pistons. The use of two or three old feeler blades will be helpful in preventing the rings dropping into empty grooves*

14 Scrape all traces of carbon from the top of the piston. A hand-held wire brush or a piece of fine emery cloth can be used, once the majority of the deposits have been scraped away. Do not, under any circumstances, use a wire brush mounted in a drill motor to remove deposits from the pistons – the piston material is soft, and may be eroded away by the wire brush.

15 Use a piston ring groove-cleaning tool to remove carbon deposits from the ring grooves. If a tool isn't available, but replacement rings have been found, a piece broken off the old ring will do the job. Be very careful to remove only the carbon deposits – don't remove any metal, and do not nick or scratch the sides of the ring grooves **(see illustrations)**. Protect your fingers – piston rings are sharp.

16 Once the deposits have been removed, clean the piston/rod assemblies with solvent,

and dry them with compressed air (if available). Make sure the oil return holes in the back sides of the ring grooves, and the oil hole in the lower end of each rod, are clear.

17 If the pistons and cylinder walls aren't damaged or worn excessively and if the cylinder block/crankcase is not rebored, new pistons won't be necessary. Normal piston wear appears as even vertical wear on the piston thrust surfaces, and slight looseness of the top ring in its groove.

18 Carefully inspect each piston for cracks around the skirt, at the pin bosses, and at the ring lands (between the ring grooves).

19 Look for scoring and scuffing on the thrust faces of the skirt, holes in the piston crown, and burned areas at the edge of the crown. If the skirt is scored or scuffed, the engine may have been suffering from overheating and/or abnormal combustion, which caused excessively-high operating temperatures. The cooling and lubrication systems should be checked thoroughly. A hole in the piston crown is an indication that abnormal combustion (pre-ignition) was occurring. Burned areas at the edge of the piston crown are usually evidence of spark knock (detonation). If any of the above problems exist, the causes must be corrected, or the damage will occur again. The causes may include intake air leaks, incorrect fuel/air mixture, incorrect ignition timing, or EGR system malfunctions.

20 Corrosion of the piston, in the form of small pits, indicates that coolant is leaking into the combustion chamber and/or the crankcase. Again, the cause must be corrected, or the problem may persist in the rebuilt engine.

21 Check the piston-to-rod clearance by twisting the piston and rod in opposite directions. Any noticeable play indicates excessive wear, which must be corrected. The piston/connecting rod assemblies should be taken to a Ford dealer or engine reconditioning specialist to have the pistons, gudgeon pins and rods checked, and new components fitted as required.

22 On petrol engines, the gudgeon pin is an interference fit in the connecting rod. If new pistons are to be fitted to existing connecting rods, the work should be carried out by a Ford

9.15a The piston ring grooves can be cleaned with a special tool, as shown here . . .

9.15b . . . or a section of a broken piston ring, if available

9.23a Insert a small screwdriver into the slot (arrowed) and prise out the circlips . . .

9.23b . . . then push out the gudgeon pin to separate the piston and the connecting rod

dealer or similar engine reconditioning specialist. Due to the special heating equipment, press, mandrels and supports required to do the job. If the piston/connecting rod assemblies do require this sort of work, have the connecting rods checked for bend and twist, since only such engine repair specialists will have the facilities for this purpose.

23 On diesel engines, remove the circlips, push out the gudgeon pin, and separate the piston from the connecting rod **(see illustrations)**. Discard the circlips as new items must be fitted on reassembly. If the pin proves difficult to remove, heat the piston to 60°C with hot water – the resulting expansion will then allow the two components to be separated. Take note of the fitment of the piston to the connecting rod, so that it can be refitted in the same position.

24 Check the connecting rods for cracks and

other damage. Temporarily remove the big-end bearing caps and the old bearing shells, wipe clean the rod and cap bearing recesses, and inspect them for nicks, gouges and scratches. After checking the rods, refit the old shells, slip the caps into place, and tighten the bolts finger-tight.

10 Crankshaft – removal and inspection

Caution: Refer to the Caution and Note in Sections 1 and 2 on models fitted with petrol engines.

Removal

Note: *The crankshaft can be removed only after the engine/transmission has been*

removed from the vehicle. It is assumed that the transmission and flywheel/driveplate, timing chain, lower crankcase, cylinder head, sump, oil pump pick-up/strainer pipe and oil baffle, main oil seal, oil pump, and piston/connecting rod assemblies, have already been removed. The crankshaft oil seal carrier must be unbolted from the cylinder block/crankcase before proceeding with crankshaft removal.

1 Before the crankshaft is removed, check the endfloat. Mount a DTI (Dial Test Indicator, or dial gauge) with the probe in line with the crankshaft and just touching the crankshaft **(see illustration)**.

2 Push the crankshaft fully away from the gauge, and zero it. Next, lever the crankshaft towards the gauge as far as possible, and check the reading obtained. The distance that the crankshaft moved is its endfloat; if it is greater than specified, check the crankshaft thrust surfaces for wear. If no wear is evident, new thrustwashers should correct the end-float. On 4-cylinder models, the thrust control bearing is part of the No 3 (centre) main bearing **(see illustration)**. On V6 models, the thrust control bearing consists of the No 4 (rear) lower main bearing half and a washer that fits into the cylinder block.

3 If a dial gauge is not available, feeler gauges can be used. Gently lever or push the crankshaft all the way towards the right-hand end of the engine. Slip feeler gauges between the crankshaft and the right-hand face of the No 3 (centre) main bearing to determine the clearance **(see illustration)**.

4 On 4-cylinder models, check the main bearing caps, to see if they are marked to indicate their locations. They should be numbered consecutively from the timing chain end of the engine – if not, mark them with number-stamping dies or a centre-punch. The caps will also have an embossed arrow pointing to the timing chain end of the engine **(see illustrations)**. Slacken the cap bolts a quarter-turn at a time each, starting with the left- and right-hand end caps and working toward the centre, until they can be removed by hand.

5 On V6 models, the lower crankcase holds the lower main bearing halves and the crankshaft in the cylinder block. Conventional

10.1 Measure the crankshaft endfloat using a DTI gauge

10.2 Fitting the thrust control bearing which is part of the No 3 (centre) main bearing (4-cylinder engines)

10.3 If a DTI gauge is not available, measure the endfloat using feeler gauges

10.4a Note the main bearing caps are numbered to indicate their locations . . .

10.4b . . . the caps may have an embossed arrow pointing to the timing chain end of the engine

main bearing caps are not used on V6 models. In addition, the interior lower crankcase bolts are the torque-to-yield design and must be renewed during reassembly. Progressively loosen the lower crankcase bolts, then remove them and separate the lower crankcase from the block. Note the position of the lower main bearing halves for reassembly reference.

6 On 4-cylinder models, gently tap the caps with a soft-faced hammer, then separate them from the cylinder block/crankcase. If necessary, use the bolts as levers to remove the caps. Take care not to drop the bearing shells as the bearing caps are removed.

7 Carefully lift the crankshaft out of the engine **(see illustration)**. It may be a good idea to have an assistant available, since the crankshaft is quite heavy. With the bearing shells in place in the cylinder block/crankcase and main bearing caps (4-cylinder engine) or lower crankcase (V6 engine), return the caps to their respective locations on the block, or refit the lower crankcase, and tighten the bolts finger-tight. Leaving the old shells in place until reassembly will help prevent the bearing recesses from being accidentally nicked or gouged. New shells should be used on reassembly.

Inspection

8 Clean the crankshaft, and dry it with compressed air if available. Be sure to clean the oil holes with a pipe cleaner or similar probe.

 Warning: Wear eye protection when using compressed air.

9 Check the main and crankpin (big-end) bearing journals carefully. If uneven wear, scoring, pitting and cracking are evident then the crankshaft should be reground (where possible) by an engineering workshop, and refitted to the engine with new undersize bearings.

10 Rather than attempt to determine the crankshaft journal sizes, and the bearing clearances, take the crankshaft to an automotive engineering workshop. Have them perform the necessary measurements, grind the journals if necessary, and supply the appropriate new shell bearings.

10.7 Carefully remove the crankshaft from the cylinder block

11 Check the oil seal journals at each end of the crankshaft for wear and damage. If either seal has worn an excessive groove in its journal, it may cause the new seals to leak when the engine is reassembled. Consult an engine overhaul specialist, who will be able to advise whether a repair is possible, or whether a new crankshaft is necessary.

11 Cylinder block/crankcase – cleaning and inspection

Caution: Refer to the Caution and Note in Sections 1 and 2 on models fitted with petrol engines.

Cleaning

1 For complete cleaning, make sure that all the external components have been removed, including lifting eyes, mounting brackets, oil cooler and filter housing, fuel injection pump mounting bracket (where applicable) and all electrical switches/sensors. Where fitted, unbolt the piston-cooling oil jets or blanking plugs **(see illustration)**. **Note:** *On some models, Ford state that the piston-cooling oil jets must be renewed whenever the engine is dismantled for full overhaul – check with Ford dealer.*

2 Remove the main bearing caps or lower crankcase, and separate the bearing shells from the caps/lower crankcase and the cylinder block. Mark or label the shells, indicating which bearing they were removed from, and whether they were in the cap or the

block (4-cylinder engine) or lower crankcase (V6 engine), then set them aside **(see illustration)**. Wipe clean the block and cap bearing recesses, and inspect them for nicks, gouges and scratches.

3 Scrape all traces of gasket from the cylinder block/lower crankcase, taking care not to damage the sealing surfaces.

4 Remove all oil gallery plugs (where fitted). The plugs are usually very tight – they may have to be drilled out and the holes retapped. Use new plugs when the engine is reassembled. Remove the core plugs by knocking them sideways in their bores with a hammer and a punch, then grasping them with large pliers and pulling them back through their holes. Alternatively, drill a small hose in the centre of each core plug, and pull them out with a car bodywork dent puller **(see illustration)**.

Caution: The core plugs (also known as freeze or soft plugs) may be difficult or impossible to retrieve if they are driven into the block coolant passages.

5 If any of the castings are extremely dirty, they should be steam-cleaned.

6 After the castings are returned from steam-cleaning, clean all oil holes and oil galleries one more time. Flush all internal passages with warm water until the water runs clear, then dry thoroughly, and apply a light film of oil to all machined surfaces, to prevent rusting. If you have access to compressed air, use it to speed the drying process, and to blow out all the oil holes and galleries.

 Warning: Wear eye protection when using compressed air.

7 If the castings are not very dirty, you can do an adequate cleaning job with hot soapy water (as hot as you can stand!) and a stiff brush. Take plenty of time, and do a thorough job. Regardless of the cleaning method used, be sure to clean all oil holes and galleries very thoroughly, and to dry all components completely; protect the machined surfaces as described above, to prevent rusting.

8 All threaded holes must be clean and dry, to ensure accurate torque readings during reassembly; now is also a good time to clean and check the threads of all principal bolts – however, note that some, such as the cylinder

11.1 Where fitted, unbolt the piston-cooling oil jets (or blanking plugs)

11.2 Felt marker pens can be used as shown to identify bearing shells without damaging them

11.4 The core plugs should be removed with a puller

11.8 All bolt holes in the block, particularly the main bearing cap and head bolt holes, should be cleaned and restored with a tap

11.9 A large socket on an extension can be used to drive the new core plugs into their bores

head, flywheel/driveplate bolts and lower crankcase inner bolts on V6 engines, must be renewed as a matter of course whenever they are disturbed. Run the proper-size tap into each of the holes, to remove rust, corrosion, thread sealant or sludge, and to restore damaged threads **(see illustration)**. If possible, use compressed air to clear the holes of debris produced by this operation. **Note:** *Take extra care to exclude all cleaning liquid from blind tapped holes, as the casting may be cracked by hydraulic action if a bolt is threaded into a hole containing liquid.*

9 When all inspection and repair procedures are complete (see below) and the block is ready for reassembly, apply suitable sealant to the new oil gallery plugs, and insert them into the holes in the block. Tighten them securely. After coating the sealing surfaces of the new core plugs with suitable sealant, install them in the cylinder block/crankcase **(see illustration)**. Make sure they are driven in straight and seated properly, or leakage could result. Special tools are available for this purpose, but a large socket with an outside diameter that will just slip into the core plug, used with an extension and hammer, will work just as well.

10 Refit the blanking plugs or (new) piston-cooling oil jets (as applicable), smear a small amount of thread locking fluid onto the retaining screws and tighten the oil jets into position **(see illustrations)**. Also refit all other external components removed, referring to the relevant Chapter of this manual for further details where required. Refit the main bearing

caps (4-cylinder engine) or lower crankcase (V6 engine), and tighten the bolts finger-tight.
11 If the engine is not going to be reassembled right away, cover it with a large plastic bag to keep it clean. Apply a thin coat of engine oil to all machined surfaces to prevent rusting.

Inspection

12 Visually check the castings for cracks and corrosion. Look for stripped threads in the threaded holes. If there has been any history of internal coolant leakage, it may be worthwhile having an engine overhaul specialist check the cylinder block/crankcase for cracks with special equipment. If defects are found, have them repaired, if possible, or renew the assembly.

13 Check each cylinder bore for scuffing and scoring. Any evidence of this kind of damage should be cross-checked with an inspection of the pistons (see Section 9 of this Chapter). If the damage is in its early stages, it may be possible to repair the block by reboring it. Seek the advice of an engineering workshop.

14 Place the cylinder block on a level surface, crankcase downwards. Use a straight-edge and set of feeler blades to measure the distortion of the cylinder head mating surface in both planes. A maximum figure is not quoted by the manufacturer, but use the figure 0.05 mm as a rough guide. If the measurement exceeds this figure, repair may be possible by machining – consult an engineering workshop for advice.

15 To allow an accurate assessment of the

wear in the cylinder bores to be made, take the cylinder block to an automotive engineering workshop, and have them carry out the measurement procedures. If necessary, they will be able to rebore the cylinders, and supply the appropriate piston kits.

16 Even if the cylinder bores are not excessively worn, the cylinder bores must be honed. This process involves using an abrasive tool to produce a fine, cross-hatch pattern on the inner surface of the bore. This has the effect of seating the piston rings, resulting in a good seal between the piston and cylinder. Again, an engineering workshop will be able to carry out the job for you at a reasonable cost.

17 Refit all the components removed in paragraph 1.

12 Main and big-end bearings – inspection

1 Even though the main and big-end bearing shells should be renewed during the engine overhaul, the old shells should be retained for close examination, as they may reveal valuable information about the condition of the engine **(see illustration)**.

2 Bearing failure occurs because of lack of lubrication, the presence of dirt or other foreign particles, overloading the engine, and corrosion. Regardless of the cause of bearing failure, it must be corrected before the engine is reassembled, to prevent it from happening again.

3 When examining the bearing shells, remove them from the cylinder block/crankcase and main bearing caps (4-cylinder models) or

11.10a Apply a small amount of thread locking fluid onto the retaining screws . . .

11.10b . . . and tighten the oil jets into position

12.1 When inspecting the main and big end bearings, look for any of these problems

lower crankcase (V6 models), and from the connecting rods and the big-end bearing caps, then lay them out on a clean surface in the same general position as their location in the engine. This will enable you to match any bearing problems with the corresponding crankshaft journal. Do not touch any shell's bearing surface with your fingers while checking it, or the delicate surface may be scratched.

4 Dirt or other foreign matter gets into the engine in a variety of ways. It may be left in the engine during assembly, or it may pass through filters or the crankcase ventilation system. It may get into the oil, and from there into the bearings. Metal chips from machining operations and normal engine wear are often present. Abrasives are sometimes left in engine components after reconditioning, especially when parts are not thoroughly cleaned using the proper cleaning methods. Whatever the source, these foreign objects often end up embedded in the soft bearing material, and are easily recognized. Large particles will not embed in the material, and will score or gouge the shell and journal. The best prevention for this cause of bearing failure is to clean all parts thoroughly, and to keep everything spotlessly-clean during engine assembly. Frequent and regular engine oil and filter changes are also recommended.

5 Lack of lubrication (or lubrication breakdown) has a number of inter-related causes. Excessive heat (which thins the oil), overloading (which squeezes the oil from the bearing face) and oil leakage (from excessive bearing clearances, worn oil pump or high engine speeds) all contribute to lubrication breakdown. Blocked oil passages, which usually are the result of misaligned oil holes in a bearing shell, will also starve a bearing of oil, and destroy it. When lack of lubrication is the cause of bearing failure, the bearing material is wiped or extruded from the shell's steel backing. Temperatures may increase to the point where the steel backing turns blue from overheating.

6 Driving habits can have a definite effect on bearing life. Full-throttle, low-speed operation (labouring the engine) puts very high loads on bearings, which tends to squeeze out the oil film. These loads cause the shells to flex, which produces fine cracks in the bearing face (fatigue failure). Eventually, the bearing material will loosen in pieces, and tear away from the steel backing.

7 Short-distance driving leads to corrosion of bearings, because insufficient engine heat is produced to drive off condensed water and corrosive gases. These products collect in the engine oil, forming acid and sludge. As the oil is carried to the engine bearings, the acid attacks and corrodes the bearing material.

8 Incorrect shell refitting during engine assembly will lead to bearing failure as well. Tight-fitting shells leave insufficient bearing running clearance, and will result in oil starvation. Dirt or foreign particles trapped

behind a bearing shell result in high spots on the bearing, which lead to failure.

9 *Do not* touch any shell's internal bearing surface with your fingers during reassembly; there is a risk of scratching the delicate surface, or of depositing particles of dirt on it.

10 As mentioned at the beginning of this Section, the bearing shells should be renewed as a matter of course during an engine overhaul. To do otherwise is false economy.

13 Engine overhaul – reassembly sequence

1 Before reassembly begins, ensure that all new parts have been obtained, and that all necessary tools are available. Read through the entire procedure, to familiarise yourself with the work involved, and to ensure that all items necessary for reassembly of the engine are at hand. In addition to all normal tools and materials, thread-locking compound will be needed. A suitable tube of sealant will also be required for certain joint faces that are without gaskets. It is recommended that the manufacturers own products are used, which are specially formulated for this purpose. ***Caution: Certain types of high-volatility RTV can foul the oxygen sensor and cause it to fail. Be sure that any RTV used is a low-volatility type and meets Ford specifications for use on engines equipped with an oxygen sensor.***

2 In order to save time and avoid problems, engine reassembly can be carried out in the following order:

a) *Crankshaft (Section 15).*
b) *Piston/connecting rod assemblies (Section 16).*
c) *Oil pump (Part A, B or C of this Chapter).*
d) *Sump (Part A, B or C of this Chapter).*
e) *Flywheel/driveplate (Part A, B or C of this Chapter).*
f) *Cylinder head(s) (Part A, B or C of this Chapter).*
g) *Timing chains, tensioner(s) and sprockets (Part A, B or C of this Chapter).*
h) *Intake and exhaust manifolds (Part A, B or C of this Chapter).*
i) *Engine external components and ancillaries.*

3 At this stage, all engine components should be absolutely clean and dry, with all faults repaired. All components should be neatly arranged on a completely clean work surface or in individual containers.

14 Piston rings – refitting

1 Before installing new piston rings, check the end gaps. Lay out each piston set with a piston/connecting rod assembly, and keep them together as a matched set from now on.

14.2 When checking the piston ring end gap, the ring must be square in the cylinder bore; push the ring down with the top of the piston

2 Insert the top compression ring into the first cylinder, and square it up with the cylinder walls by pushing it in with the top of the piston **(see illustration)**. The ring should be near the bottom of the cylinder, at the lower limit of ring travel.

3 To measure the end gap, slip feeler gauges between the ends of the ring, until a gauge equal to the gap width is found **(see illustration)**. The feeler gauge should slide between the ring ends with a slight amount of drag. Compare the measurement to the value given in the Specifications Section of this Chapter; if the gap is larger or smaller than specified, double-check to make sure you have the correct rings before proceeding. If you are assessing the condition of used rings, have the cylinder bores checked and measured by a Ford dealer or similar engine reconditioning specialist, so that you can be sure of exactly which component is worn, and seek advice as to the best course of action to take.

4 If the end gap is still too small, it must be opened up by careful filing of the ring ends using a fine file. If it is too large, this is not as serious, unless the specified limit is exceeded, in which case very careful checking is required of the dimensions of all components, as well as of the new parts.

5 Repeat the procedure for each ring that will be installed in the first cylinder, and for each ring in the remaining cylinders. Remember to keep rings, pistons and cylinders matched up.

6 Refit the piston rings as follows. Where the

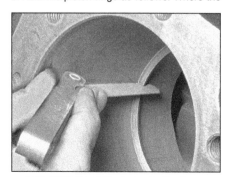

14.3 With the ring square in the bore, measure the end gap with a feeler gauge

14.6 Piston ring TOP markings

original rings are being refitted, use the marks or notes made on removal, to ensure that each ring is refitted to its original groove and the same way up. New rings generally have their top surfaces identified by markings (often an indication of size, such as STD, or the word TOP) – the rings must be fitted with such markings uppermost **(see illustration)**. **Note:** *Always follow the instructions printed on the ring package or box – different manufacturers may require different approaches. Do not mix up the top and second compression rings, as they usually have different cross-sections.*

7 The oil control ring (lowest one on the piston) is usually installed first. It is usually composed of three separate elements. Slip the spacer/expander into the groove. Next, install the lower side rail. Don't use a piston ring installation tool on the oil ring side rails, as they may be damaged. Instead, place one end of the side rail into the groove between the spacer/expander and the ring land, hold it firmly in place, and slide a finger around the piston while pushing the rail into the groove. Next, install the upper side rail in the same manner.

8 After all the oil ring components have been installed, check that both the upper and lower side rails can be turned smoothly in the ring groove.

9 The second compression (middle) ring is installed next, followed by the top compression ring – ensure their marks are uppermost. Don't expand either ring any more

than necessary to slide it over the top of the piston.

10 With all the rings in position, space the ring gaps (including the elements of the oil control ring) uniformly around the piston at 120° intervals. Repeat the procedure for the remaining pistons and rings.

15 Crankshaft – refitting

1 Crankshaft refitting is the first major step in engine reassembly. It is assumed at this point that the cylinder block/crankcase and crankshaft have been cleaned, inspected and repaired or reconditioned as necessary. Where removed, the oil jets must be refitted at this stage and their mounting bolts tightened securely.

2 Place the cylinder block on a clean, level work surface, with the crankcase facing upwards. Wipe out the inner surfaces of the main bearing caps and crankcase with a clean cloth – they must be kept spotlessly clean.

3 Clean the rear surface of the new main bearing shells with a lint free cloth. Fit the shells with an oil groove in each main bearing location in the block. On 4-cylinder models, note the thrustwashers integral with the No 3 (centre) upper main bearing shell. On V6 models, note the semi-circle shaped thrustwasher located adjacent to the No 4 (transmission end) upper main bearing. Fit the other shell from each bearing set in the corresponding main bearing cap (4-cylinder models) or lower crankcase (V6 models). Where applicable, make sure the tab on each bearing shell fits into the notch in the block or cap/lower crankcase. Also, the oil holes in the block must line up with the oil holes in the bearing shell **(see illustrations)**. Don't hammer the shells into place, and don't nick or gouge the bearing faces. It is critically important that the surfaces of the bearings are kept free from damage and contamination.

4 Clean the bearing surfaces of the shells in the block and the crankshaft main bearing journals with a clean, lint-free cloth. Check or

clean the oil holes in the crankshaft, as any dirt will become embedded in the new bearings when the engine is first started.

5 Apply a thin, uniform layer of clean molybdenum disulphide-based grease, engine assembly lubricant, or clean engine oil to each surface **(see illustration)**. Coat the thrustwasher surfaces as well.

6 Making sure the crankshaft journals are clean, lay the crankshaft back in place in the block.

7 Lubricate the crankshaft oil seal journals with molybdenum disulphide-based grease, engine assembly lubricant, or clean engine oil.

8 On 4-cylinder models, refit and tighten the main bearing caps as follows:

a) *Clean the bearing surfaces of the shells in the caps, then lubricate them. Refit the caps in their respective positions, with the arrows pointing to the timing chain end of the engine.*

b) *Working on one cap at a time, from the centre main bearing outwards (and ensuring that each cap is tightened down squarely and evenly onto the block), tighten the main bearing cap bolts to the specified torque wrench setting.*

9 On V6 models, clean the bearing surfaces of the bearings in the lower crankcase. Lubricate the bearings. Note that the No 4 bearing (transmission end) is also the thrust control bearing.

a) *Apply a 3.0 mm bead of RTV sealant to the cylinder block in the positions indicated **(see illustration)**. **Do not** apply the sealant within 6.0 mm of the rear oil seal seating.*

b) *Apply a 1.0 mm bead of RTV sealant to the cylinder block in the positions indicated **(see illustration)**. **Do not** apply the sealant within 6.0 mm of the rear oil seal seating.*

c) *Insert the lower crankcase bolts. Make sure new interior bolts are fitted. Tighten the bolts in the sequence and stages given in Specifications.*

10 Rotate the crankshaft a number of times by hand, to check for any obvious binding.

11 Check the crankshaft endfloat (see Section 10). It should be correct if the

15.3a Fitting the shells in each main bearing location

15.3b Note the thrustwashers integral with the No 3 (centre) upper main bearing shell (4-cylinder models)

15.5 Ensure the bearing shells are absolutely clean and lubricate liberally

15.9a Before refitting the lower crankcase, apply a 3.0mm bead of sealant as shown on the cylinder block . . .

15.9b . . . then apply a 1.0mm bead of sealant as shown on the cylinder block

crankshaft thrust faces aren't worn or damaged, and if the thrust control bearing(s) has been renewed.

12 Refit the crankshaft oil seal carrier, and install a new seal.

16 Piston/connecting rod assemblies – refitting

Note: *At this point, it is assumed that the crankshaft has been measured, renewed/reground as necessary, and has been fitted to the engine, as described in Section 15.*

1 Before refitting the piston/connecting rod assemblies, the cylinder bores must be perfectly clean, the top edge of each cylinder must be chamfered, and the crankshaft must be in place.

2 Remove the big-end bearing cap from No 1 cylinder connecting rod (refer to the marks noted or made on removal). Remove the original bearing shells, and wipe the bearing recesses of the connecting rod and cap with a clean, lint-free cloth. They must be kept spotlessly-clean.

3 Lubricate the cylinder bores, the pistons, piston rings and upper bearing shells with clean engine oil. Lay out each piston/connecting rod assembly in order on a clean

work surface. Take care not to scratch the crankpins and cylinder bores when the pistons are refitted.

4 Start with piston/connecting rod assembly No 1. Make sure that the piston rings are still spaced as described in Section 14, then clamp them in position with a piston ring compressor.

5 Insert the piston/connecting rod assembly into the top of cylinder No 1. Lower the big-end in first, guiding it to protect the cylinder bores. Where oil jets are located at the bottom of the bores, take particular care not to break them off when guiding the connecting rods onto the crankpins.

6 Ensure that the orientation of the piston in its cylinder is correct – the piston crown, connecting rod and big-end bearing caps should have markings, which must be aligned in the position noted on removal (see Section 9, paragraph 6).

7 Using a block of wood or hammer handle against the piston crown, tap the assembly into the cylinder until the piston crown is flush with the top of the cylinder **(see illustration).**

8 Ensure that the bearing shell is still correctly installed. Liberally lubricate the crankpin and both bearing shells with clean engine oil. Taking care not to mark the cylinder bores, tap the piston/connecting rod assembly down the bore and onto the crankpin. Where applicable, remove the insulating tape from the bolts then

oil the threads and underside of the bolt heads. Fit the big-end bearing cap, tightening its new retaining nuts/bolts finger tight at first. Note that the orientation of the bearing cap with respect to the connecting rod must be correct when the two components are reassembled **(see illustration).**

9 Tighten the retaining bolts/nuts to the specified Stage 1 torque. Tighten the retaining bolts/nuts to the specified Stage 2 torque, then finally tighten the retaining bolts/nuts to the specified Stage 3 setting (where applicable).

10 Repeat the entire procedure for the remaining piston/connecting rod assemblies.

11 After all the piston/connecting rod assemblies have been properly installed, rotate the crankshaft a number of times by hand, to check for any obvious binding or tight spots.

12 On diesel models, refit the new lower crankcase-to-cylinder block gasket. Refit the lower crankcase to the cylinder block, insert the bolts and hand-tighten. Place a straight-edge across the transmission mating surface of the cylinder block and the lower crankcase to check the lower crankcase-to-cylinder block alignment. The lower crankcase should be flush with the cylinder block. If not flush, the alignment should be within –0.05 mm overlap to a +0.05 mm gap at the rear and side of the cylinder block **(see illustrations).**

16.7 Using a hammer handle to tap the piston into its bore

16.8 Note the markings on the bearing cap with respect to the connecting rod on refitting

16.12a Place a straight-edge across the transmission mating surface of the cylinder block . . .

16.12b ... and the side of the lower crankcase-to-cylinder block alignment

16.15 Measure the piston protrusion using a DTI gauge

16.16 Note the markings (arrowed) on the cylinder head gasket (diesel engine)

13 Once the alignment is within specifications, tighten the lower crankcase bolts to the specified torque.

Diesel engines

14 If new pistons are fitted or a new short engine is installed, the projection of the piston crowns above the cylinder block upper surface at TDC must be measured, to determine the type of head gasket that should be fitted.
15 Turn the cylinder block over (so that the lower crankcase is facing downwards) and rest it on a stand or wooden blocks. Anchor a DTI gauge to the cylinder block, and zero it on the head gasket mating surface. Rest the gauge probe on No 1 piston crown and turn the crankshaft slowly by hand so that the piston reaches TDC. Measure and record the maximum projection at TDC **(see illustration)**.
16 Repeat the procedure for the remaining pistons and record the measurements. If the measurement differs from piston-to-piston, take the highest reading and use this to determine the head gasket type that must be used **(see illustration)** – refer to Chapter 2C, Section 11, for details.
17 Note that if the original pistons have been refitted, then a new head gasket of the same type as the original must be used.

All engines

18 Refer to Part A, B or C of this Chapter (as applicable) and refit the relevant assemblies.

17 Engine –
initial start-up after overhaul

1 With the engine refitted in the vehicle, double-check the engine oil and coolant levels. Make a final check that everything has been reconnected, and that there are no tools or rags left in the engine compartment.

Petrol models

2 Remove the spark plugs (see Chapter 1A).
3 Disable the ignition system by unplugging the ignition coil's electrical connector, remove the fuel pump fuse from the fusebox (see Chapter 12 – wiring diagrams).
Caution: To prevent damage to the catalytic converter, it is important to disable the fuel system.
4 Turn the engine on the starter until the oil pressure warning light goes out. If the lamp fails to extinguish after several seconds of cranking, check the engine oil level and oil filter security. Assuming these are correct, check the security of the oil pressure switch wiring – do not progress any further until you are satisfied that oil is being pumped around the engine at sufficient pressure.
5 Refit the spark plugs, and connect all the spark plug (HT) leads (Chapter 1A). Reconnect the ignition coil wiring, refit the fuel pump fuse, then switch on the ignition and listen for the fuel pump; it will run for a little longer than usual, due to the lack of pressure in the system.

Diesel models

6 Disconnect the electrical cable from the fuel cut-off solenoid at the fuel injection pump.
7 Turn the engine on the starter until the oil pressure warning light goes out. If the lamp fails to extinguish after several seconds of cranking, check the engine oil level and oil filter security. Assuming these are correct, check the security of the oil pressure switch wiring – do not progress any further until you are satisfied that oil is being pumped around the engine at sufficient pressure.
8 Reconnect the fuel cut-off solenoid cable.

All models

9 Start the engine, noting that this also may take a little longer than usual, due to the fuel system components being empty.
10 While the engine is idling, check for fuel, coolant and oil leaks. Don't be alarmed if there are some odd smells and smoke from parts getting hot and burning off oil deposits. If the hydraulic tappets have been disturbed, some valve gear noise may be heard at first; this should disappear as the oil circulates fully around the engine, and normal pressure is restored in the tappets.
11 Keep the engine idling until hot water is felt circulating through the top hose, check that it idles reasonably smoothly and at the usual speed, then switch it off.
12 After a few minutes, recheck the oil and coolant levels, and top-up as necessary (*Weekly checks*).
13 If they were tightened as described, there is no need to retighten the cylinder head bolts once the engine has first run after reassembly – in fact, Ford state that the bolts must not be retightened.
14 If new components such as pistons, rings or crankshaft bearings have been fitted, the engine must be run-in for the first 500 miles (800 km). Do not operate the engine at full-throttle, or allow it to labour in any gear during this period. It is recommended that the oil and filter be changed at the end of this period.

Chapter 3
Cooling, heating and air conditioning systems

Contents

Degrees of difficulty

Easy, suitable for novice with little experience	Fairly easy, suitable for beginner with some experience	Fairly difficult, suitable for competent DIY mechanic	Difficult, suitable for experienced DIY mechanic	Very difficult, suitable for expert DIY or professional

Specifications

Coolant
Mixture type	See Lubricants and fluids
Cooling system capacity	See Chapter 1A or 1B

System pressure
Pressure	20 psi (138 kpa)

Expansion tank filler cap
Pressure rating	18 to 21 psi (124 to 145 kpa)

Air conditioning system
Refrigerant	R134a

Torque wrench settings
	Nm	lbf ft
Air conditioning accumulator/dehydrator	8	6
Air conditioning compressor:		
1.8 and 2.0 litre petrol	25	18
2.5 litre V6	20	15
2.0 litre diesel	25	18
Air conditioning condenser	10	7
Air conditioning high pressure cut-off switch	8	6
Air conditioning low pressure cut-off switch	3	2
Oil temperature control thermostat (2.0 litre diesel)	10	7
Radiator support bracket	10	7
Refrigerant union to accumulator	8	6
Refrigerant union to air conditioning compressor	20	15
Thermostat housing:		
1.8 and 2.0 litre petrol	10	7
2.5 litre V6	18	13
2.0 diesel	23	17
Water pump:		
1.8 and 2.0 litre petrol	10	7
2.5 litre V6	10	7
2.0 litre diesel	24	18
Water pump housing (2.0 litre diesel)	10	7
Water pump pulley (1.8 and 2.0 litre petrol)	25	18

1 General information and precautions

Engine cooling system

All vehicles covered by this manual use a pressurised engine cooling system with thermostatically-controlled coolant circulation. The coolant is circulated by an impeller-type water pump, which is belt-driven from the crankshaft pulley on four-cylinder petrol engines, or belt-driven from a pulley attached to the front inlet camshaft on V6 petrol and all diesel engines.

On 1.8 and 2.0 litre petrol engines, the water pump is located on the right-hand front of the engine and is driven by the auxiliary drivebelt which also drives the alternator, power steering pump and air conditioning compressor. On the 2.5 litre V6 engine, the water pump is located on the left-hand front of the engine and is driven by a drivebelt off of the camshaft. On diesel engines, the water pump is bolted to the left-hand front of the engine cylinder block, and is driven by a drivebelt off of the camshaft, via the power steering pump which is bolted to the water pump. The drivebelt drives the power steering pump pulley, and the power steering pump drives the water pump by splines.

On 1.8 and 2.0 litre petrol engines, the thermostat is located on the right-hand rear of the cylinder block, next to the water pump. On the 2.5 litre V6 engine, the thermostat is located in the return hose from the cylinder block to the water pump, on the left-hand rear of the engine. On diesel engines, the thermostat is located in a housing on the left-hand end of the cylinder block, beneath the brake vacuum pump.

The coolant flows through the cylinder block around each cylinder; in the cylinder head(s), cast-in coolant passages direct coolant around the inlet and exhaust ports. During warm-up, the closed thermostat prevents coolant from circulating through the radiator. Instead, it returns through the coolant metal pipe running across the front of the engine to the radiator bottom hose. The supply to the heater is made from the rear of the thermostat housing. As the engine reaches normal operating temperature, the thermostat opens and allows hot coolant to travel through the radiator, where it is cooled before returning to the engine.

The radiator is of aluminium construction, and has plastic end tanks. On models with automatic transmission, the fluid cooler is incorporated in the left-hand end tank. The cooling system is sealed by a pressure-type filler cap in the expansion tank. The pressure in the system raises the boiling point of the coolant, and increases the cooling efficiency of the radiator. When the engine is at normal operating temperature, the coolant expands, and the surplus is displaced into the expansion tank. When the system cools, the surplus coolant is automatically drawn back from the tank into the radiator. One or two electric cooling fans (according to model) are mounted behind the radiator and are controlled by a thermostatic switch.

On certain diesel models, a booster heater is fitted into the heater matrix supply hose to quickly supply heat to the heater matrix while the engine is warming up. In addition to providing hot coolant to the heater, it assists the engine to reach its normal efficient temperature in as short a period as possible. The heater is located at the rear of the engine compartment, on the lower bulkhead **(see illustration)**. It is controlled by the engine management powertrain control module (PCM), and is switched on when the engine inlet air temperature is approximately 0°C. Three heating plugs are fitted to the heater housing, each one having an output of 250W (750W total).

On Scandinavian market diesel models, a fuel-fired booster heater is fitted, having an output of between 2.2kW and 5kW. A fuel pump supplies diesel fuel from the engine supply line to the evaporator section of the heater combustion chamber. The system is activated when the engine is running and the ambient temperature is lower than 5°C, or the coolant temperature is below 75°C.

Heating/ventilation system

The heating system consists of a blower fan and heater matrix (radiator) located in the heater unit, with hoses connecting the heater matrix to the engine cooling system. Hot engine coolant is circulated through the heater matrix. Incoming fresh air for the ventilation system passes through a pollen filter mounted below the windscreen cowl panel. The ventilation system air distribution is controlled by a number of electronically-operated flap doors in the heater housing. When the heater controls are operated, the flap doors open to direct the air to the chosen areas of the passenger compartment. When the blower control is operated, the blower fan forces air through the unit according to the setting selected.

On models equipped with automatic temperature control, a digital display indicates the temperature, blower speed, demist/defrost mode, and air flow direction.

1.6 Cooling system booster heater located on the lower bulkhead

Air conditioning system

See Section 10.

Precautions

⚠️ *Warning: DO NOT attempt to remove the expansion tank filler cap, or to disturb any part of the cooling system, while it or the engine is hot, as there is a very great risk of scalding. If the expansion tank filler cap must be removed before the engine and radiator have fully cooled down (even though this is not recommended) the pressure in the cooling system must first be released. Cover the cap with a thick layer of cloth, to avoid scalding, and slowly unscrew the filler cap until a hissing sound can be heard. When the hissing has stopped, showing that pressure is released, slowly unscrew the filler cap further until it can be removed; if more hissing sounds are heard, wait until they have stopped before unscrewing the cap completely. At all times, keep well away from the filler opening.*

⚠️ *Warning: Do not allow antifreeze to come in contact with your skin, or with the painted surfaces of the vehicle. Rinse off spills immediately with plenty of water. Never leave antifreeze lying around in an open container, or in a puddle in the driveway or on the garage floor. Children and pets are attracted by its sweet smell, but antifreeze is fatal if ingested.*

⚠️ *Warning: If the engine is hot, the electric cooling fan may start rotating even if the engine is not running, so be careful to keep hands, hair and loose clothing well clear when working in the engine compartment.*

⚠️ *Warning: Refer to Section 10 for precautions to be observed when working on models equipped with air conditioning.*

2 Cooling system hoses – disconnection and renewal

Note: *Refer to the warnings given in Section 1 of this Chapter before starting work.*

1 If the checks described in the appropriate part of Chapter 1 reveal a faulty hose, it must be renewed as follows.

2 First drain the cooling system (see the appropriate part of Chapter 1); if the antifreeze is not due for renewal, the drained coolant may be re-used, if it is collected in a clean container.

3 To disconnect any hose, use a pair of pliers to release the spring clamps (or a screwdriver to slacken screw-type clamps), then move them along the hose clear of the union. Carefully work the hose off its stubs. The hoses can be removed with relative ease when new – on an older car, they may have stuck.

4 If a hose proves stubborn, try to release it by rotating it on its unions before attempting to work it off. Gently prise the end of the hose with a blunt instrument (such as a flat-bladed screwdriver), but do not apply too much force, and take care not to damage the pipe stubs or hoses. Note in particular that the radiator hose unions are fragile; do not use excessive force when attempting to remove the hoses. If all else fails, cut the hose with a sharp knife, then slit it so that it can be peeled off in two pieces. While expensive, this is preferable to buying a new radiator. Check first, however, that a new hose is readily available.

5 When refitting a hose, first slide the clamps onto the hose, then work the hose onto its unions. If the hose is stiff, use soap (or washing-up liquid) as a lubricant, or soften it by soaking it in boiling water, but take care to prevent scalding.

6 Work each hose end fully onto its union, then check that the hose is settled correctly and is properly routed. Slide each clip along the hose until it is behind the union flared end, before tightening it securely.

7 Refill the system with coolant (see the appropriate part of Chapter 1).

8 Check carefully for leaks as soon as possible after disturbing any part of the cooling system.

3 Thermostat – removal, testing and refitting

Note: Refer to the warnings given in Section 1 of this Chapter before starting work.

1.8 and 2.0 litre petrol engine

Removal

1 Drain the cooling system as described in Chapter 1A. If the coolant is relatively new or in good condition, drain it into a clean container and re-use it.

2 Remove the right-hand headlamp as described in Chapter 12, Section 7.

3 Unscrew the nut and detach the power steering pump hydraulic fluid supply line support from the water pump.

4 Disconnect the wiring from the temperature sensor on the thermostat housing.

5 Note the location of the hoses on the thermostat housing, then loosen the clips and disconnect them.

6 Unscrew the bolts and remove the thermostat housing from the cylinder block. Recover the gasket/O-ring seal and discard it; obtain a new one for refitting.

7 It is not possible to separate the thermostat from the housing.

8 Thoroughly clean the surfaces of the thermostat housing and cylinder block.

Testing

9 A rough test of the thermostat may be made by suspending it with a piece of string in a container full of water so that it is immersed

3.15 Thermostat housing on the 2.5 litre V6 engine

in the water but not touching the sides or bottom of the container. Heat the water to bring it to the boil – the thermostat must open by the time the water boils. If not, renew it.

10 If a thermometer is available, the precise opening temperature of the thermostat may be determined; compare with the figures with the opening temperature marked on the thermostat.

11 A thermostat which fails to close as the water cools must also be renewed.

Refitting

12 Refitting is a reversal of removal, but fit a new gasket/O-ring seal, and tighten the mounting bolts to the specified torque. Refill the cooling system as described in Chapter 1A.

2.5 litre V6 petrol engine

Removal

13 Drain the cooling system as described in Chapter 1A. If the coolant is relatively new or in good condition, drain it into a clean container and re-use it.

14 Unbolt and remove the top cover from over the water pump pulley.

15 Loosen the clips and disconnect the hoses from the thermostat housing and cover **(see illustration)**. Where spring-type clips are fitted, use a pair of grips or, preferably, obtain a special cable-operated tool to release the clips. Remove the housing and cover assembly from the engine compartment.

16 With the assembly on the bench, unscrew the two bolts and remove the cover, then note how the thermostat is fitted and withdraw it

3.22a Unscrew the bolts . . .

3.21 Purge hose and stub on the thermostat cover

from the housing. Recover the O-ring seal from the perimeter of the thermostat and discard it; obtain a new one for refitting.

17 Thoroughly clean the surfaces of the thermostat cover and housing.

Testing

18 Refer to paragraphs 9 to 11.

Refitting

19 Refitting is a reversal of removal, but fit a new O-ring seal and tighten the bolts to the specified torque. Refill the cooling system as described in Chapter 1A.

2.0 litre diesel engine

Removal

20 Drain the cooling system as described in Chapter 1B. If the coolant is relatively new or in good condition, drain it into a clean container and re-use it.

21 Loosen the clips and disconnect the purge and radiator top hoses from the thermostat housing **(see illustration)**. Where spring-type clips are fitted, use a pair of grips or, preferably, obtain a special cable-operated tool to release the clips.

22 Unscrew the bolts and separate the cover from the thermostat housing **(see illustrations)**.

23 Note how the thermostat is fitted and withdraw it from the housing. Recover the O-ring seal and discard it; obtain a new one for refitting **(see illustrations)**.

24 If necessary, the thermostat housing may be removed from the cylinder head outlet elbow. First, disconnect the exhaust gas

3.22b . . . and separate the cover from the thermostat housing

3.23a Remove the thermostat from the housing . . .

3.23b . . . then remove the O-ring seal

3.24a Unscrew the single bolt . . .

3.24b . . . remove the housing . . .

3.24c . . . and recover the O-ring seal

recirculation (EGR) cooler hose. Unscrew the single bolt and remove the housing. Recover the O-ring seal and discard it; obtain a new one for refitting **(see illustrations)**. Withdraw the housing from the engine compartment.

4.1 Fan speed control resistor assembly

4.8 Removing the radiator lower mounting brackets

Testing

25 Refer to paragraphs 9 to 11.

Refitting

26 Refitting is a reversal of removal, but clean all sealing surfaces, fit new O-ring seals, and tighten the bolts to the specified torque. Refill the cooling system as described in Chapter 1B.

---

4 Radiator electric cooling fan assembly – testing, removal and refitting

Note: *Refer to the warnings given in Section 1 of this Chapter before starting work.*

Testing

1 The radiator cooling fan is controlled by the engine management system's ECU, acting on

4.9a Disconnect the electric cooling fan motor wiring . . .

the information received from the coolant temperature sensor. Twin fans are fitted to 2.5 litre V6 engine models, models with automatic transmission and diesel engine models. Where twin fans or two-speed fans are fitted, control is through a resistor assembly secured to the bottom left-hand corner of the fan shroud **(see illustration)** – this can be renewed separately if faulty.

2 First, check the relevant fuses and relays (see Chapter 12).

3 To test the fan motor, unplug the electrical connector and use fused jumper wires to connect the fan directly to the battery. If the fan still does not work, renew the motor.

4 If the motor proved sound, the fault lies in the coolant temperature sensor (see Section 5 for testing details), in the wiring loom (see Chapter 12 for testing details) or in the engine management system (see the appropriate part of Chapter 4).

Removal

Petrol and manual gearbox diesel engines

5 Disconnect the battery negative lead (refer to *Disconnecting the battery* at the end of this manual).

6 Apply the handbrake, then jack up the front of the vehicle and support it on axle stands (see *Jacking and vehicle support*). Where necessary, remove the engine undertray.

7 Remove the splash shield from beneath the radiator.

8 Using string or plastic cable ties, support the weight of the radiator, then unscrew the bolts securing the radiator lower mounting brackets to the front suspension subframe. Remove the brackets, noting that they are handed, and are marked to ensure correct refitting **(see illustration)**.

9 Disconnect the wiring from the cooling fan motors and release the wiring harness ties from the shroud and subframe **(see illustrations)**. Note on 2.5 litre V6 engine models, the wiring plug incorporates a spring clip which must be released.

10 Release the coolant purge hose from the clip on the shroud **(see illustration)**.

11 Unscrew the nuts retaining the cooling fan motors and shroud to the radiator. Carefully

4.9b . . . and loom connector . . .

4.9c . . . and release the wiring loom from the subframe

4.10 Release the coolant purge hose from the clip on the shroud

4.11a Unscrew the right-hand mounting nut . . .

4.11b . . . and left-hand mounting nut . . .

4.11c . . . then lower the electric cooling fan assembly from under the vehicle

slide the electric cooling fan assembly upwards from the side brackets, then lower it downwards and withdraw from under the vehicle **(see illustrations)**.

Automatic transmission diesel engine

12 Disconnect the battery negative lead (refer to *Disconnecting the battery* at the end of this manual).

13 Apply the handbrake, then jack up the front of the vehicle and support it on axle stands (see *Jacking and vehicle support*). Remove the engine undertray.

14 Remove the splash shield from beneath the radiator.

15 Using string or plastic cable ties, support the weight of the radiator, then unscrew the bolts securing the radiator lower mounting brackets to the front suspension subframe. Remove the brackets, noting that they are handed, and are marked to ensure correct refitting.

16 Disconnect the wiring from the cooling fan motors and release the wiring harness from the clip on the front suspension subframe.

17 Unscrew the nuts retaining the cooling fan motors and shroud to the radiator.

18 Carefully slide the electric cooling fan assembly upwards from the side brackets, then lower it downwards until it is possible to reach the cooling fan motor module. Unscrew the module mounting bolts, and position it within the shroud – this will provide additional clearance for removing the assembly.

19 Lower the assembly and withdraw it from under the vehicle.

Refitting

20 Refitting is a reversal of removal, but initialise the door window motors as described in Chapter 11.

---

5 Cooling system temperature sensor/sender – testing, removal and refitting

Note: *Refer to the warnings given in Section 1 of this Chapter before starting work.*

1 On 1.8 and 2.0 litre petrol and diesel engine models, the sensor is screwed into the outlet housing on the left-hand end of the cylinder head.

2 On models with the 2.5 litre V6 engine, the sensor is at the front of the bypass housing on the left-hand end of the engine **(see illustration)**.

Testing

3 If the coolant temperature gauge is inoperative, check the fuses first (see Chapter 12).

4 If the gauge indicates 'hot' at any time, consult the *Fault finding* Section at the end of this manual, to assist in tracing possible cooling system faults.

5 If the gauge indicates 'hot' shortly after the engine is started from cold, unplug the coolant temperature sender's electrical connector. If the gauge reading now drops, renew the sender. If the reading remains high, the wiring to the gauge may be shorted to earth, or the gauge is faulty.

6 If the gauge fails to indicate after the engine has been warmed up and the fuses are known to be sound, switch off the engine. Unplug the sender's electrical connector, and use a jumper wire to connect the white/red wire to a clean earth point (bare metal) on the engine. Switch on the ignition without starting the engine. If the gauge now indicates 'hot', renew the sender.

7 If the gauge still does not work, the circuit may be open, or the gauge may be faulty. See Chapter 12 for additional information.

Removal

8 Drain the cooling system (see Chapter 1A or 1B) and remove the engine top cover.

9 On 1.8 and 2.0 litre petrol engine models, remove the ignition coil pack (see Chapter 5B).

10 On 2.5 litre V6 and diesel engine models, remove the water pump drivebelt cover. Refer

5.2 Coolant temperature sender on the 2.5 litre V6 engine

to the appropriate part of Chapter 4 and disconnect the air inlet hose from the air cleaner housing. Access will be made easier if the battery is also removed (see Chapter 5A).
11 Unplug the electrical connector from the sender.
12 Unscrew the sender and withdraw it.

Refitting

13 Clean any traces of old sealant from the sender location, then apply a light coat of sealant to the sender's threads. Screw in the sender and tighten it securely, and reconnect the wiring.
14 Refill the cooling system as described in Chapter 1A or 1B and run the engine. Check for leaks.

6 Radiator and expansion tank – removal, inspection and refitting

Note: *Refer to the warnings given in Section 1 of this Chapter before starting work.*

Radiator

Removal

Note: *If leakage is the reason for removing the radiator, bear in mind that minor leaks can often be cured using a radiator sealant added to the coolant with the radiator in situ.*

1 Drain the cooling system as described in Chapter 1A or 1B. If the coolant is relatively new or in good condition, drain it into a clean container and re-use it.

2 Remove the radiator electric cooling fan assembly as described in Section 4. This procedure includes removing the radiator bottom mounting brackets.
3 Loosen the clips and disconnect the top and bottom hoses from the radiator **(see illustration)**. Where spring-type clips are fitted, use a pair of grips or, preferably, obtain a special cable-operated tool to release the clips.
4 Loosen the clip and disconnect the expansion tank hose from the radiator **(see illustration)**.
5 On diesel engine models, position a suitable container beneath the oil cooler coolant hose on the radiator, then loosen the clip and disconnect the hose. Also, release the oil cooler hose from the retaining clip and remove the clip from the front suspension subframe.
6 Support the weight of the air conditioning condenser with plastic cable ties or string, then unscrew the bolts securing it to the radiator **(see illustrations)**.

 Warning: Do not disconnect any of the refrigerant hoses.

7 Release the plastic ties, then carefully lower the radiator and withdraw from under the vehicle **(see illustration)**. Take care not to damage the radiator fins, as they are easily bent.
8 Remove the rubber radiator mounting bushes from the top and bottom brackets, and inspect them for wear and damage **(see illustration)**. If worn excessively, obtain and fit new ones before refitting the radiator.

Inspection

9 With the radiator removed, it can be inspected for leaks and damage. If it needs repair, have a radiator specialist or dealer service department perform the work, as special techniques are required.
10 Insects and dirt can be removed from the radiator with a garden hose or a soft brush. Take care not to bend the cooling fins.

Refitting

11 Refitting is the reverse of the removal procedure, but refill the cooling system as described in Chapter 1A or 1B.

Expansion tank

Removal

12 With the engine completely cool, remove the expansion tank filler cap to release any pressure, then syphon all of the coolant from the tank. If the antifreeze is not due for renewal, the drained coolant may be re-used, if it is kept clean.
13 Disconnect all the hoses from the tank.
14 Unscrew the tank's two mounting bolts and withdraw it, unplugging the coolant low level switch electrical connector (where fitted).
15 Wash out the tank, and inspect it for cracks and chafing – renew it if damaged.

Refitting

16 Refitting is the reverse of the removal procedure. Refill the cooling system with the proper mixture of antifreeze and water with reference to Chapter 1A or 1B.

6.3 Disconnecting the radiator top hose

6.4 Expansion tank hose on the radiator

6.6a Support the air conditioning condenser with cable ties . . .

6.6b . . . then unscrew the condenser mounting bolts

6.7 Lowering the radiator from under the vehicle

6.8 Check the radiator mounting bushes

7.6a Using a pulley holder when removing the water pump pulley (1.8 and 2.0 litre petrol engine)

7.6b Removing the water pump pulley (1.8 and 2.0 litre petrol engine)

7.7a Unscrew the mounting bolts . . .

7 Water pump – removal and refitting

Note: *Refer to the warnings given in Section 1 of this Chapter before starting work.*

Removal

1.8 and 2.0 litre petrol engines

1 Drain the cooling system as described in Chapter 1A. If the coolant is relatively new or in good condition, drain it into a clean container and re-use it.

2 Before removing the auxiliary drivebelt, loosen the water pump pulley mounting bolts by half a turn. Alternatively, they may be loosened later if a suitable pulley holder is available.

3 Apply the handbrake, then jack up the front of the vehicle and support it on axle stands (see *Jacking and vehicle support*). Remove the right-hand front roadwheel.

4 Working under the right-hand front wheel arch, undo the bolts and remove the splash shield for access to the right-hand end of the engine.

5 Note the routing of the auxiliary drivebelt. Turn the tensioner clockwise, then slip the drivebelt from the pulleys and remove from the engine compartment. If the belt is to be re-used, mark its direction of fitting.

6 Fully unscrew the bolts and remove the pulley from the water pump **(see illustrations)**.

7 Progressively unscrew the three mounting bolts and remove the water pump from the engine. Remove the O-ring seal and discard it **(see illustrations)**. Obtain a new one for the refitting procedure, and note that Ford state that the seal should be lubricated with 'Merpol' grease.

2.5 litre V6 petrol engine

8 Drain the cooling system as described in Chapter 1A. If the coolant is relatively new or in good condition, drain it into a clean container and re-use it.

9 Remove the air cleaner as described in the appropriate part of Chapter 4.

10 Remove the thermostat housing as described in Section 3.

7.7b . . . remove the water pump . . .

11 Remove the water pump drivebelt by turning the tensioner clockwise with a socket **(see illustration)**. Slip the drivebelt from the pulleys and remove from the engine compartment. If the belt is to be re-used, mark its direction of fitting.

12 Progressively unscrew the three mounting bolts securing the water pump to the left-hand end of the engine **(see illustration)**. **Note:** *The impeller is secured to the housing by the remaining five bolts. Neither the impeller nor its gasket is available separately.*

13 Loosen the clips and disconnect the hoses, then withdraw the pump from the engine.

2.0 litre diesel engine

14 Drain the cooling system as described in Chapter 1B. If the coolant is relatively new or in good condition, drain it into a clean container and re-use it.

7.11 Water pump and drivebelt (2.5 litre V6 engine)

7.7c . . . and remove the O-ring seal (1.8 and 2.0 litre petrol engine)

15 Remove the engine plastic top cover.

16 Remove the air intake pipe. To do this, first release the coolant pipe from the clip, then loosen the clips and withdraw the intake pipe.

17 Unscrew the air intake pipe and exhaust gas recirculation (EGR) tube mounting bolts.

18 Using a suitable square drive in the special hole, turn the tensioner clockwise, then slip the drivebelt from the power steering pump pulley **(see illustration)**. If the belt is to be re-used, mark its direction of fitting. Remove the drivebelt from the engine compartment.

19 Remove the inlet manifold from the engine as described in the appropriate part of Chapter 2.

20 Unscrew the mounting bolt and position the power steering fluid reservoir to one side.

21 Unscrew the bolt securing the power steering fluid line support bracket to the cylinder head.

7.12 Water pump mounting bolts (2.5 litre V6 engine)

7.18 Removing the drivebelt from the power steering pump pulley

7.22 Power steering pump-to-water pump mounting bolts (diesel engine)

7.23 Disconnecting the hoses from the water pump (diesel engine)

7.24a Unscrew the water pump housing-to-block bolts . . .

7.24b . . . withdraw the assembly . . .

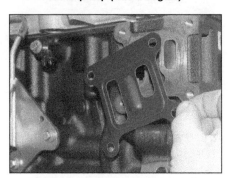

7.24c . . . and remove the gasket

22 Unscrew the bolts securing the power steering pump to the water pump, and position it to one side **(see illustration)**.
23 Loosen the clips and disconnect the hoses from the water pump. Where spring-type clips are fitted, use a pair of grips or, preferably, obtain a special cable-operated tool to release the clips **(see illustration)**.
24 Unscrew and remove the water pump housing-to-block bolts, noting the location of the wiring harness on the lower bolts. Withdraw the pump sufficient to disconnect the remaining hose. Remove the gasket and discard it **(see illustrations)**. Obtain a new one for the refitting procedure.
25 Unbolt the engine oil temperature control thermostat from the water pump housing and discard the O-ring seal **(see illustrations)**. Obtain a new one for the refitting procedure.

Refitting

26 Refitting is a reversal of removal, but tighten the mounting bolts/nuts to the specified torque. Refill the cooling system with reference to Chapter 1A or 1B.

7.25a Unscrew the bolt . . .

7.25b . . . and remove the oil temperature control thermostat from the water pump housing

8 Heater/ventilation components – removal and refitting

Heater blower motor

Removal

1 Unclip and remove the passenger footwell lower trim panel **(see illustration)**.
2 Remove the glovebox as described in Chapter 11.
3 Disconnect the wiring from the heater blower motor **(see illustration)**.
4 Undo the retaining screws and lower the blower motor from the heater casing **(see illustrations)**.

Refitting

5 Refitting is a reversal of removal.

8.1 Removing the passenger footwell lower trim panel

8.3 Disconnect the wiring . . .

8.4a . . . then undo the retaining screws . . .

8.4b . . . and lower the heater blower motor from its housing

8.8 Disconnecting the hoses from the matrix stubs on the bulkhead

8.10a Undo the lower screws . . .

8.10b . . . and single rear screw . . .

8.10c . . . and remove the rear footwell air guide

Heater matrix

Removal

6 Apply the handbrake, then jack up the front of the vehicle and support it on axle stands (see *Jacking and vehicle support*). On diesel models, remove the engine undertray.

7 Drain the cooling system as described in Chapter 1A or 1B. If the coolant is relatively new or in good condition, drain it into a clean container and re-use it.

8 On the engine side of the bulkhead, loosen the clips and disconnect the coolant hoses from the matrix stubs **(see illustration)**. Identify the locations of the hoses for correct refitting. Also disconnect the water drain hose from the drain connection on the matrix.

9 Remove the centre console as described in Chapter 11.

10 Undo the two lower and single rear screws securing the rear footwell air guide to the matrix housing, then release the clips and remove the air guide **(see illustrations)**. If the clips are tight, press upwards on the guide while releasing them.

11 Remove the front clips, then release the side clips and lower the matrix and housing to the floor **(see illustrations)**. Withdraw it from inside the vehicle.

12 With the matrix on the bench, remove the rubber seal from the stubs **(see illustration)**.

13 Undo the screw and remove the plastic clamp, then remove the matrix from its housing **(see illustrations overleaf)**. Be prepared for some spillage of coolant by placing cloth rags on the floor of the vehicle.

Refitting

14 Refitting is a reversal of removal. Refill the cooling system with reference to Chapter 1A or 1B.

8.11a Remove the front clips . . .

8.11c . . . and lower the matrix and housing to the floor

Heater housing

Removal and refitting

15 The heater housing removal and refitting procedure is similar to that for the air

8.11b . . . release the side clips . . .

8.12 Removing the rubber seal from the matrix stubs

8.13a Undo the screw . . .

8.13b . . . remove the plastic clamp . . .

8.13c . . . then remove the matrix from its housing

conditioning heater/evaporator housing described in Section 11.

Pollen filter

Removal and refitting

16 Refer to Chapter 1A or 1B.

9 Heater/air conditioning controls – removal and refitting

Removal

1 Disconnect the battery negative lead (refer to *Disconnecting the battery* at the end of this manual).
2 Remove the centre console and radio/cassette audio unit as described in Chapter 12.
3 Use a screwdriver to carefully prise the accessory switches from the heater control trim panel. Prevent damage to the facia by placing card beneath the screwdriver. Disconnect the wiring from the switches.
4 Undo the screws securing the heater control trim panel to the facia. There are two screws located in the accessory switch apertures, two screws located in the top corners of the radio/cassette aperture, and two screws located at the bottom of the panel.

5 Release the three upper clips, and remove the heater control trim panel from the facia. From the rear of the panel, disconnect the wiring for the liftgate release switch, heated front seat switch, auxiliary climate/heater control switches, and clock.
6 With the heater control trim panel on the bench, undo the screws and withdraw the heater control unit.
7 If necessary, the heater blower motor rheostat may be removed from the heater control unit by undoing the retaining screw (see illustrations).

Refitting

8 Refitting is a reversal of removal.

10 Air conditioning system – general information and precautions

General information

The air conditioning system consists of a condenser mounted in front of the radiator, an evaporator mounted adjacent to the heater matrix, a compressor driven by an auxiliary drivebelt, an accumulator/dehydrator, and the pipes connecting all of

the above components (see illustration opposite).

The cooling side of the system works in the same way as a domestic refrigerator. Refrigerant gas at low pressure is drawn into a belt-driven compressor and passes into a condenser mounted on the front of the radiator, where it loses heat and becomes liquid. The liquid passes through an expansion valve to an evaporator, where it changes from liquid under high pressure to gas under low pressure. This change is accompanied by a drop in temperature, which cools the evaporator. The refrigerant returns to the compressor, and the cycle begins again.

Air blown through the evaporator passes to the air distribution unit, where it is mixed with hot air blown through the heater matrix to achieve the desired temperature in the passenger compartment.

The heating side of the system works in the same way as on models without air conditioning.

Precautions

⚠ *Warning: The air conditioning system is under high pressure. Do not loosen any fittings or remove any components until after the system has been discharged. Air conditioning refrigerant should be properly discharged*

9.7a Undo the retaining screw . . .

9.7b . . . and remove the heater blower motor rheostat from the heater control unit into an approved type of container, at a dealer service department or an automotive air conditioning repair facility capable of handling R134a refrigerant. Always wear eye protection when disconnecting air conditioning system fittings.

When an air conditioning system is fitted, it is necessary to observe the following special precautions whenever dealing with any part of the system, its associated components, and any items which necessitate disconnection of the system:

a) While the refrigerant used – R134a – is less damaging to the environment than the previously-used R12, it is still a very dangerous substance. It must not be allowed into contact with the skin or eyes, or there is a risk of frostbite. It must also not be discharged in an enclosed space – while it is not toxic, there is a risk of suffocation. The refrigerant is heavier than air, and so must never be discharged over a pit.

b) The refrigerant must not be allowed to come in contact with a naked flame, otherwise a poisonous gas will be created – under certain circumstances, this can form an explosive mixture with air. For similar reasons, smoking in the presence of refrigerant is highly dangerous, particularly if the vapour is inhaled through a lighted cigarette.

c) Never discharge the system to the atmosphere – R134a is not an ozone-depleting ChloroFluoroCarbon (CFC) like R12, but is instead a hydrofluorocarbon, which causes environmental damage by contributing to the 'greenhouse effect' if released into the atmosphere.

d) R134a refrigerant must not be mixed with R12; the system uses different seals (now green-coloured, previously black) and has different fittings requiring different tools, so that there is no chance of the two types of refrigerant becoming mixed accidentally.

e) If for any reason the system must be disconnected, entrust this task to your Ford dealer or a refrigeration engineer.

f) It is essential that the system be professionally discharged prior to using any form of heat – welding, soldering, brazing, etc – in the vicinity of the system, before having the vehicle oven-dried at a temperature exceeding 70°C after repainting, and before disconnecting any part of the system.

10.1 Air conditioning system components

1 Evaporator matrix orifice
2 Evaporator core connections
3 Air conditioning compressor
4 Condenser matrix connections
5 Suction accumulator/ dehydrator
6 Low pressure cut-off switch
7 High pressure cut-off switch

11 Air conditioning system components – removal and refitting

Warning: The air conditioning system is under high pressure. Do not loosen any fittings or remove any components until after the system has been discharged. Air conditioning refrigerant should be properly discharged into an approved type of container, at a dealer service department or an automotive air conditioning repair facility capable of handling R134a refrigerant. Cap or plug the pipe lines as soon as they are disconnected, to prevent the entry of moisture. Always wear eye protection when disconnecting air conditioning system fittings.

Note: This Section refers to the components of the air conditioning system itself – refer to Sections 8 and 9 for details of components common to the heating/ventilation system.

Condenser

Removal

1 Have the refrigerant discharged at a dealer service department or an automotive air conditioning repair facility.
2 On models fitted with the 5-speed automatic transmission, secure the radiator at both sides with plastic cable ties or string.
3 Apply the handbrake, then jack up the front of the vehicle and support it on axle stands (see Jacking and vehicle support).
4 Remove the radiator lower splash shield.
5 Disconnect the refrigerant lines from the condenser, and immediately cap the openings to prevent the entry of dirt and moisture (see illustrations). Discard the O-ring seals and obtain new ones for the refitting procedure.

11.5a Disconnect the refrigerant line upper . . .

11.5b ... and lower retaining nuts

6 On models fitted with the 5-speed automatic transmission, unbolt the radiator lower mounting bracket from the subframe, then mark the automatic transmission fluid cooler hoses for position. Position a suitable container beneath the fluid cooler, then disconnect the hoses and allow the fluid to drain into the container.

7 Unscrew the bolts securing the air conditioning condenser to the radiator, then carefully lower it and withdraw from under the vehicle.

Refitting

8 Refitting is a reversal of removal, but fit new O-ring seals. The O-ring seals must be coated with clean refrigerant oil before refitting them. Have the system evacuated, charged and leak-tested by the specialist who discharged it.

Heater/evaporator housing

Note: *Special tool 412-081 will be required for this work.*

Removal

9 Have the refrigerant discharged at a dealer service department or an automotive air conditioning repair facility.

10 Apply the handbrake, then jack up the front of the vehicle and support it on axle stands (see *Jacking and vehicle support*). On diesel models, remove the engine undertray.

11 Disconnect the battery negative lead (refer to *Disconnecting the battery* at the end of this manual).

12 Drain the cooling system as described in Chapter 1A or 1B. If the coolant is relatively

11.24 Air conditioning refrigerant line spring lock coupling locking clips

new or in good condition, drain it into a clean container and re-use it.

13 On the engine side of the bulkhead, loosen the clips and disconnect the coolant hoses from the matrix stubs. Identify the locations of the hoses for correct refitting.

14 Disconnect the water drain hose from the drain connection on the matrix.

15 Remove the facia as described in Chapter 11.

16 Remove the air duct, then pull back the weatherstrip from the right-hand door opening and remove the cowl side trim panel.

17 Unbolt the earth cable from the A-pillar, disconnect the main electrical connector and disconnect the two wiring plugs from the generic electronic module (GEM).

18 Release the wiring harness from the heater/evaporator matrix housing. Also unclip and disconnect the vent actuator wiring harness.

19 Disconnect the blower motor and resistor wiring. Also disconnect the temperature sensor and handbrake warning light wiring.

20 Disconnect the adaptive restraint module and central junction box wiring.

21 Undo the screws and remove the windscreen air duct.

22 For models built up to 05/2001, remove the blanking caps and unscrew the bulkhead cross-beam mounting bolts from the A-pillar on both sides.

23 On 2.5 litre V6 engine models, remove the ignition coil.

24 Remove the refrigerant line spring lock coupling locking clips **(see illustration)**.

25 Using the special tool 412-081, disconnect the left- and right-hand refrigerant lines from the evaporator matrix. Discard the O-ring seals.

26 Unscrew and remove the heater/evaporator matrix housing mounting nut from the bulkhead.

27 Unclip the wiring harness, and remove the bulkhead cross-beam from inside the vehicle.

28 Withdraw the heater/evaporator housing from inside the vehicle. Be prepared for some spillage of coolant by placing cloth rags on the floor of the vehicle.

Refitting

29 Refitting is a reversal of removal, but fit new O-ring seals. The O-ring seals must be coated with clean refrigerant oil before refitting them. Have the system evacuated, charged and leak-tested by the specialist who discharged it.

Compressor

Removal

30 Have the refrigerant discharged at a dealer service department or an automotive air conditioning repair facility.

31 Apply the handbrake, then jack up the front of the vehicle and support it on axle stands (see *Jacking and vehicle support*). Remove the radiator lower splash guard. On diesel models, remove the engine undertray.

32 On 2.5 litre V6 models, unbolt and remove the compressor heat shield.

33 On diesel models with common rail fuel injection, loosen the clip and disconnect the intercooler outlet hose from the exhaust gas EGR return valve. Also disconnect the wiring from the mass air flow (MAF) sensor, and remove the intercooler outlet hose after loosening the clips.

34 On diesel models, remove the radiator as described in Section 6.

35 Disconnect the wiring from the air conditioning compressor. Note on diesel models, it is easier to disconnect the wiring as the compressor is being withdrawn from the engine.

36 Remove the auxiliary drivebelt as described in Chapter 1A or 1B.

37 Unscrew the bolt and disconnect the union block from the compressor. Discard the O-ring seals and obtain new ones for the refitting procedure. Tape over or plug the compressor apertures and line ends to prevent entry of dust and dirt.

38 Support the air conditioning compressor, then unscrew the mounting bolts. Lower the compressor from the engine. **Note:** *Keep the compressor level during handling and storage. If the compressor has seized, or if you find metal particles in the refrigerant lines, the system must be flushed out by an air conditioning technician, and the accumulator/dehydrator must be renewed.*

Refitting

39 Refitting is a reversal of removal, but fit new O-ring seals after coating them with clean refrigerant oil, and tighten the mounting bolts to the specified torque. Have the system evacuated, charged and leak-tested by the specialist that discharged it.

Accumulator/dehydrator

Note: *Special tool 412-069 will be required for this work.*

Removal

40 Have the refrigerant discharged at a dealer service department or an automotive air conditioning repair facility.

41 Apply the handbrake, then jack up the front of the vehicle and support it on axle stands (see *Jacking and vehicle support*). Remove the right-hand front roadwheel. Remove the radiator lower splash guard. On diesel models, remove the engine undertray.

42 Remove the wheel arch liner from under the right-hand front wing.

43 Disconnect the wiring from the low-pressure cut-off switch **(see illustration)**.

44 Unscrew the union and disconnect the lower refrigerant line from the accumulator **(see illustration)**. Discard the O-ring seals and obtain new ones for the refitting procedure.

45 Using the Ford special tool 412-069, disconnect the upper refrigerant line from the accumulator. Discard the O-ring seals and obtain new ones for the refitting procedure.

Tape over or plug the accumulator apertures and line ends to prevent entry of dust and dirt.
46 Unbolt the windscreen washer fluid reservoir from the inner wing panel, and position to one side. If required, the front bumper can be removed to provide additional working room (see Chapter 11).
47 Unscrew the mounting bolts and remove the accumulator/dehydrator from beneath the wing **(see illustration)**.

Refitting

48 Refitting is a reversal of removal, but fit new O-ring seals after coating them with clean refrigerant oil, and tighten the mounting bolts to the specified torque. Have the system evacuated, charged and leak-tested by the specialist who discharged it.

Low pressure cut-off switch

 Warning: This work is best carried out by a dealer service department or an automotive air conditioning repair facility.

Removal

49 Apply the handbrake, then jack up the front of the vehicle and support it on axle stands (see *Jacking and vehicle support*).
50 Unscrew the lower and front bolts securing the right-hand wheel arch liner, and tie the liner to one side for access to the lower pressure cut-off switch.
51 Disconnect the wiring from the switch.
52 Connect a 20 amp fuse rated jumper wire between Pin 1 and Pin 4 of the switch wiring, then start the engine and turn the air conditioning switch to ON.
Caution: The air conditioning compressor MUST run during removal of the lower pressure cut-off switch.
53 Unscrew and remove the switch and discard the O-ring seals. **Note:** *Check that the low pressure cut-off switch valve closes completely after removal of the switch, to prevent loss of refrigerant.* Obtain new seals for the refitting procedure.

Refitting

54 Refitting is a reversal of removal, but fit new O-ring seals after coating them with clean refrigerant oil, and tighten the switch **only** to the specified torque.

11.43 Air conditioning low pressure cut-off switch

High pressure cut-off switch

Removal

55 The high pressure cut-off switch is located in the engine compartment, next to the power steering hydraulic fluid reservoir.
56 Disconnect the wiring from the switch.
57 Unscrew and remove the switch and discard the O-ring seals. **Note:** *Check that the high pressure cut-off switch valve closes completely after removal of the switch, to prevent loss of refrigerant.* Obtain new seals for the refitting procedure.

Refitting

58 Refitting is a reversal of removal, but fit new O-ring seals after coating them with clean refrigerant oil, and tighten the switch **only** to the specified torque.

12 Heater/evaporator housing – dismantling and reassembly

Dismantling

1 With the housing on the bench, undo the four screws and remove the blend door actuator assembly.
2 Undo the three screws and remove the air inlet blend door actuator.
3 Remove the heater matrix with reference to Section 8.
4 Undo the two screws and remove the evaporator matrix upper housing.
5 Remove the rubber seal, then undo the evaporator matrix retaining bolt.

11.44 Lower refrigerant line connection to the accumulator/dehydrator

11.47 Undo the accumulator/dehydrator mounting bolts

6 Undo the screws and remove the evaporator matrix lower housing.
7 Remove the evaporator matrix.
8 Remove the heater blower motor as described in Section 8.
9 Undo the screw and remove the heater blower motor resistor.
10 Release the clips and retaining tabs, and remove the heater blower motor upper housing.
11 Remove the gasket and release the retaining tabs, then separate the motor upper housing.
12 Remove the clips and release the retaining tabs, then separate the evaporator matrix housing.
13 Remove the clip and release the retaining tabs, then separate the heater and evaporator matrix housings.
14 Note their location, then pull out the three blend doors and shafts.

Reassembly

15 Reassembly is a reversal of dismantling.

Chapter 4 Part A:
Fuel and exhaust systems – petrol models

Contents

Degrees of difficulty

Easy, suitable for novice with little experience	**Fairly easy,** suitable for beginner with some experience	**Fairly difficult,** suitable for competent DIY mechanic	**Difficult,** suitable for experienced DIY mechanic	**Very difficult,** suitable for expert DIY or professional

Specifications

General

System type	Sequential multi-point Fuel injection (SFi)
Recommended fuel (minimum octane rating)	95 RON unleaded
Idle speed:	
4-cylinder engines	700± 50 rpm
V6 engine	725± 50 rpm
Idle mixture (CO level):	
4-cylinder engines	0.5% maximum
V6 engine	0.5% maximum

Intake air temperature sensor

Resistance:	
At –40°C	approximately 880 k ohms
At –20°C	approximately 272 k ohms
At 0°C	approximately 95 k ohms
At 20°C	approximately 38 k ohms
At 40°C	approximately 16 k ohms
At 60°C	approximately 7.5 k ohms
At 80°C	approximately 3.8 k ohms
At 100°C	approximately 2.2 k ohms
At 120°C	approximately 1.2 k ohms

Torque wrench settings

	Nm	lbf ft
Camshaft position sensor bolts (4-cylinder engines)	6	4
Crankshaft speed/position sensor:		
Sensor-to-bracket screw	8	6
Bracket-to-cylinder block crankcase screw	21	15
Exhaust system nuts and bolts	46	34
Fuel filter retaining bolts	10	7
Fuel pressure regulator bolts	6	4
Fuel pressure relief valve (V6 engine)	8	6
Fuel pump/gauge sender unit locking ring	85	63
Fuel rail:		
4-cylinder engines	25	18
V6 engine	10	7
Fuel tank support strap retaining bolts	25	18
Idle air control valve bolts	10	7
Intake air temperature sensor (V6 engine)	23	17
Intake manifold tuning valve	10	7
Throttle housing-to-inlet manifold screws	10	7

2.3a Fuel pressure relief valve cap on the fuel rail on the V6 engine

2.3b ... and on 4-cylinder engines

it dies through lack of fuel. Turn the engine over once or twice on the starter to ensure that all pressure is released, then switch off the ignition. Do not forget to refit the fuse when work is complete.

6 Note that, once the fuel system has been depressurised, it may take longer to restart the engine – perhaps several seconds of cranking – before the system is refilled and pressure restored.

1 General information and precautions

The fuel system consists of a plastic tank (mounted under the body, beneath the rear seats), fuel hoses and metal lines, an electric fuel pump mounted in the fuel tank, and an electronic fuel injection system.

The exhaust system consists of an exhaust manifold (or two on the V6 engine), front downpipe, catalytic converter(s) and a rear section incorporating two or three silencers. The service replacement exhaust system consists of three or four sections. The system is suspended throughout its entire length by rubber mountings.

Extreme caution should be exercised when dealing with either the fuel or exhaust systems. Fuel is a primary element for combustion. Be very careful! The exhaust system is an area for exercising caution, as it operates at very high temperatures. Serious burns can result from even momentary contact with any part of the exhaust system, and the fire risk is ever-present. The catalytic converter in particular runs at very high temperatures.

When removing the powertrain control module (PCM), do not touch the terminals as there is a chance that static electricity may damage the internal electronic components.

 Warning: Many of the procedures in this Chapter require the removal of fuel lines and

3.3 Disconnect fuel line quick-release coupling

connections, which may result in some fuel spillage. Before carrying out any operation on the fuel system, refer to the precautions given in 'Safety first!' at the beginning of this manual, and follow them implicitly. Petrol is a highly-dangerous and volatile liquid, and the precautions necessary when handling it cannot be overstressed.

2 Fuel system – depressurisation

 Warning: Refer to the warning note in Section 1 before proceeding.

1 The fuel system referred to in this Chapter is defined as the fuel tank and tank-mounted fuel pump/fuel gauge sender unit, the fuel filter, the fuel injectors and the pressure regulator in the injector rail, and the metal pipes and flexible hoses of the fuel lines between these components. All these contain fuel, which will be under pressure while the engine is running and/or while the ignition is switched on.

2 The pressure will remain for some time after the ignition has been switched off, and must be relieved before any of these components is disturbed for servicing work.

3 The Ford method of depressurisation is to use service tool 23-033 fitted to the fuel rail pressure test/release fitting. The fitting consists of a Schrader-type valve with a plastic cap located on the fuel rail (see illustrations), and the tool acts as a tap by depressing the valve core.

4 To release the pressure without using the service tool, use a suitable container and rag wrapped around the fitting to catch the fuel. Do not simply depress the valve core without wrapping rag around it, as fuel will spray out, with the consequent risk of fire, and personal injury.

5 An alternative method is simply to disconnect the fuel pump's electrical supply while the engine is running, by removing the fuel pump fuse (see Chapter 12, wiring diagrams), and to allow the engine to idle until

3 Fuel lines and fittings – general information

 Warning: Refer to the warning note in Section 1 before proceeding.

1 Quick-release couplings are employed at all unions in the fuel feed and return lines. **Note:** *Fuel supply line connectors are identified by white quick-release coupling connector and the return lines are identified by a red quick-release coupling connector.*

2 Before disconnecting any fuel system component, relieve the pressure in the system as described in Section 2, and equalise tank pressure by removing the fuel filler cap.

3 Release the protruding locking lugs on each fuel line union, by squeezing them together and carefully pulling the coupling apart **(see illustration)**. Use rag to soak up any spilt fuel. Where the unions are colour-coded, the pipes cannot be confused. Where both unions are the same colour, note carefully which pipe is connected to which, and ensure that they are correctly reconnected on refitting.

4 If there are no locking lugs on the fuel line union, then a special tool to release the quick-release fitting is required – the tool expands the internal coil spring so that the two sections of the fitting can be disconnected. A home-made tool can be made out of a coiled piece of plastic around the fuel pipe, which may then be slid along the fuel pipe into the union to release the coil spring.

5 To reconnect one of these couplings, press them together until they are locked. Switch the ignition on to pressurise the system, and check for any sign of fuel leakage around the disturbed coupling before attempting to start the engine.

6 Checking procedures for the fuel lines are included in Chapter 1A.

7 Always use genuine fuel lines and hoses when renewing sections of the fuel system. Do not fit substitutes constructed from inferior or inappropriate material, or you could cause a fuel leak or a fire.

8 Before disconnecting any part of the fuel system, note the routing of all hoses and pipes, and the orientation of all clamps and clips to ensure correct refitting.

4 Air cleaner assembly and ducts – removal and refitting

Air cleaner assembly

4-cylinder engines

1 Disconnect the battery negative (earth) lead (refer to *Disconnecting the battery* at the end of this manual).
2 Undo the retaining clip and disconnect the air outlet pipe and breather hose from the air cleaner upper housing **(see illustration)**.
3 Withdraw the air cleaner assembly, lifting it upwards out of its grommets, and releasing it from the air intake pipe under the inner wing panel.
4 Refitting is the reverse of the removal procedure. Ensure that the housing pegs seat correctly in their grommets, and that the air intake pipe is fully engaged with the air cleaner housing.

V6 engine

5 Disconnect the battery negative (earth) lead (refer to *Disconnecting the battery* at the end of this manual).
6 Disconnect the wiring from the air flow sensor **(see illustration overleaf)**.
7 Disconnect the air bypass hose and the crankcase ventilation hoses from the air cleaner assembly.
8 Loosen the securing clip and disconnect the air outlet hose from the air cleaner housing.
9 Lift the air cleaner from its location grommets, and at the same time disconnect the intake pipe from the left-hand side.
10 Refitting is the reverse of the removal procedure. Ensure that the housing pegs seat correctly in their grommets, and that the air intake pipe and ventilation hoses are fully engaged with the air cleaner housing assembly.

J35123

4.2 Air cleaner assembly and ducts (4-cylinder engines)

1 Air cleaner outlet pipe	4 Air cleaner housing	7 Air Intake resonator box
2 Air cleaner housing cover	5 Air intake tuning pipe	8 Air cleaner intake pipe
3 Air cleaner element	6 Air cleaner intake pipe	

Air intake resonator

4-cylinder engine

11 Remove the air cleaner housing as described at the beginning of this Section.

12 Undo the air intake pipe upper retaining bolt from the left-hand inner wing.

13 Chock the rear wheels, then jack up the front of the vehicle and support on axle stands (see *Jacking and vehicle support*).

14 Remove the left-hand front wheel and inner wheel arch liner (Chapter 11).

15 From under the left-hand front wing, withdraw the upper intake pipe and tuning pipe from the resonator box.

16 Undo the retaining bolts and remove the resonator box from under the left-hand wing. Where applicable, disconnect the foglight's wiring block connector from the clip on the resonator box.

17 To remove the lower air intake pipe, remove the radiator grille as described in Chapter 11.

18 Refitting is the reverse of the removal procedure.

Air intake pipes

V6 engine

19 Carry out the procedures for removing and refitting of the resonator box on the 4-cylinder engines in this Section, except in paragraph 16, undo the retaining bolts and remove the air intake pipes from under the left-hand wing.

20 Refitting is the reverse of the removal procedure.

---

5 Accelerator cable –
removal and refitting

4-cylinder engine

Removal

1 Unclip the breather hose from the engine upper plastic cover, then unclip the cover from the top of the engine.

4.6 Air cleaner assembly and ducts (V6 engine)

1 Air cleaner outlet pipe	3 Air cleaner housing cover	5 Air cleaner housing
2 Mass air flow sensor	4 Air cleaner element	6 Air intake tuning pipe
		7 Air cleaner intake pipes

J35124

5.2a Unclip the accelerator inner cable from the throttle linkage . . .

5.2b . . . then twist the outer cable to release it from the bracket

5.3 Release the cable (arrowed) from the slot in the top of the pedal

2 Unclip the accelerator inner cable from the throttle linkage, then twist the outer cable to release it from the bracket **(see illustrations)**. Release the cable from any securing clips or ties.

3 Working in the passenger compartment, reach up to the top of the accelerator pedal. Pull the end fitting and collar out of the pedal, then release the cable inner wire through the slot in the pedal **(see illustration)**. Tie a length of string to the end of the cable.

4 Returning to the engine compartment, pull the cable through the bulkhead until the string can be untied and the cable removed.

Refitting

5 Refitting is the reverse of the removal procedure; use the string to draw the cable through the bulkhead.

V6 engine

Note: *While the following procedure deals with the complete cable, the pedal-to-actuator and actuator-to-throttle housing sections of the cable are available separately, and can be removed and refitted individually. If doing this, modify the procedure as required.*

Removal

6 The accelerator cable consists of a primary and secondary cable. The primary cable is attached to the accelerator pedal and traction control unit actuator. The secondary cable is attached to the traction control unit actuator and throttle housing quadrant.

7 Pull out the clip and lift the secondary outer cable from the support bracket **(see illustration)**.

8 Disconnect the inner cable from the quadrant or lever on the throttle housing. Where necessary, prise off the spring clip first **(see illustrations)**.

9 Unhook the secondary cable from the front support clip.

10 Disconnect the wiring from the traction control motor.

11 Carefully remove the cover from the traction control motor.

12 Disconnect the secondary inner cable from the motor upper quadrant, then detach the secondary cable from the bracket on the motor.

13 Release the cable tie, and disconnect the primary inner cable from the motor lower

quadrant. Detach the primary cable from the bracket on the motor.

14 Inside the car, disconnect the primary inner cable from the accelerator pedal. Tie a length of string to the end of the cable.

15 Returning to the engine compartment, pull the cable through the bulkhead until the string can be untied and the pedal-to-actuator cable removed.

Refitting

16 Refitting is the reverse of the removal procedure. Use the string to draw the pedal-to-actuator cable through the bulkhead. Ensure that each cable end is connected to the correct actuator quadrant.

Adjustment

Note: *Both sections of the cable must be adjusted together, even if only one has been disturbed.*

17 Remove the metal clip from the adjuster

5.7 Outer cable and adjustment ferrule

of each cable section **(see illustration)**, and lubricate the adjusters' grommets with soapy water.

18 Remove any slack by pulling both outer cables as far as possible out of their respective adjusters.

19 Unplug the TCS throttle actuator's electrical connector, and prise off its cover. Lock both pulleys together by pushing a locking pin (a pin punch or a similar tool of suitable size) into their alignment holes. Disconnect the actuator-to-throttle housing cable's end nipple from the throttle linkage.

20 Have an assistant depress the accelerator pedal fully. The pedal-to-actuator cable outer will move back into the adjuster; hold it there, and refit the clip.

21 Connect the actuator-to-throttle housing cable end nipple to the throttle linkage, and check that the outer cable grommet is correctly secured in the housing bracket.

5.8a Prise off the spring clip . . .

5.8b . . . and disconnect the inner cable from the lever

5.17 Location of TCS throttle actuator-to-throttle housing cable adjuster (arrowed)

6.2 Undo the retaining nuts and bolt (arrowed) to remove the accelerator pedal assembly

22 Again have the assistant depress the accelerator pedal fully. The actuator-to-throttle housing cable outer will move back into the adjuster; hold it there, and refit the clip.

23 Remove the locking pin from the pulleys. Check that the throttle valve moves smoothly and easily from the fully-closed to the fully-open position and back again, as the assistant depresses and releases the accelerator pedal. Re-adjust the cable(s) if required.

24 When the setting is correct, refit the TCS throttle actuator's cover and electrical connector.

6 Accelerator pedal – removal and refitting

Removal

1 Working in the driver's footwell, reach up to the top of the accelerator pedal. Pull the end fitting and collar out of the pedal, then release the inner cable from the slot in the pedal.

2 Undo the retaining nuts and bolt, then withdraw the pedal assembly **(see illustration)**.

Refitting

3 Refitting is a reversal of removal. On V6 models, check the correct fitment of the accelerator cable as described in Section 5.

J35125

8.2 Ford service tool used to release the fuel pump/sender locking ring

7 Fuel pump/fuel pressure – check

⚠ *Warning: Refer to the warning note in Section 1 before proceeding.*

Fuel pump operation check

1 Switch on the ignition and listen for the fuel pump (the sound of an electric motor running, audible from beneath the rear seats). Assuming there is sufficient fuel in the tank, the pump should start and run for several seconds, then stop. **Note:** *If the pump runs continuously all the time the ignition is switched on, the electronic control system is running in the back-up (or 'limp-home') mode referred to by Ford as 'Limited Operation Strategy' (LOS). This almost certainly indicates a fault in the Powertrain Control Module (PCM) itself, and the vehicle should therefore be taken to a Ford dealer for a full test of the complete system, using the correct diagnostic equipment; do not waste time trying to test the system without such facilities.*

2 Listen for fuel return noises from the fuel pressure regulator. It should be possible to feel the fuel pulsing in the regulator and in the feed hose from the fuel filter. If the pump does not run at all, check the fuse, relay and wiring (see Chapter 12).

Fuel pressure check

3 A fuel pressure gauge, equipped with an adaptor to suit the Schrader-type valve on the fuel rail pressure test/release fitting (identifiable by its blue plastic cap, and located on the union of the fuel feed line and the fuel rail) is required for the following procedure. If the Ford special tool 23-033 is available (see Section 2), the tool can be attached to the valve, and a conventional-type pressure gauge attached to the tool.

4 If using the service tool, ensure that its tap is turned fully anti-clockwise, then attach it to the valve. Connect the pressure gauge to the service tool. If using a fuel pressure gauge with its own adaptor, connect it in accordance with its maker's instructions.

5 Start the engine and allow it to idle. Note the gauge reading as soon as the pressure stabilises, and compare it with the manufacturer's recommendations.

   a) *If the pressure is high, check for a restricted fuel return line. If the line is clear, where fitted renew the pressure regulator.*

   b) *If the pressure is low, pinch the fuel return line. If the pressure now goes up, where fitted renew the fuel pressure regulator. If the pressure does not increase, check the fuel feed line, the fuel pump and the fuel filter.*

6 Where applicable, detach the vacuum hose from the fuel pressure regulator; the pressure shown on the gauge should increase. Note the increase in pressure, and compare it with manufacturer's recommendations. If the pressure increase is not as specified, check the vacuum hose and pressure regulator.

7 Reconnect the regulator vacuum hose, and switch off the engine. Verify that the fuel pressure stays at the specified level for five minutes after the engine is turned off.

8 Carefully disconnect the fuel pressure gauge. Be sure to cover the fitting with a rag before slackening it. Mop up any spilt petrol.

9 Run the engine, and check that there are no fuel leaks.

8 Fuel pump/gauge sender unit – removal and refitting

⚠ *Warning: Refer to the warning note in Section 1 before proceeding.*

Note: *Ford specify the use of their service tool 310-069 (a large box spanner with projecting teeth to engage the fuel pump/sender unit retaining ring's slots) for this task. While alternatives are possible, as shown below, in view of the difficulty experienced in removing and refitting the pump/sender unit, owners are strongly advised to obtain this tool before starting work. The help of an assistant will be required.*

Removal

1 Remove the fuel tank as described in Section 9.

2 Release the fuel pump/sender unit's retaining ring by turning it anti-clockwise. As noted above, Ford recommend the use of service tool 310-069. For those without access to such equipment, a hammer and drift, or a pair of slip-jointed pliers, may serve as a substitute **(see illustration)**.

3 Rotate the fuel pump/fuel gauge sender unit anti-clockwise and withdraw it from the fuel tank, taking care not to damage the float arm. The float arm is mounted on a spring-loaded extension, to hold it closely against the bottom of the tank. Note the sealing ring; this must be renewed whenever it is disturbed.

Refitting

4 On refitting, ensure that the sender unit is not damaged, and that the gauze filter over the base of the pump pick-up is clean.

5 Insert the fuel pump/sender unit into the fuel tank so that the arrows on the fuel tank and pump/sender unit are correctly aligned.

6 Use a new sealing ring, when refitting the fuel pump/sender unit's retaining ring (Ford service tool provides the best way of holding the ring square to the tank and turning it at the same time).

7 The remainder of the fuel tank refitting procedure is the reverse of removal as described in Section 9.

9 Fuel tank –
removal, inspection and refitting

⚠️ **Warning: Refer to the warning note in Section 1 before proceeding.**

Removal

1 A fuel tank drain plug is not provided, therefore it is preferable to carry out the removal operation when the tank is nearly empty **(see illustration)**. First depressurise the fuel system as described in Section 2, and equalise the tank pressure by removing the fuel filler cap.

2 Syphon or hand-pump the remaining fuel from the tank. Alternatively, position a clean container beneath the fuel filter, then disconnect the feed pipe and connect a length of hose from the filter to the container. Switch on the ignition and allow the fuel pump to empty the tank into the container. Be sure to take all necessary precautions to prevent the risk of fire. Reconnect the hose after draining the tank.

3 Make sure the ignition is switched off.

4 Unbolt or fold forwards (as appropriate) the rear seat base cushion (see Chapter 11). Prise the grommet from the floor for access to the fuel pump/sender unit **(see illustration)**.

5 Disconnect the wiring from the fuel pump/sender unit, also disconnect the fuel supply and return pipes from the unit **(see illustration)**. If the fuel lines are not marked, clearly label them, and their respective unions. Plug the hoses, to prevent leakage and contamination of the fuel system.

6 Chock the front wheels, then jack up the rear of the vehicle and support on axle stands (see *Jacking and vehicle support*).

7 Remove the fuel filter as described in Chapter 1A.

8 Unhook the exhaust system rubber mountings. Lower the system onto a suitable support, so that the front downpipe-to-exhaust manifold joint is not strained, or remove it completely as described in Section 14.

9 Unscrew the retaining nuts, and withdraw the exhaust system's rear heat shield from the underbody.

10 On models with headlamp levelling sensor fitted, remove the sensor as described in Chapter 12.

11 Unbolt the rear suspension anti-roll bar connecting links. Lower the bar down as far as possible – if preferred, remove the bar completely (see Chapter 10).

12 Support the tank with a trolley jack and block of wood.

13 Unscrew the bolt at the front of each retaining strap, then rotate the straps (twist them through 90°) at the other end to release them from the vehicle. Check that the straps and their locations in the underbody are in good condition.

9.1 Fuel tank – system layout

1 Fuel pump/sender unit
2 Fuel tank
3 Filler pipe lower retaining bolts
4 Filler pipe upper retaining bolt
5 Fuel tank filler pipe
6 Filler pipe breather hose
7 Heat shield – Estate models
8 Fuel tank heat shield
9 Heat shield retaining clips
10 Fuel tank support straps
11 Support strap retaining bolts
12 Support strap insulator
13 Fuel filter – petrol models
14 Fuel pump – diesel models (engine code D6BA)

9.4 Prise the grommet from the floor to access to the fuel pump/sender unit wiring

9.5 Note the fuel line ends may be colour-coded to enable refitting

10.3 Fuel cut-off switch retaining screws (arrowed)

14 Lower the tank enough to disconnect the charcoal canister's vapour hose from the union at the top rear of the tank. Release the locking lugs and disconnect the fuel filler pipe neck from the fuel tank.

15 Make sure there are no fuel pipes or wiring connectors still connected. Remove the tank from the vehicle, releasing it from the filler neck stub.

Caution: Take care when lowering the fuel tank, as there will still be some fuel left inside. This will cause the weight of the tank to alter as the fuel moves around the tank.

16 If required the fuel tank filler neck can be removed. It is secured by a single screw in the filler opening, and by two bolts to the underbody. **Note:** *On some models it may be necessary to lower the rear crossmember slightly, to give access for the filler neck to be removed (see Chapter 10, for information on the rear crossmember).*

Inspection

17 Check the fuel tank for damage. Any sediment inside the tank should be removed, either by swilling out with clean fuel or by steam cleaning.

18 Any repairs to the fuel tank or filler neck should be carried out by a professional who has experience in this critical and potentially-dangerous work. Even after cleaning and flushing of the fuel system, explosive fumes can remain and ignite during repair of the tank.

Refitting

19 Refitting is a reversal of removal.

10 Fuel cut-off switch – removal and refitting

Removal

1 Disconnect the battery negative (earth) lead (refer to *Disconnecting the battery* at the end of this manual).

2 Remove the trim panel from the left-hand footwell.

3 Peel back the sound-insulating material from the switch, and undo the two retaining screws **(see illustration)**.

4 Disconnect the wiring, and withdraw the switch.

Refitting

5 Refitting is the reverse of the removal procedure. Ensure that the switch is reset by depressing its red button.

11 Fuel injection system – general description

1 All petrol models are equipped with a Sequential Electronically-controlled Fuel Injection system. The engine management system on the 1.8 and 2.0 litre engines, control the sequential multi-point fuel injection (SFI), the electrically-heated thermostat and the electronically-controlled water-cooled exhaust gas recirculation (EGR) valve.

Fuel supply and air induction

2 An electric fuel pump located inside the fuel tank supplies fuel under pressure to the fuel rail, which distributes fuel to the injectors. A filter between the fuel pump and the fuel rail protects the components of the system. A pressure regulator controls the system pressure in relation to inlet depression. From the fuel rail, fuel is injected into the inlet ports, just above the inlet valves, by four fuel injectors.

3 The amount of fuel supplied by the injectors is precisely controlled by the Powertrain Control Module (PCM). The PCM uses the signals from the engine speed/crankshaft position sensor and the camshaft position sensor, to trigger each injector separately in cylinder firing order (sequential injection).

4 The air induction system consists of an air filter housing, a Mass Air Flow (MAF) sensor on V6 engines, a Temperature and Manifold Absolute Pressure (T-MAP) sensor on 4-cylinder engines, intake ducting, and a throttle housing. The MAF and T-MAP sensors are information-gathering devices for the PCM. The MAF sensor measures the volume and temperature of the air passing through the air intake pipe into the engine. The T-MAP sensor measures the air pressure

11.6a Location of principal fuel injection, ignition and emissions control system components on 4-cylinder models

1 *Camshaft position sensor*	4 *Idle air control valve*
2 *Engine coolant temperature sensor*	5 *Intake manifold tuning valve*
3 *Throttle position sensor*	6 *Temperature and manifold absolute pressure sensor*

and temperature in the intake manifold. The PCM uses these signals to calculate the mass/pressure of the air entering the engine.
5 The throttle valve inside the throttle housing is controlled by the driver, through the accelerator pedal. As the valve opens, the

quantity of air entering the engine increases. The throttle potentiometer is attached to the throttle valve and informs the PCM of the throttle position. The PCM calculates the relevant period of injection, and controls the injector opening times.

Electronic control system

6 The 'Black Oak' engine management system controls the fuel injection by means of a microcomputer known as the PCM (Power-train Control Module) (see illustrations). The

11.6b Location of principal fuel injection, ignition and emissions control system components on V6 models

1   Ignition coil
2   Electronic vacuum regulator
3   Idle air control valve (IAC)
4   Exhaust Gas Recirculation (EGR) valve
5   Electronic differential pressure sensor (DPFE)
6   Intake air temperature sensor (IAT)

7   Air cleaner
8   Battery junction box
9   Mass air flow sensor (MAF)
10 Coolant temperature sensor (ECT)
11 Throttle housing and throttle position sensor (TP)
12 Water pump drivebelt cover
13 Heated oxygen sensor (HO2S)

14 Front catalytic converter (rear on rear exhaust manifold)
15 Inlet manifold runner control (IMRC)
16 Upper inlet manifold
17 Camshaft position sensor (CMP)
18 Crankshaft position sensor (CKP)

19 Hydraulic engine mounting
20 Right-hand engine mounting
21 Power steering pressure switch (PSPS)
22 Power train control module (PCM) or Electronic control unit (ECU)
23 Service plug (octane adjustment)

PCM receives signals from a number of sensors, which monitor the intake air mass/pressure and temperature, coolant temperature, camshaft and crankshaft position, throttle position, and exhaust gas oxygen content. The signals are processed by the PCM to determine the injection duration necessary for the optimum air/fuel ratio. The sensors and associated PCM-controlled relays are located throughout the engine compartment.

7 In the event of a sensor malfunction, a back-up circuit will take over, to provide driveability until the problem is identified and fixed. The following paragraphs describe the components of the electronic control system.

Powertrain Control Module

8 This component is the heart of the entire engine management system, controlling the fuel injection, ignition and emissions control systems. It also controls sub-systems such as the radiator cooling fan, air conditioning and automatic transmission, where appropriate.

Mass Air Flow sensor

V6 engine

9 This uses a 'hot-wire' system, sending the PCM a constantly-varying (analogue) voltage signal corresponding to the mass of air passing into the engine. Since air mass varies with temperature (cold air being denser than warm), measuring air mass provides the PCM with a very accurate means of determining the correct amount of fuel required to achieve the ideal air/fuel mixture ratio.

Temperature and Manifold Absolute Pressure sensor

4-cylinder engines

10 The T-MAP sensor measures the temperature and air pressure in the intake manifold. The PCM then uses these signals to calculate the pressure of the air in the manifold. Manifold absolute pressure is calculated from the formula:

Atmospheric Pressure minus Manifold Pressure = Manifold Absolute Pressure

When the manifold vacuum is high (eg, engine at idle), manifold absolute pressure is low and the PCM provides less fuel. When the manifold vacuum is low (eg, throttle wide open), manifold absolute pressure is high and the PCM provides more fuel.

Crankshaft speed/position sensor

11 This is an inductive pulse generator bolted to the timing chain cover. The sensor scans cut-outs machined on a timing disc located on the timing chain end of the crankshaft. The ridge between the 35th and 36th holes (corresponding to 50° BTDC) is missing – this step in the incoming signals is used by the PCM to determine crankshaft (ie, piston) position.

Camshaft position sensor

12 On 4-cylinder models the camshaft position sensor is bolted to the front left-hand end of the camshaft cover, and is triggered by a high-point on the inlet camshaft. On V6 models, the camshaft position sensor is mounted on the right-hand side of the front cylinder head and is triggered by a high-point on the front inlet camshaft. The sensor functions in the same way as the crankshaft speed/position sensor, producing a series of pulses. This gives the PCM a reference point, to enable it to determine the firing order, and operate the injectors in the appropriate sequence.

Coolant temperature sensor

13 This component, which is screwed into the coolant housing on the left-hand end of the cylinder head on 4-cylinder models or into the coolant crossover on V6 models, is an NTC (Negative Temperature Coefficient) thermistor – that is, a semi-conductor whose electrical resistance decreases as its temperature increases. It provides the PCM with a constantly-varying (analogue) voltage signal, corresponding to the temperature of the engine coolant. This is used to refine the calculations made by the PCM, when determining the correct amount of fuel required to achieve the ideal air/fuel mixture ratio.

Intake air temperature sensor

14 On 4-cylinder models, this component is part of the temperature and manifold absolute pressure (T-MAP) sensor which is fitted into the intake manifold. On V6 models it is located in the air cleaner housing cover with the mass air flow (MAF) sensor. The sensor is an NTC thermistor – see the previous paragraph – providing the PCM with a signal corresponding to the temperature of air passing into the engine. This is used to refine the calculations made by the PCM, when determining the correct amount of fuel required to achieve the ideal air/fuel mixture ratio.

Throttle potentiometer

15 This is mounted on the end of the throttle valve spindle, to provide the PCM with a constantly-varying (analogue) voltage signal corresponding to the throttle opening. This allows the PCM to register the driver's input when determining the amount of fuel required by the engine.

Vehicle speed sensor

16 This component is a Hall-effect generator, mounted on the transmission's speedometer drive. It supplies the PCM with a series of pulses corresponding to the vehicle's road speed, enabling the PCM to control features such as the fuel shut-off on the overrun, and to provide information for the trip computer, adaptive damping and cruise control systems (where fitted).

Power steering pressure switch

17 This is a pressure-operated switch, screwed into the power steering system's high-pressure pipe. Its contacts are normally closed, opening when the system reaches the specified pressure – on receiving this signal, the PCM increases the idle speed, to compensate for the additional load on the engine.

Air conditioning system

18 Two pressure-operated switches and the compressor clutch solenoid are connected to the PCM, to enable it to determine how the system is operating. The PCM can increase idle speed or switch off the system, as necessary, so that normal vehicle operation and driveability are not impaired. Fault diagnosis and repair should be left to a dealer service department or air conditioning specialist.

Idle air control valve

19 The idle air control (IAC) valve maintains a stable idle speed by varying the quantity of air entering the engine through an auxiliary air passage. The valve is activated by a signal from the PCM.

Intake manifold runner control actuator

4-cylinder engines

20 The intake manifold runner control (IMRC) actuator, operates four (one for each cylinder) plates in the passageways of the intake manifold. These plates are called swirl plates and reduce the cross-section of the intake passages at low speeds, this increases the intake air swirl to make the mixture ignite more efficiently around the spark plug area. This in turn will reduce exhaust emissions and fuel consumption.

Intake manifold tuning valve

4-cylinder engines

21 The intake manifold tuning (IMT) valve controls the intake manifold runner control actuator via a vacuum pipe, this will then give the correct position of the swirl plates depending on the vacuum in the intake manifold.

Automatic transmission sensors

22 In addition to the driver's controls, the 4-speed transmission has a speed sensor, a fluid temperature sensor (built into the solenoid valve unit), and a selector lever position sensor. All of these are connected to the PCM, to enable it to control the transmission through the solenoid valve unit. On 5-speed transmissions, there is a selector lever position sensor and a Transmission Control Module (TCM). See Chapter 7B for further details.

Exhaust gas oxygen sensor

23 The oxygen sensor in the exhaust system provides the PCM with constant feedback – 'closed-loop' control – which enables it to adjust the mixture to provide the best possible conditions for the catalytic converter to operate. Refer to Chapter 4C for more information.

12 Fuel injection system – checking and fault diagnosis

 Warning: Refer to the warning note in Section 1 before proceeding.

Checking

1 Check all earth wire connections for tightness. Check all wiring and electrical connectors that are related to the system. Loose electrical connectors and poor earth connections can cause many problems that resemble more serious malfunctions.

2 Check that the battery is fully-charged and its leads tightened correctly. The PCM and sensors depend on an accurate supply voltage to properly meter the fuel.

3 Check the air filter element – a dirty or partially-blocked filter will severely impede performance and economy (see Chapter 1A).

4 Referring to the information given in Chapter 12 and in the wiring diagrams at the back of this manual, check that all fuses protecting the circuits related to the engine management system are in good condition. Fit new fuses if required, and at the same time check that all relays are securely plugged into their sockets.

5 Check the air intake ducts for leaks. Also check the condition of the vacuum hoses connected to the inlet manifold.

6 Disconnect the air ducting from the throttle housing, and check the throttle valve for dirt, carbon or residue. **Note:** *A warning label on the housing states specifically that the housing bore and the throttle valve have a special coating, and must not be cleaned using carburettor cleaner, as this may damage it.*

7 With the engine running, place a screwdriver or a stethoscope against each injector, one at a time. Listen for a clicking sound, indicating correct operation.

8 If an injector is not operating correctly, turn off the engine, and unplug the electrical connector from the injector. Check the resistance across the terminals of the injector, and compare your reading with the relevant Ford specifications. If the resistance is not as specified, renew the injector.

9 A rough idle, diminished performance and/or increased fuel consumption could also be caused by clogged or fouled fuel injectors. Fuel additives to clean fouled injectors are available at car accessory shops.

10 If these checks fail to reveal the cause of the problem, the vehicle should be taken to a suitably-equipped Ford dealer for testing. A wiring block connector is incorporated in the engine management circuit, into which a special electronic diagnostic tester can be plugged. The tester will locate the fault quickly and simply, alleviating the need to test all the system components individually, which is a time-consuming operation that also carries a risk of damaging the PCM.

Powertrain Control Module

11 Do not attempt to 'test' the PCM with any kind of equipment. If it is thought to be faulty, take the vehicle to a Ford dealer for the entire electronic control system to be checked using the proper diagnostic equipment. Only if all other possibilities have been eliminated should the PCM be considered at fault, and renewed.

Mass air flow sensor

12 Testing of this component is beyond the scope of the DIY mechanic, and should be left to a Ford dealer.

Temperature and Manifold Absolute Pressure sensor

13 Testing of this component is beyond the scope of the DIY mechanic, and should be left to a Ford dealer.

Crankshaft speed/position sensor

14 Unplug the electrical connector from the sensor.

15 Using an ohmmeter, measure the resistance between the sensor terminals. Compare this reading to the one Ford specify, if the indicated resistance is not within the specified range, renew the sensor.

16 Plug in the sensor's electrical connector on completion.

Camshaft position sensor

17 The procedure is as described in paragraphs 14 to 16 above.

Coolant temperature sensor

18 Refer to Chapter 3.

Intake air temperature sensor

19 Unplug the electrical connector from the sensor.

20 Using an ohmmeter, measure the resistance between the sensor terminals. Depending on the temperature of the sensor tip, the resistance measured will vary, but it should be within the broad limits given in the Specifications Section of this Chapter. If the sensor's temperature is varied – by placing it in a freezer for a while, or by warming it gently – its resistance should alter accordingly.

21 If the results obtained show the sensor to be faulty, renew it.

Throttle potentiometer

22 Remove the engine plastic cover, where necessary and unplug the potentiometer's electrical connector.

23 Using an ohmmeter, measure the resistance between the unit's terminals – first between the centre terminal and one of the outer two, then from the centre to the remaining outer terminal. The resistance should be within the limits given in Ford specifications, and should alter smoothly as the throttle valve is moved from the fully-closed (idle speed) position to fully open and back again.

24 If the resistance measured is significantly different from the specified value, if there are any breaks in continuity, or if the reading fluctuates erratically as the throttle is operated, the potentiometer is faulty, and must be renewed.

Vehicle speed sensor

25 Testing of this component is beyond the scope of the DIY mechanic, and should be left to a Ford dealer.

Power steering pressure switch

26 Unplug the electrical connector from the sensor.

27 Using an ohmmeter, measure the resistance between the switch terminals. With the engine switched off, or idling with the roadwheels in the straight-ahead position, little or no resistance should be measured. With the engine running and the steering on full-lock, the pressure increase in the system should open the switch contacts, so that infinite resistance is now measured.

28 If the results obtained show the switch to be faulty, renew it.

Idle air control valve

29 Disconnect the wiring from the idle speed control valve, then connect a 12 volt supply to the valve terminals – positive to terminal 37 and negative to terminal 21. A distinct click should be heard each time contact is made and broken. If not, measure the resistance between the terminals. If the resistance is not as specified, renew the valve.

Intake manifold runner control actuator

30 The intake manifold runner control actuator is vacuum operated, check the vacuum pipe for splits and correct fitting, also check to make sure the pipes are not blocked. Check the actuator linkage to the swirl plates for free movement. **Note:** *The swirl plates should be in the closed position, when the engine is switched off.*

Intake manifold tuning valve

31 The intake manifold tuning valve is electrically operated and controls the vacuum, check the vacuum pipes for splits and correct fitting, also check to make sure the pipes are not blocked.

Fault diagnosis

32 The various components of the fuel, ignition and emissions control systems (not forgetting the same PCM's control of sub-systems such as the radiator cooling fan, air conditioning and automatic transmission, where appropriate) are so closely interlinked that diagnosis of a faulty component may be almost impossible to trace using traditional methods.

33 To quickly and accurately find faults, the PCM is provided with a built-in self-diagnosis facility, which detects malfunctions in the system's components. When a fault occurs, the PCM identifies the fault and stores it in its memory, and (in most cases) runs the system using back-up values preprogrammed ('mapped') into its memory. Good driveability is thus maintained, to enable the vehicle to be driven to a garage for attention.

34 Any faults that may have occurred are stored in the PCM, when the system is connected (via the built-in diagnosis socket) to special Ford diagnostic equipment (FDS2000) – this points the user in the direction of the faulty circuit, so that further tests can pinpoint the exact location of the fault.

35 Given below is the procedure that would be followed by a Ford technician to trace a fault from scratch. Should your vehicle's engine management system develop a fault, read through the procedure and decide how much you can attempt, depending on your skill and experience and the equipment available to you, or whether it would be simpler to have the vehicle attended to by your local Ford dealer.

 a) *Preliminary checks.*
 b) *Fault code or description read-out*.*
 c) *Check ignition timing and base idle speed. Recheck fault codes to establish whether fault has been cured or not*.*
 d) *Carry out basic check of ignition system components. Recheck fault codes to establish whether fault has been cured or not*.*
 e) *Carry out basic check of fuel system components. Recheck fault codes to establish whether fault has been cured or not*.*
 f) *If fault is still not located, carry out system test*.*

* Operations marked with an asterisk require special test Ford diagnostic equipment.

Preliminary checks

Note: *When carrying out these checks to trace a fault, remember that if the fault has appeared only a short time after any part of the vehicle has been serviced or overhauled, the first place to check is where that work was carried out, however unrelated it may appear, to ensure that no carelessly-refitted components are causing the problem.*

36 If you are tracing the cause of a 'partial' engine fault, such as lack of performance, in addition to the checks outlined below, check the compression pressures (see the relevant Part of Chapter 2) and bear in mind the possibility that, on V6 models, one of the hydraulic tappets might be faulty, producing an incorrect valve clearance. Check also that the fuel filter has been renewed at the recommended intervals.

37 If the system appears to be completely dead, remember the possibility that the alarm/inhibitor system may be responsible.

38 The first check for anyone without special test equipment is to switch on the ignition, and to listen for the fuel pump (the sound of an electric motor running, audible from beneath the rear seats); assuming there is sufficient fuel in the tank, the pump should start and run for approximately one or two seconds, then stop. If the pump runs continuously all the time the ignition is switched on, the electronic control system is running in the back-up (or 'limp-home') mode referred to by Ford as 'Limited

Operation Strategy' (LOS). This almost certainly indicates a fault in the PCM itself, and the vehicle should therefore be taken to a Ford dealer for a full test of the complete system using the correct diagnostic equipment; do not waste time trying to test the system without such facilities.

39 After checking the fuel pump, a considerable amount of fault diagnosis is still possible without special test equipment. Refer to the information given at the beginning of this Section.

40 Working methodically around the engine compartment, check carefully that all vacuum hoses and pipes are securely fastened and correctly routed, with no signs of cracks, splits or deterioration to cause air leaks, or of hoses that are trapped, kinked, or bent sharply enough to restrict air flow. Check all connections and sharp bends, and renew any damaged or deformed lengths of hose.

41 Working from the fuel tank, via the filter, to the fuel rail (and including the feed and return), check the fuel lines, and renew any that are found to be leaking, trapped or kinked.

42 Check that the accelerator cable is correctly secured and adjusted; renew the cable if there is any doubt about its condition, or if it appears to be stiff or jerky in operation. Refer to the Section 5 for further information, if required.

43 If there is any doubt about the operation of the throttle, remove the air ducting from the throttle housing, and check that the throttle valve moves smoothly and easily from the fully-closed to the fully-open position and back again, as an assistant depresses the accelerator pedal. If the valve shows any sign of stiffness, sticking or otherwise-inhibited movement (and the accelerator cable is known to be in good condition), spray the throttle linkage with penetrating lubricant, allow time for it to work, and repeat the check.

44 Run the engine at idle speed. Working from the air intake at the inner wing panel, check the air inlet ducting for air leaks. Usually, these will be revealed by sucking or hissing noises. If a leak is found at any point, tighten the fastening clamp and/or renew the faulty components, as applicable.

45 Check the exhaust system for leaks with reference to Section 14.

46 It is possible to make a further check of the electrical connections by wiggling each electrical connector of the system in turn as the engine is idling; a faulty connector will be immediately evident from the engine's response as contact is broken and remade.

47 Switch off the engine. If the fault is not yet identified, the next step is to check the ignition voltages, using an engine analyser with an oscilloscope – without such equipment, the only tests possible are to remove and check each spark plug in turn, to check the spark plug (HT) lead connections and resistances, and to check the connections and resistances of the ignition coil. Refer to the relevant Sections of Chapters 1A and 5B.

48 The final step in these preliminary checks would be to use an exhaust gas analyser to measure the CO level at the exhaust tailpipe. This check cannot be made without special test equipment – see your local Ford dealer for details.

Fault diagnostic equipment

Note: *The Ford FDS 2000 tester must be used, this tester will display the fault without reference to a fault code.*

Caution: Do not use the STAR tester – only use the FDS2000 tester.

49 The preliminary checks outlined above should eliminate the majority of faults from the engine management system. If the fault is not yet identified, the next step is to connect the (FDS2000) Ford diagnostic equipment. This will guide the technician through a procedure, then direct him to a specific area for investigation and to rectify the fault.

Basic check of fuel system

50 If the checks so far have not eliminated the fault, the next step is to carry out a basic check of the fuel system components.

51 Assuming that the preliminary checks have established that the fuel pump is operating correctly, that the fuel filter is unlikely to be blocked, and also that there are no leaks in the system, the next step is to check the fuel pressure (see Section 7). If this is correct, check the injectors (see beginning of this Section) and the Positive Crankcase Ventilation system.

Idle speed and mixture

52 Both the idle speed and mixture are under the control of the PCM, and cannot be adjusted. The settings can only be checked using special diagnostic equipment.

53 If the idle speed and mixture are thought to be incorrect, take the vehicle to a Ford dealer for the complete system to be tested.

---

13 Fuel injection system components – removal and refitting

 Warning: Refer to the warning note in Section 1 before proceeding.

Powertrain Control Module

Caution: The PCM is fragile. Take care not to drop it or subject it to any other kind of impact, and do not subject it to extremes of temperature, or allow it to get wet. Do not touch the PCM terminals as there is a chance that static electricity may damage the internal electronic components.

Note: *If renewing the powertrain control module, note that it must be reprogrammed for the specific model by a Ford dealer using the FDS2000 diagnostic equipment. Failure to do so will result in the PCM assuming its limited operating strategy (LOS) settings giving poor performance and economy.*

1 Disconnect the battery negative (earth) lead (refer to *Disconnecting the battery* at the end of this manual).
2 Unclip the plastic cover and remove the three retaining nuts from the right-hand strut top mounting. **Note: *DO NOT** jack up the front of the vehicle, while these nuts are removed.*
3 Undo the four retaining bolts from the right-hand strut top mounting brace and remove it from the vehicle.
4 A security shield is riveted over the PCM and it will be necessary to drill out the rivet(s) to remove the shield and earth cable.
Caution: The PCM earth cable is connected behind the security shield rivet. Take care not to damage the earth cable when drilling through the rivet.
5 Unclip the wiring harness from along the right-hand inner wing panel.
6 Undo the retaining bolt and release the wiring connector from the PCM – to prevent dust and dirt entering the multi-plug, cover it with a polythene bag.
7 From inside the vehicle, unclip the generic electronic module (GEM) from the PCM bracket (as described in Chapter 12).
8 Undo the retaining nut and withdraw the PCM and mounting bracket from the driver's side footwell.
9 Refitting is the reverse of the removal procedure. Whenever the PCM (or battery) is disconnected, the information relating to idle speed control and other operating values will be lost from its memory until the unit has reprogrammed itself; until then, there may be surging, hesitation, erratic idle and a generally-inferior level of performance. To allow the PCM to relearn these values, start the engine and run it as close to idle speed as possible until it reaches its normal operating temperature, then run it for approximately two minutes at 1200 rpm. Next, drive the vehicle as far as necessary – approximately 5 miles of varied driving conditions is usually sufficient – to complete the relearning process.

Mass air flow sensor

V6 engine

10 Disconnect the battery negative (earth) lead (refer to *Disconnecting the battery* at the end of this manual).
11 Disconnect the wiring connector from the mass air flow sensor **(see illustration)**.
12 Remove the air cleaner assembly as described in Section 4. Unscrew and remove the sensor mounting bolts and withdraw the sensor from the air cleaner cover.
13 Refitting is the reverse of the removal procedure. Ensure that the sensor and air cleaner cover are seated correctly and securely fastened, so that there are no air leaks.

Temperature and Manifold Absolute Pressure sensor

4-cylinder engines

14 Disconnect the battery negative (earth)

13.11 Disconnecting the wiring connector from the mass air flow sensor (V6 engine)

lead (refer to *Disconnecting the battery* at the end of this manual). Unclip the breather hose from the engine upper plastic cover, then unclip the cover from the top of the engine.
15 Disconnect the wiring connector from the temperature and manifold absolute pressure sensor **(see illustration 11.6a)**.
16 Undo the retaining screw and withdraw the sensor from the intake manifold **(see illustration)**.

Crankshaft speed/position sensor

17 Disconnect the battery negative (earth) lead (refer to *Disconnecting the battery* at the end of this manual).
18 Apply the handbrake, then jack up the front of the vehicle and support it on axle stands (see *Jacking and vehicle support*).

13.20a Disconnecting the wiring connector from the crankshaft position sensor (4-cylinder engines)

13.23a Disconnecting the wiring connector from the camshaft position sensor (4-cylinder engines)

13.16 Undo the retaining screw (arrowed) to remove the T-MAP sensor (4-cylinder engines)

19 Remove the right-hand front roadwheel, undo the retaining bolts and withdraw the wheel arch liner (see Chapter 11).
20 Disconnect the wiring from the sensor **(see illustrations)**.
21 Undo the retaining bolt and withdraw the sensor.
22 Refitting is the reverse of the removal procedure.

Camshaft position sensor

23 The camshaft sensor is located on the front left-hand end of the camshaft cover on 4-cylinder models. On V6 models, the sensor is located in the timing chain cover, adjacent to the front intake camshaft sprocket **(see illustration)**.
24 On 4-cylinder models, unclip the breather

13.20b On V6 engines, the crankshaft position sensor (arrowed) is to the right of the crankshaft pulley

13.23b On V6 engines, the camshaft position sensor is at the top front edge of the timing chain cover

13.28 Intake air temperature sensor (arrowed) is screwed into the underside of the air intake resonator

13.33a Disconnecting the wiring from the throttle potentiometer on a 4-cylinder engine

13.33b Disconnecting the wiring from the throttle potentiometer on a V6 engine

hose from the engine upper plastic cover, then unclip the cover from the top of the engine.

25 Disconnect the sensor's electrical connector. Remove the retaining bolt, and withdraw the sensor from the camshaft cover (4-cylinder engines) or timing chain cover (V6 engines); be prepared for slight oil loss.

26 Refitting is the reverse of the removal procedure, noting the following points:
a) Apply petroleum jelly or clean engine oil to the sensor's sealing O-ring.
b) Locate the sensor fully in the camshaft cover/timing chain cover, and wipe off any surplus lubricant before securing it.
c) Tighten the screw to the specified torque wrench setting.

Coolant temperature sensor

27 Refer to Chapter 3.

Intake air temperature sensor

V6 engine

28 Remove the mass air flow sensor to gain access to the temperature sensor **(see illustration)**.

29 Releasing its clip, unplug the sensor's electrical connector, then unscrew the sensor from the resonator, air inlet duct or air cleaner housing.

30 Refitting is the reverse of the removal procedure. Tighten the sensor to the specified torque wrench setting. If it is over-tightened, its tapered thread may crack the resonator, duct or air cleaner housing.

Throttle position sensor (potentiometer)

31 On 4-cylinder models, unclip the breather hose from the engine upper plastic cover, then unclip the cover from the top of the engine.

32 On V6 models, remove the water pump pulley shield. If necessary, remove the PCV hose from the air inlet duct.

33 Disconnect the wiring plug. Remove the retaining screws, and withdraw the unit from the throttle housing **(see illustrations)**. Do not force the sensor's centre to rotate past its normal operating sweep, otherwise the unit will be seriously damaged.

34 Refitting is the reverse of the removal procedure, noting the following points:

a) Ensure that the sensor is correctly orientated, by locating its centre on the D-shaped throttle shaft (throttle closed), and aligning the sensor body so that the bolts pass easily into the throttle housing.
b) Tighten the screws securely (but do not overtighten them, or the sensor body will be cracked).

Vehicle speed sensor

35 The speed sensor is located in the transmission casing above the right-hand driveshaft, it is operated electronically. Refer to the relevant Section of Chapter 7A or 7B, as applicable.

Power steering pressure switch

36 The pressure switch is located in the high pressure pipe from the power steering pump. Disconnect the wiring connector and unscrew the switch from the pipe.

Throttle housing

4-cylinder engines

37 Disconnect the battery negative (earth) lead (refer to *Disconnecting the battery* at the end of this manual).

38 Unclip the breather hose from the engine upper plastic cover, then unclip the cover from the top of the engine. Slacken the retaining clips and remove the air intake pipe from the throttle housing.

39 Disconnect the accelerator cable from the throttle linkage (see Section 5). Where fitted, also disconnect the cruise control actuator cable (see Sections 15).

40 Disconnect the wiring plug from the throttle position sensor's electrical connector.

41 Remove the throttle housing mounting screws **(see illustration)**, then detach the throttle housing and gasket from the inlet manifold. Discard the gasket – this must be renewed whenever it is disturbed.

42 Using a soft brush and a suitable liquid cleaner, thoroughly clean the exterior of the throttle housing, then blow out all passages with compressed air.

Caution: Do not clean the throttle housing's bore, the throttle valve, or the throttle position sensor, either by scraping or with a solvent. Just wipe them over carefully with a clean soft cloth.

43 Refitting is the reverse of the removal procedure. Fit a new gasket, and tighten the housing screws to the specified torque.

V6 engine

44 Disconnect the battery negative (earth) lead (refer to *Disconnecting the battery* at the end of this manual).

45 Remove the air cleaner and air inlet duct (see Section 4). Also remove the water pump pulley shield.

46 Disconnect the wiring from the throttle position sensor and detach the wiring from the stud. Position the wiring to one side.

47 Disconnect the accelerator cable and speed control cable (if fitted) from the throttle housing.

48 Unscrew the mounting bolts and nut, and withdraw the throttle housing from the upper inlet manifold **(see illustration)**. Recover the gasket.

13.41 Undo the retaining bolts and remove the throttle housing (4-cylinder engines)

13.48 Undo the retaining bolts (arrowed) and remove the throttle housing (V6 engine)

13.51 Fuel rail and injector assembly

1 *Fuel pulse damper*
2 *Fuel pulse damper snap-ring*
3 *Fuel rail*

4 *Fuel rail spacers*
5 *Fuel injector retaining clip (models up to 03/2002)*

6 *Fuel injector*
7 *Fuel injector O-ring seals*

49 Using a soft brush and a suitable liquid cleaner, thoroughly clean the exterior of the throttle housing, then blow out all passages with compressed air.
Caution: Do not clean the throttle housing's bore, the throttle valve, or the throttle position sensor, either by scraping or with a solvent. Just wipe them over carefully with a clean soft cloth.
50 Refitting is the reverse of the removal procedure. Fit a new gasket, and tighten the housing bolts and nut to the specified torque.

Fuel rail and injectors

4-cylinder engines

Note: *The following procedure describes the*

removal of the fuel rail assembly, complete with the injectors and pulse damper, to enable the injectors to be serviced individually on a clean work surface (see illustration).
51 Depressurise the fuel system as described in Section 2. Also equalise tank pressure by removing the fuel filler cap.
52 Disconnect the battery negative (earth) lead (refer to *Disconnecting the battery* at the end of this manual).
53 Unclip the breather hose from the engine upper plastic cover, then unclip the cover from the top of the engine.
54 Disconnect the wiring from the four fuel injector electrical connectors.
55 Disconnect the fuel supply line at the quick-release coupling from the end of the

fuel rail (see Section 3), use rag to soak up any spilt fuel **(see illustration)**.
56 Disconnect the vacuum pipe from the fuel pulse damper **(see illustration)**.
57 Unscrew the bolts securing the fuel rail, and withdraw the rail, complete with the injectors out of the cylinder head. Drain any remaining fuel into a suitable clean container.
58 Recover the fuel rail spacers from the cylinder head **(see illustration)**.
59 Clamp the rail carefully in a vice fitted with soft jaws. On models up to 03/2002, slide the retaining clips sideways from the top of the injectors, to withdraw the injectors from the fuel rail. On models built after 03/2002 release the locking tangs at the top of the injector, to

13.55 Disconnect fuel line quick-release coupling

13.56 Disconnect the vacuum pipe (arrowed) from the fuel pulse damper

13.58 Recover the fuel rail spacers from the cylinder head

13.59a On models up to 03/2002, slide the retaining clips sideways . . .

13.59b . . . and on models after 03/2002 unclip the locking tangs, to withdraw the injectors

13.60a Withdraw the injectors from the fuel rail . . .

13.60b . . . and remove the O-ring seals

withdraw the injectors from the fuel rail. Place the injectors in a clean storage container **(see illustrations)**.

60 Discard the seals/O-rings from the fuel injectors and obtain new ones **(see illustrations)**.

61 Further testing of the injectors is beyond the scope of the home mechanic. If you are in doubt as to the status of any injector, it can be tested at a dealer service department.

62 Refitting is the reverse of the removal procedure, noting the following points:

a) Lubricate each (new) seal/O-ring with clean engine oil before refitting.

b) Locate each injector carefully in the fuel rail recess, ensuring that the retaining clips are located correctly on the top of the injectors.

c) Tighten the fuel rail bolts to the torque wrench setting specified.

d) Reconnect the fuel feed quick-release coupling as described in Section 3.

e) Ensure that the breather hose, vacuum hose and wiring are routed correctly, and secured on reconnection by any clips or ties provided.

f) On completion, switch the ignition on to activate the fuel pump and pressurise the system, without cranking the engine. Check for signs of fuel leaks around all disturbed unions and joints before attempting to start the engine.

V6 engine

63 Depressurise the fuel system as described in Section 2. Also equalise tank pressure by removing the fuel filler cap.

64 Disconnect the battery negative (earth) lead (refer to *Disconnecting the battery* at the end of this manual).

65 Remove the upper intake manifold as described in Chapter 2B.

66 Disconnect the wiring harnesses from the injectors, and position to one side **(see illustrations)**.

67 Disconnect the fuel supply line at the quick-release coupling from the end of the fuel rail (see Section 3).

68 Unscrew the mounting bolts and remove the fuel rail from the lower intake manifold **(see illustrations)**. The injectors may come away with the rail or they may remain in the intake manifold.

69 Where applicable, carefully ease the injectors from the lower intake manifold or fuel rail and place them in a clean container.

70 Remove and discard all O-ring seals. Further testing of the injectors is beyond the scope of the home mechanic. If you are in doubt as to the status of any injector, it can be tested at a dealer service department.

71 Refitting is the reverse of the removal procedure, noting the following points:

a) Lubricate each (new) O-ring seal with clean engine oil before refitting, and refit the injectors in the lower inlet manifold before fitting the fuel rail to them **(see illustration)**.

b) Tighten the fuel rail bolts to the specified torque.

c) On completion, switch the ignition on to activate the fuel pump and pressurise the system, without cranking the engine. Check for signs of fuel leaks around the unions and joints before attempting to start the engine.

13.66a Use a small screwdriver to release the injector wiring securing clips . . .

13.66b . . . then move the wiring harness to one side

13.68a Unscrew the mounting bolts . . .

13.68b . . . and remove the fuel rail

Fuel pressure regulator

72 Depressurise the fuel system as described in Section 2. Also equalise tank pressure by removing the fuel filler cap.
73 Disconnect the battery negative (earth) lead (refer to *Disconnecting the battery* at the end of this manual).
74 On V6 models, remove the upper inlet manifold as described in Chapter 2B.
75 Disconnect the vacuum hose from the regulator. Remove the two regulator screws and remove the regulator. Recover the O-ring seal. Soak up spilled fuel using a clean rag.
76 Refitting is the reverse of the removal procedure, noting the following points:
  a) *Renew the regulator sealing O-ring whenever the regulator is disturbed. Lubricate the new O-ring with clean engine oil on installation.*
  b) *Locate the regulator carefully, and tighten the bolts to the specified torque wrench setting.*
  c) *On completion, switch the ignition on and off five times, to activate the fuel pump and pressurise the system, without cranking the engine. Check for signs of fuel leaks around all disturbed unions and joints before attempting to start the engine.*

Idle air control valve

77 Disconnect the battery negative (earth) lead (refer to *Disconnecting the battery* at the end of this manual).
78 On 4-cylinder engines, unclip the breather hose from the engine upper plastic cover, then unclip the cover from the top of the engine.
79 Disconnect the wiring from the idle air control valve **(see illustrations)**.
80 Unscrew the two retaining bolts (4-cylinder) or nuts (V6), and withdraw the valve from the intake manifold **(see illustration)**. Recover the gasket.
81 Since the valve's individual components are not available separately, and the complete assembly must be renewed if it is thought to be faulty, there is nothing to be lost by attempting to flush out the passages, using carburettor cleaner or similar solvent. This won't take much time or effort, and may well cure the fault.
82 Refitting is the reverse of the removal procedure, noting the following points:
  a) *Clean the mating surfaces carefully, and always fit a new gasket whenever the valve is disturbed.*
  b) *Tighten the bolts evenly and to the specified torque wrench setting.*
  c) *Once the wiring and battery are reconnected, start the engine and allow it to idle. When it has reached normal operating temperature, check that the idle speed is stable, and that no induction (air) leaks are evident. Switch on all electrical loads (headlights, heated rear window, etc), and check that the idle speed is still correct.*

13.71 Inserting the injectors in the lower inlet manifold

13.79b Disconnecting the wiring from the idle air control valve (V6 engine)

Intake manifold runner control actuator

4-cylinder engines

83 Remove the throttle housing as described in paragraphs 37 to 42 in this Section.
84 Disconnect the actuator arm from the intake manifold swirl plate linkage **(see illustration)**.
85 Disconnect the vacuum pipe from the intake manifold runner control actuator **(see illustration)**.
86 Undo the three retaining screws and withdraw the intake manifold runner control actuator from the intake manifold.
87 Refitting is the reverse of the removal procedure, noting the following points:
  a) *Clean the mating surfaces carefully, and always fit a new gasket.*
  b) *Tighten the bolts evenly.*

13.84 Disconnect the actuator arm (arrowed) from the linkage

13.79a Disconnecting the wiring from the idle air control valve (4-cylinder engines)

13.80 Unscrew the two retaining bolts (arrowed) (4-cylinder engines)

  c) *Once the wiring and battery are reconnected, start the engine and allow it to idle. When it has reached normal operating temperature, check that the idle speed is stable, and that no induction (air) leaks are evident. Switch on all electrical loads (headlights, heated rear window, etc), and check that the idle speed is still correct.*

V6 engine

88 Undo the retaining bolts and remove the plastic cover from the front camshaft cover.
89 Disconnect the wiring connector from the intake manifold runner control unit **(see illustration)**.
90 Undo the three retaining bolts and withdraw the intake manifold runner control unit from the camshaft cover **(see illustration)**.

13.85 Disconnect the vacuum pipe (arrowed) from the actuator

13.89 Disconnecting the wiring connector from the intake manifold runner control unit

13.90 Undo the three retaining bolts (arrowed) and withdraw the control unit

13.96 Disconnect the vacuum pipes (arrowed) from the valve

91 Disconnect the operating cable from the throttle housing linkage.
92 Refitting is the reverse of the removal procedure

Intake manifold tuning valve

4-cylinder engines

93 Disconnect the battery negative (earth) lead (refer to *Disconnecting the battery* at the end of this manual).
94 Unclip the breather hose from the engine upper plastic cover, then unclip the cover from the top of the engine.
95 Disconnect the wiring connector from the intake manifold tuning valve.

96 Disconnect the vacuum pipes from the intake manifold tuning valve **(see illustration)**.
97 Undo the two retaining bolts and withdraw the valve from the intake manifold.
98 Refitting is the reverse of the removal procedure, noting the following points:
a) Clean the mating surfaces carefully, and always fit a new gasket.
b) Tighten the bolts evenly and to the specified torque wrench setting.
c) Once the wiring and battery are reconnected, start the engine and allow it to idle. When it has reached normal operating temperature, check that the idle speed is stable, and that no induction (air) leaks are

evident. Switch on all electrical loads (headlights, heated rear window, etc), and check that the idle speed is still correct.

14 Exhaust system – general description and component renewal

⚠️ **Warning: Inspection and repair of exhaust system components should be done only after the system has cooled completely. This applies particularly to the catalytic converter, which runs at very high temperatures.**

J35132

14.1 Exhaust system (4-cylinder engines)

1 Flexible pipe
2 Catalytic converter
3 Heated oxygen sensor
4 Silencer and tailpipe assembly
5 Bracket mounting on Estate only

General description

1 4-cylinder models are fitted with an exhaust system consisting of a manifold connecting to a front flexible downpipe, catalytic converter, and a rear section incorporating two silencers **(see illustration opposite)**.
2 On V6 models, the exhaust system consists of two exhaust manifolds (one from each bank) with a connecting Y-piece, catalytic converter, and a rear section incorporating three silencers **(see illustration)**.
3 The exhaust system on all models is suspended throughout its entire length by rubber mounting rings.

Component renewal

4 If any section of the exhaust is damaged or deteriorated, excessive noise and vibration will occur.
5 Carry out regular inspections of the exhaust system, to check security and condition. Look for any damaged or bent parts, open seams, holes, loose connections, excessive corrosion, or other defects which could allow exhaust fumes to enter the vehicle. Deteriorated sections of the exhaust system should be renewed.
6 If the exhaust system components are extremely corroded or rusted together, it may not be possible to separate them. In this case, simply cut off the old components with a hacksaw, and remove any remaining corroded pipe with a cold chisel. Be sure to wear safety glasses to protect your eyes, and wear gloves to protect your hands.
7 Here are some simple guidelines to follow when repairing the exhaust system:
a) Work from the back to the front when removing exhaust system components.
b) Apply penetrating fluid to the flange nuts before unscrewing them.
c) Use new gaskets and rubber mountings when installing exhaust system components.
d) Apply anti-seize compound to the threads of all exhaust system studs during reassembly.
e) Note that on some models, the downpipe is secured to the manifold by two coil springs, spring seats and a self-locking nut on each. Where fitted, tighten the nuts until they stop on the bolt shoulders; the pressure of the springs will then be sufficient to make a leak-proof connection. Do not over tighten the nuts to cure a leak – the studs will shear. Renew the gasket and the springs if a leak is found.
f) Be sure to allow sufficient clearance between newly-installed parts and all points on the underbody, to avoid overheating the floorpan, and possibly damaging the interior carpet and insulation. Pay particularly close attention to the catalytic converter and its heat shield.

14.2 Exhaust system (V6 engine)

1 Dual flexible pipe/Y-pipe
2 Catalytic converter
3 Heated oxygen sensor
4 Silencer and tailpipe assembly

Notes

Chapter 4 Part B:
Fuel and exhaust systems – diesel models

Contents

Degrees of difficulty

Easy, suitable for novice with little experience	**Fairly easy,** suitable for beginner with some experience	**Fairly difficult,** suitable for competent DIY mechanic	**Difficult,** suitable for experienced DIY mechanic	**Very difficult,** suitable for expert DIY or professional

Specifications

General

System type	Electronic fuel injection, controlled by an EEC V PCM
Application:	
2.0 litre Duratorq – DI engine	D5BA (66kW)
2.0 litre Duratorq – DI engine	D6BA (85kW)
2.0 litre Duratorq – DCI (common rail) engine	H7BA, BB or BC (85kW)
2.0 litre Duratorq – DCI (common rail) engine	FMBA (96kW)
Firing order	1 – 3 – 4 – 2 (No 1 at timing chain end)
Idle speed	900 rpm (regulated by 'Black Oak' engine management system – no adjustment possible)

Glow plugs

Maximum preheat time	8 seconds
Maximum after-glow phase (less than 2500rpm)	30 seconds
Engine above 80°C	No preheating

Fuel

Fuel type	Commercial diesel fuel for road vehicles (DERV)

Injection pump

Make and type:	
D5BA	Bosch VP-30
D6BA	Bosch VP-44
All other engines	Bosch VP-44
Rotation (viewed from crankshaft pulley end)	Clockwise
Drive	Twin chain via crankshaft and camshaft sprockets

Turbocharger

Type:	
D5BA	Fixed vane turbocharger – integral with exhaust manifold
All other engines	Variable vane turbocharger – integral with exhaust manifold

Torque wrench settings

	Nm	lbf ft
Catalytic monitor sensor	46	34
Catalytic converter support bracket	46	34
Catalytic converter to front pipe	46	34
Catalytic converter-to-manifold nuts (renew)	46	34
Crankshaft position sensor bolt	7	5
Cylinder head temperature sensor	11	8
EGR cooler securing nut and bolt	10	7
EGR cooler to exhaust manifold bolts	37	27
EGR pipe union	23	17
Exhaust heat shield fasteners	10	7
Exhaust manifold	40	30
Fuel injection pump:		
D5BA and D6BA:		
Supply union	24	18
Return union	24	18
All other engines		
Supply union	36	27
Fuel injection pump mounting bolts	22	16
Fuel injection pump mounting bracket bolts	22	16
Fuel injection pump sprocket retaining bolts	32	24
Injector pipe unions	35	26
Injectors	52	38
Intake manifold	16	12
Oxygen sensor	48	35
Turbocharger oil supply pipe bolt	14	10
Turbocharger oil return pipe flange bolts	10	7

1 General information and precautions

General information

The fuel system consists of a fuel tank (mounted under the body, beneath the rear seats), fuel filter, electronic fuel injection pump with pump control unit, injectors, fuel lines and hoses, fuel gauge sender unit mounted in the fuel tank, and EEC-V PCM (powertrain control module).

Fuel is drawn from the tank (via an electrically-operated lift pump, on the common rail engines), it then passes through the fuel filter located in the engine bay, where foreign matter and water are removed. The injection pump is driven from the crankshaft via a twin-row chain and supplies fuel under very high pressure to each injector in turn as it is needed. The camshafts are also driven from the same chain.

The Duratorq-DI engine is very much a 'state-of-the-art' unit, in that it features a full electronic engine management system. An extensive array of sensors are fitted, which supply information on many different parameters to the PCM.

Information on crankshaft position and engine speed is generated by a crankshaft position sensor. The inductive head of the sensor runs just above the engine flywheel, and scans a series of 36 protrusions on the flywheel periphery. As the crankshaft rotates, the sensor transmits a pulse every time a protrusion passes it. There is one missing protrusion in the flywheel periphery at a point corresponding to 50° BTDC. The PCM recognises the absence of a pulse from the crankshaft position sensor at this point to establish a reference mark for crankshaft position. Similarly, the time interval between absent pulses is used to determine engine speed.

Information on the quantity and temperature of the intake air is derived from the T-MAP sensor. The temperature and manifold absolute pressure (or T-MAP) sensor is located in the top of the air intake duct that runs along the front of the engine subframe below the radiator. It measures the temperature and the pressure of the air in the intake system. The temperature and quantity of air has a direct bearing on the quantity of fuel to be injected for optimum efficiency.

The traditional coolant temperature sensor has been superseded by a cylinder head temperature sensor. The new sensor is seated in a blind hole in the cylinder head, and measures the temperature of the metal directly. Information on engine temperature is critical for accurate fuelling calculations, and is also used to control the preheating system for cold starts.

The clutch pedal sensor informs the PCM whether the clutch is engaged or disengaged. When the clutch pedal is depressed, the quantity of fuel injected is momentarily reduced, to make gearchanging smoother.

The stop-light switch and separate brake pedal sensor inform the PCM when the brakes are applied – when this signal is received, the PCM puts the engine into idle mode until a signal is received from the accelerator position sensor.

The amount of fuel delivered is determined by the pump's internal quantity and timing solenoid valves, which are controlled by the pump control unit (PCU), mounted on top of the pump. The pump is internally equipped with a pulse ring fitted to the main rotor, and an angle sensor determines the pump rotor's position and speed, in much the same way as the crankshaft position sensor and engine flywheel, except that there are four gaps in the pump rotor 'teeth' – one for each cylinder. The pump control unit is supplied with information from the 'main' powertrain control module (PCM), and from this, is able to calculate the most appropriate values for injection timing and quantity (injection duration). The electronically-controlled pump internals enable these calculated values to be delivered with great accuracy, for improved efficiency and reduced emissions.

No accelerator cable is fitted on the Duratorq engines – instead, a sensor located next to the accelerator pedal informs the PCM of the accelerator position, and this information is used to determine the most appropriate fuelling requirements from the injection pump. The engine idle speed is also controlled by the PCM, and cannot be adjusted. From the signals it receives from the various sensors, the PCM can control the idle speed very accurately, compensating automatically for additional engine loads or unfavourable ambient/engine temperatures.

Rigid pipes connect the pump to the four injectors, on the D5BA and D6BA engines. On the FMBA engine there are four pipes from the injectors to the fuel supply manifold and one from the supply manifold down to the fuel pump. Each injector disperses the fuel evenly, and sprays fuel directly into the combustion chamber as its piston approaches TDC on the compression stroke. This system is known as direct injection. The pistons have a recess machined into their crowns, the shape of which has been calculated to improve 'swirl' (fuel/air mixing). Lubrication is provided by allowing a small quantity of fuel to leak back past the injector internal components. The leaked-back fuel is returned to the pump and then to the fuel tank.

Cold-starting performance is automatically controlled by the PCM. Under cold start conditions, the cylinder head temperature (CHT) sensor informs the PCM on the engine temperature, this determines the preheat time. The glow plugs are located in the side of the cylinder head, one to each cylinder, and are electrically-heated. A warning light illuminates when the ignition is switched on, showing that the glow plugs are in operation. When the light goes out, preheating is complete and the engine can be started. The glow plugs have an after-glow phase which only operates under 2500 rpm, and below temperatures of 50°C . This helps the engine to run more smoothly during idling, and reduces exhaust emissions through more efficient combustion just after starting.

The fuel system has a built-in 'strategy' to prevent it from drawing in air, should the car run low on fuel. The PCM monitors the level of fuel in the tank, via the gauge sender unit. After switching on the low fuel level warning light, it will eventually induce a misfire as a further warning to the driver, and lower the engine's maximum speed until the engine stops.

The fuel system on diesel engines is normally very reliable. Provided that clean fuel is used and the specified maintenance is conscientiously carried out, no problems should be experienced. The injection pump and injectors may require overhaul after a high mileage has been covered, but this cannot be done on a DIY basis.

Precautions

⚠️ **Warning: It is necessary to take certain precautions when working on the fuel system components, particularly the fuel injectors. Before carrying out any operations on the fuel system, refer to the precautions given in 'Safety first!' at the beginning of this manual, and to any additional warning notes at the start of the relevant Sections. In particular, note that the injectors on direct injection diesel engines operate at extremely high pressures, making the injector spray extremely hazardous.**

2 Fuel system – priming and bleeding

1 As this system is intended to be 'self-bleeding', no hand-priming pump or separate bleed screws/nipples are fitted.
2 When any part of the system has been disturbed therefore, air must be purged from the system by cranking the engine on the starter motor until it starts. When it has started, keep the engine running for approximately 5 minutes to ensure that all air has been removed from the system. To minimise the strain on the battery and starter motor when trying to start the engine, crank it in 10 second bursts, pausing for 30 seconds each time, until the engine starts.
3 Depending on the work that has been carried out, it may be possible to partially prime the system so as to spare the battery by reducing as much as possible the amount of cranking time required to start the engine. To spare the battery, fill the filter with clean fuel via its vent screw opening (where applicable), but it is essential that no dirt is introduced into the system and that no diesel fuel is poured over vulnerable components when doing this.
4 On models with a Bosch VP-30 injection pump, if a hand-operated vacuum pump is available, this can be connected to the pump's fuel return union and used to suck fuel through the supply lines and filter. This will obviously save the battery a good deal of work. If a long length of clear plastic tubing is used to connect the vacuum pump to the injection pump union, it will be easier to see when fuel emerges free from air bubbles. Turn the ignition switch to position II so that fuel can pass through the pump.
5 On models with a Bosch VP-44 injection pump, A clear plastic T-piece will need to be connected into the return line (across the front of the timing chain cover) with one piece going into a container. Remove the left-hand side front trim panel to access the inertia fuel cut-off switch (IFS). Disconnect the 3-pin wiring connector and using a fused (15 amp) jumper wire, supply a battery feed to pin No 1 in the wiring connector. This will start the fuel lift pump and supply fuel through the circuit,

3.1 Disconnect the wiring plug (arrowed) from the mass airflow sensor

check for air in the clear plastic T-piece. When no more air is visible, disconnect the jumper wire, remove the T-piece and reconnect the return pipe.

3 Air cleaner assembly and air intake components – removal and refitting

Air cleaner assembly

1 Disconnect the wiring from the mass air flow (MAF) sensor **(see illustration)**.
2 Release the hose clips and disconnect the air intake duct. Note that the hose clip may not be of the screw type, and will have to be separated by prising the crimped section with a small screwdriver. The clip can be re-used if care is taken, but it may be preferable to fit a screw-drive clip when refitting.
3 Disconnect the breather hose leading to the intake cleaner housing.
4 Lift and remove the air cleaner assembly to release it from the rubber grommets **(see illustration overleaf)**.
5 Check the rubber grommets for deterioration and renew them if necessary.
6 Refitting is the reverse of the removal procedure. Ensure that the air cleaner pegs seat fully in their rubber grommets.

Air intake components

7 If removing the intake duct between the air cleaner and turbocharger, first ensure that the engine is cool. Release the hose clip and carefully ease the duct off the turbocharger. Note that the hose clip may not be of the screw type, and will have to be separated by prising the crimped section with a small screwdriver. The clip can be re-used if care is taken, but it may be preferable to fit a screw-drive clip when refitting.
8 To remove the upper air intake pipe attached to the air cleaner base, first remove the air cleaner assembly as described in paragraphs 1 to 4.
9 Undo the air intake pipe upper retaining bolt from the left-hand inner wing.
10 Chock the rear wheels and apply the handbrake, jack up the front of the vehicle and support it on axle stands (see *Jacking and vehicle support*).
11 Remove the left-hand front wheel and inner wheel arch liner (Chapter 11).
12 From under the left-hand front wing, withdraw the upper intake pipe from the middle intake pipe.
13 Undo the retaining bolts and remove the middle intake pipe from under the left-hand wing. Where applicable, disconnect the foglight's wiring block connector from the clip on the intake pipe.
14 To remove the lower air intake pipe, remove the radiator grille as described in Chapter 11.
15 Refitting is the reverse of the removal procedure.

3.4 Air cleaner assembly layout

1 Air cleaner outlet pipe
2 Mass air flow sensor (MAF)
3 Air cleaner housing cover
4 Air cleaner element
5 Air cleaner housing
6 Air cleaner intake pipe blanking cap
7 Air cleaner intake pipe
8 Charge air cooler

4 Accelerator pedal – removal and refitting

Removal

1 Remove the retaining screws and take out the trim panel above the driver's footwell to gain access to the accelerator pedal; where applicable, unclip the datalink connector plug from the panel as it is removed.
2 Disconnect the wiring plug from the accelerator position sensor, then unscrew the bolts and remove the accelerator pedal assembly.

Refitting

3 Refit in the reverse order of removal. On completion, check the action of the pedal with the engine running.

5 Fuel tank – removal, inspection and refitting

Note: Refer to the warning note in Section 1 before proceeding.
1 Refer to Chapter 4A, Section 9. The basic procedure for tank removal on diesel models is much the same as that for petrol versions, but ignore the references to the charcoal canister and the fuel filter. On models fitted with a Bosch VP-44 injection pump, the electric fuel lift pump at the right-hand side of the fuel tank will need to be removed first, as described in Section 7.

6 Fuel gauge sender unit – removal and refitting

Note: Refer to the warning note in Section 1 before proceeding. Ford technicians use a special wrench to unscrew the pump/sender unit retaining ring, but ordinary tools can be used successfully.

7.4 Fuel pump connections

1 *Fuel pump*
2 *Fuel pump to fuel tank return line*
3 *Fuel tank to fuel pump supply line*
4 *Fuel pump to fuel filter supply line*

1 The fuel gauge sender unit is located in the top face of the fuel tank. The unit can only be detached and withdrawn from the tank after the tank is released and lowered from under the vehicle.

2 Removing the fuel gauge sender unit is a very similar procedure to that for removing the combined fuel pump and sender unit fitted to petrol models, described in Chapter 4A, Section 8.

7 Fuel lift pump – removal and refitting

Note: *Refer to the warning note in Section 1 before proceeding.*

1 Disconnect the battery negative (earth) lead (refer to *Disconnecting the battery* at the end of this manual).

2 Loosen the right-hand rear wheel nuts, then firmly apply the handbrake. Jack up the rear of the car, and support it on axle stands (see *Jacking and vehicle support*). Remove the right-hand rear wheel.

3 Release the retaining nut and screw, then unclip the air deflector from below the fuel lift pump.

4 Disconnect the three fuel lines from the pump. Fuel pump supply to fuel filter line, fuel tank supply to fuel pump line and fuel pump to fuel tank return line **(see illustration)**. Be prepared with a container for the loss of fuel.

5 Disconnect the wiring connector from the fuel lift pump.

6 Undo the three retaining bolts/nuts from the mounting bracket and remove from under the vehicle, complete with the fuel lift pump.

7 Refitting is a reversal of removal, ensuring that the wiring plug and fuel lines are securely reconnected. Run the engine and check the disturbed unions for leaks, there should be no need to bleed the system (Section 2).

8 Diesel injection system – checking

Note: *Refer to the warning note in Section 1 before proceeding.*

1 If a fault appears in the diesel injection system, first ensure that all the system wiring connectors are securely connected and free of corrosion. Then ensure that the fault is not due to poor maintenance; ie, check that the air cleaner filter element is clean, the valve clearances are correct, the cylinder compression pressures are correct, the fuel filter has been drained (or changed) and the engine breather hoses are clear and undamaged, referring to Chapter 1B or Chapter 2C.

2 If these checks fail to reveal the cause of the problem, the vehicle should be taken to a suitably-equipped Ford dealer for testing. A diagnostic connector is incorporated in the engine management system wiring harness, into which dedicated electronic test equipment can be plugged (the connector is located in the driver's side lower facia). The test equipment is capable of 'interrogating' the powertrain control module (PCM) electronically and accessing its internal fault log (reading fault codes).

3 Fault codes can only be extracted from the PCM using a dedicated fault code reader. A Ford dealer will obviously have such a reader, but they are also available from other suppliers. It is unlikely to be cost-effective for the private owner to purchase a fault code reader, but a well-equipped local garage or auto-electrical specialist will have one.

4 Using this equipment, faults can be pinpointed quickly and simply, even if their occurrence is intermittent. Testing all the

9.5a Unscrew the mounting bolt (arrowed) . . .

9.5b . . . and withdraw the sensor

9.7 The cylinder head temperature sensor (arrowed)

system components individually in an attempt to locate the fault by elimination is a time-consuming operation that is unlikely to be fruitful (particularly if the fault occurs dynamically), and carries a high risk of damage to the PCM's internal components.

5 Experienced home mechanics equipped with a diesel tachometer or other diagnostic equipment may be able to check the engine idle speed; if found to be out of specification, the vehicle must be taken to a suitably-equipped Ford dealer for assessment. The engine idle speed is not manually adjustable; incorrect test results indicate the need for maintenance (possibly, injector cleaning or recalibration) or a fault within the injection system.

6 If excessive smoking or knocking is evident, it may be due to a problem with the fuel injectors. Proprietary treatments are available which can be added to the fuel, in order to clean the injectors. Injectors deteriorate with prolonged use, however, and it is reasonable to expect them to need reconditioning or renewal after 60 000 miles (100 000 km) or so. Accurate testing, overhaul and calibration of the injectors must be left to a specialist.

9 Diesel injection system electronic components – removal and refitting

1 Disconnect the battery negative (earth) lead (refer to *Disconnecting the battery* at the end of this manual).
2 Withdraw the oil level dipstick and unclip the engine plastic cover.

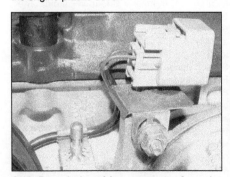

9.10 Detach the wiring connector from the retaining bracket

Crankshaft position sensor

3 The sensor is located in the top of the bellhousing to the rear.
4 For better access remove the air cleaner assembly as described in Section 3.
5 Disconnect the wiring plug, then unscrew the mounting bolt and withdraw the sensor **(see illustrations)**. **Note:** *Before removing the sensor, mark the position of the retaining bolt, so that it can be refitted in the same place.*
6 Refitting is a reversal of removal.

Cylinder head temperature sensor

7 The switch is screwed into the left-hand (flywheel) end of the cylinder head, behind the power steering pump pulley **(see illustration)**.
8 To improve access to the switch, it will be necessary to remove the power steering pump pulley, referring to Chapter 2C, Section 10.
9 It may also be helpful to release the air intake hoses and move them to one side, as described in Section 3.
10 Trace the wiring from the sensor, and disconnect it at the plug, which is clipped to the brake vacuum pump **(see illustration)**.
11 The sensor can now be unscrewed and removed **(see illustration)**. However, access to the sensor because of the length of wiring, may make it difficult getting a tool to fit onto it. Ultimately, it may be necessary to cut the sensor wiring, unscrew the sensor using a thin-wall socket or box spanner, then remake the wiring after fitting, using a suitable connector.
12 Refitting is a reversal of removal. Clean

9.11 Unscrew the sensor (arrowed) – note the wiring is part of the sensor

the threads of the sensor and mounting hole, then refit the sensor and tighten it to the specified torque.

Vehicle speed sensor

13 Refer to Chapter 7A or 7B.

Temperature and manifold absolute pressure sensor

14 The T-MAP sensor is mounted on the air intake duct which runs along the front of the engine subframe, below the radiator.
15 Disconnect the wiring plug from the sensor.
16 Unscrew and remove the two mounting bolts, and withdraw the sensor from the intake duct.
17 Refitting is a reversal of removal, ensuring that the wiring plug is securely reconnected and the sensor is fitted securely to the intake duct.

Fuel metering valve

18 The fuel metering valve is integral with the injection pump, and cannot be separated from it. If a new injection pump is fitted, the pump control unit (PCU) must be electronically 'matched' to the powertrain control module (PCM), otherwise the pump will not function correctly (or even at all, if the immobiliser function is not correctly set up) – this is a task for a Ford dealer, as specialised electronic equipment is required.

EGR valve

19 Refer to Chapter 4C, Section 4.

Clutch pedal position switch

20 Remove the trim panel above the driver's footwell to gain access to the clutch pedal; unclip the datalink connector plug from the panel as it is removed.
21 Reach up and disconnect the wiring from the clutch switch at the top of the pedal bracket. Slide the retaining clip (where fitted) down to release the switch, then twist the switch anti-clockwise and remove it from the pedal bracket.
22 Refitting is a reversal of removal. **Note:** *A new retaining clip will be required.*

Brake pedal position switch

23 Remove the trim panel above the driver's footwell to gain access to the brake pedal;

unclip the datalink connector plug from the panel as it is removed.

24 Reach up and disconnect the wiring from the switch at the top of the pedal; there are two switches and if both switches are removed at once, take care to note which wiring plug serves which switch.

25 Slide the retaining clip down to release the switch, then twist the switch through 90° and remove it from the pedal bracket.

26 Refitting is a reversal of removal. **Note:** *A new retaining clip will be required.*

Accelerator pedal sensor

27 The accelerator pedal sensor is integral with the pedal assembly, which is removed as described in Section 4.

Injection pump control unit

28 The pump control unit is integral with the injection pump, and cannot be separated from it. *If a new injection pump is fitted, the PCU must be electronically 'matched' to the powertrain control module (PCM), otherwise the pump will not function correctly (or even at all, if the immobiliser function is not correctly set up) – this is a task for a Ford dealer, as specialised electronic equipment is required.*

Powertrain Control Module

Caution: The PCM is fragile. Take care not to drop it or subject it to any other kind of impact, and do not subject it to extremes of temperature, or allow it to get wet. Do not touch the PCM terminals as there is a chance that static electricity may damage the internal electronic components.

Note: *If renewing the powertrain control module, note that it must be reprogrammed for the specific model by a Ford dealer using the FDS2000 diagnostic equipment. Failure to do so will result in the PCM assuming its 'limited operating strategy' (LOS) settings giving poor performance and economy.*

29 Disconnect the battery negative (earth) lead (refer to *Disconnecting the battery* at the end of this manual).

30 Unclip the plastic cover and remove the three retaining nuts from the right-hand strut top mounting. **Note: *DO NOT** jack up the front of the vehicle, while these nuts are removed.*

31 Unclip the cover from the right-hand strut top mounting brace and undo the retaining nuts and bolts, then remove it from the vehicle.

32 A security shield is riveted over the PCM and it will be necessary to drill out the rivet(s) to remove the shield and earth cable **(see illustration).**

Caution: The PCM earth cable is connected behind the security shield rivet. Take care not to damage the earth cable when drilling through the rivet.

33 Unclip the wiring harness from along the right-hand inner wing panel.

34 Undo the retaining bolt and release the

9.32 Powertrain control module (PCM) location

wiring connector from the PCM – to prevent dust and dirt entering the multi-plug, cover it with a polythene bag.

35 From inside the vehicle, unclip the generic electronic module (GEM) from the PCM bracket (as described in Chapter 12).

36 Undo the retaining nut and withdraw the PCM and mounting bracket from the driver's side footwell.

37 Refitting is the reverse of the removal procedure. Whenever the PCM (or battery) is disconnected, the information relating to idle speed control and other operating values will be lost from its memory until the unit has reprogrammed itself; until then, there may be surging, hesitation, erratic idle and a generally-inferior level of performance. To allow the PCM to relearn these values, start the engine and run it as close to idle speed as possible until it reaches its normal operating temperature, then run it for approximately two minutes at 1200 rpm. Next, drive the vehicle as far as necessary – approximately 5 miles of

varied driving conditions is usually sufficient – to complete the relearning process.

Injector driver module

38 The module is located under the front, of the left-hand front wing (as viewed from the driver's seat).

39 Remove the front bumper as described in Chapter 11.

40 Undo the retaining bolts and remove the intake pipe from under the left-hand wing **(see illustration).** Where applicable, disconnect the foglight's wiring block connector from the clip on the intake pipe.

41 Remove the shear bolts and detach the IDM unit from the housing cover **(see illustration).**

42 Support the IDM unit and disconnect the wiring connectors from the unit.

43 The IDM must be electronically 'config-ured' to the powertrain control module (PCM), this must be done by your Ford Dealer, as specialised electronic equipment is required.

9.40 Undo the retaining bolts (arrowed) to remove the air intake pipe

9.41 Remove the shear bolts (arrowed) to release the injector driver module

10.5 Removing the damper from the engine mounting

10.8a A 6 mm drill bit (arrowed) locating fuel pump sprocket in the 1 o'clock position (timing chain cover removed for clarity)

Mass air flow (MAF) sensor

44 Disconnect the battery negative (earth) lead (see Chapter 5A).

45 Remove the air cleaner assembly as described in Section 3. Unscrew and remove the sensor mounting bolts and withdraw the sensor from the air cleaner cover.

46 Refitting is the reverse of the removal procedure. Ensure that the sensor and air cleaner cover are seated correctly and securely fastened, so that there are no air leaks.

---

10 Fuel injection pump – removal, refitting and adjustment

Caution: Be careful not to allow dirt into the injection pump or injector pipes during this procedure.

10.10 Disconnect the wiring connectors (arrowed) – 'common rail' engine

10.6 Using a home-made tool to remove the access cover (engine mounting removed for clarity)

10.8b Ford special tool locating flywheel in the 50° BTDC position (transmission removed for clarity)

Note: *If a new injection pump is fitted, there is a possibility that the engine may not run properly (or even at all) until both the powertrain control module (PCM) and the new pump control unit have been electronically 'configured' using Ford diagnostic equipment. In particular, the immobiliser may not function correctly, leading to the engine not starting.*

Note: *Ford special tools will be required for the removal and refitting procedure of the fuel injection pump – see text*

Removal

1 Disconnect the battery negative (earth) lead (refer to *Disconnecting the battery* at the end of this manual).

2 Withdraw the oil level dipstick and unclip the engine plastic cover.

3 Undo the retaining bolts and move the coolant expansion bottle to one side.

10.13 Removing the fuel line bracket retaining bracket

4 Undo the retaining bolt(s) and move the power steering reservoir to one side.

5 Undo the two damper retaining bolts and detach the damper from the engine mounting **(see illustration)**.

6 Using the Ford special tool (303-679), remove the access cover from the timing chain cover. A tool was made up using a three-legged puller and three bolts **(see illustration)**.

7 Remove the crankshaft position sensor as described in Section 9.

Warning: Do not turn the engine when the special tool is located in the flywheel, as it will damage the crankshaft position sensor housing

8 Turn the engine in the normal direction of rotation, until it gets to 50° BTDC, then insert the Ford special tool (303-675) into the crankshaft position sensor hole and locate it in the flywheel. The hole in the fuel pump sprocket will now be in the 1 o'clock position **(see illustrations)**.

9 Remove the intake manifold as described in Chapter 2C.

10 Release the securing clips and disconnect the wiring connector(s) from the fuel injection pump **(see illustration)**.

Caution: As with any ECU, take care while the wiring connector is unplugged that the pump control unit is not damaged by static discharge across the exposed wiring pins – it may be advisable to cover the pins with a strip of paper, taped in place (do not use tape directly, as this may contaminate the pins).

11 Remove the fuel injection pipes as described in Section 11.

12 Noting their positions for refitting, prise out the plastic retaining clips and disconnect the fuel supply and return lines from the connections at the pump. The supply line connector is marked with a white band, and the return line connector has a red band.

13 Undo the retaining bolt and nut and remove the fuel line bracket from the cylinder head **(see illustration)**.

14 Access the fuel pump retaining bolts, through the holes provided in the fuel pump sprocket **(see illustration)**. **Note:** *The bolts cannot be completely removed.*

15 Using the Ford special tool (303-681), lock

10.14 Access holes (arrowed) to fuel pump retaining bolts (timing chain cover removed for clarity)

10.15 Special tool used to lock the pump sprocket in place

10.17 Unbolt the rear support bracket (arrowed) – 'common rail' engine

10.22 Fitting new gasket – note the cut out (arrowed)

the fuel injection pump sprocket in place. Undo the four sprocket retaining bolts, making sure the tool stays in place to lock the sprocket to the timing chain cover **(see illustration)**.

16 On the D5BA engine remove the fuel injection pump damper from the rear of the pump.

17 Unbolt and the injection pump rear support bracket from the cylinder block **(see illustration)**.

18 Remove the fuel injection pump from the cylinder block, discard the gasket, a new one will be required on refitting.

19 If not already removed, unbolt the fuel supply and return pipes from the fuel pump.

Refitting

20 Ensure that the engine timing setting is still set at 50° BTDC, using the information in Chapter 2C, Section 3, if necessary.

21 Using a 6 mm pin (drill bit), align the hole in the pump drive pulley with the cut-out provided in the pump rotor mounting face. With the cut-out aligned, remove the 6 mm pin.

22 Offer the pump into position, with a new gasket **(see illustration)**, and fit the support bracket mounting bolts, do not tighten them at this stage.

23 With the fuel pump in position remove the Ford special tool (303-681) from locking the fuel injection pump sprocket in place.

24 Access the fuel pump retaining bolts, through the holes provided in the fuel pump sprocket and tighten them to their specified torque setting.

25 Install the four sprocket retaining bolts, do not tighten them at this stage.

26 With the hole in the fuel pump sprocket aligned with the cut-out in the pump mounting face **(see illustration 10.22)**, insert the 6 mm pin (drill bit).

27 The four sprocket retaining bolts can now be tightened to their specified torque setting.

28 On the D5BA engine refit the fuel injection pump damper to the rear of the pump.

29 The support bracket mounting bolts at the rear of the fuel pump can now be tightened to their specified torque setting.

30 Remove the 6 mm pin (drill bit) from the fuel injection pump sprocket.

31 Using a suitable paint, mark the position of the crankshaft pulley in relation to the timing chain cover, then remove the special tool from the crankshaft sensor hole.

32 Rotate the engine in the normal direction of rotation, turning it two complete revolutions.

⚠ *Warning: Do not turn the engine while any of the special tools are in the fitted position.*

33 The engine timing setting should still be set at 50° BTDC, using the information in Chapter 2C, Section 3, if necessary.

34 Insert the Ford special tool (303-675) back into the crankshaft position sensor hole to locate in the flywheel.

35 The hole in the fuel pump sprocket should be aligned with the cut-out in the pump mounting face, insert the 6 mm pin (drill bit).

36 With the timing re-aligned, remove the special tool from the crankshaft sensor hole and refit the crankshaft sensor with reference to Section 9.

37 Remove the 6 mm pin (drill bit) from the fuel injection pump sprocket.

38 Using the Ford special tool (303-679) or the home-made tool, refit the access cover to the timing chain cover.

39 Reconnect the wiring plug to the pump control unit, and secure it in position with the locking catch.

40 Refit the new fuel injection pipes as described in Section 11.

41 Refit the fuel supply line (colour-coded white) to the injection pump, and secure it by pressing the plastic retaining clip fully home.

42 Before reconnecting the return pipe, the injection pump should be primed with fuel, to reduce the length of time spent cranking the engine at start-up. If a new pump has been fitted (or the old pump has been off the engine for some time), priming with fuel is essential, as the fuel lubricates the pump internals, which may otherwise be dry. Follow the procedures in Section 2. If a vacuum pump is not available, a new pump can be partially primed by pouring in clean fuel via the fuel supply and return connections – take precautions against fuel spillage on delicate components by covering the surrounding area with clean rags, and be very careful not to introduce dirt into the pump.

43 Refit the fuel return pipe (colour-coded red) to the injection pump, and secure by pressing the plastic retaining clip fully home.

44 Refit the retaining bolt and nut and secure the fuel line bracket to the cylinder head.

45 Refit the intake manifold as described in Chapter 2C.

46 Refit the damper to the engine mounting.

47 Refit the power steering reservoir back into place.

48 Refit the coolant expansion bottle back into place.

49 Refit the engine plastic cover and insert the oil level dipstick.

50 Reconnect the battery negative (earth) lead.

51 Start the engine, and let it idle, noting that it may take a while before a stable idle speed is achieved, as the powertrain control module (PCM) may have to relearn some of the 'adaptive' values. As the engine warms-up, check for signs of leakage from the fuel unions. If no leakage is evident, take the car for a short journey (of at least 5 miles) to allow the PCM to complete its 'learning' process.

52 If required, bleed the system as described in Section 2.

53 If a new injection pump has been fitted, refer to the Note at the start of this Section.

11 Injection pipes – removal and refitting

Caution: Be careful not to allow dirt into the injection system during this procedure.

Removal

1 The fuel injection pipes should be removed as a set. At the time of writing, it is not clear whether individual pipes are available.

2 Disconnect the battery negative (earth) lead (refer to *Disconnecting the battery* at the end of this manual).

3 Clean around the pipe unions at the injectors, supply manifold (common rail engines) and at the pump.

4 Using a spanner to hold the injectors in position, slacken the fuel supply pipes. Note the position of the fuel supply pipes **(see illustration)**.

11.4 Using two spanners, one to hold the injectors in position

11.7 On common rail engines, disconnect the fuel pump pipe from the fuel supply manifold (manifold removed for clarity)

5 On D5BA and D6BA engines, slacken the fuel supply pipes from the fuel injection pump.
6 On 'common rail' engines, slacken the fuel supply pipes from the supply manifold (see illustration).
7 On 'common rail' engines, slacken the supply pipe unions from the pump to the supply manifold (see illustration).
8 With all the unions slackened, the fuel pipes can now be completely disconnected and removed.
9 Fit blanking plugs to the injectors (see illustration), supply manifold (common rail engines) and fuel pump unions, to prevent dirt ingress.
10 Discard the fuel injection pipes, as Ford recommend that new pipes must always be used when refitting.

Refitting

11 When refitting, make sure that all the

11.6 Disconnecting the injector pipe from the fuel supply manifold – 'common rail' engine

11.9 Fitting blanking plugs to the injectors

anti-rattle clips (where fitted) are in place. Do not bend or strain the pipes and make sure they are kept clean and free from any contamination.
12 Refit the pipe assemblies to the injectors, supply manifold (common rail engines) and injection pump, initially hand-tightening the union nuts. With all the fuel injection pipes in place, fully tighten the nuts to the specified torque.
Caution: The injectors are not to turn from their position in the cylinder head, a special tool is used to align the injectors – see Section 12
13 Reconnect the battery negative (earth) lead.
14 If only the pipes have been removed, there should be no need to bleed the system (Section 2).
15 Run the engine and check the disturbed unions for leaks.

12.3 Slacken the locking sleeve and remove the fuel injectors

12.4 Remove the O-ring seals and discard them

12 Fuel injectors – removal, testing and refitting

⚠️ *Warning: Exercise extreme caution when working on the fuel injectors. Never expose the hands or any part of the body to injector spray, as the high working pressure can cause the fuel to penetrate the skin, with possibly fatal results. You are strongly advised to have any work which involves testing the injectors under pressure carried out by a dealer or fuel injection specialist.*
Caution: Be careful not to allow dirt into the injection system during this procedure.
Note: Ford special tools will be required for the refitting procedure of the fuel injectors – see text

Removal

1 Disconnect the battery negative (earth) lead (refer to *Disconnecting the battery* at the end of this manual). Clean around the injectors and the injection pipe unions.
2 Remove the camshaft cover as described in Chapter 2C.
3 Slacken the fuel injector locking sleeves until they are all the way off, then remove the fuel injectors from the cylinder head (see illustration). *Note: The injectors may be tight, carefully work them until they can be withdrawn.*
4 Recover the sealing washers and O-rings from each injector (see illustration), and discard them – new washers/O-rings must be used on reassembly.
5 Take care not to drop the injectors, nor allow the needles at their tips to become damaged.

Testing

6 Testing of injectors requires a special high-pressure test rig, and is best left to a professional. If the skin is exposed to spray from the injectors, the pressure is high enough for diesel fuel to penetrate the skin, with potentially fatal results.
7 Defective injectors should be renewed or professionally repaired. DIY repair is not a practical proposition.

12.8 Replace the injector sealing washer (A) and O-ring seal (B)

Refitting

8 Commence refitting by inserting new washers to the injector bores and fitting O-ring seals to the injectors **(see illustration)**.

9 Insert the injectors, using the Ford Special tool (303-711) to align the injectors in the cylinder head **(see illustration)**. **Note:** *A flat bar, with two cut-outs can be fabricated, to lock two of the injectors to prevent them from turning.*

10 With the injectors held in position, tighten the locking sleeve to the correct torque setting, using Ford special socket (303-677).

11 Refit the camshaft cover (Chapter 2C).

12 Check the position of the injectors using the Ford Special tool (303-711) **(see illustration)**, when refitting the fuel pipes.

13 Reconnect the battery negative (earth) lead.

13 Turbocharger – general information, removal and refitting

General information

1 The turbocharger increases engine efficiency by raising the pressure in the intake manifold above atmospheric pressure. Instead of the air simply being sucked into the cylinders, it is forced in. Additional fuel is supplied by the injection pump, in proportion to the increased amount of air.

2 Energy for the operation of the turbo-

12.9 Aligning the injectors using a flat metal bar with two cut-outs

charger comes from the exhaust gas. The gas flows through a specially-shaped housing (the turbine housing) and in so doing, spins the turbine wheel. The turbine wheel is attached to a shaft, at the end of which is another vaned wheel, known as the compressor wheel. The compressor wheel spins in its own housing, and compresses the inducted air on the way to the intake manifold.

3 Between the turbocharger and the intake manifold, the compressed air passes through an intercooler (see Section 14 for details). The purpose of the intercooler is to remove from the inducted air some of the heat gained in being compressed. Because cooler air is denser, removal of this heat further increases engine efficiency.

4 Boost pressure (the pressure in the intake manifold) is limited by a wastegate, which

12.12 Checking the position of the injectors using the Ford Special tool

diverts the exhaust gas away from the turbine wheel in response to a pressure-sensitive actuator.

5 The turbo shaft is pressure-lubricated by its own dedicated oil feed pipe. The shaft 'floats' on a cushion of oil. Oil is returned to the sump via a return pipe that connects to the sump.

6 The turbocharger on the Duratorq engine is integral with the exhaust manifold, and is not available separately. There are two types of turbocharger fitted to the Duratorq engine. A fixed vane type is fitted to the D5BA engine, and a variable vane type is fitted to the other engines **(see illustration)**. On the fixed vane type there is a wastegate control valve, which opens a flap at high engine speeds. On the variable vane type, as the engine speed increases the guide vanes in the turbine housing are progressively opened.

13.6a Fixed vane turbocharger

1 Exhaust manifold heat shield 4 Oil return tube
2 Exhaust manifold 5 Turbocharger
3 Oil supply tube 6 Wastegate control valve

13.6b Variable vane turbocharger

1 Exhaust manifold heat shield 4 Oil return tube
2 Exhaust manifold 5 Turbocharger
3 Oil supply tube 6 Vacuum diaphragm unit

14.6 Slacken the hose clip (arrowed) and disconnect the intercooler air intake pipes (right-hand side)

14.7a Remove the retaining bolt (one each side) . . .

14.7b . . . and remove the intercooler from the vehicle

7 The turbocharger is part of the exhaust manifold assembly. Removal and refitting of the exhaust manifold/turbocharger is covered in Chapter 2C, Section 20.

Precautions

8 The turbocharger operates at extremely high speeds and temperatures. Certain precautions must be observed to avoid premature failure of the turbo, or injury to the operator.
• *Do not operate the turbo with any parts exposed. Foreign objects falling onto the rotating vanes could cause excessive damage and (if ejected) personal injury.*
• *Cover the turbocharger air intake ducts to prevent debris entering, and clean using lint-free cloths only.*
• *Do not race the engine immediately after start-up, especially if it is cold. Give the oil a few seconds to circulate.*
• *Always allow the engine to return to idle speed before switching it off – do not blip the throttle and switch off, as this will leave the turbo spinning without lubrication.*
• *Allow the engine to idle for several minutes before switching off after a high-speed run.*
• *Observe the recommended intervals for oil and filter changing, and use a reputable oil of the specified quality. Neglect of oil changing, or use of inferior oil, can cause carbon formation on the turbo shaft and subsequent failure. Thoroughly clean the area around all oil pipe unions before disconnecting them, to prevent the ingress of dirt. Store dismantled components in a sealed container to prevent contamination.*

14 Intercooler –
general information,
removal and refitting

General information

1 The intercooler is effectively an 'air radiator', used to cool the pressurised intake air before it enters the engine.
2 When the turbocharger compresses the intake air, one side-effect is that the air is heated, causing the air to expand. If the intake

air can be cooled, a greater effective volume of air will be inducted, and the engine will produce more power.
3 The compressed air from the turbocharger, which would normally be fed straight into the intake manifold, is instead ducted forwards around the left side of the engine to the base of the intercooler. The intercooler is mounted at the front of the car, in the airflow. The heated air entering the base of the unit rises upwards, and is cooled by the airflow over the intercooler fins, much as with the radiator. When it reaches the top of the intercooler, the cooled air is then ducted rearwards into the intake manifold.

Removal

4 Disconnect the battery negative lead, and position the lead away from the battery (refer to *Disconnecting the battery* at the end of this manual).
5 Remove the front bumper as described in Chapter 11.
6 Slacken the hose clips and disconnect the intercooler air intake pipes from each end of the intercooler **(see illustration)**.
7 Remove the two bolts (one each side) securing the intercooler to the engine compartment front panel. Lift the intercooler away from front panel, and place it somewhere safe (remember that the intercooler fins are just as vulnerable to damage as those on the radiator) **(see illustrations)**.

Refitting

8 Refitting is a reversal of removal. Check the intake and outlet pipes for signs of damage, and make sure that the pipe clips are securely tightened.

15 Exhaust system –
general information
and component renewal

⚠️ *Warning: Inspection and repair of exhaust system components should be done only after the system has cooled completely. This applies particularly to the catalytic converter, which runs at very high temperatures.*

General information

1 The catalytic converter (see Chapter 4C) is mounted at an angle, directly below the exhaust manifold. Immediately below the converter is a short flexible section of pipe, connecting to the factory-fitted one-piece rear section, which contains the centre and rear silencers **(see illustration)**. To renew either silencer, the original rear section must be cut through mid-way between the centre and rear silencers.
2 Before making any cut, offer up the replacement exhaust section for comparison, and if necessary, adjust the cutting points as required. Bear in mind that there must be some 'overlap' allowance, as the original and replacement sections are sleeved together.
3 The system is suspended throughout its entire length by rubber mountings, with a rigid support bracket fitted below the catalytic converter.
4 To remove a part of the system, first jack up the front or rear of the car, and support it on axle stands (see *Jacking and vehicle support*). Alternatively, position the car over an inspection pit, or on car ramps.
5 Ford recommend that all nuts (such as flange joint nuts, clamp joint nuts, or converter-to-manifold nuts) are renewed on reassembly – given that they may be in less-than-perfect condition as a result of corrosion, this seems a good idea, especially as it will make subsequent removal easier.
6 At least on the car seen in our workshop, no gaskets appear to be used on the exhaust system mating surfaces. Make sure that the mating faces of the exhaust system joints are cleaned thoroughly before assembling.

Component renewal

7 If any section of the exhaust is damaged or deteriorated, excessive noise and vibration will occur.
8 Carry out regular inspections of the exhaust system, to check security and condition. Look for any damaged or bent parts, open seams, holes, loose connections, excessive corrosion, or other defects which could allow exhaust fumes to enter the vehicle. Deteriorated sections of the exhaust system should be renewed.

15.1 Exhaust system layout

1 *Catalytic converter*

2 *Exhaust flexible pipe*

3 *Silencer and tailpipe assembly*

9 If the exhaust system components are extremely corroded or rusted together, it may not be possible to separate them. In this case, simply cut off the old components with a hacksaw, and remove any remaining corroded pipe with a cold chisel. Be sure to wear safety glasses to protect your eyes, and wear gloves to protect your hands.

10 Here are some simple guidelines to follow when repairing the exhaust system:
  a) *Work from the back to the front when removing exhaust system components.*
  b) *Apply penetrating fluid to the flange nuts before unscrewing them.*
  c) *Use new gaskets and rubber mountings when installing exhaust system components.*
  d) *Apply anti-seize compound to the threads*

of all exhaust system studs during reassembly.
  e) *Note that on some models, the downpipe is secured to the manifold by two coil springs, spring seats and a self-locking nut on each. Where fitted, tighten the nuts until they stop on the bolt shoulders; the pressure of the springs will then be sufficient to make a leak-proof connection. Do not overtighten the nuts to cure a leak – the studs will shear. Renew the gasket and the springs if a leak is found.*
  f) *Be sure to allow sufficient clearance between newly-installed parts and all points on the underbody, to avoid overheating the floorpan, and possibly damaging the interior carpet and*

insulation. Pay particularly close attention to the catalytic converter and its heat shield.
  g) *The heat shields are secured to the underside of the body by special nuts, or by bolts. They are fitted above the exhaust, to reduce radiated heat affecting the cabin or fuel tank. Each shield can be removed separately, but note that some overlap each other, making it necessary to loosen another section first. If a shield is being removed to gain access to a component located behind it, it may prove sufficient in some cases to remove the retaining nuts and/or bolts, and simply lower the shield, without disturbing the exhaust system. Otherwise, remove the exhaust section as described earlier.*

Notes

Chapter 4 Part C:
Emission control systems

Contents

Degrees of difficulty

Easy, suitable for novice with little experience		Fairly easy, suitable for beginner with some experience		Fairly difficult, suitable for competent DIY mechanic		Difficult, suitable for experienced DIY mechanic		Very difficult, suitable for expert DIY or professional	

Specifications

Torque wrench settings	Nm	lbf ft
Catalytic converter to manifold (diesel models)	46	34
EGR cooler mounting bracket bolts	10	7
EGR cooler-to-manifold bolts	37	27
EGR tube-to-EGR valve bolts (diesel models)	10	7
EGR valve outlet tube union (1.8 and 2.0 litre petrol models)	55	41
EGR valve mounting bolts:		
Petrol models	25	18
Diesel models	20	15
Exhaust flexible pipe to catalytic converter	46	34
Exhaust flexible pipe to intermediate pipe	46	34
Heat shield retaining bolts	10	7
Oil separator retaining bolts	10	7
Oxygen sensor (nearest to engine)	48	35
Monitor sensor (furthest from engine)	46	34

1 General information

Emission control – petrol models

All petrol models are designed to use unleaded petrol, and are controlled by the Ford 'Black Oak' engine management system to give the best compromise between driveability, fuel consumption and exhaust emission production. In addition, a number of systems are fitted that help to minimise other harmful emissions. A Positive Crankcase Ventilation (PCV) control system is fitted, which reduces the release of pollutants from the engine's lubrication system, and a catalytic converter is fitted which reduces exhaust gas pollutants. An exhaust gas recirculation (EGR) system is fitted, to further reduce emissions. Also an evaporative emission control system is fitted which reduces the release of gaseous hydrocarbons from the fuel tank.

Positive Crankcase Ventilation

On 4-cylinder petrol models, the crankcase ventilation system main components are the oil separator mounted on the front (radiator) side of the cylinder block/crankcase behind the intake manifold, and the Positive Crankcase Ventilation (PCV) valve set in a rubber grommet in the separator's left-hand upper end. The associated pipework consists of a crankcase breather pipe and two flexible hoses connecting the PCV valve to a union on the left-hand end of the inlet manifold, and a crankcase breather hose connecting the cylinder head cover to the air cleaner assembly. On V6 models, the system is similar but the oil separator is located on top of the cylinder block between the cylinder heads, below the intake manifold. A small foam filter in the air cleaner prevents dirt from being drawn directly into the engine.

The function of these components is to reduce the emission of unburned hydro-carbons from the crankcase, and to minimise the formation of oil sludge. By ensuring that a depression is created in the crankcase under most operating conditions, particularly at idle, and by positively inducing fresh air into the system, the oil vapours and 'blow-by' gases collected in the crankcase are drawn from the crankcase, through the oil separator, into the inlet tract, to be burned by the engine during normal combustion.

The system requires no attention other than to check at regular intervals that the hoses, valve and oil separator are free of blockages and in good condition.

Exhaust emission control

The exhaust gases of any petrol engine (however efficient or well-tuned) consist largely (approximately 99%) of nitrogen (N_2), carbon dioxide (CO_2), oxygen (O_2), other inert gases and water vapour (H_2O). The remaining 1% is made up of the noxious materials (CO_2 apart) which are currently seen as the major polluters of the environment. These are carbon monoxide (CO), unburned hydrocarbons (HC), oxides of nitrogen (NO_x) and some solid matter, including a small lead content. Left to themselves, most of these pollutants are thought eventually to break down naturally (CO and NO_x, for example, break down in the upper atmosphere to release CO_2) having first caused ground-level environmental problems. The massive increase world-wide in the use of motor vehicles, and the current popular concern for the environment has caused the introduction in most countries of legislation, in varying degrees of severity, to combat the problem.

The device most commonly used to clean up vehicle exhausts is the catalytic converter. It is fitted into the vehicle's exhaust system, and uses precious metals (platinum and palladium or rhodium) as catalysts to speed up the reaction between the pollutants and the oxygen in the vehicle's exhaust gases, CO and HC being oxidised to form H_2O and CO_2 and (in the three-way type of catalytic converter) NO_x being reduced to N_2. **Note:** *The catalytic converter is not a filter in the physical sense. Its function is to promote a chemical reaction, but it is not itself affected by that reaction.* The converter consists of an element (or 'substrate') of ceramic honeycomb, coated with a combination of precious metals in such a way as to produce a vast surface area over which the exhaust gases must flow, the whole being mounted in a stainless-steel box. A simple 'oxidation' (or 'two-way') catalytic converter can deal with CO and HC only, while a 'reduction' (or 'three-way') catalytic converter can deal with CO, HC and NO_x. Three-way catalytic converters are further sub-divided into 'open-loop' (or 'uncontrolled') converters which can remove 50 to 70% of pollutants and 'closed-loop' (also known as 'controlled' or 'regulated') converters which can remove over 90% of pollutants. The catalytic converter fitted to the Mondeo models covered in this manual is of the three-way closed-loop type.

The oxygen sensor has a built-in heating element, controlled by the Powertrain Control Module (PCM) through the oxygen sensor relay, to quickly bring the sensor's tip to its optimum operating temperature. The sensor's tip is sensitive to oxygen, and sends a voltage signal to the PCM that varies according on the amount of oxygen in the exhaust gas. If the inlet air/fuel mixture is too rich, the exhaust gases are low in oxygen so the sensor sends a low-voltage signal, the voltage rising as the mixture weakens and the amount of oxygen

rises in the exhaust gases. Peak conversion efficiency of all major pollutants occurs if the inlet air/fuel mixture is maintained at the chemically-correct ratio for the complete combustion of petrol of 14.7 parts (by weight) of air to 1 part of fuel (the stoichiometric ratio). The sensor output voltage alters in a large step at this point, the PCM using the signal change as a reference point and correcting the inlet air/fuel mixture accordingly by altering the fuel injector pulse width. Some later models are fitted with two sensors, one before and one after the converter. This allows a more accurate monitoring of the exhaust gas, and a faster reaction time from the PCM; the efficiency of the converter can also be monitored.

Exhaust Gas Recirculation

To reduce oxides of nitrogen (NO_x) emissions, some of the exhaust gases are recirculated through the EGR valve to the inlet manifold. This has the effect of lowering combustion temperatures. The system consists of the EGR valve, the EGR exhaust gas pressure differential sensor, the EGR solenoid valve, the PCM, and various sensors. The PCM is programmed to produce the ideal EGR valve lift for all operating conditions. On petrol 4-cylinder models, the EGR valve is mounted on the transmission end of the cylinder head, on V6 models, an EGR vacuum regulator is located on the bulkhead.

On diesel engines the EGR system is fitted with an EGR cooler fitted across the rear of the engine below the exhaust manifold, it is then supplied from the engine cooling system. The EGR valve is located on the transmission end of the cooler (except vehicles with 5-speed automatic transmission, the EGR valve is then located on the front of the engine at the timing chain end).

Evaporative Emissions Control

The evaporative emission control (EVAP) system fitted to petrol models consists of the purge valve, the activated charcoal filter canister and a series of connecting vacuum hoses. Little is possible by way of routine maintenance, except to check that the vacuum hoses are clear and undamaged. Careless servicing work may lead to the hoses becoming crushed – always take care to route these and other hoses correctly. This system is fitted to minimise the escape of unburned hydrocarbons into the atmosphere.

The fuel tank filler cap is sealed, and a charcoal canister is mounted to the rear of the fuel tank. The canister stores petrol vapours generated in the tank when the vehicle is parked. When the engine is running, the vapours are cleared from the canister under the control of the PCM via the canister-purge solenoid valve. The vapours are drawn into the inlet manifold, to be burned by the engine during normal combustion.

To ensure that the engine runs correctly when it is cold and/or idling, and to protect the

catalytic converter from the effects of an over-rich mixture, the canister-purge solenoid valve is not opened by the PCM until the engine is fully warmed-up and running under part-load. The solenoid valve is then switched on and off, to allow the stored vapour to pass into the inlet manifold. The purge valve is located on a bracket by the ignition coil, at the left-hand rear of the engine on 4-cylinder engines (left as seen from the driver's seat), and on the rear cylinder head cover on V6 engines.

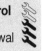

2 Evaporative emission control system (petrol models) – testing and component renewal

Testing

1 Poor idle, stalling and poor driveability can be caused by an inoperative canister-purge solenoid valve, a damaged canister, split or cracked hoses, or hoses connected to the wrong fittings. Check the fuel filler cap for a damaged or deformed gasket.

2 Fuel loss or fuel odour can be caused by liquid fuel leaking from fuel lines, a cracked or damaged canister, an inoperative canister-purge solenoid valve, and disconnected, incorrectly routed, kinked or damaged vapour or control hoses.

3 Inspect each hose attached to the canister for kinks, leaks and cracks along its entire length. Repair or renew as necessary.

4 Inspect the canister. If it is cracked or damaged, renew it. Look for fuel leaking from the bottom of the canister. If fuel is leaking, renew the canister, and check the hoses and hose routing.

5 If the canister-purge solenoid valve is thought to be faulty, unplug its electrical connector and disconnect its vacuum hoses. Connect a 12 volt battery directly across the valve terminals. Check that air can flow through the valve passages when the solenoid is energised, and that nothing can pass when the solenoid is not energised. Alternatively, connect an ohmmeter to measure the resistance across the solenoid terminals, and compare this reading to Ford's recommendations. Renew the solenoid valve if it is faulty.

6 Further testing should be left to a dealer service department.

Purge solenoid valve renewal

7 Disconnect the battery negative (earth) lead (refer to *Disconnecting the battery* at the end of this manual). On 4-cylinder models, unclip the breather hose from the engine upper plastic cover, then unclip the cover from the top of the engine.

8 Disconnect the hose(s) from the solenoid valve, noting their positions for refitting.

9 Disconnect the valve's electrical connector, then unclip the solenoid valve from the bracket **(see illustrations)**.

10 Refitting is the reverse of the removal procedure.

Charcoal canister renewal

Saloon and Hatchback models

Note: *Read through this procedure carefully before starting work, and ensure that the equipment is available that is required to carry it out safely and with minimum risk of damage, and to align the crossmember with sufficient accuracy on reassembly.*

11 Chock the front wheels, then jack up the rear of the vehicle and support on axle stands (see *Jacking and vehicle support*).

12 Remove the exhaust system as described in (Chapter 4A)

13 Where fitted, remove the headlamp levelling sensor as described in Chapter 12.

14 Ensure that the rear of the vehicle's body is supported securely on axle stands, then support the rear suspension crossmember with a jack. Remove the roadwheels and unscrew the rear suspension strut top mounting bolts (two per side).

15 Use white paint or similar (do not use a sharp-pointed scriber, which might break the underbody protective coating and cause rusting) to mark the exact relationship of the crossmember to the underbody. Unscrew the four mounting bolts. Lower the crossmember approximately 75 mm on the jack, and support it securely.

 Warning: Take care when lowering the crossmember as to not place any strain on the brake hoses and suspension components.

16 Unscrew the two rearmost canister bracket retaining bolts.

17 Disconnect the two hoses from the canister assembly, noting which way round they are fitted.

18 Unscrew the canister assembly's front retaining bolt. Withdraw the canister assembly.

19 Unclip the water separator box cover, then release the canister by pushing it to one side and unclipping it from the canister bracket **(see illustrations)**.

20 On reassembly, refit the canister to its bracket and refit the assembly to the vehicle, tightening the retaining bolts securely, and ensuring that the two hoses are securely reconnected to their original unions.

21 Offer up the crossmember and refit the

2.9a Disconnecting the wiring connector from the purge-valve (4-cylinder petrol models) . . .

crossmember bolts, tightening them only lightly at this stage. The crossmember must now be aligned on the underbody. Ford specify the use of service tool 15-097-A, which is a pair of tapered guides, with attachments to hold them in the crossmember as it is refitted. However, since the working diameter of these tools is 20.4 mm, and since the corresponding aligning holes in the crossmember and underbody are 21 mm and 22 mm in diameter, there is a significant in-built tolerance possible in the crossmember's alignment, even if the correct tools are used.

22 If these tools are not available, align the crossmember by eye, centring the crossmember aligning holes on those of the underbody, and using the marks made on removal for assistance. Alternatively, use a tapered drift such as a clutch-aligning tool, or a deep socket spanner of suitable size. Once the crossmember is aligned as precisely as possible, tighten its bolts to the specified torque (see Chapter 10 Specifications) without disturbing its position. Recheck the alignment once all the bolts are securely tightened.

23 The remainder of the refitting procedure is the reverse of removal.

24 Remember that, if the rear suspension crossmember has been disturbed, the wheel alignment and steering angles must be checked fully and carefully as soon as possible, with any necessary adjustments being made. This operation is best carried out by an experienced mechanic using proper checking equipment; the vehicle should therefore be taken to a Ford dealer or similar for attention.

2.9b . . . then unclip the valve from the bracket (V6 models)

Estate models

25 Disconnect the battery negative (earth) lead (refer to *Disconnecting the battery* at the end of this manual)..

26 Chock the front wheels, then jack up the rear of the vehicle and support on axle stands (see *Jacking and vehicle support*).

27 Disconnect the two hoses from the canister assembly, noting which way round they are fitted.

28 Unscrew the canister assembly retaining bolts and withdraw the assembly, unclipping it from the front mounting **(see illustration)**.

29 Unclip the water separator box cover, then release the canister by pushing it to one side and unclipping it from the canister bracket **(see illustration 2.19a and 2.19b)**.

30 On refitting, secure the canister to its bracket, and refit the assembly to the vehicle. Tighten the retaining bolt securely, and ensure that the two hoses are securely reconnected to their original unions.

---

3 Crankcase emission system (petrol models) – component renewal

PCV valve

1 The valve is plugged into the oil separator which is bolted to the cylinder block, remove the intake manifold as described in Chapter 2A (4-cylinder engines) or 2B (V6 engines).

2.19a Unclip the water separator box cover . . .

2.19b . . . and pushing it to one side, unclip the canister from the bracket

2.28 Undo the retaining bolts (arrowed) to remove the canister assembly

3.2a Using a screwdriver to release the clips . . .

3.2b . . . then pull the valve upwards to remove it from the oil separator

3.4 Unbolt and withdraw the oil separator from the cylinder block

3.6 Make sure the peg (arrowed) on the new gasket is located correctly

3.10 Oil separator on V6 models

4 Exhaust Gas Recirculation (EGR) system – testing and component renewal

Testing

EGR valve

1 Start the engine and allow it to idle.
2 Detach the vacuum hose from the EGR valve, and attach a hand vacuum pump in its place.
3 Apply vacuum to the EGR valve. Vacuum should remain steady, and the engine should run poorly or stall.
   a) If the vacuum doesn't remain steady and the engine doesn't run poorly, renew the EGR valve and recheck it.
   b) If the vacuum remains steady but the engine doesn't run poorly, remove the EGR valve, and check the valve and the inlet manifold for blockage. Clean or renew parts as necessary, and recheck.

EGR system

4 Any further checking of the system requires special tools and test equipment. Take the vehicle to a dealer service department for checking.

EGR valve renewal – petrol models

4-cylinder models

5 Disconnect the battery negative (earth) lead (refer to *Disconnecting the battery* at the end of this manual).
6 Unclip the breather hose from the engine upper plastic cover, then unclip the cover from the top of the engine.
7 Drain the cooling system as described in Chapter 3.
8 Undo the retaining clips and remove the air intake pipe from the throttle body to the air filter housing **(see illustration)**.
9 Disconnect the electrical connector from the EGR valve **(see illustration)**.
10 Detach the coolant hose from the EGR valve.
11 Remove the two valve mounting bolts, and withdraw the valve from the transmission end of the cylinder head **(see illustration)**.

Oil separator

4-cylinder models

3 Remove the intake manifold (see relevant Part of Chapter 2A).
4 Unbolt the oil separator from the cylinder block/crankcase, and withdraw it. Remove and discard the gasket **(see illustration)**.
5 Flush out or renew the oil separator, as required.
6 On reassembly, fit a new gasket, and tighten the bolts securely **(see illustration)**.
7 The remainder of the refitting procedure is the reverse of removal.

V6 models

8 Remove the intake manifold on V6 engines (see relevant Part of Chapter 2B).
9 Either disconnect the hose leading to the separator, or pull out the PCV valve.
10 Unscrew the bolts and remove the separator from the top of the cylinder block (between the cylinder heads), recover the gasket **(see illustration)**.
11 If not already done, remove the PCV valve from the separator. Wash out the oil separator using a suitable solvent (such as engine degreaser), and ensure that its passages are clear.
12 Refitting is a reversal of removal. Use a new gasket, and tighten the retaining bolts securely.

PCV hose(s)

13 The hoses are a push-fit onto the PCV valve and intake manifold, and can only be replaced once the intake manifold has been removed (see relevant parts of Chapter 2).
14 Wash the oil separator and valve in suitable solvent (such as engine degreaser), and ensure that all passages are clear. Check the hoses for signs of damage, especially at the hose ends. Where an O-ring is used to seal the valve into its location, check the condition of the O-ring before refitting.
15 Refitting is a reversal of removal. Make sure that the hoses are securely and correctly refitted, and that the hoses are routed as before.

4.8 Remove the air intake pipe from the throttle body

4.9 Disconnecting the wiring connector from the EGR valve

4.11 Undo the two mounting bolts and withdraw the EGR valve

4.14 Refitting the EGR valve together with a new gasket

V6 models

12 Disconnect the battery negative (earth) lead (refer to *Disconnecting the battery* at the end of this manual).

13 Remove the mass air flow sensor and remove the idle air control valve as described in Chapter 4A, Section 13.

14 Detach the vacuum hose, unscrew the sleeve nut securing the EGR pipe to the valve, remove the two valve mounting bolts, and withdraw the valve from the intake manifold **(see illustration)**. Ensure that the end of the pipe is not damaged or distorted as the valve is withdrawn, and note the valve's gasket; this must be renewed whenever the valve is disturbed.

15 Note that the metal pipe from the valve to the manifold itself should not be disturbed – it is not available separately from the manifold. However, check whenever the manifold is removed that the pipe's end fitting is securely fastened **(see illustration)**.

16 Check the valve for sticking and heavy carbon deposits. If such is found, clean the valve or renew it.

17 Refitting is the reverse of the removal procedure. Apply a smear of anti-seize compound to the sleeve nut threads, fit a new gasket, and tighten the valve bolts to the specified torque wrench setting.

EGR pipe renewal

V6 models

18 Disconnect the idle air control valve tube from the air cleaner and upper inlet manifold.

19 Unscrew the EGR tube sleeve nut from the EGR valve and disconnect the tube.

20 Chock the front wheels, then jack up the rear of the vehicle and support on axle stands (see *Jacking and vehicle support*). Remove the front left-hand wheel and the wheel arch liner.

21 Remove the EGR tube nut from the rear exhaust manifold and remove the tube **(see illustration)**.

22 Refitting is a reversal of removal. Apply anti-seize compound to the nuts on both ends of the tube.

Exhaust gas pressure differential sensor

V6 models

23 This component measures the difference

in pressure of the exhaust gases across a venturi (restriction) in the Exhaust Gas Recirculation (EGR) system's pipe, and sends the PCM a voltage signal corresponding to the pressure difference.

24 Testing of this component is beyond the scope of the DIY mechanic, and should be left to a Ford dealer.

Component renewal

25 The differential pressure sensor is located next to the EGR solenoid on the left-hand end of the rear cylinder head.

26 Note the positions of the vacuum hoses for refitting (they are of different diameter), then disconnect them from the ports on the sensor.

27 Disconnect the sensor wiring plug, then unscrew the sensor mounting bolts and remove the sensor from its location **(see illustration)**.

4.15 Check end fitting of EGR pipe into inlet manifold whenever manifold is removed, but do not disturb

4.27 Disconnecting the wiring plug from the exhaust gas pressure differential sensor

28 Refitting is a reversal of removal, making sure that the hoses are correctly refitted. *Note: Check the condition of both hoses and renew them if necessary.*

EGR valve outlet tube renewal

Diesel models

29 Disconnect the battery negative (earth) lead (refer to *Disconnecting the battery* at the end of this manual). Remove the engine upper cover.

30 Disconnect the wiring connector from the mass air flow sensor, slacken the air intake hose retaining clips and remove the complete air cleaner housing from the vehicle (see Chapter 4B).

31 Undo the two retaining bolts and disconnect the outlet tube from the EGR valve **(see illustration)**, renew the gasket on refitting.

4.21 Removing the EGR tube on V6 models

4.31 Undo the two retaining bolts (arrowed) to disconnect the outlet tube

4.32 Slacken the securing clips and remove the air intake pipe

4.33 Slacken the securing clip (arrowed) and disconnect the charge air cooler hose

4.34 Undo the retaining bolts (arrowed) and remove the outlet tube

32 Unclip the coolant hose, slacken the securing clips and remove the air intake pipe from the outlet tube (see illustration).
33 Slacken the securing clip and disconnect the charge air cooler hose from the outlet tube (see illustration).
34 Undo the retaining bolts and remove the outlet tube from across the top of the transmission unit (see illustration).
35 Refitting is a reversal of removal, making sure that the hoses are correctly refitted. Note: Check the condition of the hoses and renew them if necessary.

EGR valve renewal – diesel models

Manual transmission

36 Remove the EGR valve outlet tube as described in paragraphs 29 to 35.
37 Disconnect the vacuum pipe from the EGR valve (see illustration).

38 On vehicles without common rail fuel injection, disconnect the electrical connector from the EGR valve.
39 Undo the two retaining nuts and remove the EGR valve from the cooler (see illustration), renew the gasket on refitting.
40 Refitting is a reversal of removal.

Automatic transmission

41 Remove the engine upper cover, undo the two retaining nuts and detach the EGR valve tube from the EGR valve, renew the gasket on refitting.
42 Slacken the securing clip and disconnect the charge air cooler hose from the EGR valve.
43 Disconnect the vacuum pipe from the EGR valve.
44 Undo the two retaining bolts and remove the EGR valve from the intake manifold, renew the gasket on refitting.
45 Refitting is a reversal of removal.

EGR tube/cooler renewal

Diesel models

46 The EGR system on diesel models are fitted with a cooler (supplied from the cooling system), which reduces the temperature of the exhaust gas being recycled; the cooler is effectively a water jacket around the pipe connecting the exhaust manifold and the EGR valve.
47 Remove the EGR valve outlet tube and (EGR valve on manual transmission vehicles) as described in paragraphs 29 to 40.
48 Drain the cooling system as described in Chapter 3.
49 To gain better access, remove the catalytic converter as described in Section 6.
50 Slacken the securing clips and disconnect the coolant hose from the thermostat housing and EGR cooler.
51 Undo the retaining nut and bolts and remove the cooler (see illustrations), renew the gasket on refitting.
52 Refitting is a reversal of removal, making sure that the hoses are correctly refitted. Note: Check the condition of the hoses and renew them if necessary, top-up the cooling system as required.
53 Depending on model and transmission unit fitted, the EGR cooler tube routing will vary. Follow the tube and undo the retaining nuts and release any retaining clips to remove the tube.

4.37 Disconnect the vacuum pipe (arrowed) from the EGR valve

4.39 Undo the two retaining nuts (arrowed) and lift the EGR valve from the cooler

---

5 Oxygen sensor –
testing and
component renewal

Testing

1 Testing the oxygen sensor is only possible by connecting special diagnostic equipment to the sensor wiring, and checking that the voltage varies from low to high values when the engine is running. **Do not** attempt to 'test' any part of the system with anything other than the correct test equipment. This is beyond the scope of the DIY mechanic, and should be left to a Ford dealer. Note: Some models are fitted with two sensors – one before and one after the catalytic converter.

4.51a Undo the retaining nut and bolt (arrowed) . . .

4.51b . . . and the two bolts (arrowed), then remove the cooler

5.3a Disconnecting the oxygen sensor wiring block connector

5.3b The rear sensor wiring connector is clipped to the rear of the subframe

5.4 Removing the oxygen sensor from the exhaust manifold on V6 models

This enables more efficient monitoring of the exhaust gas, allowing a faster response time. The overall efficiency of the converter itself can also be checked. The sensor after the catalytic converter is sometimes known as a monitor sensor.

Component renewal

Note: *The sensor is delicate, and will not work if it is dropped or knocked, or if any cleaning materials are used on it.*

2 Where applicable, remove the bolts securing the heat shield fitted over the exhaust manifold, and lift away the heat shield for access to the sensor.

3 Trace the wiring from the sensor body back to its wiring plug, and disconnect it. On models with two sensors, the wiring plug for the rearmost sensor is clipped to the rear of the subframe under the car **(see illustrations)**. Note how the wiring is routed, as it must not come into contact with hot exhaust components.

4 Raise and support the front of the vehicle if required to remove the sensor from underneath. Unscrew the sensor from the exhaust system front downpipe on 4-cylinder models or from each exhaust manifold on V6 models **(see illustration)**. Recover the gasket (where fitted).

5 It may be beneficial to clean the sensor before refitting it, especially if the sensor tip appears to be contaminated. However, great care must be exercised, as the tip will be damaged by any abrasives, and by certain solvents. Seek the advice of a Ford dealer before cleaning the sensor.

6 Refitting is a reversal of removal, noting the following points:

a) *Apply a little anti-seize compound to the sensor threads, taking care not to allow any on the sensor tip, and tighten the sensor to the specified torque.*

b) *Reconnect the wiring, ensuring that it is routed clear of any hot exhaust components.*

c) *If required, proof that the sensor is working can be gained by having the exhaust emissions checked, and compare it with the figure that Ford recommends. Remember that a faulty sensor will have generated a fault code – if this code is still*

logged in the PCM electronic memory, then see your Ford dealer to read the fault code still in the memory.

6 Catalytic converter – general information, removal and refitting

General information

1 The catalytic converter reduces harmful exhaust emissions by chemically converting the more poisonous gases to ones which (in theory at least) are less harmful. The chemical reaction is known as an 'oxidising' reaction, or one where oxygen is 'added'.

2 Inside the converter is a honeycomb structure, made of ceramic material and coated with the precious metals palladium, platinum and rhodium (the 'catalyst' which promotes the chemical reaction). The chemical reaction generates heat, which itself promotes the reaction – therefore, once the car has been driven several miles, the body of the converter will be very hot.

3 The ceramic structure contained within the converter is understandably fragile, and will not withstand rough treatment. Since the converter runs at a high temperature, driving through deep standing water (in flood conditions, for example) is to be avoided, since the thermal stresses imposed when plunging the hot converter into cold water may well cause the ceramic internals to fracture, resulting in a 'blocked' converter – a common cause of failure. A converter which has been damaged in this way can be checked by shaking it (do not strike it) – if a rattling noise is heard, this indicates probable failure. **Note:** *Checking the operation of a catalytic converter requires expensive and sophisticated diagnostic equipment, starting with a high-quality exhaust gas analyser. If the level of CO in the exhaust gases is too high, a full check of the engine management system must be carried out to eliminate all other possibilities before the converter is suspected of being faulty. The vehicle should be taken to a Ford dealer for this work to be carried out using the correct diagnostic equipment. Do not waste time trying to test the system without such facilities.*

Precautions

4 The catalytic converter is a reliable and simple device which needs no maintenance in itself, but there are some facts of which an owner should be aware if the converter is to function properly for its full service life:

Petrol models

a) *DO NOT use leaded petrol (or lead-replacement petrol) in a car equipped with a catalytic converter – the lead (or other additives) will coat the precious metals, reducing their converting efficiency and will eventually destroy the converter.*

b) *Always keep the ignition and fuel systems well-maintained in accordance with the manufacturer's schedule (see Chapter 1A).*

c) *If the engine develops a misfire, do not drive the car at all (or at least as little as possible) until the fault is cured.*

d) *DO NOT push- or tow-start the car – this will soak the catalytic converter in unburned fuel, causing it to overheat when the engine does start.*

e) *DO NOT switch off the ignition at high engine speeds – i.e., do not 'blip' the throttle immediately before switching off the engine.*

Petrol and diesel models

5 The catalytic converter fitted to diesel models is simpler than that fitted to petrol models, but it still needs to be treated with respect to avoid problems:

a) *DO NOT use fuel or engine oil additives – these may contain substances harmful to the catalytic converter.*

b) *DO NOT continue to use the car if the engine burns (engine) oil to the extent of leaving a visible trail of blue smoke.*

c) *Remember that the catalytic converter operates at very high temperatures. DO NOT, therefore, park the car in dry undergrowth, over long grass or piles of dead leaves after a long run.*

d) *As mentioned above, driving through deep water should be avoided if possible. The sudden cooling effect will fracture the ceramic honeycomb, damaging it beyond repair.*

6.13 Removing the heat shield from the top of the exhaust manifold

6.14 Remove the four nuts (arrowed) to remove the catalytic converter

6.17 Support bracket (arrowed) fitted to the lower part of the catalytic converter

6.18 Lowering the converter downwards from the manifold

Removal and refitting

Note: *Do not over bend the front exhaust flexible pipe as it is removed or it will get damaged. Support the flexible pipe with a support wrap or a splint.*

Petrol models

6 Disconnect the battery negative (earth) lead (refer to *Disconnecting the battery* at the end of this manual).

7 Chock the rear wheels, then jack up the front of the vehicle and support it on axle stands (see *Jacking and vehicle support*).

8 Disconnect the wiring connector(s) from the oxygen sensor(s), unclip the wiring loom from under the vehicle, where required.

9 Undo the two retaining nuts and disconnect the flexible pipe from the catalytic converter, discard the gasket. To prevent possible damage to the flexible section of pipe behind the flange joint, Ford technicians cable-tie two strips of thick metal on either side, down the length of the flexible section.

10 Undo the two retaining nuts and

e) *Remember that the catalytic converter is FRAGILE – do not strike it with tools during servicing work, and take care handling it when removing it from the car for any reason.*

f) *If a substantial loss of power is experienced, remember that this could be due to the converter being blocked. This can occur simply as a result of high mileage, but may be due to the ceramic element having fractured and collapsed internally (see paragraph 3). A new converter is the only cure in this instance.*

g) *The catalytic converter, used on a well-maintained and well-driven car, should last for between 50 000 and 100 000 miles – if the converter is no longer effective, it must be renewed.*

h) *In some cases, a sulphurous smell (like that of rotten eggs) may be noticed from the exhaust. This is common to many catalytic converter-equipped cars, and has more to do with the sulphur content of the brand of fuel being used than the converter itself.*

disconnect the catalytic converter from the exhaust intermediate pipe, discard the gasket.

11 Refitting is a reversal of removal. Use new nuts, bolts and gaskets as necessary, and tighten all fasteners to the specified torque.

Note: *Exhaust sealant paste should not be used on any part of the exhaust system upstream of the catalytic converter (between the engine and the converter) – even if the sealant does not contain additives harmful to the converter, pieces of it may break off and foul the element, causing local overheating.*

Diesel models

12 Disconnect the battery negative (earth) lead (refer to *Disconnecting the battery* at the end of this manual).

13 Undo the retaining bolts and remove the heat shield from the top of the exhaust manifold **(see illustration)**.

14 Remove the four nuts securing the top of the catalytic converter to the exhaust manifold **(see illustration)**.

15 Chock the rear wheels, then jack up the front of the vehicle and support it on axle stands (see *Jacking and vehicle support*).

16 Undo the two retaining nuts and disconnect the flexible pipe from the bottom of the catalytic converter, discard the gasket. To prevent possible damage to the flexible section of pipe behind the flange joint, Ford technicians cable-tie two strips of thick metal on either side, down the length of the flexible section.

17 Support the converter, then remove the retaining bolts from the support bracket at the base of the converter. Alternatively, remove the support bracket completely **(see illustration)**.

18 With the converter supported, lower the converter downwards under the vehicle, taking great care not to drop it or knock it, as the internals are fragile **(see illustration)**. The converter is a bulky component, and it may be necessary to rotate it as it is withdrawn.

19 Refitting is a reversal of removal. Use new nuts, bolts and gaskets as necessary, and tighten all fasteners to the specified torque.

Note: *Exhaust sealant paste should not be used on any part of the exhaust system upstream of the catalytic converter (between the engine and the converter) – even if the sealant does not contain additives harmful to the converter, pieces of it may break off and foul the element, causing local overheating.*

Chapter 5 Part A:
Starting and charging systems

Contents

Degrees of difficulty

Easy, suitable for novice with little experience	Fairly easy, suitable for beginner with some experience	Fairly difficult, suitable for competent DIY mechanic 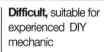	Difficult, suitable for experienced DIY mechanic	Very difficult, suitable for expert DIY or professional

Specifications

General
System type .... 12 volt, negative earth

Battery
Type .... Lead-calcium
Rating .... 60 to 70 Ah (depending on model)

Starter motor
Type .... Motorcraft, pre-engaged

Torque wrench settings

	Nm	lbf ft
Alternator mounting:		
Bolts	47	35
Nuts (diesel engines)	47	35
Studs (diesel engines)	15	11
Starter motor mounting bolts:		
4-cylinder engines	25	18
V6 engine	35	26

1 General information, precautions and battery disconnection

General information

The engine electrical systems include all ignition, charging and starting components. Because of their engine-related functions, these components are discussed separately from body electrical devices such as the lights, the instruments, etc (which are included in Chapter 12).

Precautions

Always observe the following precautions when working on the electrical system:

a) Be extremely careful when servicing engine electrical components. They are easily damaged if checked, connected or handled improperly.

b) Never leave the ignition switched on for long periods of time when the engine is not running.

c) Don't disconnect the battery leads while the engine is running.

d) Maintain correct polarity when connecting a battery lead from another vehicle during jump starting – see the 'Jump starting' Section at the front of this manual.

e) Always disconnect the negative lead first, and reconnect it last, or the battery may be shorted by the tool being used to loosen the lead clamps.

It's also a good idea to review the safety-related information regarding the engine electrical systems shown in the Safety first! section at the front of this manual, before beginning any operation included in this Chapter.

Battery disconnection

Note: Also refer to 'Disconnecting the battery' at the end of this manual.

Several systems fitted to the vehicle require battery power to be available at all times, either to ensure their continued operation (such as the clock) or to maintain control unit memories (such as that in the Powertrain Control Module – PCM) which would be wiped if the battery were to be disconnected. Whenever the battery is to be disconnected therefore, first note the following, to ensure that there are no unforeseen consequences of this action:

a) First, on any vehicle with central locking, it is a wise precaution to remove the key from the ignition, and to keep it with you, so that it does not get locked in if the central locking should engage accidentally when the battery is reconnected!

b) The engine management system's PCM will lose the information stored in its memory – referred to by Ford as the 'KAM' (Keep-Alive Memory) – when the battery is disconnected. This includes idling and operating values, and any fault

2.2 Always disconnect battery – negative (earth) lead first – to prevent the possibility of short-circuits

codes detected – in the case of the fault codes, if it is thought likely that the system has developed a fault for which the corresponding code has been logged, the vehicle must be taken to a Ford dealer for the codes to be read, using the special diagnostic equipment necessary for this (see Chapter 4A). Whenever the battery is disconnected, the information relating to idle speed control and other operating values will have to be reprogrammed into the unit's memory. The PCM does this by itself, but until then, there may be surging, hesitation, erratic idle and a generally inferior level of performance. To allow the PCM to relearn these values, start the engine and run it as close to idle speed as possible until it reaches its normal operating temperature, then run it for approximately two minutes at 1200 rpm. Next, drive the vehicle as far as necessary – approximately 5 miles of varied driving conditions is usually sufficient – to complete the relearning process.

c) If the battery is disconnected while the alarm system is armed or activated, the alarm will remain in the same state when the battery is reconnected. The same applies to the engine immobiliser system (where fitted).

d) If a trip computer is in use, any information stored in memory will be lost.

e) If a Ford 'Keycode' audio unit is fitted, and the unit and/or the battery is disconnected, the unit will not function again on reconnection until the correct security code

2.3 Unscrew hold-down nuts (one of two arrowed)

is entered. Details of this procedure, which varies according to the unit and model year, are given in the 'Ford Audio Systems Operating Guide' supplied with the vehicle when new, with the code itself being given in a 'Radio Passport' and/or a 'Keycode Label' at the same time. Ensure you have the correct code before you disconnect the battery. For obvious security reasons, the procedure is not given in this manual. If you do not have the code or details of the correct procedure, but can supply proof of ownership and a legitimate reason for wanting this information, the vehicle's selling dealer may be able to help.

Devices known as 'memory-savers' (or 'code-savers') can be used to avoid some of the above problems. Precise details vary according to the device used. Typically, it is plugged into the cigarette lighter, and is connected by its own wires to a spare battery; the vehicle's own battery is then disconnected from the electrical system, leaving the 'memory-saver' to pass sufficient current to maintain audio unit security codes and PCM memory values, and also to run permanently-live circuits such as the clock, all the while isolating the battery in the event of a short-circuit occurring while work is carried out.

⚠️ **Warning: Some of these devices allow a considerable amount of current to pass, which can mean that many of the vehicle's systems are still operational when the main battery is disconnected. If a 'memory-saver' is used, ensure that the circuit concerned is actually 'dead' before carrying out any work on it.**

2 Battery –
removal and refitting

Note: See also the relevant Sections of Chapter 1.

Removal

1 Unclip the battery cover and withdraw it from the top of the battery.

2 Disconnect the battery negative (earth) lead (refer to Disconnecting the battery at the end of this manual) **(see illustration)**.

3 Undo the two retaining nuts and remove the battery hold-down clamp **(see illustration)**.

4 Lift out the battery.

Caution: Be careful, the battery is heavy.

5 While the battery is out, inspect the tray for corrosion (see Weekly checks).

6 If you are renewing the battery, make sure that you get one that's identical, with the same dimensions, amperage rating, cold cranking rating, etc. Dispose of the old battery in a responsible fashion. Most local authorities have facilities for the collection and disposal of such items – batteries contain sulphuric acid and lead, and should not be simply thrown out with the household rubbish.

Refitting

7 Refitting is the reverse of the removal procedure. **Note:** After the battery has been disconnected, the engine management system requires approximately 5 miles of driving to relearn its optimum settings. During this period, the engine may not perform normally.

3 Battery –
testing

Testing

Traditional and low maintenance battery

1 If the vehicle covers a small annual mileage, it is worthwhile checking the specific gravity of the electrolyte every three months to determine the state of charge of the battery. Use a hydrometer to make the check and compare the results with the following table. Note that the specific gravity readings assume an electrolyte temperature of 15°C (60°F); for every 10°C (18°F) below 15°C (60°F) subtract 0.007. For every 10°C (18°F) above 15°C (60°F) add 0.007.

Ambient temperature:

	above 25°C (77°F)	below 25°C (77°F)
Fully-charged	1.210 to 1.230	1.270 to 1.290
70% charged	1.170 to 1.190	1.230 to 1.250
Discharged	1.050 to 1.070	1.110 to 1.130

2 If the battery condition is suspect, first check the specific gravity of electrolyte in each cell. A variation of 0.040 or more between any cells indicates loss of electrolyte or deterioration of the internal plates.

3 If the specific gravity variation is 0.040 or more, the battery should be renewed. If the cell variation is satisfactory but the battery is discharged, it should be charged as described later in this Section.

Maintenance-free battery

4 In cases where a 'sealed for life' maintenance-free battery is fitted, topping-up and testing of the electrolyte in each cell is not possible. The condition of the battery can therefore only be tested using a battery condition indicator or a voltmeter.

5 Certain models may be fitted with a 'Delco' type maintenance-free battery, with a built-in charge condition indicator. The indicator is located in the top of the battery casing, and indicates the condition of the battery from its colour. If the indicator shows green, then the battery is in a good state of charge. If the indicator turns darker, eventually to black, then the battery requires charging, as described in Chapter 1A or 1B. If the indicator shows clear/yellow, then the electrolyte level in the battery is too low to allow further use, and the battery should be renewed. **Do not** attempt to charge, load or jump start a battery when the indicator shows clear/yellow.

All battery types

6 If testing the battery using a voltmeter, connect the voltmeter across the battery. The test is only accurate if the battery has not been subjected to any kind of charge for the previous six hours. If this is not the case, switch on the headlights for 30 seconds, then wait four to five minutes before testing the battery after switching off the headlights. All other electrical circuits must be switched off, so check that the doors and tailgate are fully shut when making the test.

7 If the voltage reading is less than 12.2 volts, then the battery is discharged, whilst a reading of 12.2 to 12.4 volts indicates a partially-discharged condition.

8 If the battery is to be charged, remove it from the vehicle (Section 2) and charge it as described in Chapter 1A or 1B.

4 Charging system – general information and precautions

General information

The charging system includes the alternator, an internal voltage regulator, a no-charge (or 'ignition') warning light, the battery, and the wiring between all the components. The charging system supplies electrical power for the ignition system, the lights, the radio, etc. The alternator is driven by the auxiliary drivebelt at the right-hand end of the engine.

The purpose of the voltage regulator is to limit the alternator's voltage to a preset value. This prevents power surges, circuit overloads, etc, during peak voltage output.

The charging system doesn't ordinarily require periodic maintenance. However, the drivebelt, battery and wires and connections should be inspected at the intervals outlined in Chapter 1A or 1B.

The dashboard warning light should come on when the ignition key is turned to positions II or III, then should go off immediately the engine starts. If it remains on, or if it comes on while the engine is running, there is a malfunction in the charging system. If the light does not come on when the ignition key is turned, and the bulb is sound (see Chapter 12), there is a fault in the alternator.

Precautions

Be very careful when making electrical circuit connections to a vehicle equipped with an alternator, and note the following:

a) *When reconnecting wires to the alternator from the battery, be sure to note the polarity.*
b) *Before using arc-welding equipment to repair any part of the vehicle, disconnect the wires from the alternator and the battery terminals.*
c) *Never start the engine with a battery charger connected.*
d) *Always disconnect both battery leads before using a battery charger.*
e) *The alternator is driven by an engine drivebelt which could cause serious injury if your hand, hair or clothes become entangled in it with the engine running.*
f) *Because the alternator is connected directly to the battery, it could arc or cause a fire if overloaded or shorted-out.*
g) *Wrap a plastic bag over the alternator, and secure it with rubber bands, before steam-cleaning or pressure-washing the engine (do not forget to remove, before restarting the engine).*
h) *Never disconnect the alternator terminals while the engine is running.*

5 Charging system – testing

1 If a malfunction occurs in the charging circuit, don't automatically assume that the alternator is causing the problem. First check the following items:

a) *Check the tension and condition of the auxiliary drivebelt – renew it if it is worn or deteriorated (see Chapter 1A or 1B).*
b) *Ensure the alternator mounting bolts and nuts are tight.*
c) *Inspect the alternator wiring harness and the electrical connections at the alternator; they must be in good condition, and tight.*
d) *Check the large main fuses in the engine compartment (see Chapter 12). If any is blown, determine the cause, repair the circuit and renew the fuse (the vehicle won't start and/or the accessories won't work if the fuse is blown).*
e) *Start the engine and check the alternator for abnormal noises – for example, a shrieking or squealing sound may indicate a badly-worn bearing or bush.*
f) *Make sure that the battery is fully-charged – one bad cell in a battery can cause overcharging by the alternator.*
g) *Disconnect the battery leads (negative first, then positive). Inspect the battery posts and the lead clamps for corrosion. Clean them thoroughly if necessary (see 'Weekly checks'). Reconnect the lead to the negative terminal.*
h) *With the ignition and all accessories switched off, insert a test light between the battery negative post and the disconnected negative lead clamp:*
   1)   If the test light does not come on, re-attach the clamp and proceed to the next step.
   2)   If the test light comes on, there is a short in the electrical system of the vehicle. The short must be repaired before the charging system can be checked.
   3)   To find the short, disconnect the alternator wiring harness. If the light goes out, the alternator is at fault. If the light stays on, remove each fuse until it goes out – this will tell you which component is short-circuited.

2 Using a voltmeter, check the battery voltage with the engine off. It should be approximately 12 volts.

3 Start the engine and check the battery voltage again. Increase engine speed until the voltmeter reading remains steady; it should now be approximately 13.5 to 14.6 volts.

4 Switch on as many electrical accessories (eg, the headlights, heated rear window and heater blower) as possible, and check that the alternator maintains the regulated voltage at around 13 to 14 volts. The voltage may drop and then come back up; it may also be necessary to increase engine speed slightly, even if the charging system is working properly.

5 If the voltage reading is greater than the specified charging voltage, renew the voltage regulator.

6 If the voltmeter reading is less than that specified, the fault may be due to worn brushes, weak brush springs, a faulty voltage regulator, a faulty diode, a severed phase winding, or worn or damaged slip-rings. The brushes and slip-rings may be checked, but if the fault persists, the alternator should be renewed or taken to an auto-electrician for testing and repair.

6 Alternator – removal and refitting

Removal

1 Disconnect the battery negative (earth) lead (refer to *Disconnecting the battery* at the end of this manual).

2 On 4-cylinder engines, remove the upper plastic cover from the engine, and undo the alternator upper retaining bolt **(see illustrations)**. Remove the wiring harness support bracket.

3 Apply the handbrake, then jack up the front of the vehicle and support it on axle stands (see *Jacking and vehicle support*). Remove the right-hand front wheel and wheel arch liner(s).

4 Where applicable, remove the engine undershield.

6.2a Removing the alternator upper retaining bolt (4-cylinder models) . . .

6.2b . . . and unclip the wiring harness bracket

6.7 Disconnect the wiring terminals from the alternator

5 Remove the auxiliary drivebelt as described in Chapter 1A or 1B.
6 On 4-cylinder engines, release the retaining clips and remove the cooling duct from the rear of the alternator **(see illustration)**.

7.2 Remove three screws and withdraw end cover (Bosch alternator). . .

7.4b Regulator/brushholder retaining screws (Motorcraft alternator)

6.6 Removing the cooling duct from the rear of the alternator (4-cylinder models)

6.10 Withdrawing the alternator through the right-hand front wheel arch

7 Unplug the wiring connector from the rear of the alternator, then undo the nut to disconnect the wiring terminal from the alternator **(see illustration)**.
8 Undo the retaining nut and disconnect the

7.4a . . . then remove regulator/brushholder assembly (secured by two screws)

7.7 Check that the slip-rings are clean

track rod end as described in Chapter 10.
9 On V6 engines, undo the alternator upper retaining bolt and unclip the wiring harness support bracket.
10 Remove the two lower mounting bolts and remove the alternator out through the right-hand wheel arch **(see illustration)**. Note: *On diesel engines the alternator is fastened by studs and nuts, the studs will need to be removed from the cylinder block to allow the alternator to be removed.*
11 If required, undo the four retaining nuts and remove the plastic cover from the rear of the alternator.
12 If you are renewing the alternator, take the old one with you. Make sure that the new or rebuilt unit is identical to the old alternator. Look at the terminals – they should be the same in number, size and location as the terminals on the old alternator. Finally, look at the identification markings – they will be stamped in the housing, or printed on a tag or plaque affixed to the housing. Make sure that these numbers are the same on both alternators and the pulleys are identical.

Refitting

13 Refitting is the reverse of the removal procedure, referring where necessary to the relevant Chapters of this manual. Tighten all nuts and bolts to the specified torque wrench settings.

---

7 Alternator brushes and voltage regulator – renewal

Note: *This procedure assumes that parts of the correct type have been obtained. At the time of writing, no individual alternator components were available as separate replacement Ford parts. An auto-electrical specialist should be able to supply parts such as brushes.*

1 Remove the alternator from the vehicle (see Section 6) and place it on a clean workbench.

Removal

2 Undo the retaining screws/nuts, and withdraw the alternator end cover **(see illustration)**.
3 Remove the two voltage regulator/brushholder mounting screws and where applicable ease the wire from the connector.
4 Remove the regulator/brushholder from the end frame **(see illustrations)**.
5 Measure the exposed length of each brush, and compare it to the manufacturer's Specifications. If the length of either brush is less than the specified minimum, renew the assembly.
6 Make sure that each brush moves smoothly in the brushholder.
7 Check that the slip-rings – the ring of copper on which each brush bears – are clean **(see illustration)**. Wipe them with a solvent-moistened cloth; if either appears scored or

blackened, take the alternator to a repair specialist for advice.

Refitting

8 Fit the voltage regulator/brushholder **(see illustration)**. Ensure the brushes bear correctly on the slip-rings, and that they compress into their holders. Tighten the screws securely and where applicable, refit the wire to its connector
9 Install the rear cover, and tighten the screws/nuts securely.
10 Refit the alternator (see Section 6).

8 Starting system – general information and precautions

General information

The sole function of the starting system is to turn over the engine quickly enough to allow it to start.

The starting system consists of the battery, the starter motor, the starter solenoid, and the wires connecting them. The solenoid is mounted directly on the starter motor.

The solenoid/starter motor assembly is installed on the rear upper part of the transmission on V6 engines, and on the front of the cylinder block – next to the transmission bellhousing, on 4-cylinder engines.

When the ignition key is turned to position III, the starter solenoid is actuated through the starter control circuit. The starter solenoid then connects the battery to the starter. The battery supplies the electrical energy to the starter motor, which does the actual work of cranking the engine.

The starter motor on a vehicle equipped with automatic transmission can be operated only when the selector lever is in Park or Neutral (P or N).

If the alarm system is armed or activated, the starter motor cannot be operated. The same applies with the engine immobiliser system (where fitted).

Precautions

Always observe the following precautions when working on the starting system:
a) Excessive cranking of the starter motor can overheat it, and cause serious damage. Never operate the starter motor for more than 15 seconds at a time without pausing to allow it to cool for at least two minutes. Excessive starter operation will also risk unburned fuel collecting in the catalytic converter's element, causing it to overheat when the engine does start.
b) The starter is connected directly to the battery, and could arc or cause a fire if mishandled, overloaded or shorted-out.
c) Always detach the lead from the negative terminal of the battery before working on the starting system (see Section 1).

7.8 Insert a rod through the special hole to retain the brushes in their retracted position

9 Starting system – testing

Note: *Before diagnosing starter problems, make sure that the battery is fully-charged, and ensure that the alarm/engine immobiliser system is not activated.*
1 If the starter motor does not turn at all when the switch is operated, make sure that, on automatic transmission models, the selector lever is in Park or Neutral (P or N).
2 Make sure that the battery is fully-charged, and that all leads, both at the battery and starter solenoid terminals, are clean and secure.
3 If the starter motor spins but the engine is not cranking, the overrunning clutch or (when applicable) the reduction gears in the starter motor may be slipping, in which case the starter motor must be overhauled or renewed. (Other possibilities are that the starter motor mounting bolts are very loose, or that teeth are missing from the flywheel/driveplate ring gear.)
4 If, when the switch is actuated, the starter motor does not operate at all but the solenoid clicks, then the problem lies with either the battery, the main solenoid contacts, or the starter motor itself (or the engine is seized).
5 If the solenoid plunger cannot be heard to click when the switch is actuated, the battery is faulty, there is a fault in the circuit, or the solenoid itself is defective.
6 To check the solenoid, connect a fused jumper lead between the battery (+) and the ignition switch terminal (the small terminal) on the solenoid. If the starter motor now operates, the solenoid is OK, and the problem is in the ignition switch, selector lever position sensor (automatic transmission) or in the wiring.
7 If the starter motor still does not operate, remove it. The brushes and commutator may be checked, but if the fault persists, the motor should be renewed, or taken to an auto-electrician for testing and repair.
8 If the starter motor cranks the engine at an abnormally-slow speed, first make sure that the battery is charged, and that all terminal

connections are tight. If the engine is partially-seized, or has the wrong viscosity oil in it, it will crank slowly.
9 Run the engine until normal operating temperature is reached, then switch off and disable the ignition system by unplugging the ignition coil's electrical connector; remove the fuel pump fuse – see wiring diagrams in Chapter 12.
10 Connect a voltmeter positive lead to the battery positive terminal, and connect the negative lead to the negative terminal.
11 Crank the engine, and take the voltmeter readings as soon as a steady figure is indicated. Do not allow the starter motor to turn for more than 15 seconds at a time. A reading of 10.5 volts or more, with the starter motor turning at normal cranking speed, is normal. If the reading is 10.5 volts or more but the cranking speed is slow, the solenoid contacts are burned, the motor is faulty, or there is a bad connection. If the reading is less than 10.5 volts and the cranking speed is slow, the starter motor is faulty or there is a problem with the battery.

10 Starter motor – removal and refitting

1 Disconnect the battery negative (earth) lead (refer to *Disconnecting the battery* at the end of this manual).

4-cylinder models

Removal

2 Apply the handbrake, then jack up the front of the vehicle and support it on axle stands (see *Jacking and vehicle support*).
3 Where applicable, remove the engine undershield.
4 Remove the splash shield from across the front of the vehicle under the radiator.
5 On diesel models, undo the retaining bolts and securing clips and remove the charge air cooler intake pipe from across the front subframe.
6 Undo the two retaining nuts and release the wiring bracket from the starter motor retaining studs/bolts **(see illustration)**.

10.6 Remove the wiring harness bracket from the starter motor retaining studs/bolts

10.7 Disconnecting the wiring from the starter/solenoid terminals

10.8 Undo the retaining bolt (arrowed) from the rear support bracket (petrol models)

10.9 Unscrew the two starter motor mounting bolts/studs (arrowed)

10.12 Disconnecting the wiring and support bracket from the starter motor

10.14a Unscrew the mounting bolts . . .

10.14b . . . and withdraw the starter motor from the transmission

7 Unscrew the nuts to disconnect the wiring from the starter/solenoid terminals **(see illustration)**.

8 On petrol models, undo the retaining bolt and remove the starter motor rear support bracket **(see illustration)**.

9 Unscrew the two starter motor mounting studs/bolts, and remove the starter motor **(see illustration)**.

Refitting

10 Refitting is the reverse of the removal procedure. Tighten the bolts to the specified torque wrench settings.

V6 models

Removal

11 Release the retaining clips from the air intake hoses, disconnect the mass air flow (MAF) sensor and remove the air cleaner and air cleaner mounting bracket.

12 Disconnect the wiring from the starter motor. Also remove the two nuts and bolt securing the support bracket to the starter motor and transmission housing. Remove the bracket **(see illustration)**.

13 On manual transmission models, disconnect the wiring from the reversing light switch.

14 Unscrew the mounting bolts from the starter motor, then release the starter motor from the dowels on the transmission housing and withdraw from the engine compartment **(see illustrations)**.

Refitting

15 Refitting is a reversal of removal. Tighten the bolts to the specified torque wrench settings.

11 Starter motor –
testing and overhaul

Note: *At the time of writing, no individual starter motor components were available as separate Ford parts. An auto-electrical specialist should be able to supply and fit parts such as brushes.*

If the starter motor is thought to be defective, it should be removed from the vehicle (as described in Section 10) and taken to an auto-electrician for assessment. In the majority of cases, new starter motor brushes can be fitted at a reasonable cost. However, check the cost of repairs first as it may prove more economical to purchase a new or exchange motor.

Chapter 5 Part B:
Ignition system

Contents

Degrees of difficulty

Easy, suitable for novice with little experience	Fairly easy, suitable for beginner with some experience	Fairly difficult, suitable for competent DIY mechanic	Difficult, suitable for experienced DIY mechanic	Very difficult, suitable for expert DIY or professional

Specifications

Ignition timing .... Not adjustable – PCM (Powertrain Control Module) controlled

Ignition coil
Primary resistances – measured at coil connector terminal pins ...... 0.50 ± 0.05 ohms

Torque wrench settings	Nm	lbf ft
Knock sensor:		
4-cylinder models	20	15
V6 models	34	25

1 Ignition system – general information and precautions

General information

The ignition system includes the ignition switch, the battery, the crankshaft speed/position sensor, the coil, the primary (low tension/LT) and secondary (high tension/HT) wiring circuits, and the spark plugs. On models with CD4E automatic transmission, a separate ignition module is also fitted, its functions being incorporated in the PCM on models with manual transmission. The ignition system is controlled by the engine management system's Powertrain Control Module (PCM). Using data provided by information sensors which monitor various engine functions (such as engine speed and piston position, intake air mass and temperature, engine coolant temperature, etc), the PCM ensures a perfectly-timed spark under all conditions (see Chapter 4A). **Note:** *The ignition timing is under the full control of the PCM, and cannot be adjusted – see Chapter 4A for further details.*

The basic operation is as follows; the module supplies a voltage to the input stage of the ignition coil which causes the primary windings in the coil to be energised. The supply voltage is periodically interrupted by the PCM and this results in the collapse of the primary magnetic field, which then induces a much larger voltage in the secondary windings, called the High Tension (HT) voltage. This voltage is directed, via the HT leads, to the spark plugs. The spark plug electrodes form a gap small enough for the HT voltage to arc across, and the resulting spark ignites the fuel/air mixture in the cylinder. The timing sequence of events is critical and is regulated by the PCM.

Precautions

When working on the ignition system, take the following precautions:
a) Do not keep the ignition switch on for more than 10 seconds if the engine will not start.
b) If a separate tachometer is ever required for servicing work, consult a dealer service department before buying a tachometer for use with this vehicle – some tachometers may be incompatible with this ignition system – and always connect it in accordance with the equipment manufacturer's instructions.
c) Never connect the ignition coil terminals to earth. This could result in damage to the coil and/or the PCM or ignition module (whichever is fitted).
d) Do not disconnect the battery when the engine is running.
e) Make sure that the ignition module (where fitted) is properly earthed.
f) Refer to the warning at the beginning of the next Section concerning HT voltage.

2 Ignition system – testing

⚠ **Warning: Extreme care must be taken when working on the system with the ignition switched on; it is possible to get a substantial electric shock from a vehicles ignition system. Persons with cardiac pacemaker devices should keep well clear of the ignition circuits, components and test equipment. Always switch off the ignition before disconnecting or connecting any component and when using a multi-meter to check the resistances.**

⚠ **Warning: Because of the high voltage generated by the ignition system, extreme care should be taken whenever an operation is performed involving ignition components also. This not only includes the ignition module/PCM, coil and spark plug (HT) leads, but related components such as electrical connectors, tachometer and other test equipment also.**

3.8 Disconnecting the wiring connector for the ignition coil (4-cylinder engine)

3.9 Undo Torx-type screws (arrowed) to release ignition coil assembly

Note the suppressor is held on by two of the screws

General

Note: *This is an initial check of the 'ignition part' of the main engine management system, to be carried out as part of the preliminary checks of the complete engine management system (see Chapter 4A).*

1 Most ignition system faults are likely to be due to loose or dirty connections or to tracking (unintentional earthing) of the HT voltage due to dirt, dampness or damaged insulation, rather than by the failure of any of the systems components. Always check all the wiring thoroughly before condemning an electrical component and work methodically to eliminate all the other possibilities before deciding that a particular component is faulty.

2 The practise of checking for a spark by holding the live end of an HT lead a short distance away from the engine is definitely not recommended, because of the risk of personal injury, or of damage to the PCM/ignition module.

Engine will not start

3 If the engine either will not turn over at all, or only turns very slowly, check the battery and the starter motor. Connect a voltmeter across the battery terminals (meter positive probe to battery positive terminal), then disable the ignition by disconnecting the wiring from the coil. Note the voltage reading obtained while turning the engine over on the starter for a maximum of 10 seconds. If the reading obtained is less than approximately 10 volts, first check the battery, starter motor and charging systems (see Chapter 5A).

Checking HT leads and coil

4 Disconnect the (HT) lead from any spark plug, and attach it to a calibrated tester (available at most automotive accessory shops). Connect the clip on the tester to a good earth – a bolt or metal bracket on the engine. If you're unable to obtain a calibrated ignition tester, have the check carried out by a Ford dealer service department or similar. Any other form of testing (such as jumping a spark from the end of

an HT lead to earth) is not recommended (see Warnings above and in Section 1).

5 Crank the engine and watch the end of the tester to see if bright blue, well-defined sparks occur.

6 If sparks occur, sufficient voltage is reaching the plug to fire it. Repeat the check at the remaining plugs, to ensure that all leads are sound and that the coil is serviceable. However, the plugs themselves may be fouled or faulty, so remove and check them as described in Chapter 1A.

7 If no sparks or intermittent sparks occur, the spark plug lead(s) may be defective.

8 If there's still no spark, check the coil's electrical connector, to make sure it's clean and tight. Check for full battery voltage to the coil, at terminal 2, on 4-cylinder engines and at terminal 4, on V6 engines. The coil is earthed through the PCM – do not attempt to check this. Check the coil itself (see Section 3). Make any necessary repairs, then repeat the check again.

9 The remainder of the system checks should be left to a dealer service department or other qualified repair facility, as there is a chance that the PCM may be damaged if tests are not performed properly.

---

3 Ignition coil –
check, removal and refitting

Caution: see Warnings in Section 2 of this Chapter, before proceeding with any work on the ignition system.

Check

1 Having checked that full battery voltage is available at the coil's electrical connector (see Section 2), disconnect the battery negative (earth) lead (refer to *Disconnecting the battery* at the end of this manual).

2 Unplug the coil's electrical connector, if not already disconnected.

3 Using an ohmmeter, measure the

resistance of the coil's primary windings, connecting the meter between the coil's terminal pins as follows. Measure first from one outer pin to the centre pin, then from the other outer pin to the centre. Compare your readings with the coil primary resistance listed in the Specifications Section at the beginning of this Chapter.

4 Disconnect the spark plug (HT) leads – note their connections or label them carefully, as described in Chapter 1A. Use the meter to check that there is continuity between each pair of (HT) lead terminals. On 4-cylinder models, coil terminals 1 and 4 are connected by their secondary windings as are terminals 2 and 3. On V6 models, terminals 1 and 5 are connected, terminals 3 and 4 are connected and terminals 2 and 6 are connected. Now switch to the highest resistance scale, and check that there is no continuity between either pair of terminals and the other – ie, on 4-cylinder vehicles, there should be infinite resistance between terminals 1 and 2 or 3 and 4 – also between any terminal and earth.

5 If either of the above tests yield resistance values outside the specified amount, or results other than those described, renew the coil. Any further testing should be left to a dealer service department or other qualified repair facility.

Removal and refitting

4-cylinder models

Note: *On 4-cylinder models, the ignition coil is mounted on the coolant housing located at the left-hand end of the cylinder head.*

6 Disconnect the battery negative (earth) lead (refer to *Disconnecting the battery* at the end of this manual).

7 Unclip the breather hose from the engine upper plastic cover, then unclip the cover from the top of the engine.

8 Unplug the electrical connector from the coil, then disconnect the spark plug (HT) leads – note their connections or label them carefully, as described in Chapter 1A **(see illustration)**.

3.12a Disconnecting the wiring from the ignition coil . . .

3.12b . . . and the suppressor (V6 engines)

3.13 Note the location of the HT leads on the ignition coil – each one is marked with its corresponding cylinder number

9 Undo the four (Torx-type) screws securing the coil to the top of the coolant housing **(see illustration)**. Withdraw the coil assembly from the cylinder head. **Note:** *The suppressor on the side of the coil can also be removed, disconnect the wiring connector if required.*

10 Refitting is the reverse of the removal procedure. Ensure that the spark plug (HT) leads are correctly reconnected, and tighten the coil screws securely.

V6 models

Note: *On V6 models, the ignition coil is mounted on the rear valve cover.*

11 Disconnect the battery negative (earth) lead (refer to *Disconnecting the battery* at the end of this manual).

12 Disconnect and unclip the wiring from the ignition coil and suppressor **(see illustrations)**.

13 Note their location, then disconnect the spark plug (HT) leads from the ignition coil. Label the wires for location to ensure correct refitting, each lead is marked with its corresponding cylinder number **(see illustration)**.

14 Unscrew the mounting screws and remove the coil, noting that an earth wire is

attached to one of the mounting bolts and the suppressor is attached to two of the bolts **(see illustrations)**.

15 Refitting is a reversal of removal. Make sure the earth wire is attached to one of the coil mounting screws. Also, ensure that the spark plug (HT) leads are connected correctly.

4 Ignition module (CD4E automatic transmission) – removal and refitting

Removal

1 Disconnect the battery negative (earth) lead (refer to *Disconnecting the battery* at the end of this manual).

2 If better access is required, remove the air intake resonator (see Chapter 4A, Section 4).

3 Unplug the electrical connector from the module **(see illustration)**.

4 Remove the retaining screws, and detach the module from the bulkhead mounting bracket.

Refitting

5 Refitting is a reversal of removal.

3.14a An earth wire is attached to one of the ignition coil mounting bolts . . .

5 Ignition timing – adjusting and checking

The ignition timing is controlled entirely by the PCM (acting with the ignition module, on models with CD4E automatic transmission), and cannot be adjusted. Not only can the ignition timing not be adjusted, it cannot be checked either, except with the use of special diagnostic equipment – this makes it a task for a Ford dealer service department.

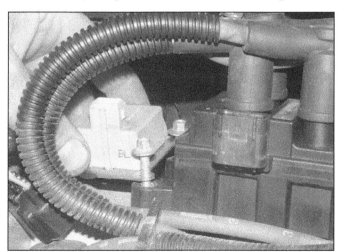

3.14b . . . and a suppressor to two of the mounting bolts

4.3 Separate ignition module is fitted to CD4E automatic transmission models only – note electrical connector (A) and retaining screws (B)

6.1a On 4-cylinder engines, the knock sensor (arrowed) is bolted above the oil separator

6.1b On V6 engines, the knock sensor (arrowed) is bolted to the rear of the engine

6.4 On 4-cylinder engines, remove the knock sensor from the front of the cylinder block (cylinder head removed for clarity)

6 Knock sensors – removal and refitting

Removal

1 On 4-cylinder engines, the knock sensor is bolted to the front of the cylinder block under the intake manifold. On V6 engines, it is bolted to the rear of the engine above the right-hand intermediate driveshaft **(see illustrations)**. **Note:** *On some V6 engines there may be a second knock sensor fitted to the front bank of cylinders.*

2 On 4-cylinder engines, remove the intake manifold as described in Chapter 2A.

3 Follow the wiring from the knock sensor and disconnect its wiring block connector, where applicable, unclip the wiring from the cable ties.

4 Unscrew the centre bolt and remove the knock sensor from the cylinder block **(see illustration)**.

Refitting

5 Refitting is the reversal of the removal procedure; noting the following points:
  a) *Clean the sensor and its location on the cylinder block.*
  b) *On 4-cylinder models, rotate the sensor as far anti-clockwise as possible, without touching the cylinder head/block or oil separator **(see illustration)**.*
  c) *The sensor bolt **must** be tightened to the specified torque, as this is critical to the sensor's correct operation.*

6.5 Leave a gap (arrowed) between the cylinder head and the knock sensor (4-cylinder engines)

Chapter 5 Part C:
Preheating system – diesel models

Contents

Degrees of difficulty

Easy, suitable for novice with little experience		**Fairly easy,** suitable for beginner with some experience		**Fairly difficult,** suitable for competent DIY mechanic		**Difficult,** suitable for experienced DIY mechanic		**Very difficult,** suitable for expert DIY or professional	

Specifications

Torque wrench setting	Nm	lbf ft
Glow plugs	13	10

---

1 Preheating system components – general information

General information

Cold-starting performance is automatically controlled by the PCM. Under cold start conditions, the cylinder head temperature (CHT) sensor informs the PCM on the engine temperature, this determines the preheat time.

Each cylinder of the engine is fitted with a heater plug (commonly called a glow plug) screwed into the cylinder head. The plugs are electrically-operated before and during start-up when the engine is cold. Electrical feed to the glow plugs is controlled via the powertrain control module (PCM).

A warning light in the instrument panel tells the driver that preheating is taking place. When the light goes out, the engine is ready to be started. The voltage supply to the glow plugs continues for several seconds after the light goes out. If no attempt is made to start, the timer then cuts off the supply, in order to avoid draining the battery and overheating the glow plugs.

The glow plugs have an after-glow phase which only operates under 2500 rpm, and below temperatures of 50°C. This helps the engine to run more smoothly during idling, and reduces exhaust emissions through more efficient combustion just after starting.

Component locations

1 The preheating is controlled by the powertrain control module (PCM) which is located on the rear right-hand side of the engine compartment (as seen from the driver's seat) where it is mounted with the generic electronic module (GEM). Refer to Chapter 4B, Section 9, for removal and refitting details.

2 The cylinder head temperature switch is screwed into the transmission end of the cylinder head. Refer to Chapter 4B, Section 9, for removal and refitting details.

3 The glow plug relay is located in the fusebox in the engine compartment in front of the battery. Refer to Chapter 12 for further details.

2.12 Disconnect the wiring connector (arrowed) – Common Rail engines

2.13 Unscrew the retaining nut (two of four arrowed) from each glow plug – intake manifold removed for clarity

2.14 Remove the glow plug from the cylinder head – intake manifold removed for clarity

2 Glow plugs –
testing, removal and refitting

Testing

1 If the system malfunctions, testing is ultimately by substitution of known good units, but some preliminary checks may be made as follows.

2 Connect a voltmeter or 12 volt test light between the glow plug supply cable and earth (engine or vehicle metal). Make sure that the live connection is kept clear of the engine and bodywork.

3 Have an assistant switch on the ignition and check that voltage is applied to the glow plugs. Note that, after a certain number of seconds, the system cuts out automatically if the engine is not started, to prevent battery drain. Switch off the ignition.

4 If an ammeter of suitable range (0 to 50 amp approx) is available, connect it between the glow plug feed wire and the busbar (the wire which connects the four plugs together). During the preheating period, the ammeter should show a current draw of approximately 8 amps per working plug, ie, 32 amps if all four plugs are working. If one or more plugs appear not to be drawing current, remove the busbar and check each plug separately with a continuity tester or self-powered test light.

5 If there is no supply at all to the glow plugs, the associated wiring may be at fault. Otherwise, this points to a defective cylinder head temperature sensor (see Chapter 4B, Section 9), or to a problem with the powertrain control module (PCM).

6 To locate a defective glow plug, disconnect the main feed wire and the interconnecting busbar from the top of the glow plugs. Be careful not to drop the nuts and washers.

7 Use a continuity tester, or a 12 volt test light connected to the battery positive terminal, to check for continuity between each glow plug terminal and earth. The resistance of a glow plug in good condition is very low (less than 1 ohm), so if the test light does not come on or the continuity tester shows a high resistance, the glow plug is certainly defective.

8 If an ammeter is available, the current draw of each glow plug can be checked. After an initial surge of around 15 to 20 amps, each plug should draw around 10 amps. Any plug which draws much more or less than this is probably defective.

9 As a final check the glow plugs can be removed and inspected as described below.

Removal

⚠ *Warning: If the glow plug (preheating) system has just been energised, or if the engine has recently been running, the glow plugs may be extremely hot.*

10 Disconnect the battery negative lead, and position the lead away from the battery (also see *Disconnecting the battery*).

11 Withdraw the oil level dipstick and unclip the engine plastic cover.

12 On common rail models, disconnect the wiring connector from the camshaft position sensor **(see illustration)**.

13 Unscrew the nut securing each glow plug connector, then lift the wiring away from the plugs **(see illustration)**. Note that the wiring need not be removed completely for access to the plugs.

14 Unscrew the glow plugs, and remove them from the engine for inspection **(see illustration)**.

15 Inspect the glow plug stems for signs of damage. A badly burned or charred stem may be an indication of a faulty fuel injector – consult a diesel specialist for advice if necessary. Otherwise, if one plug is found to be faulty and the engine has completed a high mileage, it is probably worth renewing all four plugs as a set.

Refitting

16 Refitting is a reversal of removal, noting the following points:
  a) Apply a little anti-seize compound (or copper brake grease) to the glow plug threads.
  b) Make sure when remaking the glow plug wiring connections that the contact surfaces are clean.
  c) Tighten the glow plugs to the specified torque.

Chapter 6
Clutch

Contents

Degrees of difficulty

| Easy, suitable for novice with little experience | | Fairly easy, suitable for beginner with some experience | | Fairly difficult, suitable for competent DIY mechanic | | Difficult, suitable for experienced DIY mechanic | | Very difficult, suitable for expert DIY or professional | |

Specifications

General

Type	Single dry plate, hydraulically-operated with automatic adjustment
Disc diameter:	
Petrol engines:	
1.8 and 2.0 litre	228 mm
2.5 litre	240 mm
Diesel engines	228 mm
Lining thickness:	
New 6.8 mm	
Minimum (worn)	6.0 mm

Torque wrench settings

	Nm	lbf ft
Clutch cover to flywheel	29	21
Clutch master/slave cylinder mounting nuts/bolts	10	7
Clutch pedal retaining nut	23	17

1 General information

Vehicles with manual transmission are fitted with a pedal-operated single dry plate clutch system. When the clutch pedal is depressed, effort is transmitted to the clutch release mechanism hydraulically, via a master cylinder. The release mechanism transfers effort to the pressure plate diaphragm spring, which withdraws from the flywheel and releases the friction disc.

The flywheel is mounted on the crankshaft, with the pressure plate bolted to it. Removal of the flywheel is described in the appropriate part of Chapter 2.

Since many of the procedures covered in this Chapter involve working under the vehicle, make sure that it is securely supported on axle stands placed on a firm, level floor (see Jacking and vehicle support).

⚠ **Warning: The fluid used in the system is hydraulic fluid, which is poisonous. Take care to keep it off bare skin, and in particular not to get splashes in your eyes. The fluid also attacks paintwork, and may discolour carpets, etc – keep spillages to a minimum, and wash any off immediately with cold water. Finally, hydraulic fluid is highly inflammable, and should be handled with the same care as petrol.**

2 Clutch – description and checking

Description

1 All manual transmission models are equipped with a single dry plate diaphragm spring clutch assembly. The cover assembly consists of a steel cover (dowelled and bolted to the rear face of the flywheel), the pressure plate, and a diaphragm spring.

2 The clutch friction disc is free to slide along the splines of the gearbox input shaft, and is held in position between the flywheel and the pressure plate by the pressure of the diaphragm spring. Friction lining material is bonded or riveted to the friction disc (driven plate), which has a spring-cushioned hub, to absorb transmission shocks and help ensure a smooth take-up of the drive.

3 The centrally-mounted clutch release bearing contacts the fingers of the diaphragm spring. Depressing the clutch pedal pushes the release bearing against the diaphragm fingers, so moving the centre of the diaphragm spring inwards. As the centre of the spring is pushed inwards, the outside of the spring pivots outwards, so moving the pressure plate backwards and disengaging its grip on the friction disc.

4 When the pedal is released, the diaphragm spring forces the pressure plate back into contact with the linings on the clutch friction

2.5 Clutch master cylinder and related fittings

1 Fluid supply (low-pressure) hose
2 Hose retaining clip
3 High-pressure fluid pipe
4 Master cylinder mounting nuts
5 Master cylinder-to-pedal circlip

2.6 Clutch slave cylinder/thrust bearing (arrowed) is a complete assembly

disc. The disc is now firmly held between the pressure plate and the flywheel, thus transmitting engine power to the gearbox.

5 The clutch is hydraulically-operated and has a master cylinder mounted behind the clutch pedal, it takes its hydraulic fluid supply from a chamber in the brake fluid reservoir **(see illustration)**.

6 Depressing the clutch pedal operates the master cylinder pushrod, and the fluid pressure is transferred along the fluid lines to a slave cylinder mounted inside the bellhousing **(see illustration)**.

7 The slave cylinder is incorporated into the release bearing – when the slave cylinder operates, the release bearing moves against the diaphragm spring fingers and disengages the clutch.

8 The hydraulic clutch is self-adjusting.

Checking

9 The following checks may be performed to diagnose a clutch problem:

a) Check the fluid lines from the clutch master cylinder into the bellhousing for damage, signs of leakage, or for kinks or dents which might restrict fluid flow.

b) Slow or poor operation may be due to air being present in the fluid. The system can be bled of air as described in Section 7.

c) Check the clutch pedal for excessive wear of the bushes (where applicable), and for any obstructions which may restrict the pedal movement.

3 Clutch master cylinder – removal and refitting

Note: Refer to the warning in Section 1 concerning the dangers of hydraulic fluid before proceeding.

Removal

1 Disconnect the battery negative (earth) lead (refer to Disconnecting the battery at the end of this manual).

2 Working inside the vehicle, move the driver's seat fully to the rear, to allow maximum working area. Remove the fasteners securing the driver's side lower facia trim panel, and remove the panel from the car.

3 Twist the clutch pedal position switch(es) and detach it from the pedal bracket, then remove the clutch pedal spring from the bracket **(see illustration)**.

4 Before proceeding, anticipate some spillage of hydraulic (brake) fluid – most will occur on the engine compartment side.

However, if sufficient fluid comes into contact with the carpet, it may be discoloured or worse. Place a good quantity of clean rags below the clutch pedal, and have a container ready in the engine compartment.

5 Remove the brake fluid reservoir cap, and then tighten it down over a piece of polythene or cling film, to obtain an airtight seal. This may help to reduce the spillage of fluid when the lines are disconnected.

6 To gain access to the fluid connections where they pass through the engine compartment bulkhead, move any wiring and hoses to one side as necessary. On four-cylinder models, remove the air cleaner inlet hose and plenum chamber as described in the relevant Part of Chapter 4. On V6 models, it may be necessary to remove the upper section of the inlet manifold as described in Chapter 2B.

7 Working in the engine compartment, release the hose clip and disconnect the (upper) fluid supply hose from the clutch master cylinder **(see illustration)**. Plug or clamp the hose end if possible, to reduce fluid loss and to prevent dirt entry.

8 To remove the (lower) fluid pipe, pull out the spring clip to the side, then pull the pipe fitting out of the base of the cylinder **(see illustration)**. Again, plug or tape over the pipe end, to avoid losing fluid, and to prevent dirt entry.

3.3 Unhook the clutch pedal spring (arrowed) from the bracket

3.7 Release the hose clip (arrowed) and disconnect the fluid supply hose

3.8 Withdraw the spring clip (arrowed) and disconnect the pipe

9 Returning to the driver's footwell, undo the two mounting nuts from the clutch master cylinder **(see illustration)**.

10 Undo the clutch pedal retaining nut **(see illustration)** and remove the pedal complete with the clutch master cylinder. Release the retaining clip and detach the master cylinder from the clutch pedal. Take care to avoid spilling any remaining fluid onto the interior fittings.

Refitting

11 Refitting is a reversal of removal, noting the following points:
  a) *Tighten the mounting nuts to the specified torque.*
  b) *Use new clips when refitting the fluid feed hose.*
  c) *Refit any components removed for access.*
  d) *Remove the polythene from under the fluid reservoir cap, and top-up the fluid level (see 'Weekly checks').*
  e) *Refer to Section 7 and bleed the clutch hydraulic system.*
  f) *If the fluid level in the reservoir fell sufficiently, it may be necessary to bleed the braking system also – refer to Chapter 9.*

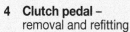

4 Clutch pedal –
removal and refitting

Removal

1 Disconnect the battery negative (earth) lead (refer to *Disconnecting the battery* at the end of this manual).

2 Working inside the vehicle, move the driver's seat fully to the rear, to allow maximum working area. Remove the fasteners securing the driver's side lower facia trim panel, and remove the panel from the car.

3 Twist the clutch pedal position switch and detach it from the pedal bracket, then release the clutch pedal spring from the retaining bracket **(see illustration 3.3)**.

4 Where possible, prise off the circlip which secures the clutch master cylinder to the clutch pedal. **Note:** *It may be necessary to remove the pedal complete with master cylinder as described in Section 3.*

5 Undo the clutch pedal retaining nut and remove the pedal from the pivot shaft **(see illustration 3.10)**.

Refitting

6 Prior to refitting the pedal, apply a little grease to the pivot shaft.

7 Refitting is a reversal of the removal procedure, making sure that any bushes or spacers (where applicable) are correctly located.

8 If the master cylinder was removed with the clutch pedal, refit as described in Section 3.

3.9 Undo the two clutch master cylinder mounting nuts (arrowed)

5 Clutch components –
removal, inspection and refitting

⚠ *Warning: Dust created by clutch wear and deposited on the clutch components may contain asbestos, which is a health hazard. DO NOT blow it out with compressed air, and do not inhale any of it. DO NOT use petrol or petroleum-based solvents to clean off the dust. Brake system cleaner or methylated spirit should be used to flush the dust into a suitable receptacle. After the clutch components are wiped clean with rags, dispose of the contaminated rags and cleaner in a sealed, marked container.*

Removal

1 Access to the clutch may be gained in one of two ways. The engine/transmission unit can be removed, as described in Chapter 2D, and the transmission separated from the engine on the bench. Alternatively, the engine may be left in the vehicle and the transmission removed independently, as described in Chapter 7A.

2 Having separated the transmission from the engine, check if there are any marks identifying the relation of the clutch cover to the flywheel. If not, make your own marks using a dab of paint or a scriber. These marks will be used if the original cover is refitted, and will help to maintain the balance of the unit. A new cover may be fitted in any position allowed by the locating dowels.

3 Unscrew and remove the six clutch cover

5.3a Unscrewing the clutch cover bolts . . .

3.10 Undo the clutch pedal retaining nut (arrowed)

retaining bolts, working in a diagonal sequence, and slackening the bolts only a turn at a time. If necessary, the flywheel may be held stationary using a home-made locking tool **(see illustrations)** or a wide-bladed screwdriver, inserted in the teeth of the starter ring gear and resting against part of the cylinder block.

4 Ease the clutch cover off its locating dowels. Be prepared to catch the friction disc, which will drop out as the cover is removed. Note which way round the disc is fitted.

Inspection

5 The most common problem which occurs in the clutch is wear of the friction disc. However, all the clutch components should be inspected at this time, particularly if the engine has covered a high mileage. Unless the clutch components are known to be virtually new, it is worth renewing them all as a set (disc, pressure plate and release bearing). Renewing a worn friction disc by itself is not always satisfactory, especially if the old disc was slipping and causing the pressure plate to overheat.

6 Examine the linings of the friction disc for wear, and the disc hub and rim for distortion, cracks, broken torsion springs, and worn splines. The surface of the friction linings may be highly glazed, but as long as the friction material pattern can be clearly seen (and the thickness of the lining is within the specifications at the beginning of this Chapter), this is satisfactory. The disc must be renewed if the lining thickness has worn down to the minimum thickness in the specifications.

5.3b . . . using a home-made locking tool, to hold the flywheel

5.8 Examine the fingers of the diaphragm spring for wear or scoring

5.11 Using a clutch-aligning tool to centralise the clutch friction disc

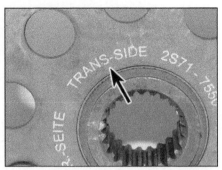

5.12 Transmission side TRANS-SIDE marking on the clutch friction disc

7 If there is any sign of oil contamination, indicated by shiny black discoloration, the disc must be renewed, and the source of the contamination traced and rectified. This will be a leaking crankshaft oil seal or gearbox input shaft oil seal. The renewal procedure for the former is given in the relevant Part of Chapter 2. Renewal of the gearbox input shaft oil seal is given in the relevant Part of Chapter 7A.

8 Check the machined faces of the flywheel and pressure plate. If either is grooved, or heavily scored, renewal is necessary. The pressure plate must also be renewed if any cracks are apparent, or if the diaphragm spring is damaged or its pressure suspect. Pay particular attention to the tips of the spring fingers **(see illustration)**, where the release bearing acts upon them.

9 With the gearbox removed, it is also advisable to check the condition of the release bearing, as described in Section 6. Having got this far, it is almost certainly worth renewing it.

Refitting

10 It is important that no oil or grease is allowed to come into contact with the friction material of the clutch disc or the pressure plate and flywheel faces. To ensure this, it is advisable to refit the clutch assembly with clean hands, and to wipe down the pressure plate and flywheel faces with a clean dry rag before assembly begins.

11 Ford technicians use a special tool for centralising the friction disc at this stage. The tool holds the disc centrally on the pressure plate, and locates in the middle of the diaphragm spring fingers **(see illustration)**. If the tool is not available, it will be necessary to centralise the disc after assembling the cover loosely on the flywheel, as described in the following paragraphs.

12 Place the friction disc against the flywheel, ensuring that it is the right way round. It should be marked TRANSMISSION – SIDE, but if not, position it so that the raised hub with the cushion springs is facing away from the flywheel **(see illustration)**.

13 Place the clutch cover over the dowels. Refit the retaining bolts, and tighten them finger-tight so that the friction disc is gripped lightly, but can still be moved.

14 The friction disc must now be centralised so that, when the engine and transmission are mated, the splines of the gearbox input shaft will pass through the splines in the centre of the disc hub.

15 Centralisation can be carried out by inserting a round bar through the hole in the centre of the friction disc, so that the end of the bar rests in the hole in the rear end of the crankshaft. Move the bar sideways or up-and-down, to move the disc in whichever direction is necessary to achieve centralisation. Centralisation can then be checked by removing the bar and viewing the friction disc hub in relation to the diaphragm spring fingers, or by viewing through the side apertures of the cover, and checking that the disc is central in relation to the outer edge of the pressure plate.

16 An alternative and more accurate method of centralisation is to use a commercially-available clutch-aligning tool, obtainable from most accessory shops **(see illustration 5.11)**.

17 Once the clutch is centralised, progressively tighten the cover bolts in a diagonal sequence to the torque setting given in the Specifications.

18 Ensure that the input shaft splines, clutch disc splines and release bearing guide sleeve are clean. Apply a thin smear of high melting-point grease to the input shaft splines.

19 Refit the transmission to the engine as described in Chapter 7A.

6 Clutch release bearing (and slave cylinder) – removal, inspection and refitting

Note: *Refer to the warning in Section 1 concerning the dangers of hydraulic fluid before proceeding.*

Removal

1 Remove the transmission as described in Chapter 7A.

2 The release bearing and slave cylinder are combined into one unit, which is located in the bellhousing of the transmission.

3 Remove the bleed screw dust cap, and prise out the grommet from the top of the transmission housing **(see illustrations)**.

4 Remove the three mounting bolts, and withdraw the slave cylinder and release bearing from the transmission input shaft **(see illustrations)**.

6.3a Take off the bleed screw cap ...

6.3b ... then prise out the grommet from the transmission housing

6.4a Remove the three mounting bolts (arrowed) ...

6.4b . . . and withdraw the slave cylinder/release bearing assembly

6.7a Renew the large O-ring on the slave cylinder . . .

6.7b . . . and of the smaller pipe connection O-rings

Inspection

5 Check the bearing for smoothness of operation, and renew it if there is any sign of harshness or roughness as the bearing is spun. Do not attempt to dismantle, clean or lubricate the bearing.

6 Repair kits are not available from Ford. If a fault develops, the complete cylinder/release bearing must be renewed. **Note:** *Cylinder assemblies should be supplied with an input shaft seal already fitted. If not, refer to Chapter 7A and fit a new seal.*

7 Check the condition of all seals, and renew if necessary **(see illustrations)**. Considering the difficulty in gaining access to some of the seals if they fail, it would be wise to renew these as a precaution.

Refitting

8 Refitting of the clutch release bearing is a reversal of the removal procedure, noting the following points:
a) *Renew the cylinder-to-transmission casing O-ring seal.*
b) *Tighten the mounting bolts to the specified torque.*
c) *Refit the transmission as described in Chapter 7A.*

d) *Bleed the system as described in Section 7.*

7 Clutch hydraulic system – bleeding

Note: *Refer to the warning in Section 1 concerning the dangers of hydraulic fluid before proceeding.*

1 The clutch hydraulic system will not normally require bleeding, and this task should only be necessary when the system has been opened for repair work. However, as with the brake pedal, if the clutch pedal feels at all soggy or unresponsive in operation, this may indicate the need for bleeding.

2 The system bleed screw is located on top of the transmission bellhousing.

3 Where applicable, remove the battery as described in Chapter 5A, and the air cleaner as described in the relevant Part of Chapter 4. Move the pipework and wiring harness to one side as necessary to reach the access cover.

4 Remove the bleed screw cap **(see illustration 6.3a)**.

5 Bleeding the clutch is much the same as

bleeding the brakes – refer to Chapter 9. Ensure that the level in the brake fluid reservoir is maintained well above the MIN mark at all times, otherwise the clutch and brake hydraulic systems will both need bleeding.

6 If conventional bleeding does not work, it may be necessary to use a vacuum pump kit: Ford tool – 416-D001 (23-036A). Syphon some of the fluid out of the reservoir until the level is at the MIN mark, remove the bleed screw dust cap and connect the hose from the hand pump. Fill the hand pump reservoir with new hydraulic fluid, open the bleed screw, and pump the fluid backwards through the slave cylinder/release bearing up to the reservoir until it reaches its MAX mark.

7 On completion, tighten the bleed screw securely, and top-up the brake fluid level to the MAX mark. If possible, test the operation of the clutch before refitting all the components removed for access.

8 Failure to bleed correctly may point to a leak in the system, or to a worn master or slave cylinder. At the time of writing, it appears that the master and slave cylinders are only available as complete assemblies – overhaul is not possible.

Chapter 7 Part A:
Manual transmission

Contents

Degrees of difficulty

| Easy, suitable for novice with little experience | | Fairly easy, suitable for beginner with some experience | | Fairly difficult, suitable for competent DIY mechanic | | Difficult, suitable for experienced DIY mechanic | | Very difficult, suitable for expert DIY or professional | |

Specifications

General

Type	Manual, five forward gears and reverse. Synchromesh on all forward gears
Identification code	MTX-75

Torque wrench settings	**Nm**	**lbf ft**
Gear change linkage to selector shaft	23	17
Gear lever assembly to floor	10	7
Transmission filler/drain plugs	45	33
Transmission to engine	44	32
Vehicle speed sensor	8	6

1 General information

1 The manual transmission is a compact, two-piece, lightweight aluminium alloy housing, containing both the transmission and differential assemblies. The manual transmission code name is MTX-75, MT standing for Manual Transmission, X for transaXle (front-wheel-drive), and 75 being the distance between the input and output shafts in mm **(see illustration)**.

2 Because of the complexity, possible unavailability of parts and special tools necessary, internal repair procedures for the manual transmission are not recommended for the home mechanic. For readers who wish to tackle a transmission rebuild, exploded views and brief notes on overhaul are provided in Section 10. The bulk of the information in this Chapter is devoted to removal and refitting procedures.

J35143

1.1 Sectional diagram of the manual transmission

1 Clutch housing	4 Output shaft	7 4th gear	11 5th/reverse synchro
2 Transmission housing	5 Distance between shaft centres = 75 mm	8 Needle roller bearing	12 Differential
3 Input shaft	6 Taper roller bearings	9 3rd/4th synchro	13 Driveshafts
		10 1st/2nd synchro	14 Shims

2.3 Ford special tool 16-097 used to lock the gear lever in neutral

2.5 Disengage the red plastic locking slider (arrowed) to adjust the cable

2 Gearchange cables – adjustment

Note: *The special Ford tool 308-436 (16-097) will be required in order to carry out the following adjustment. This tool locks the gear lever in the neutral position during adjustment. If the tool is not available, adjustment is still possible by proceeding on a trial-and-error basis, preferably with the help of an assistant to hold the gear lever in the neutral position.*

1 Disconnect the battery negative (earth) lead (refer to *Disconnecting the battery* at the end of this manual) and check the gear lever is the neutral position.
2 Inside the car, release the gear change lever gaiter and trim from the centre console and remove the insulation pad.
3 Lock the gear lever in neutral using the special tool **(see illustration)**.
4 Apply the handbrake, then jack up the front of the vehicle and support it on axle stands (see *Jacking and vehicle support*).
5 On the transmission, release the adjusters on the cables by disengaging the red plastic locking sliders from the cable **(see illustration)**.

6 Make sure that the levers on the transmission are both in the neutral position, then lock the red plastic locking sliders by pressing them back into the cable.
7 Remove the special tool, and check the gear lever can select all the gears.
8 Refit the gaiter and trim to the gearchange lever.
9 Reconnect the battery negative (earth) lead.

3 Gearchange lever – removal and refitting

Removal

1 Disconnect the battery negative (earth) lead (refer to *Disconnecting the battery* at the end of this manual).
2 Apply the handbrake, then jack up the front of the vehicle and support it on axle stands (see *Jacking and vehicle support*).
3 Where applicable, remove the engine undershield.
4 If required, remove the relevant front part of the exhaust (as described in Chapter 4A or 4B), to gain access to the underside of the gear lever

5 On petrol models, remove the exhaust front heat shield, disconnecting the oxygen sensor cable on removal.
6 Unscrew the retaining nuts and release the lever assembly from the floor **(see illustration)**.
7 Inside the car, release the gearchange lever gaiter and trim from the centre console and remove the insulation pad.
8 Press the side button in to release the cable end fittings from the gear lever stubs- note their fitted locations, then detach the cable ferrules from the bracket by turning the serrated collars clockwise **(see illustrations)**.
9 Withdraw the gearchange linkage/lever assembly out from the centre console **(see illustration overleaf)**.

Refitting

10 Refitting is a reversal of removal, noting the following points:
a) Fit new gasket between the gear lever assembly and the floor.
b) Fit new gear lever assembly retaining nuts.
c) If required, adjust the cables as described in Section 2.

3.6 Unscrew the retaining nuts (arrowed) to release the lever assembly

3.8a Press the side button (arrowed) in . . .

3.8b . . . and release the cable from the gear lever stub

3.9 Gearchange lever and housing

1 Gearshift lever knob
2 Compression spring
3 Spring damper
4 Reverse gear release
5 Gearshift lever/linkage
6 Selector lever
7 Self-tapping screws
8 Gearshift linkage lower housing

4 Gearchange cables – removal and refitting

Removal

1 Disconnect the battery negative (earth) lead (refer to *Disconnecting the battery* at the end of this manual).

2 Apply the handbrake, then jack up the front of the vehicle and support it on axle stands (see *Jacking and vehicle support*).

3 At the transmission, remove the cables (gearchange cable coloured white – selector cable coloured black) from the support brackets by twisting the spring-loaded knurled collars anti-clockwise. Press the retaining button at the end of the cables and release them from the transmission lever balljoints – note their fitted locations. Withdraw the cables downwards from the engine compartment **(see illustrations)**.

4 Detach the cables from the retaining clips on the subframe.

5 Remove the centre console as described in Chapter 11.

6 Remove the gearchange lever assembly as described in Section 3.

7 Pull the carpet to one side (the carpet and insulation may need to be cut slightly to gain access to the cable retaining plate). Unscrew the nuts and release the adapter from the floor, then withdraw the cables through the bulkhead and into the car **(see illustration)**. **Note:** *Do not bend or kink the cables as damage to the cables may occur.*

Refitting

8 Refitting is a reversal of removal. **Note:** *If required, adjust the cables as described in Section 2.*

4.3a Twist the spring-loaded knurled collar anti-clockwise . . .

4.3b . . . and withdraw the outer cable from the retaining bracket . . .

4.3c . . . then press the button and release the cable from the transmission lever balljoints

5 Vehicle speed sensor – removal and refitting

Removal

1 Apply the handbrake, then jack up the front of the vehicle and support it on axle stands (see *Jacking and vehicle support*).

2 Disconnect the wiring connector from the vehicle speed sensor.

3 Unscrew the retaining bolt and remove the sensor from the transmission **(see illustration)**.

4 On some models the speed sensor may be held in place by a roll pin and not a retaining bolt. Using a pair of grips, pull out the retaining roll pin from the transmission casing to remove the speed sensor.

Refitting

5 Refitting is a reversal of the removal procedure. Where applicable, fit a new O-ring to the speed sensor.

6 Oil seals – renewal

Differential oil seals

1 The differential oil seals are located at the sides of the transmission, where the driveshafts enter the transmission. If leakage

4.3d Gearchange mechanism and cables

1 Shift lever	4 Selector cable	6 Gearshift lever
2 Selector lever	5 Gearshift cable	7 Gearshift linkage
3 Shift cable (white)	bushing	

at the seal is suspected, raise the vehicle and support it securely on axle stands. If the seal is leaking, oil will be found on the side of the transmission below the driveshaft.

2 Refer to Chapter 8 and remove the appropriate driveshaft. If removing the right-hand driveshaft, it will be necessary to remove the intermediate shaft as well.

3 Using a large screwdriver or lever, carefully prise the oil seal out of the transmission casing, taking care not to damage the transmission casing **(see illustration)**.

Note: *To improve access for the right-hand oil seal, it may be helpful to remove the front section of exhaust pipe (see relevant part of Chapter 4)*

4 Wipe clean the oil seal seating area in the transmission casing.

5 Apply a smear of grease to the outer lip of the new oil seal. Ensure the seal is correctly positioned, then press it a little way into the casing by hand, making sure that it is square to its seating.

6 Using suitable tubing or a large socket,

4.7 The cables pass through a rubber adapter in the lower part of the bulkhead

5.3 Unscrew the retaining bolt (arrowed) to remove the sensor from the transmission

6.3 Prise out the oil seal with a suitable lever

6.6 Using a socket to drive in the new seal

6.10 Prise the input shaft oil seal from the rear of the slave cylinder

6.11 Using a socket to drive in the new seal

carefully drive the oil seal into the casing until it contacts the seating **(see illustration)**.
7 Refit the driveshaft with reference to Chapter 8.
8 Check the oil level in the transmission as described in Chapter 1A or 1B.

Input shaft oil seal

9 The input shaft oil seal is fitted into the rear of the clutch slave cylinder/release bearing. Remove the clutch slave cylinder/release bearing as described in Chapter 6, Section 6.
10 Carefully prise the oil seal out of the slave cylinder using a flat-bladed screwdriver **(see illustration)**.
11 Wipe clean the oil seal seating area in the slave cylinder. Using suitable tubing or a large socket, carefully drive the oil seal into the casing until it contacts the seating **(see illustration)**.
12 Refit the slave cylinder/release bearing with reference to Chapter 6, Section 6.

Vehicle speed sensor O-ring

13 This procedure is covered in Section 5 of this Chapter.

7 Reversing light switch – removal and refitting

Removal

1 The reversing light circuit is controlled by a switch mounted on the gearchange bracket located on the top of the transmission casing.
2 Remove the air cleaner and the mass air flow sensor as described in Chapter 4A or 4B.
3 Disconnect the wiring leading to the reversing light switch on the top of the gearchange bracket **(see illustration)**.
4 Unscrew the reversing light switch from the cover housing on the transmission.

Refitting

5 Refitting is a reversal of the removal procedure.

8 Transmission – removal and refitting

Note: *Read through this procedure before starting work to see what is involved, particularly in terms of lifting equipment. Depending on the facilities available, the home mechanic may prefer to remove the engine and transmission together, then separate them on the bench, as described in Chapter 2D.*

Removal

1 Disconnect the battery negative (earth) lead (refer to *Disconnecting the battery* at the end of this manual). For better access, the battery may be removed completely. Remove the upper plastic cover from the top of the engine.
2 If necessary, the bonnet may be removed as described in Chapter 11 for better access, and for fitting the engine lifting hoist.
3 Hold the radiator in its raised position by using cable ties to fasten it to the upper crossmember. This is necessary to retain the radiator when the subframe is removed.
4 Remove the mass air flow sensor and air inlet duct with reference to Chapter 4A or 4B. On V6 models, remove the water pump pulley cover.
5 Remove the air cleaner assembly as described in Chapter 4A or 4B.
6 Unclip the plastic covers from the top of the suspension struts on both sides of the vehicle, then slacken the top mounting retaining nuts by approximately four turns each **(see illustrations)**.
7 Disconnect the wiring from the reversing light switch on the transmission.
8 Unscrew the bolt, and remove the earth terminal from the top of the transmission **(see illustration)**.
9 Using a small screwdriver, prise out the retaining clip and disconnect the clutch hydraulic pipe from the transmission (use a suitable clamp on the hydraulic flexible hose to prevent leak) **(see illustrations)**. Cover both the union and the pipe ends to minimise

7.3 Disconnecting the wiring connector from the reversing light switch (arrowed)

8.6a Unclip the plastic covers . . .

8.6b . . . then slacken the retaining nuts by approximately four turns each

8.8 Undo the retaining bolt and remove the earth terminals

8.9a Prise out the retaining clip (arrowed) . . .

8.9b . . . and disconnect the clutch hydraulic pipe

8.16 Removing the centre retaining nut from the left-hand transmission mounting

fluid loss and prevent the entry of dirt into the hydraulic system. **Note:** *Whilst the hydraulic hose/pipe is disconnected, DO NOT depress the clutch pedal.*

10 Apply the handbrake, and chock the rear wheels. Slacken both front roadwheel retaining bolts and where accessible the driveshaft hub bolts.

11 Jack up the front of the vehicle and support it on axle stands. There must be sufficient clearance below the vehicle for the transmission to be lowered and removed. Remove both front roadwheels and, where fitted, remove the engine undertray.

12 Drain the transmission or be prepared for some oil loss as the transmission is removed.

13 The engine and transmission must now be supported, as the left-hand mounting must be disconnected. Ford technicians use a support bar which locates in the tops of the inner wing panels – proprietary engine support bars are available from tool outlets.

14 If a support bar is not available, an engine hoist should be used. With an engine hoist the engine/transmission can be manoeuvred more easily and safely, balancing the engine on a jack is not recommended.

15 Remove the front subframe as described in Chapter 10.

16 Support the transmission with a trolley jack from below, then undo the retaining nut from the left-hand transmission mounting **(see illustration),** then undo the four retaining bolts and remove the mounting bracket from the top of the transmission housing.

17 Remove the gearchange cables from the support brackets by twisting the spring-loaded knurled collars anti-clockwise (see Section 4). Press the retaining clips at the end of the cables and release them from the transmission lever balljoints – note their fitted locations.

18 Remove the starter motor as described in Chapter 5A.

19 On diesel models, undo the three retaining bolts and remove the vacuum regulator solenoid valve assembly from the front of the transmission housing **(see illustration)**.

20 Disconnect the wiring connector from the vehicle speed sensor.

21 Remove the driveshafts as described in

Chapter 8. Plug the transmission to prevent dirt ingress (or oil loss, if the oil has not been drained).

Caution: Make sure the inner joints of the driveshaft do not bend more than 18° and the outer joints do not bend more than 45° when removing the driveshafts.

22 Working your way around the transmission casing, slacken and remove the transmission-to-engine securing bolts. Disconnect any wiring loom brackets, where applicable. On diesel models, undo the two retaining bolts and detach the coolant pipe from under the transmission housing **(see illustration)**.

23 With the help of an assistant, withdraw the transmission squarely from the engine, taking care not to allow its weight to hang on the clutch friction disc. Once the transmission is free, lower the transmission on the jack and manoeuvre the unit out from under the vehicle.

24 The clutch components can now be inspected with reference to Chapter 6, and renewed if necessary. (Unless they are virtually new, it is worth renewing the clutch components as a matter of course, even if the transmission has been removed for some other reason.)

Refitting

25 With the transmission secured on the trolley jack as on removal, raise it into position, and then carefully slide it onto the rear of the engine, at the same time engaging the input shaft with the clutch friction disc

splines. Do not use excessive force to refit the transmission – if the input shaft does not slide into place easily, readjust the angle of the transmission so that it is level, and/or turn the input shaft so that the splines engage properly with the disc. If problems are still experienced, check that the clutch friction disc is correctly centred (Chapter 6).

26 The transmission is refitted by a reversal of the removal procedure, bearing in mind the following points:

a) *Tighten all nuts and bolts to the specified torque (where given).*

b) *If required, renew the differential oil seals as described in Section 6.*

c) *Refit the driveshafts as described in Chapter 8.*

d) *Refit the front subframe as described in Chapter 10*

e) *Check the oil level in the transmission as described in Chapter 1A or 1B.*

f) *If required, adjust the gearchange cables as described in Section 2.*

27 Make a final check that all connections have been made, and all bolts tightened fully. Road test the vehicle to check for proper transmission operation, then check the transmission visually for leakage of oil.

9 Transmission mounting – checking and renewal

This procedure is covered in Chapter 2A, 2B or 2C.

8.19 Undo the bolts (arrowed) to remove the vacuum regulator solenoid valve assembly (diesel models)

8.22 On diesel models, detach the coolant pipe (arrowed) under the transmission housing

10 Transmission overhaul – general information

1 Overhauling a manual transmission is a difficult job for the do-it-yourself home mechanic. It involves the dismantling and reassembly of many small parts. Numerous clearances must be precisely measured and, if necessary, changed with selected spacers and circlips. As a result, if transmission problems arise, while the unit can be removed and refitted by a competent do-it-yourselfer, overhaul should be left to a transmission specialist. Rebuilt transmissions may be available – check with your dealer parts department, motor factors, or transmission specialists. At any rate, the time and money involved in an overhaul is almost sure to exceed the cost of a rebuilt unit.

2 Nevertheless, it's not impossible for an inexperienced mechanic to rebuild a transmission, providing the special tools are available, and the job is done in a deliberate step-by-step manner so nothing is overlooked.

3 The tools necessary for an overhaul include: internal and external circlip pliers, a bearing puller, a slide hammer, a set of pin punches, a dial test indicator, and possibly a hydraulic press. In addition, a large, sturdy workbench and a vice or transmission stand will be required.

4 During dismantling of the transmission, make careful notes of how each part comes off, where it fits in relation to other parts, and what holds it in place. Exploded views are included (see illustrations) to show where the parts go – but actually noting how they are fitted when you remove the parts will make it much easier to get the transmission back together.

5 Before taking the transmission apart for repair, it will help if you have some idea what area of the transmission is malfunctioning. Certain problems can be closely tied to specific areas in the transmission, which can make component examination and replacement easier. Refer to the *Fault finding* Section at the end of this manual for information regarding possible sources of trouble.

H.23938

10.4a Manual transmission input shaft components

1 Taper roller bearing	4 2nd gear	7 3rd/4th synchro-ring	10 4th/5th synchro-ring	13 5th gear
2 Input shaft	5 Needle roller bearing	8 3rd/4th synchro-hub	11 Needle roller bearing	14 Snap-ring
3 1st gear	6 3rd gear	9 Snap-ring	12 4th gear	15 Taper roller bearing

10.4b Manual transmission output shaft 5th and reverse components

| 1 | Taper roller bearing | 3 | Needle roller bearing | 5 | Snap-ring | 7 | 5th gear | 9 | Output shaft |
| 2 | Reverse gear | 4 | Reverse synchro-ring | 6 | 5th synchro-ring | 8 | Needle roller bearing | | |

10.4c Manual transmission output shaft 1st/2nd components

1	Taper roller bearing	4	1st gear	7	Snap-ring	10	2nd gear	12	4th gear
2	Snap-ring	5	Needle roller bearing	8	1st/2nd synchro-hub	11	Needle roller bearing	13	3rd gear
3	Output pinion	6	1st synchro-ring	9	2nd synchro-ring			14	Output shaft

11 Transmission oil – draining and refilling

1 This operation is much more efficient if the car is first taken on a journey of sufficient length to warm the engine/transmission up to normal operating temperature.
Caution: If the procedure is to be carried out on a hot transmission unit, take care not to burn yourself on the hot exhaust or the transmission/engine unit.
2 Park the car on level ground, switch off the ignition and apply the handbrake firmly. Jack up the front of the car and support it securely on axle stands. Undo the retaining bolts/nuts and remove the undertray (where applicable) from beneath the engine/transmission unit.
3 Wipe clean the area around the drain plug and position a suitable container underneath.
4 Unscrew the drain plug and allow the transmission oil to drain into the container **(see illustration)**.
5 Allow the oil to drain completely into the container. If the oil is hot, take precautions against scalding.

11.4 Removing the drain plug for the transmission oil to drain

6 Once the oil has finished draining, ensure the drain plug is clean and refit it to the transmission with a new washer. Tighten the drain plug to the specified torque. Lower the vehicle to the ground.
7 The transmission is refilled through the level plug hole on the front of the transmission casing **(see illustration)**. Wipe clean the area around the level plug and unscrew it from the casing. Refill the transmission with the specified type and

11.7 Oil level plug (arrowed) is on the front of the transmission casing

amount of oil given in the specifications, until the oil begins to trickle out of the level hole. Refit the plug and tighten it to the specified torque.
8 Take the vehicle on a short journey so that the new oil is distributed fully around the transmission components.
9 On your return, park on level ground and check the transmission oil level as described in Chapter 1A or 1B. Refit the engine/ transmission undertray.

Chapter 7 Part B:
Automatic transmission

Contents

Degrees of difficulty

| Easy, suitable for novice with little experience | | Fairly easy, suitable for beginner with some experience | | Fairly difficult, suitable for competent DIY mechanic | | Difficult, suitable for experienced DIY mechanic | | Very difficult, suitable for expert DIY or professional | |

Specifications

General

Transmission type:
2.0 litre petrol	CD4E (4-speed)
2.5 litre V6 petrol	5F31J (5-speed)
2.0 litre diesel	5F31J (5-speed)

Torque wrench settings

	Nm	lbf ft
Fluid cooler pipes to transmission:		
CD4E	23	17
5F31J	40	30
Selector cable adaptor/grommet	9	7
Selector lever cable cover (5F31J)	22	16
Selector lever position sensor:		
CD4E	12	9
5F31J	6	4
Selector lever to floor	9	7
Speed sensors (CD4E)	13	10
Torque converter to driveplate	36	27
Transmission drain plug:		
CD4E	27	20
5F31J	45	33
Transmission earth cable	20	15
Transmission mounting centre nut	133	98
Transmission mounting to inner wing	48	35
Transmission to engine	48	35

3.3a Cable end fitting arrowhead markings in locked (closed) position

1 General information

CD4E automatic transmission

This transmission is controlled electronically by the engine management electronic control unit. There are two operational modes (Economy and Sport), and a driver-operated overdrive inhibit switch prevents the 4th gear from operating when required during certain conditions. With the Economy mode selected, gearchanges occur at low engine speeds, whereas with the Sport mode selected, the changes occur at high engine speeds.

The transmission incorporates a chain drive between the planetary gear sets and the final drive. The transmission fluid is cooled by a cooler located within the radiator.

There is no kickdown switch, as kickdown is controlled by the throttle position sensor in the engine management system.

The electronic control system has a fail-safe mode, which gives the transmission

3.3b Remove the retaining bolts (arrowed) to remove cover

limited operation in order to drive the vehicle home or to a repair garage.

5F31J automatic transmission

This transmission was introduced in May 2002, and also known under the name Durashift 5-tronic (it was developed by Jatco TransTechnology – a Japanese automatic transmission manufacturer). It is a fully automatic and electronically-controlled design for front-wheel-drive vehicles.

The transmission ratios are achieved with three planetary gearsets on two shafts. The individual components are driven or held by means of four multi-plate clutches, two multi-plate brakes, one brake band and two roller-type one-way clutches. A torque converter lock-up clutch (TCC) ensures that fuel consumption is optimised. It is engaged by the transmission control unit depending on the vehicle speed and the engine load.

The transmission has a control unit (which is located in the passenger compartment behind the facia) it calculates the gearshift timing according to the personal driving style of the driver. Additional driving restrictions (such as towing a trailer or driving uphill/downhill in mountains or steep hills) are also taken into account when calculating the gearshift timing. Gears can be selected either automatically (selector lever position D) or manually by the driver (selected-shift mode). The automatic transmission range or the manually selected gear (select-shift mode) is displayed in the instrument panel.

In the event of failure of any electronic components a hydraulic emergency running programme provides restricted operation of the transmission. If the transmission control unit can no longer ensure that the correct gearshifts are performed, then it will automatically switch into emergency running mode. When in the emergency running mode, two horizontal lines are indicated on the instrument display panel.
The vehicle will then be able to drive on, giving the following restrictions:

a) *In selector lever position D (or in the select-shift gate) – 4th gear is permanently engaged.*

b) *In selector lever position R – reverse gear can be selected.*

c) *There is maximum hydraulic line pressure applied – giving harsh gearchange.*

All transmissions

As a safety measure, it is necessary for the ignition to be switched to position 2 and for the brake pedal to be depressed in order to move the selector from position P. If the vehicle battery is discharged, the selector lever release solenoid will not function; if it is required to move the vehicle in this state, remove the cover in the centre console next to the selector lever and insert a key or a similar small instrument into the aperture. Push the locking lever down to allow the selector lever to be moved out of the park P position.

2 Fault finding – general

In the event of a fault occurring on the transmission, first check that the fluid level is correct (see Chapter 1A or 1B). If there has been a loss of fluid, check the oil seals as described in Section 7. Also check the hoses to the fluid cooler in the radiator for leaks. The only other checks possible for the home mechanic are the adjustment of the selector cable (Section 3) and the selector lever position sensor (Section 6).

If the fault still persists, it is necessary to determine whether it is of an electrical, mechanical or hydraulic nature; to do this, special test equipment is required. It is therefore essential to have the work carried out by an automatic transmission specialist or Ford dealer if a transmission fault is suspected.

Do not remove the transmission from the vehicle for possible repair before professional fault diagnosis has been carried out, since most tests require the transmission to be in the vehicle.

3 Selector cable – removal, refitting and adjustment

Removal

1 Unclip the breather hose from the engine upper plastic cover, then unclip the cover from the top of the engine.

2 Remove the air cleaner assembly (Chapter 4A or 4B) in order to gain access to the selector cable, which is located on the side of the transmission.

3 Detach the selector inner cable end fitting outwards from the lever on the side of the transmission. Turn the outer cable locking ring anti-clockwise to remove the cable from the bracket **(see illustration)**. **Note:** *On the 5F31J transmissions, remove the selector lever cable cover, before removing the cable* ***(see illustration)***.

4 Apply the handbrake, then jack up the front of the vehicle and support it on axle stands (see *Jacking and vehicle support*).

5 Working beneath the vehicle (on petrol models), remove the heat shield from above the catalytic converter, disconnect the wiring connector for the oxygen sensor.
Caution: The catalytic converter operates at very high temperatures, if there is any chance that the system may be still hot, wear suitable safety clothing/gloves.

6 Working along the outer cable, unclip the cable from the retaining clips under the bulkhead.

7 Move the selector lever in the vehicle to the D (drive) position.

8 Remove the centre console as described in Chapter 11.

9 Detach the selector cable retaining clip from the selector lever, pull out the retaining pin and push the cable out from the selector lever.
10 Pull the carpet to one side (the carpet and insulation may need to be cut slightly to gain access to the cable retaining plate).
11 Undo the retaining screw and detach the heater air duct from under the centre of the facia panel.
12 Unscrew the retaining nuts and release the adapter/grommet from the floor, then withdraw the cable through the bulkhead and into the car. **Note:** *Before pulling the cable through the bulkhead, tie a piece of guide-wire to the transmission end of the selector cable and pull it through with the cable. Disconnect the guide-wire leaving it through the bulkhead for refitting.*

Refitting

13 Refitting is a reversal of the removal procedure, but adjust the cable as follows:

Adjustment

CD4E

14 Check that the selector lever in the vehicle is still in the drive D position.
15 With the inner cable disconnected from the lever on the transmission, check that the lever is in the D position on the transmission. To do this, it will be necessary to move the lever slightly up-and-down until it is positioned correctly **(see illustration)**.
16 Check that the cable locking ring on the transmission end is still unlocked (ie, turned anti-clockwise by 90°).
17 With the selector lever inside the vehicle in position D and the lever on the transmission also in position D, refit the cable end fitting to the transmission lever, then turn the locking ring 90° clockwise to lock it in the selector bracket.

18 With the handbrake applied, start the engine and move the selector lever through all the ranges, allowing enough time for each position to engage.
19 Road test the vehicle to check the transmission for correct operation.

5F31J

20 Check that the selector lever in the vehicle is still in the drive D position.
21 With the selector lever cover removed, release the yellow locking clip from the selector lever cable adjustment mechanism **(see illustration)**.
22 Move the selector lever on the transmission until it is in the drive D position **(see illustration)**. **Note:** *The dot on the transmission casing must align with the hole on the selector lever when it is in the drive D position.*
23 With the selector in the drive D position, press the yellow locking clip back into the selector lever cable to lock the adjustment mechanism. Refit the selector lever cable cover.
24 With the handbrake applied, start the engine and move the selector lever through all the ranges, allowing enough time for each position to engage.
25 Road test the vehicle to check the transmission for correct operation.

4 Selector lever assembly – removal and refitting

Removal

1 Remove the centre console as described in Chapter 11.
2 Detach the selector cable retaining clip from the selector lever, pull out the retaining

3.15 Lever positions on transmission

1 First gear　　4 Neutral
2 Second gear　5 Reverse
3 Drive　　　　6 Park

pin and push the cable out from the selector lever.
3 Apply the handbrake, then jack up the front of the vehicle and support it on axle stands (see *Jacking and vehicle support*).
4 Working beneath the vehicle (on petrol models), remove the heat shield from above the catalytic converter, disconnect the wiring connector for the oxygen sensor.
Caution: The catalytic converter operates at very high temperatures, if there is any chance that the system may be still hot, wear suitable safety clothing/gloves.
5 Unscrew the mounting nuts securing the selector lever assembly to the floor.
6 Disconnect the selector lever wiring connector, then withdraw the selector lever assembly from inside the vehicle. Where applicable, recover the gasket.

Refitting

7 Refitting is a reversal of the removal procedure, but adjust the selector cable as described in Section 3.

3.21 Release the locking clip (arrowed) from the selector lever cable

3.22 Align the dot (arrowed) on the transmission housing with the hole in the lever to select the D (drive) position

1 Park　　2 Reverse　　3 Neutral　　4 Drive

5 Speed sensors – removal and refitting

Note: *The following removal and refitting procedure is for the CD4E transmission. At the time of writing there was no information available for the speed sensors in the 5F31J transmission unit (The following information can be used as a typical sensor removal and refitting procedure).*

Note: *In the CD4E transmission, there are two speed sensors* **(see illustration 5.2)**, *one is the vehicle or output shaft speed sensor (OSS) and the other is the turbine shaft speed sensor (TSS). The output shaft speed sensor is located in the differential next to the driveshaft and the turbine shaft speed sensor is located in the transmission end cover. The procedure for the removal and refitting of both speed sensors are the same.*

Removal

1 Apply the handbrake, then jack up the front of the vehicle and support it on axle stands (see *Jacking and vehicle support*).
2 Disconnect the wiring connector from the speed sensor **(see illustration)**. **Note:** *The output shaft speed sensor connector is coloured black and the turbine shaft speed sensor connector is coloured white.*
3 Unscrew the retaining bolt and withdraw the vehicle speed sensor from the transmission.
4 Using a small screwdriver, remove the rubber O-ring from the sensor and discard it; obtain a new one for reassembly.
5 Wipe clean the speed sensor and the seating bore in the transmission casing.

Refitting

6 Refitting is a reversal of the removal procedure noting the following points:
  a) *Lightly lubricate the new O-ring with petroleum jelly before inserting the assembly in the transmission casing.*
  b) *Tighten the clamp bolt to the specified torque setting.*
  c) *With the handbrake applied, start the engine and move the selector lever through all the ranges, allowing enough time for each position to engage.*
  d) *Select the park P position and check the transmission fluid level as described in Chapter 1A or 1B.*

6 Selector lever position sensor – removal, refitting and adjustment

Removal

1 Remove the battery as described in Chapter 5A. Undo the retaining bolts and remove the battery tray.
2 In order to gain better access to the selector lever position sensor, which is located on top of the transmission **(see illustration 5.2)**. Remove the air cleaner assembly as described in Chapter 4A or 4B.
3 Move the selector lever to the N (neutral) position.
4 Disconnect the wiring multi-plug from the position sensor **(see illustration)**.
5 Unscrew the mounting bolts, and remove the sensor.

Refitting and adjustment

6 Refitting is a reversal of the removal procedure, but check the alignment of the sensor as follows before fully tightening the mounting bolts.
7 Check that the transmission is in the N (neutral) position (see Section 3).

J35151

5.2 Sensors fitted to the CD4E transmission

1 *Selector lever position sensor*   2 *Output speed sensor (OSS)*   3 *Turbine shaft speed sensor (TSS)*

6.4 Multi-plug (arrowed) for the selector lever position sensor

6.8a Alignment tool for the selector lever position sensor
(selector in position N) (CD4E transmission)

1 Sensor   2 Alignment tool (pegs arrowed)

8 There is a Ford special tool for aligning the sensor, it consists of a metal plate with pegs to engage with the cut-outs in the sensor and shaft (see illustrations).
9 Twist the sensor on the transmission until the special tool is aligned, this is the neutral N position in the transmission. With the sensor correctly aligned, tighten the bolts, then remove the alignment tool.
10 Reconnect the wiring multi-plug to the position sensor.
11 Refit the battery as described in Chapter 5A, and the air cleaner assembly as described in Chapter 4A or 4B.
12 As a further check, with the handbrake applied, move the selector lever to position park P or neutral N, the engine should start. Note: The vehicle should not be able to start if any other gear is selected. When reverse R is selected the reversing lights should illuminate.

7 Oil seals – renewal

Differential side gear oil seals

1 The procedure is the same as that for the manual transmission (refer to Chapter 7A). Note: Ford use a special puller tool, to remove the differential seal from the transmission casing.

Speed sensor oil seals

2 The procedure is covered in Section 5.

8 Transmission – removal and refitting

Note: Read through this procedure before starting work, to see what is involved, particularly in terms of lifting equipment. Depending on the facilities available, the home

mechanic may prefer to remove the engine and transmission together, then separate them on the bench, as described in Chapter 2D.

Removal

1 Disconnect the battery negative (earth) lead (refer to Disconnecting the battery at the end of this manual). For better access, the battery may be removed completely. Remove the upper plastic cover from the top of the engine.
2 If necessary, remove the bonnet (Chapter 11) for better access, and for fitting the engine lifting hoist.

3 Raise the radiator, and hold it in the raised position by using cable ties through the holes in the upper crossmember. This is necessary to retain the radiator when the subframe is removed.
4 Unclip the plastic covers from the top of the suspension struts on both sides of the vehicle, then slacken the top mounting retaining nuts by approximately four turns each (see illustrations).
5 Remove the air cleaner assembly as described in Chapter 4A or 4B. On diesel models disconnect the turbocharger air intake pipe.

6.8b Alignment tool for the selector lever position sensor (5F31J transmission)

1 Selector lever position sensor   2 Alignment tool

8.4a Unclip the plastic covers . . .

8.4b . . . then slacken the top strut mounting retaining nuts

8.7 Earth lead attachment (arrowed) on the transmission

6 Drain the cooling system as described in Chapter 1A or 1B.

7 Where applicable, detach the battery earth lead from the transmission **(see illustration)**.

8 Pull the selector cable end fitting from the lever on the transmission and unbolt the support bracket. **Note:** *On the 5F31J transmissions, remove the selector lever cable cover, before removing the cable (see Section 3).*

9 Apply the handbrake, and chock the rear wheels. Slacken both front roadwheel retaining bolts and where accessible the driveshaft hub bolts.

10 Jack up the front of the vehicle and support it on axle stands. There must be sufficient clearance below the vehicle for the transmission to be lowered and removed. Remove both front roadwheels and where fitted, remove the engine undertray.

11 Remove the front lower cover from under the radiator, by prising out the side clips and unscrewing the retaining bolts.

12 Drain the transmission fluid into a suitable container. Where fitted discard the washer/gasket, refit the plug with a new washer/gasket and tighten to the specified torque setting on completion.

13 On diesel models undo the retaining bolts, and remove the charge air cooler intake hose from across the underside of the engine/transmission.

14 The engine and transmission must now be supported. Ford technicians use a support bar which locates in the tops of the inner wing panels – proprietary engine support bars are available from tool outlets.

15 If a support bar is not available, an engine hoist should be used. With an engine hoist the engine/transmission can be manoeuvred more easily and safely, balancing the engine on a jack is not recommended.

16 Remove the front subframe as described in Chapter 10.

17 Remove the driveshafts as described in Chapter 8. Plug the transmission to prevent dirt ingress (or oil loss, if the oil has not been drained).

Caution : Make sure the inner joints of the driveshaft do not bend more than 18° and the outer joints do not bend more than 45° when removing the driveshafts.

18 Support the transmission with a trolley jack from below, then undo the retaining nut from the left-hand transmission mounting, then undo the four retaining nuts and remove the mounting from the inner wing panel **(see illustrations)**.

19 On CD4E transmissions, disconnect the wiring connectors from the output speed sensor (OSS), the turbine shaft speed sensor (TSS) and (where fitted) the headlamp levelling sensor wiring connector.

20 On the 5F31J transmissions, disconnect the three multi-plug wiring connectors from the transmission housing. Also disconnect the vent hose from the top of the transmission.

21 Unscrew the union nut securing the automatic transmission fluid cooler pipe to the left-hand side of the transmission and also the cooler return pipe to the transmission. Unclip the pipes, and move them to one side. Plug the end of the pipes,

to prevent dust and dirt entering the hydraulic system.

22 Remove the starter motor as described in Chapter 5A.

23 Disconnect the wiring connectors from the selector lever position sensor. On CD4E transmissions, disconnect the transmission control electrical connector from the top of the transmission.

24 On CD4E transmissions, remove the rubber cover from the starter motor recess in the transmission bellhousing, for access to the torque converter retaining bolts.

25 On the 5F31J transmissions, remove the cover in the lower section of the transmission casing to gain access to the torque converter retaining bolts.

26 Unscrew and remove the torque converter retaining bolts. It will be necessary to turn the engine, using the crankshaft pulley bolt, so that each of the four nuts can be unscrewed through the aperture.

27 Undo the retaining nuts/bolts and remove transmission mounting bracket from the top of the transmission housing.

28 With the weight of the transmission supported on a trolley jack. Use safety chains or make up a cradle to steady the transmission on the jack.

29 Working your way around the transmission casing, slacken and remove the transmission-to-engine securing bolts. Disconnect any wiring loom brackets, where applicable.

30 With the help of an assistant, withdraw the transmission squarely from the engine, making sure that the torque converter comes away with the transmission, and does not stay in contact with the driveplate. If this precaution is not taken, there is a risk of the torque converter falling out and being damaged.

31 Lower the transmission to the ground.

Refitting

32 Clean the contact surfaces of the driveplate and torque converter.

33 Check that the torque converter is fully entered in the transmission, to do this, place a straight-edge across the transmission flange. *On CD4E transmissions (2.0 litre petrol engines), check that the torque converter*

8.18a Undo the retaining nut (arrowed) . . .

8.18b . . . then undo the four retaining nuts (arrowed)

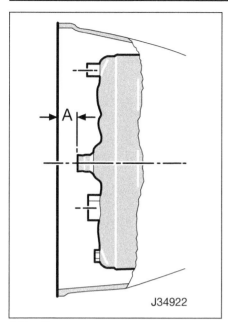

J34922

8.33a Torque converter centre spigot must be at least 14mm below the transmission flange (dimension A) (CD4E transmission)

centre spigot is 14 mm below the straight-edge (see illustration).
On 5F31J transmissions, check the drive plate studs (see illustration) are:
a) *21 mm below the straight-edge on diesel engines.*
b) *15.5 mm below the straight-edge on 2.5 litre V6 petrol engines.*
Apply a thin layer of high-temperature grease to the centre spigot on the torque converter.
Caution: This procedure is important, to ensure that the torque converter is fully engaged with the fluid pump. If it is not fully engaged, serious damage will occur.

34 With the help of an assistant, raise the transmission, and locate it on the rear of the driveplate. Ensure the transmission is correctly aligned with the locating dowels, before pushing it fully into engagement with the engine. **Note:** *The torque converter must remain in full engagement with the fluid pump at the correct installation depth throughout the fitting procedure.*
35 Working your way around the transmission casing, refit the transmission-to-engine bolts. Do not fully tighten the retaining bolts until all the bolts are in place, then tighten to the specified torque setting.
36 Using four new retaining nuts, tighten the torque converter retaining nuts to the specified torque. Turn the engine as required to bring each of the nuts into view. **Note:** *Insert all of the new nuts before fully tightening them to the specified torque.*

37 The remainder of the refitting procedure is a reversal of the removal procedure, noting the following special points:
a) *Tighten all retaining bolts to their specified torque wrench setting (where given).*
b) *Reconnect and adjust the selector cable, as described in Section 3.*
c) *Renew the transmission fluid as described in Chapter 1A or 1B.*
d) *If a new unit has been fitted, depending on the transmission type, it may be necessary to have the transmission ECU 'matched' to the engine management PCM electronically, to ensure correct operation – seek the advice of your Ford dealer or automatic transmission specialist.*
e) *After running the engine, recheck the transmission fluid level, and top-up if necessary (refer to Chapter 1).*
f) *Road test the vehicle to check the transmission for correct operation.*

9 Transmission fluid – renewal

1 Refer to Chapter 1A or 1B.

10 Transmission overhaul – general information

In the event of a fault occurring, it will be necessary to establish whether the fault is electrical, mechanical or hydraulic in nature, before repair work can be contemplated. Diagnosis requires detailed knowledge of the transmission's operation and construction, as well as access to specialised test equipment, and so is deemed to be beyond the scope of this manual. It is therefore essential that problems with the automatic transmission are referred to a Ford dealer or automatic transmission specialist for assessment.

A faulty transmission should not be removed before the vehicle has been assessed by a dealer or specialist, as fault diagnosis is carried out with the transmission connected up to the vehicle. Refer to the information given in Section 2 before removing the unit.

Note that, if the vehicle is still within the warranty period, in the event of a fault it is important to take it to a Ford dealer, who will carry out a comprehensive diagnosis procedure using specialist equipment. Failure to do this will invalidate the warranty.

J35154

8.33b Torque converter drive plate stud depth (2) must be measured using a straight-edge (1) (5F31J transmission)

1   Straight-edge
2   Depth:
     21 mm – diesel engines
     15.5 mm – 2.5 litre V6 petrol engines

11 Transmission control module (5F31J) – removal and refitting

Note: *The transmission control module (TCM) which is fitted to the 5F31J transmissions, is located on the inner bulkhead behind the facia panel.*

Removal

1 Remove the facia panel as described in Chapter 11.
2 Undo the retaining bolts and remove the vehicle cross-beam from across the inside of the bulkhead.
3 Disconnect the wiring connector from the transmission control module.
4 The control module is riveted to a bracket on the inner bulkhead, drill out the rivets and remove the control module from the vehicle.

Refitting

5 Refitting is a reversal of the removal procedure, fit new rivets to the control module retaining bracket.
Caution: Check the correct transmission control module (TCM) for the vehicle is installed, or irregular driving conditions may occur.

Chapter 8
Driveshafts

Contents

Degrees of difficulty

| Easy, suitable for novice with little experience | | Fairly easy, suitable for beginner with some experience | | Fairly difficult, suitable for competent DIY mechanic | | Difficult, suitable for experienced DIY mechanic | | Very difficult, suitable for expert DIY or professional | |

Specifications

General

Inner CV joint grease quantity:
  1.8 and 2.0 litre petrol models . . . . 155 grams
  2.5 litre V6 and all diesel models . . . . 165 grams
Outer CV joint grease quantity:
  1.8 and 2.0 litre petrol models . . . . 100 grams
  2.5 litre V6 and all diesel models . . . . 115 grams

Torque wrench settings

	Nm	lbf ft
Anti-roll bar link and mounting	48	35
Driveshaft/hub retaining nut	290	214
Front suspension lower arm balljoint clamp bolt	83	61
Front suspension strut top mount to body	30	22
Front suspension subframe mounting bolts	142	105
Front suspension subframe rear bracket	10	7
Intermediate shaft centre bearing bracket to block	48	35
Intermediate shaft centre bearing retaining nut	25	18
Roadwheel nuts	85	63
Steering column flexible coupling to steering gear pinion shaft (renew)	25	18
Steering column-to-flexible coupling clamp bolt (renew)	20	15

J35155

1.1 Exploded view of the driveshafts (1.8 and 2.0 litre engine)

1 *Driveshaft with fixed outer CV joint*
2 *Large gaiter retaining clamp*
3 *Gaiter*
4 *Small gaiter retaining clamp*
5 *Inner joint tripod retaining circlip*
6 *Inner joint tripod*

7 *Inner joint housing*
8 *Driveshaft inner retaining circlip*
9 *Intermediate shaft*
10 *Right-hand driveshaft-to-intermediate
     shaft retaining circlip*

1 General information

Drive is transmitted from the transmission differential to the front wheels by means of two driveshafts, each incorporating two constant velocity (CV) joints. The right-hand driveshaft is in two sections, and incorporates a support bearing **(see illustration)**. On 2.5 litre V6 and all diesel engine models, the driveshaft is of solid design, however, on 1.8 and 2.0 litre petrol models it is of tubular design.

Each driveshaft consists of three main components: the sliding (tripod type) inner joint, the actual driveshaft, and the outer (fixed ball) joint. The inner (male) end of the left-hand tripod joint is secured in the differential side gear by the engagement of a circlip. The inner (female) end of the right-hand driveshaft is held on the intermediate shaft by the engagement of a circlip. The intermediate shaft is held in the transmission by the support bearing, which in turn is supported by a bracket bolted to the rear of the cylinder block. The outer CV joint on both driveshafts is of fixed ball-bearing type, and is secured in the front hub by the hub nut.

Caution: When removing the driveshafts, the inner CV joint must not be bent by more than 18° and the outer CV joint must not be bent by more than 45°. The outer CV joint must not be dismantled from the driveshaft, as it is a press-fit.

2 Driveshafts –
removal and refitting

Note: *Read the Caution in Section 1 before proceeding. This procedure includes partially lowering the front suspension subframe.*

Removal

1 Position the front wheels in the straight-ahead position, and centralise the steering wheel. Remove the wheel cover (or centre cover) from the relevant wheel, apply the handbrake, and engage 1st gear (manual transmission) or P (automatic transmission). Loosen the hub nut about half a turn.
Caution: This nut is very tight, and can only be re-used a maximum of 4 times. Mark the nut as an indication.
2 Loosen the front wheel retaining nuts. Jack up the front of the vehicle and support it on axle stands (see *Jacking and vehicle support*). Remove both front wheels. On diesel models, remove the engine undertray.
3 Working inside the car, unscrew and remove the clamp bolt securing the steering inner column to the splined pinion shaft of the steering gear. Rotate the clamp plate clockwise and detach the clamp from the pinion shaft. Discard the bolt as a new one must be fitted on reassembly.
4 With the bonnet open, unclip the cover from the top of the relevant front suspension strut, then unscrew each of the three mounting nuts four turns only.
5 Unscrew and remove the hub nut **(see illustration).**

2.5 Removing the hub nut

2.23 Using a lever to remove the left-hand driveshaft from the transmission

2.24 Removing the outer end of the driveshaft from the steering knuckle

2.26 Removing the circlip from the inner end of the left-hand driveshaft

6 Undo the screws and remove the splash shield from under the radiator position.

7 At the front of the engine compartment, use cable ties to support the radiator on both sides. Alternatively, pins may be inserted through the holes in the radiator upper location tubes. Access to the tubes is gained through the apertures in the front crossmember.

8 Under the front of the car, unbolt the hose bracket (where fitted) next to the left-hand radiator support bracket, then unbolt and remove both radiator support brackets.

9 On diesel models, loosen the clips and disconnect the air intake hose and turbocharger outlet hose near the front of the subframe.

10 Working beneath each wheel arch in turn, unbolt the anti-roll bar link from the suspension strut.

11 On 1.8 and 2.0 litre petrol engines, and all diesel engines, remove the exhaust flexible pipe from the front of the exhaust system with reference to the appropriate part of Chapter 4.

12 On the 2.5 litre petrol engine, remove the exhaust dual converter Y-pipe with reference to the appropriate part of Chapter 4.

13 Remove the engine rear support/link with reference to the appropriate part of Chapter 2.

14 On petrol models, disconnect the catalytic converter monitor sensor wiring, and unclip the wiring from the subframe.

15 On models with xenon headlamps, release the ties and detach the headlamp leveling sensor wiring harness from the subframe.

16 Release the radiator cooling fan wiring harness from the subframe.

17 Support the front suspension subframe on one or two trolley jacks. If necessary, enlist the help of an assistant.

18 Note which way round the front suspension lower arm balljoint clamp bolts are fitted on each side, then unscrew and remove each one from the knuckle assembly. *Caution: Do not pull down on the lower arms at this stage, as the rear hydro-bushes will be damaged.*

19 Carefully mark the position of the front suspension subframe on the underbody to ensure correct refitting. **Note:** *Ford*

technicians use special alignment pins to locate the subframe accurately when refitting – it is recommended that these pins are obtained for the refitting procedure. Unscrew and remove the subframe rear mounting bolts, then unbolt the rear brackets from the subframe.

20 Unscrew and remove the subframe front mounting bolts.

21 Lower the subframe uniformly approximately 150 mm, making sure that the lower arm rear hydro-bushes are not strained or damaged.

22 Detach the lower arm balljoints from the steering knuckles, and remove the heat shields. If they are tight, carefully tap down the outer ends of the arms with a mallet, or drive a thin metal wedge into the knuckle clamps. Take care not to damage the balljoint rubber boots.

Left-hand driveshaft

23 Insert a lever between the inner driveshaft joint and the transmission case, with a thin piece of wood against the case. Prise free the inner joint from the differential **(see illustration)**. If it proves reluctant to move, strike the lever firmly with the palm of the hand. Be careful not to damage adjacent components, and in particular, make sure that the driveshaft oil seal in the differential is not damaged. Be prepared for some oil spillage from the transmission. Support the inner end of the driveshaft on an axle stand.

24 Press the outer end of the driveshaft through the front hub and steering knuckle **(see illustration)**. If necessary, use a universal

puller located on the hub flange.

25 Withdraw the driveshaft from under the vehicle.

26 Extract the circlip from the groove on the inner end of the driveshaft, and obtain a new one **(see illustration)**.

Right-hand driveshaft

Note: *The right-hand driveshaft may either be removed complete with the intermediate shaft from the transmission, or it may be disconnected from the outer end of the intermediate shaft.*

27 Press the outer end of the driveshaft through the front hub and steering knuckle – if necessary, use a universal puller located on the hub flange. Tie the steering knuckle to one side, and support the outer end of the driveshaft on an axle stand.

28 To disconnect the driveshaft from the outer end of the intermediate shaft, insert a lever between the inner driveshaft joint and the intermediate bearing housing, with a thin piece of wood against the housing. Prise free the inner joint from the bearing housing; this will release the internal circlip. Alternatively, use a soft-faced mallet to drive off the housing **(see illustrations)**.

29 To remove the intermediate shaft, unscrew the nuts securing the driveshaft support bearing to the rear of the bracket on the cylinder block, and, where fitted, remove the exhaust heat shield. Mark the cap with the normal direction of rotation to ensure correct refitting **(see illustrations)**.

30 Withdraw the intermediate shaft from the transmission **(see illustration)**.

2.28a Using a mallet to drive off the right-hand driveshaft housing

2.28b Disconnecting the right-hand driveshaft from the intermediate shaft

2.29a Mark the cap with the normal direction of rotation . . .

2.29b . . . then remove the cap . . .

2.29c . . . and withdraw the bearing from the bracket

2.29d Intermediate shaft support bearing (2.5 litre V6 engine)

2.29e Exhaust heat shield (2.0 litre engine)

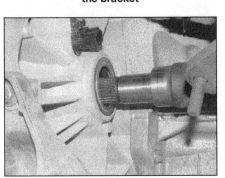

2.30 Withdraw the intermediate shaft from the transmission

31 Where the driveshaft has been disconnected from the intermediate shaft, extract the circlip from the groove on the splined outer end of the intermediate shaft, and obtain a new one **(see illustration)**.

Both sides

32 Check the condition of the differential oil seals, and if necessary renew them as described in Chapter 7A (manual transmission) or

Chapter 7B (automatic transmission) **(see illustrations)**. Check the support bearing, and if necessary renew it as described in Section 5.

Refitting

Left-hand driveshaft

33 Fit the new circlip to the groove on the inner end of the driveshaft, making sure it is correctly seated.

34 Keeping the driveshaft level, insert the splined inner end into the transmission and engage with the splines in the differential sun gear. Take care not to damage the transmission oil seal. Press in the driveshaft until the circlip is fully engaged.

35 Pull the knuckle outwards, and insert the outer end of the driveshaft through the hub. Turn the driveshaft as necessary to engage the splines in the hub, and fully push on the hub. If necessary, use a wooden mallet to tap the hub onto the driveshaft splines until it is possible to screw on the hub nut several threads.

Right-hand driveshaft

36 If the complete driveshaft and intermediate shaft have been removed, insert the inner end of the intermediate shaft into the transmission and engage it with the splines on the differential sun gear, taking care not to damage the oil seal. Locate the intermediate shaft centre bearing on its bracket, refit the cap, and tighten the retaining nuts to the specified torque.

37 Where the intermediate shaft was left in position, locate a new circlip in the groove on

2.31 Removing the circlip from the groove on the intermediate shaft

2.32a Prising out the old oil seal

2.32b Locate the new oil seal . . .

2.32c . . . and drive it fully into the transmission casing

the outer end of the intermediate shaft, then locate the driveshaft on the intermediate shaft splines, and push it on until the internal circlip is heard to engage with the groove in the shaft.

38 Pull the knuckle outwards, and insert the outer end of the driveshaft through the hub. Turn the driveshaft as necessary to engage the splines in the hub, and fully push on the hub. If necessary, use a wooden mallet to tap the hub onto the driveshaft splines until it is possible to screw on the hub nut several threads.

Both sides

39 Locate the front suspension lower arm balljoint stubs in the bottom of the knuckles together with the heat shields. Insert the clamp bolts from the rear (heads facing rearwards), screw on the nuts, and tighten it to the specified torque.

40 Raise the subframe against the underbody, and position it accurately with the marks made during removal. If available, use the special Ford alignment pins. Refit the rear brackets, then insert the mounting bolts and tighten to the specified torque. Make sure the subframe does not move when tightening the bolts.

41 Refit the radiator cooling fan wiring harness to the subframe.

42 On models with xenon headlamps, attach the headlamp leveling sensor wiring harness to the subframe using cable ties.

43 On petrol models, reconnect the catalytic converter monitor sensor wiring, and secure the wiring to the subframe.

44 Refit the engine rear support/link insulator with reference to the appropriate part of Chapter 2.

45 On 1.8 and 2.0 litre petrol engines, and all diesel engines, refit the exhaust flexible pipe to the front of the exhaust system with reference to the appropriate part of Chapter 4.

46 On the 2.5 litre petrol engine, refit the exhaust dual converter Y-pipe with reference to the appropriate part of Chapter 4.

47 Refit the anti-roll bar link to the suspension strut and tighten the nut to the specified torque.

48 On diesel models, reconnect the air intake hose and turbocharger outlet hose near the front of the subframe, and tighten the clips.

49 Under the front of the car, refit the hose bracket and the radiator support brackets, making sure that the rubber mountings are located on the radiator correctly, then tighten the bolts. Remove the temporary cable ties or pins from the radiator.

50 Refit the splash shield beneath the radiator and tighten the screws.

51 Tighten the hub nut moderately at this stage.

52 Tighten the front suspension strut upper mounting nuts to the specified torque, then refit the plastic cover.

53 Working inside the car, refit the steering column clamp to the steering gear pinion shaft taking care not to turn the column from its straight-ahead position. Turn the clamp plate anti-clockwise and insert the **new** clamp bolt. Tighten the bolt to the specified torque.

54 On diesel models, refit the engine undertray.

55 Check, and if necessary top-up of transmission oil (manual) or fluid (automatic) with reference to Chapter 1A or 1B.

56 Refit both front wheels, then lower the front of the car to the ground and tighten the wheel retaining nuts to the specified torque.

57 Tighten the hub nut to the specified torque. Finally, refit the wheel cover (or centre cover).

3 Driveshaft inner CV joint gaiter – renewal

Note: *Read the Caution in Section 1 before proceeding.*

1 Although it is possible to renew the gaiter by just disconnecting the inner end of the driveshaft from the transmission (LH) or intermediate shaft (RH), it is recommended that the driveshaft be removed completely and the work carried out on the bench. If the work is carried out working beneath the car, the CV joints may inadvertently be articulated beyond the maximum angles described in Section 1. Note that if both the inner and outer gaiters are being renewed at the same time, the outer gaiter is removed from the inner end of the driveshaft.

2 Remove the driveshaft as described in Section 2, and mount it in a vice.

3 Mark the driveshaft in relation to the joint housing, to ensure correct refitting.

4 Note the fitted location of both of the inner joint gaiter retaining clips, then release the clips from the gaiter, and slide the gaiter back along the driveshaft a little way **(see illustrations)**.

5 Withdraw the inner joint housing from the tripod. As the housing is being removed, be prepared for some of the bearing rollers to fall out – identify them for position with a dab of paint and tape **(see illustrations)**. Scoop out the grease from the joint and gaiter.

6 Check that the inner end of the driveshaft is marked in relation to the splined tripod hub. If not, carefully centre-punch the two items, to ensure correct refitting. Alternatively, use dabs of paint on the driveshaft and one end of the tripod.

7 Extract the circlip retaining the tripod on the driveshaft **(see illustration)**.

8 Using a puller, remove the tripod from the

3.4a Remove the inner joint gaiter large clip . . .

3.5a . . . and withdraw the inner joint housing from the tripod

3.4b . . . and small clip, release the gaiter . . .

3.5b Identify the rollers for position

3.7 Removing the circlip retaining the inner tripod on the driveshaft

3.8 Using a puller to remove the tripod

3.11a Slide on the small clip . . .

3.11b . . . followed by the gaiter and large clip

3.11c Checking the distance between the inner and outer gaiters

3.12a Drive the tripod fully onto the driveshaft splines . . .

3.12b . . . and fit the new circlip

end of the driveshaft, and slide off the gaiter (see illustration).
9 If the outer gaiter is also to be renewed, remove it and fit the new one with reference to Section 4.

10 Clean the driveshaft, and obtain a new joint retaining circlip. The gaiter retaining clips must also be renewed.
11 Slide the new gaiter on the driveshaft, together with new clips. Make sure that the

gaiter is located at its previously-noted position on the driveshaft, then tighten the small diameter clip (see illustrations). The distance between the inner and outer gaiters must be:

1.8 and 2.0 litre manual transmission models, 180.0 mm
2.0 litre automatic transmission models, 160.0 mm
2.5 litre V6 and all diesel models, 165.5 mm

12 Refit the tripod on the driveshaft splines, if necessary using a soft-faced mallet and a suitable metal tube to drive it fully onto the splines. It must be fitted with the chamfered edge leading (towards the driveshaft), and with the previously-made marks aligned. Secure it in position using a new circlip. Ensure that the circlip is fully engaged in its groove (see illustrations).
13 Locate the bearing rollers on the tripod in their previously-noted positions, using grease to hold them in place (see illustration).
14 Pack the specified amount of CV joint grease to the tripod and joint housing (see illustration).
15 Guide the joint housing onto the tripod fully, and locate the gaiter in the special groove, ensuring it is not twisted or distorted (see illustrations).
16 Insert a small screwdriver under the lip of the gaiter at the housing end. This will allow trapped air to escape, then withdraw the joint housing by 20.0 mm from its fully-in position – this is the normal operating position (see illustrations).
17 Fit and tighten the retaining clips. If possible, use the special tool to tighten the

3.13 Fit the rollers in their previously-noted position . . .

3.14 . . . and pack the joint housing with the specified amount of CV joint grease

3.15a Guide the housing onto the tripod . . .

3.15b . . . and locate the gaiter in the special groove

3.16a Use a screwdriver to release the trapped air . . .

3.16b . . . then withdraw the joint housing by 20.0 mm

3.17 Using the special tool to tighten the gaiter clips

clips, otherwise, use pincers **(see illustration)**.

18 Refit the driveshaft with reference to Section 2.

4 Driveshaft outer CV joint gaiter – renewal

Note: *Read the Caution in Section 1 before proceeding. The outer CV joint is pressed onto the driveshaft and must not be removed.*

1 The outer CV joint gaiter is removed by first

removing the inner gaiter as described in Section 3.

2 Clean the exposed part of the driveshaft to facilitate removal of the balance weight (where fitted) and the outer gaiter.

3 Mark the position of the balance weight (where fitted) and the outer gaiter on the driveshaft. The balance weight is pressed onto the driveshaft, and ideally a puller or press is required to remove it. However, if the weight is supported in a vice, the driveshaft may be driven through it, using a soft-faced mallet on the inner end of the driveshaft.

4 Note the location of both of the outer gaiter

retaining clips, then release them. Release the gaiter from the outer CV joint, then slide it off of the inner end of the driveshaft together with the clips **(see illustrations)**. Scoop out the grease from the outer CV joint.

5 Slide the new gaiter, together with the new clips, onto the driveshaft until it is near the outer CV joint.

6 Pack the outer CV joint with the specified amount of CV joint grease, then slide the gaiter fully onto its previously-noted position on the driveshaft and CV joint housing. Ensure the gaiter is not twisted or distorted.

7 Temporarily insert a small screwdriver under the lip of the gaiter at the housing end. This will allow trapped air to escape.

8 Tighten the gaiter retaining clips.

9 Where a balance weight is fitted, measure its length and add 125.0 mm to determine the correct fitting position on the driveshaft. The distance must be measured from the inner end of the driveshaft to the further (smaller diameter) edge of the weight **(see illustration)**. Press or drive the weight onto the driveshaft, however, do not exceed a force of 10 kN if supporting the outer end of the driveshaft otherwise the outer CV joint may be damaged.

10 Refit the inner gaiter with reference to Section 3.

4.4a Remove the small clip . . .

4.4b . . . and large clip from the outer joint . . .

4.4c . . . and slide the gaiter off the inner end of the driveshaft

4.9 The fitting position of the balance weight (x) = the length of the weight + 125.0 mm

5 Driveshafts – inspection and joint renewal

Note: *Read the Caution in Section 1 before proceeding.*

1 If any of the checks described in the appropriate part of Chapter 1 reveal apparent excessive wear or play in any driveshaft joint, first remove the wheel cover (or centre cover), and check that the hub nut (driveshaft outer nut) is tightened to the specified torque. Repeat this check on the hub nut on the other side.

2 Road test the vehicle, and listen for a metallic clicking from the front as the vehicle is driven slowly in a circle on full-lock. If a clicking noise is heard, this indicates wear in the outer constant velocity joint, which means that the driveshaft and outer joint must be renewed; it is not possible to renew the joint separately.

3 If vibration, consistent with road speed, is felt through the car when accelerating, there is a possibility of wear in the inner tripod joints. To renew an inner joint, remove the driveshaft as described in Section 2, then separate the joint from the driveshaft with reference to Section 3.

4 Continual noise from the right-hand driveshaft, increasing with road speed, may indicate wear in the support bearing. To renew this bearing, the driveshaft and intermediate shaft must be removed (see Section 2), and the bearing extracted using a puller.

5 Remove the bearing dust cover, and obtain a new one.

6 Drive or press on the new bearing, applying the pressure to the inner race only. Similarly drive or press on the new dust cover.

7 Refit the driveshaft and intermediate shaft with reference to Section 2.

Chapter 9
Braking system

Contents

Degrees of difficulty

Easy, suitable for novice with little experience	Fairly easy, suitable for beginner with some experience	Fairly difficult, suitable for competent DIY mechanic	Difficult, suitable for experienced DIY mechanic	Very difficult, suitable for expert DIY or professional

Specifications

Front brakes

Type	Ventilated disc, with single-piston floating caliper
Minimum front brake pad lining thickness	1.5 mm
Disc diameter	300.0 mm
Disc thickness:	
New	24.0 mm
Minimum	22.0 mm
Maximum disc run-out (fitted)	0.15 mm
Maximum disc thickness variation	0.015 mm
Front hub face maximum run-out	0.05 mm

Rear disc brakes

Type	Solid disc, with single-piston floating caliper
Minimum rear brake pad lining thickness	1.5 mm
Disc diameter	280.0 mm
Disc thickness:	
New	12.0 mm
Minimum	10.2 mm
Maximum disc thickness variation	0.015 mm

Torque wrench settings

	Nm	lbf ft
Front brakes		
ABS hydraulic unit	25	18
Brake line union nuts to ABS hydraulic unit	15	11
Brake pedal bracket	25	18
Brake pedal cross-shaft	25	18
Brake pipe unions to master cylinder	20	15
Caliper guide pin bolts	30	22
Caliper mounting bracket	130	96
In-line brake union nuts	17	13
Master cylinder	20	15
Vacuum servo:		
Bracket to body	25	18
Mounting nuts	20	15
Vacuum pump (diesel models)	22	16
Thermostat housing (diesel models)	22	16
Rear brakes		
Caliper guide pin bolts	30	22
Caliper mounting bracket	80	59
Rear hub retaining bolts	90	66
ESP components		
Steering wheel rotation sensor	1	0.7
Handbrake		
Handbrake lever assembly to floor	20	15
Roadwheels		
Roadwheel nuts	85	63

1 General information and precautions

The braking system is of diagonally-split, dual-circuit design, with ventilated discs at the front, and solid discs at the rear. The front and rear calipers are of single-piston, floating design. Models with steel wheels have standard brake discs, whereas models with alloy wheels have anti-corrosion coated brake discs.

The rear brake caliper is located on the front of the knuckle on Saloon and Hatchback models, and on the rear of the knuckle on Estate models.

All models are fitted with a low-pressure anti-lock braking system (ABS) which uses the basic conventional brake system, together with an ABS hydraulic unit fitted between the master cylinder and the four wheel brakes. If wheel lock-up is detected on a wheel when the vehicle speed is above 3 mph, the valve opens, releasing pressure to the relevant brake, until the wheel regains a rotational speed corresponding to the speed of the vehicle. The cycle can be repeated many times a second. In the event of a fault in the ABS system, the conventional braking system is not affected. Diagnosis of a fault in the ABS system requires the use of special equipment, and this work should therefore be left to a Ford dealer.

The traction control system (TCS) is fitted as an option to some models, and uses the basic ABS system, with an additional pump and valves fitted to the hydraulic actuator. If wheelspin is detected at a speed below 30 mph, one of the valves opens, to allow the pump to pressurise the relevant brake, until the spinning wheel slows to a rotational speed corresponding to the speed of the vehicle. This has the effect of transferring torque to the wheel with most traction. At the same time, the throttle plate is closed slightly, to reduce the torque from the engine.

The Electronic Stability Program (ESP) adds another function to the ABS system. Sensors measure the position of the steering wheel, the pressure in the brake master cylinder, the yaw velocity/rate, and the lateral acceleration. With this information, the system can compare the driver's intention with the vehicle's movement, and apply the appropriate corrective action.

The handbrake is cable-operated, with a short primary cable and two rear main cables. The cable self-adjustment mechanism is incorporated into the handbrake lever, and consists of a large clock spring, drum and spring-tensioned brake rod. The primary cable is wound around the drum which operates in a similar manner to a one-way clutch, so that all slack is removed from both the primary and secondary cables. Handbrake lever movement remains consistent at all times, and no adjustment is necessary or possible.

⚠ **Warning: When servicing any part of the system, work carefully and methodically; also observe scrupulous cleanliness when overhauling any part of the hydraulic system. Always renew brake pads in axle sets. Note the warnings given in 'Safety first!' concerning the dangers of asbestos dust and hydraulic fluid. Hydraulic fluid is poisonous; wash off immediately and thoroughly in the case of skin contact, and seek immediate medical advice if any fluid is swallowed or gets into the eyes. Also, brake fluid is highly inflammable, and should be handled with the same care as petrol. When topping-up or renewing the hydraulic fluid, always use fluid from a new container.**

2 Front brake pads – renewal

⚠ **Warning: Disc brake pads must be renewed on BOTH front wheels at the same time – never renew the pads on only one wheel, as uneven braking may result. DO NOT use petroleum-based solvents to clean brake parts; use brake cleaner or methylated spirit only. DO NOT allow any brake fluid, oil or grease to contact the brake pads or disc.**

Note: *Refer to the warnings given in Section 1 before proceeding.*

1 Apply the handbrake, then jack up the front of the vehicle and support it on axle stands (see *Jacking and vehicle support*). Remove both front roadwheels. Work on one brake assembly at a time, using the assembled brake for reference if necessary.

2 Push the piston into its bore by pulling the caliper outwards.

3 Unscrew and remove the caliper lower guide pin bolt, using a slim open-ended spanner to prevent the guide pin itself from rotating **(see illustration)**.
4 Pivot the caliper away from the brake pads and mounting bracket, and tie it to the suspension strut using a suitable piece of wire. If the upper guide pin bolt is also removed, do not allow the caliper to hang down by the hose **(see illustration)**.
5 Withdraw the two brake pads from the caliper mounting bracket **(see illustration)**.
6 First measure the thickness of each brake pad lining **(see illustration)**. If either pad is worn at any point to the specified minimum thickness or less, all four pads must be renewed. Note that the pads are fitted with audible warning springs, which are designed to make a warning noise when the linings have reached their minimum thickness. The pads should also be renewed if any are fouled with oil or grease; note that there is no satisfactory way of degreasing friction material, once worn unevenly, or fouled with oil or grease, trace and rectify the cause before reassembly.
7 If the brake pads are still serviceable, carefully clean them using a clean, fine wire brush or similar, paying particular attention to the sides and back of the metal backing. Clean out the grooves in the friction material, and pick out any large embedded particles of dirt or debris. Carefully clean the pad locations in the caliper mounting bracket.
8 Prior to fitting the pads, check that the guide pins are free to slide easily in the caliper mounting bracket, and check that the rubber guide pin gaiters are undamaged. Brush the dust and dirt from the caliper and piston, but **do not** inhale it, as it is a health hazard. Scrape any corrosion from the edge of the disc, taking care not to damage the friction surface and inspect the disc for scoring and cracks. Inspect the dust seal around the piston for damage, and the piston for evidence of fluid leaks, corrosion or damage. If attention to any of these components is necessary, refer to Sections 3 and 4.
9 If new brake pads are to be fitted, the caliper piston must be pushed back into the cylinder to make room for them. Either use a G-clamp or similar tool, or use suitable pieces

2.3 Unscrewing the caliper lower guide pin bolt

2.5 Removing the brake pads from the mounting bracket

of wood as levers; take care not to damage the piston seals **(see illustration)**. Provided that the master cylinder reservoir has not been overfilled with hydraulic fluid, there should be no spillage, but keep a careful watch on the fluid level while retracting the piston. If the fluid level rises above the MAX level line at any time, the surplus should be syphoned off or ejected via a plastic tube connected to the bleed screw. **Note:** *Do not syphon the fluid by mouth, as it is poisonous; use a syringe or an old antifreeze tester.*
10 Smear a little high-melting point brake grease to the metal contact points of each brake pad **(see illustration)**.
11 Ensuring that the friction material of each pad is against the brake disc, fit the pads to the caliper mounting bracket **(see illustration)**.
12 Locate the caliper over the pads, then fit the guide pin bolts and tighten them to the

2.4 Removing the caliper from the front brake pads

2.6 Measuring the thickness of the front brake pad linings

specified torque while retaining the guide pin with an open-ended spanner.
13 Depress the brake pedal repeatedly, until the pads are pressed into firm contact with the brake disc, and normal pedal pressure is restored.
14 Repeat the above procedure on the remaining front brake caliper.
15 Refit the roadwheels, then lower the vehicle to the ground and tighten the road-wheel nuts to the specified torque setting.
16 Check the hydraulic fluid level as described in *Weekly checks*.

 HAYNES HiNT *New pads will not give full braking efficiency until they have bedded-in. Be prepared for this, and avoid hard braking as far as possible for the first hundred miles or so after pad renewal.*

2.9 Using a special tool to retract the caliper piston

2.10 Apply a little high-melting point brake grease to the contact points of each brake pad

2.11 The outer pad located in the carrier bracket

3.6 Front brake caliper mounting bracket bolts

3 Front brake caliper – removal, overhaul and refitting

Note: *Refer to the warnings given in Section 1 before proceeding.*

Removal

1 Apply the handbrake, then jack up the front of the vehicle and support it on axle stands (see *Jacking and vehicle support*). Remove the appropriate front roadwheel.
2 Fit a brake hose clamp to the flexible hose leading to the front brake caliper. This will minimise brake fluid loss during subsequent operations.
3 Loosen the union on the caliper end of the flexible brake hose. Once loosened, do not try to unscrew the hose at this stage.

4 Remove the caliper guide pin bolts as described in Section 2.
5 Support the caliper in one hand, and prevent the hydraulic hose from turning with the other hand. Unscrew the caliper from the hose, making sure that the hose is not twisted unduly or strained. Once the caliper is detached, plug the open hydraulic unions in the caliper and hose, to keep out dust and dirt.
6 If required, the pads can be removed and the caliper mounting bracket can be unbolted and removed from the steering knuckle **(see illustration)**.

Overhaul

7 With the caliper on the bench, brush away all traces of dust and dirt, but take care not to inhale any dust, as it may be injurious to health.
8 Pull the dust-excluding rubber seal from the end of the piston.
9 Apply low air pressure to the fluid inlet union, and eject the piston. Only low air pressure is required for this, such as is produced by a foot-operated tyre pump.
Caution: The piston may be ejected with some force. Position a thin piece of wood between the piston and the caliper body, to prevent damage to the end face of the piston, in the event of it being ejected suddenly.
10 Using a suitable blunt instrument, prise the piston seal from the groove in the cylinder bore. Take care not to scratch the surface of the bore.
11 Clean the piston and caliper body with

methylated spirit, and allow to dry. Examine the surfaces of the piston and cylinder bore for wear, damage and corrosion. If either the cylinder bore or piston is unserviceable, the complete caliper must be renewed. The seals must be renewed, regardless of the condition of the other components.
12 Coat the piston and seals with clean brake fluid, then manipulate the piston seal into the groove in the cylinder bore.
13 Push the piston squarely into its bore.
14 Fit the dust-excluding rubber seal onto the piston and caliper, then depress the piston fully.
15 Release the dust-excluding rubber boots and remove the guide pin components from the mounting bracket. Thoroughly clean the components and examine them for wear and damage. Renew as necessary, and reassemble using a reversal of the removal procedure, using high-melting point grease to lubricate the guide pins **(see illustrations)**.

Refitting

16 Refit the caliper, and where applicable the pads and mounting bracket, by reversing the removal operations. Make sure that the flexible brake hose is not twisted. Tighten the mounting bolts and wheel nuts to the specified torque.
17 Bleed the brake circuit as described in Section 12, remembering to remove the brake hose clamp from the flexible hose. Make sure there are no leaks from the hose connections. Test the brakes carefully before returning the vehicle to normal service.

3.15a Front brake caliper mounting bracket components

3.15b Apply high-melting point grease to the bracket bore . . .

3.15c . . . fit the rubber dust cover . . .

3.15d . . . locate the rubber bush on the lower guide pin . . .

3.15e . . . grease the guide pin . . .

3.15f . . . and refit the guide pin

4 Front brake disc –
inspection, removal and refitting

Note: *To prevent uneven braking, BOTH front brake discs should be renewed or reground at the same time.*

Inspection

1 Apply the handbrake. Loosen the relevant wheel nuts, jack up the front of the vehicle and support it on axle stands. Remove the appropriate front wheel.

2 Unscrew the two bolts securing the brake caliper mounting bracket to the steering knuckle, then slide the caliper and brake pads off of the brake disc. Tie the caliper and bracket to the front suspension strut coil spring, taking care not to strain the flexible hydraulic hose.

3 Temporarily refit three of the wheel nuts, with the flat sides of the nuts against the disc. Tighten the nuts progressively, to hold the disc firmly.

4 Scrape any corrosion from the disc. Rotate the disc, and examine it for deep scoring, grooving or cracks. Using a micrometer, measure the thickness of the disc in several places **(see illustration)**. The minimum thickness is stamped on the disc hub. Light wear and scoring is normal, but if excessive, the disc should be removed, and either reground by a specialist, or renewed. If regrinding is undertaken, the minimum thickness must be maintained. Obviously, if the disc is cracked, it must be renewed.

5 Using a dial gauge or a flat metal block and feeler gauges, check that the disc run-out 10 mm from the outer edge does not exceed the limit given in the Specifications **(see illustration)**. To do this, fix the measuring equipment, and rotate the disc, noting the variation in measurement as the disc is rotated. The difference between the minimum and maximum measurements recorded is the disc run-out.

6 If the run-out is greater than the specified amount, check for variations of the disc thickness as follows. Mark the disc at eight positions 45° apart, then using a micrometer, measure the disc thickness at the eight positions, 15 mm in from the outer edge. If the variation between the minimum and maximum readings is greater than the specified amount, the disc should be renewed.

7 The hub face run-out can also be checked in a similar way. First remove the disc as described later in this Section, fix the measuring equipment, then slowly rotate the hub, and check that the run-out does not exceed the amount given in the Specifications. If the hub face run-out is excessive, this should be corrected (by renewing the hub bearings – see Chapter 10) before rechecking the disc run-out.

4.4 Checking the thickness of the front brake disc with a micrometer

4.10a Remove the special washers . . .

Removal

8 With the wheel and caliper removed, remove the wheel nuts which were temporarily refitted in paragraph 3.

9 Mark the disc in relation to the hub, if it is to be refitted.

10 Remove the two special washers (where fitted), and withdraw the disc over the wheel studs **(see illustrations)**.

Refitting

11 Make sure that the disc and hub mating surfaces are clean, then locate the disc on the wheel studs. Align the previously-made marks if the original disc is being refitted.

12 Refit the two special washers, where fitted.

13 Refit the brake caliper and mounting bracket with reference to Section 3.

5.2 Disconnecting the handbrake inner cable from the rear caliper lever

4.5 Using a dial gauge to check the brake disc run-out

4.10b . . . and withdraw the brake disc over the wheel studs

14 Refit the wheel, and lower the vehicle to the ground.

15 Test the brakes carefully before returning the vehicle to normal service.

5 Rear brake pads –
renewal

Note: *Refer to the warnings given in Section 1 before proceeding.*

1 Work on one brake assembly at a time, using the assembled brake for reference if necessary. Chock the front wheels then jack up the rear of the vehicle and support on axle stands (see *Jacking and vehicle support*). Remove the rear wheels, then release the handbrake lever.

2 To enable the caliper to pivot upwards for pad removal, the handbrake cable must be disconnected from the caliper. First push the lever forwards, then release the end of the inner cable from the fitting on the lever **(see illustration)**.

3 Release the handbrake outer cable from the caliper bracket and position it to one side. Where a plastic ferrule is fitted to the outer cable, it will be necessary to compress the plastic tangs in order to release it from the bracket. Where a spring clip is fitted, pull it from the outer cable **(see illustration)**.

4 Unscrew and remove the caliper lower guide pin bolt **(see illustration)**. Swivel the caliper upwards leaving the upper guide pin still entered in the caliper mounting bracket.

5.3 Disconnecting the handbrake cable from the caliper bracket

5.4 Remove the caliper lower guide pin bolt and swivel the caliper upwards

5.5a Remove the inner disc pad . . .

5.5b . . . followed by the outer disc pad

5.7 Apply a little copper-based brake grease to the contact areas on the pad backing plates

5.8 The self-adjusting piston must be retracted into the caliper to allow room for the new pads

5 Remove the pads from the mounting bracket, noting their fitted positions **(see illustrations)**. Brush all dust and dirt from the caliper, pads and disc, but do not inhale it, as it may be harmful to health. Scrape any corrosion from the edge of the disc.

6 Inspect the rear brake disc as described in Section 7.

7 Apply a little copper-based brake grease to the contact areas on the pad backing plates **(see illustration)**, taking care not to get any on the friction material. Fit the new pads onto the mounting bracket, with the friction material facing the brake disc.

8 The self-adjusting piston must be retracted into the caliper to allow room for the new pads **(see illustration)**. To do this, use an Allen key to turn the piston fully into the caliper whilst also applying pressure to it. On Estate models, turn the piston anti-clockwise when working on the left-hand rear caliper, and clockwise when working on the right-hand rear caliper. On Saloon and Hatchback models, turn the piston anti-clockwise when working on the right-hand rear caliper, and clockwise when working on the left-hand rear caliper. At the time of writing, there appeared to be some models manufactured which

required turning the piston in the directly opposite direction, however, it will be obvious which is the correct direction from the movement of the piston itself.

Caution: Brake fluid will be displaced into the master cylinder reservoir, so check first that there is enough space to accept the fluid. If necessary, syphon off some of the fluid.

9 With the piston screwed in fully, centralize the correct cut-out on the piston with the raised mark on the caliper as shown **(see illustrations)**. On the left-hand rear caliper, the 'short' cut-out must align with the mark,

J35157

5.9a On the left-hand rear caliper, the 'short' cut-out must align with the raised mark . . .

J35158

5.9b . . . but, on the right-hand rear caliper, the 'long' cut-out must align with the mark whereas, on the right-hand rear caliper, the 'long' cut-out must align with the mark. Note that the 'pips' on the outer faces of the brake pads locate in these cut-outs.

10 Swivel the caliper down. Apply a little locking fluid to the threads of the lower guide pin bolt, then tighten it to the specified torque.

11 Refit the handbrake outer cable to the bracket, making sure that it is locked firmly in position.

12 Push the handbrake lever forwards, then hook the inner cable on the fitting, and release the lever.

13 Repeat the procedure on the remaining rear brake, then refit the rear wheels and lower the car to the ground. Tighten the wheel nuts to the specified torque.

14 Firmly depress the brake pedal a few times, to bring the pads to their normal working position. Check the level of the brake fluid in the reservoir, and top-up if necessary.

15 Give the vehicle a road test, to make sure that the brakes are functioning correctly, and to bed-in the new linings to the contours of the disc. Remember that full braking efficiency will not be obtained until the new linings have bedded-in.

6 Rear brake caliper –
removal, overhaul and refitting

Note: *Refer to the warnings given in Section 1 before proceeding.*

Removal

1 Remove the rear caliper lower guide pin bolt as described in Section 5.

2 Fit a brake hose clamp to the flexible hose leading to the rear brake caliper. This will minimise brake fluid loss during subsequent operations.

3 Loosen the union on the caliper end of the flexible hose, but do not completely unscrew it at this stage.

4 Unscrew the upper guide pin bolt, remove the caliper, and support it to one side. Do not allow it to hang down unsupported, as this will strain the brake hose.

5 Unscrew the caliper from the hydraulic hose, making sure that the hose is not twisted or strained unduly. Tape over or plug the open hydraulic unions and ports to keep dust and dirt out.

6 Remove the pads and the mounting bracket from the knuckle if necessary.

Overhaul

7 No overhaul procedures were available at the time of writing, so check availability of spares before dismantling the caliper. In principle, the overhaul information given for the front brake caliper will apply, noting that it will be necessary to unscrew the piston from the handbrake mechanism before being able to expel the piston from the caliper. On reassembly, push the piston fully into the

5.9c Piston alignment on the left-hand rear caliper . . .

caliper, and screw it back onto the handbrake mechanism. Do not attempt to dismantle the handbrake mechanism; if the mechanism is faulty, the complete caliper assembly must be renewed.

8 Release the rubber boots, and slide the guide pins from the mounting bracket. Thoroughly clean the guide pins and their locations in the bracket, then inspect the boots for wear or damage. Renew the boots as necessary. Apply some high temperature copper grease (or brake grease) to the guide pins and insert them in the carrier. Locate the boots on the bracket and guide pins.

Refitting

9 Refit the mounting bracket to the knuckle and tighten the bolts to the specified torque. Fit the pads.

10 Remove the temporary plugs, then screw the caliper fully onto the hose.

11 Locate the caliper on the mounting bracket and refit the upper guide pin bolt. Tighten the bolt to the specified torque.

12 Fully tighten the hydraulic flexible hose union. Check that the hose is not twisted; if necessary remove the caliper from the mounting bracket and reposition it.

13 Remove the brake hose clamp from the flexible hose.

14 Refit the lower guide pin bolt with reference to Section 5.

15 Bleed the brake circuit with reference to Section 12. Make sure there are no leaks from the hose connections. Test the brakes carefully before returning the vehicle to normal service.

8.3 Low fluid level warning light multi-plug

5.9d . . . and right-hand rear caliper

7 Rear brake disc –
inspection, removal and refitting

Refer to Section 4 (front disc inspection). Once the rear caliper is removed, the procedure is the same.

8 Master cylinder –
removal and refitting

⚠ *Warning: Do not fit a standard brake master cylinder to a vehicle equipped with Emergency Brake Assist.*

Note: *Refer to the warnings given in Section 1 before proceeding.*

Removal

1 Exhaust the vacuum in the servo by pressing the brake pedal a few times, with the engine switched off.

2 Unclip and disconnect the vacuum pipe from the one-way/check valve on the brake servo unit.

3 Disconnect the low fluid level warning light multi-plug from the fluid reservoir **(see illustration)**. Unscrew and remove the filler cap.

4 Draw off the hydraulic fluid from the reservoir, using an old battery hydrometer or a poultry baster. If preferred, to reduce fluid spillage, completely drain the fluid as described in the following paragraph.

⚠ *Warning: Do not syphon the fluid by mouth; it is poisonous.*

5 To completely drain the hydraulic fluid from the reservoir and master cylinder, it is necessary to connect a bleed tube to each front brake caliper in turn. Apply the handbrake, then jack up the front of the vehicle and support it on axle stands (see *Jacking and vehicle support*). With the steering on the left-hand lock, connect the tube to the left-hand caliper bleed screw. Loosen the screw and have an assistant depress the footbrake pedal repeatedly until the hydraulic fluid is completely drained from

8.8 Brake master cylinder

the reservoir. Retighten the bleed screw. Now turn the steering on the right-hand lock and connect the tube to the right-hand caliper bleed screw. Loosen the screw and have the assistant depress the footbrake pedal several times in order to drain the remaining fluid from the reservoir and master cylinder.

6 On manual transmission models, release the clip and disconnect the clutch fluid hose from the brake fluid reservoir. Tape over or plug the hose and reservoir openings.

7 Place rags beneath the master cylinder to catch spilt hydraulic fluid. Identify the locations of the brake pipes on the master cylinder, then unscrew the union nuts and carefully move the pipes to one side without bending them excessively. If the nuts are tight, a split ring spanner should be used in preference to an open-ended spanner. Plug or cap open unions, to keep dust and dirt out.

8 Unscrew the mounting nuts, and withdraw

the master cylinder together with the fluid reservoir from the studs on the front of the servo unit **(see illustration)**. Recover the gasket ring.

9 Carefully prise the fluid reservoir from the rubber grommets on the top of the master cylinder, then prise out the grommets and gaskets.

10 If the master cylinder is faulty, it must be renewed. It is not possible to obtain new internal seals.

Refitting

11 Locate the rubber grommets and gaskets in the master cylinder inlet ports.

12 Apply a little brake fluid to the grommets, then press the fluid reservoir fully into position.

13 Clean the contact surfaces of the master cylinder and servo, and fit a new gasket ring.

14 Position the master cylinder on the studs on the servo unit. Refit and tighten the nuts to the specified torque.

15 Carefully insert the hydraulic lines in the apertures in the master cylinder, then tighten the union nuts. Make sure that the nuts enter their threads correctly.

16 On manual transmission models, reconnect the clutch fluid supply hose, then fill the reservoir with fresh brake fluid.

17 Bleed the brake hydraulic system as described in Section 12. On manual transmission models, if fluid has been lost, bleed the clutch hydraulic system as described in Chapter 6.

18 Refit the reservoir filler cap, and reconnect

the multi-plug for the low fluid level warning light.

19 Reconnect the vacuum pipe to the one-way/check valve on the brake servo unit.

20 Test the brakes carefully before returning the vehicle to normal service.

9 Brake pedal and bracket – removal and refitting

Removal

1 On models with manual transmission, fit a hose clamp to the hydraulic fluid supply hose to the clutch master cylinder on the bulkhead. Alternatively, disconnect the hose from the brake fluid reservoir and plug its end. Loosen the clips and disconnect both hoses from the clutch master cylinder.

2 Working inside the vehicle, move the driver's seat fully to the rear, to allow maximum working area. Undo the screws, release the clip, and remove the lower facia panel on the driver's side.

3 Unscrew the nut and detach the cross-link (RHD) or vacuum servo (LHD) pushrod from the brake pedal **(see illustration)**.

4 Remove the brake pedal position switch retaining clip and discard it **(see illustration)**. A new one must be fitted on reassembly. Disconnect the wiring, then twist the switch anti-clockwise and remove it from the pedal bracket.

5 On manual transmission models, remove the clutch pedal position switch from the pedal bracket **(see illustration)**. To do this, twist the switch anti-clockwise.

6 Release the brake pedal position switch wiring from the bracket.

7 Unhook the accelerator cable from the top of the accelerator pedal **(see illustration)**.

8 On right-hand drive models only, undo the two pedal bracket mounting nuts from the bulkhead inside the car, then, working in the engine compartment, undo the two mounting nuts from the engine side of the bulkhead **(see illustration)**.

9 On left-hand drive models only, undo the pedal bracket mounting nuts from the bulkhead inside the car **(see illustration)**.

9.3 Pushrod-to-brake pedal nut (RHD)

9.4 Brake pedal position switch (RHD)

9.5 Clutch pedal position switch (RHD)

9.7 Accelerator cable connection to the top of the pedal (RHD)

9.8 Pedal bracket top mounting nuts (RHD)

10 Remove the brake pedal and bracket from inside the car and recover the seal and spacer.
11 On manual transmission models, unhook the return spring from the top of the clutch pedal, then unscrew the nut and slide the clutch pedal from the pivot bolt.
12 Unscrew and remove the pivot bolt and remove the brake pedal from the bracket.

Refitting

13 Refitting is a reversal of the removal procedure, but fit a new brake pedal position switch retaining clip, and bleed the clutch hydraulic system as described in Chapter 6.

10 Brake pedal-to-servo cross-link (RH drive models) – removal and refitting

Removal

1 Disconnect the battery negative lead (refer to *Disconnecting the battery* at the end of this manual).
2 Remove the master cylinder and the vacuum servo unit as described in Sections 8 and 13.
3 Working inside the car, turn the brake pedal

cross-link to release the tension on the return spring, then unhook it, noting how it is fitted.
4 Unscrew the nut and detach the cross-link pushrod from the brake pedal.
5 Loosen the brake vacuum servo mounting nuts.
6 Unscrew and remove the brake pedal bracket mounting nuts.
7 Unscrew and remove the cross-link bracket mounting bolts **(see illustration)**.
8 Move the vacuum servo mounting bracket towards the left-hand side of the engine compartment.
9 Move the cross-link to the right then pull it forward and remove from the engine compartment.
10 Clean the cross-link components, and examine the bushes for wear. Renew the bushes if necessary.

Refitting

11 Refitting is a reversal of the removal procedure.

11 Hydraulic pipes and hoses – inspection, removal and refitting

Note: *Refer to the warnings given in Section 1 before proceeding.*

Inspection

1 Jack up the front and rear of the vehicle, and support on axle stands.
2 Check for signs of leakage at the pipe unions, then examine the flexible hoses for signs of cracking, chafing and fraying.
3 The brake pipes should be examined carefully for signs of dents, corrosion or other damage. Corrosion should be scraped off, and if the depth of pitting is significant, the pipes renewed. This is particularly likely in those areas underneath the vehicle body where the pipes are exposed and unprotected.
4 Renew any defective brake pipes and/or hoses.

Removal

5 If a section of pipe or hose is to be removed, loss of brake fluid can be reduced by unscrewing the filler cap, and completely sealing the top of the reservoir with cling film

J34923

9.9 Brake pedal and bracket components (LHD automatic transmission)

1 *Pedal and bracket assembly*	3 *Speed control inhibitor*	5 *Pedal pad*
2 *Upper support bracket*	4 *Stop-light switch*	6 *Screw*
		7 *Nut*

10.7 Brake pedal-to-servo cross-link

or adhesive tape. Alternatively, the reservoir can be emptied as described in Section 8.

6 To remove a section of pipe, hold the adjoining hose union nut with a spanner to prevent it from turning, then unscrew the union nut at the end of the pipe, and release it. Repeat the procedure at the other end of the pipe, then release the pipe by pulling out the clips attaching it to the body.

7 Where the union nuts are exposed to the full force of the weather, they can sometimes be quite tight. If an open-ended spanner is used, burring of the flats on the nuts is not un-common, and for this reason, it is preferable to use a split ring (brake) spanner, which will engage all the flats. If such a spanner is not available, self-locking grips may be used as a last resort; these may well damage the nuts, but if the pipe is to be renewed, this does not matter.

8 To minimise the loss of fluid when disconnecting a downstream rigid pipe from a flexible brake hose, clamp the hose using a brake hose clamp or a pair of self-locking grips with protected jaws.

9 To remove a flexible hose, first clean the ends of the hose and the surrounding area, then unscrew the union nuts from the hose ends. Remove the spring clip, and withdraw the hose from the serrated mounting in the support bracket. Where applicable, unscrew the hose from the caliper.

10 Brake pipes supplied with flared ends and union nuts can be obtained individually or in sets from Ford dealers or accessory shops. The pipe is then bent to shape, using the old pipe as a guide. Be careful not to kink or crimp the pipe when bending it; ideally, a proper pipe-bending tool should be used.

Refitting

11 Refitting of the pipes and hoses is a reversal of removal. Make sure that all brake pipes are securely supported in their clips, and ensure that the hoses are not twisted. Check also that the hoses are clear of all suspension components and underbody fittings, and will remain clear during movement of the suspension and steering.

12 On completion, bleed the brake hydraulic system as described in Section 12, and where applicable, the clutch hydraulic system as described in Chapter 6.

13.3 The vacuum servo unit

12 Hydraulic system – bleeding

Caution: Using a pressure bleeding kit to bleed the hydraulic system on models with ABS is NOT recommended, although a vacuum bleeding kit may be used.
Note: *Refer to the warnings given in Section 1 before proceeding.*

1 Disconnect the battery negative lead (refer to *Disconnecting the battery* at the end of this manual).

2 If the master cylinder or ABS unit has been disconnected and reconnected, then the complete system (both circuits) must be bled of air. If a single component of one circuit has been disturbed, then only that particular circuit need be bled.

3 Bleeding should commence on one front brake, followed by the diagonally-opposite rear brake. The remaining front brake should then be bled, followed by its diagonally-opposite rear brake.

4 There are a variety of do-it-yourself 'one-man' brake bleeding kits available from motor accessory shops, and it is recommended that one of these kits be used wherever possible, as they greatly simplify the bleeding operation. Follow the kit manufacturer's instructions in conjunction with the following procedure.

5 During the bleeding operation, do not allow the brake fluid level in the reservoir to drop below the minimum mark. If the level is allowed to fall so far that air is drawn in, the whole procedure will have to be started again from scratch. Only use new fluid for topping-up, preferably from a freshly-opened container. Never re-use fluid bled from the system.

6 Before starting, check that all rigid pipes and flexible hoses are in good condition, and that all hydraulic unions are tight. Take care not to allow hydraulic fluid to come into contact with the vehicle paintwork, otherwise the finish will be seriously damaged. Wash off any spilt fluid immediately with cold water.

7 If a brake bleeding kit is *not* being used, gather together a clean jar, a length of plastic or rubber tubing which is a tight fit over the bleed screw, and a new container of the specified brake fluid (see *Lubricants and fluids*). The help of an assistant will also be required.

8 Clean the area around the bleed screw on the front brake unit to be bled (it is important that no dirt be allowed to enter the hydraulic system), and remove the dust cap. Connect one end of the tubing to the bleed screw, and immerse the other end in the jar, which should be filled with sufficient brake fluid to keep the end of the tube submerged.

9 Open the bleed screw by one or two turns, and have the assistant depress the brake pedal to the floor. Tighten the bleed screw at the end of the downstroke, then have the assistant release the pedal. Continue this procedure until clean brake fluid, free from air bubbles, can be seen flowing into the jar.

Finally tighten the bleed screw with the pedal in the fully-depressed position.

10 Remove the tube, and refit the dust cap. Top-up the master cylinder reservoir as necessary, then repeat the procedure on the diagonally-opposite rear brake.

11 Repeat the procedure on the remaining circuit, starting with the front brake, and followed by the diagonally-opposite rear brake.

12 Check the feel of the brake pedal – it should be firm. If it is spongy, there is still some air remaining in the system, and the bleeding procedure should be repeated.

13 When bleeding is complete, top-up the master cylinder reservoir and refit the cap.

14 On completion, check the operation or the hydraulically-operated clutch; if necessary, bleed the clutch hydraulic system as described in Chapter 6.

15 Reconnect the battery negative lead (refer to *Disconnecting the battery* at the end of this manual).

13 Vacuum servo unit – testing, removal and refitting

 Warning: Do not fit a standard vacuum servo unit to a vehicle equipped with Emergency Brake Assist.

Testing

1 To test the operation of the servo unit, depress the footbrake four or five times to dissipate the vacuum, then start the engine while keeping the footbrake depressed. As the engine starts, there should be a noticeable 'give' in the brake pedal as vacuum builds-up. Allow the engine to run for at least two minutes, and then switch it off. If the brake pedal is now depressed again, it should be possible to hear a hiss from the servo when the pedal is depressed. After four or five applications, no further hissing should be heard, and the pedal should feel harder.

2 Before assuming that a problem exists in the servo unit itself, inspect the check valve as described in the next Section.

Removal

3 Refer to Section 8 and remove the master cylinder **(see illustration)**.

4 Unclip the plastic cover from the top of the left-hand front suspension strut.

5 With the weight of the car on the front suspension, unscrew and remove the three mounting nuts from the top of the strut.

6 Unbolt the top mount brace from the bulkhead and inner wing panel.

7 On right-hand drive models, unscrew the nuts securing the brake vacuum servo to its mounting bracket on the left-hand side of the bulkhead **(see illustration)**, then extract the clip and pull out the pin attaching the cross-link to the vacuum servo pushrod. If necessary, have an assistant hold the brake pedal depressed to improve access.

8 On left-hand drive models, working inside the car, unscrew the nut securing the pedal trunnion to the servo unit pushrod, then unscrew the vacuum servo mounting nuts from the inside of the bulkhead.

9 Remove the brake servo unit from the engine compartment.

10 Note that the servo unit cannot be dismantled for repair or overhaul and, if faulty, must be renewed.

Refitting

11 Refitting is a reversal of the removal procedure. Refer to Section 8 for details of refitting the master cylinder.

14 Vacuum servo unit vacuum hose and check valve – removal, testing and refitting

Removal

1 With the engine switched off, depress the brake pedal four or five times, to dissipate any remaining vacuum from the servo unit.

2 Disconnect the vacuum hose adaptor at the servo unit **(see illustration)**, by pulling it free from the rubber grommet. If it is reluctant to move, prise it free, using a screwdriver with its blade inserted under the flange.

3 Detach the vacuum hose from the inlet manifold connection, pressing in the collar to disengage the tabs, then withdrawing the collar slowly.

4 If the hose or the fixings are damaged or in poor condition, they must be renewed.

Testing

5 Examine the check valve for damage and signs of deterioration, and renew it if necessary. The valve may be tested by blowing through it in both directions. It should only be possible to blow from the servo end towards the inlet manifold.

Refitting

6 Refitting is a reversal of the removal procedure. If fitting a new check valve, ensure that it is fitted the correct way round.

15 Vacuum pump (diesel engine models) – removal and refitting

Removal

1 Unclip the plastic cover from the top of the engine.

2 Drain the cooling system as described in Chapter 1B.

3 Disconnect the wiring plug for the cylinder head temperature sensor at the power steering hydraulic fluid line support bracket.

4 Unbolt the power steering line support bracket from the brake vacuum pump on the left-hand end of the cylinder head.

5 Loosen the clip and disconnect the crankcase ventilation hose from the valve cover.

6 Disconnect the vacuum hose from the rear of the vacuum pump **(see illustration)**.

7 Release the clip, and disconnect the coolant hose from the vacuum pump. If the

13.7 Vacuum servo unit mounting nuts

original clip is fitted, use a pair of grips to release it.

8 Disconnect the exhaust gas recirculation coolant hose from the thermostat housing.

9 Unbolt the thermostat housing from the brake vacuum pump and recover the O-ring seal.

10 Unscrew the mounting bolts and withdraw the brake vacuum pump from the end of the cylinder head **(see illustrations)**. Discard the gasket and obtain a new one.

11 Thoroughly clean the mating surfaces of the vacuum pump, cylinder head and thermostat housing.

Refitting

12 Locate a new gasket on the vacuum pump, then refit the pump to the cylinder head, making sure that the drive dog engages correctly with the end of the camshaft **(see illustrations)**. Insert the mounting bolts and tighten to the specified torque.

14.2 Vacuum hose adaptor at the servo unit

15.6 Vacuum hose connection on the vacuum pump

15.10a Brake vacuum pump mounting bolts

15.10b Removing the vacuum pump and housing from the cylinder head

15.12a Fit a new vacuum pump housing gasket on the cylinder head

15.12b Drive dogs on the end of the camshaft

17.5 ABS hydraulic unit location

13 Refit the thermostat housing to the brake vacuum pump using a new O-ring seal, and tighten the mounting bolts to the specified torque.

14 Reconnect the exhaust gas recirculation coolant hose to the thermostat housing.

15 Reconnect the coolant hose to the vacuum pump and tighten the clip.

16 Reconnect the vacuum hose to the rear of the vacuum pump.

17 Reconnect the crankcase ventilation hose to the valve cover.

18 Refit the power steering line support bracket and tighten the bolts.

19 Reconnect the wiring plug for the cylinder head temperature sensor.

20 Refill the cooling system with reference to Chapter 1B.

21 Refit the plastic cover to the top of the engine.

16 Vacuum pump (diesel engine models) – testing and overhaul

1 The operation of the braking system vacuum pump can be checked using a vacuum gauge.

2 Disconnect the vacuum pipe from the pump, and connect the gauge to the pump union using a suitable length of hose.

3 Start the engine and allow it to idle, then measure the vacuum created by the pump. As a guide, after one minute, a minimum of approximately 500 mm Hg should be

recorded. If the vacuum registered is significantly less than this, it is likely that the pump is faulty. However, seek the advice of a Ford dealer before condemning the pump.

4 Overhaul of the vacuum pump is not possible, since no components are available separately for it. If faulty, the complete pump assembly must be renewed.

17 ABS hydraulic unit – removal and refitting

Note 1: Refer to the warnings given in Section 1 before proceeding.
Note 2: If any part of the ABS hydraulic unit is defective, with the exception of the ESP hydraulic pressure transducer, the unit must be renewed complete.

Removal

1 Disconnect the battery negative lead (refer to *Disconnecting the battery* at the end of this manual).

2 Remove the air cleaner as described in the appropriate part of Chapter 4.

3 Remove the brake vacuum servo unit as described in Section 13.

4 Disconnect the wiring from the ABS hydraulic unit.

5 Make a note of the brake line positions on the ABS hydraulic unit and in-line connectors as an aid to refitting **(see illustration)**.

6 Unscrew the union nuts and disconnect the three brake lines from the ABS hydraulic unit at the in-line connectors.

7 Unscrew the union nuts and disconnect the six brake lines from the ABS hydraulic unit. Tape over or plug the ends of the lines and the apertures in the unit to prevent entry of dust and dirt.

8 Release the brake, clutch and fuel lines from their supports on the bulkhead.

9 On manual transmission models, push the clutch master cylinder hydraulic hose and grommet from its support bracket over the transmission and position to one side.

10 Unscrew the four mounting bolts and remove the ABS hydraulic unit and mounting bracket from the bulkhead.

11 Note the position of the insulator pad,

then remove the side clip and separate the hydraulic unit from the bracket.

Refitting

12 Refitting is a reversal of removal referring to Section 13 and the appropriate part of Chapter 4 as necessary, but make sure that the insulator pad is positioned correctly on the bottom of the hydraulic unit. Tighten all union nuts securely.

18 ABS wheel sensor – testing, removal and refitting

Testing

1 Checking of the sensors is done before removal, connecting a voltmeter to the disconnected sensor multi-plug. Using an analogue (moving coil) meter is not practical, since the meter does not respond quickly enough. A digital meter having an AC facility may be used to check that the sensor is operating correctly.

2 To do this, raise the relevant wheel then disconnect the wiring to the ABS sensor and connect the meter to it.

3 Spin the wheel and check that the output voltage is between 1.5 and 2.0 volts, depending on how fast the wheel is spun.

4 Alternatively, an oscilloscope may be used to check the output of the sensor – an alternating current will be traced on the screen, of magnitude depending on the speed of the rotating wheel.

5 If the sensor output is low or zero, renew the sensor.

Removal

Front wheel sensor

6 Apply the handbrake, then jack up the front of the vehicle and support it on axle stands (see *Jacking and vehicle support*). Remove the relevant wheel.

7 Disconnect the wiring from the sensor located on the steering knuckle **(see illustration)**.

8 Unscrew the mounting bolt and withdraw the sensor **(see illustrations)**.

18.7 Disconnect the wiring . . .

18.8a . . . then unscrew the bolt . . .

18.8b . . . and withdraw the ABS front wheel sensor

Rear wheel sensor

9 Chock the front wheels and engage 1st gear (or P), then jack up the rear of the vehicle and support on axle stands (see *Jacking and vehicle support*).

10 Disconnect the wiring from the sensor located on the inner end of the hub. Access is through the hole in the rear suspension lower arm.

11 Unscrew the mounting bolt, and withdraw the sensor.

Refitting

12 Refitting is a reversal of the removal procedure.

---

19 Electronic Stability Program (ESP) components – removal and refitting

Yaw Rate Sensor

⚠️ **Warning: Never fit a damaged yaw rate sensor, as the vehicle may react dangerously in the event of an emergency. The yaw rate sensor will be damaged if dropped.**

Removal

1 Disconnect the battery negative lead (refer to *Disconnecting the battery* at the end of this manual).

2 On automatic transmission models, unclip and remove the selector lever surround trim panel.

3 On manual transmission models, unclip and remove the gearshift lever surround panel, then remove the insulation pad.

4 Remove the centre console side trim panels as follows. Unscrew the front mounting screws, then carefully prise out the trim panels to release the retaining clips.

5 Disconnect the wiring from the yaw rate sensor.

6 Unscrew and remove the left-hand mounting nut for the sensor. Note the arrow on the top of the sensor faces towards the front of the vehicle.

7 On manual transmission models, prise the gear linkage rod from the balljoint, then rotate the linkage through 90°.

8 Unscrew and remove the right-hand mounting nut, then lift the sensor from the left-hand locating stud, tilt it clockwise, and remove it from the right-hand locating stud **(see illustration)**.

Refitting

9 Refitting is a reversal of removal, but make sure that the sensor is fitted with the arrow facing the front of the vehicle.

Steering wheel rotation sensor

⚠️ **Warning: Never fit a damaged steering wheel rotation sensor, as the vehicle may react dangerously in the event of an emergency. Do not use excessive force when removing or refitting the sensor.**

Removal

10 Remove the steering column complete as described in Chapter 10.

11 With the steering column on the bench, undo the three screws and carefully withdraw the sensor from the bottom of the column.

12 Thoroughly check the sensor drive pins and pin locations in the sensor for damage, wear and looseness **(see illustrations)**. The pins must be located correctly in the sensor hub. If necessary, obtain a new sensor otherwise the vehicle may react dangerously in the event of an emergency.

Refitting

13 Carefully locate the sensor over the bottom of the column and onto the base of the upper column. Insert the screws, making sure they are centralised, then tighten them to the specified torque, the screw on the flat edge first, followed by the two screws on the curved edge. Check the vertical alignment of the sensor as shown **(see illustration).**

19.8 Yaw rate sensor removal

1 *Lift the sensor from the left-hand stud . . .*
2 *. . . tilt it clockwise . . .*
3 *. . . and remove it from the right-hand stud*

Hydraulic pressure transducer

Note: *Refer to the warnings given in Section 1 before proceeding.*

Removal and refitting

14 The hydraulic pressure transducer is screwed into the side of the ABS hydraulic unit on the left-hand side of the engine compartment, and can be obtained separately. First, disconnect the wiring from the transducer.

15 Have the new transducer ready to fit, then unscrew the old one using suitable grips, and immediately screw in the new one and tighten securely. If the new unit is not immediately available, plug the hydraulic unit aperture.

16 Bleed the complete brake hydraulic circuit as described in Section 12.

19.12a Drive pins on the steering column intermediate shaft upper UJ . . .

19.12b . . . and the corresponding locations in the steering wheel rotation sensor

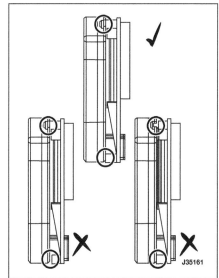

19.13 Make sure that the sensor is correctly positioned on the base of the upper steering column

21.6a Release the catalytic converter wiring from the heat shield . . .

21.6b . . . then remove the heat shields

20 Stop-light switch – removal, refitting and adjustment

Removal

1 The stop-light switch is located on the pedal bracket. The switch is the lower of the two switches mounted over the brake pedal; the upper switch is the brake pedal position switch or the cruise control inhibitor switch.
2 Pull out the switch retaining clip and discard it. A new one must be fitted on reassembly.
3 Disconnect the wiring from the switch.
4 Twist the switch 90° anti-clockwise and withdraw it from the pedal bracket.

Refitting and adjustment

5 Fit a new retaining clip to the bracket.
6 Fully extend the switch plunger.

7 Depress the brake pedal and hold it in this position while refitting the switch.
8 Insert the switch in the pedal bracket and turn it 90° clockwise to lock it.
9 Release the brake pedal; this will automatically adjust the switch plunger.
10 Reconnect the wiring to the switch.

21 Handbrake lever – removal and refitting

Note: *The handbrake lever is only available as a complete assembly which includes the cable self-adjustment mechanism.*

Removal

1 Chock the front wheels then jack up the rear of the vehicle and support on axle stands (see *Jacking and vehicle support*). For improved access to the underbody, also raise the front of the vehicle and support on axle stands. Fully release the handbrake lever.
2 On models fitted with a petrol engine, for additional working room it is recommended that the catalytic converter is unbolted from the exhaust front pipe (see Chapter 4C) and supported on an axle stand. However, it is possible to reach the underside of the hand-brake lever with the exhaust still *in situ* provided care is taken not to damage the catalytic con-verter wiring when removing the heat shields.
3 On models fitted with a diesel engine, unbolt the flexible downpipe from the front exhaust pipe (see Chapter 4B) and support the front pipe on an axle stand. To prevent damage to the flexible pipe, it is recommended that a splint is attached to it. Two or three lengths of wood attached to the pipe with cable ties will be sufficient.
4 It is recommended that the exhaust gaskets, sealing rings and nuts are all renewed on reassembly.
5 Support the exhaust system, then release the front and intermediate rubber hangers and lower it as far as possible from the underbody. Support the exhaust on an axle stand.
6 Undo the special nuts and remove the intermediate and rear exhaust heat shields from the underbody for access to the handbrake lever mounting nuts **(see illustrations)**.
7 Hold the equalizer bar at the end of the primary handbrake cable stationary, then disconnect both secondary cables by pulling them slightly forwards and unhooking them **(see illustration)**.
8 Unscrew the nuts securing the handbrake lever assembly to the floor/underbody and remove the plate **(see illustrations)**.
9 Working inside the car, remove the centre console as described in Chapter 11. Take care to release the handbrake warning light switch wiring from the clip inside the console before lifting it.
10 Disconnect the wiring from the warning light switch on the handbrake lever assembly **(see illustration)**.
11 Pull the primary cable and equalizer bar through the hole in the floor and withdraw the lever assembly from inside the car **(see illustration)**. If necessary, have an assistant

21.7 Disconnecting the handbrake secondary cables from the equalizer bar

21.8a Unscrew the nuts . . .

21.8b . . . and remove the plate

21.10 Disconnecting the wiring from the handbrake warning light switch

21.11 Pull the primary cable and equalizer bar through the hole in the floor

21.13a Pull on the equalizer bar while depressing the spring

21.13b Handbrake lever self-adjusting lock spring

guide the bar through the hole from underneath. Undo the screw and remove the warning light switch.

12 The self-adjustment mechanism consists of a large clock spring, drum and spring-tensioned brake rod. If these parts are worn or faulty, the complete assembly must be renewed. The primary cable may be renewed as described in Section 22.

Refitting

13 Before refitting the handbrake lever, make sure that there is maximum slack in the primary cable to allow it to enter the hole in the floor. Mount the assembly in a vice (screw nuts on the mounting studs and grip the nuts in the vice) and pull on the equalizer bar while at the same time pulling on the brake rod or depressing the side spring (see illustrations). Release the rod, then make sure that the small side spring locks the drum to hold the primary cable in its fully extended position. The drum is released later (paragraph 21) after the assembly is tightened in position.

14 Refit the warning light switch and tighten the mounting screw.

15 Position the handbrake assembly on the floor, and insert the equalizer and cable through the hole in the floor. Make sure that the insulation pad is in position, and that the mounting studs are entered through the holes.

16 Press the cable rubber grommet into the floor.

17 Reconnect the wiring to the warning light switch.

18 Refit the centre console with reference to Chapter 11. Make sure that the warning light switch wiring is located in the clip on the inside of the console.

19 Working under the car, refit and tighten the nuts securing the handbrake lever assembly to the floor/underbody.

20 Reconnect the secondary inner cables to the equalizer bar by pulling them slightly forwards.

21 Pull the primary cable rearwards to

release the internal brake drum, then allow the main clock spring to pull the primary cable forwards and take up the slack. Check the operation of the handbrake lever.

22 Refit the intermediate and rear exhaust heat shields and tighten the mounting nuts.

23 Lift the exhaust system and reconnect the front and intermediate rubber hangers.

24 Refit the exhaust front downpipe using new gaskets, sealing rings and nuts with reference to Chapter 4A or 4B. On diesel models, remove the temporary splint. Coat the threads of the catalytic converter flange studs with copper grease.

25 Apply the handbrake, then lower the car to the ground. Apply the handbrake several times to operate the self-adjustment mechanism.

22 Handbrake cables – removal and refitting

Removal

Primary (front)

1 Remove the handbrake lever assembly as described in Section 21.

2 Mount the assembly in a vice (screw nuts on the mounting studs and grip the nuts in the vice) and pull on the equalizer bar while at the same time pulling on the brake rod or depressing the brake spring. Release the rod, then make sure that the small side spring locks the drum to hold the primary cable in its fully extended position.

Caution: Make sure that the side spring locks the drum firmly. If the spring is released with the primary cable disconnected, the drum will rotate at high speed and possibly cause personal injury.

3 Unhook the primary cable end fitting from the drum and remove it together with the rubber grommet.

Secondary (rear)

4 Chock the front wheels then jack up the rear of the vehicle and support on axle stands (see Jacking and vehicle support). For improved access to the underbody, also raise the front of the vehicle and support on axle stands. Remove the relevant rear wheel, then fully release the handbrake lever.

5 On models fitted with a petrol engine, unbolt the catalytic converter from the exhaust front pipe (see Chapter 4C) and support the converter on an axle stand.

6 On models fitted with a diesel engine, unbolt the flexible downpipe from the front exhaust pipe (see Chapter 4B) and support the front pipe on an axle stand. To prevent damage to the flexible pipe, it is recommended that a splint is attached to it. Two or three lengths of wood attached to the pipe with cable ties will be sufficient.

7 It is recommended that the exhaust gaskets, sealing rings and nuts are all renewed on reassembly.

8 Support the exhaust system, then release the front and intermediate rubber hangers and lower it as far as possible from the underbody. Support the exhaust on an axle stand.

9 Undo the special nuts and remove the intermediate and rear exhaust heat shields from the underbody for access to the handbrake cables.

10 Hold the equalizer bar at the end of the primary handbrake cable stationary, then disconnect the secondary cable by pulling it slightly forwards and unhooking it.

11 Unbolt the tie bar bracket cover at the rear of the handbrake cable.

12 At the rear brake caliper, push the lever forwards then unhook the inner cable from the fitting (see illustration).

13 Release the handbrake outer cable from the caliper bracket. Where a plastic ferrule is fitted to the outer cable, it will be necessary to compress the plastic tangs in order to release it from the bracket. Where a spring clip is

22.12 Unhooking the inner cable from the rear brake caliper fitting

22.13 Pull out the spring clip securing the handbrake cable to the caliper bracket

22.14 Compress the plastic tangs to release the handbrake outer cable from the support

fitted, pull the clip from the end of the outer cable **(see illustration)**.

14 Release the front end of the outer cable from the underbody support by compressing the plastic tangs **(see illustration)**.

15 Release the outer cable from the support clips and withdraw from under the car **(see illustrations)**.

Refitting

Front and rear cables

16 Refitting is a reversal of the removal procedure, but apply the handbrake several times to operate the self-adjustment mechanism. Before lowering the car to the ground, fully apply the handbrake and check that both rear wheels are locked firmly. Fully release the handbrake and check that both rear wheels are free to turn.

22.15a Handbrake cable underbody support clip

22.15b Cable tie securing the handbrake cable to the rear suspension trailing arm

Chapter 10
Suspension and steering

Contents

Degrees of difficulty

Easy, suitable for novice with little experience		Fairly easy, suitable for beginner with some experience		Fairly difficult, suitable for competent DIY mechanic		Difficult, suitable for experienced DIY mechanic		Very difficult, suitable for expert DIY or professional	

Specifications

Front wheel alignment (at kerb weight)

Toe setting:
Tolerance allowed before resetting required . . . . 0.0 mm ± 2.5 mm (0°00' ± 0°21' or 0.00° ± 0.35°)
Adjustment setting (if required) . . . . 0.0 mm ± 1.0 mm (0°00' ± 0°08' or 0.00° ± 0.14°)

Rear wheel alignment (at kerb weight)

Toe setting:
Tolerance allowed before resetting required . . . . 3.2 mm toe-in ± 2.5 mm (0°27' toe-in ± 0°20' or 0.45° toe-in ± 0.34°)
Adjustment setting (if required) . . . . 2.0 mm toe-in ± 1.0 mm (0°17' toe-in ± 0°08' or 0.28° toe-in ± 0.14°)

Roadwheels and tyres

Wheel size . . . . 16 x 6.5, 17 x 6.5 or 18 x 7
    Spare . . . . Temporary weight-saving type
Tyre sizes (depending on model) . . . . 205/55R16, 205/50R17 or 225/40R18
    Spare T125/85R16
Tyre pressures . . . . See end of *Weekly checks*

Torque wrench settings	Nm	lbf ft
Front suspension		
Coolant hose support bracket to subframe	10	7
Crossmember mounting bolts	120	89
Engine rear mounting link	80	59
Front anti-roll bar clamp bolts	48	35
Front anti-roll bar link	48	35
Front brake caliper mounting bracket to steering knuckle	130	96
Front subframe rear mounting brackets to underbody	10	7
Front subframe to underbody	142	105
Hub/driveshaft nut	290	214
Lower arm balljoint to lower arm (service replacement, bolted on)	58	43
Lower arm balljoint-to-steering knuckle pinch-bolt	83	61
Lower arm front bolt:		
Stage 1	80	59
Stage 2	Angle-tighten by 60°	
Lower arm rear bolt:		
Stage 1	90	66
Stage 2	Angle-tighten by 60°	
Radiator mounting bracket to subframe	25	18
Steering knuckle-to-suspension strut pinch-bolt	83	61
Suspension strut thrust bearing (centre) retaining nut	59	44
Suspension strut top mount to body	30	22
Track rod end to steering arm	40	30
Rear suspension (Saloon/Hatchback)		
ABS sensor to hub	7	5
Front and rear lower arm to crossmember	103	76
Front and rear lower arm to knuckle	120	89
Rear anti-roll bar link	48	35
Rear anti-roll bar to crossmember	25	18
Rear brake caliper mounting bracket to knuckle/tie-bar	80	59
Rear crossmember to underbody	120	89
Rear hub to suspension knuckle/tie-bar	70	52
Rear strut mounting bolts	25	18
Rear strut to knuckle	85	63
Suspension strut thrust bearing retaining nut	50	37
Tie-bar bracket to underbody	120	89
Tie-bar to bracket	103	76
Tie-bar to knuckle	103	76
Rear suspension (Estate)		
Note: Same as for Saloon/Hatchback, except for the following.		
Front lower arm to tie-bar/knuckle	84	62
Rear anti-roll bar mounting	25	18
Rear anti-roll bar to rear lower arm	48	35
Rear lower arm to crossmember	103	76
Rear lower arm to tie-bar/knuckle	84	62
Shock absorber lower mounting bolt	120	89
Shock absorber lower mounting to tie-bar/knuckle	120	89
Shock absorber upper mounting bolt	84	62
Shock absorber upper mounting to crossmember	84	62
Tie-bar/knuckle front mounting bracket to underbody	120	89
Tie-bar/knuckle front mounting to bracket	103	76
Upper arm to crossmember	84	62
Upper arm to knuckle	120	89
Upper arm to tie-bar/knuckle	120	89
Steering (general)		
Flexible coupling to steering gear pinion shaft (renew)	25	18
Power steering pipe unions to valve body	23	17
Steering column mounting bolts	24	18
Steering column-to-flexible coupling clamp bolt (renew)	20	15
Steering gear mounting bolts (renew)	130	96
Steering wheel	45	33
Track rod end to steering knuckle (renew)	40	30
Track rod end-to-track rod locknut	40	30

Torque wrench settings (continued)

	Nm	lbf ft
Steering (1.8 and 2.0 litre engines)		
Power steering hydraulic fluid reservoir mounting stud/bolts	9	7
Power steering pump high pressure outlet union nut	65	48
Power steering pump mounting bolts/studs	18	13
Steering (2.5 litre engine)		
Power steering pump elbow	10	7
Power steering pump high pressure outlet union nut	17	13
Power steering pump mounting bolts	48	35
Power steering pump outlet union	65	48
Power steering pump pulley	25	18
Retaining plate to power steering pump:		
Nuts	10	7
Bolts	25	18
Right-hand engine mounting	83	61
Steering (diesel engine)		
Power steering pump high pressure outlet union nut	23	17
Power steering pump mounting bolts	16	12
Power steering pump pulley	10	7
Roadwheel nuts	85	63

1 General information

The independent front suspension is of MacPherson strut type, incorporating coil springs, integral telescopic shock absorbers, and an anti-roll bar. The struts are attached to steering knuckles at their lower ends, and the knuckles are in turn attached to the lower suspension arm by balljoints. The rear bushes of the front lower suspension arms are of hydraulic type, and must not be articulated downwards excessively; all procedures involving the lower arms include cautions against excessive movement of the arms. It is not possible to renew the bushes separate to the lower arm. The anti-roll bar is bolted to the rear of the subframe, and is connected to the front suspension struts by links **(see illustration)**.

On Saloon/Hatchback models, the independent rear suspension is of 'Quadralink' type, having four mounting points on each side of the vehicle. The two lower arms are attached to the rear suspension knuckle at their outer ends, and to the rear crossmember at their inner ends. A tie-bar, located between the bottom of the knuckle and the floor, counteracts braking and acceleration forces on each side **(see illustration)**.

On Estate models, the independent rear suspension is of 'SLA' (Short and Long Arm) type. This allows a larger load area, since there are no suspension points projecting into the luggage area. There are three side arms on each side: one forged upper arm, and two pressed-steel lower side arms. A tie-bar on each side supports the rear suspension knuckles. The coil springs are separate from the shock absorbers **(see illustration)**.

J35307

1.1 Front suspension components

1	Anti-roll bar	5	ABS wheel speed	8	Balljoint heat shield
2	Link		sensor	9	Front suspension lower
3	Front coil spring	6	Knuckle		arm
4	Front suspension strut	7	Hub	10	Subframe

A rear anti-roll bar is fitted to all models. Self-levelling rear shock absorbers are available on Estate models.

A variable-ratio type rack-and-pinion steering gear is fitted, together with a conventional column and telescopic coupling, incorporating two universal joints. Power-

assisted steering is fitted to all models. A power steering system fluid cooler is fitted, in front of the cooling system radiator on the crossmember. On models with adaptive damping, a steering position sensor with sensor disc is located above the upper universal joint.

⚠️ *Warning: Never, under any circumstances, rely on a jack alone to support the vehicle while working beneath it. When jacking up the vehicle, do not lift or support it beneath the front subframe or rear crossmember (see 'Jacking and vehicle support').*

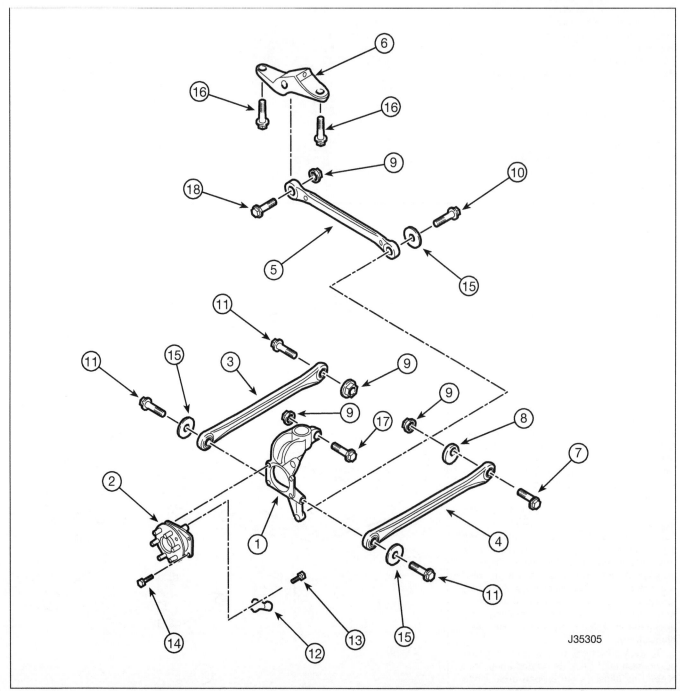

1.2 Rear suspension components – less strut (Saloon and Hatchback models)

1 Knuckle	6 Front mounting bracket	10 Bolt	14 Bolt
2 Hub	7 Eccentric bolt	11 Bolt	15 Washer
3 Front lower arm	8 Eccentric cam	12 ABS wheel speed sensor	16 Bolt
4 Rear lower arm	9 Nut	13 Bolt	17 Bolt
5 Tie-bar			18 Bolt

1.3 Rear suspension components – less spring and shock absorber (Estate models)

1 Rear suspension tie-bar/knuckle
2 Rear suspension upper arm
3 Rear suspension rear lower arm
4 Rear suspension upper arm
5 Brace
6 Rear hub
7 ABS wheel speed sensor
8 Bracket
9 Bolt
10 Bolt
11 Bolt
12 Bolt
13 Bolt
14 Bolt
15 Nut
16 Nut
17 Cam
18 Eccentric bolt
19 Bolt
20 Bolt

J35306

2 Steering knuckle and hub assembly – removal and refitting

Caution: The subframe MUST be lowered when removing the steering knuckle, otherwise damage will occur to the lower arm rear hydro-bush.

Removal

1 Remove the wheel cover (or centre cover) from the wheel, apply the handbrake, and engage 1st gear or P. Loosen the hub nut about half a turn.
Caution: This nut is very tight, and can only be re-used a maximum of 4 times. Mark the nut as an indication.
2 Working inside the engine compartment, remove the plastic cover from the top of the front suspension strut. Retain the suspension strut piston with an Allen key, then loosen the strut thrust bearing retaining nut by five complete turns. Do not remove the nut completely.
3 Loosen the front wheel nuts, then jack up the front of the vehicle and support it on axle stands (see *Jacking and vehicle support*). Remove the front wheel, then unscrew and remove the hub nut.
4 Disconnect the wiring from the ABS wheel speed sensor located at the top of the steering knuckle.
5 Loosen the track rod end balljoint nut several turns, then use a balljoint removal tool to release the balljoint from the steering arm. If necessary, use a 5 mm Allen key to hold the balljoint spindle while loosening the nut. With the balljoint released, unscrew the nut and disconnect the balljoint from the steering arm. Discard the nut as a new one must be fitted on reassembly.

6 Unscrew the two bolts securing the brake caliper mounting bracket to the steering knuckle, then slide the caliper and brake pads off of the brake disc. Tie the caliper and bracket to the front suspension strut coil spring, taking care not to strain the flexible hydraulic hose.
7 Undo the screws securing the front splash undershield to the subframe. On diesel engine models, remove the engine undershield complete.
8 Support the subframe next to the relevant lower suspension arm using a trolley jack.
Note: *Only one side of the subframe needs to be lowered to detach the lower arm balljoint from the steering knuckle.*
9 Carefully mark the position of the front suspension subframe on the underbody to ensure correct relocation. **Note:** *Ford technicians use special alignment pins to locate the subframe accurately.*
10 Unbolt and remove the subframe-to-underbody rear mounting bracket on the side being worked on. Loosen the bolts of the remaining rear mounting bracket by five turns only.

11 Unscrew and remove the subframe front mounting bolt on the side being worked on. Loosen the remaining front mounting bolt by five turns.
12 Note which way round the front suspension lower arm balljoint pinch-bolt is fitted, then unscrew and remove it from the knuckle assembly **(see illustration)**.
Caution: Do not pull down on the lower arm at this stage, as the rear hydro-bush will be damaged.
13 Lower the subframe on the side being worked on, sufficient to access the top of the lower arm rear mounting bolt; this will give the necessary room to disconnect the lower arm balljoint. Check that the steering inner column is free to move through the bulkhead.
14 Detach the lower arm balljoint from the steering knuckle, and remove the heat shield **(see illustration)**. If it is tight, carefully tap down the outer end of the arm with a mallet, or prise open the knuckle clamp using a wedge-shaped tool. Take care not to damage the balljoint rubber boot.
15 Remove the brake disc with reference to Chapter 9.

2.12 Removing the balljoint pinch-bolt

2.14 Removing the lower arm balljoint from the steering knuckle

2.17a Prise open the clamp with a cold chisel . . .

2.17b . . . and release the knuckle from the strut

2.18 Locate the knuckle over the tab on the strut

16 Using a universal puller located on the hub flange, press the outer end of the drive-shaft through the front hub and steering knuckle. It will help if the knuckle is turned at an angle.
Caution: The driveshaft inner CV joint must not be bent by more than 18° and the outer CV joint must not be bent by more than 45°.
17 Unscrew and remove the pinch-bolt securing the steering knuckle assembly to the front suspension strut, noting which way round it is fitted. Prise open the clamp using a wedge-shaped tool, and release the knuckle from the strut **(see illustrations)**. If necessary, tap the knuckle downwards with a soft-headed mallet to separate the two components. Remove the knuckle from the car.

Refitting

18 Thoroughly clean the bottom end of the strut and its location in the knuckle. Locate the knuckle onto the strut and over the tab, then insert the pinch-bolt and tighten to the specified torque **(see illustration)**.
19 Pull out the knuckle and insert the end of the driveshaft through the front hub. Refit the driveshaft/hub nut, and tighten it moderately at this stage. Final tightening of the nut is made with the vehicle lowered to the ground.
20 Refit the brake disc with reference to Chapter 9.
21 Locate the heat shield on the bottom of the knuckle, then position the knuckle over the lower arm balljoint and lift the balljoint until the spindle is fully entered in the clamp. Tap up the end of the lower arm to make sure it is fully entered. Insert the pinch-bolt from the

rear of the knuckle and tighten it to the specified torque.
22 Raise the subframe against the under-body, and position it accurately with the marks made during removal. If available, use the special Ford alignment pins. Refit the rear bracket, then insert the mounting bolts. Tighten all of the subframe and rear bracket bolts to the specified torque. Make sure the subframe does not move when tightening the bolts. If applicable, remove the Ford alignment pins.
23 On diesel models, refit the complete engine undershield. On all models insert and tighten the screws securing the front splash undershield to the subframe.
24 Locate the brake caliper complete with mounting bracket to the steering knuckle, while guiding the brake pads over the brake disc. Insert the bolts and tighten them to the specified torque.
25 Locate the track rod end balljoint on the steering arm. Screw on a new nut and tighten to the specified torque. If necessary, use a 5 mm Allen key to hold the balljoint spindle while tightening the nut.
26 Reconnect the wiring to the ABS wheel speed sensor on the steering knuckle.
27 Have an assistant apply the brakes, then tighten the hub nut to a pre-load setting of 100 Nm (74 lbf ft).
28 Refit the front wheel and lower the car to the ground. Fully tighten the wheel nuts, then fully tighten the hub nut to the specified torque. Refit the wheel cover (or centre cover) to the wheel.
29 Hold the suspension strut piston stationary with an Allen key, then tighten the

upper mount thrust bearing (centre) nut to the specified torque. The nut can be tightened initially with a ring spanner while the piston rod is being held, then a torque wrench can be used for the final tightening.
30 Refit the plastic cover to the top of the front suspension strut.

3 Front hub and bearings – inspection and renewal

Inspection

1 The front hub bearings are non-adjustable, and are supplied already greased.
2 To check the bearings for excessive wear, apply the handbrake, then jack up the front of the vehicle and support it on axle stands (see *Jacking and vehicle support*).
3 Grip the front wheel at top and bottom, and attempt to rock it. If excessive movement is noted, it may be that the hub bearings are worn. Do not confuse wear in the driveshaft outer joint or front suspension lower arm balljoint with wear in the bearings. Hub bearing wear will show up as roughness or vibration when the wheel is spun; it will also be noticeable as a rumbling or growling noise when driving.

Renewal

Note: *The ABS wheel speed sensor is integral with the hub bearing.*
4 Remove the steering knuckle and hub assembly as described in Section 2.
5 Undo the screw and remove the ABS wheel speed sensor from the knuckle.
6 The hub must now be removed from the bearing. It is preferable to use a press to do this **(see illustration)**, but it is possible to drive out the hub using a length of metal tube of suitable diameter. Part of the inner race will remain on the hub, and the remaining bearing will remain in the knuckle. The bearing will be rendered unserviceable by removing it, and **must not** be re-used.
7 With the hub removed, remove the bearing cage, oil seal and the old bearing inner race by supporting the race and pressing the hub down through it. Alternatively use a puller to withdraw the race **(see illustrations)**. Do not use heat to remove the race.

3.6 Using a press to remove the front hub from the bearings

3.7a Remove the bearing cage (and oil seal) . . .

3.7b . . . then use a puller . . .

3.7c . . . to remove the old bearing inner race

3.8 Pressing out the old bearing

8 Press or drive the bearing from the steering knuckle, using a length of metal tube of suitable diameter **(see illustration)**.
9 Clean the bearing seating surfaces on the steering knuckle and hub.
10 Press the new bearing into the knuckle until it contacts the shoulder **(see illustration)**, using a length of metal tube of diameter slightly less than the outer race. The wheel speed sensor ring may be damaged if the bearing is driven into position, therefore it is recommended that a press is used. Do not apply any pressure to the inner race.
Caution: The bearing must be fitted with the ABS wheel speed sensor ring, coloured black, towards the wheel speed sensor end of the knuckle. The ABS wheel speed sensor ring must not be subjected to any magnetic force.
11 Support the bearing inner race on a length of metal tube, then press or drive the hub fully into the bearing **(see illustration)**. Alternatively, support the hub and press the bearing inner race onto it.
12 Refit the ABS wheel speed sensor and tighten the screw.
13 Refit the steering knuckle and hub assembly as described in Section 2.

---

4 Front suspension strut – removal and refitting

Caution: The subframe MUST be lowered when removing the front suspension strut, otherwise damage will occur to the lower arm rear hydro-bush.

Removal

1 Apply the handbrake, then jack up the front of the vehicle and support it on axle stands (see *Jacking and vehicle support*). Remove the front wheel.
2 Unbolt the brake hydraulic hose support bracket from the strut **(see illustration)**. Alternatively, unclip the hose from the bracket.
3 Unscrew the nut and disconnect the anti-roll bar link from the strut. If necessary, use a

3.10 Pressing in the new bearing . . .

5 mm Allen key to hold the spindle while the nut is loosened.
4 Unscrew the two bolts securing the brake caliper mounting bracket to the steering knuckle, then slide the caliper and brake pads off of the brake disc. Tie the caliper and bracket to one side or support on an axle stand, making sure that the flexible hose is not strained.
5 Undo the screws securing the front splash undershield to the subframe. On diesel engine models, remove the engine undershield complete.
6 Support the subframe on the relevant side using a trolley jack. **Note:** *Only one side of the subframe needs to be lowered to detach the lower arm balljoint from the steering knuckle.*
7 Carefully mark the position of the front suspension subframe on the underbody to ensure correct relocation. **Note:** *Ford*

4.2 Removing the hydraulic hose support bracket from the strut

3.11 . . . then press the hub through the inner race

technicians use special alignment pins to locate the subframe accurately.
8 Unbolt and remove the subframe-to-underbody rear mounting bracket on the side being worked on. Loosen the bolts of the remaining rear mounting bracket by five turns only.
9 Unscrew and remove the subframe front mounting bolt on the side being worked on. Loosen the remaining front mounting bolt by five turns.
10 Lower the subframe on the side being worked on, sufficient to access the top of the lower arm rear mounting bolt; this will give the necessary room to disconnect the strut from the knuckle without damaging the lower arm rear mounting hydro-bush. Check that the steering inner column is free to move through the bulkhead.
11 Note which way round the front suspension lower arm balljoint pinch-bolt is fitted, then unscrew and remove it from the knuckle assembly.
12 Detach the lower arm balljoint from the steering knuckle, and remove the heat shield. If it is tight, carefully tap down the outer end of the arm with a mallet, or prise open the knuckle clamp using a wedge-shaped tool. Take care not to damage the balljoint rubber boot.
Caution: Do not press down on the lower arm, as the rear hydro-bush will be damaged.
13 Unscrew and remove the pinch-bolt securing the steering knuckle assembly to the front suspension strut, noting which way round it is fitted.

4.15a Removing the plastic cover from the top of the strut

4.15b The arrow and white line on the top mount must face the front of the vehicle

4.16 Unscrewing the front suspension strut top mount nuts

14 Prise open the clamp using a wedge-shaped tool, and release the knuckle from the strut. If necessary, tap the knuckle downwards with a soft-headed mallet to separate the two components. Support the knuckle on an axle stand, taking care not to bend the driveshaft joints excessively.

Caution: The driveshaft inner CV joint must not be bent by more than 18° and the outer CV joint must not be bent by more than 45°.

15 Working inside the engine compartment, remove the plastic cover from the top of the front suspension strut. Note the arrow and white line on the top mount are facing the front of the vehicle **(see illustrations)**.

16 Support the strut, then unscrew the three top mount nuts **(see illustration)**. Lower the strut and withdraw from under the wheel arch.

Refitting

17 Lift the suspension strut into position, and insert the studs through the holes in the body, making sure that the arrow and white line on the top mount are facing the front of the vehicle. Screw on the nuts and tighten them to the specified torque.

18 Refit the plastic cover to the top of the strut.

19 Thoroughly clean the bottom end of the strut and its location in the knuckle. Locate the knuckle onto the strut, then insert the pinch-bolt and tighten to the specified torque.

20 Locate the heat shield on the bottom of the knuckle, then position the knuckle over the lower arm balljoint and lift the balljoint until the spindle is fully entered in the clamp. Tap up the end of the lower arm to make sure it is fully entered. Insert the pinch-bolt from the rear of the knuckle and tighten it to the specified torque.

21 Raise the subframe against the underbody, and position it accurately with the marks made during removal. If available, use the special Ford alignment pins. Refit the rear bracket, then insert the mounting bolts. Tighten all of the subframe and rear bracket bolts to the specified torque. Make sure the subframe does not move when tightening the bolts. If applicable, remove the Ford alignment pins.

22 On diesel models, refit the complete engine undershield. On all models insert and tighten the screws securing the front splash undershield to the subframe.

23 Locate the brake caliper complete with mounting bracket to the steering knuckle, while guiding the brake pads over the brake disc. Insert the bolts and tighten them to the specified torque.

24 Refit the anti-roll bar link to the strut. Screw on the nut and tighten to the specified torque. If necessary, use a 5 mm Allen key to hold the spindle.

25 Refit the brake hydraulic hose support bracket to the strut and tighten the nut to the specified torque.

26 Refit the front wheel and lower the vehicle to the ground.

5 Front suspension strut – overhaul

⚠ *Warning: Before attempting to dismantle the front suspension strut, a spring compressor tool is required to hold the coil spring in compression. Do not attempt to use makeshift methods. Uncontrolled release of the spring could cause damage and personal injury.*

1 If the front suspension struts exhibit signs of wear (leaking fluid, loss of damping capability, sagging or cracked coil springs) then they should be dismantled and overhauled as necessary. The struts themselves cannot be serviced, and should be renewed if faulty, but the springs and related components can be renewed. To maintain balanced characteristics on both sides of the vehicle, the components on both sides should be renewed at the same time.

2 With the strut removed from the vehicle, clean away all external dirt, then mount it in a vice **(see illustration)**.

3 Fit the coil spring compressor tools (ensuring they are fully engaged), and compress the spring until all tension is relieved from the upper mounting.

4 Hold the strut piston with an Allen key, and unscrew the thrust bearing retaining nut with a ring spanner **(see illustration)**.

5 Withdraw the top mounting, thrust bearing, bump stop and upper spring seat, gaiter and coil spring **(see illustrations)**.

5.2 Front suspension strut and coil spring removed from the vehicle

5.4 Hold the piston with an Allen key while unscrewing the retaining nut

5.5a Remove the nut . . .

6 If a new spring is to be fitted, the original spring must now be carefully released from the compressor. If it is to be re-used, the spring can be left in compression.

7 With the strut assembly now completely dismantled, examine all the components for wear and damage, and check the bearing for smoothness of operation. Renew components as necessary.

8 Examine the strut for signs of fluid leakage. Check the strut piston for signs of pitting along its entire length, and check the strut body for signs of damage.

9 Test the operation of the strut, while holding it in an upright position, by moving the piston through a full stroke, and then through short strokes of 50 to 100 mm. In both cases, the resistance felt should be smooth and continuous. If the resistance is jerky, uneven, or if there is any visible sign of wear or damage to the strut, renewal is necessary.

10 Reassembly is a reversal of dismantling, noting the following points:
  a) *Make sure that the coil spring ends are correctly located in the upper and lower seats before releasing the compressor* **(see illustration)**.
  b) *Check that the thrust bearing is correctly fitted to the upper mounting.*
  c) *Tighten the thrust bearing retaining nut to the specified torque.*

6 Front anti-roll bar and links – removal and refitting

Removal

1 Apply the handbrake, then jack up the front of the vehicle and support it on axle stands (see *Jacking and vehicle support*). Turn the steering to the straight-ahead position and lock it. Remove both front wheels.

2 Working in the driver's footwell, undo the retaining screws and unclip the lower facia panel from under the steering column. Where applicable, disconnect the wiring from the electronic automated temperature control (EATC) sensor located on the panel.

3 Where applicable, remove the insulation pad from over the foot pedals.

4 Unscrew and remove the clamp bolt securing the steering inner column to the flexible coupling on the steering gear. Rotate the clamp plate clockwise and detach the clamp from the coupling. Note that the coupling stub has a triangular shape and the shaft may only be fitted in one of three positions. Discard the bolt as a new one must be fitted on reassembly.

⚠ *Warning: Make sure that the steering wheel remains locked in its straight-ahead position while the clamp is disconnected from the flexible coupling. Failure to do this may result in damage to the airbag and clock spring, and subsequent personal injury in the event of an accident.*

5.5b . . . followed by the top mounting . . .

5.5d . . . bump stop and upper spring seat . . .

5.5f . . . and coil spring (with compressor tool)

5 Hold the radiator in the upper mountings using split pins inserted through the holes in the upper location pins. Access to the holes is gained through the apertures in the front crossmember.

6 Undo the screws and remove the splash shield from under the radiator position. On diesel models, also remove the engine under-tray and left-hand wheel arch lower liner.

7 Under the front of the car, unbolt the hose bracket (where fitted) next to the left-hand radiator support bracket, then unbolt and remove both radiator support brackets.

8 Unscrew the nuts and disconnect the anti-roll bar links from the front suspension struts. If necessary, use a 5 mm Allen key to hold the spindles while the nuts are loosened.

9 On 1.8 and 2.0 litre petrol engines, and all diesel engines, remove the exhaust flexible pipe from the front of the exhaust system with reference to the appropriate part of Chapter 4.

5.5c . . . thrust bearing . . .

5.5e . . . gaiter . . .

5.10 Make sure that the coil spring ends are located against the spring seats

10 On the 2.5 litre petrol engine, remove the exhaust dual converter Y-pipe with reference to the appropriate part of Chapter 4.

11 Remove the engine rear support/link with reference to the appropriate part of Chapter 2.

12 On all models except diesel models, disconnect the catalytic converter monitor sensor wiring, and unclip the wiring from the subframe.

13 On models with xenon headlamps, release the ties and detach the headlamp levelling sensor wiring harness from the subframe.

14 Release the radiator cooling fan wiring harness from the subframe.

15 Support the front suspension subframe on one or two trolley jacks. If necessary, enlist the help of an assistant.

16 Carefully mark the position of the front suspension subframe on the underbody to ensure correct refitting. **Note:** *Ford technicians*

6.21 Anti-roll bar mounting clamp

6.22 The anti-roll bar mounting rubbers are located on flats

6.23 Press the clamps onto the mounting rubbers in a vice, using a 10 mm thick metal bar as a spacer

use special alignment pins to locate the subframe accurately when refitting. Unscrew and remove the subframe rear mounting bolts, then unbolt the rear brackets from the subframe.

17 Unscrew and remove the subframe front mounting bolts.

18 Lower the subframe uniformly approximately 150 mm, making sure that the lower arm rear hydro-bushes are not strained or damaged.

19 Unscrew the nuts and disconnect the anti-roll bar links from the anti-roll bar. If necessary, use a 5 mm Allen key to hold the spindles while the nuts are loosened.

20 Unbolt the steering gear from the subframe, then use cable ties to suspend the steering gear from the underbody.

21 Unscrew the mounting clamp bolts on both sides **(see illustration)**, then remove the anti-roll bar from the subframe and withdraw from one side of the vehicle. Remove the clamps.

22 With the anti-roll bar on the bench, mark the location of the mounting rubbers and note how they are fitted to the flats on the bar, then remove them **(see illustration)**. Examine the rubbers for wear and damage, and renew them if necessary.

Refitting

23 Before refitting the anti-roll bar, the mounting rubbers and clamps must be pressed into position. Grip the anti-roll bar in a vice, and use a 10 mm thick metal bar measuring 30 mm by 100 mm as a spacer to press on the clamps **(see illustration)**.

24 Refitting is a reversal of the removal procedure, but tighten the nuts and bolts to the specified torques. When refitting the subframe, raise it against the underbody, and position it accurately with the marks made during removal. If available, use the special Ford alignment pins. Refit the rear brackets, then insert the mounting bolts and tighten to the specified torque. Make sure the subframe does not move when tightening the bolts. Always fit a new steering column-to-flexible coupling clamp bolt.

25 Have the front suspension wheel alignment checked and adjusted at the earliest opportunity.

26 If on completion, the car pulls to one side, or abnormal tyre wear is noted, have the subframe alignment checked by a Ford dealer.

7 Front suspension lower arm – removal and refitting

Caution: The subframe MUST be lowered when removing the front suspension lower arm, otherwise damage will occur to the lower arm rear hydro-bush.

Removal

1 Apply the handbrake, then jack up the front of the vehicle and support it on axle stands (see *Jacking and vehicle support*). Remove the relevant wheel.

2 Undo the screws securing the front splash undershield to the subframe. On diesel engine

models, remove the engine undershield complete.

3 On models with xenon headlamps, a headlamp levelling sensor is located on the left-hand lower suspension arm. If removing this arm, remove the sensor by first disconnecting the wiring, then releasing the connecting rod and unbolting the sensor.

4 Support the subframe next to the relevant lower suspension arm using a trolley jack. **Note:** *Only one side of the subframe needs to be lowered to remove the lower arm.*

5 Carefully mark the position of the front suspension subframe on the underbody to ensure correct relocation. **Note:** *Ford technicians use special alignment pins to locate the subframe accurately.*

6 Unbolt and remove the subframe-to-underbody rear mounting bracket on the side being worked on. Loosen the bolts of the remaining rear mounting bracket by five turns only.

7 Unscrew and remove the subframe front mounting bolt on the side being worked on. Loosen the remaining front mounting bolt by five turns.

8 Note which way round the front suspension lower arm balljoint pinch-bolt is fitted, then unscrew and remove it from the knuckle assembly.

Caution: Do not pull down on the lower arm at this stage, as the rear hydro-bush will be damaged.

9 Lower the subframe on the side being worked on, sufficient to access the top of the lower arm rear mounting bolt; this will give the necessary room to disconnect the lower arm balljoint without damaging the rear hydro-bush.

10 Detach the lower arm balljoint from the steering knuckle, and remove the heat shield. If it is tight, carefully tap down the outer end of the arm with a mallet, or prise open the knuckle clamp using a wedge-shaped tool. Take care not to damage the balljoint rubber boot.

11 Support the lower arm, then unscrew and remove the front bolt and the rear mounting nut and bolt, and withdraw the arm from the subframe **(see illustrations)**. Take care not to damage the rear hydro-bush. Discard the bolts and nut, and obtain new ones.

12 The front suspension lower arm is

7.11a Front suspension lower arm front mounting . . .

7.11b . . . and rear mounting

supplied complete with the rubber mountings and the balljoint, and it is not possible to obtain the mountings and balljoint separately.

Refitting

13 Refit the lower arm to the subframe and insert the new bolts and nut finger-tight at this stage. Final tightening is carried out with the weight of the vehicle on the suspension.

14 Locate the heat shield on the bottom of the knuckle, then position the knuckle over the lower arm balljoint and lift the balljoint until the spindle is fully entered in the clamp. Tap up the end of the lower arm to make sure it is fully entered. Insert the pinch-bolt from the rear of the knuckle and tighten it to the specified torque.

15 Raise the subframe against the underbody, and position it accurately with the marks made during removal. If available, use the special Ford alignment pins. Refit the rear bracket, then insert the mounting bolts. Tighten all of the subframe and rear bracket bolts to the specified torque. Make sure the subframe does not move when tightening the bolts. If applicable, remove the Ford alignment pins.

16 On models with xenon headlamps, refit the sensor to the lower arm and tighten the bolts. Reconnect the connecting rod and the wiring. **Note:** *After refitting, the headlamp levelling system must be initialised by a Ford dealer using a special setting instrument.*

17 Refit the wheel and lower the vehicle to the ground.

18 With the weight of the vehicle on its suspension, tighten the lower arm front and rear bolts to the specified torques.

19 Raise and support the front of the vehicle on axle stands again.

20 On diesel models, refit the complete engine undershield. On all models insert and tighten the screws securing the front splash undershield to the subframe.

21 Lower the vehicle to the ground.

22 Have the front suspension wheel alignment checked and adjusted at the earliest opportunity. On models with xenon headlamps, have the levelling system initialised by a Ford dealer.

23 If on completion, the car pulls to one side, or abnormal tyre wear is noted, have the subframe alignment checked by a Ford dealer.

8.2 Front suspension lower arm balljoint rivets

8 Front suspension lower arm balljoint – renewal

Note: *If the lower arm balljoint is worn, it appears at the time of writing that the complete lower arm must be renewed (see Section 7), although the balljoint was available separately on earlier models. Seek the advice of your Ford dealer or parts supplier to establish whether the balljoint is available separately. If the balljoint has already been renewed, it will be bolted in position; if the original balljoint is being renewed, then it will be riveted in position. This Section describes the renewal of a riveted balljoint.*

1 Remove the front suspension lower arm as described in Section 7. It is not recommended that the balljoint be renewed with the lower arm in position on the vehicle; the accurate drilling necessary may not be possible, and the holes in the arm may be enlarged.

2 With the lower arm on the bench, use a 3 mm drill to make a pilot hole through each of the three rivets **(see illustration)**. Now use a 9 mm drill to drill the rivets to a depth of 12 mm, then use a 7 or 8 mm drift to drive the rivets out of the arm.

3 Clean any rust or dirt from the rivet holes.

4 The new balljoint is supplied with a protective plastic cover over the rubber boot and stub, and it is recommended that this remains in position until it is time to connect the balljoint to the steering knuckle.

5 Locate the new balljoint on the lower arm,

8.5 Location lug (1) and bolt hole (2) in the front suspension lower arm balljoint

and use three new bolts to secure it, inserting the bolts from the top of the arm. Tighten the nuts to the specified torque. Make sure that the location lug on the balljoint engages the hole in the lower arm **(see illustration)**.

6 Refit the front suspension lower arm as described in Section 7.

9 Front suspension subframe – removal and refitting

Removal

1 Apply the handbrake, then jack up the front of the vehicle and support it on axle stands (see *Jacking and vehicle support*). Turn the steering to the straight-ahead position and lock it. Remove both front wheels.

2 Working inside the car, unscrew and remove the clamp bolt securing the steering inner column to the flexible coupling on the steering gear. Rotate the clamp plate clockwise and detach the clamp from the coupling. Discard the bolt as a new one must be fitted on reassembly.

 Warning: Make sure that the steering wheel remains locked in its straight-ahead position while the clamp is disconnected from the flexible coupling. Failure to do this may result in damage to the airbag and clock spring.

3 Hold or tie the radiator in the upper mountings – where necessary, use split pins inserted through the holes in the radiator upper location pins. Access to the holes is gained through the apertures in the front crossmember.

4 Undo the screws and remove the splash shield from under the radiator position. On diesel models, also remove the engine undertray.

5 Under the front of the car, unbolt the hose bracket (where fitted) next to the left-hand radiator support bracket, then unbolt and remove both radiator support brackets.

6 Unscrew the nuts and disconnect the anti-roll bar links from the front suspension struts. If necessary, use a 5 mm Allen key to hold the spindles while the nuts are loosened **(see illustrations)**.

7 On 1.8 and 2.0 litre petrol engines, and all

9.6a Use a 5 mm Allen key to hold the spindles while the nuts are loosened . . .

9.6b . . . then disconnect the anti-roll bar links from the struts

9.7a On 1.8 and 2.0 litre petrol engines, and all diesel engines, remove the bracket . . .

9.7b . . . unhook the rubber mountings . . .

9.7c . . . then remove the flexible pipe . . .

9.7d . . . and recover the gasket

9.9 Removing the engine rear support/link

diesel engines, remove the exhaust flexible pipe from the front of the exhaust system with reference to the appropriate part of Chapter 4 **(see illustrations)**.

8 On the 2.5 litre petrol engine, remove the exhaust dual converter Y-pipe with reference to the appropriate part of Chapter 4.

9 Remove the engine rear support/link with reference to the appropriate part of Chapter 2 **(see illustration)**.

10 On all non-diesel models, disconnect the catalytic converter monitor sensor wiring, and

unclip the wiring from the subframe.

11 On models with xenon headlamps, disconnect the wiring from the headlamp levelling sensor then release the ties and detach the wiring harness from the subframe.

12 Release the radiator cooling fan wiring harness from the subframe **(see illustration)**.

13 Support the front suspension subframe on one or two trolley jacks. If necessary, enlist the help of an assistant **(see illustration)**.

14 Carefully mark the position of the front suspension subframe on the underbody to ensure correct refitting. **Note:** *Ford technicians use special alignment pins to locate the subframe accurately when refitting.* Unscrew and remove the subframe rear mounting bolts, then unbolt the rear brackets from the subframe **(see illustrations)**.

15 Unscrew and remove the subframe front mounting bolts **(see illustration)**.

9.12 Removing the radiator cooling fan wiring from the subframe

9.13 Support the subframe adequately

9.14a Mark the position of the subframe to ensure correct refitting

9.14b Subframe rear bracket

9.14c Using the special subframe alignment tool

9.15 Removing the subframe front mounting bolts

9.17 Removing the front suspension lower arm balljoint pinch-bolts

9.18 Removing the lower balljoint heat shields

9.19 Power steering hose and pipe union on the steering gear

16 Lower the subframe uniformly approximately 150 mm, making sure that the lower arm rear hydro-bushes are not strained or damaged.
17 Note which way round the front suspension lower arm balljoint pinch-bolts are fitted, then unscrew and remove them from the knuckle assemblies on both sides **(see illustration)**.
18 Detach the lower arm balljoints from the steering knuckles, and remove the heat shields **(see illustration)**. If they are tight, carefully tap down the outer ends of the arms with a mallet, or prise open the knuckle clamps using a wedge-shaped tool. Take care not to damage the balljoint rubber boots.
19 Unbolt the steering gear from the subframe, then use cable ties to suspend the steering gear from the underbody. Alternatively, the steering gear may be left on the subframe if the power steering hose and pipe union is disconnected first **(see illustration)**. If this latter method is used, fit a hose clamp to the hydraulic flexible fluid lines to reduce fluid loss. Recover the O-ring seals.
20 Lower the subframe to the ground.
21 Unscrew the mounting clamp bolts on both sides, then remove the anti-roll bar from the subframe.
22 Remove the lower suspension arms from the subframe with reference to Section 7. If necessary, the subframe mounting bushes may be renewed using a suitable puller **(see illustration)**.
23 If applicable, unbolt and remove the steering gear from the subframe.

Refitting

24 Refit the lower suspension arms to the subframe with reference to Section 7.
25 Refit the anti-roll bar and tighten the mounting clamp bolts to the specified torque with reference to Section 6.
26 Raise and support the subframe to approximately 150 mm below the underbody.
27 Refit the steering gear and tighten the mounting bolts to the specified torque. Where applicable, refit the power steering hydraulic pipe union using new seals, and tighten to the specified torque **(see illustration)**. Remove the hose clamp.
28 Working on each side separately, locate the heat shield on the bottom of the knuckle, then position the knuckle over the lower arm

balljoint and lift the balljoint until the spindle is fully entered in the clamp. Tap up the end of the lower arm to make sure it is fully entered. Insert the pinch-bolt from the rear of the knuckle and tighten to the specified torque.
29 Raise the subframe against the underbody, and position it accurately with the marks made during removal. If available, use the special Ford alignment pins. Refit the rear bracket, then insert the mounting bolts. Tighten all of the subframe and rear bracket bolts to the specified torque. Make sure the subframe does not move when tightening the bolts. If applicable, remove the Ford alignment pins.
30 Use a cable tie to attach the radiator cooling fan wiring harness to the subframe.
31 On models with xenon headlamps, reconnect the wiring to the headlamp levelling sensor, then use cable ties to attach the wiring harness to the subframe.
32 On all non-diesel models, reconnect the catalytic converter monitor sensor wiring, and clip the wiring to the subframe.
33 Refit the engine rear support/link with reference to the appropriate part of Chapter 2.
34 On the 2.5 litre petrol engine, refit the exhaust dual converter Y-pipe with reference to the appropriate part of Chapter 4.
35 On 1.8 and 2.0 litre petrol engines, and all diesel engines, refit the exhaust flexible pipe to the front of the exhaust system with reference to the appropriate part of Chapter 4.
36 Reconnect the anti-roll bar links to the struts and tighten the nuts to the specified torque. If necessary, use a 5 mm Allen key to hold the spindles while tightening the nuts.
37 Refit the radiator support brackets and

9.22 Subframe mounting bush

hose bracket to the subframe and tighten to the specified torque.
38 On diesel models, refit the complete engine undershield. On all models insert and tighten the screws securing the front splash undershield to the subframe.
39 Remove the temporary retaining split pins from the radiator upper location pins.
40 Refit the steering inner column to the flexible coupling on the steering gear, rotate the clamp plate anti-clockwise, then insert a new clamp bolt and tighten to the specified torque.
41 Refit the front wheels and lower the car to the ground. Fully tighten the wheel nuts to the specified torque. Refit the wheel cover (or centre cover) to the wheels.
42 Have the front suspension wheel alignment checked and adjusted at the earliest opportunity. On models with xenon headlamps, have the levelling system initialised by a Ford dealer.
43 If on completion, the car pulls to one side, or abnormal tyre wear is noted, have the subframe alignment checked by a Ford dealer.

10 Rear hub and bearings – inspection, removal and refitting

Inspection

1 The rear hub bearings are non-adjustable, and are supplied complete with the hub and ABS wheel sensor ring. It is not possible to renew the bearings separately from the hub.
2 To check the bearings for excessive wear,

9.27 Fitting new O-ring seals to the power steering hydraulic union

10.3 Assessing rear wheel bearing play

10.7a Disconnect the wiring . . .

10.7b . . . then undo the mounting screw . . .

10.7c . . . and withdraw the sensor

10.8a Unbolt the caliper from the bracket . . .

10.8b . . . then remove the plastic covers . . .

chock the front wheels then jack up the rear of the vehicle and support on axle stands (see *Jacking and vehicle support*). Fully release the handbrake.

3 Grip the rear wheel at the top and bottom,

and attempt to rock it **(see illustration)**. If excessive movement is noted, or if there is any roughness or vibration felt when the wheel is spun, it is indicative that the hub bearings are worn.

Removal

4 Remove the rear wheel.

5 Disconnect the handbrake cable from the rear brake caliper as follows. First push the lever forwards, then release the end of the inner cable from the fitting on the lever.

6 Release the handbrake outer cable from the caliper bracket and position it to one side. Where a plastic ferrule is fitted to the outer cable, it will be necessary to compress the plastic tangs in order to release it from the bracket.

7 Disconnect the wiring from the ABS wheel speed sensor located on the inner end of the hub. Access is gained through the hole in the rear suspension lower arm. Undo the mounting screw, and withdraw the sensor **(see illustrations)**.

8 Remove the plastic covers, then unscrew the two bolts securing the brake caliper mounting bracket to the lower arm, and slide the caliper and brake pads off of the brake disc. Alternatively, remove the brake pads first and unbolt the caliper from the bracket, then unbolt the bracket **(see illustrations)**. Note the dampers/spacers located beneath the bolts. Tie or support the caliper and bracket as necessary to one side, taking care not to strain the flexible hydraulic hose.

9 Remove the rear brake disc with reference to Chapter 9.

10 Using a socket through the holes in the hub drive flange, unscrew the bolts securing the hub to the suspension lower arm. Withdraw the hub and backplate from the vehicle **(see illustrations)**.

10.8c . . . unscrew the bolts and remove the dampers/spacers . . .

10.8d . . . and withdraw the bracket from the lower arm

10.10a Using a Torx socket through the holes in the hub drive flange . . .

10.10b . . . remove the bolts . . .

10.10c . . . then withdraw the hub . . .

10.10d . . . and backplate

10.13 Apply locking fluid to the threads of the mounting bracket retaining bolts

Refitting

11 Clean the contact surfaces of the hub and lower arm, then refit the hub and backplate, insert the bolts and tighten them to the specified torque.

12 Refit the rear brake disc with reference to Chapter 9.

13 Refit the caliper and brake pads, together with the mounting bracket, onto the brake disc, insert the two bolts, and tighten them to the specified torque. Apply a little locking fluid to the threads of the mounting bracket retaining bolts before refitting them **(see illustration)**.

14 Refit the ABS wheel speed sensor and tighten the bolt, then reconnect the wiring.

15 Refit the handbrake outer cable to the caliper bracket, then reconnect the inner cable to the caliper lever fitting.

16 Refit the rear wheel and lower the vehicle to the ground.

11 Rear suspension knuckle (Saloon/Hatchback models) – removal and refitting

Removal

1 Remove the rear hub and backplate as described in Section 10.

2 Unbolt the front and rear lower arms from the rear suspension knuckle, and move them to one side.

3 Unscrew the bolt and disconnect the rear of the tie-bar downwards from the bottom of the knuckle.

4 Unscrew the nut and disconnect the anti-roll bar link lower end from the anti-roll bar.

5 Support the knuckle, then unscrew and remove the clamp bolt securing the knuckle to the strut.

6 Prise the top of the knuckle apart carefully using a large flat-bladed tool, and withdraw the knuckle downwards from the strut. If necessary, tap the knuckle downwards with a soft-faced mallet. Withdraw the knuckle from under the rear wheel arch.

Refitting

7 Locate the knuckle fully on the strut, then

insert the clamp bolt and tighten to the specified torque.

8 Refit the anti-roll bar link to the anti-roll bar, and tighten the nut to the specified torque.

9 Refit the tie-bar to the bottom of the knuckle, and insert the bolt finger-tight at this stage.

10 Refit the front and rear lower arms to the knuckle, and insert the bolts finger-tight at this stage.

11 Refit the rear hub and backplate with reference to Section 10.

12 With the weight of the vehicle on the suspension, fully tighten the mounting bolts for the tie-bar and lower arms.

12 Rear suspension strut (Saloon/Hatchback models) – removal and refitting

Removal

1 Remove the rear suspension knuckle as described in Section 11.

2 Unscrew the nut and disconnect the upper end of the anti-roll bar link from the rear suspension strut.

3 The bottom of the strut rests on a suspension crossmember ledge/bump stop when fully extended. Using a trolley jack, lift the strut above the ledge, move it outwards and lower it fully.

4 Reach up into the wheel housing and unscrew the strut mounting bolts. Lower the strut and withdraw it from under the vehicle.

Refitting

5 Lift the strut into position, insert the mounting bolts and tighten to the specified torque.

6 Position the trolley jack under the strut, then raise the strut, move it inwards, and lower it onto the crossmember ledge/bump stop. The bump stop is tapered inwards, and the strut bracket should be fully engaged with it before releasing the jack.

7 Reconnect the anti-roll bar link on the strut and tighten the nut to the specified torque.

8 Refit the rear suspension knuckle with reference to Section 11.

13 Rear suspension strut (Saloon/Hatchback models) – overhaul

Warning: Before attempting to dismantle the rear suspension strut, a spring compressor tool is required to hold the coil spring in compression. Do not attempt to use makeshift methods. Uncontrolled release of the spring could cause damage and personal injury.

1 If the rear suspension struts exhibit signs of wear (leaking fluid, loss of damping capability, sagging or cracked coil springs) then they should be dismantled and overhauled as necessary. The struts themselves cannot be serviced, and should be renewed if faulty, but the springs and related components can be renewed. To maintain balanced characteristics on both sides of the vehicle, the components on both sides should be renewed at the same time.

2 With the strut removed from the vehicle, clean away all external dirt, then mount it in a vice.

3 Fit the coil spring compressor tools (ensuring they are fully engaged), and compress the spring until all tension is relieved from the upper mounting.

4 Hold the strut piston with an Allen key, and unscrew the top mounting/thrust bearing retaining nut with a ring spanner.

5 Withdraw the retaining cup, top mounting, upper spring seat and spring, followed by the gaiter and bump stop **(see illustration overleaf)**.

6 If a new spring is to be fitted, the original spring must now be carefully released from the compressor. If it is to be re-used, the spring can be left in compression.

7 With the strut assembly now completely dismantled, examine all the components for wear and damage, and check the bearing for smoothness of operation. Renew components as necessary.

8 Examine the strut for signs of fluid leakage. Check the strut piston for signs of pitting along its entire length, and check the strut body for signs of damage.

9 Test the operation of the strut, while

J35167

13.5 Rear suspension strut components

1 Top mounting/bearing retaining nut	3 Top mounting/ bearing	5 Rear suspension strut
2 Retaining cup	4 Upper spring seat	6 Gaiter
		7 Bump stop

holding it in an upright position, by moving the piston through a full stroke, and then through short strokes of 50 to 100 mm. In both cases, the resistance felt should be smooth and continuous. If the resistance is jerky, uneven, or if there is any visible sign of wear or damage to the strut, renewal is necessary.

10 Reassembly is a reversal of dismantling, noting the following points:

a) *Make sure that the coil spring ends are correctly located in the upper seat and strut before releasing the compressor.*

b) *Tighten the thrust bearing retaining nut to the specified torque.*

---

14 Rear anti-roll bar and links (Saloon/Hatchback models) – removal and refitting

Removal

1 Chock the front wheels then jack up the rear of the vehicle and support on axle stands (see *Jacking and vehicle support*). Remove the rear wheel.

2 Unscrew the nuts securing the anti-roll bar links to the rear suspension struts on both sides.

3 Unscrew the bolts securing the anti-roll bar mounting clamps to the rear suspension crossmember **(see illustration)**, then unhook the clamps and withdraw the anti-roll bar from under the vehicle. Identify the left- and right-hand sides of the bar to ensure correct refitting.

4 Unscrew the nuts and remove the links from the anti-roll bar.

5 Examine the rubber bushes for the mounting clamps and links, and if necessary renew them. The links are available individually.

14.3 Rear anti-roll bar mounting clamp bolts

Refitting

6 Locate the anti-roll bar on the rear crossmember, hook the mounting clamps in position, and insert the bolts. Tighten the bolts to the specified torque.

7 Locate the anti-roll bar links on the struts and bar. Refit the nuts and tighten them to the specified torque.

8 Refit the rear wheels, and lower the vehicle to the ground.

---

15 Rear suspension lower arms (Saloon/Hatchback models) – removal and refitting

Removal

1 Chock the front wheels then jack up the rear of the vehicle and support on axle stands (see *Jacking and vehicle support*). Remove the relevant rear wheel.

Front lower arm

2 On models with xenon headlamps, a headlamp levelling sensor is located on the front left-hand lower suspension arm. If removing this arm, remove the sensor by first disconnecting the wiring, then releasing the connecting rod and unbolting the sensor.

3 Release the rubber mounting supporting the intermediate exhaust system.

4 Release the rubber mounting supporting the rear exhaust system, then lower the exhaust system onto an axle stand. On models with the 2.5 litre engine, release both rear rubber mountings.

5 Carefully mark the position of the rear suspension subframe on the underbody to ensure correct relocation. **Note:** *Ford technicians use special alignment pins to locate the subframe accurately.*

6 Support the rear subframe using a trolley jack and block of wood.

7 Unscrew and remove the subframe mounting bolts.

8 Lower the subframe sufficient to access the front lower arm retaining nut and bolt.

9 Check the markings on the lower arm to ensure correct refitting.

10 Unscrew the outer bolt securing the lower arm to the knuckle, then unscrew the inner bolt securing the lower arm to the subframe. Withdraw the arm from under the vehicle.

Rear lower arm

11 Check the markings on the lower arm to ensure correct refitting.

12 Unscrew the outer bolt securing the lower arm to the knuckle, then unscrew the inner bolt securing the lower arm to the subframe. Withdraw the arm from under the vehicle.

Refitting

13 Refitting is a reversal of the removal procedure, noting the following points:

a) *The arm mounting bolts should be finger-tightened initially, and only fully tightened after the vehicle is lowered to the ground, so that its weight is on the rear suspension. Note that the rear lower arm is marked TOP for correct refitting (see illustration).*

b) *The rear toe setting should be checked, and if necessary adjusted, at the earliest opportunity.*

16 Rear suspension tie-bar (Saloon/Hatchback models) – removal and refitting

Removal

1 Chock the front wheels then jack up the rear of the vehicle and support on axle stands (see *Jacking and vehicle support*). Remove the relevant rear wheel.
2 Unbolt the cover from over the tie-bar.
3 Where applicable, unhook the exhaust mounting rubber from the tie-bar front mounting bracket.
4 On models with xenon headlamps, the levelling sensor wiring is attached to the left-hand tie-bar. Release the wiring from the clips.
5 Release the handbrake cable from the clips on the tie-bar.
6 Release the ABS rear wheel speed sensor wiring from the tie-bar.
7 Unscrew and remove the bolt securing the tie-bar to the bottom of the knuckle.
8 At the front of the tie-bar, unscrew and remove the two bolts securing the mounting bracket to the underbody. Withdraw the tie-bar from under the car.
9 With the tie-bar on the bench, unscrew and remove the front pivot bolt and remove the bracket from the tie-bar.
10 It is not possible to renew the rubber bushes – if they are worn excessively, the tie-bar should be renewed complete.

Refitting

11 Refitting is a reversal of the removal procedure, noting the following points:
a) *The bracket-to-underbody bolts should be fully tightened to the specified torque before lowering the vehicle.*
b) *The bolts securing the tie-bar to the bracket and knuckle should be finger-tightened initially, and only fully tightened after the vehicle is lowered to the ground, so that its weight is on the rear suspension.*

17 Rear suspension crossmember (Saloon/Hatchback models) – removal and refitting

Removal

1 Chock the front wheels then jack up the rear of the vehicle and support on axle stands (see *Jacking and vehicle support*). Remove both rear wheels.

15.13 TOP marking on the rear lower arm

2 On models with xenon headlamps, a headlamp levelling sensor is located on the left-hand lower suspension arm. Remove the sensor by first disconnecting the wiring, then releasing the connecting rod and unbolting the sensor.
3 Unscrew the nuts and disconnect the catalytic converter (petrol models) or front silencer (diesel models) from the exhaust front pipe. On diesel models the front flexible section must be protected with a temporary splint (refer to the appropriate part of Chapter 4). Recover the gasket/ring. It is recommended that the gasket/ring and nuts are renewed on refitting.
4 Release the front, intermediate and rear rubber exhaust mountings, then lower the exhaust as far as possible and support it on axle stands.
5 Unscrew the nuts and disconnect both anti-roll bar links from the anti-roll bar.
6 Reach in behind the rear hubs and disconnect the wiring from the ABS wheel speed sensors on both sides.
7 At each rear brake caliper, push the handbrake lever forwards then unhook the inner cable from the fitting.
8 Release the handbrake outer cables from the caliper brackets. Where a plastic ferrule is fitted to the outer cable, it will be necessary to compress the plastic tangs in order to release it from the bracket.
9 Working on both sides, unscrew the mounting bolts securing the brake caliper bracket to the strut, and slide the caliper complete with pads from the discs. Support the calipers to one side on axle stands, taking care not to strain the flexible brake hoses.
10 Unscrew the bolts and remove the front and rear lower arms from the knuckles on both sides.
11 Unscrew the bolts and remove each tie-bar from the bottom of the struts.
12 Working on each side in turn, use a trolley jack to raise the suspension strut and move it outwards from the ledges on the crossmember. Lower the jack to release the tension on the strut coil springs.
13 Support the crossmember using two trolley jacks. It is recommended that an assistant be available for the removal of the crossmember, as it is heavy.
14 Carefully mark the exact position of the

crossmember on the underbody to ensure correct refitting. **Note:** *Ford technicians use special alignment pins to locate the subframe accurately.*
15 Unscrew the mounting bolts (two each side) then lower the crossmember to the ground.

Refitting

16 Raise the crossmember against the underbody, and position it accurately with the marks made during removal. If available, use the special Ford alignment pins. Insert the mounting bolts and tighten to the specified torque.
17 Working on each side in turn, use a trolley jack to raise the suspension struts and position them on the crossmember ledges.
18 Refit each tie-bar to the bottom of the struts, and insert the bolts finger-tight. All suspension bolts are fully tightened with the vehicle weight on the suspension.
19 Refit the front and rear lower arms to the knuckles, and insert the bolts finger-tight.
20 Refit the brake calipers complete with pads to the struts, and tighten the mounting bracket bolts to the specified torque.
21 Refit the handbrake outer cables and hook the inner cables onto the caliper levers.
22 Reconnect the wiring to the ABS wheel speed sensors on both sides.
23 Reconnect the anti-roll bar links to the anti-roll bar, and tighten the nuts to the specified torque.
24 Relocate the exhaust system on the rubber mountings and reconnect to the front pipe using a new gasket/ring and nuts. Refer to the appropriate part of Chapter 4 if necessary, and apply anti-seize grease to the studs before refitting the nuts. On diesel models, remove the temporary splint.
25 On models with xenon headlamps, refit the sensor to the lower arm and tighten the bolts. Reconnect the connecting rod and the wiring. **Note:** *After refitting, the headlamp levelling system must be initialised by a Ford dealer using a special setting instrument.*
26 Refit the rear wheels and lower the car to the ground.
27 Fully tighten the front and rear arm and tie-bar mounting bolts/nuts to the specified torque.
28 Have the rear wheel toe setting checked and adjusted at the earliest opportunity (see Section 35).

18 Rear suspension tie-bar/knuckle (Estate models) – removal and refitting

Removal

1 Remove the rear hub as described in Section 10.
2 On models with xenon headlamps, a headlamp levelling sensor is located on the front left-hand lower suspension arm.

18.11 Position the spacer (1) as shown and raise the rear lower arm (2), when removing and refitting the rear tie-bar/knuckle (Estate)

Disconnect the wiring from the sensor and release it from the knuckle.

3 Release the ABS wheel speed sensor wiring from the tie-bar/knuckle.

4 Pull the handbrake cable through the aperture in the tie-bar/knuckle.

5 Unbolt the cover from the front of the tie-bar/knuckle.

6 Release the handbrake cable from the clip on the front of the tie-bar/knuckle.

7 Where applicable, unhook the exhaust system rubber mounting from the tie-bar/knuckle.

8 A suitable rod or bar must now be fabricated in order to hold the rear of the tie-bar/knuckle at its design height setting. This will prevent damage to the rubber mountings, and enable the mounting bolts to be tightened to their specified torque before lowering the vehicle to the ground. Fabricate a 20 mm by 186 mm long metal bar for this purpose.

9 Using a socket through the hole in the bottom of the rear lower arm, unscrew the anti-roll bar link securing nut.

10 Refer to Section 21 and remove the coil spring. Only use a purpose-made coil spring compressor to do this.

11 With the coil spring removed, raise the rear lower arm and position the bar described in paragraph 8 as shown **(see illustration)**.

12 Unbolt the front lower arm from the tie-bar/knuckle.

13 Unbolt the upper arm from the tie-bar/knuckle.

14 Unbolt the shock absorber from the tie-bar/knuckle.

15 Unbolt the rear lower arm from the tie-bar/knuckle.

16 Support the weight of the tie-bar/knuckle, then unbolt the front bracket from the under-body and lower the tie-bar/knuckle to the ground.

17 Unscrew the front pivot bolt and separate the bracket from the tie-bar/knuckle.

Refitting

18 Refitting is a reversal of the removal procedure, but tighten all nuts and bolts to the specified torque. Finally, check and if necessary adjust the rear wheel toe setting as described in Section 35.

19.3 Removing the shock absorber lower mounting bolt (Estate)

19 Rear shock absorber (Estate models) – removal, testing and refitting

Removal

1 Chock the front wheels then jack up the rear of the vehicle and support on axle stands (see *Jacking and vehicle support*). Remove the relevant rear wheel.

2 Position a trolley jack under the coil spring area of the rear lower suspension arm, to keep the coil spring in compression.

3 Unscrew and remove the shock absorber lower mounting bolt **(see illustration)**.

4 Unscrew and remove the upper mounting bolt, and withdraw the shock absorber from under the vehicle. Access to the upper bolt is difficult, and a socket drive with universal joint may be required **(see illustration)**.

Testing

5 Check the mounting rubbers for damage and deterioration. If they are worn, the complete shock absorber must be renewed, as they are not available separately.

6 Mount the shock absorber in a vice, gripping it by the lower mounting. Examine the shock absorber for signs of fluid leakage. Test the operation of the shock absorber by moving it through a full stroke, and then through short strokes of 50 to 100 mm. In both cases, the resistance felt should be smooth and continuous. If the resistance is jerky or uneven, the shock absorber should be renewed.

20.3 Rear anti-roll bar mounting clamp

19.4 Access to the shock absorber upper bolt is difficult

Refitting

7 Refitting is a reversal of the removal procedure, however, do not fully tighten the mounting bolts to the specified torque until the full weight of the vehicle is on its suspension. Note that on models fitted with load-levelling shock absorbers, the tab on the upper mounting must point outwards.

20 Rear anti-roll bar and links (Estate models) – removal and refitting

Removal

1 Chock the front wheels then jack up the rear of the vehicle and support on axle stands (see *Jacking and vehicle support*). Remove both rear wheels.

2 Unscrew the nuts securing the anti-roll bar links to the rear lower arms. The nuts are accessed through the holes in the bottom of the arms.

3 Unscrew the bolts securing the anti-roll bar mounting clamps to the rear suspension crossmember **(see illustration)**. Release the clamps, and withdraw the anti-roll bar from under the vehicle.

4 Unscrew the nuts and remove the links from the anti-roll bar **(see illustration)**.

5 Examine the rubber bushes for the mounting clamps and links, and if necessary renew them. The links are available individually, and the rubbers can be pulled from the ends of the bar.

20.4 Anti-roll bar links

Refitting

6 Where removed, fit the new rubbers in position on the bar, with their flat surfaces facing upwards. Also refit the links to the bar and tighten the upper mounting nuts to the specified torque.

7 Locate the anti-roll bar on the rear crossmember, then refit the clamps and tighten the bolts to the specified torque.

8 Refit the anti-roll bar links to the rear lower arms, and tighten the nuts to the specified torque, while holding the actual links stationary in their central position.

9 Refit the rear wheels, and lower the vehicle to the ground.

---

21 Rear coil spring (Estate models) – removal and refitting

Note: *Before attempting to remove the rear suspension coil spring, a tool to hold the coil spring in compression must be obtained. Careful use of conventional coil spring compressors will prove satisfactory.*

Removal

1 Chock the front wheels then jack up the rear of the vehicle and support on axle stands (see *Jacking and vehicle support*). Remove the relevant rear wheel.

2 With no weight on the rear suspension, the shock absorber will be fully extended and will support the lower arm. Mark the spring to ensure it is refitted correctly **(see illustration)**.

3 Fit the coil spring compressor tools (ensuring they are fully engaged), and compress the coil spring until all tension is relieved from the upper mounting.

⚠ *Warning: The coil spring will be under extreme tension; make sure that the compressor tools are fitted correctly.*

4 Release the bump stop from the crossmember, then withdraw it together with the coil spring from under the vehicle.

5 If a new coil spring is to be fitted, the original coil spring must be released from the compressor. If it is to be re-used, the coil spring can be left in compression.

21.2 Rear coil spring (Estate)

Refitting

6 Refitting is a reversal of the removal procedure, but make sure that the bump stop is located correctly on the crossmember, and that the ends of the coil spring are correctly located in the crossmember and lower arm before releasing the spring tension.

---

22 Rear suspension rear lower arm (Estate models) – removal and refitting

Removal

1 Chock the front wheels then jack up the rear of the vehicle and support on axle stands (see *Jacking and vehicle support*). Remove the relevant wheel.

2 The bolt securing the rear lower arm to the crossmember has an eccentric head and spacer, which are used to adjust the rear toe setting. Before removing this bolt, mark its position, using a scriber or similar sharp instrument.

3 Remove the rear suspension coil spring as described in Section 21.

4 A suitable rod or bar must now be fabricated in order to hold the rear of the tie-bar/knuckle at its design height setting. This will prevent damage to the rubber mountings, and enable the mounting bolts to be tightened to their specified torque before lowering the vehicle to the ground. Fabricate a 20 mm by 186 mm long metal bar for this purpose.

5 With the coil spring removed, raise the rear lower arm and position the bar as described in Section 18 **(see illustration 18.11)**.

6 Unscrew the nut securing the anti-roll bar link to the rear lower arm. The nut is accessed through the hole in the bottom of the arm **(see illustration)**.

7 On models with xenon headlamps, a headlamp levelling sensor is located on the left-hand lower suspension arm. Disconnect the wiring from the sensor and unclip it from the lower arm.

8 Unscrew and remove the bolt securing the rear lower arm to the tie-bar knuckle.

9 Unscrew and remove the eccentric bolt and withdraw the lower arm from the crossmember **(see illustration)**.

Refitting

10 Refitting is a reversal of the removal procedure, but tighten all nuts and bolts to the specified torque. Finally, check and if necessary adjust the rear wheel toe setting as described in Section 35.

---

23 Rear suspension front lower arm and brace (Estate models) – removal and refitting

Removal

1 Chock the front wheels then jack up the rear of the vehicle and support on axle stands (see *Jacking and vehicle support*). Remove the rear wheels.

2 The brace is fitted across the cross-member, between the two inner pivots of the front lower arms. To remove the brace, unscrew the two nuts and withdraw the brace from the crossmember **(see illustration)**. Do not remove the bolts from the crossmember.

3 To remove a front lower arm, first remove the brace, then remove the inner pivot bolt from the crossmember. Note which way round the mounting bolts are fitted.

4 Unscrew and remove the outer pivot bolt, and withdraw the arm from the crossmember and knuckle **(see illustration)**.

22.6 Nut securing the anti-roll bar link to the rear lower arm

22.9 Eccentric bolt securing the lower arm to the crossmember

23.2 Brace securing nut

23.4 Front lower arm outer mounting

24.3 Rear suspension upper arm (Estate)

Refitting

5 Refitting is a reversal of the removal procedure, but delay fully tightening the mounting bolts until the weight of the vehicle is on the rear suspension. Note that the bolts are fitted with their heads facing forwards.

24 Rear suspension upper arm (Estate models) – removal and refitting

Removal

1 Chock the front wheels then jack up the rear of the vehicle and support on axle stands (see *Jacking and vehicle support*). Remove the relevant wheel.
2 Support the rear suspension tie-bar/knuckle on a trolley jack. Note which way round the mounting bolts are fitted.
3 Unscrew and remove the mounting bolts, and withdraw the arm from the tie-bar/knuckle and crossmember **(see illustration)**.

Refitting

4 Refitting is a reversal of the removal procedure, but delay fully tightening the mounting bolts until the weight of the vehicle is on the rear suspension. Note that the outer bolt is fitted with its head facing forwards, whereas the inner bolt is fitted with its head facing rearwards.

25 Rear suspension crossmember (Estate models) – removal and refitting

Removal

1 Remove both rear tie-bars/knuckles as described in Section 18.
2 On models with xenon headlamps, a headlamp levelling sensor is located on the left-hand lower suspension arm. Remove the sensor by first disconnecting the wiring, then releasing the connecting rod and unbolting the sensor.
3 Working on each side in turn, remove the brake calipers and mounting brackets as described in Chapter 9, however, disconnect

the flexible hoses at the crossmember brackets instead of at the calipers. To do this, unscrew the rigid brake line union nuts, then pull out the retaining clips and remove the hoses from the crossmember. Plug or tape over the brake pipes and hoses to prevent entry of dust and dirt.
4 The bolts securing the rear lower arms to the crossmember have eccentric heads and spacers, which are used to adjust the rear toe setting. Before removing these bolts, mark their positions, using a scriber or similar sharp instrument.
5 Unscrew and remove the inner pivot bolts and disconnect the lower arms from the crossmember.
6 With the help of an assistant, support the rear crossmember on one or two trolley jacks.
7 Unscrew the three mounting bolts on each side, then carefully lower the crossmember to the ground. Note that guide pins are incorporated in the crossmember to ensure correct refitting.
8 If necessary, remove the suspension components from the crossmember as described in the appropriate Sections of this Chapter.

Refitting

9 Refitting is a reversal of the removal procedure, noting the following points:
a) When raising the crossmember, locate the guide pins in the holes provided in the underbody, then insert and fully tighten the mounting bolts.
b) Delay fully tightening the suspension arm mounting bolts until the weight of the vehicle is on the rear suspension.

26.4 Unscrew the steering wheel retaining bolt . . .

c) Tighten all bolts to the specified torque.
d) Bleed the brake hydraulic system as described in Chapter 9.
e) Check, and if necessary adjust, the rear wheel toe setting as described in Section 35.

26 Steering wheel – removal and refitting

⚠ **Warning: All models are equipped with an airbag system. Make sure that the safety recommendations given in Chapter 12 are followed, to prevent personal injury.**

Removal

1 Disconnect the battery negative lead (refer to *Disconnecting the battery* at the end of this manual).

⚠ *Warning: Before proceeding, wait a minimum of one minute after disconnecting the battery, as a precaution against accidental firing of the airbag unit. This period ensures that any stored energy in the back-up capacitor is dissipated. We suggest you wait several minutes.*
2 Turn the steering wheel so that the front wheels are in the straight-ahead position.
3 Remove the airbag unit from the steering wheel as described in Chapter 12.

⚠ *Warning: Position the airbag module in a safe place, with the airbag and trim cover facing up as a precaution against accidental operation.*
4 Make sure that the steering lock is not engaged by inserting the ignition key. Identify the top of the steering wheel to aid refitting (note the steering wheel can only be fitted in three positions). Unscrew the retaining bolt from the centre of the steering wheel **(see illustration)**.
5 Remove the steering wheel from the top of the column, while feeding the horn and airbag wiring through the hole in the steering wheel hub **(see illustration)**.

Refitting

6 Make sure that the front wheels are still facing straight-ahead, then locate the steering

26.5 . . . and remove the steering wheel from the top of the column

wheel on the top of the steering column while feeding the horn and airbag wiring through the centre hole.

7 Refit the retaining bolt, and tighten it to the specified torque while holding the steering wheel. Do not tighten the bolt with the steering lock engaged, as this may damage the lock.

8 Refit the airbag unit with reference to Chapter 12.

9 Reconnect the battery negative lead (refer to *Disconnecting the battery* at the end of this manual).

27 Steering column – removal, inspection and refitting

Warning: All models are equipped with an airbag system. Make sure that the safety recommendations given in Chapter 12 are followed, to prevent personal injury.

Removal

1 Disconnect the battery negative lead (refer to *Disconnecting the battery* at the end of this manual).

Warning: Before proceeding, wait a minimum of one minute after disconnecting the battery, as a precaution against accidental firing of the airbag unit. This period ensures that any stored energy in the back-up capacitor is dissipated. We suggest you wait several minutes.

2 Turn the steering wheel so that the front wheels are in the straight-ahead position. At this stage, the steering wheel can be removed as described in Section 26, or alternatively left in position and removed together with the column.

Warning: If the steering wheel is left in situ, use adhesive tape to hold it in the straight-ahead position. Failure to do this may result in damage to the airbag and clock spring.

3 Working in the driver's footwell, undo the retaining screws and unclip the lower facia panel from under the steering column. Where applicable, disconnect the wiring from the

27.8a Disconnecting the ignition switch wiring . . .

27.9a Disconnecting the passive anti-theft system (PATS) wiring . . .

electronic automated temperature control (EATC) sensor located on the panel.

4 Where applicable, remove the insulation pad from over the foot pedals.

5 Where fitted, remove the audio control switch from the steering column lower shroud. Use a small screwdriver to release the locking tang, then lift the switch from the column and disconnect the wiring.

6 Remove the steering column upper shroud from the lower shroud by inserting a thin screwdriver between the clip on each side.

7 Undo the three screws and remove the lower shroud.

8 Disconnect the ignition switch and turn signal switch wiring connectors **(see illustrations)**.

9 On the right-hand side of the steering column, disconnect the wiring connectors for the passive anti-theft system (PATS)

27.8b . . . and turn signal switch wiring

27.9b . . . and wiper/washer switch wiring

transceiver, wiper/washer switch and airbag clock spring **(see illustrations)**.

10 Note the routing of the airbag clock spring wiring, then undo the screw and remove the spreader plate from under the column **(see illustrations)**.

11 On models with Electronic Stability Programme (ESP), disconnect the wiring from the steering wheel rotation sensor at the bottom of the column.

12 Unscrew and remove the clamp bolt securing the column intermediate shaft to the flexible coupling on the steering gear. Rotate the clamp plate through 180°, and release the shaft from the coupling **(see illustrations)**. Note that the coupling has a triangular shape and the shaft may only be fitted in one of three positions. Discard the clamp bolt and obtain a new one.

13 Support the steering column, then

27.10a Undo the screws . . .

27.10b . . . and remove the spreader plate from under the column

27.12a Unscrew the clamp bolt . . .

27.12b ... and rotate the clamp plate through 180°

27.13a Steering column mounting bolt locations

27.13b Using a Torx key to unscrew the steering column mounting bolts

27.13c Lowering the steering column from the bulkhead

unscrew the four mounting bolts with a Torx key. Slide the column upwards to disengage the retaining tab from the groove in the cross-beam then lower the column from the bulkhead crossbar bracket (see illustrations). Discard the bolts and obtain new ones.

Inspection

14 With the steering column removed, check the universal joints for wear, and examine the column upper and lower shafts for any signs of damage or distortion. Where evident, the column should be renewed complete.
15 Examine the height adjustment lever mechanism for wear and damage. Lock the mechanism before refitting the column.
16 With the steering lock disengaged, turn the inner column, and check the upper and lower bearings for smooth operation. At the time of writing it was not possible to obtain the column bearings separately, so if

excessive wear is evident, the column assembly must be renewed complete.

Refitting

17 Before refitting the steering column, the inner safety telescopic tube must be set to 70.00 mm by temporarily fitting a metal spacer. First apply some silicone grease to the inner tube and fully extend and retract the column several times. Now make up the spacer and attach it to the inner column with two plastic cable ties (see illustration).
18 Locate the steering column on its bracket, making sure that the tab slides down into the groove correctly, then insert the **new** mounting bolts and tighten to the specified torque.
19 With the front wheels and steering wheel still in their straight-ahead positions, locate the steering column shaft on the flexible coupling, swivel the clamp plate anti-

clockwise, then insert a **new** bolt and tighten to the specified torque.
20 Remove the temporary spacer from the inner column.

⚠ *Warning: Failure to remove the temporary spacer could result in personal injury in the event of an accident.*

21 On models with Electronic Stability Programme (ESP), reconnect the wiring to the steering wheel rotation sensor at the bottom of the column.
22 Make sure that the clock spring wiring loom is routed inside the spreader plate depression, then refit the spreader plate to the column and tighten the retaining screw.
23 On the right-hand side of the steering column, reconnect the wiring connectors for the passive anti-theft system (PATS) transceiver, wiper/washer switch and airbag clock spring.
24 Beneath the steering column, reconnect the ignition switch and turn signal switch wiring connectors.
25 Refit the column lower shroud and tighten the three screws.
26 Refit the column upper shroud. Press down on the shroud to engage the clips.
27 Where fitted, refit the audio control switch to the steering column, and reconnect the wiring.
28 Where applicable, refit the insulation pad over the foot pedals.
29 Refit the lower facia panel, and where applicable reconnect the wiring to the electronic automated temperature control (EATC) sensor. Insert and tighten the screws.
30 If removed, refit the steering wheel with reference to Section 26.
31 Reconnect the battery negative lead (refer to *Disconnecting the battery* at the end of this manual), and initialise the door window motors as described in Chapter 11.
32 On models with Electronic Stability Programme (ESP), have the steering wheel rotation sensor initialised by a Ford dealer.

28 Steering column flexible coupling – removal and refitting

Removal

1 Apply the handbrake, then jack up the front of the vehicle and support it on axle stands (see *Jacking and vehicle support*). Turn the steering to the straight-ahead position and lock it. Remove both front wheels.
2 Working in the driver's footwell, undo the retaining screws and unclip the lower facia panel from under the steering column. Where applicable, disconnect the wiring from the electronic automated temperature control (EATC) sensor located on the panel.
3 Where applicable, remove the insulation pad from over the foot pedals.
4 Unscrew and remove the clamp bolt

27.13d The steering column removed from the vehicle

27.17 The 70.00 mm spacer attached to the steering column with cable ties securing the steering inner column to the flexible coupling on the steering gear. Rotate the clamp plate clockwise and detach the clamp from the coupling. Note that the coupling stub has a triangular shape and the shaft may only be fitted in one of three positions. Discard the bolt as a new one must be fitted on reassembly.

⚠️ **Warning: Make sure that the steering wheel remains locked in its straight-ahead position while the clamp is disconnected from the flexible coupling. Failure to do this may result in damage to the airbag and clock spring, and subsequent personal injury in the event of an accident.**

5 Hold the radiator in the upper mountings using temporary split pins inserted through the holes in the upper location pins. Access to the holes is gained through the apertures in the front crossmember.
6 Undo the screws and remove the splash shield from under the radiator position. On diesel models, also remove the engine undertray and left-hand wheel arch lower liner.
7 Under the front of the car, unbolt the hose bracket (where fitted) next to the left-hand radiator support bracket, then unbolt and remove both radiator support brackets.
8 Unscrew the nuts and disconnect the anti-roll bar links from the front suspension struts. If necessary, use a 5 mm Allen key to hold the spindles while the nuts are loosened.
9 On 1.8 and 2.0 litre petrol engines, and all diesel engines, remove the exhaust flexible pipe from the front of the exhaust system with reference to the appropriate part of Chapter 4.
10 On the 2.5 litre petrol engine, remove the exhaust dual converter Y-pipe with reference to the appropriate part of Chapter 4.
11 Remove the engine rear support/link with reference to the appropriate part of Chapter 2.
12 On all petrol models, disconnect the catalytic converter monitor sensor wiring, and unclip the wiring from the subframe.
13 On models with xenon headlamps, release the ties and detach the headlamp levelling sensor wiring harness from the subframe.
14 Release the radiator cooling fan wiring harness from the subframe.
15 Support the front suspension subframe on one or two trolley jacks. If necessary, enlist the help of an assistant.
16 Carefully mark the position of the front suspension subframe on the underbody to ensure correct refitting. **Note:** *Ford technicians use special alignment pins to locate the subframe accurately when refitting.* Unscrew and remove the subframe rear mounting bolts, then unbolt the rear brackets from the subframe.
17 Unscrew and remove the subframe front mounting bolts.
18 Lower the subframe uniformly approximately 150 mm, making sure that the lower arm rear hydro-bushes are not strained or damaged.

19 Mark the coupling in relation to the steering gear pinion shaft to aid refitting, then use an Allen key to unscrew the clamp bolt and withdraw the coupling from the splines on the pinion shaft. Discard the bolt and obtain a new one. On right-hand drive models, also withdraw the seal from the bulkhead.

Refitting

20 On right-hand drive models, locate the seal on the bulkhead.
21 Locate the coupling on the pinion shaft splines making sure that the clamp bolt hole is aligned with the annular groove. Insert the new bolt, and tighten to the specified torque.
22 Raise the subframe against the underbody, and position it accurately with the marks made during removal. If available, use the special Ford alignment pins. Refit the rear bracket, then insert the mounting bolts. Tighten all of the subframe and rear bracket bolts to the specified torque. Make sure the subframe does not move during tightening of the bolts. If applicable, remove the Ford alignment pins.
23 Secure the radiator cooling fan wiring harness to the subframe with plastic cable ties.
24 On models with xenon headlamps, secure the headlamp levelling sensor wiring to the subframe clips.
25 On all petrol models, reconnect the catalytic converter monitor sensor wiring and secure with the clips.
26 Refit the engine rear support/link with reference to the appropriate part of Chapter 2.
27 On 1.8 and 2.0 litre petrol engines, and all diesel engines, refit the exhaust flexible pipe to the front of the exhaust system with reference to the appropriate part of Chapter 4.
28 On the 2.5 litre petrol engine, refit the exhaust dual converter Y-pipe with reference to the appropriate part of Chapter 4.
29 Reconnect the anti-roll bar links to the front suspension struts and tighten the nuts to the specified torque. If necessary, use a 5 mm Allen key to hold the spindles while the nuts are loosened.
30 Refit the hose bracket (where fitted) and the two radiator support brackets, and tighten the bolts to the specified torque.
31 Refit the splash shield under the radiator position and tighten the screws. On diesel models, also refit the engine undertray and left-hand wheel arch lower liner.
32 Remove the temporary split pins holding the radiator to its upper mountings.
33 Apply some silicone grease to the steering column inner tube and fully extend and retract the column several times. Before refitting the steering column to the flexible coupling, the inner safety telescopic tube must be set to 70.00 mm by temporarily fitting a metal spacer. Make up the spacer and attach it to the inner column with two plastic cable ties (refer to Section 27 if necessary).
34 Locate the steering column shaft on the flexible coupling, swivel the clamp plate anti-

clockwise, then insert a **new** bolt and tighten to the specified torque.
35 Remove the temporary spacer from the inner column.

⚠️ *Warning: Failure to remove the temporary spacer could result in personal injury in the event of an accident.*

36 Where applicable, refit the insulation pad over the foot pedals.
37 Refit the lower facia panel beneath the steering column, and where necessary reconnect the wiring to the electronic automated temperature control (EATC) sensor.
38 Refit the front wheels, then lower the vehicle to the ground.
39 Have the front suspension wheel alignment checked and adjusted at the earliest opportunity.
40 If on completion, the car pulls to one side, or abnormal tyre wear is noted, have the subframe alignment checked by a Ford dealer.

29 Steering gear – removal and refitting

Removal

1 Remove the steering column flexible coupling as described in Section 28. This procedure includes lowering the front suspension subframe by 150 mm.
2 Loosen the nuts securing the steering track rod ends to the knuckle steering arms on each side. Using a balljoint separator tool, release the balljoints from the steering arms. Fully unscrew the nuts and disconnect the track rod ends from the arms. If necessary, use a 5 mm Allen key to hold the balljoints stationary while the nuts are loosened. Discard the nuts as new ones must be used on refitting.
3 Remove the bulkhead seal from the steering gear pinion shaft **(see illustration)**.
4 To reduce the loss of hydraulic fluid from the power steering circuit, either syphon the fluid from the reservoir, or fit a hose clamp to the supply and return hoses.
5 Release the power steering hydraulic lines from the retaining clips on the steering gear.

29.3 Bulkhead seal on the steering gear

29.6a Hydraulic lines to the control valve on the steering gear (note the tape over the apertures to prevent entry of dust and dirt)

6 Note the location of each hydraulic line on the steering gear, then unscrew the union nuts and pull the lines a short distance away from the steering gear. Be prepared for some loss of hydraulic fluid by positioning a suitable container beneath the steering gear. Tape over or plug the lines and apertures to prevent entry of dust and dirt **(see illustrations)**. Remove and discard the O-ring seals, and obtain new ones.

7 Unscrew and remove the steering gear mounting bolts. The bolts are located on top of the steering gear, and are difficult to reach. Ideally, the special U-shaped Ford spanner should be used, but it is just possible to reach them with a normal spanner **(see illustrations)**. Discard the bolts and obtain new ones.

8 Carefully withdraw the steering gear to one side, taking care not to damage the brake lines and components on the underbody.

29.7a Steering gear right-hand mounting bolt . . .

29.7c Steering gear on the subframe

29.6b Hydraulic line to power steering ram

Refitting

9 Locate the steering gear on the subframe, and insert the two **new** mounting bolts. Tighten the bolts to the specified torque. Note that, if the special Ford tool is being used, the bottom of the tool must be turned anti-clockwise in order to tighten the mounting bolts.

10 Using new O-ring seals, reconnect the hydraulic lines to the steering gear and tighten the union nuts to the specified torque. The seals are located in grooves in the union nuts, and ideally they should be protected from the threads with a plastic tube or similar adapter. Where applicable, remove the hose clamps from the hoses.

11 Secure the hydraulic lines in the retaining clips on the steering gear.

12 Refit the bulkhead seal to the steering gear pinion shaft.

13 Refit the track rod end balljoints to the

29.7b . . . and left-hand mounting bolt

29.7d The steering gear mounting bolts are just accessible with a normal spanner

steering knuckles, and tighten the **new** nuts to the specified torque. If necessary, use a 5 mm Allen key to hold the balljoints stationary while the nuts are tightened.

14 Refit the steering column flexible coupling with reference to Section 28.

15 Fill and bleed the power steering hydraulic system as described in Section 32.

16 Have the front wheel alignment checked, and if necessary adjusted, at the earliest opportunity (refer to Section 35).

17 On models with Electronic Stability Programme (ESP), have the steering wheel rotation sensor initialised by a Ford dealer.

30 Power steering gear rubber gaiter – renewal

1 Apply the handbrake, then jack up the front of the vehicle and support it on axle stands (see *Jacking and vehicle support*). Remove the relevant wheel.

2 On diesel models, remove the engine undershield, and also remove the wheel arch lower liner from the left-hand side.

3 Remove the track rod end and its locknut from the track rod, as described in Section 31. Note the exact position of the track rod end on the track rod, in order to retain the front wheel alignment setting on refitting.

4 Wipe clean the outer surfaces of the rubber gaiter, then disconnect the breather pipe. Note the location of the breather pipe stub for correct refitting. Also clean the track rod.

5 Release the inner and outer retaining clips securing the gaiter to the steering gear and track rod. Note the position of the gaiter on the track rod.

6 Disconnect the inner end of the gaiter from the steering gear housing, then pull the outer end from the track rod.

7 Remove the gaiter clips and discard them. New clips are supplied with the new gaiter.

8 Scrape off all grease from the old gaiter, and apply to the track rod inner joint. Wipe clean the seating areas on the steering gear housing and track rod.

9 Apply a little grease to the track rod, then slide the new gaiter into position. Position the inner end on the steering gear housing, and the outer end at its previously-noted position on the track rod.

10 Position the breather pipe stub at the top as previously-noted, then refit and tighten the inner and outer retaining clips. If crimp-type clips are supplied, tighten them with a pair of pincers.

11 Reconnect the breather pipe.

12 Refit the track rod end with reference to Section 31.

13 On diesel models, refit the wheel arch lower liner and engine undershield.

14 Refit the wheel and lower the vehicle to the ground.

15 Have the front wheel alignment checked, and if necessary adjusted, at the earliest opportunity (refer to Section 35).

31.2 Steering track rod end

31.3 Loosen (only) the nut while using an Allen key to hold the balljoint shaft . . .

31.4 . . . then use a balljoint separator tool to release the balljoint from the steering arm

31 Track rod end – renewal

Removal

1 Apply the handbrake, then jack up the front of the vehicle and support it on axle stands (see *Jacking and vehicle support*). Remove the relevant front roadwheel.

2 Slacken the locknut on the track rod by a quarter-turn **(see illustration)**. Hold the track rod end stationary with another spanner engaged with the special flats while loosening the locknut.

3 Loosen the nut securing the steering track rod end to the knuckle steering arm. Do not remove the nut at this stage as it will protect the balljoint threads. If necessary, use an Allen key to hold the balljoint shaft while loosening the nut **(see illustration)**.

4 Using a balljoint separator tool, release the balljoint from the steering arm **(see illustration)**. If the balljoint is to be re-used, take care not to damage the dust cover when using the separator tool. Fully unscrew the nut and disconnect the track rod end from the arm. If necessary, use a 5 mm Allen key to hold the balljoint stationary while the nut is loosened. Discard the nut as a new one must be used on refitting.

5 Count the number of exposed threads visible on the inner section of the track rod, and record this figure.

6 Unscrew the track rod end from the track rod, counting the number of turns necessary to remove it. If necessary, hold the track rod stationary with grips.

Refitting

7 Screw the track rod end onto the track rod by the number of turns noted during removal, until it just contacts the locknut.

8 Engage the shank of the balljoint with the steering knuckle arm, and refit the **new** nut. Tighten the nut to the specified torque. If the balljoint shank turns while the nut is being tightened, use a 5 mm Allen key to hold the shank, or alternatively press down on the track rod. The tapered fit of the shank will lock it, and prevent rotation as the nut is tightened.

9 Hold the track rod stationary with one spanner, then tighten the track rod end locknut to the specified torque.

10 Refit the roadwheel, and lower the vehicle to the ground.

11 Finally check, and if necessary adjust, the front wheel alignment as described in Section 35.

32 Power steering hydraulic system – bleeding and flushing

1 Following any operation in which the power steering fluid lines have been disconnected, the power steering system must be bled, to remove any trapped air. If the vehicle has covered a high mileage and the fluid is noticeably discoloured or dirty, the old fluid must be flushed and new fluid installed.

Bleeding

2 With the front wheels in the straight-ahead position, check the power steering fluid level in the reservoir and, if low, add fresh fluid until it reaches the MAX mark. Pour the fluid slowly, to prevent air bubbles forming, and use only the specified fluid (refer to *Weekly checks* and Chapter 1A or 1B).

3 Start the engine, and allow it to run at idle speed. Check the hoses and connections for leaks.

4 Stop the engine, and recheck the fluid level. Add more if necessary, up to the MAX mark.

5 Start the engine again, allow it to idle, then bleed the system by slowly turning the steering wheel from side-to-side several times. This should purge the system of all internal air. However, if air remains in the system (indicated by the steering operation being very noisy), leave the vehicle overnight, and repeat the procedure again the next day.

6 If air still remains in the system, it may be necessary to resort to the Ford method of bleeding, which uses a hand-operated vacuum pump. Turn the steering to the right until it is near the stop, then switch off the engine. Fit the vacuum pump to the fluid reservoir, and apply 15.0 in Hg of vacuum. Maintain the vacuum for a minimum of 5 minutes, then repeat the procedure with the steering turned to the left. If

the vacuum decreases by more than 2.0 in Hg in the 5 minutes, check the hoses for leaks.

7 Keep the fluid level topped-up throughout the bleeding procedure. Note that, as the fluid temperature increases, the level will rise in the reservoir.

Flushing

Note: *This procedure involves turning the engine on the starter motor.*

8 Apply the handbrake, then jack up the front of the vehicle and support it on axle stands (see *Jacking and vehicle support*).

Petrol models

9 Remove the engine top cover.

10 Position a suitable container beneath the hydraulic fluid reservoir. Have ready a cap to fit onto the reservoir return stub. Loosen the clip and disconnect the return hose, then allow the fluid to drain from the reservoir and hose into the container. Position the cap on the reservoir return stub.

11 Disconnect the crankshaft position sensor wiring from the right-hand end of the engine (this is necessary to temporarily prevent the fuel injection and ignition systems from working). If necessary, remove the lower plastic cover from the right-hand wheel housing for access to the sensor.

12 Disconnect the HT wiring from the spark plugs, then unscrew and remove the spark plugs. Refer to Chapter 1A if necessary.

Diesel models

13 Remove the oil filler cap and the oil level dipstick, then remove the engine top cover. Refit the filler cap and dipstick to prevent dust and dirt entry into the lubrication system.

14 Remove the glow plug relay from the fusebox with reference to Chapter 12.

15 On models with common rail injection, disconnect the wiring from the injector control valves, and also disconnect the wiring from the fuel high pressure sensor and camshaft position sensor.

16 Unscrew the nuts and disconnect the wiring from the glow plugs, then unscrew and remove them (refer to the appropriate part of Chapter 5 if necessary).

17 Unclip and remove the radiator grille from the engine compartment front crossmember.

33.5 Fit a cap to the reservoir stub

33.6 Removing the plastic clip at the rear of the hydraulic fluid reservoir

18 Unscrew the mounting bolt securing the power steering fluid reservoir to the inner wheel arch panel
19 Position a suitable container beneath the hydraulic fluid reservoir. Have ready a cap to fit onto the reservoir return stub. Loosen the clip and disconnect the return hose, then allow the fluid to drain from the reservoir and hose into the container. Position the cap on the reservoir return stub.

All models

20 Pour fresh fluid into the reservoir up to the MAX mark. Do not agitate the fluid prior to pouring it, as air may be introduced.
21 An assistant will be required for this procedure. Do not allow the level of fluid to drop below the MIN mark on the reservoir.
22 While directing the fluid from the return hose into the container, have the assistant crank the engine on the starter motor for 30 seconds and turn the steering wheel slowly from lock-to-lock. **Note:** *Do not exceed 30 seconds, as the starter motor may overheat causing internal damage. Wait at least 60 seconds before activating the starter motor again.*
23 Top up the fluid to the MAX mark on the reservoir.
24 Repeat the procedure described in the last two paragraphs, using 1.0 litre of fresh fluid. Turn off the ignition switch.
25 Remove the cap from the fluid reservoir, and immediately reconnect the return hose. Tighten the retaining clip.
26 Refit and reconnect the relevant components as applicable for petrol or diesel

models, then bleed the system again as described above.

33 Power steering pump – removal and refitting

Removal

1.8 and 2.0 litre petrol models

Note: *If fitting a new power steering pump, a new drive pulley must be fitted at the same time.*

1 Disconnect the battery negative lead (refer to *Disconnecting the battery* at the end of this manual).
2 Apply the handbrake, then jack up the front of the vehicle and support it on axle stands (see *Jacking and vehicle support*). Remove the right-hand roadwheel.
3 Unbolt and remove the splash shield for access to the crankshaft pulley. Note the routing of the auxiliary drivebelt, and mark it with an arrow to indicate its normal (clockwise) rotational direction. Turn the auxiliary drivebelt tensioner clockwise using a spanner on the centre bolt, then slip the drivebelt from the pulleys and remove from under the wheel arch.
4 At this stage, removal of the power steering pump will be made easier if the pulley is first removed using a suitable puller, as this will allow access to the high pressure line union, however, it is just possible to remove the pump without loosening the union and leaving

the pulley in position. The following paragraphs describe removal leaving the pulley in position. **Note:** *If a new pump is being fitted, a tool will be required to press a new pulley onto the pump driveshaft.*

5 Syphon the hydraulic fluid from the power steering fluid reservoir. Position cloth rags beneath the pump, then loosen the clip and disconnect the fluid outlet (cooler) hose. Fit a cap to the reservoir stub and plug the hose, and tie the hose to one side **(see illustration)**. Recover the two seals.
6 Release the wiring loom from the plastic clip at the rear of the hydraulic fluid reservoir, then remove the plastic clip **(see illustration)**.
7 Unscrew the fluid reservoir mounting stud/bolts (1 rear stud and 2 side bolts), then tilt the reservoir back and remove it from the pump **(see illustrations)**. Plug the reservoir outlet and pump aperture to prevent entry of dust and dirt. Remove the O-ring seals from the reservoir and discard them; obtain new ones for refitting. **Note:** *The reservoir contains a filter which must not be contaminated. Make sure the filler cap is tightened firmly.*
8 If the pulley has not been removed, it will not be possible to unscrew the high pressure outlet union, and in this case the in-line union at the flexible hose-to-pressure switch near the pump should be unscrewed. If the pulley has been removed, unscrew the outlet union securing the high pressure pipe to the pump. Tape over or plug the line and aperture.
9 Unscrew the hydraulic line support bracket retaining nut, disconnect the wiring from the hydraulic line pressure switch, then unscrew the mounting bolts and studs and withdraw the power steering pump from the engine. Where applicable, unscrew the high pressure union nut and disconnect the line **(see illustrations)**.

2.5 litre petrol models

10 Disconnect the battery negative lead (refer to *Disconnecting the battery* at the end of this manual).
11 Apply the handbrake, then jack up the front of the vehicle and support it on axle stands (see *Jacking and vehicle support*). Remove the right-hand roadwheel.
12 Unbolt and remove the splash shield for access to the crankshaft pulley. Note the

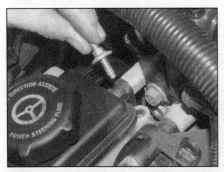

33.7a Remove the rear mounting stud ...

33.7b ... and side mounting bolts ...

33.7c ... then remove the hydraulic fluid reservoir from the power steering pump

33.9a Unscrew the hydraulic line support bracket retaining nut . . .

33.9b . . . disconnect the wiring from the pressure switch . . .

33.9c . . . then unscrew the mounting bolts . . .

33.9d . . . and studs

33.9e Power steering pump removed from the engine (2.0 litre petrol)

routing of the auxiliary drivebelt, and mark it with an arrow to indicate its normal rotational direction. Turn the auxiliary drivebelt tensioner clockwise using a spanner on the centre bolt, then slip the drivebelt from the pulleys and remove from under the wheel arch.

13 Position a suitable container beneath the power steering pump, then unscrew the union nut securing the high pressure line to the pump. Unbolt the support bracket and disconnect the hydraulic fluid high pressure line from the pump. Allow the fluid to drain, then tape over or plug the end of the line and the aperture in the pump to prevent entry of dust and dirt.

14 Syphon the hydraulic fluid from the power steering fluid reservoir, or alternatively fit a hose clamp to the reservoir hose leading to the pump. Loosen the clip and disconnect the hose.

15 Unscrew the reservoir mounting bolt from the inner wheel arch, and move the reservoir to one side.

16 Unscrew the coolant expansion tank mounting bolts from the inner wheel arch, and move the tank to one side.

17 Release the spark plug HT leads and plastic holder from the right-hand engine mounting.

18 Using a trolley jack and block of wood beneath the sump, temporarily support the weight of the engine. Make sure the engine is supported safely.

19 Unscrew the nuts securing the right-hand engine mounting bracket to the engine, and also unscrew the bolts securing the bracket to the inner wheel arch. Remove the bracket.

20 Unbolt the drive pulley from the power steering pump. If necessary, the pulley may be held stationary using an 8 mm Allen key or with a screwdriver inserted through one of the holes in the pulley.

21 At the front of the power steering pump, unscrew the mounting bracket retaining bolt.

22 Unscrew the small nuts from the retaining plate, then unscrew the two main bolts from the retaining plate.

23 Unscrew the two mounting bolts, then remove the retaining plate followed by the pump itself.

24 If fitting a new pump, unbolt the elbow and union from the old pump. Discard the O-ring seals and obtain new ones.

Diesel engine models

25 Disconnect the battery negative lead (refer to *Disconnecting the battery* at the end of this manual).

26 Undo the fasteners and remove the upper engine cover.

27 Release the coolant hose from the plastic clip, then loosen the clips and remove the air intake elbow.

28 Unscrew and remove the two bolts securing the air intake pipe and exhaust gas recirculation (EGR) tube.

29 Note the routing of the power steering pump drivebelt, and mark it with an arrow to indicate its normal rotational direction.

30 Using a suitable square tool in the special hole at the top of the drivebelt tensioner, rotate the tensioner clockwise then slip the drivebelt from the camshaft and pump pulleys. Release the tensioner.

31 Unscrew the bolt securing the fluid high-pressure line bracket to the left-hand end of the cylinder head **(see illustration)**.

32 Position a suitable container beneath the power steering pump, then loosen the clip and disconnect the return hose from the bottom of the pump. Allow the fluid to drain into the container. Alternatively, fit a hose clamp to the hose.

33 Unscrew the union and disconnect the high pressure line from the top of the pump **(see illustration)**. Be prepared for some loss of fluid. Remove the union O-ring seal and discard it; a new one must be fitted on refitting.

34 Unscrew and remove the power steering pump support bracket bolts **(see illustration)**.

35 Unscrew the mounting bolts and remove the pump from the water pump housing **(see illustrations)**.

36 If fitting a new pump, unbolt the pulley from the old unit.

33.31 Power steering hydraulic fluid high-pressure line support bracket

33.33 High pressure line to the top of the power steering pump

33.34 The power steering pump support bracket bolts

33.35a Unscrew the mounting bolts . . .

33.35b . . . and remove the power steering pump from the water pump housing bracket

Refitting

1.8 and 2.0 litre petrol models

37 If necessary, the sealing ring on the high-pressure outlet union nut should be renewed. Ideally, the special Ford sleeve should be used to prevent damage to the ring as it passes over the union threads, however, a suitable alternative can be made out of plastic tubing or by wrapping suitable tape over the threads. Note that new pumps are supplied with new unions.

38 If the drive pulley is already fitted to the pump, connect the high pressure line and screw on the union. Tighten the union to the specified torque.

39 Locate the pump on the engine, insert the mounting bolts and studs, and tighten them to the specified torque.

40 If the drive pulley has not been fitted at this stage, refit the high pressure pipe and tighten the union to the specified torque.

41 Refit the hydraulic line support bracket and tighten the retaining nut securely.

42 Fit new O-ring seals to the hydraulic fluid reservoir outlet, then refit the reservoir to the pump **(see illustrations)**. Insert the reservoir mounting stud/bolts and tighten to the specified torque.

43 Refit the plastic clip to the rear of the reservoir, then locate the wiring loom in it.

44 Reconnect the fluid outlet (cooler) hose to the reservoir and tighten the clip.

45 At this stage, if a new pump is being fitted, the new pulley should be pressed onto the pump driveshaft using the special Ford

tool or similar. The pulley must be pressed on flush with the end of the shaft.

46 Turn the auxiliary drivebelt tensioner clockwise, then locate the drivebelt on the pulleys and release the tensioner. Make sure the multi-vee serrations of the belt locate correctly on the pulleys. If the original belt is being refitted, make sure it is fitted the same way around as noted on removal.

47 Refit the crankshaft pulley splash shield, then refit the roadwheel and lower the vehicle to the ground.

2.5 litre petrol models

48 Where applicable, fit the elbow and union to the power steering pump, using new O-ring seals, and tighten the bolts and union to the specified torque.

49 Refit the retaining plate to the pump, and tighten the nuts and two main bolts to the specified torque.

50 Locate the pump on the engine, refit the mounting bolts and tighten to the specified torque. Also refit and tighten the mounting bracket retaining bolt at the front of the pump.

51 Refit the pulley and tighten to the specified torque while holding it stationary as for removal.

52 Refit the right-hand engine mounting bracket and tighten the nuts and bolts to the specified torque. Remove the trolley jack from under the engine.

53 Refit the spark plug HT leads and plastic holder to the right-hand engine mounting.

54 Refit the coolant expansion tank and tighten the mounting bolts.

55 Refit the power steering fluid reservoir and tighten the mounting bolt.

56 Reconnect the fluid hose to the pump and tighten the clip.

57 If necessary, the sealing ring on the high-pressure outlet union nut should be renewed. Ideally, the special Ford sleeve should be used to prevent damage to the ring as it passes over the union threads, however, a suitable alternative can be made out of plastic tubing or by wrapping suitable tape over the threads. Note that new pumps are supplied with new unions.

58 Reconnect the high pressure line to the pump and tighten the union to the specified torque. Refit the support bracket bolt and tighten securely.

59 Turn the auxiliary drivebelt tensioner clockwise, then locate the drivebelt on the pulleys and release the tensioner. Make sure the multi-vee serrations of the belt locate correctly on the pulleys. If the original belt is being refitted, make sure it is fitted the same way around as noted on removal.

60 Refit the crankshaft pulley splash shield, then refit the roadwheel and lower the vehicle to the ground.

Diesel models

61 Where applicable, fit the pulley to the pump and tighten the bolts to the specified torque.

62 If necessary, the sealing ring on the high-pressure outlet union nut should be renewed. Ideally, the special Ford sleeve should be used to prevent damage to the ring as it

33.42a Fit a new large diameter seal . . .

33.42b . . . and small diameter seal to the power steering hydraulic fluid reservoir outlet . . .

33.42c . . . then refit the reservoir to the pump

passes over the union threads, however, a suitable alternative can be made out of plastic tubing or by wrapping suitable tape over the threads. Note that new pumps are supplied with new unions.

63 On the rear of the pump, apply spline lubricant to the splines on the water pump drive.

64 Refit the power steering pump to the water pump housing, then insert the mounting bolts and tighten to the specified torque.

65 Refit the support bracket and tighten the bolts securely.

66 Reconnect the high pressure line and tighten the union to the specified torque.

67 Reconnect the fluid return hose and tighten the clip.

68 Refit the fluid high-pressure line bracket to the left-hand end of the cylinder head, and tighten the bolt securely.

69 Locate the auxiliary drivebelt on the camshaft and pump pulleys. Using the special tool, rotate the tensioner clockwise and position the belt on the tensioner pulley. Release the tensioner and check that the belt is correctly located on each pulley.

All models

70 Reconnect the battery negative lead (refer to *Disconnecting the battery* at the end of this manual), and finally initialise the electric window motors as described in Chapter 11.

71 Fill and bleed the power steering system with reference to Section 32.

34 Power steering fluid cooler – removal and refitting

Removal

1 Disconnect the battery negative (earth) lead (refer to *Disconnecting the battery* at the end of this manual).

2 Apply the handbrake, then jack up the front of the vehicle and support it on axle stands.

3 The fluid hoses to and from the cooler must now be disconnected. The connections at the cooler itself are inaccessible with the unit in place, so trace the hoses back from the cooler, and disconnect them at the front of the subframe. Alternatively, remove the front bumper as described in Chapter 11 for access **(see illustration)**. Have a container ready to catch spilt fluid, and plug the open hose ends quickly, to prevent fluid loss and dirt entry.

4 Unscrew and remove the cooler mounting screws, taking care not to damage the radiator (or the air conditioning condenser). Slide the cooler (and where applicable, its hoses) out of position **(see illustration)**. Handle the unit carefully, as the cooling fins are easily damaged.

Refitting

5 Refitting is a reversal of removal. It may be wise to replace the spring-type hose clips

34.3 Fluid hose connection to the power steering fluid cooler

with screw-type items when reconnecting the fluid hoses. On completion, fill and bleed the power steering system as described in Section 32.

35 Wheel alignment and steering angles – general information

1 Accurate front wheel alignment is essential to provide positive steering, and to prevent excessive tyre wear. Before considering the steering/suspension geometry, check that the tyres are correctly inflated, that the front wheels are not buckled, and that the steering linkage and suspension joints are in good order, without slackness or wear. Alignment of the front subframe is also critical to the front suspension geometry – refer to a Ford dealer for accurate setting-up.

2 Wheel alignment consists of four factors **(see illustration):**

Camber is the angle at which the front wheels are set from the vertical, when viewed from the front of the vehicle. 'Positive camber' is the amount (in degrees) that the wheels are tilted outward at the top of the vertical.

Castor is the angle between the steering axis and a vertical line, when viewed from each side of the car. 'Positive castor' is when the steering axis is inclined rearward at the top.

Steering axis inclination is the angle (when viewed from the front of the vehicle) between the vertical and an imaginary line drawn through the suspension strut upper mounting and the lower suspension arm balljoint.

Toe setting is the amount by which the distance between the front inside edges of the roadwheels (measured at hub height) differs from the diametrically-opposite distance measured between the rear inside edges of the front roadwheels.

3 With the exception of the toe setting, all other steering angles are set during manufacture, and no adjustment is possible. It can be assumed, therefore, that unless the vehicle has suffered accident damage, all the preset steering angles will be correct. Should there be some doubt about their accuracy, it

34.4 Power steering cooler mounting screw

37.2 Wheel alignment and steering angles

will be necessary to seek the help of a Ford dealer, as special gauges are needed to check the steering angles.

4 Two methods are available to the home mechanic for checking the front wheel toe setting. One method is to use a gauge to measure the distance between the front and rear inside edges of the roadwheels. The other method is to use a scuff plate, in which each front wheel is rolled across a movable plate which records any deviation, or scuff, of the tyre from the straight-ahead position as it moves across the plate. Relatively-inexpensive equipment of both types is available from accessory outlets.

5 If, after checking the toe setting using whichever method is preferable, it is found that adjustment is necessary, proceed as follows.

6 Turn the steering wheel onto full-left lock, and record the number of exposed threads on the right-hand track rod. Now turn the steering onto full-right lock, and record the number of threads on the left-hand track rod. If there are the same number of threads visible on both sides, then subsequent adjustment can be made equally on both sides. If there are more threads visible on one side than the other, it will be necessary to compensate for this during adjustment. After adjustment, there must be the same number of threads visible on each track rod. This is most important.

7 To alter the toe setting, slacken the locknut on the track rod, and turn the track rod using self-locking pliers to achieve the desired setting. When viewed from the side of the car, turning the rod clockwise will increase the toe-in, turning it anti-clockwise will increase the toe-out. Only turn the track rods by a quarter of a turn each time, and then recheck the setting.

8 After adjustment, tighten the locknuts. Reposition the steering gear rubber gaiters, to remove any twist caused by turning the track rods.

9 The rear wheel toe setting may also be checked and adjusted, but as this additionally requires alignment with the front wheels, it should be left to a Ford dealer or specialist having the required equipment.

Chapter 11
Bodywork and fittings

Contents

Degrees of difficulty

Easy, suitable for novice with little experience | **Fairly easy,** suitable for beginner with some experience | **Fairly difficult,** suitable for competent DIY mechanic | **Difficult,** suitable for experienced DIY mechanic | **Very difficult,** suitable for expert DIY or professional

Specifications

Torque wrench settings	Nm	lbf ft
Bonnet hinge to body and bonnet	25	18
Bonnet latch	8	6
Bonnet	23	17
Boot lid hinge to body	23	17
Boot lid to hinge	23	17
Bumper mounting to body	15	11
Door check strap to door	6	4
Door check strap to door pillar	23	17
Door striker	28	21
Exterior mirror	2	1
Front seat belt height adjuster	25	18
Front seat belt stalk and pretensioner	50	37
Front seats	25	18
Rear bumper to mounting bracket	20	15
Rear seat backrest (4-door)	25	18
Rear seat backrest centre hinge pin	20	15
Rear seat backrest centre locking plate	25	18
Rear seat backrest hinge bolts	55	41
Rear seat backrest latch	30	22
Rear seat belt centre stalk (4-door Saloon)	55	41
Rear seat cushion	25	18
Seat belt lower anchor	38	28
Seat belt retractor	38	28
Seat belt upper anchor	38	28
Tailgate	23	17

1 General information

The bodyshell and underframe on all models is of all-steel welded construction, incorporating progressive crumple zones at the front and rear, and a rigid centre safety cell.

The bulkhead behind the engine compartment incorporates crash grooves which determine its energy-absorption characteristics, and special beams to prevent the intrusion of the front wheels into the passenger compartment during a serious accident. All passenger doors incorporate side impact bars.

All sheet metal surfaces which are prone to corrosion are galvanised. The painting process includes a base colour which closely matches the final topcoat, so that any stone damage is not as noticeable.

The door hinges are bolted to both the door and body, and the striker plates have integral contact switches.

The front and rear bumpers have foam elements built into them, which spread the forces to the crumple zones in the event of an accident. The driver and passenger seats have a built-in active function; in the event of a rear end crash, pressure against the seat back causes the headrest to be pushed forwards and upwards. The bonnet hinges are pretensioned to avoid vibrations at high speed.

Automatic seat belts are fitted, and the front seat belt stalks are mounted on automatic tensioners. In the event of a serious front impact, the system is triggered and pulls the stalk buckle downwards to tension the seat belt. It is not possible to reset the tensioner once fired, and it must therefore be renewed. The tensioners are fired by an explosive charge similar to that used in the airbag, and are triggered via the airbag control module.

Central locking with 'double-locking' is fitted as standard. The lock mechanism is disconnected (when the system is in use) from the interior door handles, making it impossible to open any of the doors or the tailgate/boot lid from inside the vehicle. This means that, even if a thief should break a side window, he will not be able to open the door using the interior handle. In the event of a serious accident, a crash sensor unlocks all doors if they were previously locked. The central locking system is monitored and controlled by the Generic Electronic Module (GEM) which also synchronises the locking functions of the doors. If the vehicle is unlocked with the remote control but no door is opened and the ignition not switched on within 45 seconds, the GEM automatically relocks the vehicle. All windows and the sunroof may be closed by pressing the remote control locking button for approximately 2 seconds, however, the action

is interrupted if an object becomes trapped. The bonnet is locked with the ignition key.

Many of the procedures in this Chapter require the battery to be disconnected (refer to *Disconnecting the battery* at the end of this manual).

2 Maintenance – bodywork and underframe

The general condition of a vehicle's bodywork is the one thing that significantly affects its value. Maintenance is easy, but needs to be regular. Neglect, particularly after minor damage, can lead quickly to further deterioration and costly repair bills. It is important also to keep watch on those parts of the vehicle not immediately visible, for instance the underside, inside all the wheel arches, and the lower part of the engine compartment.

The basic maintenance routine for the bodywork is washing – preferably with a lot of water, from a hose. This will remove all the loose solids which may have stuck to the vehicle. It is important to flush these off in such a way as to prevent grit from scratching the finish. The wheel arches and underframe need washing in the same way, to remove any accumulated mud, which will retain moisture and tend to encourage rust. Paradoxically enough, the best time to clean the underframe and wheel arches is in wet weather, when the mud is thoroughly wet and soft. In very wet weather, the underframe is usually cleaned of large accumulations automatically, and this is a good time for inspection.

Periodically, except on vehicles with a wax-based underbody protective coating, it is a good idea to have the whole of the underframe of the vehicle steam-cleaned, engine compartment included, so that a thorough inspection can be carried out to see what minor repairs and renovations are necessary. Steam-cleaning is available at many garages, and is necessary for the removal of the accumulation of oily grime, which sometimes is allowed to become thick in certain areas. If steam-cleaning facilities are not available, there are some excellent grease solvents available which can be brush-applied; the dirt can then be simply hosed off. Note that these methods should not be used on vehicles with wax-based underbody protective coating, or the coating will be removed. Such vehicles should be inspected annually, preferably just prior to Winter, when the underbody should be washed down, and any damage to the wax coating repaired. Ideally, a completely fresh coat should be applied. It would also be worth considering the use of such wax-based protection for injection into door panels, sills, box sections, etc, as an additional safeguard against rust damage, where such protection is not provided by the vehicle manufacturer.

After washing paintwork, wipe off with a chamois leather to give an unspotted clear finish. A coat of clear protective wax polish will give added protection against chemical pollutants in the air. If the paintwork sheen has dulled or oxidised, use a cleaner/polisher combination to restore the brilliance of the shine. This requires a little effort, but such dulling is usually caused because regular washing has been neglected. Care needs to be taken with metallic paintwork, as special non-abrasive cleaner/polisher is required to avoid damage to the finish. Always check that the door and ventilator opening drain holes and pipes are completely clear, so that water can be drained out. Brightwork should be treated in the same way as paintwork. Windscreens and windows can be kept clear of the smeary film which often appears, by the use of proprietary glass cleaner. Never use any form of wax or other body or chromium polish on glass.

3 Maintenance – upholstery and carpets

Mats and carpets should be brushed or vacuum-cleaned regularly, to keep them free of grit. If they are badly stained, remove them from the vehicle for scrubbing or sponging, and make quite sure they are dry before refitting. Seats and interior trim panels can be kept clean by wiping with a damp cloth. If they do become stained (which can be more apparent on light-coloured upholstery), use a little liquid detergent and a soft nail brush to scour the grime out of the grain of the material. Do not forget to keep the headlining clean in the same way as the upholstery. When using liquid cleaners inside the vehicle, do not over-wet the surfaces being cleaned. Excessive damp could get into the seams and padded interior, causing stains, offensive odours or even rot.

Caution: If the inside of the vehicle gets wet accidentally, it is worthwhile taking some trouble to dry it out properly, particularly where carpets are involved. Do not leave oil or electric heaters inside the vehicle for this purpose.

4 Minor body damage – repair

Minor scratches

If the scratch is very superficial, and does not penetrate to the metal of the bodywork, repair is very simple. Lightly rub the area of the scratch with a paintwork renovator, or a very fine cutting paste, to remove loose paint from the scratch, and to clear the surrounding bodywork of wax polish. Rinse the area with clean water.

Apply touch-up paint to the scratch using a fine paint brush; continue to apply fine layers of paint until the surface of the paint in the scratch is level with the surrounding paintwork. Allow the new paint at least two weeks to harden, then blend it into the surrounding paintwork by rubbing the scratch area with a paintwork renovator or a very fine cutting paste. Finally, apply wax polish.

Where the scratch has penetrated right through to the metal of the bodywork, causing the metal to rust, a different repair technique is required. Remove any loose rust from the bottom of the scratch with a penknife, then apply rust-inhibiting paint to prevent the formation of rust in the future. Using a rubber or nylon applicator, fill the scratch with bodystopper paste. If required, this paste can be mixed with cellulose thinners to provide a very thin paste which is ideal for filling narrow scratches. Before the stopper-paste in the scratch hardens, wrap a piece of smooth cotton rag around the top of a finger. Dip the finger in cellulose thinners, and quickly sweep it across the surface of the stopper-paste in the scratch; this will ensure that the surface of the stopper-paste is slightly hollowed. The scratch can now be painted over as described earlier in this Section.

Dents

When deep denting of the vehicle's bodywork has taken place, the first task is to pull the dent out, until the affected bodywork almost attains its original shape. There is little point in trying to restore the original shape completely, as the metal in the damaged area will have stretched on impact, and cannot be reshaped fully to its original contour. It is better to bring the level of the dent up to a point which is about 3 mm below the level of the surrounding bodywork. In cases where the dent is very shallow anyway, it is not worth trying to pull it out at all. If the underside of the dent is accessible, it can be hammered out gently from behind, using a mallet with a wooden or plastic head. Whilst doing this, hold a suitable block of wood firmly against the outside of the panel, to absorb the impact from the hammer blows and thus prevent a large area of the bodywork from being 'belled-out'.

Should the dent be in a section of the bodywork which has a double skin, or some other factor making it inaccessible from behind, a different technique is called for. Drill several small holes through the metal inside the area – particularly in the deeper section. Then screw long self-tapping screws into the holes, just sufficiently for them to gain a good purchase in the metal. Now the dent can be pulled out by pulling on the protruding heads of the screws with a pair of pliers.

The next stage of the repair is the removal of the paint from the damaged area, and from an inch or so of the surrounding 'sound' bodywork. This is accomplished most easily by using a wire brush or abrasive pad on a

power drill, although it can be done just as effectively by hand, using sheets of abrasive paper. To complete the preparation for filling, score the surface of the bare metal with a screwdriver or the tang of a file, or alternatively, drill small holes in the affected area. This will provide a really good 'key' for the filler paste.

To complete the repair, see the Section on filling and respraying.

Rust holes or gashes

Remove all paint from the affected area, and from an inch or so of the surrounding 'sound' bodywork, using an abrasive pad or a wire brush on a power drill. If these are not available, a few sheets of abrasive paper will do the job most effectively. With the paint removed, you will be able to judge the severity of the corrosion, and therefore decide whether to renew the whole panel (if this is possible) or to repair the affected area. New body panels are not as expensive as most people think, and it is often quicker and more satisfactory to fit a new panel than to attempt to repair large areas of corrosion.

Remove all fittings from the affected area, except those which will act as a guide to the original shape of the damaged bodywork (eg headlight shells etc). Then, using tin snips or a hacksaw blade, remove all loose metal and any other metal badly affected by corrosion. Hammer the edges of the hole inwards, in order to create a slight depression for the filler paste.

Wire-brush the affected area to remove the powdery rust from the surface of the remaining metal. Paint the affected area with rust-inhibiting paint, if the back of the rusted area is accessible, treat this also.

Before filling can take place, it will be necessary to block the hole in some way. This can be achieved by the use of aluminium or plastic mesh, or aluminium tape.

Aluminium or plastic mesh, or glass-fibre matting, is probably the best material to use for a large hole. Cut a piece to the approx-imate size and shape of the hole to be filled, then position it in the hole so that its edges are below the level of the surrounding body-work. It can be retained in position by several blobs of filler paste around its periphery.

Aluminium tape should be used for small or very narrow holes. Pull a piece off the roll, trim it to the approximate size and shape required, then pull off the backing paper (if used) and stick the tape over the hole; it can be overlapped if the thickness of one piece is insufficient. Burnish down the edges of the tape with the handle of a screwdriver or similar, to ensure that the tape is securely attached to the metal underneath.

Filling and respraying

Before using this Section, see the Sections on dent, deep scratch, rust holes and gash repairs.

Many types of bodyfiller are available, but generally speaking, those proprietary kits which contain a tin of filler paste and a tube of resin hardener are best for this type of repair. A wide, flexible plastic or nylon applicator will be found invaluable for imparting a smooth and well-contoured finish to the surface of the filler.

Mix up a little filler on a clean piece of card or board – measure the hardener carefully (follow the maker's instructions on the pack), otherwise the filler will set too rapidly or too slowly. Using the applicator, apply the filler paste to the prepared area; draw the applicator across the surface of the filler to achieve the correct contour and to level the surface. As soon as a contour that approximates to the correct one is achieved, stop working the paste – if you carry on too long, the paste will become sticky and begin to 'pick-up' on the applicator. Continue to add thin layers of filler paste at 20-minute intervals, until the level of the filler is just proud of the surrounding bodywork.

Once the filler has hardened, the excess can be removed using a metal plane or file. From then on, progressively-finer grades of abrasive paper should be used, starting with a 40-grade production paper, and finishing with a 400-grade wet-and-dry paper. Always wrap the abrasive paper around a flat rubber, cork, or wooden block – otherwise the surface of the filler will not be completely flat. During the smoothing of the filler surface, the wet-and-dry paper should be periodically rinsed in water. This will ensure that a very smooth finish is imparted to the filler at the final stage.

At this stage, the 'dent' should be surrounded by a ring of bare metal, which in turn should be encircled by the finely 'feathered' edge of the good paintwork. Rinse the repair area with clean water, until all of the dust produced by the rubbing-down operation has gone.

Spray the whole area with a light coat of primer – this will show up any imperfections in the surface of the filler. Repair these imperfections with fresh filler paste or bodystopper, and once more smooth the surface with abrasive paper. Repeat this spray-and-repair procedure until you are satisfied that the surface of the filler, and the feathered edge of the paintwork, are perfect. Clean the repair area with clean water, and allow to dry fully.

 HAYNES HiNT *If bodystopper is used, it can be mixed with cellulose thinners, to form a really thin paste which is ideal for filling small holes.*

The repair area is now ready for final spraying. Paint spraying must be carried out in a warm, dry, windless and dust-free atmosphere. This condition can be created artificially if you have access to a large indoor working area, but if you are forced to work in the open, you will have to pick your day very carefully. If you are working indoors, dousing the floor in the work area with water will help to settle the dust which would otherwise be in the atmosphere. If the repair area is confined to one body panel, mask off the surrounding panels; this will help to minimise the effects of a slight mis-match in paint colours. Bodywork fittings (eg chrome strips, door handles etc) will also need to be masked off. Use genuine masking tape, and several thicknesses of newspaper, for the masking operations.

Before commencing to spray, agitate the aerosol can thoroughly, then spray a test area (an old tin, or similar) until the technique is mastered. Cover the repair area with a thick coat of primer; the thickness should be built up using several thin layers of paint, rather than one thick one. Using 400-grade wet-and-dry paper, rub down the surface of the primer until it is really smooth. While doing this, the work area should be thoroughly doused with water, and the wet-and-dry paper periodically rinsed in water. Allow to dry before spraying on more paint.

Spray on the top coat, again building up the thickness by using several thin layers of paint. Start spraying at one edge of the repair area, and then, using a side-to-side motion, work until the whole repair area and about 2 inches of the surrounding original paintwork is covered. Remove all masking material 10 to 15 minutes after spraying on the final coat of paint.

Allow the new paint at least two weeks to harden, then, using a paintwork renovator, or a very fine cutting paste, blend the edges of the paint into the existing paintwork. Finally, apply wax polish.

Plastic components

With the use of more and more plastic body components by the vehicle manufacturers (eg bumpers. spoilers, and in some cases major body panels), rectification of more serious damage to such items has become a matter of either entrusting repair work to a specialist in this field, or renewing complete components. Repair of such damage by the DIY owner is not really feasible, owing to the cost of the equipment and materials required for effecting such repairs. The basic technique

involves making a groove along the line of the crack in the plastic, using a rotary burr in a power drill. The damaged part is then welded back together, using a hot-air gun to heat up and fuse a plastic filler rod into the groove. Any excess plastic is then removed, and the area rubbed down to a smooth finish. It is important that a filler rod of the correct plastic is used, as body components can be made of a variety of different types (eg polycarbonate, ABS, polypropylene).

Damage of a less serious nature (abrasions, minor cracks etc) can be repaired by the DIY owner using a two-part epoxy filler repair material. Once mixed in equal proportions, this is used in similar fashion to the bodywork filler used on metal panels. The filler is usually cured in twenty to thirty minutes, ready for sanding and painting.

If the owner is renewing a complete component himself, or if he has repaired it with epoxy filler, he will be left with the problem of finding a suitable paint for finishing which is compatible with the type of plastic used. At one time, the use of a universal paint was not possible, owing to the complex range of plastics encountered in body component applications. Standard paints, generally speaking, will not bond to plastic or rubber satisfactorily. However, it is now possible to obtain a plastic body parts finishing kit which consists of a pre-primer treatment, a primer and coloured top coat. Full instructions are normally supplied with a kit, but basically, the method of use is to first apply the pre-primer to the component concerned, and allow it to dry for up to 30 minutes. Then the primer is applied, and left to dry for about an hour before finally applying the special-coloured top coat. The result is a correctly-coloured component, where the paint will flex with the plastic or rubber, a property that standard paint does not normally posses.

5 Major body damage – repair

Where serious damage has occurred, or large areas need renewal due to neglect, it means that complete new panels will need

welding-in; this is best left to professionals. If the damage is due to impact, it will also be necessary to check completely the alignment of the bodyshell; this can only be carried out accurately by a Ford dealer, using special jigs. If the body is left misaligned, it is primarily dangerous, as the car will not handle properly, and secondly, uneven stresses will be imposed on the steering, suspension and possibly transmission, causing abnormal wear or complete failure, particularly to items such as the tyres.

6 Bumpers – removal and refitting

Front bumper

Removal

1 Apply the handbrake, then jack up the front of the vehicle and support it on axle stands (see *Jacking and vehicle support*).
2 Release the two clips, then remove the radiator grille from the front panel.
3 Where applicable, prise the headlamp washer covers from the front bumper.
4 Undo the screws and remove the splash shield from beneath the radiator.
5 Disconnect the wiring from the low temperature warning indicator on the bumper.
6 Where applicable, disconnect the wiring from the foglights.
7 Working on both sides, undo the screws securing the wheel arch liners to the front bumper **(see illustration)**.
8 Pull out the rear edge of the bumper on both sides, and unscrew the three mounting bolts **(see illustration)**.
9 With the aid of an assistant, carefully lift the front bumper away from the vehicle, noting how the location pegs engage the bracket on the front valance **(see illustrations)**.

Refitting

10 Refitting is a reversal of removal.

Rear bumper

Removal

11 Chock the front wheels then jack up the

6.7 Undo the screws securing the wheel arch liners to the front bumper . . .

6.8 . . . then undo the mounting bolts on each side . . .

6.9a . . . then withdraw the front bumper . . .

6.9b . . . noting how the location pegs engage the bracket

6.14 Unscrew the rear bumper front mounting bolts . . .

6.15 . . . the lower side screws . . .

rear of the vehicle and support on axle stands (see *Jacking and vehicle support*).

12 Open the rear tailgate or boot lid according to model.

13 On 4-door Saloon models, unscrew the two upper retaining screws securing the rear bumper to the boot lid inner panel.

14 Working in the rear of each rear wheel arch, unscrew the rear bumper front mounting bolts. The bolts are on the rear edges of the wheel arches **(see illustration)**.

15 Undo the lower screws from the sides of the bumper **(see illustration)**.

16 Working under the vehicle, undo the nuts securing the bumper to the spare wheel well **(see illustration)**.

17 On models equipped with a parking aid, disconnect the wiring from the sensors behind the bumper.

18 With the aid of an assistant, carefully lift the front bumper away from the vehicle **(see illustration)**.

Refitting

19 Refitting is a reversal of removal.

7 Radiator grille – removal and refitting

Removal

1 Support the bonnet in the open position.

2 Release the fasteners at each upper corner of the radiator grille. Twist the fasteners a quarter turn to release them **(see illustration)**.

3 Unhook the grille from its lower mountings and withdraw from the vehicle **(see illustration)**.

Refitting

4 Refitting is a reversal of the removal procedure.

8 Bonnet – removal, refitting and adjustment

Removal

1 Open the bonnet. The help of an assistant

6.16 . . . and the nuts on the spare wheel well . . .

will be necessary when the support struts are disconnected.

2 Undo the screws and remove the plastic resonator from the bonnet **(see illustrations)**.

3 Prise out the clips from the insulator panel

7.2 Twist the fasteners through a quarter turn to remove them

8.2a Undo the screws . . .

6.18 . . . then lift the rear bumper from the vehicle

on the underside of the bonnet, for access to the windscreen washer hoses **(see illustration)**. It is not necessary to completely remove the insulator.

4 Carefully pull the hoses from the washer

7.3 Unhooking the radiator grille from the crosspanel

8.2b . . . and remove the plastic resonator from the underside of the bonnet

8.3 Prise out the clips securing the insulator panel to the bonnet

8.4 Disconnecting the hoses from the washer jets

8.5 Disconnecting the washer jet heater wiring

8.7 Support strut and bonnet bracket

8.8 Unscrewing the bonnet-to-hinge mounting bolts

8.10 Bonnet striker

jets and release them from the retaining clips **(see illustration)**.
5 Disconnect the washer jet heater wiring, and release it from the retaining clips **(see illustration)**.
6 To assist in correctly realigning the bonnet when refitting it, mark the outline of the hinges with a soft pencil.
7 While an assistant supports the bonnet in its fully open position, prise off the spring clips and disconnect the support struts **(see illustration)**.
8 With the help of an assistant, unscrew the four bolts and lift the bonnet from the vehicle **(see illustration)**.

Refitting and adjustment

9 Refitting is a reversal of the removal procedure. If the original bonnet is being refitted, and the hinge positions were carefully noted, there should be no need to carry out a

full adjustment procedure, however, if a new bonnet is being fitted, proceed as follows.
10 Before refitting the support struts, slowly close the bonnet and check that the striker enters the lock centrally. If necessary, adjust the position of the bonnet at the hinge bolts and striker **(see illustration)**. Also check that, when closed, the bonnet is level with the front wings and windscreen scuttle cowl. With the adjustment complete, reconnect the support struts.

9 Bonnet lock –
removal, refitting and adjustment

Removal

1 Remove the radiator grille as described in Section 7.

9.2 Shear-bolts securing the cylinder private lock to the housing

9.3 Top view of the bonnet lock

2 The cylinder private lock assembly is attached to the security housing by shear-bolts, and it will be necessary to drill these out for access to the lock **(see illustration)**. Obtain new shear-bolts for refitting.
3 Use a soft pencil to mark the position of the bonnet lock on the front crossmember, then unscrew the mounting bolts and remove the lock **(see illustration)**.

Refitting and adjustment

4 Refitting is a reversal of the removal procedure, but position the lock as previously noted before tightening the bolts. Check that the bonnet striker enters the lock centrally. When refitting the cylinder private lock, tighten the new shear-bolts until their heads break off. Check that the front edge of the bonnet is level with the front wings, and if necessary, align the bonnet as described in Section 8.

10 Door inner trim panel –
removal and refitting

Removal

Front door

1 Disconnect the battery negative lead (refer to *Disconnecting the battery* at the end of this manual).
2 Prise out the plastic cover, then undo the screw securing the exterior mirror trim panel to the door. Withdraw the panel and

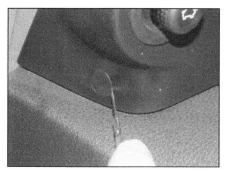

10.2a Prise out the plastic cover . . .

10.2b . . . then undo the screw . . .

10.2c . . . and disconnect the exterior mirror wiring

10.3a Prise out the plastic cover . . .

10.3b . . . then undo the screw . . .

10.3c . . . and slide off the bezel

disconnect the wiring from the control switch **(see illustrations)**.

3 Prise out the plastic cover, then use an Allen key to undo the screw securing the inner handle bezel to the door. Slide the bezel to one side over the inner door handle **(see illustrations)**.

4 Carefully prise out the cover from inside the door pocket, then undo the exposed screws securing the trim panel to the door **(see illustrations)**.

5 Undo the trim panel securing screws. There are two at the front, two at the rear and two at the bottom **(see illustration)**.

6 Lift the trim panel slightly to release the upper edge, then withdraw the panel from the door sufficiently to disconnect the wiring from the electric window switch **(see illustration)**.

7 If further dismantling of the door is required, remove the waterproof membrane as follows.

Prise out the electric window wiring loom retaining clip, then disconnect the exterior mirror wiring and slide the connector from the support. Undo the screws and remove the speaker from the door, then disconnect the

wiring. The membrane is attached to the inner door panel with adhesive; carefully pull back the membrane while using a knife to cut the adhesive **(see illustrations)**.

8 Place the membrane to one side and

10.4a Prise out the cover . . .

10.4b . . . and undo the screws

10.5 Removing the trim panel securing screws

10.6 Disconnecting the wiring from the electric window switch

10.7a Prise out the loom clip . . .

10.7b . . . disconnect the exterior mirror wiring . . .

10.7c . . . slide the connector from the support . . .

10.7d . . . remove the speaker . . .

10.7e . . . and cut the adhesive with a knife

10.10a Prise out the plastic cover . . .

10.10b . . . then undo the screw . . .

protect the adhesive from dust and dirt to enable it to be used again.

Rear door

9 Disconnect the battery negative lead (refer to *Disconnecting the battery* at the end of this manual).

10 Prise out the plastic cover, then use an Allen key to undo the screw securing the inner handle bezel to the door. Slide the bezel to one side over the inner door handle **(see illustrations)**.

11 Carefully prise out the cover from inside the door pocket, then undo the exposed screw securing the trim panel to the door **(see illustrations)**.

12 On models fitted with manual (ie, non-electric) windows, fully shut the window, and note the position of the regulator handle. Release the spring clip by inserting a clean cloth between the handle and the door trim. Using a 'sawing' action, pull the cloth against the open ends of the clip to release it, at the same time pulling the handle from the regulator shaft splines. Withdraw the handle (and where fitted, the spacer) and recover the clip.

13 Undo the trim panel securing screws. There are two at the front edge and two at the rear edge **(see illustration)**.

14 Lift the trim panel slightly to release the

10.10c . . . and remove the bezel

10.11a Prise out the cover . . .

10.11b . . . and undo the screw

10.13 Removing the trim panel securing screws

10.14 Disconnecting the wiring from the electric window switch upper edge, then withdraw the panel from the door. On models with electric windows, disconnect the wiring from the electric window switch **(see illustration)**.

15 If further dismantling of the door is required, remove the waterproof membrane as follows. Prise out the electric window wiring loom retaining clip, then undo the screws and remove the support bracket. Undo the screws and remove the speaker from the door, then disconnect the wiring. The membrane is attached to the inner door panel with adhesive; carefully pull back the membrane while using a knife to cut the adhesive **(see illustrations)**. Place the membrane to one side and protect the adhesive from dust and dirt to enable it to be used again.

Refitting

16 Refitting is a reversal of removal.

11 Door window glass – removal and refitting

Removal

Front door

1 With the ignition temporarily switched on, lower the front door window glass 160 mm from its closed position **(see illustration)**.
2 Remove the front door inner trim panel and waterproof membrane as described in Section 10 **(see illustration)**.
3 Using a socket through the inner door panel apertures, loosen the clamp bolts securing the window regulator to the glass **(see illustration)**.
4 Carefully prise out the inner glass weatherstrip from the inner door panel **(see illustration)**.
5 Lift the rear edge of the glass, then tilt the glass forwards and remove it upwards from the outside of the door **(see illustration)**.

Rear door

6 Lower the rear door window glass 160 mm from its closed position **(see illustration)**. On models with electric windows, it will be necessary to temporarily switch on the ignition.

10.15a Prise out the loom clip . . .

10.15c . . . remove the speaker . . .

7 Remove the rear door inner trim panel and waterproof membrane as described in Section 10.
8 Carefully prise out the inner glass weatherstrip from the inner door panel **(see illustration)**.

11.1 Lower the window glass 160 mm . . .

11.4 . . . remove the inner glass weatherstrip . . .

10.15b . . . remove the support bracket . . .

10.15d . . . then pull back the waterproof membrane

9 The window glass is attached to the regulator by a strong plastic clip which is quite difficult to access. Reach into the door through the openings in the inner door panel, and release the plastic clip **(see illustrations)**.

11.2 . . . remove the door inner trim panel and waterproof membrane . . .

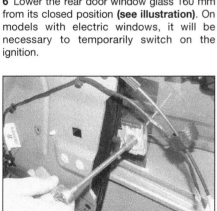

11.3 . . . loosen the clamp bolts securing the window regulator to the glass . . .

11.5 . . . and lift the glass from the outside of the front door

11.6 Lower the window glass 160 mm . . .

11.8 . . . and remove the inner glass weatherstrip

11.9a Plastic clip securing the window glass to the regulator

11.9b Reach through the two apertures to disconnect the clip

11.10a Pull back the window channel rubber weatherstrip . . .

11.10b . . . remove the glass outer weatherstrip . . .

10 On Estate models, the rear quarter light must be removed from the rear door before removing the window glass. It is suggested that the window regulator is also removed to provide additional working room. Pull back the window channel rubber weatherstrip and remove the glass outer weatherstrip, then unclip the plastic outer cover, undo the retaining screws and withdraw the quarter light from the door **(see illustrations)**.

11 Tilt the window glass forwards, and carefully lift it from the outside of the door **(see illustration)**.

Refitting

12 Refitting is a reversal of the removal procedure, but initialise the electric windows as described in Section 12.

11.10c . . . unclip the plastic outer cover . . .

11.10d . . . undo the retaining screws . . .

| 12 Door window regulator and motor – removal, refitting and initialisation |

Removal

Front door

1 Remove the front door window glass as described in Section 11.
2 Disconnect the wiring from the door window regulator **(see illustration)**.

11.10e . . . and withdraw the quarter light from the rear door

11.11 Removing the window glass from the rear door

12.2 Disconnecting the window regulator wiring

12.3a Release the plastic clip . . .

12.3b . . . then loosen the screws . . .

12.3c . . . and withdraw the regulator through the aperture in the inner door panel

12.3d Window regulator removed from the front door

12.5 Unscrew the single lower mounting bolt . . .

12.6a . . . then disconnect the wiring . . .

3 Release the plastic clip, loosen (but do not remove) the five regulator retaining screws, then lift the regulator and move the screws through the larger holes in the inner panel. Carefully withdraw the regulator from the rear aperture in the door **(see illustrations)**.

Rear door

4 Remove the rear door window glass as described in Section 11.
5 If the regulator is still mounted, loosen (but do not remove) the three upper regulator mounting bolts, then unscrew and remove the single lower mounting bolt securing the regulator to the bottom of the door **(see illustration)**.
6 Disconnect the wiring from the regulator motor, then lift the regulator and move the bolts through the larger holes in the inner panel. Carefully withdraw the regulator from the bottom aperture in the door **(see illustrations)**.

Refitting and initialisation

7 Refitting is a reversal of the removal procedure, however, tighten the mounting bolts securely and initialise each of the door window motors as follows. First, make sure that there is no obstruction in the window aperture. With the ignition switched on, press the switch close button until the window is fully closed, then hold the button in the closed position for a further second. Release the close button, then depress again two or three more times for a further one second. Press the switch open button until the window is fully open, then release. Press the switch close button to the second detent and

release. If the window does not close automatically, repeat the initialisation procedure. Repeat the initialisation for the remaining window motors.

13 Door handle and lock components – removal and refitting

Front door lock and handle

Removal

1 With the door open, prise out the grommet from the rear edge of the door. Pull out and hold the exterior handle, then loosen the handle retaining screw using an Allen key **(see illustrations)**.
2 On the driver's side, lift out the private lock cover **(see illustration)**.

13.1a Prise out the grommet . . .

12.6b . . . and withdraw the regulator from the bottom aperture of the door

3 Slide the door handle rearwards and withdraw it from the door. Recover the rubber gasket **(see illustration)**.
4 Remove the door inner trim panel and waterproof membrane as described in Section 10.

13.1b . . . pull out the exterior handle, and loosen the retaining screw with an Allen key

13.2 Remove the private lock cover from the driver's side

13.3 Removing the exterior handle rubber gasket

13.5a Undo the screw and remove the spacer . . .

13.5b . . . and release the inner door handle from the door

13.6 Disconnecting the wiring from the door lock actuator

13.7 Loosen the screw from the reinforcement plate

5 Undo the screw securing the inner door handle to the door, remove the spacer, and release the handle from the door **(see illustrations)**.

6 Disconnect the wiring from the door lock actuator **(see illustration)**.

7 Working through the aperture in the inner door panel, loosen (do not remove com-

pletely) the screw from the reinforcement plate **(see illustration)**. Slide the plate towards the front of the door and release the locking tangs from the slots in the outer door panel.

8 Unscrew the lock retaining screws from the rear edge of the door, and withdraw the lock complete with inner handle from the door **(see illustrations)**.

9 With the lock assembly on the bench, undo the screws and remove the security shield **(see illustration)**.

10 Release the clips and disconnect the connecting rods from the lock. Where necessary, rotate the rod through 90° to align the tab with the cut-out. Also disconnect the inner handle cable **(see illustrations)**.

11 Unclip the adjustment clip from the reinforcement plate. **Note:** *Ford recommend that the clip is renewed.*

12 It is not possible to remove the private lock cylinder separately.

13.8a Undo the retaining screws . . .

13.8b . . . and withdraw the lock and inner handle from the door

13.9 Undo the screws and remove the security shield

13.10a Disconnecting the rods . . .

13.10b . . . and cable

13.10c Private lock and security housing

13.15a Prise out the grommet . . .

13.15b . . . and loosen the handle retaining screw

13.16a Remove the handle and cover . . .

13.16b . . . followed by the rubber gasket

13.17a Undo the screw . . .

Refitting

13 Refitting is a reversal of removal. The adjustment clip should be fitted so that the lock is released after the exterior handle has moved approximately 22.0 mm from its closed position. There should then be approximately 5.0 to 6.0 mm of handle movement after the lock has been released. When closing the door slowly, there must be two audible clicks as the lock engages.

Rear door lock and handle

Removal

14 Remove the door inner trim panel and waterproof membrane as described in Section 10.
15 Prise out the grommet from the rear edge of the door. Pull out and hold the exterior handle, then loosen the handle retaining screw using an Allen key **(see illustrations)**.
16 Slide the door handle rearwards and withdraw it from the door. Remove the cover and rubber gasket **(see illustrations)**.

17 Undo the screw securing the inner door handle to the door, remove the spacer, and release the handle from the door **(see illustrations)**.
18 Disconnect the wiring from the door lock actuator **(see illustration)**.

19 Working through the aperture in the inner door panel, loosen (do not remove completely) the screw from the reinforcement plate. Slide the plate towards the front of the door and release the locking tangs from the slots in the door **(see illustrations)**.

13.17b . . . remove the spacer . . .

13.17c . . . and release the inner handle from the door

13.18 Disconnect the door lock actuator wiring . . .

13.19a . . . loosen the reinforcement plate screw . . .

13.19b . . . and slide the plate to release the locking tangs from the door

13.20a Unscrew the lock retaining screws . . .

13.20b . . . and withdraw the lock complete with inner handle from the door

13.21a Squeeze the plastic clip . . .

13.21b . . . and disconnect the reinforcement plate from the lock

13.22a Disconnecting the cable from the lock . . .

13.22b . . . and interior door handle

20 Unscrew the lock retaining screws from the rear edge of the door, and withdraw the lock complete with inner handle from the door (see illustrations).

21 With the lock assembly on the bench, use a pair of pliers to squeeze the plastic clip, then remove the reinforcement plate from the lock (see illustrations).

22 Release the clips and disconnect the connecting rods from the lock. Where necessary, rotate the rod through 90° to align the tab with the cut-out. Also disconnect the inner handle cable (see illustrations).

23 Unclip the adjustment clip from the connecting rod. Note: Ford recommend that the clip is renewed.

Refitting

24 Refitting is a reversal of removal. The adjustment clip should be fitted so that the lock is released after the exterior handle has moved approximately 22.0 mm from its closed position (see illustrations). There should then be approximately 5.0 to 6.0 mm of handle movement after the lock has been released. When closing the door slowly, there must be two audible clicks as the lock engages.

Strikers

Removal

25 To remove a door striker, first mark its pos-

ition with a pencil to assist refitting. Use an Allen key to undo the retaining screws and remove the striker from the door pillar (see illustration).

26 To remove the tailgate striker, first undo the screws and remove the kick panel. Mark the position of the striker with a pencil, then undo the screws and remove it from the rear valance (see illustrations).

Refitting

27 Refitting is a reversal of removal. Adjust the position of the striker so that it enters the lock centrally. Note that on Estate models the position of the striker may be adjusted without removing the kick panel (see illustration).

13.24a The lock must release with the handle 22.0 mm from its closed position

13.24b The lock adjustment clip

13.25 Front door striker on the B-pillar

13.26a Remove the kick panel . . .

13.26b . . . then unscrew the striker mounting bolts

Check straps

Removal

28 Remove the door inner trim panel as described in Section 10.

29 Using a Torx key, unscrew the bolt securing the strap to the door pillar **(see illustration)**.

30 Unscrew the mounting nuts and withdraw the check strap from inside the door.

Refitting

31 Refitting is a reversal of removal.

14 Door –
removal and refitting

13.27 The striker can be adjusted with the kick panel in position

13.29 Torx bolt securing the check strap to the door pillar

Removal

1 Disconnect the battery negative lead (refer

to *Disconnecting the battery* at the end of this manual).

2 Using a Torx key, unscrew and remove the check strap mounting screw from the door pillar **(see illustration)**.

3 Disconnect the wiring connector by twisting it anti-clockwise **(see illustration)**.

4 Extract the small circlips from the upper and lower hinge pins. The upper circlip is at the top of the pin, whereas the lower circlip is at the bottom of the pin **(see illustration)**.

5 Have an assistant support the weight of the door, then drive the hinge pins through the hinges using a small drift. Carefully lift the door from the hinges.

6 If required, the hinge brackets can be unbolted from the door and pillar **(see illustration)**. Access to the inner bolt will require the inner trim to be removed.

Refitting

7 Refitting is a reversal of the removal procedure, but check that the door lock passes over the striker centrally **(see illustration)**. If necessary, reposition the striker.

14.2 Door check strap

14.3 Wiring connector on the door pillar

14.4 Small circlip retaining the pin in the hinge brackets

14.6 Bolts securing the hinge bracket to the door pillar

14.7 Front door striker on the B-pillar

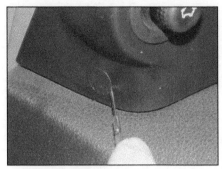

15.1a Prise out the plastic cover . . .

15.1b . . . undo the screw . . .

15.1c . . . then remove the trim and disconnect the wiring

15.2 Undo the screws . . .

15.3 . . . and withdraw the exterior mirror from the door

15.6a Depress the plastic tags to release the mirror from its base

15 Exterior mirror and glass – removal and refitting

16 Interior mirror – removal and refitting

Exterior mirror

Removal

1 Prise out the plastic cover, then undo the screw securing the inner trim and switch to the door panel. Disconnect the switch wiring and remove the trim (see illustrations). Remove the door inner trim panel as described in Section 10 and disconnect the mirror wiring.
2 Support the exterior mirror, then undo the retaining screws using an Allen key (see illustration).
3 Withdraw the mirror from the outside of the door while feeding the wiring through the hole (see illustration).

Refitting

4 Refitting is a reversal of removal.

Exterior mirror glass

Removal

5 Position the glass so that its outer edge is towards the rear of the car.
6 Using a screwdriver, carefully depress the plastic tags and release the mirror and holder from the articulated base (see illustrations).

Refitting

7 Locate the mirror on the base, and, using a wad of cloth, carefully press on the mirror until the plastic tags engage.

Removal

1 Where applicable for models with auto-dimming, disconnect the wiring from the base of the interior mirror.
2 Ford technicians use a special puller tool to release the locking tag holding the mirror joint housing on the windscreen bracket. The tool is tightened onto the housing then pushed upwards to release the locking tag, however, careful use of a screwdriver will release the tag (see illustration).
3 With the locking tag released, support the interior mirror, then, if necessary, use a wooden block and hammer to tap the housing

15.6b Plastic tag shown with the mirror removed

from the windscreen bracket (see illustration).
Caution: Only tap the bracket lightly to prevent damage/breakage to the wind-screen.

16.2 Release the tag . . .

16.3 . . . then withdraw the interior mirror

Refitting

4 Locate the mirror socket housing on the mounting bracket, and push it downwards until it locks into position. It may be necessary to use the wooden block and hammer to ensure the housing is locked onto the bracket.
5 Where applicable, reconnect the auto-dimming wiring.

17 Boot lid – removal and refitting

Removal

1 Disconnect the battery negative lead (refer to *Disconnecting the battery* at the end of this manual), and open the boot lid.
2 Have an assistant support the open boot lid, then disconnect the support strut from the ball on the hinge.
3 Where fitted, remove the trim from inside the boot lid.
4 Disconnect the wiring at the connectors visible through the boot lid inner skin aperture.
5 Attach a length of strong cord to the end of the wires in the aperture, to act as an aid to guiding the wiring through the lid when it is refitted.
6 Withdraw the wiring loom through the boot lid apertures. Untie the cord, and leave it in the boot lid.
7 Mark the position of the hinge arms with a pencil.
8 Place rags beneath each corner of the boot lid, to prevent damage to the paintwork.
9 With the help of an assistant, unscrew the mounting bolts and lift the boot lid from the car.

Refitting

10 Refitting is a reversal of the removal procedure, but check that the boot lid is correctly aligned with the surrounding bodywork, with equal clearance around its edge. Adjustment is made by loosening the hinge bolts and moving the boot lid within the elongated mounting holes. Check that the striker enters the lock centrally when the boot lid is closed. If necessary, loosen the striker retaining bolts, reposition the striker, then retighten them. If new components have been fitted, carry out the following adjustment procedure.
11 Loosen the three striker mounting bolts, then pull off the weatherstrip from the boot lid opening.
12 Unscrew and remove the bump stops from the boot lid. Have an assistant support the boot lid, then prise out the spring clips and remove the support struts.
13 Loosen the bolts securing the hinges to the body, adjust the hinges to the centre of the elongated holes, and retighten the bolts.
14 Loosen the bolts securing the hinges to the boot lid, then finger-tighten them to allow adjustment of the boot lid position.

15 Lower the boot lid and adjust its position so that equal clearances exist on each side. It should be possible to insert a 4.0 mm thick spacer between the boot lid and rear quarter panel on each side.
16 Carefully open the boot lid, taking care not to move the hinges, then fully tighten the boot lid-to-hinge bolts to the specified torque.
17 Loosen the two hinge-to-body bolts on each side, then finger-tighten them. Close the boot lid and position the boot so that it is 2.0 mm below the rear quarter panels. Carefully raise the boot lid, then fully tighten the bolts to the specified torque.
18 Refit the support struts, bump stops and weatherstrip, then check the striker as described in paragraph 10 and tighten the retaining bolts.

18 Boot lid lock – removal and refitting

Removal

1 Disconnect the battery negative lead (refer to *Disconnecting the battery* at the end of this manual).
2 With the boot lid open, remove the inner trim panels.
3 Undo the screws and remove the cover from the boot lid lock.
4 Disconnect the wiring and cable.
5 Mark the position of the lock, for use when refitting. Using a Torx key, unscrew the lock mounting screws, and withdraw the lock.

19.3b . . . and tailgate trim

Refitting

6 Refitting is a reversal of removal, but use the alignment marks made on removal to ensure that the lock is positioned accurately.

19 Tailgate – removal and refitting

Removal

1 Disconnect the battery negative lead (refer to *Disconnecting the battery* at the end of this manual).
2 With the tailgate open, undo the screws and remove the handgrip **(see illustration)**.
3 Using a wide-bladed screwdriver, carefully prise away the window surround trim, then similarly prise away the tailgate trim **(see illustrations)**. Locate the screwdriver near the retaining clips when releasing the clips.
4 Note the location and routing of the wiring loom, then disconnect it from each component in the tailgate, including the heated rear window **(see illustration)**.
5 Prise out the wiring rubber gaiter from the top edge of the tailgate, and carefully remove the wiring loom. Also disconnect and remove the tailgate washer tubing.
6 Have an assistant support the tailgate. Using a screwdriver, prise out the spring clips and disconnect the support struts from the tailgate. Lower the struts into the rear luggage compartment.

19.3a Removing the window surround trim . . .

19.4 Wiring to the heated rear window

19.2 Removing the handgrip from the tailgate

7 Use a pencil to mark the position of the hinges on the tailgate, then unscrew the bolts and lift away the tailgate **(see illustration)**.

Refitting

8 Refitting is a reversal of the removal procedure, but check that the tailgate is located centrally in the body aperture, and that the striker enters the lock centrally. If necessary, loosen the mounting bolts and reposition the tailgate as required.

20 Tailgate support strut – removal and refitting

Removal

1 Support the tailgate in its open position.
2 Prise off the upper spring clip securing the

21.1 Removing the handgrip from the tailgate trim

19.7 Bolts securing the tailgate to the hinges

strut to the tailgate, then pull the socket from the ball-stud **(see illustration)**.
3 Similarly prise off the bottom clip, and pull the socket from the ball-stud. Withdraw the strut.

Refitting

4 Refitting is a reversal of the removal procedure, but make sure that the narrow (piston) end of the strut is fitted on the tailgate (ie, upwards).

21 Tailgate lock components – removal and refitting

Private lock

Removal

1 With the tailgate open, undo the trim

20.2 Prising off the tailgate support strut upper spring clip

retaining screws, noting that some are located within the handgrips and some are beneath plastic covers **(see illustration)**.
2 Using a wide-bladed screwdriver, carefully prise away the window surround trim, then similarly prise away the tailgate trim. Locate the screwdriver near the retaining clips when releasing the clips **(see illustrations)**.
3 Disconnect the wiring from the rear of the number plate illumination cross-panel. Undo the retaining nuts and withdraw the panel from the tailgate, and at the same time disconnect the wiring from the number plate illumination lights. Disconnect the wiring and cable, then unscrew the mounting nuts and remove the private lock from the tailgate **(see illustrations)**. It is not possible to remove the lock cylinder separately.

Refitting

4 Refitting is a reversal of removal.

21.2a Removing the window surround trim . . .

21.2b . . . and the tailgate trim

21.3a Disconnect the wiring . . .

21.3b . . . then unscrew the mounting nuts . . .

21.3c . . . withdraw the number plate illumination cross-panel . . .

21.3d . . . disconnect the wiring

21.3e Unscrew the nuts . . .

21.3f . . . and remove the private lock

21.7a Disconnect the wiring and cable . . .

Tailgate lock

Removal

5 With the tailgate open, undo the screws and remove the handgrip.

6 Using a wide-bladed screwdriver, carefully prise away the window surround trim, then similarly prise away the tailgate trim. Locate the screwdriver near the retaining clips when releasing the clips.

7 Disconnect the wiring and cable, then unscrew the mounting screws and withdraw the lock through the aperture in the tailgate inner panel **(see illustrations)**.

Refitting

8 Refitting is a reversal of removal.

21.7b . . . then unscrew the mounting screws . . .

21.7c . . . and withdraw the lock

22 Windscreen and fixed windows – removal and refitting

1 The windscreen and rear window on all models are bonded in place with special mastic, as are the rear side windows on Estate models. Special tools are required to cut free the old units and fit replacements; special cleaning solutions and primer are also required. It is therefore recommended that this work is entrusted to a Ford dealer or windscreen replacement specialist.

2 Note that the windscreen contributes towards the structural strength of the vehicle as a whole, so it is important that it is fitted correctly.

23 Body side-trim mouldings and adhesive emblems – removal and refitting

Removal

1 Insert a length of strong cord (fishing line is ideal) behind the moulding or emblem concerned. With a sawing action, break the adhesive bond between the moulding or emblem and the panel.

2 Thoroughly clean all traces of adhesive from the panel using methylated spirit, and allow the location to dry.

Refitting

3 Peel back the protective paper from the rear face of the new moulding or emblem. Carefully fit it into position on the panel concerned, but take care not to touch the adhesive. When in position, apply hand pressure to the moulding/emblem for a short period, to ensure maximum adhesion to the panel.

24 Sunroof opening motor – removal and refitting

Note: *With the exception of the sunroof opening motor, work on the sunroof is considered outside the scope of the home mechanic as it involves removal of the headlining.*

Removal

1 Disconnect the battery negative lead (refer to *Disconnecting the battery* at the end of this manual).

2 Remove the overhead console as described in Section 29.

3 Disconnect the wiring from the sunroof opening motor.

4 Unscrew the three mounting bolts, then withdraw the motor.

Refitting

5 Remove the panel guide arm covers from the front of the sunroof opening.

6 Check that the left- and right-hand cable guide pins are aligned centrally between the lugs on the guides **(see illustration)**. Depress the bar in order to view the pins.

7 If adjustment of guide pins is necessary, use a screwdriver to move the cable in the required direction.

8 Refit the sunroof opening panel guide arm covers.

9 Support the motor and reconnect the wiring.

10 Reconnect the battery negative lead and the sunroof opening control switch connector.

Motor initialisation (updating)

⚠️ *Warning: The anti-trap function will not operate during initialisation. Make sure that foreign material, fingers, etc, are kept away from the sunroof opening.*

11 If refitting the original motor, carry out the following updating motor initialisation procedure. If a new motor is being fitted, proceed to paragraph 16.

24.6 Depress the bar, and check that the guide pins are aligned

25.3a Undo the bolt . . .

25.3b . . . and remove the front seat wiring connector

25.4 Removing the front mounting bolts

12 With the sunroof opening panel guide arm covers removed, close the sunroof, then position a 1.0 to 1.2 mm thick, 150.0 mm long plastic spacer between the rear edge of the sunroof panel glass and the roof panel opening.
13 Loosen the screws and adjust the rear edge of the glass so that it is flush with, or no more than 1.0 mm above the rear roof panel. Check that the glass is central in the opening, then tighten the rear retaining screws. Similarly, adjust the front edge of the glass so that it is flush with, or no more than 1.0 mm below the rear roof panel.
14 Refit the guide arm covers, then remove the plastic spacer.
15 Fully open the sunroof then release the switch. Close the sunroof and hold the switch for 30 seconds until there is a small movement of approximately 2.0 mm and the motor stops. Release the switch and immediately close the sunroof within 0.5 seconds until the

panel stops. This completes one initialisation cycle.

Motor initialisation (initial)

⚠ *Warning: The anti-trap function will not operate during initialisation. Make sure that foreign material, fingers, etc, are kept away from the sunroof opening.*

16 Align the sunroof as described in paragraphs 12 to 14.
17 Fully close the sunroof, then release the switch and immediately re-press the close switch within 0.5 seconds until the panels stops. This completes one initialisation cycle.

Motor initialisation (erasure)

Note: *This is necessary only when the motor has been detached from the sunroof panel, and must also be carried out before fitting a previously used motor (ie, before removing the used motor).*

18 With the wiring connected to the motor, operate the close switch until the motor stops, then release it.
19 Operate the close switch again and hold it for 30 seconds. The motor will turn in one direction. Release the switch, then attempt to operate the open switch – if the motor does not turn, the erasing procedure has been carried out correctly. If the motor turns, repeat the erasing procedure.

25 Seats – removal and refitting

Front seat

Removal

1 Disconnect the battery negative lead (refer to *Disconnecting the battery* at the end of this manual).

⚠ *Warning: Before proceeding, wait a minimum of one minute, as a precaution against accidental firing of the airbag unit. This period ensures that any stored energy in the back-up capacitor is dissipated.*

2 Adjust the seat fully rearwards.
3 Disconnect the wiring from under the front seat. Where applicable, unscrew the connector mounting bolt **(see illustrations)**.
4 Unscrew and remove the seat front mounting bolts **(see illustration)**.
5 Adjust the seat fully forwards.
6 Unbolt the seat belt lower anchor from the underside of the front seat **(see illustration)**.
7 Undo the screws and remove the rear mounting bolt covers **(see illustrations)**.
8 Unscrew and remove the rear mounting bolts, then carefully withdraw the seat from inside the vehicle **(see illustrations)**.

Refitting

9 Refitting is a reversal of removal, but tighten the mounting bolts to the specified torque. Initialise the door window motors as described in Section 12 after reconnecting the battery negative lead.

Rear seat

Removal

10 On Saloon and Estate models, pull out the

25.6 Unbolting the seat belt lower anchor from the front seat

25.7a Undo the screws . . .

25.7b . . . and remove the rear mounting bolt covers

25.8a Removing the rear mounting bolts

25.8b Front seat wiring connector (seat removed)

26.3 Pull back the weatherstrips from the B-pillar

26.5a Prise off the cover . . .

retaining clips from the front edge of the seat, then lift the cushion and remove from the inside of the vehicle. Ford recommend that the clips are renewed whenever removed.

11 On 5-door Hatchback models, simply raise the rear edge of the cushion, and withdraw it from inside the vehicle.

12 Position the seat belt plastic retainer approximately 200 mm up from the stop.

13 Unbolt the centre safety belt stalk from the rear floor.

14 On Saloon models, fold the rear seat backrests forwards, then unscrew the bolts securing them to the hinges. There are four on each backrest.

15 On Hatchback and Estate models, fold the rear seat backrest forwards, then unscrew the bolt from the centre hinge locking plate. Remove the backrest outer hinge retaining clip, and withdraw the backrest from inside the vehicle.

Refitting

16 Refitting is a reversal of removal, but tighten the mounting bolts to the specified torque.

26 Seat belts –
removal and refitting

Front belt and retractor

1 Move the front seat fully forwards.

2 Unbolt the seat belt anchor from the rear underside of the seat.

3 Pull back the rubber weatherstrips from each side of the door B-pillar, for access to the seat belt shoulder height adjuster (see illustration). Move the adjuster to its lowest position.

4 Carefully pull out (sideways) the lower

edges of the trim panel and release the locating tangs.

5 Prise off the cover, then undo the screw securing the top of the trim to the B-pillar (see illustrations).

6 Remove the upper section trim panel and, at the same time, feed the seat belt through the slot (see illustrations).

7 Undo the screws, then release the clips and remove the lower section of the B-pillar trim (see illustrations).

8 Undo the screws, then release the clips and remove the inner sill kick plate (see illustrations).

9 Unscrew the bolt and remove the seat belt upper anchor from the shoulder height adjuster (see illustration).

Caution: A special washer is fitted to the bolt to retain it on the anchor plate. The washer must remain on the bolt at all times with the seat belt removed.

26.5b . . . and undo the screw from the B-pillar trim

26.6a Remove the upper section of the B-pillar trim . . .

26.6b . . . and feed the seat belt through the slot

26.7a Undo the screws . . .

26.7b . . . and remove the lower section of the B-pillar trim

26.8a Remove the centre screws . . .

26.8b ... and end screws ...

26.8c ... and remove the inner sill kick plate

26.9 Bolt securing the seat belt upper anchor to the shoulder height adjuster

10 Unbolt the guide loop from the B-pillar (see illustration).

11 Unscrew the bolt and lift the retractor from inside the B-pillar (see illustration). Note the locating tang on the retractor.

12 Refitting is a reversal of removal, but tighten all bolts to the specified torque. Ensure the retractor tang is correctly located.

Front belt stalk

⚠ *Warning: Take extreme care when handling the seat belt pretensioning device. It contains a small explosive charge (pyrotechnic device), and injury may occur if the device is accidentally deployed. Once fired, the tensioner cannot be reset, and must be renewed. Note also that seat belts and associated components which have been subject to impact loads must be renewed at the same time.*

13 Remove the front seat as described in Section 25.

14 Disconnect the wiring from the seat belt buckle switch and pretensioner.

15 Note the location of the pretensioner wiring harnesses, then release them from the underside of the front seat.

16 Unscrew the mounting bolt, and remove the stalk from the front seat (see illustration). *Caution: Do not probe any of the wiring, as static electricity may activate the pretensioner.*

17 Refitting is a reversal of removal, but tighten all mounting bolts to the specified torque.

Rear outer belt

Saloon and Hatchback models

18 Pull the rear door weatherstrip from the C-pillar, and remove the rear seat cushion.

19 Using a Torx key, unscrew the bolt securing the rear seat belt anchor to the floor (see illustration).

20 Undo the screws and remove the lower trim panel from the C-pillar (see illustrations).

21 On Saloon models, prise out the plastic covers, then undo the screws and remove the rear trim panel. Feed the seat belt through the slot in the panel.

22 On Hatchback models, where necessary remove the rear shelf side panel, then prise out the plastic covers and undo the screws securing the rear upper trim panel. Release the retaining clips and withdraw the panel. If working on the right-hand seat belt, disconnect the rear window washer tube from the panel. Undo the screws securing the rear lower trim panel, then release the clip and withdraw the panel while feeding the seat belt through the slot (see illustrations).

26.10 Bolt securing the seat belt guide loop to the B-pillar

26.11 Bolt securing the seat belt retractor to the B-pillar

26.16 Front seat belt stalk mounting bolt

26.19 Rear seat belt floor anchor

26.20a Undo the screws ...

26.20b ... and remove the lower trim panel from the C-pillar

26.22a On Hatchback models, remove the rear shelf side panel . . .

26.22b . . . then remove the rear upper trim panel . . .

26.22c . . . undo the screws . . .

26.22d . . . release the clip . . .

26.22e . . . and remove the rear lower trim panel while feeding the seat belt through the slot

26.23 Rear seat belt upper anchor bolt

23 On all models, unscrew the bolt and remove the seat belt upper anchor from the C-pillar **(see illustration)**.
Caution: A special washer is fitted to the bolt to retain it on the anchor plate. The

washer must remain on the bolt at all times with the seat belt removed.
24 Unscrew the bolt and lift the retractor from inside the C-pillar **(see illustration)**. Note the locating tang on the retractor.

25 Refitting is a reversal of removal, but tighten all bolts to the specified torque. Ensure the retractor tang is correctly located.

Rear belt and stalks

Estate models

26 With the tailgate open, pull away the weatherstrip from the D-pillar trim panel **(see illustration)**.
27 Undo the screw and remove the trim panel from the D-pillar **(see illustrations)**. If removing the right-hand panel, disconnect the rear washer tube.
28 Pull away the weatherstrip from the C-pillar, then undo the screws and remove the load space upper trim panel located beneath the rear quarter window. Where necessary, disconnect the wiring for the auxiliary 12 volt supply **(see illustrations)**.
29 Using a Torx key, unscrew the seat belt

26.24 Rear seat belt retractor retaining bolt

26.26 Pull away the weatherstrip . . .

26.27a . . . then undo the screw . . .

26.27b . . . and remove the trim panel from the D-pillar

26.28a Pull away the weatherstrip . . .

26.28b ... then undo the screws ...

26.28c ... and remove the load space upper trim panel

26.28d Disconnecting the wiring from the auxiliary 12 volt supply

26.29 Bolt securing the rear seat belt lower anchor to the floor

26.30a Bolt securing the rear seat belt upper anchor bolt to the C-pillar

26.30b Removing the upper trim panel

lower anchor bolt from the floor (see illustration).

30 Prise off the cover and unscrew the seat belt upper anchor bolt from the C-pillar. If necessary, unclip and remove the upper trim panel (see illustrations).

Caution: A special washer is fitted to the bolt to retain it on the anchor plate. The washer must remain on the bolt at all times with the seat belt removed.

31 Pull back the carpet, then unscrew the mounting bolt and withdraw the retractor from the C-pillar. Note the locating tang on the retractor (see illustration).

32 To remove the centre stalk, first remove the cushion by pulling out the retaining clips, then unscrew the mounting bolt and remove the stalks (see illustration).

33 Refitting is a reversal of removal, but tighten all bolts to the specified torque. Ensure the retractor tang is correctly located.

Rear stalk and centre retractor

Saloon models

34 Pull the rear door weatherstrip from the C-pillar.

35 Prise out the plastic covers, then undo the screw and remove the lower trim panel from the C-pillar.

36 Remove the rear seat cushion.

37 Unscrew the Torx bolt and remove the centre stalk from the floor.

38 Fold down the rear seat backrests.

39 Remove the centre seat belt plastic guide.

40 Remove the backrest retaining latch trim panels.

41 Prise out the plastic covers, then undo the screws and remove the rear parcel shelf, while feeding the seat belt through the slot.

42 Unscrew the mounting bolt and remove the centre seat belt retractor.

43 Refitting is a reversal of removal, but tighten the mounting bolts to the specified torque.

Rear centre belt retractor

Hatchback and Estate models

44 Remove the rear seat backrest, then lock the backrest latch.

45 Note the location of the backrest latch cable, then remove it from the retractor.

46 Using a knife, make a cut in the carpet over the retractor mounting bolt in the backrest. Unscrew the bolt and remove the retractor while feeding the seat belt through the guide.

47 Refitting is a reversal of removal, but tighten the mounting bolt to the specified torque, and apply suitable adhesive to the rear carpet to stick it to the backrest.

27 Interior trim panels – removal and refitting

Removal

Sun visor

1 Using a Torx key, unscrew the two screws securing the sun visor to the roof/headlining, and withdraw it (see illustration).

2 Prise up the cover, unscrew the inner bracket mounting screws, and remove the bracket.

Passenger grab handle

3 Prise up the covers, then unscrew the mounting screws and remove the grab handle (see illustration).

26.31 Outer rear seat belt retractor mounting bolt (Estate)

26.32 Rear seat centre stalk mounting bolt (Estate)

27.1 Removing the sun visor

27.3 Removing the passenger grab handle

27.6a The side air curtain strap must be correctly located in the yellow plastic holder

A-pillar trim

4 Note that on models fitted with side air curtains (airbag system), the A-pillar trim is attached to the top of the A-pillar by a special yellow strap which forms part of the airbag system and retains the black cord from the air curtain. It is important that this strap is not damaged and is always refitted correctly.

5 Pull away the door weatherstrip in the area of the trim.

6 Carefully pull away the top of the trim and release the clips. Where applicable, note the location of the side air curtain cord strap, then release it from the trim. Withdraw the trim panel **(see illustrations)**.

B-pillar and cowl side trim

7 The procedure is described in Section 26 as the first part of the removal of the front seat belt.

C-pillar trim (Hatchback and Estate)

8 Pull away the rear door weatherstrip in the area of the trim.

9 On Estate models, unbolt the rear seat belt upper anchor from the C-pillar with reference to Section 26. On Hatchback models, prise out the covers and undo the trim panel retaining screws.

10 Release the retaining clips, then withdraw the C-pillar trim in a forwards and upwards direction **(see illustration)**.

C-pillar trim (Saloon)

11 Pull away the rear door weatherstrip in the area of the trim.

12 Undo the single screw and remove the lower trim panel from the C-pillar.

13 Fold down the rear seat backrests, and remove the latch covers.

14 Undo the screws and remove the parcel shelf trim panel.

15 Prise out the covers, then undo the screws securing the C-pillar trim. Where necessary, remove the rear seat belt upper anchor (see Section 26). Withdraw the trim panel.

D-pillar trim (Estate)

16 With the tailgate open, pull away the weatherstrip in the area of the trim **(see illustration)**.

17 Undo the screw securing the trim to the D-pillar **(see illustration)**.

18 Release the retaining clips, then withdraw the D-pillar trim **(see illustration)**. If removing

27.6b Releasing the bottom end of the trim panel from the A-pillar

the right-hand panel, release the rear window washer tube.

Lower facia panel

19 Remove the steering column top and bottom shrouds.

27.16 Pull away the weatherstrip . . .

27.18 . . . and remove the trim panel from the D-pillar (Estate)

27.10 Removing the C-pillar trim panel (Estate)

20 Unscrew the mounting screws from the upper corners and above the coin tray position, and withdraw the lower facia panel from the facia **(see illustrations)**. Where applicable, detach the diagnostic plug connector from the panel.

27.17 . . . then undo the screw . . .

27.20a Undo the upper screws . . .

27.20b ... and lower screws ...

27.20c ... and withdraw the lower facia panel from the facia

27.21 Removing the lower centre panels

Lower centre panels

21 Release the two screws or clips each side, and withdraw the panels from the front of the centre console (see illustrations).

28.2a Remove the gear lever trim panel ...

Refitting

22 Refitting is a reversal of the removal procedure. Where seat belt fastenings have been disturbed, make sure that they are tightened to the specified torque.

28 Centre console – removal and refitting

Removal

1 Disconnect the battery negative lead (refer to *Disconnecting the battery* at the end of this manual).
2 Remove the trim panel from around the gear lever (manual) or selector lever (automatic), with reference to Chapter 7A or 7B. On manual transmission models, remove the insulation pad beneath the panel (see illustrations). On automatic transmission models, move the selector lever to the N position.
3 Remove the floor console side panels. To do this, prise out the cover and undo the front screw located near the bulkhead, then carefully release the 5 upper clips and 1 lower clip. Withdraw the panels (see illustrations).
4 Carefully prise out the ashtray and cup holder (where applicable) from the centre console, and disconnect the wiring from the cigar lighter (see illustrations). Note on certain models, the cup holder is located in the heater control surround.
5 Undo the centre console retaining screws and bolts – there are two at the front, one in the middle, and three in the oddments box (see illustrations). Remove the insert for access to the screws.

28.2b ... then remove the insulation pad (manual)

28.3a Prise out the covers and undo the screws ...

28.3b ... then unclip the floor console side panels

28.4a Prise out the ashtray ...

28.4b ... and disconnect the wiring from the cigar lighter

28.5a The centre console is retained with two front screws ...

28.5b ... one middle screw ...

28.5c ... and three screws in the oddments box

28.7 Removing the centre console

6 Fully apply the handbrake lever and, on automatic transmission models, move the selector lever to the P position.

7 Raise the rear of the centre console and remove it from between the front seats **(see illustration)**. Where applicable, also release the handbrake warning light switch wiring from the clip inside the console.

Refitting

8 Refitting is a reversal of the removal procedure, but initialise the electric windows as described in Section 12.

29 Overhead console – removal and refitting

Removal

1 Disconnect the battery negative lead (refer to *Disconnecting the battery* at the end of this manual).

2 Using a screwdriver, carefully prise the interior lamp from the overhead console, then disconnect the wiring **(see illustration)**.

3 On models equipped with a sunroof, prise up the covers and turn the front retaining clips through 90°. Lower the front of the overhead console, then move it forwards and release the rear retaining clips. Disconnect the wiring and remove the sunroof control switch.

4 On models without a sunroof, open the storage compartment, then carefully pull down the rear of the compartment, using a screwdriver to release the retaining clips. Take

care not to damage the compartment or console.

5 On all models, carefully prise down the rear of the console, then pull it to the rear to release the front retaining clips **(see illustrations)**.

6 Release the hook loop tape and withdraw the storage compartment cover downwards.

7 On models with telematics, note the location of the microphone, then remove it from the console as follows. Release the adhesive tape from the electrical connector and wiring harness. Detach the microphone wiring connector followed by the microphone and foam pad.

Refitting

8 Refitting is a reversal of removal, but initialise the electric windows as described in Section 12. Do not refit the hook loop tape until after the storage compartment has been

29.2 Removing the interior lamp from the overhead console

29.5b Front retaining clip on the overhead console

30.1 Disconnect the damper ...

refitted; with the compartment fitted, push up the console and refit the tape.

30 Glovebox – removal and refitting

Removal

1 Open the glovebox, then disconnect the damper from the outer side of the glovebox **(see illustration)**.

2 Press in both sides of the glovebox to release the stops, and fully open the glovebox **(see illustration)**.

3 Release the bottom hinges, and withdraw the glovebox from the facia panel **(see illustration)**.

4 To remove the glovebox latch, first undo the two retaining screws. Withdraw the latch

29.5a Removing the overhead console from the headlining

30.2 ... press in both sides ...

30.3 . . . then release the hinges and withdraw the glovebox

30.4a Undo the screws . . .

30.4b . . . and disconnect the illumination light bulbholder . . .

30.4c . . . then disconnect the wiring and withdraw the latch

and disconnect the illumination light bulb-holder. Disconnect the illumination light wiring at the connector **(see illustrations)**.

Refitting

5 Refitting is a reversal of removal.

---

31 Facia –
removal and refitting

Removal

1 Disconnect the battery negative lead (refer to *Disconnecting the battery* at the end of this manual).
2 Remove the centre console as described in Section 28.
3 Remove the steering column as described in Chapter 10.

31.8a Undo the screw . . .

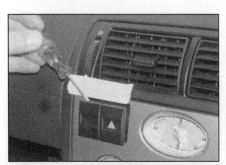

31.13a Use a strip of card to protect the facia while prising out the accessory switches

4 On models with the 2.5 litre petrol engine, and all diesel engine models, remove the driver's side lower footwell trim.
5 Where fitted, remove the passenger's side lower footwell trim.
6 Remove the glovebox as described in Section 30.
7 On models fitted with footwell illumination, disconnect the wiring, then undo the screw and remove the lamp from the lower facia.
8 Detach the data link connector (DLC) from the lower facia on the driver's side **(see illustrations)**.
9 Remove the internal temperature sensor from the lower facia on the driver's side.
10 Reach up under the facia on the passenger's side, and disconnect the wiring from the passenger airbag module.
11 Undo the two bolts securing the passenger airbag to the bulkhead cross-beam.

31.8b . . . and remove the data link connector

31.13b Removing the windscreen/rear window heater switches

Caution: The passenger airbag module retaining bolts must only be used a maximum of three times. Use a centre punch to mark the bolts.

12 Remove the radio/cassette audio unit from the centre of the facia as described in Chapter 12.
13 Use a screwdriver to carefully prise the accessory switches from the heater control trim panel. Prevent damage to the facia by placing card beneath the screwdriver. Disconnect the wiring from the switches **(see illustrations)**.
14 Undo the screws securing the heater control trim panel to the facia. There are two screws located in the accessory switch apertures, two screws located in the top corners of the radio/cassette aperture, and two screws located at the bottom of the panel **(see illustrations)**.
15 Release the three upper clips, and remove

31.13c Disconnecting the wiring from the accessory switches

31.14a Undo the screws located in the accessory switch apertures . . .

31.14b . . . in the radio/cassette aperture . . .

31.14c . . . and at the bottom of the heater control trim panel . . .

31.15a . . . then remove the panel . . .

31.15b . . . and disconnect the wiring (auxiliary climate control switch)

31.17 Removing the grille from the front of the facia (non-keyless entry antenna type)

the heater control trim panel from the facia. From the rear of the panel, disconnect the wiring for the tailgate release switch, heated front seat switch, auxiliary climate/heater control switches, and clock (see illustrations).

31.18 Removing a support bracket from the centre of the facia

16 Remove the instrument panel from the facia as described in Chapter 12.
Caution: The instrument panel must be kept upright to prevent silicone liquid leaking from the gauges.

31.19 Unscrewing the nuts/bolts securing each end of the facia to the bulkhead cross-beam

17 On models equipped with a keyless entry antenna, carefully prise out the grille from the front of the facia (beneath the windscreen) and disconnect the wiring from the sensor (see illustration). The sensor is visible on top of the grille if the keyless entry system is fitted, otherwise it is not necessary to remove the grille.
18 From the centre of the facia, undo the screws and remove the support bracket. Also in the centre, unscrew the support bracket retaining nut (see illustration).
19 Unscrew the nuts/bolts securing each end of the facia to the bulkhead cross-beam (see illustration).
20 Remove the trim panels from each A-pillar as described in Section 27.
21 Pull back the A-pillar weatherstrips in the area of the facia, then remove the side trim panels, and unscrew the facia side mounting bolts (see illustrations).

31.21a Pull back the weatherstrips . . .

31.21b . . . remove the side trim panels . . .

31.21c . . . and unscrew the facia side mounting bolts

31.23 Removing the facia

33.2 Fuel filler flap release pin and cable

33.4 Fuel filler flap release cable routed over the rear wheel arch

22 On automatic transmission models, move the selector lever to position P.

23 With the help of an assistant, carefully lift the facia away from the bulkhead and withdraw it through one side of the vehicle **(see illustration)**.

Refitting

24 Refitting is a reversal of removal, but tighten nuts and bolts to the specified torque where this is given in the appropriate Chapter. In particular, observe the refitting procedure for the passenger airbag, A-pillar trim and steering column. On completion, check the operation of all electrical components.

32 Wheel arch liner – removal and refitting

Removal

Front

1 Apply the handbrake, then jack up the front of the vehicle and support it on axle stands (see *Jacking and vehicle support*). Remove the relevant roadwheel.

2 Undo the retaining screws located on the outer edge of the wheel arch.

3 Unscrew the two bolts located on the rear lower edge of the liner.

4 Remove the three plastic fasteners by pressing out the central locking pins.

5 Remove the wheel arch liner from the vehicle, while guiding it around the front suspension strut.

Rear

6 Chock the front wheels then jack up the rear of the vehicle and support on axle stands (see *Jacking and vehicle support*). Remove the relevant roadwheel.

7 Remove the screws and clips securing the liner to the outer edge of the wheel arch.

8 Unscrew and remove the screws securing the liner to the inner wheel arch, and withdraw the liner from under the vehicle.

Refitting

9 Refitting is a reversal of the removal procedure, but tighten the wheel nuts to the specified torque.

33 Fuel filler flap release cable – removal and refitting

Removal

1 Working in the luggage compartment, remove the trim from the right-hand side for access to the fuel flap release cable.

2 Reach into the inner panel aperture and

33.6 Fuel filler flap release lever

disconnect the cable from the release pin **(see illustration)**.

3 With the filler flap open, prise out the release pin.

4 The filler flap cable is routed over the rear wheel arch and along the inner sill panel to the control lever next to the driver's seat **(see illustration)**. Remove the interior trim panels with reference to Section 27.

5 Release the cable from the retaining clips and withdraw from the vehicle.

6 The release lever is bolted to the inner sill panel with two bolts **(see illustration)**.

7 The fuel tank filler neck is retained by a single bolt to the body panel.

Refitting

8 Refitting is a reversal of removal.

Chapter 12
Body electrical system

Contents

Degrees of difficulty

Easy, suitable for novice with little experience	**Fairly easy,** suitable for beginner with some experience	**Fairly difficult,** suitable for competent DIY mechanic
Difficult, suitable for experienced DIY mechanic	**Very difficult,** suitable for expert DIY or professional	

Specifications

Fuses and relays
Refer to the wiring diagrams at the end of this Chapter
Note: *Fuse ratings and circuits are liable to change from year to year.*
Consult the handbook supplied with the vehicle, or consult a Ford dealer, for the latest information.

Bulbs	Wattage	Type
Direction indicator lights	21	Bayonet
Footwell	5	Wedge
Front foglight:		
Standard	55	H11 Halogen
Sports	55	H3 Halogen
Glove compartment	5	Wedge
Headlight:		
Main beam	55	H1 Halogen
Dipped beam	55	H7 Halogen
High-level stop-light (5x)	5	Wedge
Interior light	10	Festoon
Luggage compartment	10	Festoon
Number plate light	5	Festoon
Reading light	5	Wedge
Rear fog/tail lights (Estate)	21/4	Bayonet
Rear foglight (Saloon)	21	Bayonet
Rear tail light (Saloon and Hatchback)	5	Bayonet
Reversing light	21	Bayonet
Sidelight	5	Wedge
Side repeater light	5	Wedge
Sun visor	5	Wedge

Torque wrench settings

	Nm	lbf ft
Airbag control module	7	5
Driver's airbag	5	4
Front crash sensor	8	6
Front suspension strut top mounting brace:		
to cowl	8	6
to inner wing panel	25	18
Front suspension strut upper mounting	30	22
Passenger's airbag	7	5
Side impact sensor	7	5
Windscreen wiper motor crank to motor shaft	26	19
Windscreen wiper motor linkage/bracket to bulkhead	8	6
Windscreen wiper motor to bracket	8	6
Wiper arm nuts	22	16

J35170

1.3 Airbag and safety belt pretensioner supplemental restraint system (SRS)

1 Passenger airbag module
2 Occupant classification sensor
3 Driver airbag module
4 Airbag control module
5 Side air curtain module
6 Side impact sensor
7 Seat position sensor
8 Safety belt buckle switch
9 Crash sensor

1 General information

⚠️ *Warning: Before carrying out any work on the electrical system, read through the precautions given in 'Safety first!' at the beginning of this manual.*

The electrical system is of 12 volt negative earth type. Power for the lights and all electrical accessories is supplied by a lead-calcium or lead-acid battery which is charged by the alternator. The lead-calcium battery is identified by the letters 'Ca' on the information label, and the manufacturers recommend that an identical battery is fitted when renewing the battery.

This Chapter covers repair and service procedures for the various electrical components not associated with the engine. Information on the battery, alternator, and starter motor can be found in Chapter 5A; the ignition system is covered in Chapter 5B.

All models are fitted with a driver's airbag, which is designed to prevent serious chest and head injuries to the driver during a direct front accident within 30° from the left or right of the vehicle centre line. A similar bag for the front seat passenger is also available. On some models, side curtain airbags are fitted on each side of the roof headlining. The control unit for the airbag system is located under the centre console, and performs continual system diagnostics **(see illustration)**. A crash sensor is located at the front of the vehicle and the side impact sensor is located under the centre console. A seat lateral-position sensor is fitted to the driver's seat track, and, where applicable, a seat occupancy sensor is fitted to the passenger seat. The occupancy sensor forms part of the seat cushion and cannot be renewed separately. Together with the airbag system, the seat belt pretensioners are deployed in the event of an accident – refer to Chapter 11 for more details.

Models equipped with both driver's and passenger's airbags can also be specified with side airbags, which are built into the sides of the front seats. The intention of the side airbags is principally to offer greater passenger protection in a side impact. Although the side airbags are linked to the 'front' airbags, a separate sensor for the side airbags (below the driver's side carpet) is used to detect lateral movement.

The sensor and electronic unit for the airbag is located next to the steering column inside the vehicle, and contains a back-up capacitor, crash sensor, decelerometer, safety sensor, integrated circuit and microprocessor. The airbag is inflated by a gas generator, which forces the bag out of the module cover in the centre of the steering wheel. A 'clock spring' ensures that a good electrical connection is maintained with the airbag at all times – as the steering wheel is turned in each direction, the spring winds and unwinds.

⚠️ *Warning: When working on the airbag system, always wait at least one minute after disconnect the battery, as a precaution against accidental deployment of the airbag unit. This period ensures that any stored energy in the back-up capacitor is dissipated. Do not use battery-operated radio key code savers, as this may cause the airbag to be deployed, with the possibility of personal injury.*

On models with xenon dipped headlights, an automatic headlight levelling system is fitted to comply with current legislation. The system consists of sensors fitted to the front and rear axles, a master control module on the left-hand headlight housing, a slave control module fitted on the right-hand headlight housing, and headlight levelling motors fitted to both headlight housings. When the ignition is switched on, the system automatically adjusts the headlight beam to avoid dazzling of oncoming traffic. Note that the system must be initialised whenever a sensor is removed, or after disconnecting the system electrical wiring. Note that xenon bulbs are designed to last the life of the vehicle.

All UK models are fitted with an alarm system incorporating an engine immobiliser. On Saloon and Hatchback models, the alarm system horn is located on the left-hand side of the luggage compartment, but on Estate models, it is on the right-hand side.

Some models are fitted with a headlight levelling system, which is controlled by a knob on the facia. On position 0, the headlights are in their base position, and on position 5, the headlights are in their maximum inclined angle.

It should be noted that, when portions of the electrical system are serviced, the lead should be disconnected from the battery negative terminal, to prevent electrical shorts and fires (refer to *Disconnecting the battery* at the end of this manual).

2 Electrical fault finding – general information

Note: *Refer to the precautions given in 'Safety first!' and in Section 1 of this Chapter before starting work. The following tests relate to testing of the main electrical circuits, and should not be used to test delicate electronic circuits (such as engine management systems, anti-lock braking systems, etc), particularly where an electronic control unit (ECU) is used.*

General

A typical electrical circuit consists of an electrical component, any switches, relays, motors, fuses, fusible links or circuit breakers related to that component, and the wiring and connectors which link the component to both the battery and the body. To help pinpoint a problem in an electrical circuit, wiring diagrams are included at the end of this Chapter.

Before attempting to diagnose an electrical fault, first study the appropriate wiring diagram, to obtain a complete understanding of the components included in the particular circuit concerned. The possible sources of a fault can be narrowed down by noting if other components related to the circuit are operating properly. If several components or circuits fail at one time, the problem is likely to be related to a shared fuse or earth connection.

Electrical problems usually stem from simple causes, such as loose or corroded connections, a faulty earth connection, a blown fuse, a melted fusible link, or a faulty relay (refer to Section 3 for details of testing relays). Visually inspect the condition of all fuses, wires and connections in a problem circuit before testing the components. Use the wiring diagrams to determine which terminal connections will need to be checked in order to pinpoint the trouble spot.

The basic tools required for electrical fault finding include a circuit tester or voltmeter (a 12 volt bulb with a set of test leads can also be used for certain tests), an ohmmeter (to measure resistance and check for continuity), a battery and set of test leads, and a jumper wire (preferably with a circuit breaker or fuse incorporated), which can be used to bypass suspect wires or electrical components. Before attempting to locate a problem with test instruments, use the wiring diagram to determine where to make the connections.

To find the source of an intermittent wiring fault (usually due to a poor or dirty connection, or damaged wiring insulation), a 'wiggle' test can be performed on the wiring. This involves wiggling the wiring by hand to see if the fault occurs as the wiring is moved. It should be possible to narrow down the source of the fault to a particular section of wiring. This method of testing can be used in conjunction with any of the tests described in the following sub-Sections.

Apart from problems due to poor connections, two basic types of fault can occur in an electrical circuit – open-circuit, or short-circuit.

Open circuit faults are caused by a break somewhere in the circuit, which prevents current from flowing. An open circuit fault will prevent a component from working, but will not cause the relevant circuit fuse to blow.

Short circuit faults are caused by a 'short' somewhere in the circuit, which allows the current flowing in the circuit to 'escape' along an alternative route, usually to earth. Short circuit faults are normally caused by a breakdown in wiring insulation, which allows a feed wire to touch either another wire, or an earthed component such as the bodyshell. A short circuit fault will normally cause the relevant circuit fuse to blow.

3.1 Main fusebox and relay location behind the glovebox

3.2 Auxiliary fusebox in the engine compartment

Finding an open-circuit

To check for an open circuit, connect one lead of a circuit tester or the negative lead of a voltmeter either to the battery negative terminal or to a known good earth.

Connect the other lead to a connector in the circuit being tested, preferably nearest to the battery or fuse.

Switch on the circuit, bearing in mind that some circuits are live only when the ignition switch is moved to a particular position.

If voltage is present (indicated either by the tester bulb lighting or a voltmeter reading, as applicable), this means that the section of the circuit between the relevant connector and the switch is problem-free.

Continue to check the remainder of the circuit in the same fashion.

When a point is reached at which no voltage is present, the problem must lie between that point and the previous test point with voltage. Most problems can be traced to a broken, corroded or loose connection.

Finding a short-circuit

To check for a short circuit, first disconnect the load(s) from the circuit (loads are the components which draw current from a circuit, such as bulbs, motors, heating elements, etc).

Remove the relevant fuse from the circuit, and connect a circuit tester or voltmeter to the fuse connections.

Switch on the circuit, bearing in mind that some circuits are live only when the ignition switch is moved to a particular position.

If voltage is present (indicated either by the

tester bulb lighting or a voltmeter reading, as applicable), this means that there is a short circuit.

If no voltage is present during this test, but the fuse still blows with the load(s) reconnected, this indicates an internal fault in the load(s).

Finding an earth fault

The battery negative terminal is connected to 'earth' – the metal of the engine/transmission unit and the vehicle body – and many systems are wired so that they only receive a positive feed, the current returning via the metal of the car body. This means that the component mounting and the body form part of that circuit. Loose or corroded mountings can therefore cause a range of electrical faults, ranging from total failure of a circuit, to a puzzling partial failure. In particular, lights may shine dimly (especially when another circuit sharing the same earth point is in operation), motors (eg, wiper motors or the radiator cooling fan motor) may run slowly, and the operation of one circuit may have an apparently unrelated effect on another. Note that on many vehicles, earth straps are used between certain components, such as the engine/transmission and the body, usually where there is no metal-to-metal contact between components, due to flexible rubber mountings, etc.

To check whether a component is properly earthed, disconnect the battery and connect one lead of an ohmmeter to a known good earth point. Connect the other lead to the wire or earth connection being tested. The resistance reading should be zero; if not, check the connection as follows.

If an earth connection is thought to be faulty, dismantle the connection, and clean back to bare metal both the bodyshell and the wire terminal or the component earth connection mating surface. Be careful to remove all traces of dirt and corrosion, then use a knife to trim away any paint, so that a clean metal-to-metal joint is made. On reassembly, tighten the joint fasteners securely; if a wire terminal is being refitted, use serrated washers between the terminal and the bodyshell, to ensure a clean and secure connection. When the connection is remade, prevent the onset of corrosion in the future by applying a coat of petroleum jelly or silicone-based grease, or by spraying on (at regular intervals) a proprietary ignition sealer or a water dispersant lubricant.

3 Fuses and relays – testing and renewal

1 Fuses are designed to break a circuit when a predetermined current is reached, in order to protect components and wiring which could be damaged by excessive current flow. Any excessive current flow will be due to a fault in the circuit, usually a short-circuit. The main fusebox, which also carries some relays, is located inside the vehicle behind the glovebox (see illustration); remove the glovebox, or simply disconnect the damper and fully open the glovebox as described in Chapter 11.

2 The auxiliary fusebox is located in the engine compartment, on the left-hand side of the battery (see illustration), and is accessed by first unclipping and removing the battery cover, then releasing the catch and lifting the fusebox cover. The auxiliary fusebox also contains some relays. Each circuit is identified on the outside of the removed glovebox and on the inside of the auxiliary fusebox cover. Plastic tweezers are attached to the inside face of the auxiliary fusebox, to remove and fit the fuses.

3 To remove a fuse, use the tweezers provided or pliers to pull it out of the holder. Slide the fuse sideways from the tweezers. The wire within the fuse is clearly visible, and it will be broken if the fuse is blown (see illustrations).

4 Always renew a fuse with one of an

3.3a Removing a fuse

GOOD   J35171   BLOWN

3.3b The fuses can be checked visually to determine if they are blown

3.3c Using the special tweezers to remove a fuse

4.1 Disconnecting the battery negative lead

4.7a Undo the screw . . .

4.7b . . . and remove the Passive Anti-Theft System (PATS) transceiver

identical rating. Never substitute a fuse of a higher rating, or make temporary repairs using wire or metal foil; more serious damage, or even fire, could result. The fuse rating is stamped on top of the fuse. Never renew a fuse more than once without tracing the source of the trouble.

5 Spare fuses of various current ratings are provided in the cover of the auxiliary fusebox.

6 Relays are electrically-operated switches, which are used in certain circuits. The various relays can be removed from their respective locations by carefully pulling them from the sockets.

7 If a component controlled by a relay becomes inoperative and the relay is suspect, listen to the relay as the circuit is operated. If the relay is functioning, it should be possible to hear it click as it is energised. If the relay proves satisfactory, the fault lies with the components or wiring of the system. If the relay is not being energised, then either the relay is not receiving a switching voltage, or the relay itself is faulty. Do not overlook the relay socket terminals when tracing faults. Testing is by the substitution of a known good unit, but be careful; some relays are identical in appearance and in operation, others look similar, but perform different functions.

8 To renew a relay first ensure that the ignition switch is off. The relay can then simply be pulled out from the socket and the new relay pressed in.

4.8a Release the clips . . .

2 With the front wheels in the straight-ahead position, remove the steering wheel as described in Chapter 10.

Caution: Make sure that the airbag clock spring is retained in its straight-ahead position using tape.

3 Undo the screws then unclip the lower facia panel from around the steering column.

4 Where fitted, remove the audio control switch from the steering column lower shroud. To do this, use a small screwdriver to release the plastic locking clip. Disconnect the wiring.

5 Remove the steering column upper shroud from the lower shroud by inserting a thin screwdriver between the clip on each side.

6 Undo the three screws and remove the lower shroud.

7 Undo the screw and remove the Passive Anti-Theft System (PATS) transceiver from the ignition/steering lock **(see illustrations)**.

8 Using a screwdriver, release the clips and remove the ignition switch **(see illustrations)**.

4.8b . . . and remove the ignition switch

Disconnect the wiring connector.

9 Insert the ignition key and turn it to position I, then, using a small screwdriver, depress the detent in the lock housing and withdraw the lock cylinder **(see illustration)**.

Refitting

10 Refitting is a reversal of removal, with reference to Chapter 10 when refitting the steering wheel. Also initialise the door window motors as described in Chapter 11.

Wiper/washer switch

Removal

11 Remove the steering column upper shroud from the lower shroud by inserting a thin screwdriver between the clip on each side.

12 Undo the three screws and remove the lower shroud.

13 Disconnect the wiring at the multi-plug **(see illustration)**.

4 Switches –
removal and refitting

Ignition switch and lock

Removal

1 Disconnect the battery negative lead (refer to *Disconnecting the battery* at the end of this manual) **(see illustration)**.

⚠️ *Warning: Before proceeding, wait a minimum of one minute after disconnecting the battery, as a precaution against accidental firing of the airbag unit. This period ensures that any stored energy in the back-up capacitor is dissipated. We suggest you wait several minutes.*

4.9 Removing the ignition lock cylinder

4.13 Disconnect the wiring . . .

4.14a . . . then release the clip . . .

14 Using a screwdriver, release the clip then slide the windscreen wiper/washer multi-function switch up from the steering column (see illustrations).

4.16a Removing the lower facia panel . . .

4.16b . . . and vent

4.20 Prise the switch from the facia . . .

4.14b . . . and slide the windscreen wiper multi-function switch up from the steering column

Refitting

15 Refitting is a reversal of removal.

Lights and foglights switch

Removal

16 Open the coin box lid, then undo the screws and unclip the lower facia panel from around the steering column. Also remove the vent located above the switch position (see illustrations).
17 Reach up behind the facia and carefully press out the combination switch (see illustration). The retaining plastic clips should release, however, it may be necessary to squeeze them together.
18 Disconnect the wiring from the rear of the switch (see illustration).

Refitting

19 Refitting is a reversal of removal.

4.17 Press out the main lights and foglights combination switch from the facia . . .

4.21 . . . and disconnect the wiring

Heated window switches

Removal

20 Using a small screwdriver, carefully prise the switch from the facia, using a screwdriver against a cloth pad to prevent damage to the facia (see illustration).
21 Disconnect the wiring plug from the rear of the switch (see illustration).

Refitting

22 Refitting is a reversal of removal.

Heated seats, luggage compartment release and electronic stability program switches

Removal

23 Using a small screwdriver, carefully prise the switch from the facia, using a screwdriver against a cloth pad to prevent damage to the facia.
24 Disconnect the wiring plug from the rear of the switch.

Refitting

25 Refitting is a reversal of removal.

Hazard flasher switch and airbag deactivation light

Removal

26 Using a small screwdriver, carefully prise the switch/light from the facia, using a screwdriver against a cloth pad to prevent damage to the facia (see illustration).

4.18 . . . then disconnect the wiring

4.26 Prise the switch from the facia . . .

27 Disconnect the wiring plug from the rear of the switch/light (see illustration).

Refitting

28 Refitting is a reversal of removal.

Door mirror control switch

Removal

29 Prise the plastic cover from the door mirror inner trim, then undo the retaining screw.
30 Remove the trim and disconnect the wiring from the mirror control switch.
31 Carefully push the switch from the trim.

Refitting

32 Refitting is a reversal of removal.

Indicator and main/dip switch

Removal

33 Where fitted, remove the audio control switch from the steering column lower shroud. Use a small screwdriver to release the locking tang, then lift the switch from the column and disconnect the wiring.
34 Remove the steering column upper shroud from the lower shroud by inserting a thin screwdriver between the clip on each side.
35 Undo the three screws and remove the lower shroud.
36 Disconnect the multi-plug, the depress the retaining lug and withdraw the switch assembly (see illustrations).
37 With the switch assembly removed, pull out the direction indicator relay (flasher unit) if required.

4.27 . . . then disconnect the wiring

Refitting

38 Refitting is a reversal of removal.

Horn switch

Removal

39 Remove the airbag unit from the steering wheel as described in Section 28.
40 On models with cruise control, remove the switch components as described in Section 22.
41 Disconnect the wiring connector, then (where applicable) remove the two securing screws and carefully prise out the switch assembly.

Refitting

42 Refitting is a reversal of removal.

Radio remote control switch

Removal

43 Remove the audio control switch from the

steering column lower shroud. Use a small screwdriver to release the locking tang, then lift the switch from the column shroud (see illustrations).
44 Disconnect the wiring and remove the switch.

Refitting

45 Refitting is a reversal of removal.

Cruise control switches

46 Refer to Section 22.

Electric window switch

Removal

47 Carefully prise out the switch from the door inner trim panel, using a cloth pad to prevent damage to the trim.
48 Disconnect the multi-plug and remove the switch.

Refitting

49 Refitting is a reversal of removal.

Handbrake-on warning switch

Removal

50 Remove the centre console as described in Chapter 11.
51 Disconnect the wiring, then remove the screw and withdraw the switch from the handbrake lever mounting bracket (see illustration).

Refitting

52 Refitting is a reversal of removal.

4.36a Disconnect the wiring . . .

4.36b . . . then release the clip . . .

4.36c . . . and slide the direction indicator/dipped beam multi-function switch up from the steering column

4.43a Release the locking tang . . .

4.43b . . . and lift the switch from the shroud

4.51 Removing the handbrake-on warning switch from the handbrake lever

5.3 Removing the cover for access to the headlight bulb

5.4a Disconnect the wiring connector . . .

5.4b . . . then release the spring clip . . .

5.4c . . . and withdraw the headlight main beam bulb

5.8a Disconnect the wiring connector . . .

5.8b . . . then release the spring clip . . .

5 Bulbs (exterior lights) – renewal

1 Whenever a bulb is renewed, note the following points:

a) Switch off all exterior lights and the ignition.
b) Remember that if the light has just been in use, the bulb may be extremely hot.
c) Always check the bulb contacts and holder, ensuring that there is clean metal-to-metal contact.
d) Where bayonet-type bulbs are fitted, ensure that the contact springs bear firmly against the bulb contacts.
e) Always ensure that the new bulb is of the correct rating and that it is completely clean before fitting it.

f) Do not touch the glass of halogen-type bulbs (headlights, front foglights, reversing lights) with the fingers, as this may lead to premature failure of the new bulb; if the glass is accidentally touched, clean it with methylated spirit.

⚠ **Warning: Ford recommend the wearing of protective gloves and safety glasses when renewing xenon headlamp bulbs. Do not switch on the headlamps with the bulb removed – high voltages are present which could cause personal injury.**

Headlight (main beam)

2 Remove the headlight unit as described in Section 7.
3 With the headlight unit on the bench, release the plastic clips and remove the cover for access to the headlight bulb **(see illustration)**. On models with xenon bulbs,

undo the screws and release the locking tab to remove the cover.
4 Disconnect the wiring connector from the headlight main beam bulb (the inner one), then release the spring clip and withdraw the bulb, noting how it is fitted **(see illustrations)**.
5 Fit the new bulb using a reversal of the removal procedure.

Headlight (dipped beam)

6 Remove the headlight unit as described in Section 7.
7 With the headlight unit on the bench, release the plastic clips and remove the cover for access to the headlight bulb. On models with xenon bulbs, undo the screws and release the locking tab to remove the cover.
8 Disconnect the wiring connector from the headlight dipped beam bulb (the outer one), then release the spring clip and withdraw the bulb, noting how it is fitted **(see illustrations)**.
9 Fit the new bulb using a reversal of the removal procedure.

Front sidelight

10 Remove the headlight unit as described in Section 7.
11 With the headlight unit on the bench, twist the cover anti-clockwise to remove it **(see illustration)**.
12 Prise out the bulbholder, if necessary using a screwdriver **(see illustration)**.
13 Pull out the wedge-type bulb **(see illustration)**.
14 Fit the new bulb using a reversal of the removal procedure.

5.8c . . . and withdraw the headlight dipped beam bulb

5.11 Twist the cover anti-clockwise and remove it . . .

5.12 ... then prise out the bulbholder ...

5.13 ... and pull out the wedge-type front sidelight bulb

5.16 Turn the front direction indicator bulbholder anti-clockwise to remove it from the headlight unit

5.17 Depress and twist the bulb to remove it from the bulbholder

5.19a Press down the ends of the side repeater lens ...

5.19b ... then pull it out from the front wing

Front direction indicator

15 Remove the headlight unit as described in Section 7.
16 With the headlight unit on the bench, turn the bulbholder anti-clockwise and remove it together with the bulb from the rear of the headlight unit **(see illustration)**.
17 Depress and twist the bulb to remove it from the bulbholder **(see illustration)**.

18 Fit the new bulb using a reversal of the removal procedure.

Side repeater

19 Carefully press down on the ends of the side repeater lens, then pull it out from the front wing **(see illustrations)**.
20 Twist the bulbholder anti-clockwise and remove it from the lens **(see illustration)**.
21 Pull out the wedge-type bulb from the bulbholder **(see illustration)**.
22 Fit the new bulb using a reversal of the removal procedure.

Front foglight

Standard bumper

23 Using a screwdriver or similar tool, carefully prise the foglight bezel from the front bumper **(see illustration)**. Take care not to damage the paintwork.
24 Undo the three crosshead screws and withdraw the foglight from the bumper sufficient to access the bulbholder **(see illustration)**.
25 Disconnect the wiring then twist the bulbholder anti-clockwise and pull out the bulb, noting the three location cut-outs in the housing **(see illustrations)**.
26 Fit the new bulb using a reversal of the removal procedure.

Sports bumper

27 Undo the single screw then carefully prise out the foglight bezel.
28 Undo the two crosshead screws, and pull out the foglight from the front bumper.

5.20 Twist the bulbholder anti-clockwise from the lens ...

5.21 ... then pull out the wedge-type bulb

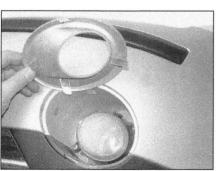

5.23 Remove the foglight bezel from the front bumper ...

5.24 ... and remove the three crosshead screws

5.25a Disconnect the wiring . . .

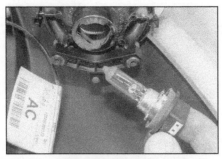

5.25b . . . then twist the bulbholder anti-clockwise and pull out the bulb, noting the three location cut-outs

5.31a Twist off the fasteners . . .

5.31b . . . and remove the rear light cluster cover . . .

5.32a . . . then squeeze together the red tabs . . .

5.32b . . . and remove the bulbholder assembly

5.33a Removing a bulb

Direction indicator 21 watt
Reversing light H1 halogen bulb
Tail light 5 watt
Tail light 5 watt
Rear fog light 21 watt
Brake/tail light 21/4 watt

J35172

5.33b Rear light cluster bulb locations (Saloon and Hatchback)

29 Disconnect the wiring then pull out the bulb, noting the three location cut-outs in the housing.
30 Fit the new bulb using a reversal of the removal procedure.

Rear light cluster

Saloon and Hatchback

31 Open the boot lid and turn the fasteners anti-clockwise to remove the relevant rear light cluster cover (see illustrations).
32 Squeeze together the two red tabs to separate the bulbholder assembly from the light housing (see illustrations).
33 Depress and twist the relevant bulb to remove it (see illustrations).
34 Fit the new bulb using a reversal of the removal procedure.

Estate

35 With the tailgate open, remove the upper

and lower rear light cluster covers – on some models, the lower one is secured with Velcro (see illustrations).
36 Support the rear light cluster from outside, then unscrew and remove the upper and lower wing nuts from inside the cover

5.35a Remove the upper cover . . .

apertures (see illustration). Take care not to drop the nuts inside the inner cavity.
37 Withdraw the rear light cluster from outside (see illustration).
38 Twist the relevant bulbholder anti-clockwise from the rear of the light cluster,

5.35b . . . and lower cover, for access to the rear light cluster retaining wing nuts (Estate)

5.36 Unscrew the wing nuts . . .

5.37 . . . and withdraw the rear light cluster from the outside

5.38a Twist the bulbholder from the light cluster . . .

5.38b . . . then depress and twist the bulb to remove it

Brake light 21 watt

Direction indicator 21 watt, orange

Reversing light 21 watt, halogen bulb

Rear fog light/Tail light 21/4 watt

J35173

5.38c Rear light cluster bulb locations (Estate)

then depress and twist the bulb to remove it **(see illustrations)**.
39 Fit the new bulb using a reversal of the removal procedure.

Number plate light

40 Undo the retaining screws and lower the number plate light unit from the tailgate/boot lid.

41 Remove the festoon-type bulb from the contact springs.
42 Fit the new bulb using a reversal of the removal procedure. Make sure that the tension of the contact springs is sufficient to hold the bulb firmly.

High-level stop-light

43 On Saloon models, carefully pull off the cover.
44 On Estate and Hatchback models, open the tailgate then undo the screws and remove the high-level stop-light and cover **(see illustrations)**.
45 On all models, disconnect the wiring connector and prise out the high-level stop-light unit with a screwdriver **(see illustrations)**.
46 Depress the catches and remove the cover, then pull out the relevant wedge-type bulb **(see illustrations)**.

5.44a Undo the screws . . .

5.44b . . . and remove the high-level stop-light and cover

5.45a Disconnect the wiring . . .

5.45b . . . and prise out the light unit

5.46a Remove the cover . . .

47 Fit the new bulb using a reversal of the removal procedure.

6 Bulbs (interior lights) – renewal

1 Whenever a bulb is renewed, note the following points:
a) *Switch off all interior lights.*
b) *Remember that if the light has just been in use, the bulb may be extremely hot.*
c) *Always check the bulb contacts and holder, ensuring that there is clean metal-to-metal contact.*
d) *Where bayonet-type bulbs are fitted, ensure that the contact springs bear firmly against the bulb contacts.*
e) *Always ensure that the new bulb is of the*

5.46b . . . and pull out the wedge-type bulb

correct rating and that it is completely clean before fitting it.

Sun visor/vanity mirror light

2 Pull down the sun visor.

6.3 Prise out the sun visor/vanity light from the headlining . . .

6.4 . . . then pull out the wedge-type bulb

6.6 Prise out the map reading light . . .

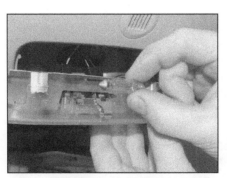

6.7 . . . and release the festoon-type bulb from the contact springs

6.12 Press the bulbholder into the top of the glovebox latch

6.13 Removing the luggage compartment light from the headlining

3 Using a screwdriver, prise out the light from the headlining **(see illustration)**.
4 Pull out the wedge-type bulb from the light **(see illustration)**.
5 Fit the new bulb using a reversal of the removal procedure.

Map reading light

6 Prise out the map reading light using a small screwdriver inserted in the recess opposite the switch **(see illustration)**.
7 Release the festoon-type bulb from the contact springs **(see illustration)**.
8 Fit the new bulb using a reversal of the removal procedure. Make sure that the tension of the contact springs is sufficient to hold the bulb firmly.

Glovebox light

9 Remove the glovebox as described in Chapter 11.
10 Reach up under the glovebox latch, and pull out the wedge-type bulb from the bulbholder **(see illustration)**.
11 Fit the new bulb using a reversal of the removal procedure.
12 If the bulbholder becomes detached from the latch, remove the latch as follows. Undo the retaining screws and withdraw the glovebox latch and bulbholder from the facia. Press the bulbholder into the hole on top of the latch, then refit the latch **(see illustration)**.

Luggage compartment light

13 Prise out the light from the headlining using a small screwdriver **(see illustration)**.

6.10 Removing the glovebox illumination bulb

6.14a Disconnect the wiring, if necessary . . .

14 Where applicable, unclip the reflector from the light unit, and if necessary, disconnect the wiring and remove the light unit from the headlining **(see illustrations)**.

15 Release the festoon-type bulb from the contact springs **(see illustration)**.

16 Fit the new bulb using a reversal of the removal procedure. Make sure that the tension of the contact springs is sufficient to hold the bulb firmly.

Footwell illumination light

17 Remove the driver's side lower facia panel.

18 Pull the bulb out of its holder to remove.

19 Fit the new bulb using a reversal of removal procedure.

Instruments and warning lights

20 Remove the instrument panel as described in Section 11.

21 Twist the bulbholder anti-clockwise to remove it **(see illustration)**.

22 Pull out the wedge-type bulb **(see illustration)**. **Note:** *The Ford bulb is only available together with the bulbholder.*

23 Fit the new bulb using a reversal of the removal procedure.

Cigar lighter illumination

24 Carefully prise out the ashtray and cup holder from the centre console, and disconnect the wiring from the cigar lighter.

25 Use a screwdriver to release the tag, then pull the bulbholder from the side of the cigar lighter **(see illustrations)**.

26 Pull the wedge-type bulb from the bulbholder **(see illustration)**.

27 Fit the new bulb using a reversal of the removal procedure.

Automatic transmission selector illumination

28 Select position N, then prise out the panel from the centre console.

29 Disconnect the bulbholder and pull out the wedge-type bulb.

30 Fit the new bulb using a reversal of the removal procedure.

Heater control illumination

31 Remove the centre console as described in Chapter 11.

32 Remove the radio/cassette audio unit from the centre of the facia as described in Section 24.

33 Use a screwdriver to carefully prise the accessory switches from the heater control trim panel. Prevent damage to the facia by placing card beneath the screwdriver. Disconnect the wiring from the switches.

34 Undo the screws securing the heater control trim panel to the facia. There are two screws located in the accessory switch apertures, two screws located in the top corners of the radio/cassette aperture, and two screws located at the bottom of the panel.

6.14b . . . and unclip the reflector

6.15 Removing the festoon-type bulb from the luggage compartment light

6.21 Twist the bulbholder anti-clockwise to remove it . . .

6.22 . . . then pull out the wedge-type bulb

35 Release the three upper clips, and remove the heater control trim panel from the facia. From the rear of the panel, disconnect the wiring for the liftgate release switch, heated front seat switch, auxiliary climate/heater control switches, and clock.

36 Using pliers, twist the illumination bulbholder anti-clockwise from the rear of the auxiliary climate/heater control panel **(see illustration)**.

6.25a Release the tag . . .

6.25b . . . then pull the bulbholder from the cigar lighter

6.26 Pull the wedge-type bulb from the bulbholder

6.36 Twist the bulbholder anti-clockwise to remove it from the control panel . . .

6.37 . . . then pull out the wedge-type bulb

37 Pull the wedge-type bulb from the bulbholder **(see illustration)**.
38 Fit the new bulb using a reversal of the removal procedure.

7.3a To remove the headlight, pull up the inner . . .

7 Exterior light units – removal and refitting

1 Before removing any light unit, note the following points:
  a) *Ensure that the light is switched off.*
  b) *Remember that if the light has just been in use, the bulb and lens may be extremely hot.*

Headlight and indicator unit

2 Remove the radiator grille as described in Chapter 11. The two retaining fasteners are located next to the headlight units.
3 Pull up the two headlight locking bars, then carefully withdraw the headlight unit from the front of the car. The inner bar is located next to the radiator grille fastener bracket, and the outer bar is located near the wing panel **(see illustrations)**.
4 Disconnect the wiring multi-plug from the rear of the headlight unit **(see illustration)**.
5 Refitting is a reversal of the removal procedure. Have the beam alignment checked or adjusted as described in the next Section.

Front foglight

6 Using a screwdriver or similar tool, carefully prise the foglight bezel from the front bumper. Take care not to damage the paintwork.
7 Undo the three crosshead screws and withdraw the foglight from the bumper sufficient to access the bulbholder.

8 Disconnect the wiring and remove the foglight.
9 Refitting is a reversal of the removal procedure. Note that the foglight reflector is marked TOP to ensure correct location in the front bumper **(see illustration)**. Have the beam alignment checked as described in the next Section.

Rear light cluster

Saloon and Hatchback

10 Open the boot lid and turn the fasteners anti-clockwise to remove the relevant rear light cluster cover.
11 Squeeze together the two red tabs to separate the bulbholder assembly from the light housing.
12 Support the rear light cluster, then undo the retaining screws and remove the unit from the rear of the car. Recover the gasket **(see illustrations)**.
13 Refitting is a reversal of removal. Check the condition of the gasket, and renew it if necessary.

Estate

14 With the tailgate open, remove the upper and lower rear light cluster covers – on some models, the lower one is secured with Velcro.
15 Support the rear light cluster from outside, then unscrew and remove the upper and lower wing nuts from inside the cover apertures **(see illustration)**. Take care not to drop the nuts inside the inner cavity.
16 Withdraw the rear light cluster from

7.3b . . . and outer locking bars . . .

7.3c . . . and withdraw the headlight

7.4 Disconnecting the wiring from the headlight unit

7.9 TOP mark on the front foglight

7.12a Undo the retaining screws . . .

7.12b . . . and withdraw the rear light cluster (Hatchback)

outside, then twist the bulbholders anti-clockwise and remove them from the light cluster unit (see illustration).

17 Refitting is a reversal of removal.

Number plate light

18 Undo the retaining screws and lower the number plate light unit from the tailgate/boot lid.

19 Disconnect the wiring and remove the number plate light.

20 Refitting is a reversal of removal.

High-level stop-light

21 On Saloon models, carefully pull off the cover.

22 On Estate and Hatchback models, open the tailgate then undo the screws and remove the high-level stop-light and cover.

23 On all models, disconnect the wiring connector and prise out the high-level stop-light unit with a screwdriver.

24 Depress the catches and remove the cover.

25 Refitting is a reversal of removal.

8 Headlight and front foglight beam alignment – checking and adjustment

1 Accurate adjustment of the headlight or front foglight beams is only possible using optical beam-setting equipment. This work should therefore be carried out by a Ford dealer, or other service station with the necessary facilities.

2 Temporary adjustment as follows can be made as an emergency measure if the alignment is incorrect following accident damage.

Headlight adjustment

3 Position the unladen vehicle on a level surface, with the tyres at the correct pressure. Bounce the front of the vehicle a few times.

4 On models fitted with load-levelling shock absorbers, leave the vehicle to settle for at least one minute.

5 Switch on the ignition and operate the headlamp levelling system several times, then set it to position 0. Switch off the ignition.

6 Ideally, headlamp beam alignment equipment should now be positioned in front of the headlamps, however, this equipment is not usually available to the average home mechanic. Alternatively, to make a temporary adjustment, position the vehicle 5 metres in front of a wall or garage door, and make a horizontal line at the height of the headlight centres. Mark this line with the position of the headlights as a focal point to make the main beam adjustment. Make a further line slightly below

7 Switch on the headlights and select main beam. Check that the area of light concentration is centred on the main beam focal points marked on the wall.

7.15 Unscrew the wing nuts . . .

8 Now switch the headlights on dipped beam, and check that the beam boundary line touches the lower line on the wall, with the 15° riser commencing directly beneath the main beam mark.

9 If adjustment is necessary, use a screwdriver inserted onto the two adjustment knobs from the top of the unit. These rotate the adjustment turnwheels on the rear of the headlight units. Note that the 'inner' headlights are the main beams, and the 'outer' headlights are the dipped beams.

10 Note that on models equipped with xenon dipped headlights, adjustment is possible for driving on the left or right-hand side of the road, however, this adjustment must be carried out by a Ford dealer.

Front foglight adjustment

11 Position the unladen vehicle on a level surface, with the tyres at the correct pressure. Bounce the front of the vehicle a few times.

12 On models fitted with load-levelling shock absorbers, leave the vehicle to settle for at least one minute.

13 Ideally, foglight beam alignment equipment should now be positioned in front of the foglights, however, this equipment is not usually available to the average home mechanic. Alternatively, to make a temporary adjustment, position the vehicle 5 metres in front of a wall or garage door, and make a horizontal line slightly below the height of the foglight centres. Mark this line with the position of the foglights as a focal point to make the beam adjustment.

9.3 Headlight levelling motor

7.16 . . . and withdraw the rear light cluster

14 Carefully prise out the bezel from the front of the foglight, for access to the single adjustment screw.

15 Switch on the foglights and check that the beam boundary line touches the line on the wall, with the 15° riser commencing at the positional mark.

16 If necessary, turn the adjustment screw as required.

9 Headlight levelling motor – removal and refitting

Removal

1 Remove the headlight as described in Section 7.

2 With the headlight unit on the bench, release the plastic clips and remove the rear cover.

3 Twist or undo the screws and disconnect the pushrod ball from the socket (see illustration). Remove the motor from the headlight.

Refitting

4 Refitting is a reversal of removal.

10 Headlight levelling sensor – removal and refitting

Note: On models with xenon headlamps, headlamp leveling sensors are fitted to the front and rear suspension.

Removal

1 Raise the relevant front or rear of the vehicle, and support on axle stands (see Jacking and vehicle support). Remove the roadwheel.

2 Disconnect the wiring from the headlight levelling sensor. Note that the sensor is connected to the suspension arm by a short link.

3 Disconnect the link from the sensor arm by prising it from the ball.

4 Undo the mounting screws and withdraw the sensor.

11.4 Removing the steering column upper shroud

11.5a Undo the screws . . .

11.5b . . . and remove the lower shroud

Refitting

5 Refitting is a reversal of removal. On completion, have the headlight levelling system initialised by a Ford dealer.

---

11 Instrument panel – removal and refitting

> ⚠ **Warning: The instrument panel must be kept in an upright position at all times, otherwise silicone liquid will leak from the gauges.**

Note: *If a new instrument panel is being fitted, the existing instrument panel configuration must first be uploaded so that the new unit can be programmed with the same configuration. This can only be carried out by a Ford dealer using specialised equipment. Note that Ford* operate a 'new for old' scheme whereby the old instrument panel can be exchanged.

Removal

1 Disconnect the battery negative lead (refer to *Disconnecting the battery* at the end of this manual).

> ⚠ **Warning: Before proceeding, wait a minimum of one minute after disconnecting the battery, as a precaution against accidental firing of the airbag unit. This period ensures that any stored energy in the back-up capacitor is dissipated. We suggest you wait several minutes.**

2 Working in the driver's footwell, undo the retaining screws and unclip the lower facia panel from under the steering column. Where applicable, disconnect the wiring from the electronic automated temperature control (EATC) sensor located on the panel.

3 Where fitted, remove the audio control switch from the steering column. Use a small screwdriver to release the locking tang, then lift the switch from the column and disconnect the wiring.
4 Remove the steering column upper shroud from the lower shroud by inserting a thin screwdriver between the clip on each side **(see illustration)**.
5 Undo the three screws and remove the lower shroud **(see illustrations)**.
6 Undo the screws and remove the instrument panel surround **(see illustrations)**.
7 Undo the two lower screws and withdraw the instrument panel from the facia sufficient for access to the wiring. Pull out the top of the panel first, before removing it **(see illustrations)**.
8 Release the locking tang, and disconnect the wiring from the rear of the instrument panel **(see illustration)**.
9 Withdraw the instrument panel from the facia, and to one side of the steering wheel.

Refitting

10 Refitting is a reversal of removal.

---

12 Instrument panel components – general information, removal and refitting

General information

1 The instrument panel is connected to the powertrain control module (PCM), anti-lock brake system (ABS), traction control system

11.6a Undo the screws . . .

11.6b . . . and remove the instrument panel surround

11.7a Undo the screws . . .

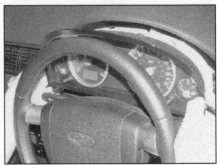

11.7b . . . and withdraw the instrument panel

11.8 Disconnecting the wiring from the instrument panel

13.1a Prise out the ashtray . . .

13.1b . . . and disconnect the wiring from the cigar lighter

13.2a Release the tang . . .

13.2b . . . and remove the cigar lighter illumination light bulbholder

13.3a Release the clip . . .

13.3b . . . and remove the holder from the ashtray

(TCS), and electronic stability program (ESP), by a control area network (CAN) bus. When the ignition is switched on, a display test is carried out to verify that all warning and indicator bulbs are functioning correctly.

2 The instrument panel incorporates a self-diagnosis mode. To enter the mode, depress and hold the tripmeter reset button, then turn the ignition switch to position II. When TEST is displayed, release the tripmeter reset button; the self-diagnosis test will now commence. Press the reset button to navigate through or skip any of the options. To cancel the test, depress and hold the reset button for 5 seconds, or switch off the ignition.

Removal and refitting

3 Remove the warning light and illumination bulbs by twisting them anti-clockwise.
4 At the time of writing, no procedures were available for the removal and refitting of the instrument panel gauges or printed circuit.

13 Cigar lighter –
removal and refitting

Removal

1 Using a screwdriver, carefully prise out the ashtray (and cup holder, where applicable) from the centre console, and disconnect the wiring from the cigar lighter **(see illustrations)**.
2 From the rear of the unit, release the tang and remove the illumination light bulbholder **(see illustrations)**.

3 Remove the cigar lighter element, then use a screwdriver to release the clip, and remove the holder from the ashtray **(see illustrations)**.
4 Release the clip and remove the plastic illumination ring **(see illustration)**.

Refitting

5 Refitting is a reversal of removal.

14 Clock –
removal and refitting

Removal

1 Disconnect the battery negative lead (refer to *Disconnecting the battery* at the end of this manual).
2 Remove the centre console as described in

13.4 Removing the plastic illumination ring

Chapter 11. Remove the radio/cassette audio unit from the centre of the facia as described in Section 24.

3 Use a screwdriver to carefully prise the accessory switches from the heater control trim panel. Prevent damage by placing card beneath the screwdriver. Disconnect the wiring from the switches.
4 Undo the screws securing the heater control trim panel to the facia. There are two screws located in the accessory switch apertures, two screws located in the top corners of the radio/cassette aperture, and two screws located at the bottom of the panel.
5 Release the three upper clips, and remove the heater control trim panel from the facia. From the rear of the panel, disconnect the wiring for the tailgate release switch, heated front seat switch, auxiliary climate/heater control switches, and clock **(see illustration)**.

14.5 Disconnecting the clock wiring

14.6 Clock mounting screws

15.2 Twin horns are fitted to some models

15.4 Horn and mounting bracket

6 With the heater control trim panel on the bench, undo the screws and withdraw the clock **(see illustration)**.

Refitting

7 Refitting is a reversal of removal. Reset the clock on completion.

15 Horn – removal and refitting

Removal

1 Apply the handbrake, then jack up the front of the vehicle and support it on axle stands (see *Jacking and vehicle support*).
2 Remove the undertray/splash shield for access to the horns located on the front valance **(see illustration)**.

16.3a Using a puller to release the wiper arm from its taper

16.3b Removing a wiper arm

3 Disconnect the wiring from the horn terminal.
4 Unscrew the mounting bolt, and withdraw the horn with its mounting bracket from under the vehicle **(see illustration)**.

Refitting

5 Refitting is a reversal of the removal procedure. Tighten the horn unit mounting bolt securely.

16 Wiper arms – removal and refitting

Removal

1 With the wipers 'parked' (ie, in the normal at-rest position), mark the positions of the blades on the screen/rear window, using a wax crayon or strips of masking tape.
2 Lift up the plastic cap from the bottom of the wiper arm, and loosen the nut one or two turns.
3 Lift the wiper arm, and release it from the taper on the spindle by easing it from side to side. If necessary use a puller to release it **(see illustrations)**.
4 Completely remove the nut, and withdraw the wiper arm from the spindle. If necessary, remove the blade from the arm as described in *Weekly checks* at the beginning of this Manual.

Refitting

5 Refitting is a reversal of the removal

17.3a Undo the screws . . .

procedure. Make sure that the arm is fitted in its previously-noted position before tightening the nut to the specified torque.

17 Windscreen wiper motor and linkage – removal and refitting

Removal

1 Make sure that the ignition is switched off. Be aware, however, that there is a live wire supply in the wiring connector to the windscreen wiper motor, which operates the 'park' function. Provided the connector is positioned to one side when the wiper motor is being removed, there is no need to disconnect the battery, as this would entail recoding the radio and initialising the electric windows, etc.
2 Remove the wiper arms as described in Section 16.
3 Undo the screws securing the plastic cowls in front of the windscreen, then lift the rear of the cowl from the retaining groove **(see illustrations)**.
4 Disconnect the wiring from the wiper motor **(see illustration)**.
5 Unscrew the three bolts and remove the wiper motor complete with linkage from the bulkhead **(see illustrations)**.
6 Mark the wiper crank in relation to the motor bracket to ensure correct refitting, then unscrew the retaining nut and remove the crank from the splines on the motor shaft **(see illustration)**.

17.3b . . . then remove the left-hand cowl . . .

17.3c . . . and right-hand cowl

17.4 Disconnect the wiring . . .

17.5a . . . then unscrew the mounting bolts . . .

7 Undo the three mounting bolts and remove the motor from the bracket.

Refitting

8 Refitting is a reversal of the removal procedure, but tighten the nuts/bolts to the specified torque. Make sure that the crank is refitted in its previously-noted position, and also make sure that the wiper motor is in its 'parked' position.

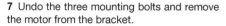

18 Tailgate wiper motor assembly – removal and refitting

Removal

1 Make sure that the ignition is switched off. Be aware, however, that there is a live wire supply in the wiring connector to the rear

17.5b . . . and remove the wiper motor and linkage

17.6 The wiper motor crank

window wiper motor, which operates the 'park' function. Provided the connector is positioned to one side when the wiper motor is being removed, there is no need to disconnect the battery, as this would entail recoding the radio and initialising the electric windows, etc.

2 Remove the tailgate wiper arm as described in Section 16 **(see illustration)**.

3 Open the tailgate, then undo the trim panel retaining screws, noting that some are located beneath plastic covers. On Hatchback models remove the lock cover first. On Estate models, some of the screws are located in the handgrip recesses **(see illustrations)**.

4 Using a wide-bladed screwdriver, carefully prise the trim panel from the tailgate. Insert the screwdriver next to the retaining clips to prevent damage from the clip being torn from the panel.

5 Disconnect the wiring from the wiper motor **(see illustration)**.

6 Undo the mounting screws and withdraw the wiper motor from the tailgate, while guiding the spindle through the rubber grommet **(see illustrations)**.

18.2 Removing the tailgate wiper arm

18.3a Where necessary, prise out the plastic cover . . .

18.3b . . . for access to the screws

18.3c Retaining screws located in the handgrip recesses on Estate models

18.3d Removing the lock cover on Hatchback models

18.5 Disconnect the wiring . . .

18.6a . . . then undo the mounting screws . . .

18.6b . . . and withdraw the wiper motor from the tailgate

18.6c Wiper motor on the bench

18.7 Wiper motor rubber grommet in the tailgate

7 If necessary, remove the rubber grommet from the tailgate **(see illustration)**.

Refitting

8 Refitting is a reversal of the removal procedure. Make sure that the wiper motor is in its 'parked' position before fitting the wiper arm.

19 Generic electronic module – general information, testing, removal and refitting

Note: *The Generic electronic module is also known as the Central timer unit.*

General information

1 As from early 2001, a generic electronic module (GEM) is fitted to control the following functions:
 a) *Direction indicator/hazard warning light control.*
 b) *Interior light control.*
 c) *Instrument panel dimmer control.*
 d) *Heated windscreen and rear window deactivation control.*
 e) *Wiper interval and washer control.*
 f) *Lights-on warning.*
 g) *Door not closed warning.*
 h) *Automatic transmission PRNDL warning.*
 i) *Generation of warning and confirmation tones.*
 j) *Battery protection function (switching off interior lights after a predetermined delay).*
 k) *Window/sunroof closing system control.*

 l) *Checking that doors and tailgate are closed, and activating a warning buzzer.*
 m) *Window regulator and sliding roof closing control.*
 n) *Vehicle static condition monitoring (anti-theft warning system).*

2 The generic electronic module will automatically activate the rear wiper if reverse gear is engaged when the windscreen wipers are switched on. The mode of operation is adapted to the windscreen wipers; if the windscreen wipers are in continual mode, the rear wiper will also be in continual mode, and similarly, if the windscreen wipers are in intermittent mode, likewise the rear wiper will be in intermittent mode. Note, however, that the rear wiper has only one intermittent speed.
3 The remote central locking aerial is attached to the generic electronic module and is located in the wiring harness along the facia carrier.
4 Fault diagnosis of the GEM can be performed by a Ford dealer using a WDS diagnostic instrument, however, it is possible to carry out a limited check of the system as described below.
5 The GEM is programmable and includes a self-diagnosis function. If a new unit is fitted, it must be programmed specifically for the vehicle, as otherwise functions which are not available are recognised as faults and are stored in the memory.

Testing

6 The GEM self-diagnosis system can be activated either by a Ford dealer using the WDS equipment, or by using the integrated

service mode. To enable the integrated service mode, first switch off the ignition and all electrical systems, apply the handbrake, engage neutral (or P on automatic transmission models), and close all doors.
7 Note that if the anti-theft alarm sounds, the service mode cannot be activated. First switch the ignition on then off. Press and hold the rear window heater switch, then switch on the ignition and release the rear window heater switch. At this point, a signal sounds and the indicator lights come on to indicate that the service mode has been entered.
8 Switch the wiper switch to the 'off' position to test the input signals, then check the following components (in no particular order). An acoustic signal sounds and the direction indicator lights flash to indicate receipt of each input signal by the GEM:
 a) *Direction indicators (right, left, hazard warning lights).*
 b) *Sidelights.*
 c) *Intermittent wipe, windscreen.*
 d) *Wash/wipe system, windscreen.*
 e) *Rear wiper.*
 f) *Wash/wipe system, rear window.*
 g) *Doors open/closed.*
 h) *Remote release switch in the centre console for the tailgate/luggage compartment lid.*
 i) *Tailgate/luggage compartment lid release button in the tailgate/luggage compartment lid.*
 j) *Open the tailgate/luggage compartment lid with a key.*
 k) *Locking key on the remote control (the ignition key must not be in the ignition during the test).*
 l) *Release key on the remote control (the ignition key must not be in the ignition during the test).*
 m) *Tailgate/luggage compartment lid release key on the remote control (the ignition key must not be in the ignition during the test).*
 n) *Bonnet open/closed (in vehicles equipped with an anti-theft alarm system).*
 o) *Heated rear window.*
 p) *Heated windscreen (where fitted).*
 q) *Ignition on.*
 r) *Automatic transmission, selector lever position P.*

9 Switch the wiper switch to the 'intermittent'

position to test the output signals – pressing the rear window heater switch activates or deactivates the output signals in the following order:

a) *Front wipers (a signal sounds and the direction indicator lights flash when the Park position is reached).*
b) *Rear window heater.*
c) *Interior lights (the switch for the interior lights must be in the 'door contact' setting).*
d) *'Door ajar' warning light in the instrument panel.*
e) *Rear window wiper.*
f) *Windscreen heater (when the engine is running only).*

10 The GEM automatically exits the service mode 20 seconds after the last input or if the vehicle is driven. This is indicated by three acoustic signals and by the direction indicator lights flashing.

11 If a fault is indicated, first check all wiring and connectors for damage, then if necessary check the component.

Removal

Note: *The GEM must be initialised by a Ford dealer after refitting.*

12 The GEM is located on top of the engine management powertrain control module (PCM) behind the right-hand side of the facia.

13 On left-hand drive models, remove the passenger side lower facia trim. Open the glovebox and disconnect the damper, then squeeze the top of the glovebox and detach the hinges to remove it from the facia.

14 On right-hand drive models, remove the facia lower trim panel.

15 Note the location of the five wiring connectors, then disconnect them from the GEM unit **(see illustration)**.

16 Depress the clip and slide the GEM from the top of the PCM.

Refitting

17 Refitting is a reversal of removal, but have the GEM initialised by a Ford dealer as soon as possible.

20 Telematics control module – general information, removal and refitting

General information

1 The telematics system allows the driver to select the following functions:
a) *Emergency calls.*
b) *Roadside assistance service.*
c) *GPS location of the vehicle.*
d) *Voice communications.*
e) *Route finder system.*
f) *Traffic information.*
g) *Ordering services (hotel, theatre, car parking, etc).*

2 The microphone for the telematics system is attached to the overhead console.

19.15 The generic electronic module (GEM)

3 The control module is located beneath the right-hand side of the facia, and includes a SIM (subscriber identification module), GSM module, GPS receiver, and telematics processor.

Removal

4 On left-hand drive models, remove the passenger side lower facia trim. Open the glovebox and disconnect the damper, then squeeze the top of the glovebox and detach the hinges to remove it from the facia.

5 On right-hand drive models, remove the facia lower trim panel.

6 Unscrew the telematics control module support bracket mounting screw.

7 Push the module retaining bracket from the support bracket for access to the top mounting screw, then undo all the mounting screws and lower the control module.

8 Disconnect the wiring from the module, then disconnect the GPS and GSM aerial leads.

9 Withdraw the module from inside the vehicle.

Refitting

10 Refitting is a reversal of removal.

21 Anti-theft alarm system – general information

1 All UK models are fitted with an anti-theft alarm system, incorporating an engine immobiliser. The system is activated when the vehicle is locked, and has both active and passive capabilities. The active section includes the generic electronic module (GEM – described in Section 19), door and luggage compartment lock actuators, bonnet latch, audio unit security, and the alarm horn. The passive section includes the ignition key transponder, passive anti-theft system (PATS) transceiver and LED, starter relay, fuel injection pump control unit (diesel models), and the powertrain control module (PCM).

2 When activating the anti-theft alarm system, there is a 20 second delay during which time it is still possible to open the

vehicle without triggering the alarm. After the 20 second delay, the system monitors all doors, bonnet and tailgate, provided they are closed. If one of these items is closed later, the system will monitor if after the 20 second delay.

3 If the alarm is triggered, the alarm horn will sound for a period of 30 seconds, and the hazard lights will flash for a period of 5 minutes. An attempt to start the engine or remove the radio automatically triggers the alarm horn.

4 To deactivate the alarm system, the driver's door must be unlocked with the ignition key or remote control. The tailgate may be unlocked with the ignition key or remote control with the alarm system still activated, however, the alarm is again reactivated when the tailgate is locked.

5 The PATS includes a start inhibitor circuit, which makes it impossible to start the engine with the system armed. The immobiliser is deactivated by a transponder chip built into the ignition key.

6 The PATS transceiver unit is fitted around the ignition switch, and it 'reads' the code from a microchip in the ignition key. This means that any replacement or duplicate keys must be obtained through a Ford dealer – any cut locally will not contain the microchip, and will therefore not disarm the immobiliser.

7 If an attempt is made to remove the audio/cassette unit while the alarm is active, the alarm will sound.

22 Cruise control system – general information and component renewal

General information

1 Cruise control is available as an option on some models **(see illustration overleaf)**.

2 The system is active at road speeds above 25 mph (all models except TDCi) or 38 mph (TDCi models).

3 The system comprises an electronic speed control unit with integral actuator and switches mounted in the engine compartment with a control cable connected to the throttle valve actuator, driver-operated switches, brake and clutch pedal switches, an indicator light, and the vehicle speed sensor.

4 The driver-operated switches are mounted on the steering wheel, and allow the driver to control the various functions.

5 The vehicle speed sensor is mounted on the transmission, and generates pulses which are fed to the speed control unit.

6 The brake stop-light switch and clutch pedal switches are used to disable the cruise control system.

7 An indicator light on the instrument panel is illuminated when the system is in operation.

Steering wheel switches

Removal

8 Remove the airbag unit from the steering wheel as described in Section 28.

9 Disconnect the wiring plugs from the horn switch, noting the location of each plug and how the wiring is routed for refitting.

10 Remove the two screws each side securing the operating switches, and remove them as required from the steering wheel.

11 If required (for access to the horn switch, for example), the switch contact plates and springs can be removed, after unscrewing the two retaining screws each side.

Refitting

12 Refitting is a reversal of removal.

Brake and clutch pedal switches

Removal

13 Remove the lower facia panel from under the steering column.

14 Disconnect the multi-plugs from the clutch switch, brake pedal switch and stop-light switch.

15 To remove the clutch and brake pedal switches, twist them anti-clockwise. To remove the stop-light switch, twist it clockwise.

Refitting

16 Refitting is the reverse of removal. To ensure correct operation of the switches, reset the switch by fully extending its plunger. Fully depress the pedal and hold it in this position, then clip the switch securely into position and slowly release the pedal. This will automatically set the position of the switch.

Speed control actuator

Removal

17 Detach the crankcase ventilation hose and vacuum hose from the clips on the engine top cover. Remove the top cover.

18 Remove the cover from the left-hand front suspension strut top mounting brace, then unscrew the three nuts securing the strut to the body and brace.

19 Unscrew the nuts from the cowl and inner wing panel, then remove the strut top mounting brace.

20 Disconnect the speed control cable from the throttle linkage, then unclip the speed control cable from the throttle body.

21 Note the routing and fixing of the speed control cable around the air cleaner and left-hand suspension strut tower, then release it.

22 Behind the left-hand suspension strut tower, unscrew and remove the speed control actuator retaining bolt.

23 Detach the speed control actuator inwards from the retaining bracket, then disconnect the wiring plug.

24 Withdraw the actuator outwards from the engine compartment.

25 To detach the cable from the actuator, press and hold the locking clip, and turn the cap anti-clockwise 90°. Carefully release the locking spring, then push the cable out of the pulley slot.

Refitting

26 Engage the inner cable with the pulley slot in the actuator, then pull the inner cable to ensure there is no free play at the actuator end of the cable.

27 Refit the cable cap and rotate it 90° to secure.

28 Locate the actuator on the bulkhead and reconnect the wiring.

29 Insert and tighten the mounting bolt, then locate the cable in its clips and reconnect it to the throttle body and linkage.

30 Refit the strut top mounting brace and tighten the bolts to the specified torque.

31 Refit the nuts securing the strut to the mounting brace and tighten to the specified torque. Refit the cover.

32 Refit the engine top cover, then locate the crankcase ventilation hose and vacuum hose in their clips.

23 Windscreen/tailgate washer system components – removal and refitting

Removal

Washer reservoir and pump

1 Apply the handbrake and loosen the right-hand front wheel nuts. Jack up the front of the car and support on axle stands. Remove the front wheel.

22.1 Cruise control system components

1 Speed control status indicator
2 Speed control resume switch
3 Speed control set/accelerate and tap up switch
4 Speed control coast and tap down switch
5 Speed control de-activator switch (clutch pedal)
6 Speed control de-activator switches (brake pedal)
7 Speed control de-activate switch
8 Speed control activate switch

J35174

2 Unscrew the bolts, and release the clips to remove the radiator lower cover. Release the wheel arch liner fasteners as necessary for access to the reservoir.

3 Unscrew the two mounting bolts, and pull the reservoir forwards slightly **(see illustrations)**. For better access, it may be necessary to remove the front bumper.

4 Disconnect the multi-plugs for the windscreen washer pump and fluid level sensor **(see illustration)**.

5 Disconnect the hoses from the windscreen washer pump and (where applicable) from the headlight washer pump. Anticipate some loss of fluid by placing a container beneath the reservoir. The pump is attached to the inner face of the reservoir.

6 Withdraw the reservoir from the vehicle.

7 Pull the level sensor, the windscreen washer pump, and (where applicable) the headlight washer pump, from the reservoir.

8 Remove the rubber seals.

Washer nozzle (windscreen)

9 With the bonnet supported in its open position, remove the screws and fasteners, and withdraw the sound deadening cover and material from the area beneath the washer nozzles. Disconnect the washer tube from the bottom of the nozzle **(see illustrations)**.

10 Using a screwdriver and working from under the bonnet, carefully prise out the nozzle. Where necessary, disconnect the wiring for the nozzle heater **(see illustrations)**.

Washer nozzle (rear window)

11 With the tailgate open, carefully pull off

23.3a Washer reservoir front mounting bolts . . .

23.3b . . . and rear mounting bolt

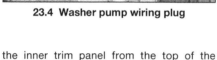

23.4 Washer pump wiring plug

23.9a Remove the sound deadening cover . . .

the inner trim panel from the top of the tailgate.

12 Pull the washer tube from the bottom of the nozzle.

13 Carefully prise the nozzle out of the tailgate glass **(see illustration)**, then prise out the rubber grommet. Where necessary, disconnect the wiring for the nozzle heater.

23.9b . . . and material . . .

23.9c . . . then disconnect the washer tube . . .

23.10a . . . disconnect the jet heater wiring . . .

23.10b . . . and prise out the washer nozzle

23.10c Removing the nozzle from the bonnet

23.13 Removing the rear window washer nozzle

24.6 Using the U-shaped rods to remove the radio/cassette unit

24.9a Disconnecting the wiring . . .

24.9b . . . and aerial from the radio/cassette unit

Washer nozzle (headlight)

14 Remove the front bumper as described in Chapter 11.

15 Disconnect the washer tube from the base of the nozzle.

> **HAYNES HiNT** *To make disconnecting the washer tubes easier, gently heat the tube where it connects to the nozzle, using a hot-air gun or hairdryer. This will soften the tube, making it easier to prise off the tube.*

16 Pull off the nozzle retaining clip and withdraw the nozzle from the bumper.

Refitting

17 Refitting is a reversal of the removal procedure, noting the following points:
  a) In the case of the screen washer nozzles, press them in until they are fully engaged.
  b) The rear window washer nozzle must rest against the rubber seal.
  c) After refitting the headlight washer nozzle, refit the front bumper (see Chapter 11).

24 Radio/cassette player – removal and refitting

Note: *Special tools are required to remove the radio.*

1 If a Ford 'Keycode' unit is fitted, and the unit and/or the battery is disconnected, the unit will not function again on reconnection until the correct security code is entered. Details of this procedure are given in the 'Ford Audio Systems Operating Guide' supplied with the vehicle when new, with the code itself being given in a 'Radio Passport' and/or a 'Keycode Label' at the same time.

2 For obvious security reasons, the recoding procedure is not given in this manual – if you do not have the code or details of the correct procedure, but can supply proof of ownership and a legitimate reason for wanting this information, the vehicle's selling dealer may be able to help.

3 Note that these units will allow only ten attempts at entering the code – any further

attempts will render the unit permanently inoperative until it has been reprogrammed by Ford themselves. At first, three consecutive attempts are allowed; if all three are incorrect, a 30-minute delay is required before another attempt can be made. Each of any subsequent attempts (up to the maximum of ten) can be made only after a similar delay.

Removal

4 Disconnect the battery negative lead (refer to *Disconnecting the battery* at the end of this manual).

5 Where fitted, prise the cover/surround from the front of the radio/cassette player.

6 On models without the satellite navigation system, in order to release the radio retaining clips, two U-shaped rods must be inserted into the special holes on each side of the radio **(see illustration)**. If possible, it is preferable to obtain purpose-made rods from an audio specialist, as these have cut-outs which snap firmly into the clips so that the radio can be pulled out.

7 On models with the satellite navigation system, two special removal keys are required to remove the audio unit – these are handed, left and right, and are unlikely to be available anywhere other than from a Ford dealer.

8 Pull the unit squarely from its aperture, or it may jam. If the unit proves difficult to withdraw, remove the cassette tray (or where applicable, the CD player) from beneath the unit, then reach through the aperture and ease it out from behind.

9 With the radio partly withdrawn, disconnect the feed, earth, aerial and speaker leads **(see illustrations)**. Where applicable, also detach

26.2 Undo the mounting screws, and withdraw the speaker . . .

and remove the plastic support bracket from the rear of the unit.

Refitting

10 Refitting is a reversal of removal. With the leads reconnected to the rear of the unit, press it into position until the retaining clips are felt to engage. Reactivate the unit by entering the correct code in accordance with the maker's instructions.

25 Compact disc player and autochanger – removal and refitting

CD player

1 The procedure is identical to that for the radio/cassette player described in Section 24.

Autochanger

Removal

2 A compact disc (CD) changer is available as an optional extra on most models. It is located beneath the passenger front seat.

3 Disconnect the battery negative lead (refer to *Disconnecting the battery* at the end of this manual).

4 Remove the passenger seat as described in Chapter 11.

5 Lay the passenger seat on its back, then undo the mounting screws from each side and remove the CD autochanger from the bracket.

6 Disconnect the wiring and withdraw the unit from inside the car.

Refitting

7 Refitting is a reversal of removal, but initialise the electric window motors as described in Chapter 11.

26 Speakers – removal and refitting

Removal

1 To remove the door-mounted speakers, first remove the door trim panel as described in Chapter 11.

2 Unscrew the cross-head screws, and withdraw the speaker from the door inner panel **(see illustration)**.
3 Disconnect the wiring and remove the speaker **(see illustration)**.

Refitting

4 Refitting is a reversal of the removal procedure.

27 Radio aerial and lead –
removal and refitting

Removal

1 If just the aerial mast is to be removed, this can be unscrewed from the base, from outside.
2 To remove the aerial base, first remove the overhead console as described in Chapter 11, then unbolt the lead and remove the base from the roof **(see illustration)**.
3 To remove the complete aerial lead, remove the radio/cassette player (Section 24) and overhead console (Chapter 11), then unbolt the aerial lead from the aerial base. Remove the right-hand A-pillar trim panel and the right-hand centre console trim panel, then lift up the right-hand front door weatherstrip and remove the right-hand cowl trim. Remove the right-hand rear door weatherstrip, cowl panel, B-pillar trim panel, and remove the carpet from the right-hand front footwell. Detach the aerial lead from the floor, then attach a piece of string to the roof end of the aerial lead. Pull the aerial lead down the A-pillar, disconnect the string, and remove it from inside the vehicle.

Refitting

4 Refitting is a reversal of the removal procedure.

28 Airbag units –
removal and refitting

⚠ *Warning: Handle any airbag unit with extreme care, as a precaution against personal injury, and always hold it with the cover facing away from the body. If in doubt concerning any proposed work involving an airbag unit or its control circuitry, consult a Ford dealer or other qualified specialist. Stand the airbag with the cover uppermost, and do not expose it to heat sources in excess of 100°C. Do not attempt to open or repair an airbag unit, or apply any electrical current to it. Do not use any airbag unit which is visibly damaged or which has been tampered with. It is recommended that safety glasses are worn when working on the airbag unit.*

26.3 . . . then disconnect the wiring

28.3 Unscrew the mounting bolts . . .

28.4b . . . and airbag wiring

Driver's airbag

1 Disconnect the battery negative lead (refer to *Disconnecting the battery* at the end of this manual).

⚠ *Warning: Before proceeding, wait a minimum of one minute, as a precaution against accidental firing of the airbag unit. This period ensures that any stored energy in the back-up capacitor is dissipated.*

2 Rotate the steering wheel so that one of the airbag mounting bolt holes (at the rear of the steering wheel boss) is visible above the steering column upper shroud. Alternatively, remove the multi-function switches as described in Section 4.
3 Unscrew and remove the first mounting bolt, then turn the steering wheel through 180° and remove the remaining mounting bolt **(see illustration)**.

27.2 Aerial mounting bolt on the roof

4 Carefully withdraw the airbag unit from the steering wheel far enough to disconnect the airbag and horn push wiring, then remove it from inside the vehicle **(see illustrations)**.
5 If a new airbag module is being fitted, the horn switch must be transferred from the old unit. Disconnect the wiring from the switch, then detach the connectors, undo the nuts and remove the switch and contact plate from the module.

⚠ *Warning: The module should only be inverted while the switch and contact plate are being removed. Position it with the cover uppermost after.*

6 Refitting is a reversal of the removal procedure, but tighten the bolts to the specified torque, and initialise the electric window motors as described in Chapter 11.

Passenger's airbag

7 Disconnect the battery negative lead (refer

28.4a . . . then disconnect the horn wiring . . .

28.4c Driver's airbag module removed from the steering wheel

28.9 Disconnecting the wiring from the passenger's airbag

28.10 Unscrewing the passenger's airbag mounting bolts

28.12 The curtain airbag module is located behind the rear luggage compartment side panel

to *Disconnecting the battery* at the end of this manual).

⚠ *Warning: Before proceeding, wait a minimum of one minute, as a precaution against accidental firing of the airbag unit. This period ensures that any stored energy in the back-up capacitor is dissipated.*

8 Remove the glovebox and latch as described in Chapter 11.

9 Disconnect the wiring from the passenger airbag module **(see illustration)**. To do this, slide the clips away from the module.

10 Unscrew the retaining bolts and remove the airbag module from the bulkhead cross-beam **(see illustration)**.

⚠ *Warning: The retaining bolts must only be used a maximum of three times. Centre punch them to indicate the number of times they have been unscrewed.*

29.3 Airbag control module located beneath the centre console

30.3a Removing the large coil spring

11 Refitting is a reversal of the removal procedure, but tighten the bolts to the specified torque, and initialise the electric window motors as described in Chapter 11.

Side airbag and curtain airbag

12 Removal of the side airbag and curtain airbag units requires work which is not considered to be within the scope of the home mechanic. The vehicle should be taken to a Ford dealer for this work to be undertaken **(see illustration)**.

29 Airbag control module – removal and refitting

Caution: New airbag modules must be configured following installation. This work must be carried out by a Ford dealer, using specialist equipment.

Removal

1 Disconnect the battery negative lead (refer to *Disconnecting the battery* at the end of this manual).

⚠ *Warning: Before proceeding, wait a minimum of one minute, as a precaution against accidental firing of the airbag unit. This period ensures that any stored energy in the back-up capacitor is dissipated.*

2 Remove the centre console as described in Chapter 11.

3 Disconnect the wiring from the airbag control module **(see illustration)**.

30.3b Use adhesive tape to keep the clock spring in its straight-ahead position

4 Unscrew the nuts and remove the module from the floor. Note the forward pointing arrow on the upper face of the module.

Refitting

5 Refitting is a reversal of the removal procedure, but tighten the mounting nuts to the specified torque. Initialise the electric window motors as described in Chapter 11.

30 Airbag clock spring – removal and refitting

Removal

1 Disconnect the battery negative lead (refer to *Disconnecting the battery* at the end of this manual).

⚠ *Warning: Before proceeding, wait a minimum of one minute, as a precaution against accidental firing of the airbag unit. This period ensures that any stored energy in the back-up capacitor is dissipated.*

2 Remove the lower trim panel from beneath the steering column. There are 4 screws and 2 clips.

3 Remove the steering wheel as described in Chapter 10, then remove the large coil spring. Make sure the front wheels are in their straight-ahead position. Ensure the airbag clock spring remains in its straight-ahead position using adhesive tape **(see illustrations)**.

4 Where fitted, remove the audio control switch from the steering column lower shroud using a thin screwdriver to release the locking tang. Disconnect the wiring.

5 Using a screwdriver, release the clips and remove the steering column upper shroud, then undo the screws and remove the lower shroud.

6 Remove both multi-function switches from the steering column as described in Section 4.

7 If necessary, undo the screw and remove the spreader plate from under the steering column and position it to one side. Note that it is possible to remove the clock spring leaving the plate in position.

8 Disconnect the wiring from the clock spring **(see illustration)**.

9 Using a screwdriver, carefully release the plastic locking clips and withdraw the clock spring from the steering column **(see illustrations)**.

Refitting

10 Refitting is a reversal of removal, but make sure that all wiring is connected correctly. If the spreader plate was removed, ensure that the clock spring wiring is routed down the special depression. **Note:** *The clock spring must be fitted in its central position, with the special alignment arrows aligned (see illustration). To check for this position, turn the clock spring housing anti-clockwise until resistance is felt, then turn in the opposite direction by two-and-a-half turns. The front wheels must still be in their straight-ahead position before refitting the clock spring.* Finally, initialise the electric window motors as described in Chapter 11.

31 Airbag side impact sensor – removal and refitting

Removal

1 Disconnect the battery negative lead (refer to *Disconnecting the battery* at the end of this manual).

⚠ **Warning: Before proceeding, wait a minimum of one minute, as a precaution against accidental firing of the airbag unit. This period ensures that any stored energy in the back-up capacitor is dissipated.**

2 With the relevant side doors open, pull the rubber weatherstrips away from the B-pillar for access to the trim panel.

3 Adjust the seat belt height to its lowest position. Prise out the cover and undo the uppermost screw, then unclip the trim panel from the B-pillar. Undo the screws and unclip the lower trim panel from the B-pillar.

4 Undo the screws then unclip the sill inner trim panel.

5 Disconnect the wiring from the side impact sensor located at the bottom of the B-pillar.

6 Unscrew the bolt and withdraw the sensor **(see illustration)**.

31.6 Airbag side impact sensor mounting bolt

30.8 Disconnect the wiring from the airbag clock spring

30.9b . . . then withdraw the clock spring from the steering column

Refitting

7 Refitting is a reversal of removal, but tighten the mounting bolt to the specified torque. Initialise the electric window motors as described in Chapter 11.

32 Front crash sensor – removal and refitting

Removal

1 Disconnect the battery negative lead (refer to *Disconnecting the battery* at the end of this manual).

⚠ **Warning: Before proceeding, wait a minimum of one minute, as a precaution against accidental firing of the airbag unit. This period ensures that any stored energy in the back-up capacitor is dissipated.**

2 Remove the radiator grille as described in Chapter 11.

3 Disconnect the wiring from the crash sensor located below the bonnet lock **(see illustration)**.

4 Unscrew the bolt and withdraw the sensor.

Refitting

5 Refitting is a reversal of removal, but tighten the mounting bolt to the specified torque. Initialise the electric window motors as described in Chapter 11.

30.9a Use a screwdriver to release the plastic locking clips . . .

30.10 Airbag clock spring alignment arrows

33 Parking sensor system – general information

Where fitted as an option, the park reverse aid is an ultrasonic proximity detection system, intended to help avoid rear collisions when reversing.

The system consists of four ultrasonic sensors mounted in the rear bumper, a display/buzzer unit mounted in the C-pillar trim panel, and an ECU mounted behind the left-hand side trim panel in the luggage compartment.

The system is only operational when reverse gear is engaged; changing audible and visual signals warn the driver of impending contact as the car reverses towards an object in its path.

The sensors in the bumper can be

32.3 The crash sensor is located beneath the bonnet lock

unclipped and disconnected once the rear bumper is removed, and the display/buzzer unit can be removed after removal of the C-pillar trim panel. Refer to Chapter 11 for this procedure.

The system ECU can be disconnected once the luggage area left-hand trim panel is removed.

34 Ice/frost warning sender unit – removal and refitting

Removal

1 Remove the front bumper as described in Chapter 11.
2 Unclip the sender unit and disconnect the wiring **(see illustration)**.

Refitting

3 Refitting is a reversal of removal.

35 Satellite navigation system – general information

The satellite navigation system uses Global Positioning System (GPS) satellites to track the car against a digital map stored on CD. The antenna for the AM/FM radio and telematics system (where applicable) is also used for the satellite navigation system. The system receives input signals from the reversing lamp switch and the ABS hydraulic control unit. The reversing lamp switch allows the system module to determine whether the vehicle is moving forward or backward. The ABS rear wheel sensors provide the system with data on how far the vehicle has travelled, and a compass is fitted. The CD autochanger is the communication link from the navigation module to the display panel on the radio/cassette unit. The digital map is stored on a CD, which is read by the navigation module. The navigation module is the heart of the system, processing all data received from the antenna, wheel sensors, compass and map CD, and providing instructions which are displayed on the radio/cassette display panel.

Any problems with the system should be referred to a Ford dealer for diagnosis.

36 Electric seat components – removal and refitting

Heated seats

1 If heated seats are fitted, both driver's and front passenger seats have heating elements built into the seat cushion and backrest.
2 No repairs can be made to the heating elements without dismantling the seat and removing the seat fabric – therefore this work should be left to a Ford dealer or other specialist.
3 The heated seat switches are removed as described in Section 4.

Seat adjustment components

4 Only the driver's seat is equipped with

34.2 Unclipping the ice/frost warning sender unit from the front bumper

motors, and only the highest specification models have anything other than a height adjustment motor.
5 To gain access to the motors, remove the driver's seat as described in Chapter 11.
6 The motors are bolted to a mounting frame, which in turn is bolted to the seat base. Before removing a motor, trace its wiring back from the motor to its wiring plug, and disconnect it.
7 Remove the mounting frame bolts or the motor mounting bolts, as applicable, and remove the components from the seat base.
8 Refitting is a reversal of removal. It is worth periodically greasing the worm-drive components and seat runners, to ensure trouble-free operation.
9 For further diagnosis of any problems with the system, refer to Sections 2 and 3, and to the wiring diagrams at the end of this Chapter.

FORD MONDEO 2000 on wiring diagrams

Diagram 1

Key to symbols

Bulb	⊗
Switch	
Multiple contact switch (ganged)	
Fuse/fusible link and current rating	F5 30A
Resistor	
Variable resistor	
Connecting wires	
Plug and socket contact	
Item no.	2
Pump/motor	M
Earth point and location	E12
Gauge/meter	
Diode	
Wire splice or soldered joint	
Solenoid actuator	
Light emitting diode (LED)	
Wire colour and wire size (brown with black tracer, 4mm^2)	Br/Sw 4
Screened cable	

Dashed outline denotes part of a larger item, containing in this case an electronic or solid state device.
2 - unspecified connector pin 2.
182 1 - Connector C182, pin 1.

Earth points

E1	Battery earth	**E8**	RH front door sill
E2	LH front door sill	**E9**	RH 'A' pillar bottom
E3	LH rear wing	**E10**	LH 'A' pillar bottom
E4	LH front engine compartment	**E11**	LH engine near battery fuse box
E5	RH front engine compartment	**E12**	Center of dash board
E6	RH 'A' pillar bottom	**E13**	RH engine rear
E7	RH 'A' pillar middle		

Key to circuits

Diagram 1	Information for wiring diagrams
Diagram 2	Front and rear wash/wipe, and airbags
Diagram 3	Central locking, ABS, cigarette lighter and rear power point
Diagram 4	Interior lights, clock, horn non xenon headlights and non xenon headlight leveling
Diagram 5	Xenon headlights, xenon headlight leveling, brake lights, reversing lights and licence plate lights
Diagram 6	Electric mirrors, sidelights, dimming rear view mirror, foglights, direction indicators and hazard lights
Diagram 7	Electric windows, heated windows and mirrors
Diagram 8	Sunroof, radio and engine cooling
Diagram 9	Air conditioning
Diagram 10	Cruise control and automatic transmission
Diagram 11	Instrument module, instrument and switch illumination

Fuse table

Battery fuse box

Fuses	Rating	Circuit protected
F1	30A	ABS
F2	50A	Ignition relay
F3	60A	Diesel engine heater
F4	30A	Heated rear window
F6	40A	Heater blower relay
F7	50A	Main power
F8	60A	Engine cooling, pre-glow relay
F9	20A	PCM relay
F10	40A	Engine cooling
F11	30A	Heated windscreen
F13	30A	Heated windscreen
F15	3A	Heated windscreen
F16	20A	LH xenon headlight
	7.5A	LH headlight without xenon
F17	10A	Automatic transmission
F18	20A	RH xenon headlight
	7.5A	RH headlight without xenon
F20	20A	ABS
F21	15A	Light switch
F22	20A	Headlight cleaning relay
F23	7.5A	Battery backup sounder (petrol)
	15A	Injection relays, booster heater (diesel)
F24	20A	Central timer unit
F25	15A	Central timer unit
F26	20A	Horn relay
F27	15A	Fuel pump relay, windscreen heater
F28	20A	Ignition switch
F29	30A	Starter relay
F30	7.5A	Alternator
F31	7.5A	Air conditioning
F32	3A	Automatic transmission, engine control module
F37	15A	Oxygen sensor
F40	7.5A	Engine
F42	10A	Engine

Central junction box

Fuses	Rating	Circuit protected
F60	25A	Electric windows
F61	25A	Electric windows
F62	15A	Light switch
F63	7.5A	Direction indicators
F64	7.5A	Direction indicators
F65	7.5A	Air conditioning
F66	30A	Drivers power seat
F67	7.5A	Alarm
F68	15A	Cigarette lighter
F69	7.5A	Radio, instrument cluster
F70	15A	RH rear power point
F72	20A	Radio
F73	20A	Sunroof
F74	20A	Trailer
F75	7.5A	Electric mirrors
F76	7.5A	Air conditioning
F77	7.5A	ABS, traction control
F78	7.5A	Instrument cluster, airbag
F80	7.5A	Automatic transmission, reverse lights
F81	7.5A	Temperature sensor, automatic transmission, seat sensor
F82	7.5A	Air conditioning, windscreen washer heater, booster heater, cruise control
F83	15A	Heated seats
F84	20A	Light switch
F85	7.5A	LH headlight
F86	7.5A	RH headlight
F88	15A	Low beam relay, light switch
F89	7.5A	Airbag
F90	15A	Rear wiper motor
F91	7.5A	Electric windows, dimming mirror, sunroof
F92	10A	Trailer
F93	10A	Headlights, brake lights, heater blower
F94	20A	Wash/wipe
F95	7.5A	Low beam headlights
F97	7.5A	Licence plate lights, glove box light, central timer unit
F98	7.5A	Electric mirrors, heated mirrors
F99	7.5A	Interior lights
F100	7.5A	Multimedia module
F101	3A	CD changer

H32678

Wire colours

Br	Brown	**Gr**	Grey
Bl	Blue	**Or**	Orange
Ro	Red	**Pu**	Purple
Ge	Yellow	**Sw**	Black
Gn	Green	**Ws**	White

Key to items

1 Battery
2 Battery fuse box
3 Central junction box
4 Ignition switch
5 Ignition relay
6 Windscreen wiper relay
7 Rear wiper relay
8 Windscreen wiper motor
9 Headlight cleaning relay
10 Wash/wipe switch
11 Central timer unit
12 LH windscreen washer heater
13 RH windscreen washer heater
14 Washer pump
15 Headlight washer pump
16 Rear wiper motor
17 Diagnostic connector
18 Airbag control module
19 Drivers head airbag
20 Passenger head airbag
21 Passenger seat sensor
22 Drivers seat position sensor
23 Impact sensor
24 Passenger seatbelt
     pre tensioner
25 Drivers seatbelt
     pre tensioner
26 Passengers seatbelt switch
27 Drivers seatbelt switch
28 LH side airbag sensor
29 RH side airbag sensor
30 LH side airbag
31 RH side airbag
32 Passengers airbag
33 Clock spring
34 Drivers airbag
35 Airbag dissabled light

Diagram 2

MTS
H32679

Wash/wipe

Airbags

Wire colours

Br	Brown	**Gr**	Grey
Bl	Blue	**Or**	Orange
Ro	Red	**Pu**	Purple
Ge	Yellow	**Sw**	Black
Gn	Green	**Ws**	White

MTS
H32680

Key to items

1	Battery	39	LH rear door switch
2	Battery fuse box	40	Aerial
4	Ignition switch	41	Passenger door lock
11	Central timer unit	42	Driver door lock
17	Diagnostic connector	43	LH rear door lock
36	LH front door switch	44	RH rear door lock
37	RH front door switch	45	Tailgate motor
38	RH rear door switch	46	Tailgate release interior switch

47	Tailgate external release switch
48	ABS or Stability module
49	Brake light switch
50	Yaw velocity sensor
51	Steering position sensor
52	Traction control switch
53	Brake pressure sensor

54	LH front wheel sensor
55	LH rear wheel sensor
56	RH front wheels sensor
57	RH rear wheel sensor
58	Cigarette lighter
59	RH rear socket
∗	Stability control only

Diagram 3

Central locking

ABS

Cigarette lighter and rear power point

Wire colours

Br Brown   Gr Grey
Bl Blue   Or Orange
Ro Red   Pu Purple
Ge Yellow Sw Black
Gn Green   Ws White

MTS
H32681

Key to items

1 Battery
2 Battery fuse box
3 Central junction box
4 Ignition switch
11 Central timer unit
33 Clock spring
36 LH front door switch
37 RH front door switch
38 RH rear door switch
39 LH rear door switch
45 Tailgate motor
60 Battery saver relay
61 LH front footwell light
62 RH front footwell light
63 Rear dome light
64 Front dome light
65 Boot light
66 LH vanity mirror light
67 RH vanity mirror light
68 Light switch
69 Glove box light
70 Glove box light switch
71 Horn switch
72 Horn relay
73 Hi pitch horn
74 Lo pitch horn
75 Low beam relay
76 LH headlight
   a) low beam
   b) high beam
77 RH headlight
   (as 76)

Diagram 4

78 High beam relay
79 Indicator switch
80 Clock

* Estate only
** 4 & 5 door only

Interior lights

Clock

Headlights without xenon

Headlight leveling without xenon

Horn

Wire colours

Br	Brown	**Gr**	Grey
Bl	Blue	**Or**	Orange
Ro	Red	**Pu**	Purple
Ge	Yellow	**Sw**	Black
Gn	Green	**Ws**	White

MTS
H32682

Key to items

1	Battery	68	Light switch	78	High beam relay
2	Battery fuse box	75	Low beam relay	79	Indicator switch
3	Central junction box	76	LH headlight	81	Xenon headlight relay
4	Ignition switch		a) low beam	82	Xenon headlight
5	Ignition relay		b) high beam		calibration connector
11	Central timer unit	77	RH headlight	83	Rear headlight level sensor
17	Diagnostic connector		(as 76)	84	Front headlight level sensor
49	Brake light switch				

85	LH tail light	89	RH licence plate light
	a) brake light	90	LH licence plate light
	b) reverse light		
86	RH tail light		
	(as 85)		
87	High level brake light	*	4 door only
88	Reverse light switch	**	5 door only

Diagram 5

Xenon headlights

Xenon headight leveling

Brake lights

Reversing lights

Licence plate lights

Diagram 6

Wire colours

Br	Brown	**Gr**	Grey
Bl	Blue	**Or**	Orange
Ro	Red	**Pu**	Purple
Ge	Yellow	**Sw**	Black
Gn	Green	**Ws**	White

MTS
H32683

Key to items

1	Battery	76	LH headlight	84	Front headlight
2	Battery fuse box		c) side light		level sensor
3	Central junction box		d) direction indicator	85	LH tail light
4	Ignition switch	77	RH headlight		c) tail light
5	Ignition relay		(as 76)		d) fog light
11	Central timer unit	79	Indicator switch		e) direction indicator
68	Light switch	83	Rear headlight	86	RH tail light
			level sensor		(as 85)

88	Reverse light switch	97	Mirror folding module
91	LH front foglight	98	Drivers mirror
92	RH front foglight	99	Passengers mirror
93	LH side indicator	100	Dimming rear view mirror
94	RH side indicator		
95	Hazard warning	*	without xenon
	light switch	**	xenon only
96	Electric mirror switch		

Side and tail lights

Electric mirrors

Dimming rear view mirror

Direction indicators and hazard warning lights

Fog lights

Wire colours

Br	Brown	**Gr**	Grey
Bl	Blue	**Or**	Orange
Ro	Red	**Pu**	Purple
Ge	Yellow	**Sw**	Black
Gn	Green	**Ws**	White

MTS
H32684

Key to items

1	Battery	98	Drivers mirror
2	Battery fuse box	99	Passengers mirror
3	Central junction box	100	Dimming rear view mirror
4	Ignition switch	101	Windscreen heater relay
5	Ignition relay	102	LH windscreen heater
11	Central timer unit	103	RH windscreen heater

104	Windscreen heater switch	110	Passenger window switch
105	Rear window heater relay	111	Passenger window motor
106	Rear window heater switch	112	LH rear window switch
107	Rear window heater	113	LH rear window motor
108	Drivers window switch	114	RH rear window switch
109	Drivers window motor	115	RH rear window motor

Diagram 7

Electric windows

Heated windows and mirrors

Diagram 8

Wire colours

Br	Brown	Gr	Grey
Bl	Blue	Or	Orange
Ro	Red	Pu	Purple
Ge	Yellow	Sw	Black
Gn	Green	Ws	White

MTS
H32685

Key to items

1 Battery
2 Battery fuse box
3 Central junction box
4 Ignition switch
5 Ignition relay
11 Central timer unit
116 Sunroof switch
117 Sunroof module
118 Sunroof motor
119 Radio
120 LH front speaker
121 RH front speaker
122 LH rear speaker
123 RH rear speaker
124 Aerial
125 Remote control switch
126 Starter relay
127 Starter motor
128 Alternator
129 PCM relay
130 High speed engine
    cooling fan relay
131 Engine cooling
    fan relay
132 Engine coolant
    temperature sensor
133 Engine cooling
    fan resistor
134 Engine cooling fan
    motor
135 Second cooling
    fan motor

* 1.8l & 2.0l only
** diesel only

Sunroof

Radio

Starting and charging

Engine cooling

Wire colours

Br	Brown	**Gr**	Grey
Bl	Blue	**Or**	Orange
Ro	Red	**Pu**	Purple
Ge	Yellow	**Sw**	Black
Gn	Green	**Ws**	White

MTS
H32686

Key to items

1 Battery
2 Battery fuse box
3 Central junction box
4 Ignition switch
5 Ignition relay
17 Diagnostic connector
129 PCM relay

136 Air conditioning
  wide open throttle relay
137 Heater blower relay
138 A/C clutch solenoid
139 A/C compressor
  cycling switch
140 Dual pressure switch

141 Heater blower motor
142 Heater blower resistor pack
143 Heater blower switch
144 Air conditioning module
145 Floor air temperature sensor
146 Recirculation door motor

147 Defrost mode actuator
148 Panel/floor mode actuator
149 Air temperature mode actuator

Diagram 9

Typical air conditioning

Wire colours

Br	Brown	**Gr**	Grey
Bl	Blue	**Or**	Orange
Ro	Red	**Pu**	Purple
Ge	Yellow	**Sw**	Black
Gn	Green	**Ws**	White

Key to items

1 Battery
2 Battery fuse box
3 Central junction box
4 Ignition switch
5 Ignition relay
17 Diagnostic connector
33 Clock spring
49 Brake light switch
129 PCM relay
150 Cruise control module
151 Vehicle speed sensor
152 Brake pedal position switch
153 Clutch pedal position switch
154 Transmission control unit
155 Transmission range sensor
156 Transmission hardware unit
157 Brake pressure switch
158 Reverse light relay
159 Gearshift lever unit

Diagram 10

MTS
H32687

* diesel only

Automatic transmission

Cruise control

Engine control module

See diagram 11
Light switch

See diagram 11
Instrument module

See diagram 11
Instrument module

Engine control module

See diagram 8
Starter relay

Wire colours

Br	Brown	**Gr**	Grey
Bl	Blue	**Or**	Orange
Ro	Red	**Pu**	Purple
Ge	Yellow	**Sw**	Black
Gn	Green	**Ws**	White

MTS
H32688

Key to items

1 Battery
2 Battery fuse box
3 Central junction box
4 Ignition switch
5 Ignition relay
11 Central timer unit
17 Diagnostic connector
68 Light switch
79 Indicator switch
159 Gearshift lever unit
160 Instrument module
    a) instrument illumination
161 Outside temperature
    thermostat switch
162 Booster heater
163 Brake fluid level switch
164 Handbrake switch
165 Oil pressure switch
166 Fuel tank sender unit

Diagram 11

* diesel only
** petrol only

Dimensions and weights

Note: *All figures are approximate, and vary according to model. Refer to manufacturer's data for exact figures*

Dimensions

Overall length:
    Saloon .... 4731 mm
    Hatchback .... 4753 mm
    Estate .... 4804 mm (4831 mm with body styling kit)
Overall width – including mirrors .... 1931 mm
Overall height – at kerb weight:
    Saloon/Hatchback .... 1429 to 1459 mm
    Estate:
        Including roof rails .... 1481 to 1514 mm
        Without roof rails .... 1441 to 1474 mm
Wheelbase .... 2754 mm
Track width:
    Front .... 1522 mm
    Rear .... 1537 mm

Weights

	Hatchback	Saloon	Estate
Kerb weight:			
1.8 (81 kW) petrol	1384 to 1416 kg	1374 to 1404 kg	1432 to 1465 kg
1.8 (92 kW) petrol	1384 to 1440 kg	1373 to 1430 kg	1431 to 1488 kg
2.0 petrol:			
Manual transmission	1388 to 1444 kg	1376 to 1433 kg	1435 to 1491 kg
Automatic transmission	1421 to 1476 kg	1409 to 1465 kg	1467 to 1523 kg
2.5 V6 petrol	1467 to 1518 kg	1458 to 1510 kg	1518 to 1567 kg
2.0 (66 kW) diesel	1492 to 1519 kg	1485 to 1511 kg	1545 to 1574 kg
2.0 (85/96 kW) diesel	1498 to 1547 kg	1491 to 1541 kg	1551 to 1600 kg

Maximum roof rack load:
    Estate .... 100 kg
    All others .... 75 kg
Maximum towing weight:
    Hatchback/Saloon:
        Petrol models .... 1875 to 1950 kg
        Diesel models .... 1975 to 1980 kg
    Estate:
        Petrol models .... 2030 to 2105 kg
        Diesel models .... 2140 kg
Trailer nose weight limit .... 75 kg

Length (distance)

Inches (in)	x 25.4	= Millimetres (mm)	x 0.0394	= Inches (in)
Feet (ft)	x 0.305	= Metres (m)	x 3.281	= Feet (ft)
Miles	x 1.609	= Kilometres (km)	x 0.621	= Miles

Volume (capacity)

Cubic inches (cu in; in³)	x 16.387	= Cubic centimetres (cc; cm³)	x 0.061	= Cubic inches (cu in; in³)
Imperial pints (Imp pt)	x 0.568	= Litres (l)	x 1.76	= Imperial pints (Imp pt)
Imperial quarts (Imp qt)	x 1.137	= Litres (l)	x 0.88	= Imperial quarts (Imp qt)
Imperial quarts (Imp qt)	x 1.201	= US quarts (US qt)	x 0.833	= Imperial quarts (Imp qt)
US quarts (US qt)	x 0.946	= Litres (l)	x 1.057	= US quarts (US qt)
Imperial gallons (Imp gal)	x 4.546	= Litres (l)	x 0.22	= Imperial gallons (Imp gal)
Imperial gallons (Imp gal)	x 1.201	= US gallons (US gal)	x 0.833	= Imperial gallons (Imp gal)
US gallons (US gal)	x 3.785	= Litres (l)	x 0.264	= US gallons (US gal)

Mass (weight)

Ounces (oz)	x 28.35	= Grams (g)	x 0.035	= Ounces (oz)
Pounds (lb)	x 0.454	= Kilograms (kg)	x 2.205	= Pounds (lb)

Force

Ounces-force (ozf; oz)	x 0.278	= Newtons (N)	x 3.6	= Ounces-force (ozf; oz)
Pounds-force (lbf; lb)	x 4.448	= Newtons (N)	x 0.225	= Pounds-force (lbf; lb)
Newtons (N)	x 0.1	= Kilograms-force (kgf; kg)	x 9.81	= Newtons (N)

Pressure

Pounds-force per square inch (psi; lbf/in²; lb/in²)	x 0.070	= Kilograms-force per square centimetre (kgf/cm²; kg/cm²)	x 14.223	= Pounds-force per square inch (psi; lbf/in²; lb/in²)
Pounds-force per square inch (psi; lbf/in²; lb/in²)	x 0.068	= Atmospheres (atm)	x 14.696	= Pounds-force per square inch (psi; lbf/in²; lb/in²)
Pounds-force per square inch (psi; lbf/in²; lb/in²)	x 0.069	= Bars	x 14.5	= Pounds-force per square inch (psi; lbf/in²; lb/in²)
Pounds-force per square inch (psi; lbf/in²; lb/in²)	x 6.895	= Kilopascals (kPa)	x 0.145	= Pounds-force per square inch (psi; lbf/in²; lb/in²)
Kilopascals (kPa)	x 0.01	= Kilograms-force per square centimetre (kgf/cm²; kg/cm²)	x 98.1	= Kilopascals (kPa)
Millibar (mbar)	x 100	= Pascals (Pa)	x 0.01	= Millibar (mbar)
Millibar (mbar)	x 0.0145	= Pounds-force per square inch (psi; lbf/in²; lb/in²)	x 68.947	= Millibar (mbar)
Millibar (mbar)	x 0.75	= Millimetres of mercury (mmHg)	x 1.333	= Millibar (mbar)
Millibar (mbar)	x 0.401	= Inches of water (inH₂O)	x 2.491	= Millibar (mbar)
Millimetres of mercury (mmHg)	x 0.535	= Inches of water (inH₂O)	x 1.868	= Millimetres of mercury (mmHg)
Inches of water (inH₂O)	x 0.036	= Pounds-force per square inch (psi; lbf/in²; lb/in²)	x 27.68	= Inches of water (inH₂O)

Torque (moment of force)

Pounds-force inches (lbf in; lb in)	x 1.152	= Kilograms-force centimetre (kgf cm; kg cm)	x 0.868	= Pounds-force inches (lbf in; lb in)
Pounds-force inches (lbf in; lb in)	x 0.113	= Newton metres (Nm)	x 8.85	= Pounds-force inches (lbf in; lb in)
Pounds-force inches (lbf in; lb in)	x 0.083	= Pounds-force feet (lbf ft; lb ft)	x 12	= Pounds-force inches (lbf in; lb in)
Pounds-force feet (lbf ft; lb ft)	x 0.138	= Kilograms-force metres (kgf m; kg m)	x 7.233	= Pounds-force feet (lbf ft; lb ft)
Pounds-force feet (lbf ft; lb ft)	x 1.356	= Newton metres (Nm)	x 0.738	= Pounds-force feet (lbf ft; lb ft)
Newton metres (Nm)	x 0.102	= Kilograms-force metres (kgf m; kg m)	x 9.804	= Newton metres (Nm)

Power

Horsepower (hp)	x 745.7	= Watts (W)	x 0.0013	= Horsepower (hp)

Velocity (speed)

Miles per hour (miles/hr; mph)	x 1.609	= Kilometres per hour (km/hr; kph)	x 0.621	= Miles per hour (miles/hr; mph)

Fuel consumption*

Miles per gallon, Imperial (mpg)	x 0.354	= Kilometres per litre (km/l)	x 2.825	= Miles per gallon, Imperial (mpg)
Miles per gallon, US (mpg)	x 0.425	= Kilometres per litre (km/l)	x 2.352	= Miles per gallon, US (mpg)

Temperature

Degrees Fahrenheit = (°C x 1.8) + 32   Degrees Celsius (Degrees Centigrade; °C) = (°F - 32) x 0.56

It is common practice to convert from miles per gallon (mpg) to litres/100 kilometres (l/100km), where mpg x l/100 km = 282

Spare parts are available from many sources, including maker's appointed garages, accessory shops, and motor factors. To be sure of obtaining the correct parts, it will sometimes be necessary to quote the vehicle identification number. If possible, it can also be useful to take the old parts along for positive identification. Items such as starter motors and alternators may be available under a service exchange scheme – any parts returned should be clean.

Our advice regarding spare parts is as follows.

Officially appointed garages

This is the best source of parts which are peculiar to your car, and which are not otherwise generally available (eg, badges, interior trim, certain body panels, etc). It is also the only place at which you should buy parts if the vehicle is still under warranty.

Accessory shops

These are very good places to buy materials and components needed for the maintenance of your car (oil, air and fuel filters, light bulbs, drivebelts, greases, brake pads, touch-up paint, etc). Components of this nature sold by a reputable shop are of the same standard as those used by the car manufacturer.

Besides components, these shops also sell tools and general accessories, usually have convenient opening hours, charge lower prices, and can often be found close to home. Some accessory shops have parts counters where components needed for almost any repair job can be purchased or ordered.

Motor factors

Good factors will stock all the more important components which wear out comparatively quickly, and can sometimes supply individual components needed for the overhaul of a larger assembly (eg, brake seals and hydraulic parts, bearing shells, pistons, valves). They may also handle work such as cylinder block reboring, crankshaft regrinding, etc.

Tyre and exhaust specialists

These outlets may be independent, or members of a local or national chain. They frequently offer competitive prices when compared with a main dealer or local garage, but it will pay to obtain several quotes before making a decision. When researching prices, also ask what 'extras' may be added – for instance fitting a new valve and balancing the wheel are both commonly charged on top of the price of a new tyre.

Other sources

Beware of parts or materials obtained from market stalls, car boot sales or similar outlets. Such items are not invariably sub-standard, but there is little chance of compensation if they do prove unsatisfactory. In the case of safety-critical components such as brake pads, there is the risk not only of financial loss, but also of an accident causing injury or death.

Second-hand components or assemblies obtained from a car breaker can be a good buy in some circumstances, but his sort of purchase is best made by the experienced DIY mechanic.

Vehicle identification

Modifications are a continuing and unpubliscised process in vehicle manufacture, quite apart from major model changes. Spare parts manuals and lists are compiled upon a numerical basis, the individual vehicle identification numbers being essential to correct identification of the component concerned.

When ordering spare parts, always give as much information as possible. Quote the car model, year of manufacture, body and engine numbers as appropriate.

The *vehicle identification plate* is located on the lower section of the right-hand front door pillar (see illustration). In addition to many other details, it carries the Vehicle Identification Number, maximum vehicle weight information, and codes for interior trim and body colours.

The *Vehicle Identification Number* is given on the vehicle identification plate. It is also stamped on the engine compartment bulk-head, and on a tag on the left-hand side of the facia, so that it can be seen through the bottom left-hand corner of the windscreen (see illustrations). A symbol on the tag indicates how many air bags are fitted to the vehicle.

The *engine number* is stamped on the cylinder block/crankcase. On 16-valve petrol engines, it is also on a sticker attached to the timing chain cover. On the 24-valve V6 engine, it is at the front of the engine compartment and on the left-hand cam cover. On diesel engines, it is on the right-hand side, adjacent to the timing chain cover (see illustration).

Engine codes are as follows:
Petrol engines
1.8 litre   CGBA (81 kW) and CHBA (92 kW)
2.0 litre   CJBA (107 kW)
2.5 litre   LCBD (125 kW)

Diesel engines
Duratorq-DI direct injection   D5BA (66 kW)
Duratorq-DI direct injection   D6BA (85 kW)
Duratorq-DCI common rail   FMBA (96 kW)

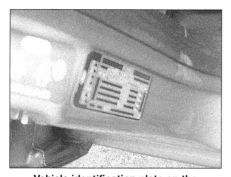

Vehicle identification plate on the right-hand front door pillar

Vehicle identification number stamped on the engine compartment bulkhead

Vehicle identification number visible through the bottom left-hand corner of the windscreen

Engine number (diesel)

Whenever servicing, repair or overhaul work is carried out on the car or its components, observe the following procedures and instructions. This will assist in carrying out the operation efficiently and to a professional standard of workmanship.

Joint mating faces and gaskets

When separating components at their mating faces, never insert screwdrivers or similar implements into the joint between the faces in order to prise them apart. This can cause severe damage which results in oil leaks, coolant leaks, etc upon reassembly. Separation is usually achieved by tapping along the joint with a soft-faced hammer in order to break the seal. However, note that this method may not be suitable where dowels are used for component location.

Where a gasket is used between the mating faces of two components, a new one must be fitted on reassembly; fit it dry unless otherwise stated in the repair procedure. Make sure that the mating faces are clean and dry, with all traces of old gasket removed. When cleaning a joint face, use a tool which is unlikely to score or damage the face, and remove any burrs or nicks with an oilstone or fine file.

Make sure that tapped holes are cleaned with a pipe cleaner, and keep them free of jointing compound, if this is being used, unless specifically instructed otherwise.

Ensure that all orifices, channels or pipes are clear, and blow through them, preferably using compressed air.

Oil seals

Oil seals can be removed by levering them out with a wide flat-bladed screwdriver or similar implement. Alternatively, a number of self-tapping screws may be screwed into the seal, and these used as a purchase for pliers or some similar device in order to pull the seal free.

Whenever an oil seal is removed from its working location, either individually or as part of an assembly, it should be renewed.

The very fine sealing lip of the seal is easily damaged, and will not seal if the surface it contacts is not completely clean and free from scratches, nicks or grooves. If the original sealing surface of the component cannot be restored, and the manufacturer has not made provision for slight relocation of the seal relative to the sealing surface, the component should be renewed.

Protect the lips of the seal from any surface which may damage them in the course of fitting. Use tape or a conical sleeve where possible. Where indicated, lubricate the seal lips with oil before fitting and, on dual-lipped seals, fill the space between the lips with grease.

Unless otherwise stated, oil seals must be fitted with their sealing lips toward the lubricant to be sealed.

Use a tubular drift or block of wood of the appropriate size to install the seal and, if the seal housing is shouldered, drive the seal down to the shoulder. If the seal housing is unshouldered, the seal should be fitted with its face flush with the housing top face (unless otherwise instructed).

Screw threads and fastenings

Seized nuts, bolts and screws are quite a common occurrence where corrosion has set in, and the use of penetrating oil or releasing fluid will often overcome this problem if the offending item is soaked for a while before attempting to release it. The use of an impact driver may also provide a means of releasing such stubborn fastening devices, when used in conjunction with the appropriate screwdriver bit or socket. If none of these methods works, it may be necessary to resort to the careful application of heat, or the use of a hacksaw or nut splitter device. Before resorting to extreme methods, check that you are not dealing with a left-hand thread!

Studs are usually removed by locking two nuts together on the threaded part, and then using a spanner on the lower nut to unscrew the stud. Studs or bolts which have broken off below the surface of the component in which they are mounted can sometimes be removed using a stud extractor.

Always ensure that a blind tapped hole is completely free from oil, grease, water or other fluid before installing the bolt or stud. Failure to do this could cause the housing to crack due to the hydraulic action of the bolt or stud as it is screwed in.

For some screw fastenings, notably cylinder head bolts or nuts, torque wrench settings are no longer specified for the latter stages of tightening, "angle-tightening" being called up instead. Typically, a fairly low torque wrench setting will be applied to the bolts/nuts in the correct sequence, followed by one or more stages of tightening through specified angles.

When checking or retightening a nut or bolt to a specified torque setting, slacken the nut or bolt by a quarter of a turn, and then retighten to the specified setting. However, this should not be attempted where angular tightening has been used.

Locknuts, locktabs and washers

Any fastening which will rotate against a component or housing during tightening should always have a washer between it and the relevant component or housing.

Spring or split washers should always be renewed when they are used to lock a critical component such as a big-end bearing retaining bolt or nut. Locktabs which are folded over to retain a nut or bolt should always be renewed.

Self-locking nuts can be re-used in non-critical areas, providing resistance can be felt when the locking portion passes over the bolt or stud thread. However, it should be noted that self-locking stiffnuts tend to lose their effectiveness after long periods of use, and should then be renewed as a matter of course.

Split pins must always be replaced with new ones of the correct size for the hole.

When thread-locking compound is found on the threads of a fastener which is to be re-used, it should be cleaned off with a wire brush and solvent, and fresh compound applied on reassembly.

Special tools

Some repair procedures in this manual entail the use of special tools such as a press, two or three-legged pullers, spring compressors, etc. Wherever possible, suitable readily-available alternatives to the manufacturer's special tools are described, and are shown in use. In some instances, where no alternative is possible, it has been necessary to resort to the use of a manufacturer's tool, and this has been done for reasons of safety as well as the efficient completion of the repair operation. Unless you are highly-skilled and have a thorough understanding of the procedures described, never attempt to bypass the use of any special tool when the procedure described specifies its use. Not only is there a very great risk of personal injury, but expensive damage could be caused to the components involved.

Environmental considerations

When disposing of used engine oil, brake fluid, antifreeze, etc, give due consideration to any detrimental environmental effects. Do not, for instance, pour any of the above liquids down drains into the general sewage system, or onto the ground to soak away. Many local council refuse tips provide a facility for waste oil disposal, as do some garages. You can find your nearest disposal point by calling the Environment Agency on 08708 506 506 or by visiting www.oilbankline.org.uk.

Note: It is illegal and anti-social to dump oil down the drain. To find the location of your local oil recycling bank, call 08708 506 506 or visit www.oilbankline.org.uk.

Jacking and vehicle support REF•5

The jack supplied with the vehicle tool kit should only be used for changing the roadwheels – see *Wheel changing* at the front of this manual. When carrying out any other kind of work, raise the vehicle using a hydraulic trolley jack, and always supplement the jack with axle stands positioned under the vehicle jacking points.

If the front of the vehicle is to be raised, first apply the handbrake, and/or place chocks behind the rear wheels. Either place the jack head under the front jacking points on the door sill, with a block of wood to prevent damage, or use the two front support points, and lift the vehicle evenly **(see illustrations)**.

Note that the front jacking point is located approximately 27.0 cm from the front end of the sills; the height of this Haynes Manual is approximately 27.0 cm.

To raise the rear of the vehicle, chock the front wheels and engage a gear (or select P). Use the two rear jacking points on the door sill, with a block of wood to prevent damage **(see illustration)**. The rear jacking points are located approximately 10.0 cm from the rear end of the sills; approximately half the width of a page in this Haynes Manual.

To raise the side of the vehicle, prepare the vehicle as described for front AND rear lifting. Place the jack head under the appropriate point. If a trolley jack or similar is used on the points provided for the vehicle's jack, make up a wooden spacer with a groove cut in it to accept the underbody flange, so that there is no risk of the jack slipping or buckling the flange.

Do not attempt to jack the vehicle under the front crossmember, the sump, or any of the suspension components. Also, take care not to damage the air deflectors located under the vehicle when using a trolley jack.

⚠ **Warning: Never work under, around, or near a raised vehicle, unless it is adequately supported in at least two places.**

Jacking and supporting points

1 *Jacking points for vehicle jack in roadside use. May also be used as support points with axle stands*
2 *Jacking points for trolley jack. May be used as additional support points with axle stands*

Using the front jacking point and support point (with wooden blocks) to raise the front of the car

Using the rear jacking point to raise the rear of the car

Radio/cassette unit anti-theft system

The radio/cassette unit fitted may be equipped with a built-in security code, to deter thieves. If the power source to the unit is cut, the anti-theft system will activate. Even if the power source is immediately reconnected, the radio/cassette unit will not function until the correct security code has been entered. Therefore if you do not know the correct security code for the unit, **do not** disconnect the battery negative lead, or remove the radio/cassette unit from the vehicle.

If the security code is lost or forgotten, seek the advice of your Ford dealer. On presentation of proof of ownership, a Ford dealer will be able to provide you with a new security code.

Disconnecting the battery

Note: *When reconnecting the battery, the electric windows will need to be re-initialised (see Chapter 11, Section 12).*

Several systems fitted to the vehicle require battery power to be available at all times, either to ensure their continued operation (such as the clock), or to maintain electronic memory settings which would otherwise be erased. Whenever the battery is to be disconnected, first note the following points, to ensure there are no unforeseen consequences:

a) *First, on any vehicle with central door locking, it is a wise precaution to remove the key from the ignition, and to keep it with you, so that it does not get locked in if the central locking engages when the battery is reconnected.*

b) *If a security-coded audio unit is fitted, and the unit and/or the battery is disconnected, the unit will not function again on reconnection until the correct security code is entered. Details of this procedure, which varies according to the unit fitted and vehicle model, are given in the vehicle owner's handbook. Where necessary, ensure you have the correct code before you disconnect the battery. If you do not have the code or details of the correct procedure, but can supply proof of ownership and a legitimate reason for wanting this information, a Ford dealer may be able to help.*

Devices known as 'memory-savers' or 'code-savers' can be used to avoid some of the above problems. Precise details of use vary according to the device used. Typically, it is plugged into the cigar lighter socket, and is connected by its own wiring to a spare battery; the vehicle battery is then disconnected from the electrical system, leaving the memory- saver to pass sufficient current to maintain audio unit security codes and other memory values, and also to run permanently-live circuits such as the clock.

⚠ **Warning: Some of these devices allow a considerable amount of current to pass, which can mean that many of the vehicle's systems are still operational when the main battery is disconnected. If a 'memory-saver' is used, ensure that the circuit concerned is actually 'dead' before carrying out any work on it!**

Introduction

A selection of good tools is a fundamental requirement for anyone contemplating the maintenance and repair of a motor vehicle. For the owner who does not possess any, their purchase will prove a considerable expense, offsetting some of the savings made by doing-it-yourself. However, provided that the tools purchased meet the relevant national safety standards and are of good quality, they will last for many years and prove an extremely worthwhile investment.

To help the average owner to decide which tools are needed to carry out the various tasks detailed in this manual, we have compiled three lists of tools under the following headings: *Maintenance and minor repair*, *Repair and overhaul*, and *Special*. Newcomers to practical mechanics should start off with the *Maintenance and minor repair* tool kit, and confine themselves to the simpler jobs around the vehicle. Then, as confidence and experience grow, more difficult tasks can be undertaken, with extra tools being purchased as, and when, they are needed. In this way, a *Maintenance and minor repair* tool kit can be built up into a *Repair and overhaul* tool kit over a considerable period of time, without any major cash outlays. The experienced do-it-yourselfer will have a tool kit good enough for most repair and overhaul procedures, and will add tools from the *Special* category when it is felt that the expense is justified by the amount of use to which these tools will be put.

Maintenance and minor repair tool kit

The tools given in this list should be considered as a minimum requirement if routine maintenance, servicing and minor repair operations are to be undertaken. We recommend the purchase of combination spanners (ring one end, open-ended the other); although more expensive than open-ended ones, they do give the advantages of both types of spanner.

☐ *Combination spanners:*
Metric - 8 to 19 mm inclusive
☐ *Adjustable spanner - 35 mm jaw (approx.)*
☐ *Spark plug spanner (with rubber insert) - petrol models*
☐ *Spark plug gap adjustment tool - petrol models*
☐ *Set of feeler gauges*
☐ *Brake bleed nipple spanner*
☐ *Screwdrivers:*
Flat blade - 100 mm long x 6 mm dia
Cross blade - 100 mm long x 6 mm dia
Torx - various sizes (not all vehicles)
☐ *Combination pliers*
☐ *Hacksaw (junior)*
☐ *Tyre pump*
☐ *Tyre pressure gauge*
☐ *Oil can*
☐ *Oil filter removal tool (if applicable)*
☐ *Fine emery cloth*
☐ *Wire brush (small)*
☐ *Funnel (medium size)*
☐ *Sump drain plug key (not all vehicles)*

Repair and overhaul tool kit

These tools are virtually essential for anyone undertaking any major repairs to a motor vehicle, and are additional to those given in the *Maintenance and minor repair* list. Included in this list is a comprehensive set of sockets. Although these are expensive, they will be found invaluable as they are so versatile - particularly if various drives are included in the set. We recommend the half-inch square-drive type, as this can be used with most proprietary torque wrenches.

The tools in this list will sometimes need to be supplemented by tools from the *Special* list:

☐ *Sockets to cover range in previous list (including Torx sockets)*
☐ *Reversible ratchet drive (for use with sockets)*
☐ *Extension piece, 250 mm (for use with sockets)*
☐ *Universal joint (for use with sockets)*
☐ *Flexible handle or sliding T "breaker bar" (for use with sockets)*
☐ *Torque wrench (for use with sockets)*
☐ *Self-locking grips*
☐ *Ball pein hammer*
☐ *Soft-faced mallet (plastic or rubber)*
☐ *Screwdrivers:*
Flat blade - long & sturdy, short (chubby), and narrow (electrician's) types
Cross blade – long & sturdy, and short (chubby) types
☐ *Pliers:*
Long-nosed
Side cutters (electrician's)
Circlip (internal and external)
☐ *Cold chisel - 25 mm*
☐ *Scriber*
☐ *Scraper*
☐ *Centre-punch*
☐ *Pin punch*
☐ *Hacksaw*
☐ *Brake hose clamp*
☐ *Brake/clutch bleeding kit*
☐ *Selection of twist drills*
☐ *Steel rule/straight-edge*
☐ *Allen keys (inc. splined/Torx type)*
☐ *Selection of files*
☐ *Wire brush*
☐ *Axle stands*
☐ *Jack (strong trolley or hydraulic type)*
☐ *Light with extension lead*
☐ *Universal electrical multi-meter*

Sockets and reversible ratchet drive

Brake bleeding kit

Torx key, socket and bit

Hose clamp

Angular-tightening gauge

Special tools

The tools in this list are those which are not used regularly, are expensive to buy, or which need to be used in accordance with their manufacturers' instructions. Unless relatively difficult mechanical jobs are undertaken frequently, it will not be economic to buy many of these tools. Where this is the case, you could consider clubbing together with friends (or joining a motorists' club) to make a joint purchase, or borrowing the tools against a deposit from a local garage or tool hire specialist.

The following list contains only those tools and instruments freely available to the public, and not those special tools produced by the vehicle manufacturer specifically for its dealer network. You will find occasional references to these manufacturers' special tools in the text of this manual. Generally, an alternative method of doing the job without the vehicle manufacturers' special tool is given. However, sometimes there is no alternative to using them. Where this is the case and the relevant tool cannot be bought or borrowed, you will have to entrust the work to a dealer.

☐ Angular-tightening gauge
☐ Valve spring compressor
☐ Valve grinding tool
☐ Piston ring compressor
☐ Piston ring removal/installation tool
☐ Cylinder bore hone
☐ Balljoint separator
☐ Coil spring compressors (where applicable)
☐ Two/three-legged hub and bearing puller
☐ Impact screwdriver
☐ Micrometer and/or vernier calipers
☐ Dial gauge
☐ Tachometer
☐ Fault code reader
☐ Cylinder compression gauge
☐ Hand-operated vacuum pump and gauge
☐ Clutch plate alignment set
☐ Brake shoe steady spring cup removal tool
☐ Bush and bearing removal/installation set
☐ Stud extractors
☐ Tap and die set
☐ Lifting tackle

Buying tools

Reputable motor accessory shops and superstores often offer excellent quality tools at discount prices, so it pays to shop around.

Remember, you don't have to buy the most expensive items on the shelf, but it is always advisable to steer clear of the very cheap tools. Beware of 'bargains' offered on market stalls, on-line or at car boot sales. There are plenty of good tools around at reasonable prices, but always aim to purchase items which meet the relevant national safety standards. If in doubt, ask the proprietor or manager of the shop for advice before making a purchase.

Care and maintenance of tools

Having purchased a reasonable tool kit, it is necessary to keep the tools in a clean and serviceable condition. After use, always wipe off any dirt, grease and metal particles using a clean, dry cloth, before putting the tools away. Never leave them lying around after they have been used. A simple tool rack on the garage or workshop wall for items such as screwdrivers and pliers is a good idea. Store all normal spanners and sockets in a metal box. Any measuring instruments, gauges, meters, etc, must be carefully stored where they cannot be damaged or become rusty.

Take a little care when tools are used. Hammer heads inevitably become marked, and screwdrivers lose the keen edge on their blades from time to time. A little timely attention with emery cloth or a file will soon restore items like this to a good finish.

Working facilities

Not to be forgotten when discussing tools is the workshop itself. If anything more than routine maintenance is to be carried out, a suitable working area becomes essential.

It is appreciated that many an owner-mechanic is forced by circumstances to remove an engine or similar item without the benefit of a garage or workshop. Having done this, any repairs should always be done under the cover of a roof.

Wherever possible, any dismantling should be done on a clean, flat workbench or table at a suitable working height.

Any workbench needs a vice; one with a jaw opening of 100 mm is suitable for most jobs. As mentioned previously, some clean dry storage space is also required for tools, as well as for any lubricants, cleaning fluids, touch-up paints etc, which become necessary.

Another item which may be required, and which has a much more general usage, is an electric drill with a chuck capacity of at least 8 mm. This, together with a good range of twist drills, is virtually essential for fitting accessories.

Last, but not least, always keep a supply of old newspapers and clean, lint-free rags available, and try to keep any working area as clean as possible.

Micrometers

Dial test indicator ("dial gauge")

Oil filter removal tool (strap wrench type)

Compression tester

Bearing puller

This is a guide to getting your vehicle through the MOT test. Obviously it will not be possible to examine the vehicle to the same standard as the professional MOT tester. However, working through the following checks will enable you to identify any problem areas before submitting the vehicle for the test.

It has only been possible to summarise the test requirements here, based on the regulations in force at the time of printing. Test standards are becoming increasingly stringent, although there are some exemptions for older vehicles.

An assistant will be needed to help carry out some of these checks.

The checks have been sub-divided into four categories, as follows:

1 Checks carried out **FROM THE DRIVER'S SEAT**

2 Checks carried out **WITH THE VEHICLE ON THE GROUND**

3 Checks carried out **WITH THE VEHICLE RAISED AND THE WHEELS FREE TO TURN**

4 Checks carried out on **YOUR VEHICLE'S EXHAUST EMISSION SYSTEM**

---

1 Checks carried out **FROM THE DRIVER'S SEAT**

Handbrake (parking brake)

☐ Test the operation of the handbrake. Excessive travel (too many clicks) indicates incorrect brake or cable adjustment.

☐ Check that the handbrake cannot be released by tapping the lever sideways. Check the security of the lever mountings.

☐ If the parking brake is foot-operated, check that the pedal is secure and without excessive travel, and that the release mechanism operates correctly.

☐ Where applicable, test the operation of the electronic handbrake. The brake should engage and disengage without excessive delay. If the warning light does not extinguish when the brake is disengaged, this could indicate a fault which will need further investigation.

Footbrake

☐ Depress the brake pedal and check that it does not creep down to the floor, indicating a master cylinder fault. Release the pedal,

wait a few seconds, then depress it again. If the pedal travels nearly to the floor before firm resistance is felt, brake adjustment or repair is necessary. If the pedal feels spongy, there is air in the hydraulic system which must be removed by bleeding.

☐ Check that the brake pedal is secure and in good condition. Check also for signs of fluid leaks on the pedal, floor or carpets, which would indicate failed seals in the brake master cylinder.

☐ Check the servo unit (when applicable) by operating the brake pedal several times, then keeping the pedal depressed and starting the engine. As the engine starts, the pedal will move down slightly. If not, the vacuum hose or the servo itself may be faulty.

Steering wheel and column

☐ Examine the steering wheel for fractures or looseness of the hub, spokes or rim.

☐ Move the steering wheel from side to side and then up and down. Check that the steering wheel is not loose on the column, indicating wear or a loose retaining nut. Continue moving the steering wheel as before, but also turn it slightly from left to right.

☐ Check that the steering wheel is not loose on the column, and that there is no abnormal movement of the steering wheel, indicating wear in the column support bearings or couplings.

☐ Check that the ignition lock (where fitted) engages and disengages correctly.

☐ Steering column adjustment mechanisms (where fitted) must be able to lock the column securely in place with no play evident.

Windscreen, mirrors and sunvisor

☐ The windscreen must be free of cracks or other significant damage within the driver's field of view. (Small stone chips are acceptable.) Rear view mirrors must be secure, intact, and capable of being adjusted.

☐ The driver's sunvisor must be capable of being stored in the "up" position.

Seat belts and seats

Note: *The following checks are applicable to all seat belts, front and rear.*

☐ Examine the webbing of all the belts (including rear belts if fitted) for cuts, serious fraying or deterioration. Fasten and unfasten each belt to check the buckles. If applicable, check the retracting mechanism. Check the security of all seat belt mountings accessible from inside the vehicle, ensuring any height adjustable mountings lock securely in place.

☐ Seat belts with pre-tensioners, once activated, have a "flag" or similar showing on the seat belt stalk. This, in itself, is not a reason for test failure.

☐ The front seats themselves must be securely attached and the backrests must lock in the upright position.

Doors

☐ Both front doors must be able to be opened and closed from outside and inside, and must latch securely when closed.

Bonnet and boot/tailgate

☐ The bonnet and boot/tailgate must latch securely when closed.

2 Checks carried out WITH THE VEHICLE ON THE GROUND

Vehicle identification

☐ Number plates must be in good condition, secure and legible, with letters and numbers correctly spaced – spacing at (A) should be 33 mm and at (B) 11 mm. At the front, digits must be black on a white background and at the rear black on a yellow background. Other background designs (such as honeycomb) are not permitted.

☐ The VIN plate and/or homologation plate must be permanently displayed and legible.

Electrical equipment

☐ Switch on the ignition and check the operation of the horn.

☐ Check the windscreen washers and wipers, examining the wiper blades; renew damaged or perished blades. Also check the operation of the stop-lights.

☐ Check the operation of the sidelights and number plate lights. The lenses and reflectors must be secure, clean and undamaged.

☐ Check the operation and alignment of the headlights. The headlight reflectors must not be tarnished and the lenses must be undamaged.

☐ Switch on the ignition and check the operation of the direction indicators (including the instrument panel tell-tale) and the hazard warning lights. Operation of the sidelights and stop-lights must not affect the indicators - if it does, the cause is usually a bad earth at the rear light cluster. Indicators should flash at a rate of between 60 and 120 times per minute – faster or slower than this could indicate a fault with the flasher unit or a bad earth at one of the light units.

☐ Check the operation of the rear foglight(s), including the warning light on the instrument panel or in the switch.

☐ The ABS warning light must illuminate in accordance with the manufacturers' design. For most vehicles, the ABS warning light should illuminate when the ignition is switched on, and (if the system is operating properly) extinguish after a few seconds. Refer to the owner's handbook.

Footbrake

☐ Examine the master cylinder, brake pipes and servo unit for leaks, loose mountings, corrosion or other damage. If ABS is fitted, this unit should also be examined for signs of leaks or corrosion.

☐ The fluid reservoir must be secure and the fluid level must be between the upper (**A**) and lower (**B**) markings.

☐ Inspect both front brake flexible hoses for cracks or deterioration of the rubber. Turn the steering from lock to lock, and ensure that the hoses do not contact the wheel, tyre, or any part of the steering or suspension mechanism. With the brake pedal firmly depressed, check the hoses for bulges or leaks under pressure.

Steering and suspension

☐ Have your assistant turn the steering wheel from side to side slightly, up to the point where the steering gear just begins to transmit this movement to the roadwheels. Check for excessive free play between the steering wheel and the steering gear, indicating wear or insecurity of the steering column joints, the column-to-steering gear coupling, or the steering gear itself.

☐ Have your assistant turn the steering wheel more vigorously in each direction, so that the roadwheels just begin to turn. As this is done, examine all the steering joints, linkages, fittings and attachments. Renew any component that shows signs of wear or damage. On vehicles with power steering, check the security and condition of the steering pump, drivebelt and hoses.

☐ Check that the vehicle is standing level, and at approximately the correct ride height.

Shock absorbers

☐ Depress each corner of the vehicle in turn, then release it. The vehicle should rise and then settle in its normal position. If the vehicle continues to rise and fall, the shock absorber is defective. A shock absorber which has seized will also cause the vehicle to fail.

Exhaust system

☐ Start the engine. With your assistant holding a rag over the tailpipe, check the entire system for leaks. Repair or renew leaking sections.

3 Checks carried out
WITH THE VEHICLE RAISED AND THE WHEELS FREE TO TURN

Jack up the front and rear of the vehicle, and securely support it on axle stands. Position the stands clear of the suspension assemblies. Ensure that the wheels are clear of the ground and that the steering can be turned from lock to lock.

Steering mechanism

☐ Have your assistant turn the steering from lock to lock. Check that the steering turns smoothly, and that no part of the steering mechanism, including a wheel or tyre, fouls any brake hose or pipe or any part of the body structure.

☐ Examine the steering rack rubber gaiters for damage or insecurity of the retaining clips. If power steering is fitted, check for signs of damage or leakage of the fluid hoses, pipes or connections. Also check for excessive stiffness or binding of the steering, a missing split pin or locking device, or severe corrosion of the body structure within 30 cm of any steering component attachment point.

Front and rear suspension and wheel bearings

☐ Starting at the front right-hand side, grasp the roadwheel at the 3 o'clock and 9 o'clock positions and rock gently but firmly. Check for free play or insecurity at the wheel bearings, suspension balljoints, or suspension mount-ings, pivots and attachments.

☐ Now grasp the wheel at the 12 o'clock and 6 o'clock positions and repeat the previous inspection. Spin the wheel, and check for roughness or tightness of the front wheel bearing.

☐ If excess free play is suspected at a component pivot point, this can be confirmed by using a large screwdriver or similar tool and levering between the mounting and the component attachment. This will confirm whether the wear is in the pivot bush, its retaining bolt, or in the mounting itself (the bolt holes can often become elongated).

☐ Carry out all the above checks at the other front wheel, and then at both rear wheels.

Springs and shock absorbers

☐ Examine the suspension struts (when applicable) for serious fluid leakage, corrosion, or damage to the casing. Also check the security of the mounting points.

☐ If coil springs are fitted, check that the spring ends locate in their seats, and that the spring is not corroded, cracked or broken.

☐ If leaf springs are fitted, check that all leaves are intact, that the axle is securely attached to each spring, and that there is no deterioration of the spring eye mountings, bushes, and shackles.

☐ The same general checks apply to vehicles fitted with other suspension types, such as torsion bars, hydraulic displacer units, etc. Ensure that all mountings and attachments are secure, that there are no signs of excessive wear, corrosion or damage, and (on hydraulic types) that there are no fluid leaks or damaged pipes.

☐ Inspect the shock absorbers for signs of serious fluid leakage. Check for wear of the mounting bushes or attachments, or damage to the body of the unit.

Driveshafts (fwd vehicles only)

☐ Rotate each front wheel in turn and inspect the constant velocity joint gaiters for splits or damage. Also check that each driveshaft is straight and undamaged.

Braking system

☐ If possible without dismantling, check brake pad wear and disc condition. Ensure that the friction lining material has not worn excessively, (A) and that the discs are not fractured, pitted, scored or badly worn (B).

☐ Examine all the rigid brake pipes underneath the vehicle, and the flexible hose(s) at the rear. Look for corrosion, chafing or insecurity of the pipes, and for signs of bulging under pressure, chafing, splits or deterioration of the flexible hoses.

☐ Look for signs of fluid leaks at the brake calipers or on the brake backplates. Repair or renew leaking components.

☐ Slowly spin each wheel, while your assistant depresses and releases the footbrake. Ensure that each brake is operating and does not bind when the pedal is released.

□Examine the handbrake mechanism, checking for frayed or broken cables, excessive corrosion, or wear or insecurity of the linkage. Check that the mechanism works on each relevant wheel, and releases fully, without binding.

□It is not possible to test brake efficiency without special equipment, but a road test can be carried out later to check that the vehicle pulls up in a straight line.

Fuel and exhaust systems

□Inspect the fuel tank (including the filler cap), fuel pipes, hoses and unions. All components must be secure and free from leaks. Locking fuel caps must lock securely and the key must be provided for the MOT test.

□Examine the exhaust system over its entire length, checking for any damaged, broken or missing mountings, security of the retaining clamps and rust or corrosion.

Wheels and tyres

□Examine the sidewalls and tread area of each tyre in turn. Check for cuts, tears, lumps, bulges, separation of the tread, and exposure of the ply or cord due to wear or damage. Check that the tyre bead is correctly seated on the wheel rim, that the valve is sound and properly seated, and that the wheel is not distorted or damaged.

□Check that the tyres are of the correct size for the vehicle, that they are of the same size and type on each axle, and that the pressures are correct.

□Check the tyre tread depth. The legal minimum at the time of writing is 1.6 mm over the central three-quarters of the tread width. Abnormal tread wear may indicate incorrect front wheel alignment or wear in steering or suspension components.

□If the spare wheel is fitted externally or in a separate carrier beneath the vehicle, check that mountings are secure and free of excessive corrosion.

Body corrosion

□Check the condition of the entire vehicle structure for signs of corrosion in load-bearing areas. (These include chassis box sections, side sills, cross-members, pillars, and all suspension, steering, braking system and seat belt mountings and anchorages.) Any corrosion which has seriously reduced the thickness of a load-bearing area (or is within 30 cm of safety-related components such as steering or suspension) is likely to cause the vehicle to fail. In this case professional repairs are likely to be needed.

□Damage or corrosion which causes sharp or otherwise dangerous edges to be exposed will also cause the vehicle to fail.

Towbars

□Check the condition of mounting points (both beneath the vehicle and within boot/hatchback areas) for signs of corrosion, ensuring that all fixings are secure and not worn or damaged. There must be no excessive play in detachable tow ball arms or quick-release mechanisms.

4 Checks carried out on **YOUR VEHICLE'S EXHAUST EMISSION SYSTEM**

Petrol models

□The engine should be warmed up, and running well (ignition system in good order, air filter element clean, etc).

□Before testing, run the engine at around 2500 rpm for 20 seconds. Let the engine drop to idle, and watch for smoke from the exhaust. If the idle speed is too high, or if dense blue or black smoke emerges for more than 5 seconds, the vehicle will fail. Typically, blue smoke signifies oil burning (engine wear);

black smoke means unburnt fuel (dirty air cleaner element, or other fuel system fault).

□An exhaust gas analyser for measuring carbon monoxide (CO) and hydrocarbons (HC) is now needed. If one cannot be hired or borrowed, have a local garage perform the check.

CO emissions (mixture)

□The MOT tester has access to the CO limits for all vehicles. The CO level is measured at idle speed, and at 'fast idle' (2500 to 3000 rpm). The following limits are given as a general guide:

At idle speed – Less than 0.5% CO
At 'fast idle' – Less than 0.3% CO
Lambda reading – 0.97 to 1.03

□If the CO level is too high, this may point to poor maintenance, a fuel injection system problem, faulty lambda (oxygen) sensor or catalytic converter. Try an injector cleaning treatment, and check the vehicle's ECU for fault codes.

HC emissions

□The MOT tester has access to HC limits for all vehicles. The HC level is measured at 'fast idle' (2500 to 3000 rpm). The following limits are given as a general guide:

At 'fast idle' – Less then 200 ppm

□Excessive HC emissions are typically caused by oil being burnt (worn engine), or by a blocked crankcase ventilation system ('breather'). If the engine oil is old and thin, an oil change may help. If the engine is running badly, check the vehicle's ECU for fault codes.

Diesel models

□The only emission test for diesel engines is measuring exhaust smoke density, using a calibrated smoke meter. The test involves accelerating the engine at least 3 times to its maximum unloaded speed.

Note: *On engines with a timing belt, it is VITAL that the belt is in good condition before the test is carried out.*

□With the engine warmed up, it is first purged by running at around 2500 rpm for 20 seconds. A governor check is then carried out, by slowly accelerating the engine to its maximum speed. After this, the smoke meter is connected, and the engine is accelerated quickly to maximum speed three times. If the smoke density is less than the limits given below, the vehicle will pass:

Non-turbo vehicles: 2.5m-1
Turbocharged vehicles: 3.0m-1

□If excess smoke is produced, try fitting a new air cleaner element, or using an injector cleaning treatment. If the engine is running badly, where applicable, check the vehicle's ECU for fault codes. Also check the vehicle's EGR system, where applicable. At high mileages, the injectors may require professional attention.

Engine

- ☐ Engine fails to rotate when attempting to start
- ☐ Engine rotates, but will not start
- ☐ Engine difficult to start when cold
- ☐ Engine difficult to start when hot
- ☐ Starter motor noisy or excessively-rough in engagement
- ☐ Engine starts, but stops immediately
- ☐ Engine idles erratically
- ☐ Engine misfires at idle speed
- ☐ Engine misfires throughout the driving speed range
- ☐ Engine hesitates on acceleration
- ☐ Engine stalls
- ☐ Engine lacks power
- ☐ Engine backfires
- ☐ Oil pressure warning light illuminated with engine running
- ☐ Engine runs-on after switching off
- ☐ Engine noises

Cooling system

- ☐ Overheating
- ☐ Overcooling
- ☐ External coolant leakage
- ☐ Internal coolant leakage
- ☐ Corrosion

Fuel and exhaust systems

- ☐ Excessive fuel consumption
- ☐ Fuel leakage and/or fuel odour
- ☐ Excessive noise or fumes from exhaust system

Clutch

- ☐ Pedal travels to floor – no pressure or very little resistance
- ☐ Clutch fails to disengage (unable to select gears)
- ☐ Clutch slips (engine speed increases, with no increase in vehicle speed)
- ☐ Judder as clutch is engaged
- ☐ Noise when depressing or releasing clutch pedal

Manual transmission

- ☐ Noisy in neutral with engine running
- ☐ Noisy in one particular gear
- ☐ Difficulty engaging gears
- ☐ Jumps out of gear
- ☐ Vibration
- ☐ Lubricant leaks

Automatic transmission

- ☐ Fluid leakage
- ☐ Transmission fluid brown, or has burned smell
- ☐ General gear selection problems
- ☐ Transmission will not downshift (kickdown) with accelerator pedal fully depressed
- ☐ Engine will not start in any gear, or starts in gears other than Park or Neutral
- ☐ Transmission slips, shifts roughly, is noisy, or has no drive in forward or reverse gears

Driveshafts

- ☐ Vibration when accelerating or decelerating
- ☐ Clicking or knocking noise on turns (at slow speed on full-lock)

Braking system

- ☐ Vehicle pulls to one side under braking
- ☐ Noise (grinding or high-pitched squeal) when brakes applied
- ☐ Excessive brake pedal travel
- ☐ Brake pedal feels spongy when depressed
- ☐ Excessive brake pedal effort required to stop vehicle
- ☐ Judder felt through brake pedal or steering wheel when braking
- ☐ Brakes binding
- ☐ Rear wheels locking under normal braking

Suspension and steering

- ☐ Vehicle pulls to one side
- ☐ Wheel wobble and vibration
- ☐ Excessive pitching and/or rolling around corners, or during braking
- ☐ Wandering or general instability
- ☐ Excessively-stiff steering
- ☐ Excessive play in steering
- ☐ Lack of power assistance
- ☐ Tyre wear excessive

Electrical system

- ☐ Battery will not hold a charge for more than a few days
- ☐ Ignition/no-charge warning light remains illuminated with engine running
- ☐ Ignition/no-charge warning light fails to come on
- ☐ Lights inoperative
- ☐ Instrument readings inaccurate or erratic
- ☐ Horn inoperative, or unsatisfactory in operation
- ☐ Windscreen wipers inoperative, or unsatisfactory in operation
- ☐ Windscreen washers inoperative, or unsatisfactory in operation
- ☐ Electric windows inoperative, or unsatisfactory in operation
- ☐ Central locking system inoperative, or unsatisfactory in operation

Introduction

The vehicle owner who does his or her own maintenance according to the recommended service schedules should not have to use this section of the manual very often. Modern component reliability is such that, provided those items subject to wear or deterioration are inspected or renewed at the specified intervals, sudden failure is comparatively rare. Faults do not usually just happen as a result of sudden failure, but develop over a period of time. Major mechanical failures in particular are usually preceded by characteristic symptoms over hundreds or even thousands of miles. Those components which do occasionally fail without warning are often small and easily carried in the vehicle.

With any fault-finding, the first step is to decide where to begin investigations. Sometimes this is obvious, but on other occasions, a little detective work will be necessary. The owner who makes half a dozen haphazard adjustments or replacements may be successful in curing a fault (or its symptoms), but will be none the wiser if the fault recurs, and ultimately may have spent more time and money than was necessary. A calm and logical approach will be found to be more satisfactory in the long run. Always take into account any warning signs or abnormalities that may have been noticed in the period preceding the fault – power loss, high or low gauge readings, unusual smells,

etc – and remember that failure of components such as fuses or spark plugs may only be pointers to some underlying fault.

The pages which follow provide an easy-reference guide to the more common problems which may occur during the operation of the vehicle. These problems and their possible causes are grouped under headings denoting various components or systems, such as Engine, Cooling system, etc. The general Chapter which deals with the problem is also shown in brackets; refer to the relevant part of that Chapter for system-specific information. Whatever the fault, certain basic principles apply. These are as follows:

Verify the fault. This is simply a matter of being sure that you know what the symptoms are before starting work. This is particularly important if you are investigating a fault for someone else, who may not have described it very accurately.

Don't overlook the obvious. For example, if the vehicle won't start, is there fuel in the tank? (Don't take anyone else's word on this particular point, and don't trust the fuel gauge either!) If an electrical fault is indicated, look for loose or broken wires before digging out the test gear.

Cure the disease, not the symptom. Substituting a flat battery with a fully-charged one will get you off the hard shoulder, but if the underlying cause is not attended to, the new battery will go the same way. Similarly, changing oil-fouled spark plugs for a new set will get you moving again, but remember that the reason for the fouling (if it wasn't simply an incorrect grade of plug) will have to be established and corrected.

Don't take anything for granted. Particularly, don't forget that a 'new' component may itself be defective (especially if it's been rattling around in the boot for months), and don't leave components out of a fault diagnosis sequence just because they are new or recently-fitted. When you do finally diagnose a difficult fault, you'll probably realise that all the evidence was there from the start.

Consider what work, if any, has recently been carried out. Many faults arise through careless or hurried work. For instance, if any work has been performed under the bonnet, could some of the wiring have been dislodged or incorrectly routed, or a hose trapped? Have all the fasteners been properly tightened? Were new, genuine parts and new gaskets used? There is often a certain amount of detective work to be done in this case, as an apparently-unrelated task can have far-reaching consequences.

Engine

Engine fails to rotate when attempting to start

- [ ] Battery terminal connections loose or corroded (see *Weekly checks*)
- [ ] Battery discharged or faulty (Chapter 5A)
- [ ] Broken, loose or disconnected wiring in the starting circuit (Chapter 5A)
- [ ] Defective starter solenoid or ignition switch (Chapter 5A or 12)
- [ ] Defective starter motor (Chapter 5A)
- [ ] Starter pinion or flywheel ring gear teeth loose or broken (Chapter 2 or 5A)
- [ ] Engine earth strap broken or disconnected (Chapter 5A)
- [ ] Engine suffering 'hydraulic lock' (eg, from water ingested after traversing flooded roads, or from a serious internal coolant leak) – consult a Ford dealer for advice
- [ ] Automatic transmission not in position P or N (Chapter 7B)

Engine rotates, but will not start

- [ ] Fuel cut-off switch energised (Chapter 4A)
- [ ] Fuel tank empty
- [ ] Battery discharged (engine rotates slowly) (Chapter 5A)
- [ ] Battery terminal connections loose or corroded (see *Weekly checks*)
- [ ] Ignition components damp or damaged – petrol models (Chapter 1A or 5B)
- [ ] Immobiliser fault, or 'uncoded' ignition key being used (Chapter 12 or *Roadside repairs*)
- [ ] Crankshaft sensor fault (Chapter 4A or 4B)
- [ ] Broken, loose or disconnected wiring in the ignition circuit – petrol models (Chapter 1A or 5B)
- [ ] Worn, faulty or incorrectly-gapped spark plugs – petrol models (Chapter 1A)
- [ ] Preheating system faulty – diesel models (Chapter 4B)
- [ ] Fuel injection system fault (Chapter 4A or 4B)
- [ ] Air in fuel system – diesel models (Chapter 4B)
- [ ] Major mechanical failure (eg timing chain snapped) (Chapter 2A, 2B, 2C or 2D)

Engine difficult to start when cold

- [ ] Battery discharged (Chapter 5A)
- [ ] Battery terminal connections loose or corroded (see *Weekly checks*)
- [ ] Worn, faulty or incorrectly-gapped spark plugs – petrol models (Chapter 1A)
- [ ] Other ignition system fault – petrol models (Chapter 1A or 5B)
- [ ] Preheating system faulty – diesel models (Chapter 4B)
- [ ] Fuel injection system fault (Chapter 4A or 4B)
- [ ] Wrong grade of engine oil used (*Weekly checks*, Chapter 1A or 1B)
- [ ] Low cylinder compression (Chapter 2A, 2B, 2C or 2D)

Engine difficult to start when hot

- [ ] Air filter element dirty or clogged (Chapter 1A or 1B)
- [ ] Fuel injection system fault (Chapter 4A or 4B)
- [ ] Low cylinder compression (Chapter 2A, 2B, 2C or 2D)

Starter motor noisy or excessively-rough in engagement

- [ ] Starter pinion or flywheel ring gear teeth loose or broken (Chapter 2 or 5A)
- [ ] Starter motor mounting bolts loose or missing (Chapter 5A)
- [ ] Starter motor internal components worn or damaged (Chapter 5A)

Engine starts, but stops immediately

- [ ] Loose or faulty electrical connections in the ignition circuit – petrol models (Chapter 1A or 5B)
- [ ] Vacuum leak at the throttle body or inlet manifold – petrol models (Chapter 4A)
- [ ] Blocked injectors/fuel injection system fault (Chapter 4A or 4B)
- [ ] Air in fuel, possibly due to loose fuel line connection – diesel models (Chapter 4B)

Engine idles erratically

- [ ] Air filter element clogged (Chapter 1A or 1B)
- [ ] Vacuum leak at the throttle body, inlet manifold or associated hoses – petrol models (Chapter 4A)
- [ ] Worn, faulty or incorrectly-gapped spark plugs – petrol models (Chapter 1A)
- [ ] Valve clearances incorrect (Chapter 2A, 2B, 2C or 2D)
- [ ] Uneven or low cylinder compression (Chapter 2A, 2B, 2C or 2D)
- [ ] Camshaft lobes worn (Chapter 2A, 2B, 2C or 2D)
- [ ] Blocked injectors/fuel injection system fault (Chapter 4A or 4B)
- [ ] Air in fuel, possibly due to loose fuel line connection – diesel models (Chapter 4B)

Engine misfires at idle speed

- [ ] Worn, faulty or incorrectly-gapped spark plugs – petrol models (Chapter 1A)
- [ ] Faulty spark plug HT leads – petrol models (Chapter 1A)
- [ ] Vacuum leak at the throttle body, inlet manifold or associated hoses – petrol models (Chapter 4A)
- [ ] Blocked injectors/fuel injection system fault (Chapter 4A or 4B)
- [ ] Faulty injector(s) – diesel models (Chapter 4B)
- [ ] Uneven or low cylinder compression (Chapter 2A, 2B, 2C or 2D)
- [ ] Disconnected, leaking, or perished crankcase ventilation hoses (Chapter 4C)

Engine (continued)

Engine misfires throughout the driving speed range

- [ ] Fuel filter choked (Chapter 1A or 1B)
- [ ] Fuel pump faulty, or delivery pressure low – petrol models (Chapter 4A)
- [ ] Fuel tank vent blocked, or fuel pipes restricted (Chapter 4A or 4B)
- [ ] Vacuum leak at the throttle body, inlet manifold or associated hoses – petrol models (Chapter 4A)
- [ ] Worn, faulty or incorrectly-gapped spark plugs – petrol models (Chapter 1A)
- [ ] Faulty spark plug HT leads (where fitted) – petrol models (Chapter 1A)
- [ ] Faulty injector(s) – diesel models (Chapter 4B)
- [ ] Faulty ignition coil – petrol models (Chapter 5A)
- [ ] Uneven or low cylinder compression (Chapter 2A, 2B, 2C or 2D)
- [ ] Blocked injector/fuel injection system fault (Chapter 4A or 4B)
- [ ] Blocked catalytic converter (Chapter 4A or 4B)
- [ ] Engine overheating – petrol models (Chapter 3)
- [ ] Fuel tank level low – diesel models (Chapter 4B)

Engine hesitates on acceleration

- [ ] Worn, faulty or incorrectly-gapped spark plugs – petrol models (Chapter 1A)
- [ ] Vacuum leak at the throttle body, inlet manifold or associated hoses – petrol models (Chapter 4A)
- [ ] Blocked injectors/fuel injection system fault (Chapter 4A or 4B)
- [ ] Faulty injector(s) – diesel models (Chapter 4B)
- [ ] Faulty clutch pedal switch (Chapter 4A or 4B)

Engine stalls

- [ ] Vacuum leak at the throttle body, inlet manifold or associated hoses – petrol models (Chapter 4A)
- [ ] Fuel filter choked (Chapter 1A or 1B)
- [ ] Fuel pump faulty, or delivery pressure low – petrol models (Chapter 4A)
- [ ] Fuel tank vent blocked, or fuel pipes restricted (Chapter 4A or 4B)
- [ ] Blocked injectors/fuel injection system fault (Chapter 4A or 4B)
- [ ] Faulty injector(s) – diesel models (Chapter 4B)

Engine lacks power

- [ ] Air filter element blocked (Chapter 1A or 1B)
- [ ] Fuel filter choked (Chapter 1A or 1B)
- [ ] Fuel pipes blocked or restricted (Chapter 4A or 4B)
- [ ] Valve clearances incorrect (Chapter 2A, 2B, 2C or 2D)
- [ ] Worn, faulty or incorrectly-gapped spark plugs – petrol models (Chapter 1A)
- [ ] Engine overheating – petrol models (Chapter 4A)
- [ ] Fuel tank level low – diesel models (Chapter 4B)
- [ ] Accelerator cable problem – petrol models (Chapter 4A)
- [ ] Accelerator position sensor faulty – diesel models (Chapter 4B)
- [ ] Vacuum leak at the throttle body, inlet manifold or associated hoses – petrol models (Chapter 4A)
- [ ] Blocked injectors/fuel injection system fault (Chapter 4A or 4B)
- [ ] Faulty injector(s) – diesel models (Chapter 4B)
- [ ] Fuel pump faulty, or delivery pressure low – petrol models (Chapter 4A)
- [ ] Uneven or low cylinder compression (Chapter 2A, 2B, 2C or 2D)
- [ ] Blocked catalytic converter (Chapter 4A or 4B)
- [ ] Injection pump timing incorrect – diesel models (Chapter 4B)
- [ ] Brakes binding (Chapter 1A, 1B or 9)
- [ ] Clutch slipping (Chapter 6)

Engine backfires

- [ ] Vacuum leak at the throttle body, inlet manifold or associated hoses – petrol models (Chapter 4A)
- [ ] Blocked injectors/fuel injection system fault (Chapter 4A or 4B)
- [ ] Blocked catalytic converter (Chapter 4A or 4B)
- [ ] Spark plug HT leads incorrectly fitted – petrol models (Chapter 1A or 5B)
- [ ] Ignition coil unit faulty – petrol models (Chapter 5B)

Oil pressure warning light illuminated with engine running

- [ ] Low oil level, or incorrect oil grade (see *Weekly checks*)
- [ ] Faulty oil pressure sensor, or wiring damaged (Chapter 5A)
- [ ] Worn engine bearings and/or oil pump (Chapter 2A, 2B, 2C or 2D)
- [ ] High engine operating temperature (Chapter 3)
- [ ] Oil pump pressure relief valve defective (Chapter 2A, 2B, 2C or 2D)
- [ ] Oil pump pick-up strainer clogged (Chapter 2A, 2B, 2C or 2D)

Engine runs-on after switching off

- [ ] Excessive carbon build-up in engine (Chapter 2)
- [ ] High engine operating temperature (Chapter 3)
- [ ] Fuel injection system fault (Chapter 4A or 4B)

Engine noises

Pre-ignition (pinking) or knocking during acceleration or under load

- [ ] Ignition timing incorrect/ignition system fault – petrol models (Chapter 1A or 5B)
- [ ] Incorrect grade of spark plug – petrol models (Chapter 1A)
- [ ] Incorrect grade of fuel (Chapter 4)
- [ ] Knock sensor faulty – some petrol models (Chapter 4A)
- [ ] Vacuum leak at the throttle body, inlet manifold or associated hoses – petrol models (Chapter 4A)
- [ ] Excessive carbon build-up in engine (Chapter 2A, 2B, 2C or 2D)
- [ ] Blocked injector/fuel injection system fault (Chapter 4A or 4B)
- [ ] Faulty injector(s) – diesel models (Chapter 4B)

Whistling or wheezing noises

- [ ] Leaking inlet manifold or throttle body gasket – petrol models (Chapter 4A)
- [ ] Leaking exhaust manifold gasket or pipe-to-manifold joint (Chapter 4A or 4B)
- [ ] Leaking vacuum hose (Chapter 4, 5 or 9)
- [ ] Blowing cylinder head gasket (Chapter 2A, 2B, 2C or 2D)
- [ ] Partially blocked or leaking crankcase ventilation system (Chapter 4C)

Tapping or rattling noises

- [ ] Valve clearances incorrect (Chapter 2A, 2B, 2C or 2D)
- [ ] Worn valve gear or camshaft (Chapter 2A, 2B, 2C or 2D)
- [ ] Ancillary component fault (coolant pump, alternator, etc) (Chapter 3, 5A, etc)

Knocking or thumping noises

- [ ] Worn big-end bearings (regular heavy knocking, perhaps less under load) (Chapter 2D)
- [ ] Worn main bearings (rumbling and knocking, perhaps worsening under load) (Chapter 2D)
- [ ] Piston slap – most noticeable when cold, caused by piston/bore wear (Chapter 2D)
- [ ] Ancillary component fault (coolant pump, alternator, etc) (Chapter 3, 5A, etc)
- [ ] Engine mountings worn or defective (Chapter 2A, 2B, 2C or 2D)
- [ ] Front suspension or steering components worn (Chapter 10)

Cooling system

Overheating

- ☐ Insufficient coolant in system (see *Weekly checks*)
- ☐ Thermostat faulty (Chapter 3)
- ☐ Radiator core blocked, or grille restricted (Chapter 3)
- ☐ Cooling fan faulty, or resistor pack fault on models with twin fans (Chapter 3)
- ☐ Inaccurate cylinder head temperature sender (Chapter 3, 4A or 4B)
- ☐ Airlock in cooling system (Chapter 3)
- ☐ Expansion tank pressure cap faulty (Chapter 3)
- ☐ Engine management system fault (Chapter 4A or 4B)

Overcooling

- ☐ Thermostat faulty (Chapter 3)
- ☐ Inaccurate cylinder head temperature sender (Chapter 3, 4A or 4B)
- ☐ Cooling fan faulty (Chapter 3)
- ☐ Engine management system fault (Chapter 4A or 4B)

External coolant leakage

- ☐ Deteriorated or damaged hoses or hose clips (Chapter 1A or 1B)
- ☐ Radiator core or heater matrix leaking (Chapter 3)
- ☐ Expansion tank pressure cap faulty (Chapter 1A or 1B)
- ☐ Coolant pump internal seal leaking (Chapter 3)
- ☐ Coolant pump gasket leaking (Chapter 3)
- ☐ Boiling due to overheating (Chapter 3)
- ☐ Cylinder block core plug leaking (Chapter 2D)

Internal coolant leakage

- ☐ Leaking cylinder head gasket (Chapter 2A, 2B, 2C or 2D)
- ☐ Cracked cylinder head or cylinder block (Chapter 2A, 2B, 2C or 2D)

Corrosion

- ☐ Infrequent draining and flushing (Chapter 1A or 1B)
- ☐ Incorrect coolant mixture or inappropriate coolant type (see *Weekly checks*)

Fuel and exhaust systems

Excessive fuel consumption

- ☐ Air filter element dirty or clogged (Chapter 1A or 1B)
- ☐ Fuel injection system fault (Chapter 4A or 4B)
- ☐ Engine management system fault (Chapter 4A or 4B)
- ☐ Crankcase ventilation system blocked (Chapter 4C)
- ☐ Tyres under-inflated (see *Weekly checks*)
- ☐ Brakes binding (Chapter 1A, 1B or 9)
- ☐ Fuel leak, causing apparent high consumption (Chapter 1A, 1B, 4A or 4B)

Fuel leakage and/or fuel odour

- ☐ Damaged or corroded fuel tank, pipes or connections (Chapter 4A or 4B)
- ☐ Evaporative emissions system fault – petrol models (Chapter 4C)

Excessive noise or fumes from exhaust system

- ☐ Leaking exhaust system or manifold joints (Chapter 1A, 1B, 4A or 4B)
- ☐ Leaking, corroded or damaged silencers or pipe (Chapter 1A, 1B, 4A or 4B)
- ☐ Broken mountings causing body or suspension contact (Chapter 1A or 1B)

Clutch

Pedal travels to floor – no pressure or very little resistance

- ☐ Air in hydraulic system/faulty master or slave cylinder (Chapter 6)
- ☐ Faulty hydraulic release system (Chapter 6)
- ☐ Clutch pedal return spring detached or broken (Chapter 6)
- ☐ Broken clutch release bearing or fork (Chapter 6)
- ☐ Broken diaphragm spring in clutch pressure plate (Chapter 6)

Clutch fails to disengage (unable to select gears)

- ☐ Air in hydraulic system/faulty master or slave cylinder (Chapter 6)
- ☐ Faulty hydraulic release system (Chapter 6)
- ☐ Clutch disc sticking on transmission input shaft splines (Chapter 6)
- ☐ Clutch disc sticking to flywheel or pressure plate (Chapter 6)
- ☐ Faulty pressure plate assembly (Chapter 6)
- ☐ Clutch release mechanism worn or incorrectly assembled (Chapter 6)

Clutch slips (engine speed increases, with no increase in vehicle speed)

- ☐ Faulty hydraulic release system (Chapter 6)
- ☐ Clutch disc linings excessively worn (Chapter 6)
- ☐ Clutch disc linings contaminated with oil or grease (Chapter 6)
- ☐ Faulty pressure plate or weak diaphragm spring (Chapter 6)

Judder as clutch is engaged

- ☐ Clutch disc linings contaminated with oil or grease (Chapter 6)
- ☐ Clutch disc linings excessively worn (Chapter 6)
- ☐ Faulty or distorted pressure plate or diaphragm spring (Chapter 6).
- ☐ Worn or loose engine or transmission mountings (Chapter 2A, 2B, 2C or 2D)
- ☐ Clutch disc hub or transmission input shaft splines worn (Chapter 6)

Noise when depressing or releasing clutch pedal

- ☐ Worn clutch release bearing (Chapter 6)
- ☐ Worn or dry clutch pedal bushes (Chapter 6)
- ☐ Worn or dry clutch master cylinder piston (Chapter 6)
- ☐ Faulty pressure plate assembly (Chapter 6)
- ☐ Pressure plate diaphragm spring broken (Chapter 6)
- ☐ Broken clutch disc cushioning springs (Chapter 6)

Manual transmission

Noisy in neutral with engine running

- [ ] Lack of oil (Chapter 1A or 1B)
- [ ] Input shaft bearings worn (noise apparent with clutch pedal released, but not when depressed) (Chapter 7A)*
- [ ] Clutch release bearing worn (noise apparent with clutch pedal depressed, possibly less when released) (Chapter 6)

Noisy in one particular gear

- [ ] Worn, damaged or chipped gear teeth (Chapter 7A)*

Difficulty engaging gears

- [ ] Clutch fault (Chapter 6)
- [ ] Worn, damaged, or poorly-adjusted gearchange cables (Chapter 7A)
- [ ] Lack of oil (Chapter 1A or 1B)
- [ ] Worn synchroniser units (Chapter 7A)*

Jumps out of gear

- [ ] Worn, damaged, or poorly-adjusted gearchange cables (Chapter 7A)
- [ ] Worn synchroniser units (Chapter 7A)*
- [ ] Worn selector forks (Chapter 7A)*

Vibration

- [ ] Lack of oil (Chapter 1A or 1B)
- [ ] Worn bearings (Chapter 7A)*

Lubricant leaks

- [ ] Leaking driveshaft or selector shaft oil seal (Chapter 7A)
- [ ] Leaking housing joint (Chapter 7A)*
- [ ] Leaking input shaft oil seal (Chapter 7A)*

Although the corrective action necessary to remedy the symptoms described is beyond the scope of the home mechanic, the above information should be helpful in isolating the cause of the condition, so that the owner can communicate clearly with a professional mechanic.

Automatic transmission

Note: *Due to the complexity of the automatic transmission, it is difficult for the home mechanic to properly diagnose and service this unit. For problems other than the following, the vehicle should be taken to a dealer service department or automatic transmission specialist. Do not be too hasty in removing the transmission if a fault is suspected, as most of the testing is carried out with the unit still fitted. Remember that, besides the sensors specific to the transmission, many of the engine management system sensors described in Chapter 4A are essential to the correct operation of the transmission.*

Fluid leakage

- [ ] Automatic transmission fluid is usually dark red in colour. Fluid leaks should not be confused with engine oil, which can easily be blown onto the transmission by airflow.
- [ ] To determine the source of a leak, first remove all built-up dirt and grime from the transmission housing and surrounding areas using a degreasing agent, or by steam-cleaning. Drive the vehicle at low speed, so airflow will not blow the leak far from its source. Raise and support the vehicle, and determine where the leak is coming from. The following are common areas of leakage:
  a) *Fluid pan*
  b) *Dipstick tube (Chapter 1A)*
  c) *Transmission-to-fluid cooler unions (Chapter 7B)*

Transmission fluid brown, or has burned smell

- [ ] Transmission fluid level low (Chapter 1A)

General gear selection problems

- [ ] Chapter 7B deals with checking the selector cable on automatic transmissions. The following are common problems which may be

caused by a faulty cable or sensor:
a) *Engine starting in gears other than Park or Neutral.*
b) *Indicator panel indicating a gear other than the one actually being used.*
c) *Vehicle moves when in Park or Neutral.*
d) *Poor gear shift quality or erratic gear changes.*

Transmission will not downshift (kickdown) with accelerator pedal fully depressed

- [ ] Low transmission fluid level (Chapter 1A)
- [ ] Engine management system fault (Chapter 4A)
- [ ] Faulty transmission sensor or wiring (Chapter 7B)
- [ ] Incorrect selector cable adjustment (Chapter 7B)

Engine will not start in any gear, or starts in gears other than Park or Neutral

- [ ] Faulty transmission sensor or wiring (Chapter 7B)
- [ ] Engine management system fault (Chapter 4A)
- [ ] Incorrect selector cable adjustment (Chapter 7B)

Transmission slips, shifts roughly, is noisy, or has no drive in forward or reverse gears

- [ ] Transmission fluid level low (Chapter 1A)
- [ ] Faulty transmission sensor or wiring (Chapter 7B)
- [ ] Engine management system fault (Chapter 4A)

Note: *There are many probable causes for the above problems, but diagnosing and correcting them is considered beyond the scope of this manual. Having checked the fluid level and all the wiring as far as possible, a dealer or transmission specialist should be consulted if the problem persists.*

Driveshafts

Vibration when accelerating or decelerating

- [ ] Worn inner constant velocity joint (Chapter 8)
- [ ] Bent or distorted driveshaft (Chapter 8)
- [ ] Worn intermediate bearing (Chapter 8)

Clicking or knocking noise on turns (at slow speed on full-lock)

- [ ] Worn outer constant velocity joint (Chapter 8)
- [ ] Lack of constant velocity joint lubricant, possibly due to damaged gaiter (Chapter 8)
- [ ] Worn intermediate bearing (Chapter 8)

Braking system

Note: *Before assuming that a brake problem exists, make sure that the tyres are in good condition and correctly inflated, that the front wheel alignment is correct, and that the vehicle is not loaded with weight in an unequal manner. Apart from checking the condition of all pipe and hose connections, any faults occurring on the anti-lock braking system should be referred to a Ford dealer for diagnosis.*

Vehicle pulls to one side under braking

☐ Worn, defective, damaged or contaminated brake pads/shoes on one side (Chapter 1A, 1B or 9)
☐ Seized or partially-seized brake caliper piston/wheel cylinder (Chapter 1A, 1B or 9)
☐ A mixture of brake pad/shoe lining materials fitted between sides (Chapter 1A, 1B or 9)
☐ Brake caliper/backplate mounting bolts loose (Chapter 9)
☐ Worn or damaged steering or suspension components (Chapter 1A, 1B or 10)

Noise (grinding or high-pitched squeal) when brakes applied

☐ Brake pad/shoe friction lining material worn down to metal backing (Chapter 1A, 1B or 9)
☐ Excessive corrosion of brake disc/drum (may be apparent after the vehicle has been standing for some time (Chapter 1A, 1B or 9)
☐ Foreign object (stone chipping, etc) trapped between brake disc and shield (Chapter 1A, 1B or 9)

Excessive brake pedal travel

☐ Faulty master cylinder (Chapter 9)
☐ Air in hydraulic system (Chapter 1A, 1B, 6 or 9)
☐ Faulty vacuum servo unit (Chapter 9)

Brake pedal feels spongy when depressed

☐ Air in hydraulic system (Chapter 1A, 1B, 6 or 9)
☐ Deteriorated flexible rubber brake hoses (Chapter 1A, 1B or 9)
☐ Master cylinder mounting nuts loose (Chapter 9)
☐ Faulty master cylinder (Chapter 9)

Excessive brake pedal effort required to stop vehicle

☐ Faulty vacuum servo unit (Chapter 9)
☐ Faulty vacuum pump – diesel models (Chapter 9)
☐ Disconnected, damaged or insecure brake servo vacuum hose (Chapter 9)
☐ Primary or secondary hydraulic circuit failure (Chapter 9)
☐ Seized brake caliper/wheel cylinder piston (Chapter 9)
☐ Brake pads/shoes incorrectly fitted (Chapter 9)
☐ Incorrect grade of brake pads/shoes fitted (Chapter 9)
☐ Brake pad/shoe linings contaminated (Chapter 1A, 1B or 9)

Judder felt through brake pedal or steering wheel when braking

Note: *Under heavy braking on models equipped with ABS, vibration may be felt through the brake pedal. This is a normal feature of ABS operation, and does not constitute a fault*

☐ Excessive run-out or distortion of discs/drums (Chapter 1A, 1B or 9)
☐ Brake pad/shoe linings worn (Chapter 1A, 1B or 9)
☐ Brake caliper/backplate mounting bolts loose (Chapter 9)
☐ Wear in suspension or steering components or mountings (Chapter 1A, 1B or 10)
☐ Front wheels out of balance (see *Weekly checks*)

Brakes binding

☐ Seized brake caliper/wheel cylinder piston (Chapter 9)
☐ Incorrectly-adjusted handbrake mechanism (Chapter 9)
☐ Faulty master cylinder (Chapter 9)

Rear wheels locking under normal braking

☐ Rear brake pad/shoe linings contaminated or damaged (Chapter 1 or 9)
☐ Rear brake discs/drums warped (Chapter 1 or 9)
☐ Rear brake load sensing proportioning valve faulty – Estate models (Chapter 9)

Suspension and steering

Note: *Before diagnosing suspension or steering faults, be sure that the trouble is not due to incorrect tyre pressures, mixtures of tyre types, or binding brakes.*

Vehicle pulls to one side

☐ Defective tyre (see *Weekly checks*)
☐ Excessive wear in suspension or steering components (Chapter 1A, 1B or 10)
☐ Incorrect front wheel alignment (Chapter 10)
☐ Accident damage to steering or suspension components (Chapter 1A or 1B)

Wheel wobble and vibration

☐ Front wheels out of balance (vibration felt mainly through the steering wheel) (see *Weekly checks*)
☐ Rear wheels out of balance (vibration felt throughout the vehicle) (see *Weekly checks*)
☐ Roadwheels damaged or distorted (see *Weekly checks*)
☐ Faulty or damaged tyre (see *Weekly checks*)
☐ Worn steering or suspension joints, bushes or components (Chapter 1A, 1B or 10)
☐ Wheel nuts loose (Chapter 1A or 1B)

Excessive pitching and/or rolling around corners, or during braking

☐ Defective shock absorbers (Chapter 1A, 1B or 10)

☐ Broken or weak spring and/or suspension component (Chapter 1A, 1B or 10)
☐ Worn or damaged anti-roll bar or mountings (Chapter 1A, 1B or 10)

Wandering or general instability

☐ Incorrect front wheel alignment (Chapter 10)
☐ Worn steering or suspension joints, bushes or components (Chapter 1A, 1B or 10)
☐ Roadwheels out of balance (see *Weekly checks*)
☐ Faulty or damaged tyre (see *Weekly checks*)
☐ Wheel nuts loose (Chapter 1A or 1B)
☐ Defective shock absorbers (Chapter 1A, 1B or 10)

Excessively-stiff steering

☐ Seized steering linkage balljoint or suspension balljoint (Chapter 1A, 1B or 10)
☐ Broken or incorrectly-adjusted auxiliary drivebelt (Chapter 1A or 1B)
☐ Incorrect front wheel alignment (Chapter 10)
☐ Steering rack damaged (Chapter 10)

Excessive play in steering

☐ Worn steering column/intermediate shaft joints (Chapter 10)
☐ Worn track rod balljoints (Chapter 1A, 1B or 10)
☐ Worn steering rack (Chapter 10)
☐ Worn steering or suspension joints, bushes or components (Chapter 1A, 1B or 10)

Suspension and steering (continued)

Lack of power assistance

- ☐ Broken or incorrectly-adjusted auxiliary drivebelt (Chapter 1A or 1B)
- ☐ Incorrect power steering fluid level (see *Weekly checks*)
- ☐ Restriction in power steering fluid hoses (Chapter 1A or 1B)
- ☐ Faulty power steering pump (Chapter 10)
- ☐ Faulty steering rack (Chapter 10)

Tyre wear excessive

Tyres worn on inside or outside edges

- ☐ Tyres under-inflated (wear on both edges) (see *Weekly checks*)
- ☐ Incorrect camber or castor angles (wear on one edge only) (Chapter 10)
- ☐ Worn steering or suspension joints, bushes or components (Chapter 1A, 1B or 10)
- ☐ Excessively-hard cornering or braking
- ☐ Accident damage

Tyre treads exhibit feathered edges

- ☐ Incorrect toe-setting (Chapter 10)

Tyres worn in centre of tread

- ☐ Tyres over-inflated (see *Weekly checks*)

Tyres worn on inside and outside edges

- ☐ Tyres under-inflated (see *Weekly checks*)

Tyres worn unevenly

- ☐ Tyres/wheels out of balance (see *Weekly checks*)
- ☐ Excessive wheel or tyre run-out
- ☐ Worn shock absorbers (Chapter 1A, 1B or 10)
- ☐ Faulty tyre (see *Weekly checks*)

Electrical system

Note: *For problems associated with the starting system, refer to the faults listed under 'Engine' earlier in this Section.*

Battery will not hold a charge for more than a few days

- ☐ Battery defective internally (Chapter 5A)
- ☐ Battery terminal connections loose or corroded (see *Weekly checks*)
- ☐ Auxiliary drivebelt worn or incorrectly adjusted (Chapter 1A or 1B)
- ☐ Alternator not charging at correct output (Chapter 5A)
- ☐ Alternator or voltage regulator faulty (Chapter 5A)
- ☐ Short-circuit causing continual battery drain (Chapter 5A or 12)

Ignition/no-charge warning light remains illuminated with engine running

- ☐ Auxiliary drivebelt broken, worn, or incorrectly adjusted (Chapter 1A or 1B)
- ☐ Internal fault in alternator or voltage regulator (Chapter 5A)
- ☐ Broken, disconnected, or loose wiring in charging circuit (Chapter 5A or 12)

Ignition/no-charge warning light fails to come on

- ☐ Warning light bulb blown (Chapter 12)
- ☐ Broken, disconnected, or loose wiring in warning light circuit (Chapter 5A or 12)
- ☐ Alternator faulty (Chapter 5A)

Lights inoperative

- ☐ Bulb blown (Chapter 12)
- ☐ Corrosion of bulb or bulbholder contacts (Chapter 12)
- ☐ Blown fuse (Chapter 12)
- ☐ Faulty relay (Chapter 12)
- ☐ Broken, loose, or disconnected wiring (Chapter 12)
- ☐ Faulty switch (Chapter 12)

Instrument readings inaccurate or erratic

Instrument readings increase with engine speed

- ☐ Faulty instrument panel voltage regulator (Chapter 12)

Fuel or temperature gauges give no reading

- ☐ Faulty gauge sender unit (Chapter 3, 4A or 4B)
- ☐ Wiring open-circuit (Chapter 12)
- ☐ Faulty gauge (Chapter 12)

Fuel or temperature gauges give continuous maximum reading

- ☐ Faulty gauge sender unit (Chapter 3, 4A or 4B)
- ☐ Wiring short-circuit (Chapter 12)
- ☐ Faulty gauge (Chapter 12)

Horn inoperative, or unsatisfactory in operation

Horn operates all the time

- ☐ Horn push either earthed or stuck down (Chapter 12)
- ☐ Horn cable-to-horn push earthed (Chapter 12)

Horn fails to operate

- ☐ Blown fuse (Chapter 12)
- ☐ Cable or connections loose, broken or disconnected (Chapter 12)
- ☐ Faulty horn (Chapter 12)

Horn emits intermittent or unsatisfactory sound

- ☐ Cable connections loose (Chapter 12)
- ☐ Horn mountings loose (Chapter 12)
- ☐ Faulty horn (Chapter 12)

Electrical system (continued)

Windscreen wipers inoperative, or unsatisfactory in operation

Wipers fail to operate, or operate very slowly

- [ ] Wiper blades stuck to screen, or linkage seized or binding (Chapter 12)
- [ ] Blown fuse (Chapter 12)
- [ ] Battery discharged (Chapter 5A)
- [ ] Cable or connections loose, broken or disconnected (Chapter 12)
- [ ] Faulty relay (Chapter 12)
- [ ] Faulty wiper motor (Chapter 12)

Wiper blades sweep over too large or too small an area of the glass

- [ ] Wiper blades incorrectly fitted, or wrong size used (see *Weekly checks*)
- [ ] Wiper arms incorrectly positioned on spindles (Chapter 12)
- [ ] Excessive wear of wiper linkage (Chapter 12)
- [ ] Wiper motor or linkage mountings loose or insecure (Chapter 12)

Wiper blades fail to clean the glass effectively

- [ ] Wiper blade rubbers dirty, worn or perished (see *Weekly checks*)
- [ ] Wiper blades incorrectly fitted, or wrong size used (see *Weekly checks*)
- [ ] Wiper arm tension springs broken, or arm pivots seized (Chapter 12)
- [ ] Insufficient windscreen washer additive to adequately remove road film (see *Weekly checks*)

Windscreen washers inoperative, or unsatisfactory in operation

One or more washer jets inoperative

- [ ] Blocked washer jet
- [ ] Disconnected, kinked or restricted fluid hose (Chapter 12)
- [ ] Insufficient fluid in washer reservoir (see *Weekly checks*)

Washer pump fails to operate

- [ ] Broken or disconnected wiring or connections (Chapter 12)
- [ ] Blown fuse (Chapter 12)
- [ ] Faulty washer switch (Chapter 12)
- [ ] Faulty washer pump (Chapter 12)

Washer pump runs for some time before fluid is emitted from jets

- [ ] Faulty one-way valve in fluid supply hose (Chapter 12)

Electric windows inoperative, or unsatisfactory in operation

Window glass will only move in one direction

- [ ] Faulty switch (Chapter 12)

Window glass slow to move

- [ ] Battery discharged (Chapter 5A)
- [ ] Regulator seized or damaged, or in need of lubrication (Chapter 11)
- [ ] Door internal components or trim fouling regulator (Chapter 11)
- [ ] Faulty motor (Chapter 11)

Window glass fails to move

- [ ] Blown fuse (Chapter 12)
- [ ] Faulty relay (Chapter 12)
- [ ] Broken or disconnected wiring or connections (Chapter 12)
- [ ] Faulty motor (Chapter 11)

Central locking system inoperative, or unsatisfactory in operation

Complete system failure

- [ ] Remote handset battery discharged, where applicable
- [ ] Blown fuse (Chapter 12)
- [ ] Faulty relay (Chapter 12)
- [ ] Broken or disconnected wiring or connections (Chapter 12)
- [ ] Faulty motor (Chapter 11)

Latch locks but will not unlock, or unlocks but will not lock

- [ ] Remote handset battery discharged, where applicable
- [ ] Faulty master switch (Chapter 12)
- [ ] Broken or disconnected latch operating rods or levers (Chapter 11)
- [ ] Faulty relay (Chapter 12)
- [ ] Faulty motor (Chapter 11)

One solenoid/motor fails to operate

- [ ] Broken or disconnected wiring or connections (Chapter 12)
- [ ] Faulty operating assembly (Chapter 11)
- [ ] Broken, binding or disconnected latch operating rods or levers (Chapter 11)
- [ ] Fault in door latch (Chapter 11)

Note: *References throughout this index are in the form* **"Chapter number"** • **"Page number"**

Preserving Our Motoring Heritage

< The Model J Duesenberg Derham Tourster. Only eight of these magnificent cars were ever built – this is the only example to be found outside the United States of America

Almost every car you've ever loved, loathed or desired is gathered under one roof at the Haynes Motor Museum. Over 300 immaculately presented cars and motorbikes represent every aspect of our motoring heritage, from elegant reminders of bygone days, such as the superb Model J Duesenberg to curiosities like the bug-eyed BMW Isetta. There are also many old friends and flames. Perhaps you remember the 1959 Ford Popular that you did your courting in? The magnificent 'Red Collection' is a spectacle of classic sports cars including AC, Alfa Romeo, Austin Healey, Ferrari, Lamborghini, Maserati, MG, Riley, Porsche and Triumph.

A Perfect Day Out

Each and every vehicle at the Haynes Motor Museum has played its part in the history and culture of Motoring. Today, they make a wonderful spectacle and a great day out for all the family. Bring the kids, bring Mum and Dad, but above all bring your camera to capture those golden memories for ever. You will also find an impressive array of motoring memorabilia, a comfortable 70 seat video cinema and one of the most extensive transport book shops in Britain. The Pit Stop Cafe serves everything from a cup of tea to wholesome, home-made meals or, if you prefer, you can enjoy the large picnic area nestled in the beautiful rural surroundings of Somerset.

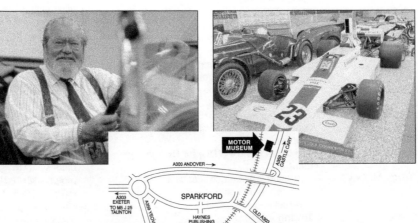

> John Haynes O.B.E., Founder and Chairman of the museum at the wheel of a Haynes Light 12.

< Graham Hill's Lola Cosworth Formula 1 car next to a 1934 Riley Sports.

The Museum is situated on the A359 Yeovil to Frome road at Sparkford, just off the A303 in Somerset. It is about 40 miles south of Bristol, and 25 minutes drive from the M5 intersection at Taunton.
Open 9.30am - 5.30pm (10.00am - 4.00pm Winter) 7 days a week, except Christmas Day, Boxing Day and New Years Day
Special rates available for schools, coach parties and outings Charitable Trust No. 292048